Lecture Notes in Artificial Intelligence 10314

Subseries of Lecture Notes in Computer Science

LNAI Series Editors

Randy Goebel
   University of Alberta, Edmonton, Canada
Yuzuru Tanaka
   Hokkaido University, Sapporo, Japan
Wolfgang Wahlster
   DFKI and Saarland University, Saarbrücken, Germany

LNAI Founding Series Editor

Joerg Siekmann
   DFKI and Saarland University, Saarbrücken, Germany

Lech Polkowski · Yiyu Yao
Piotr Artiemjew · Davide Ciucci
Dun Liu · Dominik Ślęzak
Beata Zielosko (Eds.)

Rough Sets

International Joint Conference, IJCRS 2017
Olsztyn, Poland, July 3–7, 2017
Proceedings, Part II

 Springer

Editors

Lech Polkowski
Polish-Japanese Academy of Information
  Technology
Warsaw
Poland

Yiyu Yao
University of Regina
Regina, SK
Canada

Piotr Artiemjew
University of Warmia and Mazury
Olsztyn
Poland

Davide Ciucci
University of Milano-Bicocca
Milan
Italy

Dun Liu
Southwest Jiaotong University
Chengdu
China

Dominik Ślęzak
Warsaw University
Warsaw
Poland

Beata Zielosko
Silesian University
Sosnowiec
Poland

ISSN 0302-9743   ISSN 1611-3349   (electronic)
Lecture Notes in Artificial Intelligence
ISBN 978-3-319-60839-6   ISBN 978-3-319-60840-2   (eBook)
DOI 10.1007/978-3-319-60840-2

Library of Congress Control Number: 2017944319

LNCS Sublibrary: SL7 – Artificial Intelligence

Printed on acid-free paper

This Springer imprint is published by Springer Nature
The registered company is Springer International Publishing AG
The registered company address is: Gewerbestrasse 11, 6330 Cham, Switzerland

Preface

The two-volume set of proceedings of IJCRS 2017, the 2017 International Joint Conference on Rough Sets, contains the results of the meeting of the International Rough Set Society held at the University of Warmia and Mazury in Olsztyn, Poland, during July 3–7, 2017.

Conferences in the IJCRS series are held annually and comprise four main tracks relating the topic rough sets to other topical paradigms: rough sets and data analysis covered by the RSCTC conference series from 1998, rough sets and granular computing covered by the RSFDGrC conference series since 1999, rough sets and knowledge technology covered by the RSKT conference series since 2006, and rough sets and intelligent systems covered by the RSEISP conference series since 2007. Owing to the gradual emergence of hybrid paradigms involving rough sets, it was deemed necessary to organize Joint Rough Set Symposiums, first in Toronto, Canada, in 2007, followed by Symposiums in Chengdu, China in 2012, Halifax, Canada, 2013, Granada and Madrid, Spain, 2014, Tianjin, China, 2015, where the acronym IJCRS was proposed, continuing with the IJCRS 2016 conference in Santiago de Chile.

The IJCRS conferences aim at gathering together experts from academia and industry representing fields of research in which theoretical and applicational aspects of rough set theory already find or may potentially find usage. They also provide a venue for researchers wanting to present their ideas before the rough set community, or for those who would like to learn about rough sets and find out whether they could be useful for their problems.

This year's conference, IJCRS 2017, celebrated the 35th anniversary of the seminal work by Prof. Zdzisław Pawlak published in 1982, in which the notion of a rough set emerged.

Professor Zdzisław Pawlak (1926–2006) contributed to computer science with many achievements such as addressless Pawlak machines, a random number generator, a participant in the design and production of the Polish computing machine UMC-2, and a proposition of the first genomic grammar (1965).

The emergence of the rough set idea owes much to Prof. Pawlak's deep interest in the foundations of logics and mathematics — in the 1960s he conducted seminars with the eminent logician and mathematician Prof. Andrzej Ehrenfeucht at the Mathematical Institute of the Polish Academy of Sciences. At the root of the idea of a rough set lie the mathematical notions of the lower and the upper approximation known in geometry and analysis, and the idea of an inexact concept as possessing a boundary that consists of things belonging neither in the concept nor in its complement, going back to Gottlob Frege.

The second motive for celebration was the 50th anniversary of the dissemination in the scientific world by Prof. Solomon Marcus (1924–2015) of the Pawlak model of the DNA grammar, published in 1965 in Polish, in a small popular monograph on grammar theory, intended for high schoolers. This grammar, constructed also visually by means of chains of triangles, was the precursor of visual and mosaic grammars.

The conference commemorated Prof. Pawlak with a special session on "Zdzisław Pawlak — Life and Heritage" with Prof. Grzegorz Rozenberg as the honorary chair and Professor Andrzej Skowron as the chair; there were also commemorative talks by Prof. Grzegorz Rozenberg, Sankar Kumar Pal, Lech Polkowski, Roman Słowiski, Shusaku Tsumoto, Guoyin Wang, Zbigniew Ras, and Urszula Wybraniec-Skardowska. The essay by Prof. Wybraniec-Skardowska opens the proceedings.

The conference included six keynote lectures by Prof. Rakesh Agrawal, Jan Komorowski, Eric Matson, Sankar Kumar Pal, Grzegorz Rozenberg, and Guoyin Wang as well as four plenary lectures by Profs. Tianrui Li, Son Hung Nguyen, Pradipta Maji, Amedeo Napoli, and Zbigniew Ras.

For the process of submission, review, acceptance, updating, and compilation of the proceedings, the EasyChair Pro system was used that allowed for subdivision of submissions into tracks: Rough Sets (68 submissions), Special Session on Vagueness, Rough Sets and Mereology (11 submissions), Special Session on Trends in Multi-Agent Systems (five submissions), Special Session on Formal Concept Analysis, Rough Set Theory and Their Applications (five submissions), Special Session: Software and Systems for Rough Sets (four submissions), Workshop Three-Way Decisions, Uncertainty, Granular Computing (The 5th International Workshop on Three-way Decisions, Uncertainty, and Granular Computing, TWDUG 2017; 17 submissions), Workshop: Recent Advances in Biomedical Data Analysis (three submissions), and one invited submission to the Special Session "Zdzisław Pawlak — Life and Heritage." In all, 114 (130 with invited talks) submissions were received. Submissions were allowed to be regular at 10–20 long length and short at 6–8 pages. They were reviewed by members of Program Committee (PC) and invited reviewers, each submission reviewed by at least three reviewers in certainly positive cases and by four or five reviewers in cases of conflicting reviews by the first three reviewers. Finally, the most complex cases were decided by the conference and PC chairs.

Of 114 (130) submissions, after positive reviews and decisions, 74 papers were selected to be included as regular papers and 16 as short papers in the proceedings, which comprise two volumes. Section 1, Invite Talks, contains the essay by Urszula Wybraniec Skardowska in remembrance of Prof. Pawlak, abstracts of the keynote, plenary, IRSS fellow talks and tutorials, as submitted by respective speakers, making up 16 chapters. Section 2 on "General Rough Sets" contains papers devoted to the rough set theory in its foundational and decision-theoretic aspects, collected in 44 chapters. Section 3 on "Software and Systems for Rough Sets" contains papers submitted and accepted to the special session with this title. These sections constitute the first volume of proceedings.

The second volume of proceedings opens with Section 4, which collects papers submitted and accepted to the special session on "Vagueness, Rough Sets, Mereology" is devoted to foundational concept-theoretical and logical analysis of the rough set idea, as well as papers on applications of mereology in intelligent methods of computer science, containing ten chapters. Section 5, "Workshop on Three-Way Decisions, Uncertainty, Granular Computing," comprises 17 chapters. In these papers, the classic trichotomy introduced by Prof. Pawlak into data objects with respect to a given concept as belonging certainly in the concept, certainly not belonging in the concept, and belonging into the boundary of the concept is extended to soft computing with these regions; the topic of granular computing fits naturally in this section since rough sets, from their very inception, are computed with elementary granules defined by attribute-value descriptors. In Section 6 on "Recent Advances in Biomedical Data Analysis, Trends in Multi-Agent Systems, Formal Concept Analysis, Rough Set Theory and Their Applications," we find submitted and accepted regular papers on these topics that are strongly tied to the rough set domain. Section 6 contains 13 chapters; 24 papers were rejected, i.e., 21% of submissions. In the "General Rough Sets" track, 22 papers were rejected, i.e., 32% of submissions to this track.

In addition to the proceedings, participants of the conference found in the conference sets a booklet, "The Polish Trace," consisting of four chapters dedicated to the little known yet spectacular achievements of Polish scientists in the area of computer science: on the work by Jan Czochralski, "the forefather of the silicon era"; on achievements of cryptologists Jan Kowalewski and professors of Warsaw University Stanisł aw Leśniewski, Stefan Mazurkiewicz, and Wacław Sierpiński in deciphering codes of the Red Army during the Polish–Russian war of 1918–1920; on cryptologists Marian Rejewski, Jerzy Różycki, and Henryk Zygalski, who broke the German Enigma code in the 1930s; and on the contributions of Stanisław Leśniewski, Jan Łukasiewicz, and Alfred Tarski to the theory of concepts, computing, and soft computing.

An additional booklet contained texts of talks in the Special Session devoted to the memory of Prof. Zdzisław Pawlak.

We acknowledge the acceptance of our proposal of organizing IJCRS 2017 in Poland at the University of Warmia and Mazury by authorities of the International Rough Set Society, the owner of rights to the series.

Honorary patronage of the conference was accepted by Gustaw Marek Brzezin, Marshal of the Province of Warmia and Mazury, Prof. Ryszard Górecki, Rector of the University of Warmia and Mazury, and by Dr. Piotr Grzymowicz, President of the City of Olsztyn.

Scientific patronage was given by the International Rough Set Society and by the Committee on Informatics of the Polish Academy of Science.

Many eminent scientists offered us their kind help by accepting our invitations. Thanks go to the honorary chairs of the conference, Profs. Ryszard Górecki, Sankar Kumar Pal, Roman Słowiński, Andrzej Skowron, and Jerzy Nowacki as well as Wojciech Samulowski, Director of the Olsztyn Park of Science and Technology, to Guoyin Wang, to the keynote speakers Profs. Rakesh Agrawal, Jan Komorowski, Eric Matson, Sankar Kumar Pal, Grzegorz Rozenberg, and Guoyin Wang, and to the plenary speakers, Profs. Tianrui Li, Nguyen Hung Son, Pradipta Maji, Amedeo Napoli, and Zbigniew Ras. The Steering Committee members are gratefully acknowledged for their support.

We express our gratitude to the organizers and chairs of special sessions and workshops: Profs. Mani A-, Andrzej Pietruszczak, Rafał Gruszczyński, Duoqian Miao, Georg Peters, Chien Chung Chan, Hong Yu, Bing Zhou, Nouman Azam, Nan Zhang, Sushmita Paul, Jan G. Bazan, Andrzej Skowron, Pradipta Maji, Dominik Ślęzak, Julio Vera, Grzegorz Rozenberg, Sankar Kumar Pal, Roman Słowiński, Shusaku Tsumoto, Guoyin Wang, Zbigniew Ras, Urszula Wybraniec-Skardowska, Andrzej Zbrzezny,

Agnieszka M. Zbrzezny, Magdalena Kacprzak, Jakub Michaliszyn, Franco Raimondi, Wojciech Penczek, Bożena Woźna-Szczęśniak, Mahdi Zargayouna, Jaume Baixeries, Dmitry Ignatov, Mehdi Kaytoue, Sergei Kuznetsov, Tianrui Li, Jarosław Stepaniuk, and Hung Son Nguyen.

We thank the following for the tutorials: Jan Komorowski, Piero Pagliani, Andrzej Zbrzezny, Ivo Duentsch, and Dimiter Vakarelov. Our special thanks go to Program Committee members and Program Committee chairs: Profs. Piotr Artiemjew, Davide Ciucci, Dun Liu, Dominik Ślęzak, and Beata Zielosko, for their dedicated work in reviewing and selecting papers to be accepted, and to the members of the Organizing Committee: Dr. Przemysław Górecki, Dr. Paweł Drozda, Dr. Krzysztof Sopyła, Dr. Piotr Artiemjew, Dr. Stanisław Drozda, Dr. Bartosz Nowak, Łukasz Żmudzinski, Dr. Agnieszka Niemczynowicz, Hanna Pikus, Dr. Marek Adamowicz, and Beata Ostrowska. Special thanks for their dedicated and timely work to Mr Łukasz Żmudziński, for his work on the conference website, Dr. Paweł Drozda, for taking care of the administration of conference finances, and to Dr. Przemysław Górecki, for liaising with the hosting university's administrative offices. Student volunteers should be mentioned for their help in running the conference. Thanks go to our material sponsors: the Olsztyn Park of Science and Technology, the Marshal of the Province of Warmia and Mazury, Billennium. For moral support we would like to mention the co-organizers, the Polish-Japanese Academy of Information Technology and the Polish Information Processing Society. Our host, the University of Warmia and Mazury in Olsztyn, provided ample space for the conference sessions, secured the participation of the Kortowo ensemble, and the professional help of the university services: the financial and international exchange offices and the Foundation "ŻAK" that provided the catering. Thanks go to Park Hotel in Olsztyn for hosting the participants.

Special thanks go to Alfred Hofmann of Springer, for accepting to publish the proceedings of IJCRS 2017 in the LNCS/LNAI series, and to Anna Kramer and Elke Werner for their help with the proceedings. We are grateful to Springer for the grant of 1,000 euro for the best conference papers.

April 2017

Lech Polkowski
Yiyu Yao
Piotr Artiemjew
Davide Ciucci
Dun Liu
Dominik Ślęzak
Beata Zielosko

Organization

Honorary Patronage

Gustaw Marek Brzezin   Marshal of the Warmia and Mazury Province, Olsztyn, Poland

Ryszard Górecki   Rektor, University of Warmia and Mazury in Olsztyn, Olsztyn, Poland

Piotr Grzymowicz   President of the City of Olsztyn, Olsztyn, Poland

Scientific Patronage

International Rough Set Society
Committee for Informatics of the Polish Academy of Science

Conference Committees

Honorary Chairs

Ryszard Górecki   University of Warmia and Mazury in Olsztyn, Poland
Jerzy Nowacki   Polish-Japanese Academy of IT, Poland
Sankar Kumar Pal   Indian Statistical Institute, India
Wojciech Samulowski   Olsztyn Park of Science and Technology, Poland
Roman Słowiński   Poznań University of Technology, Poland
Andrzej Skowron   Warsaw University, Poland
Guoyin Wang   Chongqing University of Posts and Telecommunications, China

Conference Chairs

Lech Polkowski   University of Warmia and Mazury in Olsztyn, Poland
Yiyu Yao   University of Regina, Canada

Steering Committee

Jerzy Grzymala-Busse (Chair)   University of Kansas at Lawrence, USA

Chien-Chung Chan   University of Akron, USA
Chris Cornelis   Ghent University, Belgium
Qinghua Hu   Tianjin University, China
Masahiro Inuiguchi   Osaka University, Japan
Tianrui Li   Southwest Jiaotong University, China
Pawan Lingras   St. Mary's University, Canada
Ernestina Menasalvas   Universidad Politecnica de Madrid, Spain
Duoqian Miao   Tongji University, China
Sushmita Mitra   Indian Statistical Institute, India

Marian Noga	AGH University of Science and Technology, Poland
Nguyen Hung Son	Warsaw University, Poland
Jerzy Stefanowski	Poznań University of Technology, Poland
Jarosław Stepaniuk	Białystok University of Technology, Poland
Zbigniew Suraj	Rzeszów University, Poland
Marcin Szczuka	Warsaw University, Poland
Shusaku Tsumoto	Matsue University, Japan
Richard Weber	Universidad de Chile, Chile
Weizhi Wu	Zhejiang Ocean University, China
Jingtao Yao	University of Regina, Canada

Chairs and Organizers of Special Sessions, Workshops, Tutorials

Special Session on Foundations of Vagueness, Rough Sets and Mereology

Mani A.	University of Calcutta, India
Rafał Gruszczyński	Nicolaus Copernicus University in Toruń, Poland
Andrzej Pietruszczak	Nicolaus Copernicus University in Toruń, Poland
Lech Polkowski	University of Warmia and Mazury in Olsztyn, Poland

Special Plenary Session: Zdzisław Pawlak Life and Heritage

| Grzegorz Rozenberg | Leiden Universiteit, The Netherlands; University of Colorado at Boulder, USA |
| Andrzej Skowron | Warsaw University, Poland |

Special Session: Trends in Multi-Agent Systems

Andrzej Zbrzezny	Jan Długosz Academy, Poland
Agnieszka M. Zbrzezny	Jan Długosz Academy, Poland
Magdalena Kacprzak	Białystok University of Technology, Poland
Jakub Michaliszyn	University of Wrocław, Poland
Wojciech Penczek	IPI PAN, Poland
Franco Raimondi	Middlesex University, UK
Bożena Woźna-Szcześniak	Jan Długosz Academy, Poland
Mahdi Zargayouna	Ifsttar Institute, University of Paris-Est, France

Special Session on Formal Concept Analysis, Rough Set Theory and Their Applications

Jaume Baixeries	Universidad Politecnica de Catalunya, Spain
Dmitry Ignatov	National Research University, School of Economics, Russia
Mehdi Kaytoue	Institut National des Sciences Appliques de Lyon, France
Sergei Kuznetsov	National Research University, School of Economics, Russia

Special Session: Software and Systems for Rough Sets

Tianrui Li	Southwest Jiaotong University, Chengdu, China
Jarosław Stepaniuk	Białystok University of Technology, Poland
Hung Son Nguyen	Warsaw University, Poland

TWDUG 2017: The 5th Workshop on Three-Way Decisions, Uncertainty and Granular Computing

Duoqian Miao	Tongji University, China
Georg Peters	University of Applied Sciences, Germany
Chien Chung Chan	Akron University, USA
Nouman Azam	National University of Computer and Emerging Sciences, Pakistan
Hong Yu	Chongqing University of Posts and Telecommunications, China
Bing Zhou	Sam Houston State University, USA
Nan Zhang	Tianjin University, China

Workshop on Recent Advances in Biomedical Data Analysis

Sushmita Paul	Indian Institute of Technology Jodhpur, India
Jan G. Bazan	University of Rzeszów, Poland
Pradipta Maji	Indian Statistical Institute, Kolkata, India
Andrzej Skowron	Warsaw University, Poland
Lech Polkowski	University of Warmia and Mazury in Olsztyn, Poland
Dominik Ślęzak	Warsaw University, Poland
Julio Vera	Friedrich Alexander University of Erlangen-Nürnberg, Germany

Tutorial Chairs

Ivo Düntsch	Brock University, Canada
Jan Komorowski	Uppsala University, Sweden
Piero Pagliani	Rome, Italy
Andrzej Zbrzezny	Jan Długosz Academy, Poland
Dimiter Vakarelov	Sofia University, Bulgaria

Organizing Committee

Przemysław Górecki (Chair)	University of Warmia and Mazury in Olsztyn, Poland
Marek Adamowicz	Polish Information Processing Society, Poland
Piotr Artiemjew	University of Warmia and Mazury in Olsztyn, Poland
Paweł Drozda	University of Warmia and Mazury in Olsztyn, Poland
Stanisław Drozda	University of Warmia and Mazury in Olsztyn, Poland
Agnieszka Niemczynowicz	University of Warmia and Mazury in Olsztyn, Poland

Bartosz Nowak	University of Warmia and Mazury in Olsztyn, Poland
Beata Ostrowska	Polish Information Processing Society, Poland
Hanna Pikus	Polish Information Processing Society, Poland
Sławomir Popowicz	University of Warmia and Mazury, Poland
Krzysztof Ropiak	University of Warmia and Mazury, Poland
Krzysztof Sopyła	University of Warmia and Mazury in Olsztyn, Poland
Łukasz Żmudziński	University of Warmia and Mazury in Olsztyn, Poland

Sponsoring Institutions

Marshal of the Warmia and Mazury Province
Olsztyn Park of Science and Technology
University of Warmia and Mazury in Olsztyn, Poland
Billennium

Program Committee

Mani A.	Calcutta University, India
Mehwish Alam	Université de Paris, Laboratoire d'Informatique de Paris-Nord, France
Natasha Alechina	University of Nottingham, UK
Piotr Artiemjew	University of Warmia and Mazury in Olsztyn, Poland
Nouman Azam	National University of Computer and Emerging Sciences
Jaume Baixeries	Universitat Politècnica de Catalunya, Spain
Mohua Banerjee	Indian Institute of Technology Kanpur, India
Jan Bazan	University of Rzeszów, Poland
Rafael Bello	Universidad Central de Las Villas, Cuba
Nizar Bouguila	Concordia University, Canada
Aleksey Buzmakov	National Research University Higher School of Economics
Jerzy Błaszczyński	Poznań University of Technology, Poland
Mihir Chakraborty	Jadavpur University, India
Shampa Chakraverty	Netaji Subhas Institute of Technology, Dwarka, India
Chien-Chung Chan	University of Akron, USA
Mu-Chen Chen	National Chiao Tung University, Taiwan
Giampiero Chiaselotti	Università della Calabria, Italy
Costin-Gabriel Chiru	Politehnica University of Bucharest, Romania
Davide Ciucci	University of Milano-Bicocca, Italy
Victor Codocedo	Laboratoire lorrain de recherche en informatique et ses applications, France
Chris Cornelis	University of Granada, Spain
Zoltán Ernö Csajbók	University of Debrecen, Hungary
Jianhua Dai	Tianjin University, China
Martine De Cock	University of Washington Tacoma, USA
Dayong Deng	Zhejiang Normal University, China

Thierry Denoeux	Universitè de Technologie de Compiegne, France
Fernando Diaz	University of Valladolid, Spain
Pawel Drozda	University of Warmia and Mazury in Olsztyn, Poland
Didier Dubois	IRIT/RPDMP, France
Ivo Düntsch	Brock University, Canada
Zied Elouedi	Institut Superieur de Gestion de Tunis, Tunisia
Victor Flores	Universidad Católica del Norte, Chile
Brunella Gerla	University of Insubria, Italy
Piotr Gnyś	Polish-Japanese Academy of Information Technology, Poland
Anna Gomolinska	University of Bialystok, Poland
Przemyslaw Górecki	University of Warmia and Mazury in Olsztyn, Poland
Salvatore Greco	Portsmouth Business School, UK
Rafał Gruszczyński	Nicolaus Copernicus University in Toruń
Jerzy Grzymala-Busse	University of Kansas, USA
Aboul Ella Hassanien	Cairo University, Egypt
Christopher Henry	University of Winnipeg, Canada
Christopher Hinde	Loughborough University, UK
Qinghua Hu	Tianjin University, China
Dmitry Ignatov	School of Data Analysis and Artificial Intelligence
Masahiro Inuiguchi	Osaka University, Japan
Ryszard Janicki	McMaster University, Canada
Andrzej Jankowski	Warsaw University of Technology, Poland
Andrzej Janusz	Warsaw University, Poland
Richard Jensen	Aberystwyth University, UK
Xiuyi Jia	Nanjing University of Science and Technology, China
Magdalena Kacprzak	Politechnika Białostocka, Poland
Janusz Kacprzyk	Systems Research Institute, Polish Academy of Sciences, Poland
Milosz Kadzinski	Poznan University of Technology, Poland
Mehdi Kaytoue	Institut National des Sciences Appliquées de Lyon, France
Michal Kepski	University of Rzeszow, Poland
Md. Aquil Khan	Indian Institute of Technology Indore, India
Yoo-Sung Kim	Inha University, South Korea
Jan Komorowski	Uppsala University, Sweden
Marzena Kryszkiewicz	Warsaw University of Technology, Poland
Yasuo Kudo	Muroran Institute of Technology, Japan
Mirosław Kurkowski	UKSW
Yoshifumi Kusunoki	Osaka University, Japan
Sergei Kuznetsov	School of Data Analysis and Artificial Intelligence
Huaxiong Li	Nanjing University, China
Tianrui Li	Southwest Jiaotong University, China
Jiye Liang	Shanxi University, China
Churn-Jung Liau	Academia Sinica, Taipei, Taiwan
Tsau Young Lin	San Jose State University, USA

Gabriela Lindemann-Von Trzebiatowski	Humboldt University of Berlin, Germany
Pawan Lingras	Saint Mary's University, UK
Caihui Liu	Gannan Normal University, China
Dun Liu	Southwest Jiaotong University, China
Guilong Liu	Beijing Language and Culture University, China
Pradipta Maji	Indian Statistical Institute, Kolkata, India
Krzysztof Marasek	Polish-Japanese Academy of Information Technology, Poland
Benedetto Matarazzo	University of Catania, Italy
Jesús Medina Moreno	University of Cádiz, Spain
Ernestina Menasalvas	Universidad Politecnica de Madrid, Spain
Claudio Meneses	Universidad Católica del Norte, Chile
Duoqian Miao	Tongji University, China
Marcin Michalak	Silesian University of Technology, Poland
Jakub Michaliszyn	University of Wroclaw, Poland
Tamás Mihálydeák	University of Debrecen, Hungary
Fan Min	Southwest Petroleum University, China
Boris Mirkin	School of Data Analysis and Artificial Intelligence, Moscow, Russia
Pabitra Mitra	Indian Institute of Technology Kharagpur, India
Sadaaki Miyamoto	University of Tsukuba, Japan
Jesús Medina Moreno	University of Cádiz, Spain
Mikhail Moshkov	KAUST
Michinori Nakata	Josai International University, Japan
Amedeo Napoli	LORIA Nancy, France
Hung Son Nguyen	Institute of Mathematics, Warsaw University, Poland
Sinh Hoa Nguyen	Polish-Japanese Academy of Information Technology, Poland
M.C. Nicoletti	FACCAMP and UFSCar
Vilem Novak	University of Ostrava, Czech Republic
Jerzy Nowacki	Polish-Japanese Academy of Information Technology, Poland
Bartosz Nowak	University of Warmia and Mazury in Olsztyn, Poland
Hannu Nurmi	University of Turku, Finland
Ewa Orlowska	Institute of Telecommunication, Warsaw, Poland
Piero Pagliani	Research Group on Knowledge and Information, Rome, Italy
Sankar Kumar Pal	Indian Statistical Institute, Kolkata, India
Krzysztof Pancerz	University of Rzeszow, Poland
Vladimir Parkhomenko	St. Petersburg State Polytechnical University, Russia
Sushmita Paul	Indian Institute of Technology, Jodhpur
Andrei Paun	University of Bucharest, Romania
Witold Pedrycz	University of Edmonton, Canada
Wojciech Penczek	ICS PAS and Siedlce University
Tatiana Penkova	Institute of Computational Modelling SB RAS

Georg Peters	Munich University of Applied Sciences and Australian Catholic University
James Peters	University of Manitoba, Winnipeg, Department of Electrical and Computer Engineering
Alberto Pettorossi	Università di Roma Tor Vergata
Andrzej Pietruszczak	Nicolaus Copernicus University in Toruń
Jonas Poelmans	KU Louvain
Lech Polkowski	Polish-Japanese Academy of Information Technology
Henri Prade	IRIT: CNRS
Yuhua Qian	Shanxi University, Taiyuan
Mohammed Quafafou	Aix-Marseille University
Franco Raimondi	Middlesex University, London
Elisabeth Rakus-Andersson	Blekinge Institute of Technology
Sheela Ramanna	Department of Applied Computer Science, University of Winnipeg
C. Raghavendra Rao	University of Hyderabad, Andhra Pradesh, India
Zbigniew Ras	University of North Carolina at Charlotte
Guido Rosales	Universitätsklinikum Erlangen
Grzegorz Rozenberg	Leiden University
Giuseppe Ruggeri	Università Mediterranea di Reggio Calabria
Leszek Rutkowski	Technical University of Czestochowa
Henryk Rybiński	Warsaw University of Technology
Wojciech Rzasa	University of Rzeszow
Hiroshi Sakai	Kyushu Institute of Technology
Gerald Schaefer	Loughborough University
Zhongzhi Shi	Institute of Computing Technology, Chinese Academy of Sciences
Marek Sikora	Silesian University of Technology
Bruno Simoes	Research foundation: Fondazione Graphitech
Andrzej Skowron	Warsaw University
Dominik Ślęzak	Warsaw University & Infobright
Roman Słowiński	Poznan University of Technology
Krzysztof Sopyła	University of Warmia and Mazury in Olsztyn
John Stell	University of Leeds
Jaroslaw Stepaniuk	Bialystok University of Technology
Zbigniew Suraj	Chair of Computer Science, University of Rzeszów, Rzeszów
Piotr Synak	Infobright Inc.
Andrzej Szałas	Warsaw University
Marcin Szczuka	Institute of Mathematics, The University of Warsaw
Marcin Szelag	Poznan University of Technology
Ryszard Tadeusiewicz	AGH University of Science and Technology, Krakow, Poland
Bala Krushna Tripathy	VIT University, India
Martin Trnecka	Palacky University, Czech Republic

Li-Shiang Tsay	North Carolina A&T State University, USA
Dimiter Vakarelov	Sofia University, Bulgaria
Dmitry Vinogradov	Federal Research Center for Computer Science and Control RAN, Russia
Guoyin Wang	Chongqing University of Posts and Telecommunications, China
Thomas Wilcockson	Lancaster University, UK
Szymon Wilk	Poznan University of Technology, Poland
Arkadiusz Wojna	Warsaw University, Poland
Marcin Wolski	Maria Curie-Sklodowska University, Poland
Bożena Wozna-Szczesniak	Jan Dlugosz University in Czestochowa, Poland
Wei-Zhi Wu	Zhejiang Ocean University, China
Yan Yang	Jiaotong University, China
Jingtao Yao	University of Regina, Canada
Yiyu Yao	University of Regina, Canada
Dongyi Ye	Fuzhou University, China
Hong Yu	Chongqing University of Posts and Telecommunications, China
Mahdi Zargayouna	Université Paris Est, Ifsttar, France
Agnieszka M. Zbrzezny	Jan Dlugosz University, Poland
Andrzej Zbrzezny	Jan Dlugosz University, Poland
Bo Zhang	Chinese Academy of Sciences, China
Nan Zhang	Yantai University, China
Qinghua Zhang	Institute of Computer Science and Technology, Chongqing University of Posts and Telecommunications, China
Yan Zhang	University of Regina, Canada
Ning Zhong	Maebashi Institute of Technology, Japan
Bing Zhou	Sam Houston State University, USA
William Zhu	Minnan Normal University, China
Wojciech Ziarko	University of Regina, Canada
Beata Zielosko	University of Silesia, Poland

Additional Reviewers

Azam, Muhammad	Krzeszowski, Tomasz
Boldak, Cezary	Melliti, Tarek
Chen, Yewang	Mondal, Ajoy
Czajkowski, Marcin	Nayak, Losiana
Garai, Partha	Szreter, Maciej
Jana, Purbita	Tripathy, B.K.
Keith, Brian	Vluymans, Sarah
Kopczynski, Maciej	

Contents – Part II

Three-Way Decisions, Uncertainty, Granular Computing

**Recent Advances in Biomedical Data Analysis, Trends
in Multi-Agent Systems, Formal Concept Analysis, Rough Set Theory
and Their Applications**

Contents – Part I

Software and Systems for Rough Sets

Vagueness, Rough Sets, Mereology

Approximations from Anywhere and General Rough Sets

A. Mani[✉]

Department of Pure Mathematics, University of Calcutta,
9/1B, Jatin Bagchi Road, Kolkata 700029, India
a.mani.cms@gmail.com
http://www.logicamani.in

Abstract. Not all approximations arise from information systems. The problem of fitting approximations, subjected to some rules (and related data), to information systems in a rough scheme of things is known as the *inverse problem*. The inverse problem is more general than the duality (or abstract representation) problems and was introduced by the present author in her earlier papers. From the practical perspective, a few (as opposed to one) theoretical frameworks may be suitable for formulating the problem itself. *Granular operator spaces* have been recently introduced and investigated by the present author in her recent work in the context of antichain based and dialectical semantics for general rough sets. The nature of the inverse problem is examined from number-theoretic and combinatorial perspectives in a higher order variant of granular operator spaces and some necessary conditions are proved. The results and the novel approach would be useful in a number of unsupervised and semi supervised learning contexts and algorithms.

Keywords: Inverse problem · Duality · Rough objects · Granular operator spaces · High operator spaces · Anti chains · Combinatorics · Hybrid methods

1 Introduction

General rough set theory specifically targets information systems as the object of study in the sense that starting from information systems, approximations are defined and rough objects of various kinds are studied [1–6]. But the focus need not always be so. In duality problems, the problem is to generate the information system (to the extent possible) from semantic structures like algebras or topological algebras associated (see for example [3, 7–11]). Logico-algebraic and other semantic structures typically capture reasoning and processes in the earlier mentioned approach.

The concept of *inverse problem* was introduced by the present author in [9] and was subsequently refined in [3]. In simple terms, the problem is a generalization of the duality problem which may be obtained by replacing the semantic

© Springer International Publishing AG 2017
L. Polkowski et al. (Eds.): IJCRS 2017, Part II, LNAI 10314, pp. 3–22, 2017.
DOI: 10.1007/978-3-319-60840-2_1

structures with parts thereof. Thus the goal of the problem is to fit a given set of approximations and some semantics to a suitable rough process originating from an information system. Examples of approximations that are not rough in any sense are common in misjudgments and irrational reasoning guided by prejudice.

The above simplification is obviously dense because it has not been formulated in a concrete setup. It also needs many clarifications at the theoretical level. At the theoretical level again a number of frameworks appear to be justified. These can be restricted further by practical considerations. All this will not be discussed in full detail in this paper (for reasons of space). Instead a specific minimalist framework called *Higher Granular Operator Space* is proposed first and the problem is developed over it by the present author. All of the results proved are from a combinatorial perspective and on the basis of these results the central question can be answered in the negative in many cases.

2   Background

A relational system is a tuple of the form $\mathfrak{S} = \langle S, R_1, R_2, \ldots, R_n \rangle$ with S being a set and R_i being predicates of arity ν_i. The type of $\mathfrak{S}$ is $(\nu_1, \nu_2, \ldots, \nu_n)$. If $\mathfrak{H} = \langle H, Q_1, Q_2, \ldots, Q_n \rangle$ is another relational system of the same type and $\varphi : S \longmapsto H$ a map satisfying for each i,

$$(R_i a_1 a_2 \ldots a_{\nu_i} \longrightarrow R_i \varphi(a_1) \varphi(a_2) \ldots \varphi(a_{\nu_i})),$$

is a *relational morphism* [12]. If φ is also bijective, then it is referred to as a *relational isomorphism*.

By an *Information System $\mathcal{I}$*, is meant a structure of the form

$$\mathcal{I} = \langle \mathbb{O}, \, At, \, \{V_a : a \in At\}, \, \{f_a : a \in At\} \rangle$$

with $\mathbb{O}$, At and V_a being respectively sets of *Objects*, *Attributes* and *Values* respectively. It is *deterministic* (or complete) if for each $a \in At$, $f_a : O \longmapsto V_a$ is a map. It is said to be *indeterministic* (or incomplete) if the valuation has the form $f_a : O \longmapsto \wp(V)$, where $V = \bigcup V_a$. These two classes of information systems can be used to generate various types of relational, covering or relator spaces which in turn relate to approximations of different types and form a substantial part of the problems encountered in general rough set theories. One way of defining an indiscernibility relation σ is as below:

For $x, \, y \in \mathbb{O}$ and $B \subseteq At$, $(x, y) \in \sigma$ if and only if $(\forall a \in B)\nu(a, x) = \nu(a, y)$. In this case σ is an equivalence relation (see [1,7,8,13]). Lower and upper approximations, rough equalities are defined over it and topological algebraic semantics can be formulated over *roughly equivalent* objects (or subsets of attributes) through extra operations. Duality theorems, proved for *pre-rough* algebras defined in [7], are specifically for structures relation isomorphic to the approximation space $(\mathbb{O}, \sigma)$. This is also true of the representation results in [8,9,14]. But these are not for information systems - optimal concepts of *isomorphic information systems* are considered by the present author in a forthcoming paper.

In fact in [9], it has been proved by the present author that

Theorem 1. *For every super rough algebra S, there exists an approximation space X such that the super rough set algebra generated by X is isomorphic to S.*

In simple terms, *granules* are the subsets (or objects) that generate approximations and *granulations* are the collections of all such granules in the context. For more on what they might be the reader may refer to [3, 15]. In this paper a variation of generalized granular operator spaces, introduced and studied by the present author in [16–18], will serve as the primary framework for most considerations. For reference, related definitions are mentioned below.

Definition 1. *A Granular Operator Space* [16] *S is a structure of the form $S = \langle \underline{S}, \mathcal{G}, l, u \rangle$ with $\underline{S}$ being a set, $\mathcal{G}$ an admissible granulation(defined below) over S and l, u being operators : $\wp(\underline{S}) \longmapsto \wp(\underline{S})$ ($\wp(\underline{S})$ denotes the power set of $\underline{S}$) satisfying the following ($\underline{S}$ is replaced with S if clear from the context. Lower and upper case alphabets may denote subsets):*

$$a^l \subseteq a \ \& \ a^{ll} = a^l \ \& \ a^u \subseteq a^{uu}$$

$$(a \subseteq b \longrightarrow a^l \subseteq b^l \ \& \ a^u \subseteq b^u)$$

$$\emptyset^l = \emptyset \ \& \ \emptyset^u = \emptyset \ \& \ \underline{S}^l \subseteq S \ \& \ \underline{S}^u \subseteq S.$$

In the context of this definition, Admissible Granulations *are granulations $\mathcal{G}$ that satisfy the following three conditions (t being a term operation formed from the set operations $\cup, \cap, {}^c, 1, \emptyset$):*

$$(\forall a \exists b_1, \ldots b_r \in \mathcal{G}) \, t(b_1, b_2, \ldots b_r) = a^l$$

$$\text{and } (\forall a) \, (\exists b_1, \ldots b_r \in \mathcal{G}) \, t(b_1, b_2, \ldots b_r) = a^u, \quad \text{(Weak RA, WRA)}$$

$$(\forall b \in \mathcal{G})(\forall a \in \wp(\underline{S})) \, (b \subseteq a \longrightarrow b \subseteq a^l), \quad \text{(Lower Stability, LS)}$$

$$(\forall a, b \in \mathcal{G})(\exists z \in \wp(\underline{S})) \, a \subset z, \, b \subset z \ \& \ z^l = z^u = z, \quad \text{(Full Underlap, FU)}$$

Remarks:

- The concept of admissible granulation was defined for RYS in [3] using parthoods instead of set inclusion and relative to RYS, **P** $=\subseteq$, $\mathbb{P}$ $=\subset$. It should be noted that the minimal assumptions make this concept more general than the idea of granulation in the precision based granular computing paradigm (and complex granules) [19, 20].
- *The conditions defining admissible granulations mean that every approximation is somehow representable by granules in a set theoretic way, that granules are lower definite, and that all pairs of distinct granules are contained in definite objects.*
- The term operation t is intended to be defined over the power set Boolean algebra in standard algebraic sense (see [21] for a detailed example).

The concept of *generalized granular operator spaces* has been introduced in [17, 22] as a proper generalization of that of granular operator spaces. The main difference is in the replacement of $\subset$ by arbitrary *part of* (**P**) relations in the axioms of admissible granules and inclusion of **P** in the signature of the structure.

Definition 2. *A* General Granular Operator Space *(GSP) S is a structure of the form $S = \langle \underline{S}, \mathcal{G}, l, u, \mathbf{P} \rangle$ with $\underline{S}$ being a set, $\mathcal{G}$ an admissible granulation(defined below) over S, l, u being operators : $\wp(\underline{S}) \longmapsto \wp(\underline{S})$ and $\mathbf{P}$ being a definable binary generalized transitive predicate (for parthood) on $\wp(\underline{S})$ satisfying the same conditions as in Definition 1 except for those on admissible granulations (Generalized transitivity can be any proper nontrivial generalization of parthood (see [20]). $\mathbb{P}$ is proper parthood (defined via $\mathbb{P}ab$ iff $\mathbf{P}ab$ & $\neg\mathbf{P}ba$) and t is a term operation formed from set operations):*

$$(\forall x \exists y_1, \ldots y_r \in \mathcal{G})\, t(y_1, y_2, \ldots y_r) = x^l$$
$$\text{and } (\forall x)\,(\exists y_1, \ldots y_r \in \mathcal{G})\, t(y_1, y_2, \ldots y_r) = x^u, \qquad \text{(Weak RA, WRA)}$$
$$(\forall y \in \mathcal{G})(\forall x \in \wp(\underline{S}))\,(\mathbf{P}yx \longrightarrow \mathbf{P}yx^l), \qquad \text{(Lower Stability, LS)}$$
$$(\forall x, y \in \mathcal{G})(\exists z \in \wp(\underline{S}))\, \mathbb{P}xz, \,\&\, \mathbb{P}yz \,\&\, z^l = z^u = z, \qquad \text{(Full Underlap, FU)}$$

2.1 Finite Posets

Let S be a finite poset with $\#(S) = n < \infty$. The following concepts and notations will be used in this paper:

- If $\mathfrak{F}$ is a collection of subsets $\{X_i\}_{i \in J}$ of a set X, then a *system of distinct representatives* SDR for $\mathfrak{F}$ is a set $\{x_i; i \in J\}$ of distinct elements satisfying $(\forall i \in J)x_i \in X_i$. Chains are subsets of a poset in which any two elements are comparable. Singletons are both chains and antichains.
- For $a, b \in S$, $a \prec b$ shall be an abbreviation for b covering a from above (that is $a < b$ and $(a \le c \le b \longrightarrow c = a$ or $c = b))$. $c(S)$ shall be the number of covering pairs in S.
- A *chain cover* of a finite poset S is a collection $\mathcal{C}$ of chains in S satisfying $\cup\mathcal{C} = S$. It is disjoint if the chains in the cover are pairwise disjoint.
- S has finite width w if and only if it can be partitioned into w number of chains, but not less.

The following results are well known:

Theorem 2. *1. A collection of subsets $\mathfrak{F}$ of a finite set S with $\#(\mathfrak{F}) = r$ has an SDR if and only if for any $1 \le k \le r$, the union of any k members of $\mathfrak{F}$ has size at least k, that is*

$$(\forall X_1, \ldots, X_k \in \mathfrak{F})\, k \le \#(\cup X_i).$$

2. Every finite poset S has a disjoint chain cover of width $w = width(S)$.

3. *If X is a partially ordered set with longest chains of length r and if it can be partitioned into k number of antichains then $r \leq k$.*
4. *If X is a finite poset with k elements in its largest antichain, then a chain decomposition of X must contain at least k chains.*

Proofs of the assertions can be found in [23, 24] for example. To prove the third, start from a chain decomposition and recursively extract the minimal elements from it to form r number of antichains. The fourth assertion is proved by induction on the size of X across many possibilities.

3   Semantic Framework

It is more convenient to use only sets and subsets in the formalism as these are the kinds of objects that may be observed by agents and such a formalism would be more suited for reformulation in formal languages. This justifies the severe variation defined below in stages:

Definition 3. *A* Higher Rough Operator Space $\mathbb{S}$ *shall be a structure of the form* $\mathbb{S} = \langle \underline{\mathbb{S}}, l, u, \leq, \bot, \top \rangle$ *with* $\underline{\mathbb{S}}$ *being a set, and* l, u *being operators* $: \underline{\mathbb{S}} \longmapsto \underline{\mathbb{S}}$ *satisfying the following (* $\underline{\mathbb{S}}$ *is replaced with* $\mathbb{S}$ *if clear from the context.):*

$$(\forall a \in \mathbb{S}) \, a^l \leq a \ \& \ a^{ll} = a^l \ \& \ a^u \leq a^{uu}$$

$$(\forall a, b \in \mathbb{S})(a \leq b \longrightarrow a^l \leq b^l \ \& \ a^u \leq b^u)$$

$$\bot^l = \bot \ \& \ \bot^u = \bot \ \& \ \top^l \leq \top \ \& \ \top^u \leq \top$$

$$(\forall a \in \mathbb{S}) \, \bot \leq a \leq \top$$

$$\mathbb{S} \, is \, a \, bounded \, poset.$$

Definition 4. *A* Higher Granular Operator Space *(SHG)* $\mathbb{S}$ *shall be a structure of the form* $\mathbb{S} = \langle \underline{\mathbb{S}}, \mathcal{G}, l, u, \leq, \vee, \wedge, \bot, \top \rangle$ *with* $\underline{\mathbb{S}}$ *being a set,* $\mathcal{G}$ *an* admissible granulation *(defined below) for* $\mathbb{S}$ *and* l, u *being operators* $: \underline{\mathbb{S}} \longmapsto \underline{\mathbb{S}}$ *satisfying the following (* $\underline{\mathbb{S}}$ *is replaced with* $\mathbb{S}$ *if clear from the context.):*

$$(\mathbb{S}, \vee, \wedge, \bot, \top) \, is \, a \, bounded \, lattice$$

$$\leq \, is \, the \, lattice \, order$$

$$(\forall a \in \mathbb{S}) \, a^l \leq a \ \& \ a^{ll} = a^l \ \& \ a^u \leq a^{uu}$$

$$(\forall a, b \in \mathbb{S})(a \leq b \longrightarrow a^l \leq b^l \ \& \ a^u \leq b^u)$$

$$\bot^l = \bot \ \& \ \bot^u = \bot \ \& \ \top^l \leq \top \ \& \ \top^u \leq \top$$

$$(\forall a \in \mathbb{S}) \, \bot \leq a \leq \top$$

Pab *if and only if* $a \leq b$ *in the following three conditions. Further* $\mathbb{P}$ *is proper parthood (defined via* $\mathbb{P}ab$ *iff* **P**ab *&* $\neg$**P**ba*) and* t *is a term operation formed from the lattice operations):*

$$(\forall x \exists y_1, \ldots y_r \in \mathcal{G}) \, t(y_1, y_2, \ldots y_r) = x^l$$
$$\text{and} \, (\forall x) \, (\exists y_1, \ldots y_r \in \mathcal{G}) \, t(y_1, y_2, \ldots y_r) = x^u, \qquad \text{(Weak RA, WRA)}$$
$$(\forall y \in \mathcal{G})(\forall x \in \mathbb{S}) \, (\mathbf{P}yx \longrightarrow \mathbf{P}yx^l), \qquad \text{(Lower Stability, LS)}$$
$$(\forall x, y \in \mathcal{G})(\exists z \in \mathbb{S}) \, \mathbb{P}xz, \, \& \, \mathbb{P}yz \, \& \, z^l = z^u = z \qquad \text{(Full Underlap, FU)}$$

Definition 5. *An element $x \in \mathbb{S}$ will be said to be* lower definite *(resp. upper definite) if and only if $x^l = x$ (resp. $x^u = x$) and* definite, *when it is both lower and upper definite. $x \in \mathbb{S}$ will also be said to be* weakly upper definite *(resp weakly definite) if and only if $x^u = x^{uu}$ (resp $x^u = x^{uu}$ & $x^l = x$). Any one of these five concepts may be chosen as a concept of* crispness.

The following concepts of *rough objects* have been either considered in the literature (see [3]) or are reasonable concepts:

- $x \in \mathbb{S}$ is a lower rough object if and only if $\neg(x^l = x)$.
- $x \in \mathbb{S}$ is a upper rough object if and only if $\neg(x = x^u)$.
- $x \in \mathbb{S}$ is a weakly upper rough object if and only if $\neg(x^u = x^{uu})$.
- $x \in \mathbb{S}$ is a rough object if and only if $\neg(x^l = x^u)$.
- *Any pair of definite elements* of the form (a, b) satisfying $a < b$.
- *Any distinct pair of elements* of the form (x^l, x^u).
- Elements in an *interval of the form* (x^l, x^u).
- Elements in an *interval of the form* (a, b) satisfying $a \leq b$ with a, b being definite elements.
- A *non-definite element in a RYS* (see [3]), that is an x satisfying $\neg\mathbf{P}x^u x^l$.

All of the above concepts of a rough object except for the last are directly usable in a higher granular operator space. Importantly, *most of the results proved in this paper can hold for many choices of concepts of roughness and crispness. The reader is free to choose suitable combinations from the 40 possibilities.*

Example 1 (No Information Tables). It should be easy to see that most examples of general rough sets derived from information tables (and involving granules and granulations) can be read as higher granular operator space. So a nontrivial example of a higher granular operator space that has not been derived from an information system is presented below:

Suppose agent X wants to complete a task and this task is likely to involve the use of a number of tools. X thinks tool-1 suffices for the task that a tool-2 is not suited for the purpose and that tool-3 is better suited than tool-1 for the same task. X also believes that tool-4 is as suitable as tool-1 for the task and that tool-5 provides more than what is necessary for the task. X thinks similarly about other tools but not much is known about the consistency of the information. X has a large repository of tools and limited knowledge about tools and their suitability for different purposes, and at the same time X might be knowing more about difficulty of tasks that in turn require better tools of different kinds.

Suppose also that similar heuristics are available about other similar tasks. The reasoning of the agent in the situation can be recast in terms of lower, upper approximations and generalized equality and questions of interest include those relating to the agent's understanding of the features of tools, their appropriate usage contexts and whether the person thinks rationally.

To see this it should be noted that the key predicates in the context are as below:

- suffices for can be read as *includes potential lower approximation of* a right tool for the task.
- is not suited for can be read as *is neither a lower or upper approximation of* any of the right tools for the task.
- better suited than can be read as *potential rough inclusion,*
- is as suitable as can be read as *potential rough equality* and
- provides more than what is necessary for is for *upper approximation* of a right tool for the task.

Example 2 (Number of Objects). Often in the design, implementation and analysis of surveys (in the social sciences in particular), a number of intrusive assumptions on the sample are done and preconceived ideas about the population may influence survey design. Some assumptions that ensure that the sample is representative are obviously good, but as statistical methods are often abused [25] a minimal approach can help in preventing errors. The idea of samples being representative translates into number of non crisp objects being at least above a certain number and below a certain number. There are also situations (as when prior information is not available or ideas of representative samples are unclear) when such bounds may not be definable or of limited interest.

Example 3 (Non-rough Approximations). Suppose $X_1, \ldots X_{24}$ are 24 colors defined by distinct frequencies and suppose the weak sensors at disposal can identify 3 of them as crisp colors. If it is required that the other 21 colors be approximated as 9 rough objects, then such a classification would not be possible in a rough scheme of things as at most three distinct pairs of crisp objects are possible. Note that using intervals of frequencies, tolerances can be defined on the set. But under the numeric restriction, 9 rough objects would not be possible.

3.1 Minimal Assumptions

For the considerations of the following sections on distribution of rough objects and on counting to be valid, a minimal set of assumptions are necessary. These will be followed unless indicated otherwise:

F1 $\mathbb{S}$ is a higher granular operator space.
F2 $\#(\mathbb{S}) = n < \infty$.
C1 $C \subseteq \mathbb{S}$ is the set of crisp objects.
C2 $\#(C) = k$.
R1 $R \subset \mathbb{S}$ is the set of rough objects not necessarily defined as in the above.
R2 $R \cup C = \mathbb{S}$.

R3 there exists a map $\varphi : R \longmapsto C^2$.
RC1 $R \cap C = \emptyset$.
RC2 $(\forall x \in R)(\exists a, b \in C)\varphi(x) = (a, b)$ & $a \subset b$.

Note that no further assumptions are made about the nature of $\varphi(x)$. It is not required that $\varphi(x) = (a, b)$ & $x^l = a$ & $x^u = b$, though this happens often.

The set of crisp objects is necessarily partially ordered. In specific cases, this order may be a lattice, distributive, relatively complemented or Boolean order. Naturally the combinatorial features associated with higher granular operator space depend on the nature of the partial order. This results in situations that are way more involved than the situation encoded by the following simple proposition.

Proposition 1. *Under all of the above assumptions, for a fixed value of* $\#(\mathbb{S}) = n$ *and* $\#(C) = k$, R *must be representable by a finite subset* $K \subseteq C^2 \setminus \Delta_C$, Δ_C *being the diagonal in* C^2.

The two most extreme cases of the ordering of the set C of crisp objects correspond to C forming a chain and $C \setminus \{\perp, \top\}$ forming an anti-chain. Numeric measures for these distributions have been defined for these in [17] by the present author. The measure gives an idea of the extent of distribution of non crisp objects over the distribution of the crisp objects and it has also been shown that such measures do not provide reasonable comparisons across diverse contexts.

4 Pre-well Distribution of Objects over Chains: PWC

Definition 6. *A distribution of rough objects relative to a chain of crisp objects* C *will be said to be a* Pre-Well Distribution of Objects over Chains *if the minimal assumptions (Subsect. 3.1) (without the condition RC1) and the following three conditions hold:*

1. *C forms a chain under inclusion order.*
2. *φ is a surjection.*
3. *Pairs of the form (x, x), with x being a crisp object, also correspond to rough objects.*

Though the variant is intended as an abstract reference case where the idea of crispness is expressed subliminally, there are very relevant practical contexts for it (see Example 4). It should also be noted that this interpretation is not compatible with the interval way of representing rough objects without additional tweaking.

Theorem 3. *Under the above assumptions, the number of crisp objects is related to the total number of objects by the formula:*

$$k \overset{i}{=} \frac{(1 + 4n)^{\frac{1}{2}} - 1}{2}.$$

In the formula $\overset{i}{=}$ *is to be read as* if the right hand side (RHS) is an integer then the left hand side is the same as RHS.

Proof. • Clearly the number of rough objects is $n - k$.
- By the nature of the surjection $n - k$ maps to k^2 pairs of crisp objects.
- So $n - k = k^2$.
- So integral values of $\dfrac{(1 + 4n)^{\frac{1}{2}} - 1}{2}$ will work.

□

This result is associated with the distribution of odd square integers of the form $4n + 1$ which in turn should necessarily be of the form $4(p^2 + p) + 1$ (p being any integer). The requirement that these be perfect squares causes the distribution of crisp objects to be very sparse with increasing values of n. The number of rough objects between two successive crisp objects increases in a linear way, but this is a misleading aspect. These are illustrated in the graphs Figs. 1 and 2.

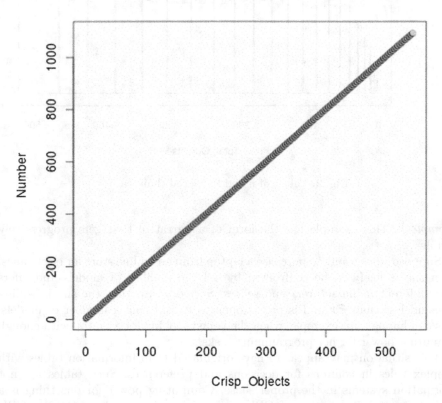

Rough and Crisp Objects: Chain Case

Fig. 1. Rough objects between crisp objects: special chain case

Crisp vs Total: Special Chain Case

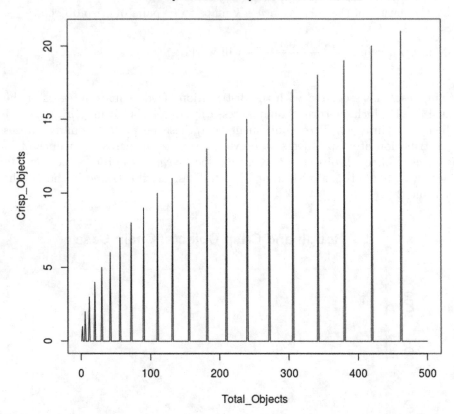

Fig. 2. Values of n and k: special chain case

Example 4. This example has the form of a narrative that gets progressively complex.

Suppose Alice wants to purchase a laptop from an on line store for electronics. Then she is likely to be confronted by a large number of models and offers from different manufacturers and sellers. Suppose also that the she is willing to spend less than €x and is pretty open to considering a number of models. This can happen, for example, when she is just looking for a laptop with enough computing power for her programming tasks.

This situation may appear to have originated from information tables with complex rules in columns for decisions and preferences. Such tables are not information systems in the proper sense. Computing power for one thing is a context dependent function of CPU cache memories, number of cores, CPU frequency, RAM, architecture of chipset, and other factors like type of hard disk storage.

Proposition 2. *The set of laptops* $\mathbb{S}$ *that are priced less than* €x *can be totally quasi ordered.*

Proof. Suppose $\prec$ is the relation defined according to $a \prec b$ if and only if price of laptop a is less than or equal to that of laptop b. Then it is easy to see that $\prec$ is a reflexive and transitive relation. If two different laptops a and b have the same price, then $a \prec b$ and $b \prec a$ would hold. So $\prec$ may not be antisymmetric. □

Suppose that under an additional constraint like CPU brand preference, the set of laptops becomes totally ordered. That is under a revised definition of $\prec$ of the form: $a \prec b$ if and only if price of laptop a is less than that of laptop b and if the prices are equal then CPU brand of b must be preferred over a's.

Suppose now that Alice has more knowledge about a subset C of models in the set of laptops $\mathbb{S}$. Let these be labeled as *crisp* and let the order on C be $\prec_{|C}$. Using additional criteria, rough objects can be indicated. Though lower and upper approximations can be defined in the scenario, the granulations actually used are harder to arrive at without all the gory details.

This example once again shows that granulation and construction of approximations from granules may not be related to the construction of approximations from properties in a cumulative way.

5 Well Distribution of Objects over Chains: WDC

Definition 7. *A distribution of rough objects relative to a chain of crisp objects C will be said to be a* Well Distribution of Objects over Chains *if the minimal assumptions (Subsect. 3.1) and the following two conditions hold:*

1. *C forms a chain under $\prec$ order.*
2. *φ is an surjection onto $C^2 \setminus \Delta_C$ (Δ_C being the diagonal of C).*

In this case pairs of the form (a, a) (with a being crisp) are not permitted to be regarded as rough objects. This amounts to requiring clearer conditions on the idea of what rough objects ought to be.

Example 5. In the example for pre-well distributions, if Alice never let a crisp object be a rough object, then the resulting example would fall under well distribution of objects over chains. In other words, the laptops would be well distributed over the crisp objects (crisp models of laptops).

Theorem 4. *When the objects are well distributed over the crisp objects, then the number of crisp objects would be related to the total number of objects by the formula:*

$$n - k = k^2 - k$$

So, it is necessary that n be a perfect square.

Proof. • Under the assumptions, an object is either rough or is crisp.
• The number of rough objects is $n - k$.
• By the nature of the surjection $n - k$ maps to $k^2 - k$ pairs of crisp objects (as the diagonal cannot represent rough objects).
• So $n - k = k^2 - k$.
• So $n = k^2$ is necessary.

$\square$

Theorem 5. *Under the assumptions of this section, if the higher granular operator space is a Boolean algebra then the cardinality of the Boolean algebra 2^x is determined by integral solutions for x in*

$$2^x = k^2.$$

Proof. As the number of elements in a finite power set must be of the form 2^x for some positive integer x, the correspondence follows. If $2^x = k^2$, then $x = 2 \log_2 k$.

$\square$

Remark 1. The previous theorem translates to a very sparse distribution of such models. In fact for $n \leq 10^8$, the total number of models is 27. Fig. 3 gives an idea of the numbers that work.

6   Relaxed Distribution of Objects over Chains: RDC

Definition 8. *A distribution of rough objects relative to a chain of crisp objects C will be said to be a α-Relaxed Distribution of Objects over Chains if the minimal assumptions (Subsect. 3.1) and the following three conditions hold.*

• *C forms a chain under $\prec$ order.*
• *φ is not necessarily a surjection and*

$$\#(\varphi(R)) \leq \alpha(k^2 - k),$$

for some rational $\alpha \in (0, 1]$ (the interpretation of α being that of a loose upper bound rather than an exact one).

Any value of α that is consistent with the inequality will be referred to as an admissible *value of α.*

Example 6. The following modifications, in the context of Example 5, are more common in practice:

• No non crisp laptops may be represented by some pairs of crisp laptops and consequently φ would not be a surjection onto $C^2 \setminus \Delta_C$ and
• an estimate of the number of rough laptops may be known (this applies when too many models are available).

These can lead to some estimate of α. *It should be noted that a natural subproblem is that of finding good values of α.*

Existence of Power Rough Sets on Chain

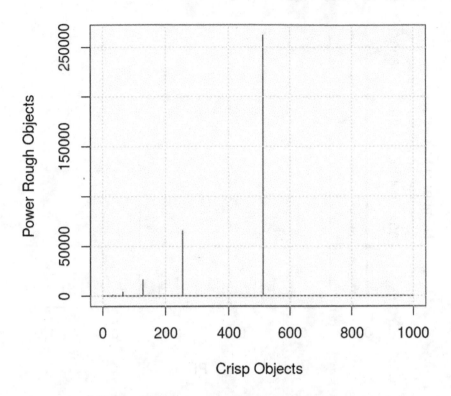

Fig. 3. Existence of power rough sets on chain

Theorem 6. *In the context of relaxed distribution of objects over chains it is provable that, for fixed n the possible values of k correspond to integral solutions of the formula:*

$$k = \frac{(\pi - 1) + \sqrt{(1 - \pi)^2 + 4n\pi}}{2\pi},$$

subject to $k \leq \lfloor \sqrt{n} \rfloor$, $\#(\varphi(R)) = \pi(k^2 - k)$ and $0 < \pi \leq \alpha$.

Proof. • When $n - k = \pi(k^2 - k)$ then $\pi = \dfrac{(n - k)}{(k^2 - k)}$

• So positive integral solutions of $k = \dfrac{(\pi - 1) + \sqrt{(1 - \pi)^2 + 4n\pi}}{2\pi}$ may be admissible.

• The expression for α means that it can only take a finite set of values given n as possible values of k must be in the set $\{2, 3, \ldots, \lfloor \sqrt{\frac{n}{\alpha}} \rfloor\}$.

$\square$

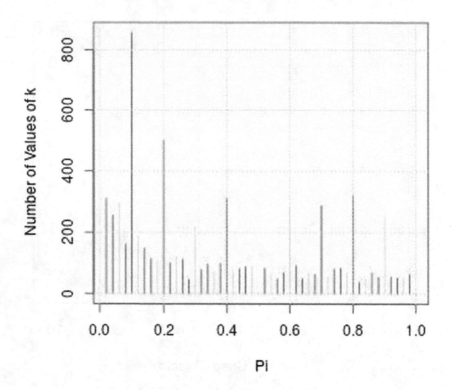

Fig. 4. Trimmed number of possible values of k

Remark 2. The bounds for k are not necessarily the best ones.

Theorem 7. *In the proof of the above theorem (Theorem 6), fixed values of n and π do not in general correspond to unique values of k and unique models.*

If the mentioned bounds on k are not imposed then it might appear that *for $\pi = 0.5$ and $n = 1000000$, the number of values of k that work seem to be 1413.* If the bounds on k are imposed then Fig. 4 gives a description of the resulting pattern of values:

Algorithms: RDC

A purely arbitrary method of supplying values of α based on *some heuristics* cannot be a tractable idea. To improve on this some algorithms for computing admissible values of *alpha* are proposed in this subsection.

RDC Algorithm-1

1. Fix the value of n.

2. Start from possible values of k less than $\sqrt{n-1}$.
3. Compute α for all of these values.
4. Suppose the computed values are $\alpha_1, \ldots \alpha_r$.
5. Check the admissibility of solutions.

RDC Algorithm-2

Another algorithm for converging to solutions is the following:

1. Start from a sequence $\{\alpha_i\}$ of possible values in the interval $(0, 1)$.
2. Check the admissibility and closeness to solutions.
3. If a solution appears to be between α_i and α_{i+1}, add an equally spaced subsequence between the two.
4. Check the admissibility and closeness to solutions.
5. Continue.
6. Stop when solution is found.

Theorem 8. *Both of the above algorithms converge in a finite number of steps.*

Proof. Convergence of the first algorithm is obvious.

Convergence of the second follows from the following construction:

- Suppose the goal is to converge to an $\alpha \in (0, 1)$.
- Let $\alpha_o = 0$, $\alpha_1 = 1$ and for a fixed positive integer n and $i = 1, \ldots, n$, let $\alpha_{1i} = \frac{i}{n}$ and $\alpha \in (\alpha_{1j}, \alpha_{1j+1})$.
- Form n number of equally spaced partitions $\{\alpha_{2i}\}$ of $(\alpha_{1j}, \alpha_{1j+1})$ and let $\alpha \in (\alpha_{2j}, \alpha_{2j+1})$.
- Clearly $(\forall \epsilon > 0 \, \exists N \, \forall r > N) \, |\alpha - \alpha_{rj}| < \epsilon$.
- So the algorithm will succeed in finding the required α.

$\square$

7   Relaxed Bounded Distribution on Chains: RBC

Definition 9. *A distribution of rough objects relative to a chain of crisp objects C will be said to be a α-Relaxed Bounded Distribution of Objects over Chains (RBC) if the minimal assumptions (Subsect. 3.1) and the following three conditions hold.*

- *C forms a chain under $\prec$ order and φ is not necessarily a surjection,*

$$\#(\varphi(R)) \le \alpha(k^2 - k),$$

for some rational $\alpha \in (0, 1]$ (the interpretation of α being that of a loose upper bound rather than an exact one) and
- *R is partitioned into disjoint subsets of size $\{r_i\}_{i=1}^g$ with $g = k^2 - k$ subject to the condition*

$$a \le r_i \le b \le n - k, \text{ with } a, b \text{ being constants.} \tag{β}$$

Any value of α that is consistent with the inequality will be referred to as an admissible value of α.

RBC differs from RDC in the explicit specification of bounds on number of objects that may be represented by a pair of crisp objects.

Proposition 3. *For $a = 0$ and $b = n - k$, every RDC is a RBC.*

Theorem 9. *If the crisp objects form a chain, then the total number of possible models B is*

$$B = \sum_{\alpha \in \pi(r)|\beta} \prod_{i=1}^{k^2-k} \alpha_i \text{ and } n_o a^{k^2-k} \le B \le n_o b^{k^2-k},$$

with the summation being over partitions $\alpha = \{\alpha_i\}$ of r subject to the condition β and n_o being the number of admissible partitions under the conditions.

Proof. • On a chain of length k, $k^2 - k$ spaces can be filled.
- The next step is to determine the partitions $\pi(r)$ of r into $k^2 - k$ distinct parts.
- The condition β eliminates many of these partitions resulting in the admissible set of partitions $\pi(r)|\beta$.
- Each of the partitions $\alpha \in \pi(r)|\beta$ corresponds to $\prod_i \alpha_i$ number of possibilities.
- So the result follows.

□

8   Distribution of Objects: General Context

Definition 10. *A distribution of rough objects relative to a poset of crisp objects C will be said to be a α-Relaxed Bounded Distribution of Objects (RBO) if the minimal assumptions (Subsect. 3.1) without the restriction R2 and the following three conditions hold:*

- $\#(\varphi(R)) = t \le n - k,$
- $t = \beta(k^2 - k)$ *and,*
- $n - k = \alpha(k^2 - k),$ *for some constants t, β, α.*

Example 7. In the context of Example 5, if Alice is not able to indicate a single criteria for the chain order, then the whole context would naturally fall under the context of this section.

This perspective can also be used in more general contexts that fall outside the scope of SHG. It is possible, in practice, that objects are neither crisp or rough. This can happen, for example, when:

- a consistent method of identifying crisp objects is not used or
- some objects are merely labeled on the basis of poorly defined partials of features or
- a sufficiently rich set of features that can provide for consistent identification is not used

For RBO, in the absence of additional information about the order structure, it is possible to rely on chain decompositions or use generalized ideals and choice functions for developing computational considerations based on the material of the earlier sections. The latter is specified first in what follows.

Definition 11. *The* lower definable scope $\mathbf{SL}(x)$ *of an element* $x \in R$ *will be the set of maximal elements in* $\downarrow (x) \cap C$, *that is*

$$\mathbf{SL}(x) = \max(\downarrow (x) \cap C).$$

The upper definable scope $\mathbf{SU}(x)$ *of an element* $x \in R$ *will be the set of minimal elements in* $\uparrow (x) \cap C$, *that is*

$$\mathbf{SU}(x) = \min(\uparrow (x) \cap C).$$

All representations of rough objects can be seen as the result of choice operations

$$\psi_x : \mathbf{SL}(x) \times \mathbf{SU}(x) \longmapsto C^2 \setminus \Delta_C.$$

Letting $\#(\mathbf{SL}(x)) = c(x)$ and $\#(\mathbf{SU}(x)) = v(x)$ formulas for possible values may be obtainable. Finding a simplification without additional assumptions remains an open problem though.

Chain Covers

Let C^* be the set of crisp objects C with the induced partial order, then by the theorem in Sect. 2.1, the order structure of the poset of crisp objects C^* permits a disjoint chain cover. This permits an incomplete strategy for estimating the structure of possible models and counting the number of models.

- Let $\{C_i : i = 1, \ldots h\}$ be a disjoint chain cover of C^*. Chains starting from a and ending at b will be denoted by $[[a, b]]$.
- Let C_1 be the chain $[[0, 1]]$ from the the smallest(empty) to the largest object.
- If C_1 has no branching points, then without loss of generality, it can be assumed that $C_2 = [[c_{2l}, c_{2g}]]$ is another chain with least element c_{2l} and greatest element c_{2g} such that $0 \prec c_{21}$, possibly $c_{2g} \prec 1$ and certainly $c_{2g} < 1$.
- If $c_{2g} < 1$, then the least element of at least two other chains ($[[c_{3l}, c_{3g}]]$ and $[[c_{4l}, c_{4g}]]$) must cover c_{2g}, that is $c_{2g} \prec c_{3l}$ and $c_{2g} \prec c_{4l}$.
- This process can be extended till the whole poset is covered.
- The first step for distributing the rough objects amongst these crisp objects consists in identifying the spaces distributed over maximal chains on the disjoint cover subject to avoiding over counting of parts of chains below branching points.

The above motivates the following combinatorial problem for solving the general problem:

Let $H = [[c_l, c_g]]$ be a chain of crisp objects with $\#(H) = \alpha$ and let c_o be a branching point on the chain with $\#([[c_l, c_o]]) = \alpha_o$. Let

$$S_C = \{(a, b) \,;\, a, b \in [[c_o, c_g]] \text{ or } c_l < a, b < c_o\}.$$

In how many ways can a subset $R_f \subseteq R$ of rough objects be distributed over S_C under $\#(R_f) = \pi$?

Theorem 10. *If the number of possible ways of distributing r rough objects over a chain of h crisp elements is $n(r, h)$, then the number of models in the above problem is*

$$n(r, h) - n(r, h_o).$$

Proof. This is because the places between crisp objects in $[[c_l, c_o]]$ must be omitted. The exact expression of $n(r, h)$ has already been described earlier.   □

Using the above theorem it is possible to evaluate the models starting with splitting of $n - k$ into atmost w partitions. *Because of this it is not necessary to use principal order filters generated by crisp objects to arrive at direct counts of the number of possible cases and a representation schematics.*

8.1   Applications: Hybrid Swarm Optimization

Many unsupervised and semi-supervised algorithms do not converge properly and steps involved may have dense and unclear meaning. The justification for using such algorithms often involve analogies that may appear to be reasonable at one level and definitely suspect in broader perspectives - typically this can be expected to happen when the independent intelligence of computational agents or potential sources of intelligence in the context are disregarded. For example, the class of ant colony algorithms (see [26]) uses probabilist assumptions and restricted scope for control at the cost of simplifying assumptions.

For example, for a set of robots to navigate unfamiliar terrain with obstacles, a swarm optimization method like the polymorphic ant colony optimization method may be used [27]. The method involves scouts, workers and other types of robots (ants). Additional information about the terrain can be used to assess the quality of paths being found through the methods developed in this paper - the guiding principle for this can be that *if the approximations of obstacles or better paths do not fit in a rough scheme of things, then the polymorphic optimization method is warranted.*

The other kind of situation where the same heuristics can apply is when the robots are not fully autonomous and under partial control as in a hacking context. More details of these applications will appear in a separate paper.

9   Interpretation and Directions

The results proved in this research are relevant from multiple perspectives. In the perspective that does not bother with issues of contamination, the results mean that the number of rough models relative to the number of other possible models of computational intelligence is low. This can be disputed as the signature of the model is restricted and categoricity does not hold.

In the perspective of the contamination problem, the axiomatic approach to granules, the results help in handling inverse problems in particular. From a minimum of information, it may be possible to deduce

- whether a rough model is possible or
- whether a rough model is not possible or
- whether the given data is part of some minimal rough extensions

The last possibility can be solved by keeping fixed the number of rough objects or otherwise. These problems apply for the contaminated approach too. It should be noted that extensions need to make sense in the first place. The results can also be expected to have many applications in hybrid, probabilist approaches and variants.

An important problem that has not been explored in this paper is the concept of isomorphism between higher granular operator spaces. This is considered in a forthcoming paper by the present author.

References

1. Pawlak, Z.: Rough Sets: Theoretical Aspects of Reasoning About Data. Kluwer Academic Publishers, Dodrecht (1991)
2. Duntsch, I., Gediga, G.: Rough Set Data Analysis: A Road to Non-invasive Knowledge Discovery. Methodos Publishers, Bangor (2000)
3. Mani, A.: Dialectics of counting and the mathematics of vagueness. In: Peters, J.F., Skowron, A. (eds.) Transactions on Rough Sets XV. LNCS, vol. 7255, pp. 122–180. Springer, Heidelberg (2012). doi:10.1007/978-3-642-31903-7_4
4. Polkowski, L.: Approximate Reasoning by Parts. Springer, Heidelberg (2011)
5. Skowron, A.: Rough sets and vague concepts. Fund. Inform. **64**(1–4), 417–431 (2005)
6. Pagliani, P., Chakraborty, M.: A Geometry of Approximation: Rough Set Theory: Logic, Algebra and Topology of Conceptual Patterns. Springer, Berlin (2008)
7. Banerjee, M., Chakraborty, M.K.: Rough sets through algebraic logic. Fundam. Informaticae **28**, 211–221 (1996)
8. Duntsch, I.: Rough sets and algebras of relations. In: Orłowska, E. (ed.) Incomplete Information and Rough Set Analysis, pp. 95–108. Physica, Heidelberg (1998). doi:10.1007/978-3-7908-1888-8_5
9. Mani, A.: Super rough semantics. Fundam. Informaticae **65**(3), 249–261 (2005)
10. Düntsch, I., Gediga, G., Orłowska, E.: Relational attribute systems II: reasoning with relations in information structures. In: Peters, J.F., Skowron, A., Marek, V.W., Orłowska, E., Słowiński, R., Ziarko, W. (eds.) Transactions on Rough Sets VII. LNCS, vol. 4400, pp. 16–35. Springer, Heidelberg (2007). doi:10.1007/978-3-540-71663-1_2
11. Duntsch, I., Gediga, G., Orlowska, E.: Relational attribute systems. Int. J. Hum. Comput. Stud. **55**(3), 293–309 (2001)
12. Malcev, A.I.: The Metamathematics of Algebraic Systems - Collected Papers. North Holland, Amsterdam (1971)

13. Banerjee, M., Chakraborty, M.K.: Algebras from rough sets - an overview. In: Pal, S.K., et al. (eds.) Rough-Neural Computing, pp. 157–184. Springer, Heidelberg (2004). doi:10.1007/978-3-642-18859-6_7

14. Duntsch, I., Orlowska, E.: Discrete duality for rough relation algebras. Fundam. Informaticae **127**, 35–47 (2013)

15. Mani, A.: Ontology, rough Y-systems and dependence. Int. J. Comput. Sci. Appl. **11**(2), 114–136 (2014). Special Issue of IJCSA on Computational Intelligence

16. Mani, A.: Antichain based semantics for rough sets. In: Ciucci, D., Wang, G., Mitra, S., Wu, W.-Z. (eds.) RSKT 2015. LNCS, vol. 9436, pp. 335–346. Springer, Cham (2015). doi:10.1007/978-3-319-25754-9_30

17. Mani, A.: Knowledge and consequence in AC semantics for general rough sets. In: Wang, G., Skowron, A., Yao, Y., Ślęzak, D. (eds.) Thriving Rough Sets: 10th Anniversary - Honoring Professor Zdzisław Pawlak's Life and Legacy & 35 Years of Rough Sets, vol. 708, pp. 237–268. Springer International Publishing, Heidelberg (2017)

18. Mani, A.: On deductive systems of AC semantics for rough sets, pp. 1–12. ArXiv Math arXiv:1610.02634v1, October 2016

19. Stepaniuk, J.: Rough - Granular Computing in Knowledge Discovery and Data Mining. Studies in Computational Intelligence, vol. 152. Springer, Heidelberg (2009)

20. Mani, A.: Algebraic semantics of proto-transitive rough sets. In: Peters, J.F., Skowron, A. (eds.) Transactions on Rough Sets XX. LNCS, vol. 10020, pp. 51–108. Springer, Heidelberg (2016). doi:10.1007/978-3-662-53611-7_3

21. Mani, A.: Towards an algebraic approach for cover based rough semantics and combinations of approximation spaces. In: Sakai, H., Chakraborty, M.K., Hassanien, A.E., Ślęzak, D., Zhu, W. (eds.) RSFDGrC 2009. LNCS, vol. 5908, pp. 77–84. Springer, Heidelberg (2009). doi:10.1007/978-3-642-10646-0_9

22. Mani, A.: Pure rough mereology and counting. In: WIECON 2016, pp. 1–8. IEEXPlore (2016)

23. Kung, J.P.S., Rota, G.C., Yan, C.H.: Combinatorics-The Rota Way. Cambridge University Press, Cambridge (2009)

24. Davey, B.A., Priestley, H.A.: Introduction to Lattices and Order, 2nd edn. Cambridge University Press, Cambridge (2002)

25. Morey, R.D., Hoekstra, R., Rouder, J.N., Lee, M.D.: The fallacy of placing confidence in confidence intervals. Technical report, August 2015

26. Dorigo, M., Blum, C.: Ant colony optimization theory: a survey. Theoret. Comput. Sci. **344**(2-3), 243–278 (2005)

27. Qing, C., Zhong, Y., Xiang, L.: Cloud database dynamic route scheduling based on polymorphic ant colony optimization algorithm. Comput. Modell. New Technol. **18**(2), 161–165 (2014)

Generalized Ideals and Co-granular Rough Sets

A. Mani[✉]

Department of Pure Mathematics, University of Calcutta,
9/1B, Jatin Bagchi Road, Kolkata (Calcutta) 700029, India
a.mani.cms@gmail.com
http://www.logicamani.in

Abstract. Lattice-theoretic ideals have been used to define and generate non granular rough approximations over general approximation spaces over the last few years by few authors. The goal of these studies, in relation based rough sets, have been to obtain nice properties comparable to those of classical rough approximations. In this research paper, these ideas are generalized in a severe way by the present author and associated semantic features are investigated by her. Granules are used in the construction of approximations in implicit ways and so a concept of co-granularity is introduced. Knowledge interpretation associable with the approaches is also investigated. This research will be of relevance for a number of logico-algebraic approaches to rough sets that proceed from point-wise definitions of approximations and also for using alternative approximations in spatial mereological contexts involving actual contact relations. The antichain based semantics invented in earlier papers by the present author also applies to the contexts considered.

Keywords: Co-granular approximations by ideals · High operator spaces · Generalized ideals · Rough objects · Granular operator spaces · Algebraic semantics · Knowledge · Mereotopology · Rough spatial mereology · GOSIH

1 Introduction

In general rough set theory that specifically targets information systems as the object of study, approximations are defined relative to information systems and rough objects of various kinds are studied [1–3]. These approximations may be defined relative to some concept of granules or they may be defined without direct reference to any concept of granules or granulations. The corresponding approximations are in general not equivalent. Among the latter class, few new approximations have been studied in [4–6] over general approximation spaces of the form (X, R) with X being a set and R being at least a reflexive relation. *In these approximations, a point is in an approximation of a subset of X if it satisfies a condition that involves lattice ideals of the Boolean power set lattice.* The formalism in the overview paper [6] makes use of a more laborious formalism - but is essentially equivalent to what has been stated in the last sentence.

© Springer International Publishing AG 2017
L. Polkowski et al. (Eds.): IJCRS 2017, Part II, LNAI 10314, pp. 23–42, 2017.
DOI: 10.1007/978-3-319-60840-2_2

The significance of the obtained results and potential application contexts are not explored in the three papers mentioned [4–6] in sufficient detail and many open problems remain hidden.

In this research paper, a definition of co-granularity of approximations is introduced, the methodology is generalized to specific modifications of granular operator spaces [7,8] (called co-granular operator spaces) and in particular to lattices generated by collections of sets and lattice ideals, connections with general approximation spaces (or adjacency spaces) are dropped, connections with granular operator spaces are established, issues in possible semantics of the generalized approach are computed, knowledge interpretation in the contexts are proposed, meaningful examples are constructed, ideal based rough approximations are shown to be natural in spatial mereological contexts and related problems are posed. One meaning that stands out in all this is that *if a property has little to do with what something is not, then that something has the property in an approximate sense.* This idea might work in some contexts - the developed/invented formalisms suggest some restrictions on possible contexts.

Ideals and filters have been used by the present author in algebraic semantics of general rough sets in some of her earlier papers like [1,9–11]. Concepts of rough ideals have also been studied by different authors in specific algebras (see for example [12,13])- these studies involve the use of rough concepts within algebras. The methodology of the present paper does not correspond to those used in the mentioned papers in a direct way.

In the next section, some of the essential background is mentioned. In Sect. 3, generalized set theoretic frameworks are introduced and properties of approximations are proved. In the following section, co-granular operator spaces are defined and studied. In Sect. 5, the meaning of the approximations and generalizations are explained for the first time and both abstract and concrete examples are constructed. Mereotopological approximations are invented/developed over very recent work on actual contact algebras in Sect. 6.

2   Background

By an *Information System* $\mathcal{I}$, is meant a tuple of the form

$$\mathcal{I} = \langle \mathbb{O}, At, \{V_a : a \in At\}, \{f_a : a \in At\}\rangle$$

with $\mathbb{O}, At$ and V_a being respectively sets of *Objects*, *Attributes* and *Values* respectively. In general the valuation has the form $f_a : O \longmapsto \wp(V)$, where $V = \bigcup V_a$ (as in indeterminate information systems). These can be used to generate various types of relational, covering or relator spaces which in turn relate to approximations of different types and form a substantial part of the problems encountered in general rough set theories. One way of defining an indiscernibility relation σ is as below:

For $x, y \in \mathbb{O}$ and $B \subseteq At, (x, y) \in \sigma$ if and only if $(\forall a \in B)\nu(a, x) = \nu(a, y)$. In this case σ is an equivalence relation. Lower and upper approximations, rough equalities are defined over it and topological algebraic semantics can be formulated over *roughly equivalent* objects (or subsets of attributes) through extra operations. Duality theorems, proved for *pre-rough* algebras defined in [14], are specifically for structures relation isomorphic to the approximation space $(\mathbb{O}, \sigma)$. This is also true of the representation results in [15–17]. But these are not for information systems - optimal concepts of *isomorphic information systems* are considered by the present author in a forthcoming paper.

In fact in [15], it has been proved by the present author that

Theorem 1. *For every super rough algebra S, there exists an approximation space X such that the super rough set algebra generated by X is isomorphic to S.*

The concept of *inverse problem* was introduced by the present author in [15] and was subsequently refined in [1]. In simple terms, the problem is a generalization of the duality problem which may be obtained by replacing the semantic structures with parts thereof. Thus the goal of the problem is to fit a given set of approximations and some semantics to a suitable rough process originating from an information system. From the practical perspective, a few (as opposed to one) theoretical frameworks may be suitable for formulating the problem itself. The theorem mentioned above is an example of a solution of the *inverse problem* in the associated context.

The definition of approximations maybe granular, point wise, abstract or otherwise. In simple terms, *granules* are the subsets (or objects) that generate approximations and *granulations* are the collections of all such granules in the context. For more details see [1,18]. In this paper a variation of generalized granular operator spaces, introduced and studied by the present author in [7,8], will serve as the main framework for most considerations. For reference, related definitions are mentioned below.

Definition 1. *A Granular Operator Space [7] GOS S is a structure of the form $S = \langle \underline{S}, \mathcal{G}, l, u \rangle$ with $\underline{S}$ being a set, $\mathcal{G}$ an admissible granulation(defined below) over S and l, u being operators : $\wp(\underline{S}) \longmapsto \wp(\underline{S})$ ($\wp(\underline{S})$ denotes the power set of $\underline{S}$) satisfying the following ($\underline{S}$ is replaced with S if clear from the context. Lower and upper case alphabets may denote subsets):*

$$a^l \subseteq a \ \& \ a^{ll} = a^l \ \& \ a^u \subseteq a^{uu}$$

$$(a \subseteq b \longrightarrow a^l \subseteq b^l \ \& \ a^u \subseteq b^u)$$

$$\emptyset^l = \emptyset \ \& \ \emptyset^u = \emptyset \ \& \ \underline{S}^l \subseteq S \ \& \ \underline{S}^u \subseteq S.$$

In the context of this definition, Admissible Granulations *are granulations $\mathcal{G}$ that satisfy the following three conditions (t is a term operation formed from the set operations $\cup, \cap, {}^c, 1, \emptyset$):*

$$(\forall a \exists b_1, \ldots b_r \in \mathcal{G}) \, t(b_1, b_2, \ldots b_r) = a^l$$

$$\text{and } (\forall a) \, (\exists b_1, \ldots b_r \in \mathcal{G}) \, t(b_1, b_2, \ldots b_r) = a^u, \qquad \text{(Weak RA, WRA)}$$

$$(\forall b \in \mathcal{G})(\forall a \in \wp(\underline{S})) \, (b \subseteq a \longrightarrow b \subseteq a^l), \qquad \text{(Lower Stability, LS)}$$

$$(\forall a, b \in \mathcal{G})(\exists z \in \wp(\underline{S})) \, a \subset z, \, b \subset z \ \& \ z^l = z^u = z, \qquad \text{(Full Underlap, FU)}$$

The concept of admissible granulation was defined for rough Y-systems RYS (a more general framework due to the present author in [1]) using parthoods instead of set inclusion and relative to RYS, $\mathbf{P} =\subseteq, \mathbb{P} =\subset$ in granular operator spaces [7]. The concept of *generalized granular operator spaces* has been introduced in [8] by the present author as a proper generalization of that of granular operator spaces. The main difference is in the replacement of $\subset$ by arbitrary *part of* ($\mathbf{P}$) relations in the axioms of admissible granules and inclusion of $\mathbf{P}$ in the signature of the structure.

Definition 2. *A General Granular Operator Space (GSP) S is a structure of the form $S = \langle \underline{S}, \mathcal{G}, l, u, \mathbf{P} \rangle$ with $\underline{S}$ being a set, $\mathcal{G}$ an* admissible granulation*(defined below) over S, l, u being operators : $\wp(\underline{S}) \longmapsto \wp(\underline{S})$ and $\mathbf{P}$ being a definable binary generalized transitive predicate (for parthood) on $\wp(\underline{S})$ satisfying the same conditions as in Definition 1 except for those on admissible granulations (Generalized transitivity can be any proper nontrivial generalization of parthood (see [11]). $\mathbb{P}$ is proper parthood (defined via $\mathbb{P}ab$ iff $\mathbf{P}ab$ & $\neg\mathbf{P}ba$) and t is a term operation formed from set operations on the powerset $\wp(S)$):*

$$(\forall x \exists y_1, \ldots y_r \in \mathcal{G})\, t(y_1, y_2, \ldots y_r) = x^l$$
$$\text{and } (\forall x)\, (\exists y_1, \ldots y_r \in \mathcal{G})\, t(y_1, y_2, \ldots y_r) = x^u, \qquad \text{(Weak RA, WRA)}$$
$$(\forall y \in \mathcal{G})(\forall x \in \wp(\underline{S}))\, (\mathbf{P}yx \longrightarrow \mathbf{P}yx^l), \qquad \text{(Lower Stability, LS)}$$
$$(\forall x, y \in \mathcal{G})(\exists z \in \wp(\underline{S}))\, \mathbb{P}xz, \,\& \mathbb{P}yz \,\&\, z^l = z^u = z, \qquad \text{(Full Underlap, FU)}$$

There are ways of defining rough approximations that do not fit into the above frameworks and the present paper is mainly about specific such cases.

2.1   Ideals on Posets

A *lattice ideal* K of a lattice $L = (L, \vee, \wedge)$ is a subset of L that satisfies the following ($\leq$ is assumed to the definable lattice order on L):

$$(\forall a \in L)(\forall b \in K)(a \leq b \longrightarrow a \in K) \qquad \text{(o-Ideal)}$$
$$(\forall a, b \in K)\, a \vee b \in K \qquad \text{(Join Closure)}$$

An ideal P in a lattice L is *prime* if and only if $(\forall a, b)(a \wedge b \in P \longrightarrow a \in P$ or $b \in P)$. $Spec(L)$ shall denote the set of all prime ideals. Maximal lattice filters are the same as ultrafilters. In Boolean algebras, any filter F that satisfies $(\forall a)a \in F$ or $a^c \in F$ is an ultra filter. *Chains* are subsets of a poset in which any two elements are comparable, while *antichains* are subsets of a poset in which no two distinct elements are comparable. Singletons are both chains and antichains.

2.2   Ideal Based Framework

The approximations in [6] are more general than the ones introduced and studied in [4,5]. A complete reformulation of the main definition and approximation is presented in this subsection. These approximations are not granular in any obvious way and need not fit into generalized granular operator spaces.

Definition 3

- Let $\langle X, R \rangle$ be a general approximation space with X being a set and R being a reflexive binary relation on X,
- $\langle \wp(X), \cup, \cap, \emptyset, X \rangle$ be the Boolean lattice on the power set of X. Any lattice ideal in the Boolean lattice would be referred to as an ideal and the collection of all ideals would be denoted by $\mathcal{I}(X)$ (this is algebraic distributive lattice ordered and the implicit σ used is the Boolean order $\subseteq$) and $\mathbb{I}$ a fixed ideal in it.
- Let $[x]^R = \{a : a \in X \ \& \ Rxa\}$ and $< x > = \bigcap\{[b]^R : b \in X \ \& \ x \in [b]^R\}$.
- $(\forall A \in \wp(X)) \ A^{l_\kappa} = \{a : a \in A \ \& \ < a > \cap A^c \in \mathbb{I}\}$
- $(\forall A \in \wp(X)) \ A^{u_\kappa} = \{a : a \in X \ \& \ < a > \cap A \notin \mathbb{I}\} \cup A$.

The approximations have properties similar to those of approximations in classical rough set theory using the point wise definition of approximations. This is mainly due to the nature of the sets of the form $< a >$.

Theorem 2. *All of the following hold for any subset $A, B \subseteq X$ in the context of the above definition:*

- $A^{l_\kappa} \subseteq A \subseteq A^{u_\kappa}$ and $\emptyset^{u_\kappa} = \emptyset, X^{l_\kappa} = X$
- $A \subset B \longrightarrow A^{l_\kappa} \subseteq B^{l_\kappa} \ \& \ A^{u_\kappa} \subseteq B^{u_\kappa}$
- $A^{l_\kappa l_\kappa} = A^{l_\kappa}, \ A^{u_\kappa u_\kappa} = A^{u_\kappa}; \ (\forall A \in \mathbb{I}) \ A^{u_\kappa} = A$
- $(A \cap B)^{l_\kappa} = A^{l_\kappa} \cap B^{l_\kappa}$ and $(A \cup B)^{l_\kappa} \supseteq A^{l_\kappa} \cup B^{l_\kappa}$
- $(A \cup B)^{u_\kappa} = A^{u_\kappa} \cup B^{u_\kappa}$ and $(A \cap B)^{u_\kappa} \subseteq A^{u_\kappa} \cap B^{u_\kappa}$
- $A^{u_\kappa} = (A^c)^{l_\kappa c}, \ A^{l_\kappa} = (A^c)^{u_\kappa c}$ and $(\forall A^c \in \mathbb{I}) \ A^{l_\kappa} = A$.

$\tau_R^* = \{A : A^{l_\kappa} = A\}$ is a topology.

3 Set-Theoretic Generalization of Ideal-Based Framework

Set theoretic generalizations of the approach in [4–6] are proposed in this section by the present author.

If R is a binary relation on a set S, then for any $x \in S$, the *successor neighborhood* $[x]_R$ generated by x is the set $[x]_R = \{a : a \in S \ \& \ Rax\}$, while the *predecessor neighborhood* $[x]^R$ is the set $[x]^R = \{a : a \in S \ \& \ Rxa\}$.

Definition 4

- Let $\langle X, R \rangle$ be a general approximation space with X being a set and R being a reflexive binary relation on X,
- $\mathcal{X}$ be a distributive lattice (a ring of subsets of X). Let $\mathcal{I}(X)$ be the lattice of lattice ideals of $\mathcal{X}$ and $\mathbb{I} \in \mathcal{I}(X)$
- Let $[x]^R = \{a : a \in X \ \& \ Rxa\}$ and $< x > = \bigcap\{[b]^R : b \in X \ \& \ x \in [b]^R\}$.
- $(\forall A \in \wp(X)) \ A^{l_k} = \{a : a \in A \ \& \ < a > \cap A^c \in \mathbb{I}\}$
- $(\forall A \in \wp(X)) \ A^{u_k} = \{a : a \in X \ \& \ < a > \cap A \notin \mathbb{I}\} \cup A$
- If $\mathcal{I}(X)$ is replaced by $Spec(X)$ in the last two statements, then the resulting lower and upper approximations will be denoted respectively by l_p and u_p.

The approximations will be referred to as Distributive set approximations by ideals *(IAD approximations). If in the second condition if $\mathcal{X}$ is an algebra of subsets of X instead, then the definitions of the approximations can be improved as below:*

- $(\forall A \in \mathcal{X})\, A^{l+} = \{a : a \in A \,\&\, <a> \setminus A \in \mathbb{I}\}$
- $(\forall A \in \mathcal{X})\, A^{u+} = \{a : a \in X \,\&\, <a> \cap A \notin \mathbb{I}\} \cup A$

These approximations will be referred to as Set difference approximations by ideals *(IASD approximations).*

When the ideals refer to a ring of subsets, the operations used in the definition of IAD approximations refer to an algebra of sets over X. IASD approximations are better behaved.

Proposition 1. *In the above, all of the following hold:*

- *For $a, b \in X$, if $a \in <b>$ then $<a> \subseteq <b>$.*
- *If τab if and only $a \in <b>$ then τ is a reflexive, transitive and weakly antisymmetric relation in the sense, if $\tau ab \,\&\, \tau ba$ then $<a> = <b>$.*

Theorem 3. *The IAD approximations are well defined and satisfy all of the following for any subsets A and B:*

$$A^{l_k} \subseteq A \subseteq A^{u_k} \tag{1}$$

$$\emptyset^{u_k} = \emptyset; \; X^{l_k} = X \tag{2}$$

$$A \subset B \longrightarrow A^{l_k} \subseteq B^{l_k} \,\&\, A^{u_k} \subseteq B^{u_k} \tag{3}$$

$$A^{l_k l_k} = A^{l_k}; \; A^{u_k u_k} = A^{u_k} \tag{4}$$

$$(A \cap B)^{l_k} = A^{l_k} \cap B^{l_k}; \; (A \cup B)^{l_k} \supseteq A^{l_k} \cup B^{l_k} \tag{5}$$

$$(A \cup B)^{u_k} = A^{u_k} \cup B^{u_k}; \; (A \cap B)^{u_k} \subseteq A^{u_k} \cap B^{u_k} \tag{6}$$

Proof

- $A^{l_k} \subseteq A \subseteq A^{u_k}$ follows from definition
- $\emptyset^{u_k} = \emptyset$ because it contains no elements. $X^{l_k} = X$ because $<x> \cap \emptyset = \emptyset$ is a trivial ideal.
-
$$\text{Let } A \subset B$$
$$\text{If } x \in A^{u_k} \text{ then } <x> \cap A \notin \mathbb{I}$$
$$\text{So } <x> \cap B \notin \mathbb{I} \text{ and } x \in B^{u_k}$$
$$\text{If } x \in A^{l_k} \text{ then } <x> \cap A^c \in \mathbb{I}$$
$$<x> \cap B^c \subset <x> \cap A^c \in \mathbb{I}$$
$$\text{and so } <x> \cap B^c \in \mathbb{I}(X) \text{ and } x \in B^{l_k}.$$

- If $a \in A^{l_k}$ then $<a> \cap A^c \in \mathbb{I}$ and $<a> \cap A^c \subseteq <a> \cap A^{l_k c}$. The converse also holds because of the definition of $<a>$. So $A^{l_k l_k} = A^{l_k}$.

- It is obvious that $A^{u_k} \subseteq A^{u_k u_k}$. If $x \in A^{u_k u_k}$, then $x \in A$ or $x \in < x > \cap A^{u_k} \notin \mathbb{I}$. As $< x > \cap A \subseteq < x > \cap A^{u_k}$, so $A^{u_k u_k} = A^{u_k}$.
- $x \in (A \cap B)^{l_k}$, if and only if $< x > \cap (A \cap B)^c \in \mathbb{I}$ and $x \in A \cap B$ if and only if $(< x > \cap A^c \in \mathbb{I}$ and $< x > \cap B^c \in \mathbb{I}$ and $x \in A \cap B$ So $(A \cap B)^{l_k} = A^{l_k} \cap B^{l_k}$.
- $x \in (A \cup B)^{l_k}$ if and only if $< x > \cap (A \cup B)^c \in \mathbb{I}$ and $x \in A \cup B$ if and only if $(< x > \cap A^c) \cap (< x > \cap B^c) \in \mathbb{I}$ and $x \in A \cup B$. This implies $(< x > \cap A^c) \in \mathbb{I}$ and $x \in A$ or $< x > \cap B^c \in \mathbb{I}$ and $x \in B$. So $(A \cup B)^{l_k} \supseteq A^{l_k} \cup B^{l_k}$.
- $x \in (A \cup B)^{u_k}$ if and only if $x \in A \cup B$ or $< x > \cap (A \cup B) \notin \mathbb{I}$. If $x \in A \cup B$, then $x \in A^{u_k} \cup B^{u_k}$. $< x > \cap (A \cup B) \notin \mathbb{I}$ if and only if $< x > \cap A \notin \mathbb{I}$ and $< x > \cap B \notin \mathbb{I}$. So it follows that $x \in A^{u_k} \cup B^{u_k}$ and conversely.
- $x \in (A \cap B)^{u_k}$ if and only if $x \in A \cap B$ or $< x > \cap (A \cap B) \notin \mathbb{I}$. If $x \in A \cap B$, then $x \in A^{u_k} \cap B^{u_k}$. $< x > \cap (A \cap B) \notin \mathbb{I}$ if and only if $< x > \cap A \notin \mathbb{I}$ or $< x > \cap B \notin \mathbb{I}$. So it follows that $(A \cap B)^{u_k} \subseteq A^{u_k} \cap B^{u_k}$.   □

Actually full complementation can be omitted and replaced with set difference. This way the approximations can be defined on subsets of the powerset.

Theorem 4. *The IASD approximations are well defined and satisfy all of the following for any subsets A and B in $\mathcal{X}$:*

$$A^{l+} \subseteq A \subseteq A^{u+}; \; \emptyset^{u+} = \emptyset; \; X^{l+} = X \tag{7}$$

$$A \subset B \longrightarrow A^{l+} \subseteq B^{l+} \; \& \; A^{u+} \subseteq B^{u+} \tag{8}$$

$$A^{l+l+} = A^{l+}; \; A^{u+u+} = A^{u+} \tag{9}$$

$$(A \cap B)^{l+} = A^{l+} \cap B^{l+}; \; (A \cup B)^{l+} \supseteq A^{l+} \cup B^{l+} \tag{10}$$

$$(A \cup B)^{u+} = A^{u+} \cup B^{u+}; \; (A \cap B)^{u+} \subseteq A^{u+} \cap B^{u+} \tag{11}$$

Proof. The proof is similar to that of the previous theorem. Relative complementation suffices.   □

Remark 1. The main advantages of the generalization are that knowledge of complementation is not required in construction of the IASD approximations, a potentially restricted collection of ideals is usable in the definition of approximations and this in turn improves computational efficiency.

4 Co-granular Operator Spaces by Ideals

Given a binary relation on a set it is possible to regard specific subsets of the set as generalized ideals relative to the relation in question. The original motivations for the approach relate to the strategies for generalizing the concept of lattice ideal to partially ordered sets (see [19–21]). It is also possible to use a binary relation on the power set to form generalized ideals consisting of some subsets of the set. Both approaches are apparently compatible with the methods used for defining approximations by ideals.

In this section the two possibilities are examined and generalizations called *co-granular operator spaces by ideals* and *higher co-granular operator spaces* are proposed.

Definition 5. *Let H be a set and σ a binary relation on H (that is $\sigma \subseteq H^2$) then*

- *The* Principal Up-set *generated by $a, b \in H$ shall be the set*

$$U(a, b) = \{x : \sigma a x \ \& \ \sigma b x\}.$$

- *The* Principal Down-set *generated by $a, b \in H$ shall be the set*

$$L(a, b) = \{x : \sigma x a \ \& \ \sigma x b\}.$$

- *$B \subseteq H$ is U-directed if and only if $(\forall a, b \in B) \, U(a, b) \cap B \neq \emptyset$.*
- *$B \subseteq H$ is L-directed if and only if $(\forall a, b \in B) \, L(a, b) \cap B \neq \emptyset$. If B is both U- and L-directed, then it is σ-directed.*
- *$K \subset H$ is a σ-ideal if and only if*

$$(\forall x \in H)(\forall a \in K)(\sigma x a \longrightarrow x \in K) \tag{12}$$

$$(\forall a, b \in K) \, U(a, b) \cap K \neq \emptyset \tag{13}$$

- *$F \subset H$ is a σ-filter if and only if*

$$(\forall x \in H)(\forall a \in F)(\sigma a x \longrightarrow x \in F) \tag{14}$$

$$(\forall a, b \in F) \, L(a, b) \cap F \neq \emptyset \tag{15}$$

- *The set of σ-ideals and σ-filters will respectively be denoted by $\mathcal{I}(H)$ and $\mathcal{F}(H)$ respectively. These are all partially ordered by the set inclusion order. If the intersection of all σ-ideals containing a subset $B \subset H$ is an σ-ideal, then it will be called the σ-ideal generated by B and denoted by $\langle B \rangle$. The collection of all principal σ-ideals will be denoted by $\mathcal{I}_p(H)$. If $\langle x \rangle$ exists for every $x \in H$, then H is said to be σ-principal (principal for short).*
- *A σ-ideal K will be said to be* prime *if and only if*

$$(\forall a, b \in H)(L(a, b) \cap K \neq \emptyset \longrightarrow a \in K \text{ or } b \in K).$$

The dual concept for filters can also be defined.
- *A subset $B \subseteq H$ will be said to be σ-convex if and only if*

$$(\forall a, b \in B)(\forall x \in H)(\sigma a x \ \& \ \sigma x b \longrightarrow x \in B)$$

Proposition 2. *All of the following hold in the context of the above definition:*

- *All σ-ideals are σ-convex and U-directed.*
- *If H is σ-directed, then all σ-ideals are σ-directed subsets.*
- *Every σ-ideal is contained in a maximal σ-ideal.*
- *If H is L-directed, K is a prime ideal and for $K_1, K_2 \in \mathcal{I}$ if $K_1 \cap K_2 \subseteq K$, then $K_1 \subseteq K_2$ or $K_2 \subseteq K_1$.*
- *If $\langle a \rangle, \langle b \rangle \in \mathcal{I}_p(H)$ and $\tau(\sigma)ab$ ($\tau(\sigma)$ being the transitive completion of σ), then $\langle a \rangle \subseteq \langle b \rangle$.*

Proof. The proofs are not too complex and may be found in [19].   □

Proposition 3. *Neighborhoods generated by points relate to bound operators according to* $(\forall x)[x]_\sigma = L_\sigma(x,x)$ & $[x]^\sigma = U_\sigma(x,x)$.

Remark 2. The connection between the two is relevant when σ is used for generating ideals and also for the neighborhoods. There are no instances of such usage in the literature as of this writing and is an open area for further investigation.

Definition 6. *In the context of Definition 5, σ will be said to be* supremal *if and only if*

$$(\forall a, b \in H)(\exists!^{>0} s(a,b) \in U(a,b))(x \in U(a,b) \longrightarrow s(a,b) = x \text{ or } \sigma s(a,b)x)(16)$$

Elements of the form $s(a,b)$ are σ-supremums of a and b.

Theorem 5. *All of the following hold:*

- *Anti symmetrical relations are uniquely supremal.*
- *σ-ideals are closed under supremal relations.*
- *If σ is supremal then $\langle K \rangle$ exists for all nonempty subsets $K \subseteq H$ in (H, σ) and is principal.*
- *If σ is supremal and $(\mathcal{I}(H), \subseteq)$ has a least element, then it is an algebraic lattice and the finitely generated σ-ideals are its compact elements.*
- *If σ is supremal, let $\mathfrak{L}, \lambda, \pi, \Sigma : \wp(H) \setminus \{\emptyset\} \longmapsto \wp(H)$ be maps such that for any $\emptyset \neq X \subseteq H$,*

$$\mathfrak{L}(X) = \{x \in H; \exists a \in X \, \sigma x a\} \text{ and } \lambda(X) = \mathfrak{L}(X) \cup X \qquad (17)$$
$$\pi(X) = \{a \in H; (\exists b, c \in X) \, a = s(b,c)\} \text{ and } \Sigma(X) = \pi(X) \cup X, \qquad (18)$$

  then $\langle X \rangle = \bigcup_1^\infty (\Sigma \lambda)^n(X)$. If σ is also reflexive, then $\langle X \rangle = \bigcup_1^\infty (\pi \mathfrak{L})^n(X)$.
- *If $(\forall a, b) \, \sigma ab$ or σba, then (H, σ) is principal, $(\forall a \in H)\langle a \rangle = \{x : \tau(\sigma)xa\}$ and $(\mathcal{I}(H), \subseteq)$ is a chain.*
- *S is principal and for each $a \in S, \langle a \rangle = \{b; \sigma ba\}$ if and only if σ is a quasi order.*

The above results mean that very few assumptions on σ suffice for reasonable properties on $\mathcal{I}(H)$.

Definition 7. *By a neighborhood granulation $\mathcal{G}$ on a set S will be meant a subset of the power set $\wp(S)$ for which there exists a map $\gamma : S \longmapsto \mathcal{G}$ such that*

$$(\forall B \in \mathcal{G})(\exists x \in S) \, \gamma(x) = B \qquad \text{(Surjectivity)}$$
$$\bigcup_{x \in S} \gamma(x) = S \qquad \text{(Cover)}$$

Definition 8. *By a* Co-Granular Operator Space By Ideals *GOSI will be meant a structure of the form* $S = \langle \underline{S}, \sigma, \mathcal{G}, l_*, u_* \rangle$ *with* $\underline{S}$ *being a set,* σ *being a binary relation on* $S, \mathcal{G}$ *a neighborhood granulation over* S *and* l_*, u_* *being *-lower and *-upper approximation operators :* $\wp(\underline{S}) \longmapsto \wp(\underline{S})$ *(* $\wp(\underline{S})$ *denotes the power set of* $\underline{S}$*) defined as below (* $\underline{S}$ *is replaced with* S *if clear from the context.* Lower and upper case alphabets may denote subsets*):*

$$(\forall X \in \wp(S)) \, X^{l_*} = \{a : a \in X \;\&\; \gamma(a) \cap X^c \in \mathcal{I}_\sigma(S)\} \qquad \text{(*-Lower)}$$

$$(\forall X \in \wp(S)) \, X^{u_*} = \{a : a \in S \;\&\; \gamma(a) \cap X \notin \mathcal{I}_\sigma(S)\} \cup X \qquad \text{(*-Upper)}$$

In general, if rough approximations are defined by expressions of the form $X^{\oplus} = \{a : \gamma(a) \odot X^* \in \mathcal{J}\}$ *with* $\oplus \in \{l, u\}, \mathcal{G} \subset \wp(S), \gamma : S \longmapsto \mathcal{G}$ *being a map,* $* \in \{c, 1\}$ *and* $\odot \in \{\cap, \cup\}$ *, then the approximation will be said to be* co-granular*.*

The definition of co-granularity can be improved/generalized in a first order language with quantifiers.

Definition 9. *By a* Higher Co-Granular Operator Space By Ideals *GOSIH will be meant a structure of the form* $S = \langle \underline{S}, \sigma, \mathcal{G}, l_o, u_o \rangle$ *with* $\underline{S}$ *being a set,* σ *being a binary relation on the powerset* $\wp(S), \mathcal{G}$ *a neighborhood granulation over* S *and* l_o, u_o *o-lower and o-upper approximation operators :* $\wp(\underline{S}) \longmapsto \wp(\underline{S})$ *(* $\wp(\underline{S})$ *denotes the power set of* $\underline{S}$*) defined by the following conditions (* $\underline{S}$ *is replaced with* S *if clear from the context.* Lower and upper case alphabets may denote subsets*):*

$$For\ a\ fixed\ \mathbb{I} \in \mathcal{I}_\sigma(\wp(S)) \qquad \text{(Ideal)}$$

$$(\forall X \in \wp(S)) \, X^{l_o} = \{a : a \in X \;\&\; \gamma(a) \cap X^c \in \mathbb{I}\} \qquad \text{(o-Lower)}$$

$$(\forall X \in \wp(S)) \, X^{u_o} = \{a : a \in S \;\&\; \gamma(a) \cap X \notin \mathbb{I}\} \cup X \qquad \text{(o-Upper)}$$

Theorem 6. *All of the following hold in a GOSI* S*:*

$$(\forall A \in \wp(S)) \, A^{l_*} \subseteq A \subseteq A^{u_*}) \qquad \text{(Inclusion)}$$

$$(\forall A \in \wp(S)) \, A^{l_* l_*} \subseteq A^{l_*} \qquad \text{(l-Weak Idempotency)}$$

$$(\forall A \in \wp(S)) \, A^{u_*} \subseteq A^{u_* u_*} \qquad \text{(u-Weak Idempotency)}$$

$$\emptyset^{l_*} = \emptyset = \emptyset^{u_*} \qquad \text{(Bottom)}$$

$$S^{l_*} = S = S^{u_*} \qquad \text{(Top)}$$

Remark 3. The proof of the above theorem is direct. Monotonicity of the approximations need not hold in general. This is because the choice of parthood is not *sufficiently coherent* with σ in general. A sufficient condition can be that σ-ideals be generated by σ that are at least quasi orders.

Proposition 4. *In a GOSI* S *all of the following hold:*

- *The granulation is not admissible*
- *The approximations* l_*, u_* *are not granular*

Proof. It is clear that both the lower and upper co-granular approximations are not representable in terms of granules using set operations alone on $\wp(S)$. So weak representability (WRA) fails.   □

The properties of approximations in a GOSIH depend on those of the ideal and the granulation operator γ. This is reflected in the next theorem:

Theorem 7. *In a GOSIH S satisfying*

- σ *is supremal,*
- σ *is a quasi order and*
- $(\forall a)a \in \gamma(a)$

then all of the following hold:

$$A^{l_o} \subseteq A \subseteq A^{u_o}; \ \emptyset^{u_o} = \emptyset; \ X^{l_o} = X \tag{19}$$

$$A \subset B \longrightarrow A^{l_o} \subseteq B^{l_o} \ \& \ A^{u_o} \subseteq B^{u_o} \tag{20}$$

$$A^{l_o l_o} = A^{l_o}; \ A^{u_o} \subseteq A^{u_o u_o} \tag{21}$$

$$(\forall A \in \mathbb{I}) \, A^{u_o} = A; \ (\forall A^c \in \mathbb{I}) \, A^{l_o} = A \tag{22}$$

Proof. Some parts are proved below:

- Monotonicity happens because the σ-ideals behave reasonably well. If $A \subset B$, then for any $z \in A^{l_o}$, it is necessary that $\gamma(z) \cap B^c \subseteq \gamma(z) \cap A^c$. This ensures that $A^{l_o} \subseteq B^{l_o}$. Again for the upper approximation, If $A \subset B$ and $z \in A^{u_o}, \gamma(z) \cap A \notin \mathcal{I}$ holds. As then $\gamma(z) \cap A \subseteq \gamma(z) \cap B$, it follows that $\gamma(z) \cap B \notin \mathcal{I}$. This ensures $A^{u_o} \subseteq B^{u_o}$.
- For proving $(\forall A \in \mathbb{I}) \, A^{u_o} = A$, note that if $z \in A^{u_o}$ then it is necessary that $\gamma(z) \cap A \notin \mathbb{I}$ or $z \in A$. It is not possible that $\gamma(z) \cap A \notin \mathbb{I}$ as A is in $\mathbb{I}$. So $A^{u_o} = A$.
- Again, if $z \in A$ and $\gamma(z) \cap A^c \in \mathbb{I}$ and $A^c \in \mathbb{I}$, then $z \in A$ and $z \in A^{l_o}$. This yields $A = A^{l_o}$.

All this shows that the ideal based approach works due to the properties of the ideals.

Definition 10. *For all of the above cases, a natural concept of A being* roughly included *in B ($A \sqsubseteq B$) if and only if $A^l \subseteq B^l$ and $A^u \subseteq B^u$ for relevant choices of l, u. A is* roughly equal *to B ($A \approx_{l,u} B$) if and only if $A \sqsubseteq B \ \& \ B \sqsubseteq A$. Quotients of the equivalence $\approx_{l,u}$ will be referred to as* rough objects.

Theorem 8. *The antichain based semantics of [7,8] applies to all of GOSI and GOSIH contexts with corresponding concepts of rough equalities.*

The proof consists in adapting the entire process of the semantics in the papers to the context. Granularity of approximations is not essential for this. More details will appear in a separate paper.

5   Meanings of Generalization and Parallel Rough Universes

The generalizations of the classical definition of approximations derived from approximation spaces and general approximation spaces using ideals differ substantially from those that have been introduced in this research paper. Both possible meanings and properties differ substantially in a perspective that is formulated below. An extended example is also used to illustrate some of the concepts introduced in this paper.

In all algebras of arbitrary finite type, ideals can be viewed in second order perspectives as subsets satisfying closure and absorption conditions. Ideals can be described through first order conditions [22] in some universal algebras with distinguished element 0 (that are *ideal determined*). In the latter case every ideal is always the 0-class of a congruence. In both cases, ideals behave like higher order zeros.

The following implication holds always in a GOSI for a point $x \in S, A \subseteq S$ and K being an ideal:

$$\gamma x \subseteq A \longrightarrow \gamma x \cap A^c = \emptyset \longrightarrow \gamma x \cap A^c \subseteq K \tag{23}$$

The same idea essentially extends to GOSIH where it is also possible to regard subsets of ideals as essential zeros.

But a *subset of an ideal need not behave like a generalized zero in general.* This statement is opposed to *the subset is part of a generalized zero.* But if every subset is contained in a minimal ideal, the restriction becomes redundant. In the absence of any contamination avoidance related impositions, the latter statement is justified only under additional conditions like *the subset is part of a specific generalized zero.* All this is behind the motivation for the definition of GOSIH. In the relational approximation contexts of [4–6], subsets of generalized zeros are generalized zeros. Apart from wide differences in properties, major differences exist on the nature of ideals. Therefore *if a property has little to do (in a structured way) with what something is not, then that something has the property in an approximate sense.* The idea of *little to do with* or *set no value of* relative operations is intended to be captured by concepts of ideals.

If σ-ideals are seen as essentially empty sets, then they have a hierarchy of their own and function like definite entities. The σ-ideals under some weak conditions permit the following association. If A is a subset then it is included in the smallest σ-ideal containing it and a set of maximal σ-ideals contained in it. These may be seen as a representation of rough objects of a parallel universe.

This motivates the following definition:

Definition 11. *In a GOSI $S = \langle \underline{S}, \sigma, \mathcal{G}, l, u \rangle$ in which σ is supremal every subset $A \subseteq S$ can be associated with a set of maximal σ-ideals ($\mu(A)$) contained in S and least σ-ideal $\Upsilon(A)$ containing it. These will be termed parallel rough approximations and pairs of the form (a, b) (with $a \in \mu(A)$ and $b = \Upsilon(A)$) will be referred to as* parallel rough objects. *Elements of $\mu(A)$ will be referred to as* lower parallel approximation *and $\Upsilon(A)$ as the* upper parallel approximation.

The lower parallel approximations can be useful for improving the concept of GOSI with additional approximations because they refer to inclusion of worthless things. This is done next.

Definition 12. *In a GOSI S with supremal σ, for any subset $A \subseteq S$, the* strong lower *and* strong upper *approximations will be as follows:*

$$A^{l_s} = \{x : x \in A \ \& \ \{\emptyset\} \subset \mu(\gamma(x) \cap A^c)\} \qquad \text{(s-lower)}$$
$$A^{u_s} = \{a : a \in S \ \& \ \gamma(a) \cap A \subset \Upsilon(\gamma(a) \cap A)\} \cup A \qquad \text{(s-upper)}$$

Proposition 5. *In a GOSI S, for any $A \subseteq S$, the following hold:*

$$A^{l_*} \subseteq A^{l_s} \subseteq A$$
$$A^{u_*} = A^{u_s}$$

Proof. If $\{\emptyset\} \subset \mu(\gamma(x) \cap A^c)$, then there is at least one nonempty σ-ideal included in $\gamma(x) \cap A^c$. This does not imply that $\gamma(x) \cap A^c$ is a σ-ideal, but the converse holds. So $A^{l_*} \subseteq A^{l_s} \subseteq A$ follows.

For the second part, as σ is supremal, $\gamma(a) \cap A \subset \Upsilon(\gamma(a) \cap A)$ ensures that $\gamma(a) \cap A$ is not a σ-ideal. The converse is also true. $A^{u_*} = A^{u_s}$ follows from this. $\qquad \square$

Often it can happen that objects/entities possessing some set of properties are not favored by objects/entities having some other set of properties. This meta phenomena suggests that anti chains on the collection of σ-ideals can help in associated exclusions and inclusions.

Definition 13. *In a GOSI S, let $\mathcal{O}$ be an antichain in $\mathcal{I}_\sigma(S)$ and $\mathcal{O}^+ = \{B : B \in \mathcal{I}_\sigma(S) \ \& \ (\exists C \in \mathcal{O}) C \subseteq B\}, \mathcal{O}^- = \mathcal{I}_\sigma(S) \setminus \mathcal{O}^+$. For any subset $X \subseteq S$, the* a-lower *and* a-upper *approximations will be as follows:*

$$X^{l_a} = \{a : a \in X \ \& \ \gamma(a) \cap X^c \in \mathcal{O}^-\} \qquad \text{(a-Lower)}$$
$$X^{u_a} = \{a : a \in S \ \& \ \gamma(a) \cap X \notin \mathcal{O}^-\} \cup X \qquad \text{(a-Upper)}$$

The resulting GOSIS of this form will be referred to as a GOSIS induced by the antichain $\mathcal{O}$.

Proposition 6. *In a GOSI S, for any $X \subseteq S$ and nontrivial antichain $\mathcal{A}$, the following hold:*

$$X^{l_a} \subseteq X^{l_*} \subseteq X$$
$$X^{u_*} \subseteq X^{u_a}$$

5.1 Abstract Examples

Let $S = \{a, b, c, e, f, g\}$, and $\sigma = \{(a, c), (a, e), (b, c), (b, e), (c, c), (c, b), (e, a), (f, f)\}$ be a binary relation on it. It is a not symmetric, transitive or

Table 1. Upper and lower bounds

Pair (x, z)	$U(x, z)$	$L(x, z)$
(a, b)	$\{e, c\}$	$\emptyset$
(a, c)	$\{c\}$	$\emptyset$
(a, e)	$\emptyset$	$\emptyset$
(b, c)	$\{c\}$	$\{c\}$
(b, e)	$\emptyset$	$\emptyset$
(c, e)	$\emptyset$	$\{a, b\}$
$(*, f)$	$\emptyset$	$\emptyset$
$(*, g)$	$\emptyset$	$\emptyset$

reflexive. In Table 1, the computed values of the set of upper bounds, lower bounds, and neighborhoods are presented. $*$ in the last two rows refers to any element from the subset $\{a, b, c, e\}$. Values of the form $U(x, x)$ and $L(x, x)$ have been kept in Table 2 because they correspond to values of neighborhoods of σ.

In Table 2, $\mathbf{U}(\mathbf{x}, \mathbf{x}) = [\mathbf{x}]^\sigma$ and $\mathbf{L}(\mathbf{x}, \mathbf{x}) = [\mathbf{x}]_\sigma$.

Table 2. Neighborhoods

$\mathbf{x}$	$\mathbf{U}(\mathbf{x}, \mathbf{x})$	$\mathbf{L}(\mathbf{x}, \mathbf{x})$	$< \mathbf{x} >$
a	$\{c, e\}$	$\{e\}$	$\{a\}$
b	$\{c, e\}$	$\{c\}$	$\{b.c\}$
c	$\{b, c\}$	$\{a, b, c\}$	$\{c\}$
e	$\{c\}$	$\{a, b\}$	$\{c, e\}$
f	$\{f\}$	$\{f\}$	$\{f\}$
g	$\emptyset$	$\emptyset$	$\emptyset$

Given the above information, it can be deduced that

Proposition 7. *In the context, the nontrivial σ- ideals are $I_1 = \{a, b, e, c\}$ and $I_2 = \{a, b, e, c, f\}$.*

If a co-granulation is defined as per $\gamma(a) = \{b\}, \gamma(b) = \{g\}, \gamma(c) = \{c, a\}, \gamma(e) = \{e\}, \gamma(f) = \{f\}, \gamma(g) = \{g, b, c\}$, then the GOSI approximations of the set $A = \{a, b\}$ can be computed to be $A_*^l = \{b\}$ and $A_*^u = \{a, b, c, g\}$. For distinct lattice ideals many approximations of A by l_k and u_k can be computed.

GOSIH related computations of approximations are bound to be cumbersome even for four element sets and so have been omitted.

5.2 Example: On Dating

Dating contexts can involve a huge number of variables and features. Expression of these depend substantially on the level of inclusion of diverse genders and sexualities in the actual context. A person's choice of pool of potential dates depends on factors including the person's sexuality.

People may decide on their potential dating pool by excluding parts of the whole pool and focusing on specific subsets. The operation of *excluding parts of the pool* often happens as a multi stage process involving progressive additions to desired features or confirmation of undesired features. This means that a person's construction of relative dating pools must be happening through rough approximations based on ideals. An ideal can include a number of features, but in general it can be impossible to collect all undesired features in a single ideal as then it would not correspond to anything remotely actualizable.

Typically actualizability depends on the reasoning strategies adopted by the person in question. It is not that everybody thinks in terms of concrete people with undesirable features and people with analogous features - abstraction can be in terms of feature sets. For example, some lesbian women prefer femme women. But concepts of femme and variants are very subjective in nature. Instances of such classification (or actualization) may depend on exclusion of many features like *muscular build*, but some features like *tattoos* may be desirable/optional. These kind of features may be in the general ideal in question.

6 Mereotopology and Approximations

In spatial mereology, spatial regions are associated with elements of a distributive lattice or a Boolean algebra and which in turn are intended to represent collections of regions with operations of aggregation and commonality. Over these binary contact relations C can be defined over them to represent instances of two regions sharing at least one point. Various constructions in the subfield are suited for the ideal based approach to rough approximations. In this section, some of the basic aspects and recent results are stated and connections with approximations are established. All this can be viewed as a new example for the theories invented/developed.

Some concepts and recent results of spatial mereology are mentioned first (see [23]).

Definition 14. *A contact relation C over a bounded distributive lattice L is a binary relation that satisfies*

$$Cab \longrightarrow 0 < a \ \& \ 0 < b \tag{C1}$$
$$Cab \longrightarrow Cba \tag{C2}$$
$$Cab \ \& \ b \leq e \longrightarrow Cae \tag{C3}$$
$$Ca(b \vee e) \longrightarrow Cab \ or \ Cae \tag{C4}$$
$$0 < a \wedge b \longrightarrow Cab \tag{C5}$$

If L is a Boolean algebra, then (L, C) is said to be a contact algebra. *If C satisfies $C1 - C4$ alone, then it is said to be a precontact relation and then (L, C) would be a* precontact algebra.

$C1$ is also written as $Cab \longrightarrow Ea$ & Eb (for contact implies existence). $C5$ is basically the statement that overlap implies contact $\mathbf{O}ab \longrightarrow Cab$. The axioms yield $C(a \vee b)e \longleftrightarrow Cae$ or Cbe and Cab & $a \leq u$ & $b \leq v \longrightarrow Cuv$.

When temporal aspects of variation of C are permitted, the predicate for ontological existence E that is defined via Ea if and only if $0 < a$ is too strong as non existence is equated with emptiness. In [24], to handle variation of existence over time, concepts of *actual existence, actual part of, actual overlap and actual contact* have been proposed and developed. The actual existence predicate AE is one that satisfies

$$AE(1) \ \& \ \neg AE(0) \tag{AE1}$$
$$AE(a) \ \& \ a \leq b \longrightarrow AE(b) \tag{AE2}$$
$$AE(a \vee b) \longrightarrow AE(a) \text{ or } AE(b) \tag{AE3}$$

Subsets of a Boolean algebra that satisfy AE1, AE2 and AE3 are called *Grills*. Every grill is a union of ultrafilters or an ultra filter.

A *discrete space with actual points* is a pair $Z = (X, X^a)$ with X being a nonempty set and $\emptyset \subset X^a \subset X$. For $H \subset X$, let $AE_Z(H)$ if and only if $H \cap X^a \neq \emptyset$. If $B(Z)$ is the Boolean algebra of all subsets over X, then $(B(Z), AE_Z)$ would be a Boolean algebra with a predicate of actual existence. It is proved in [24] that

Theorem 9. *In Boolean algebras with predicate of actual existence (B, AE), there exist a discrete space $Z = (X, X^a)$ and an isomorphic embedding $h : (B(Z), AE_Z) \longmapsto (B, AE)$.*

On a Boolean algebra with an extra predicate for actual existence, it is possible to define the *actual contact* predicate or define the latter as a predicate C^a that satisfies the following axioms:

$$C^a 11 \ \& \ C^a 00 \tag{Ca1}$$
$$C^a xb \longrightarrow C^a bx \tag{Ca2}$$
$$C^a xb \longrightarrow C^a xx \tag{Ca3}$$
$$C^a xb \ \& \ b \leq z \longrightarrow C^a xz \tag{Ca4}$$
$$C^a x(b \vee e) \longrightarrow C^a xb \text{ or } C^a xe \tag{Ca5}$$

It is also possible to define a unary predicate AC via $AC(x)$ if and only if $C^a xx$.

A subset H of a contact algebra B is a *clan* if it is a grill that satisfies CL: $(\forall a, b \in H) \, Cab$, while a subset H of a precontact algebra B is an *actual clan* if it is a grill that satisfies ACL: $(\forall a, b \in H) \, C^a ab$.

Associated collections of all clans and actual clans will respectively be denoted by $CL(B)$ and $CL^a(B)$ respectively. It can be shown that $CL^a(B) \subseteq CL(B)$ in general. If Z is the set of all ultrafilters $\mathcal{F}_u(B)$ and R^a is the canonical relation for C^a defined by

$$R^a UV \text{ if and only if } (\forall x \in U)(\forall b \in V)\, C^a xb$$

The canonical relation R for C is defined in the same way. An ultra filter U is *reflexive* if $R^a UU$ and all reflexive ultrafilters are actual clans. R^a is a nonempty, symmetric and quasi-reflexive relation while R is a reflexive and symmetric relation (Quasi reflexivity is $R^a be \longrightarrow R^a bb$). All of the following are proved in [24]:

Proposition 8

- *RUV if and only if $R^a UV$ or $U = V$.*
- *Every clan (resp. actual clan) is a union of nonempty sets of mutually R-related (resp. R^a-related) ultrafilters.*
- *All ultrafilters contained in an actual clan are reflexive ultrafilters while any ultra filter contained in a clan is an actual clan or a non-reflexive ultra filter.*
- *$C^a be$ if and only if $(\exists G \in CL_a(B))\, b, e \in G$.*

6.1 New Approximations

All of the definitions and results in this subsection are new and differ fundamentally from the approach in [25]. If (X, X^a) is the discrete space associated with a Boolean algebra with actual contact (B, C^a) and $\gamma : X \longmapsto \wp(X^a)$ is a map then approximations in B can be defined in at least two different ways (for a fixed actual clan $K \in CL_a(B)$):

$$A^{l_a} = \{x : x \in A \ \& \ \gamma(x) \cap A^c \notin K\} \qquad \text{(CG-Lower)}$$

$$A^{u_a} = \{x : x \in X \ \& \ \gamma(x) \cap A \in K\} \cup A \qquad \text{(CG-Upper)}$$

$$A^{l_g} = \bigcup\{\gamma(x) : \gamma(x) \cap A^c \notin K\} \cap A \qquad \text{(G-Lower)}$$

$$A^{u_g} = \bigcup\{\gamma(x) : \gamma(x) \cap A \in K\} \cup A \qquad \text{(G-Upper)}$$

$$A^{l_c} = \bigcup\{H : H \cap A^c \notin K\} \cap A \qquad \text{(Clan-Lower)}$$

$$A^{u_c} = \bigcup\{H : H \in K \ \& \ H \cap A \neq \emptyset\} \cup A \qquad \text{(Clan-Upper)}$$

The properties of these approximations depend to a substantial extent on the definition of γ used. One possibility is to use the actual-contact relation or a derived mereotopological relation. In the present author's view some meaningful phrases are *the things in actual contact with, the things in contact with, the most common things that become in actual contact by, the things that become in actual contact by, and the relative wholes determined by*. The first of these can be attempted with the neighborhoods generated by C^a itself in the absence of additional information about the context.

One practical context where approximations of the kind can be relevant is in the study of handwriting of people. Many kinds of variations in the handwriting of people (especially of morphological subunits and their relative placement) can be found over time, location and media used.

So if γ is defined as per $(\forall x)\, \gamma(x) = [x]_{C^a} = \{b : C^a b x\}$, then the context becomes a specific instance of a GOSI in which the ideals are also regulated by C. If instead $\gamma(x) = < x >$ holds, then it is provable that:

Theorem 10. *All of the following hold (in the context of this subsection) for any two elements of the Boolean algebra with actual contact when $\gamma(x) = < x >$*

$$A^{l_a} \subseteq A \subseteq A^{u_a}; \ \emptyset^{u_a} = \emptyset = \emptyset^{l_a}; \ X^{l_a} = X = X^{u_a} \tag{24}$$

$$A \subset B \longrightarrow A^{l_a} \subseteq B^{l_a} \ \& \ A^{u_a} \subseteq B^{u_a} \tag{25}$$

$$A^{l_a l_a} = A^{l_a}; \ A^{u_a u_a} = A^{u_a} \tag{26}$$

$$(A \cap B)^{l_a} = A^{l_a} \cap B^{l_a}; \ (A \cup B)^{l_a} \supseteq A^{l_a} \cup B^{l_a} \tag{27}$$

$$(A \cup B)^{u_a} = A^{u_a} \cup B^{u_a}; \ (A \cap B)^{u_a} \subseteq A^{u_a} \cap B^{u_a} \tag{28}$$

Proof. Note that actual clans determine specific subclasses of ideals. So all of the above properties follow from results of Sect. 3

Theorem 11. *All of the following hold (in the context of this subsection) for any two elements of the Boolean algebra with actual contact when $\gamma(x) = [x]_{C^a} = [x]$ (for short)*

$$A^{l_a} \subseteq A \subseteq A^{u_a} \tag{29}$$

$$\emptyset^{u_a} = \emptyset = \emptyset^{l_a}; \ X^{l_a} = X = X^{u_a} \tag{30}$$

$$A \subset B \longrightarrow A^{l_a} \subseteq B^{l_a} \ \& \ A^{u_a} \subseteq B^{u_a} \tag{31}$$

Proof

- $A^{l_a} \subseteq A \subseteq A^{u_a}$ follows from definition.
- $X^{l_a} = \{b : b \in X \, [b] \cap \emptyset \notin K\} = X$
- If $A \subset B$, then $(\forall b \in A^{l_a})\, [b] \cap A^c \in K^c$ and $[b] \cap B^c \subseteq [b] \cap A^c$. Since K^c is an ideal, it follows that $A^{l_a} \subseteq B^{l_a}$.
  If $b \in A^{u_a}$, then $[b] \cap A \in K$. Also $[b] \cap A \subseteq [b] \cap B$. But K is a union of ultrafilters, so $[b] \cap B \in K$ and consequently $b \in B^{u_a}$. $\qquad \square$

Since the basic duality theorems for actual contact algebras (and contact algebras in particular) are in place [24], the duality/inverse problem of such algebras enhanced with approximation operators may be solvable with ease. In the present author's opinion, the following formalism would be optimal:

Problem 1 (Inverse Problem). Given an algebraic system of the form $A = \langle B, C^a, l_a, u_a \rangle$ with B, C_a being an actual contact algebra and l_a, u_a are unary operations satisfying:

$$(\forall z)\, z^{l_a} \subseteq z \subseteq z^{u_a} \qquad (32)$$

$$0^{u_a} = 0 = 0^{l_a} \;;\; 1^{l_a} = 1 = 1^{u_a} \qquad (33)$$

$$(\forall z, v)\,(z \subset v \longrightarrow a^{l_a} \subseteq v^{l_a} \;\&\; z^{u_a} \subseteq v^{u_a} \qquad (34)$$

$$(\forall z)\, z^{l_a l_a} = z^{l_a} \qquad (35)$$

$$(\forall z)\, z^{u_a} \subseteq z^{u_a u_a} \qquad (36)$$

under what additional conditions does there exist a neighborhood operator γ and an actual clan K that permit a definition of the operators l_a, u_a according to

$$z^{l_a} = \{x : x \in z \;\&\; \gamma(x) \cap z^c \notin K\} \qquad \text{(CG-Lower)}$$

$$z^{u_a} = \{x : x \in B \;\&\; \gamma(x) \cap z \in K\} \cup z \qquad \text{(CG-Upper)}$$

Further Directions and Remarks

In this research, a relatively less explored area in the construction of point wise approximations by ideals has been investigated from new perspectives by the present author. The previously available theory has been streamlined and the meaning of approximations in the approach has been explained. A concept of co-granular approximations has been introduced to explain the generation of related approximations including the popular point wise rough approximations. Further

- the methodology is generalized to specific modifications of granular operator spaces [7,8] (called co-granular operator spaces) and in particular to lattices generated by collections of sets and lattice ideals,
- the restrictions to general approximation spaces are relaxed,
- knowledge interpretation in the contexts are proposed,
- few meaningful examples and application areas have been proposed,
- ideal based rough approximations are shown to be natural in spatial mereo-logical contexts and
- related inverse problems are posed.

In a forthcoming paper, the fine details of the mentioned antichain based semantics and other algebraic semantics will be considered by the present author.

References

1. Mani, A.: Dialectics of counting and the mathematics of vagueness. In: Peters, J.F., Skowron, A. (eds.) Transactions on Rough Sets XV. LNCS, vol. 7255, pp. 122–180. Springer, Heidelberg (2012). doi:10.1007/978-3-642-31903-7_4
2. Pagliani, P., Chakraborty, M.: A Geometry of Approximation: Rough Set Theory: Logic, Algebra and Topology of Conceptual Patterns. Springer, Berlin (2008)
3. Yao, Y., Lin, T.Y.: Generalizing rough sets using modal logics. Intell. Autom. Soft Comput. **2**(2), 103–120 (1996)

4. Abo-Tabl, A.: A comparison of two kinds of definitions of rough approximations based on a similarity relation. Inf. Sci. **181**(12), 2587–2596 (2011)
5. Allam, A., Bakeir, M., Abo-Tabl, A.: Some methods for generating topologies by relations. J. Malays. Math. Sci. Soc. **31**, 35–45 (2008)
6. Kandil, A., Yakout, M., Zakaria, A.: New approaches of rough sets via ideals. In: John, S.J. (ed.) Handbook of Research on Generalized and Hybrid Set Structures and Applications for Soft Computing, pp. 247–264. IGI Global, Hershey (2016)
7. Mani, A.: Antichain based semantics for rough sets. In: Ciucci, D., Wang, G., Mitra, S., Wu, W.-Z. (eds.) RSKT 2015. LNCS, vol. 9436, pp. 335–346. Springer, Cham (2015). doi:10.1007/978-3-319-25754-9_30
8. Mani, A.: Knowledge and consequence in AC semantics for general rough sets. In: Wang, G., Skowron, A., Yao, Y., Ślęzak, D., Polkowski, L. (eds.) Thriving Rough Sets. SCI, vol. 708, pp. 237–268. Springer, Cham (2017). doi:10.1007/978-3-319-54966-8_12
9. Mani, A.: Algebraic semantics of similarity-based bitten rough set theory. Fundamenta Informaticae **97**(1–2), 177–197 (2009)
10. Mani, A.: Contamination-free measures and algebraic operations. In: 2013 IEEE International Conference on Fuzzy Systems (FUZZ), pp. 1–8. IEEE (2013)
11. Mani, A.: Algebraic semantics of proto-transitive rough sets. In: Peters, J.F., Skowron, A. (eds.) Transactions on Rough Sets XX. LNCS, vol. 10020, pp. 51–108. Springer, Heidelberg (2016). doi:10.1007/978-3-662-53611-7_3
12. Xiao, Q., Li, Q., Guo, L.: Rough sets induced by lattices. Inf. Sci. **271**, 82–92 (2014)
13. Estaji, A., Hooshmandasl, M., Davvaz, B.: Rough set theory applied to lattice theory. Inf. Sci. **200**, 108–122 (2012)
14. Banerjee, M., Chakraborty, M.K.: Rough sets through algebraic logic. Fundamenta Informaticae **28**, 211–221 (1996)
15. Mani, A.: Super rough semantics. Fundamenta Informaticae **65**(3), 249–261 (2005)
16. Duntsch, I.: Rough sets and algebras of relations. In: Orlowska, E. (ed.) Incomplete Information and Rough Set Analysis, pp. 95–108. Physica, Heidelberg (1998). doi:10.1007/978-3-7908-1888-8_5
17. Duntsch, I., Orlowska, E.: Discrete duality for rough relation algebras. Fundamenta Informaticae **127**, 35–47 (2013)
18. Mani, A.: Ontology, rough Y-systems and dependence. Int. J. Comput. Sci. Appl. **11**(2), 114–136 (2014). Special Issue of IJCSA on Computational Intelligence
19. Duda, J., Chajda, I.: Ideals of binary relational systems. Casopis pro pestovani matematiki **102**(3), 280–291 (1977)
20. Rudeanu, S.: On ideals and filters in posets. Rev. Roum. Math. Pures. Appl. **60**(2), 155–175 (2015)
21. Venkataranasimhan, P.: Pseudo-complements in posets. Proc. Am. Math. Soc. **28**, 9–17 (1971)
22. Gumm, H., Ursini, A.: Ideals in universal algebras. Algebra Universalis **19**, 45–54 (1984)
23. Dimov, G., Vakarelov, D.: Contact algebras and region-based theory of space: a proximity approach I. Fundamenta Informaticae **74**(2–3), 209–249 (2006)
24. Vakarelov, D.: Mereotopologies with predicates of actual existence and actual contact. Fundamenta Informaticae, 1–20 (2017, forthcoming)
25. Polkowski, L.: Approximate Reasoning by Parts. Springer, Heidelberg (2011)

Certainty-Based Rough Sets

Davide Ciucci$^{(\boxtimes)}$ and Ivan Forcati

Department of Informatics, Systems and Communication (DISCo),
University of Milano–Bicocca, Milano, Italy
ciucci@disco.unimib.it, i.forcati@campus.unimib.it

Abstract. The departing point of this study is a data table with certainty values associated to attribute values. These values are deeply rooted in possibility theory, they can be obtained with standard procedures and they are efficiently manageable in databases. Our aim is to study rough set approximations and reducts in this framework. We define three categories of approximations that make use of the certainty value and generalize different aspects of the approximations: their equation, the binary relation used and the granulation. Further, new kinds of reducts aimed to make use or reduce the information provided by the certainty values are given.

Keywords: Possibility theory · Rough sets · Approximations · Reducts

1 Introduction

Since the inception of rough set theory, it was clear that data can be incomplete or uncertain. Thus, several models were proposed to tackle different forms of uncertainty. We had the pioneering work about non-deterministic information tables [8] where for a given object and attribute we do not know precisely the value but a set of possible values (with equal probability). Then, Ziarko introduced the variable precision rough set model [17], which was later generalized to the probabilistic rough set model [14], where probabilities are introduced in rough sets by means of the rough membership function.

Motivated by the recent results on possibilistic conditional tables [9,10], we suppose here that data come with a possibility distribution in the simplified form of certainty-based qualification [9] – hence the name given to the model of "certainty-based" rough set. That is, we suppose that the value assigned to a pair (object, attribute) can come with a degree of certainty. These values express an epistemic uncertainty on data, such as we are undecided if James prefers Raffaello or Tiziano paintings but we are sure that he does not like Tintoretto; or we tend to believe that Julia's car is red, but we are not sure.

For a detailed comparison and the advantages of using in this context possibility theory with respect to other approaches to uncertainty, we refer to [10]. Here, let us stress that

© Springer International Publishing AG 2017
L. Polkowski et al. (Eds.): IJCRS 2017, Part II, LNAI 10314, pp. 43–55, 2017.
DOI: 10.1007/978-3-319-60840-2_3

1. adding certainty values to attributes does not increase the computational complexity of database queries [9];
2. it is practically feasible to compute possibility distributions on data [4].

So, given a data table with associated certainty degrees for the attribute values, we want to study how rough approximations and reducts can be defined. We suppose the reader familiar with the basic notions of rough set theory, such as information table, approximations and reducts [12]. As far as notation is concerned we will denote an information table[1] as $I = (U, Att, Val, F)$ with the standard meaning, that is, U is the set of objects, Att the set of attributes, $Val = \cup_{a \in Att} Val_a$ the union of all possible values for attributes and F the mapping object-attribute onto values.

We also notice that our approach is different from Nakata and Sakai one [6,7] for two reasons. First of all, they study data with "full" possibility distributions attached, whereas we suppose to only have necessity measures (for the advantages of this approach see Sect. 2). Secondly, they adopt a possible world interpretation and convert a possibilistic table into a set of classical tables to be studied separately and then aggregate the results. Here, we do not need to split the table but we directly use the necessity measures in defining the approximations and reducts.

The paper is organized as follows: in Sect. 2 we give the basis of Possibility Theory and give an extended definition of information table. In Sect. 3 we define the lower and upper approximations taking into account the necessity measure associated to data; we will see three different approaches to give generalized approximations. In Sect. 4, new kinds of reducts based on necessity measures will be given. Finally, conclusions and future works are outlined.

2   Possibility Theory

Possibility theory is an uncertainty theory, complementary to probability, and aimed to manage incomplete information [5]. Firstly meant to provide a graded semantics to natural language statements [16], then it showed also useful in other contexts, such as preference representation or to express imprecise probabilities [5]. It relies on the notion of possibility distribution: let $S = \{s_1, \ldots, s_n\}$ be a set of states referred to a world of interest and L be a totally ordered scale with top element 1 and bottom element 0. A possibility distribution is a function $\pi : S \to L$ that associates a value of possibility to each state of S. We notice that it is not additive, contrary to probability distributions. It represents the state of knowledge of an agent about the state set S and its values express the possibility that a state shall occur. That is, if $\pi(s) = 0$ then the state s is believed as impossible; if $\pi(s) = 1$ the state s is instead believed as totally possible. The intermediate values between 0 and 1 are used to express a graded possibility:

---

[1] Let us remark that we are not using the term *information system* on purpose, since outside the rough-set community it has a different and broader meaning, as discussed in [2].

the larger the value of $\pi(s)$ is, the more possible it is believed. Moreover, a normalization condition is assumed: there exists a state s totally possible, i.e., such that $\pi(s) = 1$. In the following, we assume, for the sake of simplicity and without loss of generality, that L is the unit interval $[0, 1]$. However, also finite set of values, for instance representing linguistic labels, are a possible and simpler choice for L. Using possibility distributions, we can associate to any event two measures: the necessity and the possibility.

Definition 1. *Given a possibility distribution on a set of states S and a subset $A \subseteq S$, which represents an event, we can define possibility and necessity measures, respectively, as*

$$\Pi(A) = \sup_{s \in A} \pi(s) \qquad N(A) = \inf_{s \notin A} 1 - \pi(s) \qquad (1)$$

These two measures are dual, that is $N(A) = 1 - \Pi(A^c)$ where A^c is the complement of A. This is another main difference with probability measures P which are self-dual, that is $P(A) = 1 - P(A^c)$. Furthermore, due to the normalization condition on π:

$$\text{if} \quad N(A) > 0 \quad \text{then} \quad \forall s \in A, \pi(s) = 1 \qquad (2)$$

Now, given an information table $I = (U, Att, Val, F)$, we want to associate a possibilistic information to the data, representing their degree of confidence. In this case, for each attribute $a \in A$, the states of the world are described by the different values that can be assumed by a. So, for each object $x \in U$, we can associate a possibility distribution to the pair (x, a), pointing out which values are the most expected and which ones are unlikely to be seen.

Example 1. Let *Temperature* be an attribute with values {Low, Medium, High}. Given an object x, a possibility distribution π on x for Temperature could be $\pi_T^x(Low) = 1$, $\pi_T^x(Medium) = 0.7$, $\pi_T^x(High) = 0.2$.

This is the general case but we are not interested in having a complete possibility distribution for each attribute. Instead, we would simply like to have one measure for each pair (x, a) associated to the value $F(x, a)$. Thus, we need to define a confidence function $C : U \times Att \rightarrow [0, 1]$ using one of the two measures above. An information table on which a function C is defined can be denoted as $I = (U, Att, Val, F, C)$. Our choice is to use the necessity measure N as the confidence function in order to represent a degree of certainty about the data. Formally, if π_a^x is a possibility distribution for attribute a and object x and N_a^x is the associated necessity measure, then $C(x, a) = N_a^x(\{F(x, a)\})$.

This restriction simplifies the framework but does not lead to a trivial situation. Firstly, the information conveyed by the many possibility distributions of the general case could be hardly usable in a meaningful manner, thus we gain in intelligibility. Then, it is easy to extend the operations of relational algebra to the case where values of graded certainty are associated to the table, keeping at the same time the data complexity of a classical database [9, 10].

Example 2. We give an example of an information table, with a confidence function expressed by a necessity measure, that is referred to natural language statements made by several people regarding weather conditions in a sea location.

Table 1. Example of an information table

Person	Weather	Temperature	Wind	Humidity	Sea
x_1	Partly cloudy	Medium	Moderate	Low	Very rough
x_2	Partly cloudy	Medium	Gentle	Low	Rough
x_3	Overcast	Medium	Moderate	Medium	Very rough
x_4	Rainy	Low	Moderate	Low	Rough
x_5	Partly cloudy	Medium	Gentle	Low	Rough
x_6	Overcast	Medium	Strong	Medium	Very rough
x_7	Overcast	Low	Moderate	Low	Storm
x_8	Overcast	Low	Gentle	Low	Very rough
x_9	Partly cloudy	Medium	Moderate	Low	Very rough
x_{10}	Overcast	Medium	Strong	Medium	Very rough

The confidence function C associated with the table is shown in a tabular form in Table 2. Let us stress that, in general, we do not need to set all values with infinite precision. The unspecified confidence values can be assumed to have value 1 and the set of possible values L can be limited to a finite and small one.

Table 2. Necessity measure associated with the data of Table 1.

Person	Weather	Temperature	Wind	Humidity	Sea
x_1	0.8	0.9	0.7	0.9	0.8
x_2	0.9	0.9	0.5	1.0	0.5
x_3	1.0	0.9	0.8	0.7	1.0
x_4	0.7	0.8	0.9	0.6	0.6
x_5	0.8	1.0	0.6	0.8	0.4
x_6	1.0	0.9	0.4	0.8	0.8
x_7	1.0	0.8	0.9	0.9	0.3
x_8	0.9	0.7	0.8	0.8	0.9
x_9	0.8	0.9	1.0	1.0	0.8
x_{10}	0.8	1.0	0.7	0.7	0.9

We notice that several possibility distributions can generate the same necessity measure. Indeed, let us consider a pair (x, a) such that $F(x, a) = val$ and $C(x, a) = \alpha > 0$. Then, we know that $\pi_a^x(val) = 1$ since the degree of necessity is α and it is greater than 0 (see Eq. (2)). On the other hand, the possibility distribution for all other values $val' \in Val_a$, $val' \neq val$ is not known: we can only say that $\pi_a^x(val') \leq 1 - \alpha$, according to the definition of necessity measure given in Eq. (1). The largest of these possibility measures is of course the one assigning the greatest possible value to all alternatives, i.e. $\pi_a^x(val') = 1 - \alpha$. Indeed, this is a common choice to define a possibility distribution once given a certainty measure, see [9,10].

Example 3. With reference to the previous example, we have for the possibility distribution $\pi_W^{x_1}$ relative to the attribute Weather that $\pi_W^{x_1}(\text{Partly Cloudy}) = 1$, $\pi_W^{x_1}(\text{Overcast}) = 0.2$, $\pi_W^{x_1}(\text{Rainy}) = 0.2$.

3   Approximations

In this section, we discuss how to exploit the confidence C in the definition of the approximations. Let us recall the standard definitions of lower and upper approximations generated by a (at least serial) relation R. They are mappings $L_R, U_R : \mathcal{P}(U) \mapsto \mathcal{P}(U)$ such that for a set of objects $S \subseteq U$: $L_R(S) = \{x \in U | R(x) \subseteq S\}$ and $U_R(S) = \{x \in U | R(x) \cap S \neq \emptyset\}$ with $R(x)$ the neighbourhood of x with respect to R [13].

Remark 1. Seriality of the relation R is the condition that ensures that for all sets S we have $L_R(S) \subseteq U_R(S)$. It is debatable if this property is enough or not to characterize the two mappings as *lower* and *upper* approximations or if the stronger property $L_R(S) \subseteq S \subseteq U_R(S)$ is needed [1,3]. We decided to adopt the more general case, this choice will have an influence only in Sect. 3.3.

There are different elements playing a role in these definitions, for our scope we take into account: the formula for the approximations, the relation R and the granulation of the universe. By generalizing one of these three elements we classify different possible generalized approximations that use the confidence values.

3.1   Changing the Granulation

The standard definitions of lower and upper approximations are used, whereas the granulation of the universe generated by the relation R is changed using the confidence values.

Granulation Refinement. The granulation (partition in case of an equivalence relation) is made finer by taking into account the confidence. There are several ways that we can use to make the granulation finer: here, we will show two of them, giving reasons for their relevance.

First, we illustrate a way to bipartite the granules considering a threshold for each relevant attribute. Given a subset of attributes $A = \{a_1, \ldots a_n\} \subseteq Att$, let $s_1, \ldots, s_n \in [0, 1]$ be the chosen thresholds. In each granule, we check if all the confidence values for the elements are higher than the relative thresholds: based on the positive or negative results of these checks, we split the elements into two subsets. That is, for each granule G (that is $R(x)$ in case of neighbourhoods of a binary relation), we create the subsets G_0 and G_1 and we divide the elements $x \in G$ as follows:

$$\begin{cases} x \in G_1 & \text{if } C(x, a_i) \geq s_i \text{ for } i = 1, \ldots, n \\ x \in G_0 & \text{otherwise} \end{cases} \qquad (3)$$

This refinement can be useful when we want to assign a different relevance, based on the confidence, to each attribute and, consequently, point out those elements whose confidence values are satisfactory.

The second kind of granulation refinement considers a distance of confidence between elements: each granule is split into two subsets according to the similarity of the confidence values. Let $\epsilon \in [0, 1]$ be a threshold: given an element $y \in U$ and the granule $G = R(y)$, each element $x \in G$ is classified in the set G_1 if the distance between its confidence value $C(x)$ and the confidence value of y, that is $C(y)$, is less than ϵ; otherwise it is put into the subset G_2. So, this refinement is expressed by

$$\begin{cases} x \in G_1 & \text{if } |C(y) - C(x)| \leq \epsilon \\ x \in G_2 & \text{otherwise} \end{cases} \qquad (4)$$

This type of granulation refinement can be useful when we would like each granule to contain only those elements whose confidence values are more or less similar to the one of the element that generated the granule.

More Importance to Higher Confidence Values. It could be useful to consider from the very beginning only those elements whose confidence values are high enough. So, instead of taking into account the confidence after having established an indiscernibility relation R, we could at first bipartite the space of objects U separating the ones that have good confidence values U_{high}, i.e. above a particular threshold, from the ones that have lower confidence values U_{low}. After this step, we can proceed applying the relation R to obtain a finer granulation only for the objects in U_{high}. The objects in U_{low} will form a standalone granule.

3.2   Changing the Formula for the Approximations

There can be several ways in which the formula of the approximations can be generalized. The one we present here is based on relaxing the constraints of the set inclusion. Similarly as what is done with probabilistic rough set [14] and variable precision rough set [15,17], for the lower approximation we require a partial inclusion of $R(x)$ in X and for the upper approximation that the intersection between $R(x)$ and X shall contain a certain number of elements. In our case however, the thresholds that appear in the formulas of the approximations also depend on a single object x. As such they can be seen as a particular case of approximations obtained by granulation in rough mereology [11, Chap. 2].

Let $\underline{s}(x) \in (0, 1]$ and $\overline{s}(x) \in [0, 1)$ be two real numbers. We define the approximations as

$$\underline{R}(X) = \{x \in U \mid \frac{|R(x) \cap X|}{|R(x)|} \geq \underline{s}(x)\}$$

$$\overline{R}(X) = \{x \in U \mid \frac{|R(x) \cap X|}{|R(x)|} > \overline{s}(x)\} \tag{5}$$

under the constraint that $\underline{s}(x) > \overline{s}(x)$. These two thresholds can be defined according to the confidence values of x. The reason is the following: given two elements x_1 and x_2, with $C_A(x_1) > C_A(x_2)$, it could be reasonable to request that $\underline{s}(x_2) > \underline{s}(x_1)$ (and $\overline{s}(x_2) > \overline{s}(x_1)$) so that x_2 should have more neighbours in X than x_1 to have the right of being in the approximations of X since the values that guarantee x_2 membership in X are not as certain as the ones from $x_1{}^2$.

It is straightforward to prove that these approximations satisfy some standard properties.

Proposition 1. *Let $\underline{R}$ and $\overline{R}$ be defined as in Eq. (5). Then, the following are satisfied:*

- $\underline{R}(\emptyset) = \overline{R}(\emptyset) = \emptyset$; $\underline{R}(U) = \overline{R}(U) = U$
- $\overline{R}(X \cup Y) \supseteq \overline{R}(X) \cup \overline{R}(Y)$
- $\underline{R}(X \cap Y) \subseteq \underline{R}(X) \cap \underline{R}(Y)$
- $\overline{R}(X \cap Y) \subseteq \overline{R}(X) \cap \overline{R}(Y)$
- $\underline{R}(X \cup Y) \supseteq \underline{R}(X) \cup \underline{R}(Y)$
- $X \subseteq Y \Rightarrow \underline{R}(X) \subseteq \underline{R}(Y)$ *and* $\overline{R}(X) \subseteq \overline{R}(Y)$.

3.3   Generalizing the Relation Using the Confidence

The confidence function C expresses a graded certainty about the data. The idea is to bring this further information inside the relation R. This new kind of relation connects the elements in a graded way, so that we can associate a certainty value to each pair $(x, y) \in R$. We denote this value as $N_R(x, y)$. Furthermore, let us suppose to be able to define a possibility grade for the relation R and denote it as $\Pi_R(x, y)$ (we will explain how to define these two values in the following). Obviously, both $N_R(x, y)$ and $\Pi_R(x, y)$ shall be included in the interval $[0, 1]$.

Now, given an element $x \in U$ and a real number $\alpha \in [0, 1]$, we denote as $R_\alpha(x)$ the set of all elements y related to x for which the certainty value of $R(x, y)$ is greater than α:

$$R_\alpha(x) = \{y \in U \mid (x, y) \in R \wedge N_R(x, y) \geq \alpha\} \tag{6}$$

---

[2] By $C_A(x)$ we mean an overall confidence of x based on attributes $A \subseteq Att$, it is not specified here how to compute this value.

Similarly, given an element $x \in U$ and a real number $\beta \in [0,1]$, we denote $R^\beta(x)$ as the set of all elements $y \in U$ for which the general maximum possibility grade of being in relation with x is at least β, that is

$$R^\beta(x) = \{y \in U \mid \Pi_R(x,y) \geq \beta\} \tag{7}$$

In order to obtain meaningful approximations, Π and N must be defined such that $R_\alpha(x) \subseteq R^\beta(x)$.

Given these definitions and constraints, we can now define the approximations. The lower approximation highlights the necessity of the relation R, expressed by R_α, while the upper approximation uses the possibility of R, expressed by R^β. The definitions read as follows:

$$\begin{aligned}
\underline{R}(X) &= \{x \in U \mid R_\alpha(x) \subseteq X \wedge R_\alpha \neq \emptyset\} \\
\overline{R}(X) &= \{x \in U \mid R^\beta(x) \cap X \neq \emptyset\}
\end{aligned} \tag{8}$$

These approximations do satisfy the property $\underline{R}(X) \subseteq \overline{R}(X)$: this fact simply follows from $R_\alpha(x) \subseteq R^\beta(x)$. We notice that in the definition of the lower approximation it is necessary to specify that $R_\alpha(x)$ must not be empty since the empty set is always a subset of X: in fact there could exist an element $y \in U$ for which $R_\alpha(y) = \emptyset$ and this element would be part of the lower approximation, if there wasn't this specified restriction for R_α. This constraint is somehow similar to requesting the seriality of R in the standard case.

How to Obtain N_R and Π_R. Now, we give a possible solution to the problem of defining the necessity and possibility of the relation R given the confidence on the attributes. For the sake of simplicity, we define $N_R(x,y)$ as the minimum of all the confidence values relative to the elements x and y such that $(x,y) \in R$:

$$N_R(x,y) = \min_{a \in A}\{\{C(x,a)\} \cup \{C(y,a)\}\} \tag{9}$$

So, we have established a certainty grade $N_R(x,y)$ for every pair $(x,y) \in R$. This is enough in order to define the lower approximation according to Eq. (6). Moreover, this value of certainty represents also a value of uncertainty: indeed, it gives constraints on the possibility $\Pi_R(x,y)$ that any two elements (x,y) are in relation. It is easy to calculate this value for each pair $(x,y) \in R$ since the necessity grades $N_R(x,y)$ are available and, by Eqs. (1) and (2), if $N_R(x,y) > 0$ then $\Pi_R(x,y) = 1$. So we need only to compute $\Pi_R(x,y)$ for all the pairs $(x,y) \notin R$. At first, let us consider the following example.

Example 4. We have an information table where $U = \{x_1, x_2\}$, $Att = \{a_1, a_2\}$, $Val_{a_1} = \{b,c,d\}$, $Val_{a_2} = \{e,f,g\}$ and each cell of the Table 3 shows firstly the value of $F(x_i, a_j)$ and then the value of $C(x_i, a_j)$, for $i, j = 1, 2$.

Let R be the indiscernibility relation defined over $A = \{a_1, a_2\}$ in the standard way, so $(x_1, x_2) \notin R$.

Let us consider the attribute a_1: the value of C is higher for x_1 than x_2, so the value $F(x_1, a_1)$ is more certain than $F(x_2, a_1)$. If there is a chance for one of

Table 3. An example to show the procedure to compute Π_R.

	a_1	a_2
x_1	$(b,\ 0.9)$	$(g,\ 0.6)$
x_2	$(c,\ 0.5)$	$(f,\ 0.8)$

the elements to change its value, because of its uncertainty, this chance is surely higher for x_2: in particular, it is clear that $\Pi(F(x_2, a_1) \neq c) = 1 - C(x_2, a_1) = 1 - 0.5 = 0.5$, which is higher than $\Pi(F(x_1, a_1) \neq b) = 1 - C(x_1, a_1) = 1 - 0.9 = 0.1$. The same reasoning can be made for the attribute a_2, where $\Pi(F(x_1, a_2) \neq g) = 0.4 > \Pi(F(x_2, a_2) \neq f) = 0.2$.

We cannot know exactly what is the possibility either that $F(x_2, a_1) = b$ or $F(x_1, a_2) = f$. But we know for sure that these possibilities are bounded by the values of $C(x_2, a_1)$ and $C(x_1, a_2)$ respectively. That is, we can state that $\Pi(F(x_2, a_1) = b) \leq 1 - C(x_2, a_1) = 0.5$ and $\Pi(F(x_1, a_2) = f) \leq 1 - C(x_1, a_2) = 0.4$. So the exact values of $\Pi(F(x_2, a_1) = b)$ and $\Pi(F(x_1, a_2) = f)$ are unknown to us (unless, of course, we know the underlying possibility distribution that have generated the values of C). However, similarly to what has been explained at the end of Sect. 2, we assume the scenario with major uncertainty and set $\Pi_{\max}(F(x_2, a_1) = b) = 0.5$ and $\Pi_{\max}(F(x_1, a_2) = f) = 0.4$.

Now, by generalizing what we have just shown in the example, we obtain for $(x, y) \notin R$:

$$\Pi_{\max}(F(x, a) = F(y, a)) = 1 - \min\{C(x, a), C(y, a)\} \tag{10}$$

for each attribute $a \in A$. Supposing the independence of all these possibility values for each attribute $a \in A$, we can calculate the general maximum grade of possibility that two elements are related, using an independence product law as follows:

$$\Pi_R(x, y) = \prod_{a \in A} \Pi_{\max}(F(x, a) = F(y, a)) \tag{11}$$

for any two elements $x, y \in U$ for which $(x, y) \notin R$.

Of course, the definitions and thus the calculus of these possibility grades (both $\Pi_{\max}$ and Π_R) depend on the definition of R: in the previous paragraphs we have shown how to calculate them only for an equivalence relation. The final step is to show that these two measures are well defined, in the sense that $R_\alpha(x) \subseteq R^\beta(x)$.

Proposition 2. *Given the definitions N_R and Π_R as in Eqs. (6), (7) and the ones of R_α and R^β as in Eqs. (9), (11), then $R_\alpha(x) \subseteq R^\beta(x)$ for each $\alpha, \beta \in [0, 1]$ and for each $x \in U$.*

Proof. The proof is simple, as it follows directly from the definitions of $R_\alpha(x)$ and $R^\beta(x)$. In fact from the definition of $R_\alpha(x)$ we can state that $R_\alpha(x) \subseteq R(x)$

and from the definition of $R^\beta(x)$ we can state that $R(x) \subseteq R^\beta(x)$: these two facts together, that are valid for each $\alpha, \beta \in [0,1]$ and for each $x \in U$, lead to the initial statement.

4   Reducts

In the classical case, a reduct represents a reduction of the attributes that keeps the relation R unchanged. When considering a table with a confidence function, this classical definition holds, as the confidence is, at most, included in the definition of R. So taking as R_C one of the relations based on the confidence C defined in the previous section, we can define an attribute reduct in the standard way.

Definition 2 (Attribute reduct). *Let* (U, Att, Val, F, C) *be an information table with confidence,* $A \subseteq Att$ *a subset of attributes and* $R_{A,C} \subseteq U \times U$ *the indiscernibility relation defined over* A *and* C. *A subset of attributes* $B \subseteq A$ *is an* attribute reduct *when*

$$R_{A,C} = R_{B,C} \, and \, R_{B',C} \neq R_{A,C} \, \forall \, B' \subsetneq B \tag{12}$$

However, we can also reduce the information conveyed by the confidence function: despite the fact that the confidence values have, in general, a qualitative meaning, we can ask which are the minimal confidence values that keep the relation R unchanged. This is what we call a reduct on confidence. At first, let us define an order relation among confidence measures C, C'

$$C' \preceq C \quad \text{iff} \quad \forall x \in U, \forall a \in Att, C'(x,a) \leq C(x,a) \tag{13}$$

As usual, the strict order relation is: $C' \prec C$ iff $C' \preceq C$ and $C' \neq C$. A reduct on confidence is then defined as follows.

Definition 3 (Reduct on Confidence). *Let* (U, Att, Val, F, C) *be an information table,* $A \subseteq Att$ *a subset of attributes and* $R_{A,C} \subseteq U \times U$ *the indiscernibility relation defined over* A *and* C. *A function* $D : U \times Att \to [0,1]$ *is a reduct on confidence* when

$$R_{A,C} = R_{A,D} \, and \, R_{A,D'} \neq R_{A,C} \, \forall \, D' \prec D \tag{14}$$

This type of reduct is useful since it allows to maintain only the confidence values that are essential for the relation R. In fact, all the values that don't influence R can be set to 0.

Example 5. Given the information table about weather conditions, let $A \subseteq Att$ be a subset of attributes such that $A = \{\text{Temperature, Humidity}\}$. Let R be the equivalence relation defined over A and R_A the (equivalence) relation obtained after applying the granulation refinement specified in Eq. (3), with the thresholds $s_i = 0.8$ for both attributes in A. Thus, the granulation space is as follows:

$$U/R_A = \{\{x_1, x_2, x_5, x_9\}, \{x_3, x_{10}\}, \{x_4, x_8\}, \{x_6\}, \{x_7\}\}$$

A reduct on confidence for this case is represented by the following function D, represented in a tabular form:

Person	Weather	Temperature	Wind	Humidity	Sea
x_1	0.0	0.8	0.0	0.8	0.0
x_2	0.0	0.8	0.0	0.8	0.0
x_3	0.0	0.8	0.0	0.8	0.0
x_4	0.0	0.0	0.0	0.0	0.0
x_5	0.0	0.8	0.0	0.8	0.0
x_6	0.0	0.0	0.0	0.0	0.0
x_7	0.0	0.8	0.0	0.8	0.0
x_8	0.0	0.0	0.0	0.0	0.0
x_9	0.0	0.8	0.0	0.8	0.0
x_{10}	0.0	0.8	0.0	0.8	0.0

We can observe that the confidence values of all attributes of Att that are not included in A are set to 0, because they are not relevant to the relation R_A. Some of the confidence values of the attributes in A are set to 0 too, and this happens when one or both these values are less than the threshold. Furthermore, this is the only reduct on confidence for this case.

While the standard case keeps the relation R unchanged, we can define a reduct which preserves another property, that is the average confidence of the information table. We define this average confidence simply as an average over all the confidence values of the table. In the example we give at the end of this section, we use an arithmetic mean to calculate it, but other types of mean could also be used.

Definition 4 (Average confidence reduct). *Let $B \subseteq Att$ be a subset of attributes and $\tilde{C}(B)$ the average confidence of B. Then B is a reduct for average confidence when*

$$\tilde{C}(B) \geq \tilde{C}(Att) \, and \, \tilde{C}(B') < \tilde{C}(B) \, \forall \, B' \subset B \tag{15}$$

This reduct keeps the average confidence of data at least at the level of the initial average confidence, but it does not preserve at all the relation R.

Example 6. Let us consider again the weather example and calculate the average confidence of the whole table. As stated before, we use a simple arithmetic mean, so the average confidence is $\tilde{C}(Att) = 0.802$. Now, the average confidence of each attribute is:

- $\tilde{C}(\text{Weather}) = 0.87$
- $\tilde{C}(\text{Temperature}) = 0.88$

- $\tilde{C}(\text{Wind}) = 0.74$
- $\tilde{C}(\text{Humidity}) = 0.82$
- $\tilde{C}(\text{Sea}) = 0.70$

It is obvious that the only reducts for average confidence are:

- $B_1 = \{\text{Weather}\}$
- $B_2 = \{\text{Temperature}\}$
- $B_3 = \{\text{Humidity}\}$

As already noted, these reducts do not preserve at all the indiscernibility relation among the elements of the table.

To make this kind of reduct more significant, we can use it as a selection criterion among several already known reducts. That is, given the reducts $B_1, \ldots, B_n$, which preserve the relation R, we could keep only those whose average confidence is not lower than the initial one.

We can enunciate this *confidence criterion* as follows:

Definition 5. *Given an information table (U, Att, Val, F, C) and some reducts $B_1, \ldots, B_n$ for it, it is preferable to consider only the reducts B_i such that $\tilde{C}(B_i) \geq \tilde{C}(Att)$. If none of them satisfies this criterion, then we just keep the best reduct, that is the reduct $B_{\max}$ such that $B_{\max} = \text{argmax}_{i=1,\ldots,n}\, \tilde{C}(B_i)$.*

Of course, this criterion can be used also with reducts obtained by decision tables in order to define more confident rules.

5 Conclusions

In the present work, we have introduced the notion of information table with certainty values with the aim to take advantage of some possible information on the uncertain knowledge on data. Indeed, the consequences and usefulness of this new information in rough set theory have been explored and in particular, several kinds of approximations and reducts have been defined that use in a different manner the confidence values.

Of course this is only a preliminary step. As a future work, these new approximations and reducts should be tested and compared on real cases. In particular, when dealing with decision tables, the role of the confidence to define the rules has to be exploited. One possible solution is to use the criterion defined at the end of Sect. 4.

References

1. Ciucci, D.: Approximation algebra and framework. Fundam. Inform. **94**(2), 147–161 (2009)
2. Ciucci, D.: Back to the beginnings: Pawlak's definitions of the terms information system and rough set. In: Wang, G., Skowron, A., Yao, Y., Ślęzak, D., Polkowski, L. (eds.) Thriving Rough Sets. SCI, vol. 708, pp. 225–235. Springer International Publishing AG, Cham (2017). doi:10.1007/978-3-319-54966-8_11

3. Ciucci, D., Mihálydeák, T., Csajbók, Z.E.: On definability and approximations in partial approximation spaces. In: Miao, D., Pedrycz, W., Ślęzak, D., Peters, G., Hu, Q., Wang, R. (eds.) RSKT 2014. LNCS (LNAI), vol. 8818, pp. 15–26. Springer, Cham (2014). doi:10.1007/978-3-319-11740-9_2

4. Dubois, D., Prade, H.: Practical methods for constructing possibility distributions. Int. J. Intell. Syst. **31**(3), 215–239 (2016)

5. Dubois, D., Prade, H.: Possibility theory and its applications: where do we stand? In: Kacprzyk, J., Pedrycz, W. (eds.) Springer Handbook of Computational Intelligence, pp. 31–60. Springer, Heidelberg (2015). doi:10.1007/978-3-662-43505-2_3

6. Nakata, M., Sakai, H.: Lower and upper approximations in data tables containing possibilistic information. Trans. Rough Sets **7**, 170–189 (2007)

7. Nakata, M., Sakai, H.: Rough sets by indiscernibility relations in data sets containing possibilistic information. In: Flores, V., et al. (eds.) IJCRS 2016. LNCS, vol. 9920, pp. 187–196. Springer, Cham (2016). doi:10.1007/978-3-319-47160-0_17

8. Orlowska, E., Pawlak, Z.: Representation of nondeterministic information. Theor. Comput. Sci. **29**, 27–39 (1984)

9. Pivert, O., Prade, H.: A certainty-based model for uncertain databases. IEEE Trans. Fuzzy Syst. **23**(4), 1181–1196 (2015)

10. Pivert, O., Prade, H.: Possibilistic conditional tables. In: Gyssens, M., Simari, G. (eds.) FoIKS 2016. LNCS, vol. 9616, pp. 42–61. Springer, Cham (2016). doi:10.1007/978-3-319-30024-5_3

11. Polkowski, L., Artiemjew, P.: Granular Computing in Decision Approximation. An Application of Rough Mereology. Springer International Publishing, Cham (2015)

12. Skowron, A., Jankowski, A., Swiniarski, R.W.: Foundations of rough sets. In: Kacprzyk, J., Pedrycz, W. (eds.) Springer Handbook of Computational Intelligence, pp. 331–348. Springer, Heidelberg (2015). doi:10.1007/978-3-662-43505-2_21

13. Yao, J., Ciucci, D., Zhang, Y.: Generalized rough sets. In: Kacprzyk, J., Pedrycz, W. (eds.) Handbook of Computational Intelligence, pp. 413–424. Springer, Heidelberg (2015). doi:10.1007/978-3-662-43505-2_25

14. Yao, Y.: Probabilistic rough set approximations. Int. J. Approx. Reason. **49**(2), 255–271 (2008)

15. Yao, Y., Greco, S., Słowiński, R.: Probabilistic rough sets. In: Kacprzyk, J., Pedrycz, W. (eds.) Springer Handbook of Computational Intelligence, pp. 387–411. Springer, Heidelberg (2015). doi:10.1007/978-3-662-43505-2_24. Chap. 25

16. Zadeh, L.: Fuzzy sets as a basis for a theory of possibility. Fuzzy Set. Syst. **1**, 3–28 (1978)

17. Ziarko, W.: Variable precision rough sets model. J. Comput. Syst. Sci. **43**(1), 39–59 (1993)

The Rough Membership Function on One Type of Covering-Based Rough Sets and Its Applications

Xun Ge[1], Jianguo Tang[2], and Pei Wang[3](✉)

[1] School of Mathematical Sciences, Soochow University,
Suzhou 215006, People's Republic of China
gexun@suda.edu.cn
[2] School of Computer Science and Engineering,
Xinjiang University of Finance and Economics,
Ürümqi 830012, People's Republic of China
tjguo@126.com
[3] Department of Mathematics and Information Sciences,
Yulin Normal University, Yulin 537000, People's Republic of China
wangpei131@sina.com.cn

Abstract. In this paper, we use an example in evidence-based medicine to illustrate the practical application backgrounds of Pawlak's rough membership function in real life. By this example, we also point out the limitations of Pawlak's rough membership function in real life applications and the necessity for constructing rough membership functions for covering-based rough sets. Then, we construct covering-based rough membership function for one type of covering-based rough sets which was examined by Bonikowski et al. (Inf Sci 107:149–167, 1998), and use it to characterize the covering-based rough set approximations numerically. We not only present theoretical backgrounds for this covering-based rough membership function, but also show that this covering-based rough membership function is more realistic than Pawlak's rough membership function in applications of real life.

Keywords: Rough membership function · Covering-based rough set · Probabilistic rough set · Fuzzy set · Numerical characterization · Evidence-based medicine

1 Introduction

The concept of rough sets was originally proposed by Pawlak [8]. It is a new mathematical tool to handle uncertain knowledge, and has been successfully applied in pattern recognition, data mining, machine learning, and so on [7,11,21]. A problem with Pawlak's rough set theory is that partition or equivalence relation is explicitly used in the definition of the lower and upper approximations. However, such a partition or equivalence relation is still restrictive for

© Springer International Publishing AG 2017
L. Polkowski et al. (Eds.): IJCRS 2017, Part II, LNAI 10314, pp. 56–69, 2017.
DOI: 10.1007/978-3-319-60840-2_4

many applications because it can only deal with complete information systems [7,11,20]. To address this issue, generalizations of rough set theory were considered by scholars in order to deal with complex practical problems. One important approach was to relax the partition to a covering and obtained covering-based rough sets. Based on the mutual correspondence of the concepts of extension and intension, Bonikowski et al. proposed a type of covering-based rough sets [1]. Pomykala explored this covering-based rough set [12]. His main method included interior and closure operators from topology [12]. Zhang et al. studied axiomatic characterizations of this covering-based upper approximation operator and examined the independence of axiom sets [22]. Furthermore, the minimization of axiomatic characterizations of this covering-based upper approximation operator was investigated and more refined axiom sets were presented in [23].

The concept of rough membership functions played an important role in rough set theory for measuring the uncertainty of a set in an information system [10]. For a finite universe, a rough membership function was typically computed by Pawlak et al., and was used to present numerical characterizations of Pawlak's rough set approximations [9]. Based on the rough membership function, Yao revisited probabilistic rough set approximation operators. He also made a survey on existing studies, and gave some new results on the decision-theoretic rough set model [18]. Pawlak and Skowron interpreted rough sets by constructing membership function, weak membership function or strong membership function [10]. Greco et al. used the concept of absolute and relative rough membership functions to present a parameterized rough set model, which is a generalization of the original definition of rough sets and variable precision rough sets [3]. In addition, the relative rough membership function was an instance of a class of measures known as the Bayesian confirmation measures [2]. However, as pointed out by the authors of [5], a partition induced by equivalence relation may not provide a realistic view of relationships between elements in the real-word application although it is easy to analyze. Instead, a covering of the universe might be considered as an alternative to provide a more realistic model of rough sets [1,5,12,16]. Based on coverings of the universe, Yao and Zhang defined minimum, maximum and average rough membership functions, and studied their properties [19]. Furthermore, Intan and Mukaidono constructed minimum, maximum and average rough membership functions which are based on α-coverings of the universe, and examined their properties [4]. Xu and Zhang proposed new lower and upper approximations and constructed a covering-based rough membership function for them [16]. They also defined a measure of roughness based on the covering-based rough membership function and discussed some significant applications of this measure [16]. Based on the covering-based rough membership function defined in [16], Shi and Gong constructed similarity measure for covering rough sets, and established relationships between covering-based probabilistic rough sets and Pawlak rough sets or covering-based rough sets or Pawlak probabilistic rough sets [14]. In view that the rough membership functions studied in the above papers are described only by a single binary relation or a single covering on a given universe, which can not be applied in some practical multigranulation backgrounds, Lin et al. proposed the maximal and minimal degree of rough membership to characterize the uncertainty of covering-based multigranulation rough sets [5].

However, to the best of our knowledge, no researcher pays attention to rough membership function of covering-based rough set mentioned in the first paragraph of this section, or to the practical applications of Pawlak's rough membership function in real life. In this paper, we use an example in evidence-based medicine to illustrate the practical application backgrounds of Pawlak's rough membership function in real life. By this example, we also point out the limitations of Pawlak's rough membership function in applications of real life and the necessity of constructing rough membership functions for covering-based rough sets. Then, we construct covering-based rough membership function for the covering-based rough set. We not only present theoretical backgrounds for the covering-based rough membership function, but also show that this covering-based rough membership function is more realistic than Pawlak's rough membership function in applications of real life.

The remainder of this paper is arranged as follows: In Sect. 2, after reviewing the concept of Pawlak's rough membership function and numerical characterizations of Pawlak's rough set approximations, we present theoretical backgrounds of Pawlak's rough membership function. Then, we give an example in medical diagnosis to illustrate practical backgrounds of Pawlak's rough membership function in real life. By this example, we also point out the limitations of Pawlak's rough membership function in applications of real life. In Sect. 3, we present several fundamental concepts and basic facts needed in this paper. Section 4 is the focus of this paper. In Sect. 4, we construct covering-based rough membership function for the covering-based rough set, and present its numerical characterizations. In Sect. 5, after presenting theoretic backgrounds for the covering-based rough membership function, we use the example presented in Sect. 2 to illustrate the covering-based rough membership function is more realistic than Pawlak's rough membership function when considering practical applications. This paper concluded in Sect. 6 with remarks for future works.

2   Pawlak's Rough Sets

In this section, we first review the concept of Pawlak's rough membership function and numerical characterizations of Pawlak's rough set approximations. Then we present theoretical backgrounds of Pawlak's rough membership function. Finally, we employ an example in medical diagnosis to illustrate the practical backgrounds and limitations of Pawlak's rough membership function.

Pawlak's rough sets are defined as follows [9]:

Let U be a finite set and R be an equivalence relation on U. R will generate a partition U/R on U, and a block of the partition U/R containing the element x will be denoted as $[x]_R$. $\forall X \subseteq U$, the lower, upper approximations and the boundary region of X are defined in the following way respectively:

$$\underline{R}(X) = \{x \in U : [x]_R \subseteq X\},$$
$$\overline{R}(X) = \{x \in U : [x]_R \cap X \neq \varnothing\},$$
$$BN_R(X) = \overline{R}(X) - \underline{R}(X).$$

2.1 Definition of Rough Membership Function

Pawlak's rough membership function is a function $\mu_X^R : U \to [0,1]$, defined by $\mu_X^R(x) = \dfrac{|[x]_R \cap X|}{|[x]_R|}$, where $x \in U, X \subseteq U$ and $|X|$ denotes the cardinality of X [15].

The rough membership function expresses conditional probability that x belongs to X given by R and can be interpreted as the degree that x belongs to X in view of information about x expressed by R [9].

2.2 Numerical Characterizations

Pawlak's rough sets can be also defined by the rough membership function instead of approximation. That is, if μ_X^R be a rough membership function on U, then $\forall X \subseteq U$, the approximations and the boundary region of X can be defined as follows [9]:

$$\underline{R}(X) = \{x \in U : \mu_X^R(x) = 1\},$$
$$\overline{R}(X) = \{x \in U : \mu_X^R(x) > 0\},$$
$$BN_R(X) = \{x \in U : \mu_X^R(x) \in (0,1)\}.$$

2.3 Backgrounds of Rough Membership Function

Theoretical Backgrounds. The rough membership function may be interpreted as a special kind of fuzzy membership function. Under this interpretation, it is possible to establish the connection between Pawlak rough sets and fuzzy sets as follows [17]: $\forall X \subseteq U$,

$$\underline{R}(X) = \{x \in U : \mu_X^R(x) = 1\} = core(\mu_X^R),$$
$$\overline{R}(X) = \{x \in U : \mu_X^R(x) > 0\} = support(\mu_X^R).$$

Besides, the rough membership function, in contrast to fuzzy membership function, has a probabilistic flavor. The relationship between probabilistic rough sets and Pawlak rough sets was established as follows in [20]: If the parameters $\alpha = 1$ and $\beta = 0$, then the probabilistic lower approximation $\underline{PI}_\alpha(X)$ and upper approximation $\overline{PI}_\beta(X)$ are degenerated into the lower approximation $\underline{R}(X)$ and upper approximation $\overline{R}(X)$ in the Pawlak rough sets respectively. That is, for any $X \subseteq U$,

$$\underline{PI}_\alpha(X) = \underline{PI}_1(X) = \{x \in U : P(X|[x]_R) \geq 1\} = \{x \in U : [x]_R \subseteq X\} = \underline{R}(X),$$
$$\overline{PI}_\beta(X) = \overline{PI}_0(X) = \{x \in U : P(X|[x]_R) > 0\} = \{x \in U : [x]_R \cap X \neq \varnothing\} = \overline{R}(X),$$

where $P(X|[x]_R) = \dfrac{|[x]_R \cap X|}{|[x]_R|}$ is the conditional probability that x belongs to X given by R.

Practical Backgrounds. As we mentioned in Introduction Section, rough membership functions play an important role in Pawlak's rough sets. In the following, by means of the analysis of an example about evidence-based medical diagnosis data, we explain how we can use the Pawlak's rough membership function to determine the initial treatment of patients, in order to help doctors to make subjective diagnose. At the same time, by this example, we point out the limitations of Pawlak's rough membership function in applications of real life, and show the necessity to establish the covering-based rough membership functions. An evidence-based medical diagnosis database of a hospital is a database based on information of patients who visited the hospital and the diseases of them were diagnosed. The database consists of symptom reaction of patients and finally diagnosed illness. An evidence-based medicine database cannot be simply regarded as an 'if... then' system, since it is possible that two patients with identical symptoms were finally diagnosed with different diseases. The example consists of data of 20 patients, including 16 patients ($p_1 - p_{16}$) with diseases were identified according to their symptoms, for 2 patients (p_{17} and p_{18}) although symptoms clear, but the disease has not been identified, for the last two patients (p_{19} and p_{20}) part of the symptom reaction still not clear. The detailed information of the example is in Table 1.

Table 1. Clinical features of different types of lung cancer

Patient	Chest pain	Short breath	Local diffusion	Distant metastasis	Lung cancer
p_1	1	1	1	1	C.L.C
p_2	1	1	1	1	C.L.C
p_3	1	1	1	1	C.L.C
p_4	1	1	1	1	C.L.C
p_5	1	1	0	1	C.L.C
p_6	0	1	0	1	P.L.C
p_7	1	1	0	1	P.L.C
p_8	1	1	0	1	P.L.C
p_9	1	1	0	1	P.L.C
p_{10}	1	1	0	1	P.L.C
p_{11}	1	1	0	0	P.L.C
p_{12}	1	0	1	0	T.B.L.B.C
p_{13}	1	1	1	0	T.B.L.B.C
p_{14}	1	1	1	0	T.B.L.B.C
p_{15}	1	1	1	0	T.B.L.B.C
p_{16}	1	1	1	0	T.B.L.B.C
p_{17}	1	1	0	1	
p_{18}	1	1	1	0	
p_{19}		1		1	
p_{20}	1			0	

Example 1. In   Table 1,   {chest pain, short breath, local diffusion, distant metastasis} is a set of condition attributes, {lung cancer} is a set of decision attribute, and C.L.C, P.L.C, T.B.L.B.C denote central lung cancer, peripheral lung cancer, thin bronchuses lung bubble cancer respectively. Moreover, each row can be seen as information about a specific patient, and 1 denotes yes, 0 denotes no. The patient $p_i(i = 17, 18, 19$ and $20)$ is waiting for the hospital diagnosis, whereas the information of patient $p_i(1 \leq i \leq 16)$, which is from diagnostic database of lung cancer cases in hospital, can determine the following seven decision rules:

(1) if (chest pain, 1) and (short breath, 1) and (local diffusion, 1) and (distant metastasis, 1), then (lung cancer, central lung cancer);
(2) if (chest pain, 1) and (short breath, 1) and (local diffusion, 0) and (distant metastasis, 1), then (lung cancer, central lung cancer);
(3) if (chest pain, 0) and (short breath, 1) and (local diffusion, 0) and (distant metastasis, 1), then (lung cancer, peripheral lung cancer);
(4) if (chest pain, 1) and (short breath, 1) and (local diffusion, 0) and (distant metastasis, 1), then (lung cancer, peripheral lung cancer);
(5) if (chest pain, 1) and (short breath, 1) and (local diffusion, 0) and (distant metastasis, 0), then (lung cancer, peripheral lung cancer);
(6) if (chest pain, 1) and (short breath, 0) and (local diffusion, 1) and (distant metastasis, 0), then (lung cancer, thin bronchuses lung bubble cancer);
(7) if (chest pain, 1) and (short breath, 1) and (local diffusion, 1) and (distant metastasis, 0), then (lung cancer, thin bronchuses lung bubble cancer).

Further analysis of decision rules induced from Table 1, we can note that some rules are inconsistent, such as rule 1 and 2. This leads to patients 17 and 18 could not be easily diagnosed by these rules. One approach to overcoming this problem is using the following method based on the Pawlak's rough membership function to take the most frequent decision in the decision table.

An equivalence relation $I(C)$ can be defined on $U = \{p_i : 1 \leq i \leq 18\}$ by set of condition attributes C as follows:
$I(C) = \{(x, y) \in U \times U : f_a(x) = f_a(y), \forall a \in C\}$, where $f_a(x)$ is the value of a on $x \in U$.

For $C = \{$chest pain, short breath, local diffusion, distant metastasis$\}$, denote $C(x) = \{y \in U : (x, y) \in I(C)\}$.

By Table 1, it is easy to verify that

$C(p_1) = C(p_2) = C(p_3) = C(p_4) = \{p_1, p_2, p_3, p_4\}$;
$C(p_5) = C(p_7) = C(p_8) = C(p_9) = C(p_{10}) = C(p_{17}) = \{p_5, p_7, p_8, p_9, p_{10}, p_{17}\}$;
$C(p_6) = \{p_6\}$;
$C(p_{11}) = \{p_{11}\}$;
$C(p_{12}) = \{p_{12}\}$;
$C(p_{13}) = C(p_{14}) = C(p_{15}) = C(p_{16}) = C(p_{18}) = \{p_{13}, p_{14}, p_{15}, p_{16}, p_{18}\}$.

Thus, $U/I(C) = \{C(p_1), C(p_5), C(p_6), C(p_{11}), C(p_{12}), C(p_{13})\}$ is a partition of U. Let $\langle U, U/I \rangle$ be the Pawlak approximation space and let $X_1 = \{p_i : 1 \leq$

$i \leq 5\}, X_2 = \{p_i : 6 \leq i \leq 11\}$ and $X_3 = \{p_i : 12 \leq i \leq 16\}$. We can easily calculate values of the Pawlak's rough membership function of $p_i(i = 17, 18)$ belonging to $X_i(i = 1, 2, 3)$ with respect to $R = U/I(C)$ as follows:

$$\mu_{X_1}^R(p_{17}) = \frac{1}{6}; \ \mu_{X_1}^R(p_{18}) = 0;$$

$$\mu_{X_2}^R(p_{17}) = \frac{2}{3}; \ \mu_{X_2}^R(p_{18}) = 0;$$

$$\mu_{X_3}^R(p_{17}) = 0; \ \mu_{X_3}^R(p_{18}) = \frac{4}{5}.$$

We can make a preliminary judgement that p_{17} and p_{18} probably suffers peripheral lung cancer and thin bronchuses lung bubble cancer, respectively.

2.4 Limitations of Rough Membership Function

In Example 1, we demonstrate that how we can make frequent decisions in diagnosis of lung cancer by using the Pawlak's rough membership function when all the symptoms of illness are clear. However, in some cases, since patients are unable to describe all the symptoms of illness expressly and the clinical treatment levels of doctors are not high enough to make them clear either, the descriptions of clinical data about symptoms of patients are incomplete, such as those of patients of p_{19} and p_{20} presented in Table 1. In such cases, different of what we did in Example 1, we cannot take the most frequent decision by means of the Pawlak's rough membership function. For example, on $U = \{p_i : 1 \leq i \leq 16 \text{ or } i = 19, 20\}$, the set of condition attributes C is a covering rather than a partition, because the blocks which are formulated by condition attributes C have overlaps. Taking p_{19} for example, since the values of condition attributes chest pain and local diffusion are unknown, they can be 0 or 1. If the values are 1, then by $I(C), p_1, p_2, p_3, p_4$ and p_{19} are indiscernible. So, $\{p_1, p_2, p_3, p_4, p_{19}\}$ is a block determined by condition attributes C. If the values are 0, then by $I(C), p_6$ and p_{19} are indiscernible. So, $\{p_6, p_{19}\}$ is a block determined by condition attributes C. So, the above two blocks have a common element p_{19}, and it follows that condition attributes C is a covering instead of a partition. The condition of p_{20} is similar. Thus, the Pawlak's rough membership function based on equivalence relation can not be used to make the frequent decisions for patients p_{19} and p_{20} in Table 1. To solve this problem, the approach in presented Sect. 2.3 should be improved by using rough membership function based on covering instead of the Pawlak's rough membership function based on equivalence relation.

3 Basic Concepts

In this section, we present the basic concepts we need in this paper. To begin with, we list some definitions in probabilistic approaches to rough sets.

Definition 1 *(Probabilistic approximation space [15]). Let U be the universe of discourse, R an equivalence relation and P a probability measure on U. We call the triplet (U, R, P) a probabilistic approximation space. For every $X \subseteq U$, $0 \leq \beta < \alpha \leq 1$ and the probabilistic approximation space (U, R, P), the lower approximation and the upper approximation of X with respect to parameters α and β are defined as follows:*

$$\underline{PI}_\alpha(X) = \{x \in U : P(X|[x]_R) \geq \alpha\},$$
$$\overline{PI}_\beta(X) = \{x \in U : P(X|[x]_R) > \beta\},$$

where $P(X|[x]_R)$ is the conditional probability that x belongs to X given by R.

Then, we present some concepts about coverings to be used in this paper.

Definition 2 *(Covering [26]). Let U be the universe of discourse and C a family of nonempty subsets of U. If $\bigcup C = U, C$ is called a covering of U.*

In the following discussion, unless stated to the contrary, the universe are considered to be finite, and it follows that coverings consist of a finite number of sets.

Definition 3 *(Covering approximation space [26]). Let U be the universe of discourse and C a covering of U. We call the ordered pair $\langle U, C \rangle$ a covering approximation space.*

Definition 4 *(Minimal description [26]). Let $\langle U, C \rangle$ be a covering approximation space, $x \in U$. $Md(x) = \{K \in C : (x \in K) \wedge (\forall S \in C \wedge x \in S \wedge S \subseteq K \Rightarrow K = S)\}$ is called the minimal description of x.*

Definition 5 *(Indiscernible neighborhood [26]). Let $\langle U, C \rangle$ be a covering approximation space. $\forall x \in U, \bigcup \{K \in C : x \in K\}$ is called the indiscernible neighborhood of x and denoted as $Friends(x)$.*

Definition 6. *For a given covering C of U, the rough membership function in general are defined as follows: $\forall x \in U$ and $X \subseteq U, \mu_X^C(x) = max\{\frac{|K \cap X|}{|K|} : x \in K \in C\}$.*

The following facts about $\mu_X^C(x)$ are obvious:

Fact 1. $0 \leq \mu_X^C(x) \leq 1$;

Fact 2. $\mu_X^C(x) = 1$ if and only if there exists $K \in C$ such that $x \in K \subseteq X$;

Fact 3. $\mu_X^C(x) = 0$ if and only if for any $K \in C$ with $x \in K, K \cap X = \varnothing$.

4   Main Results

In this section, we study rough membership function on the covering-based rough set. We will address the following issues. First, we construct a rough membership function which is based on topological structures of the covering approximation operators. Then, we present numerical characterizations of the covering rough set approximations by means of the covering-based rough membership function.

4.1 Definition of the Covering-Based Rough Set and Its Rough Membership Function

Definition 7. *(CL, FH and BN_F [1]). Let C be a covering of U. The operations CL and FH: $P(U) \to P(U)$ are defined as follows: $\forall X \subseteq U$,*

$$CL(X) = \bigcup \{K \in C : K \subseteq X\},$$

$$FH(X) = CL(X) \cup (\bigcup \{\bigcup \{Md(x) : x \in X - CL(X)\}\}),$$

$$BN_F(X) = FH(X) - CL(X).$$

We call CL the covering lower approximation operation and FH the covering upper approximation operation.

Definition 7 only presents the topological characterizations of CL and FH. As it is well known, numerical characterizations are just as important to theoretical research of covering-based rough sets as topological characterizations. Meanwhile, we also found that Pawlak's rough membership function does not work with missing data. Based on the topological structures of CL and FH simultaneously, we construct a covering-based rough membership function for CL and FH, and use it not only to present numerical characterizations about CL and FH, but also to work suitably with missing data.

Definition 8. *For a given covering C of U, the rough membership function of CL and FH are defined as follows: $\forall x \in U$ and $X \subseteq U, \mu_X^C(x)_F = \lfloor \mu_X^C(x) \rfloor + \mu_X^C(x) \cdot \lfloor max\{max\{\frac{|K_1 \cap K_2|}{|K_2|} : K_1 \in Md(y), x \in K_2 \in C\} \cdot \lceil 1 - \mu_X^C(y) \rceil : y \in Friends(x) \cap X\} \rfloor \cdot \lceil 1 - \mu_X^C(x) \rceil.$*

4.2 Numerical Characterizations

Lemma 1. *$max\{\frac{|K_1 \cap K_2|}{|K_2|} : K_1, K_2 \in C\} = 1.$*

Lemma 2. *$\forall x \in U$ and $X \subseteq U, max\{max\{\frac{|K_1 \cap K_2|}{|K_2|} : K_1 \in Md(y), x \in K_2 \in C\} \cdot \lceil 1 - \mu_X^C(y) \rceil : y \in Friends(x) \cap X\} \in [0, 1].$*

Proof. We choose any $y \in Friends(x) \cap X$. By Fact 1 and Lemma 1, $\lceil 1 - \mu_X^C(y) \rceil \in \{0, 1\}$ and $max\{\frac{|K_1 \cap K_2|}{|K_2|} : K_1 \in Md(y), x \in K_2 \in C\} \in [0, 1]$. Thus, $max\{\frac{|K_1 \cap K_2|}{|K_2|} : K_1 \in Md(y), x \in K_2 \in C\} \cdot \lceil 1 - \mu_X^C(y) \rceil \in [0, 1]$. So, $max\{max\{\frac{|K_1 \cap K_2|}{|K_2|} : K_1 \in Md(y), x \in K_2 \in C\} \cdot \lceil 1 - \mu_X^C(y) \rceil : y \in Friends(x) \cap X\} \in [0, 1]$.

Lemma 3. *$\forall x \in U$ and $X \subseteq U, \mu_X^C(x)_F \in [0, 1].$*

Proof. By Fact 1 and Lemma 2, $\lceil 1 - \mu_X^C(x) \rceil \in \{0, 1\}$, and $\lfloor max\{max\{\frac{|K_1 \cap K_2|}{|K_2|} : K_1 \in Md(y), x \in K_2 \in C\} \cdot \lceil 1 - \mu_X^C(y) \rceil : y \in Friends(x) \cap X\} \rfloor \in \{0, 1\}$. Thus, $\mu_X^C(x) \cdot \lfloor max\{max\{\frac{|K_1 \cap K_2|}{|K_2|} : K_1 \in Md(y), x \in K_2 \in C\} \cdot \lceil 1 - \mu_X^C(y) \rceil : y \in$

$Friends(x) \cap X\}\rfloor \cdot \lceil 1 - \mu_X^C(x)\rceil \in [0,1]$. If $x \in U - CL(X)$, by Fact 1 and 2, then $\lfloor \mu_X^C(x)\rfloor = 0$. Thus, $\mu_X^C(x)_F = \mu_X^C(x) \cdot \lfloor max\{max\{\frac{|K_1 \cap K_2|}{|K_2|} : K_1 \in Md(y), x \in K_2 \in C\} \cdot \lceil 1 - \mu_X^C(y)\rceil : y \in Friends(x) \cap X\}\rfloor \cdot \lceil 1 - \mu_X^C(x)\rceil \in [0,1]$. If $x \in CL(X)$, by Fact 2, then $\lfloor \mu_X^C(x)\rfloor = 1$, and $\lceil 1 - \mu_X^C(x)\rceil = 0$. So, $\mu_X^C(x)_F = \lfloor \mu_X^C(x)\rfloor = 1$. Hence, $\mu_X^C(x)_F \in [0,1]$.

Theorem 1. $\forall X \subseteq U, CL(X) = \{x \in U : \mu_X^C(x)_F = 1\}$.

Proof. We choose any $x \in CL(X)$. By the proof in Lemma 3, $\mu_X^C(x)_F = 1$. Thus, $x \in \{x \in U : \mu_X^C(x)_F = 1\}$. So, by arbitrariness of $x, CL(X) \subseteq \{x \in U : \mu_X^C(x)_F = 1\}$.

We choose any $x \in \{x \in U : \mu_X^C(x)_F = 1\}$. Since $\mu_X^C(x)_F = 1, \lfloor \mu_X^C(x)\rfloor + \mu_X^C(x) \cdot \lfloor max\{max\{\frac{|K_1 \cap K_2|}{|K_2|} : K_1 \in Md(y), x \in K_2 \in C\} \cdot \lceil 1 - \mu_X^C(y)\rceil : y \in Friends(x) \cap X\}\rfloor \cdot \lceil 1 - \mu_X^C(x)\rceil = 1$. By Fact 1, $\lfloor \mu_X^C(x)\rfloor = 0$ or 1. If $\lfloor \mu_X^C(x)\rfloor = 0$, by Fact 1, then $\mu_X^C(x) \in [0,1)$ and $\lceil 1 - \mu_X^C(x)\rceil = 1$. Thus, by Lemma 2, $\mu_X^C(x)_F = \mu_X^C(x) \cdot \lfloor max\{max\{\frac{|K_1 \cap K_2|}{|K_2|} : K_1 \in Md(y), x \in K_2 \in C\} \cdot \lceil 1 - \mu_X^C(y)\rceil : y \in Friends(x) \cap X\}\rfloor \in [0,1)$. This contradicts the assumption that $\mu_X^C(x)_F = 1$. So, $\lfloor \mu_X^C(x)\rfloor = 1$. By Fact 1, $\mu_X^C(x) = 1$. Thus, by Fact 2, $x \in CL(X)$. Hence, by arbitrariness of $x, \{x \in U : \mu_X^C(x)_F = 1\} \subseteq CL(X)$.

Theorem 2. $\forall X \subseteq U, FH(X) = \{x \in U : \mu_X^C(x)_F \in (0,1]\}$.

Proof. We choose any $x \in FH(X)$. If $x \in CL(X)$, by Theorem 1, then $\mu_X^C(x)_F = 1$. So, $x \in \{x \in U : \mu_X^C(x)_F \in (0,1]\}$. If $x \in FH(X) - CL(X)$, then $x \in FH(X)$ and $x \notin CL(X)$. Since $x \notin CL(X)$, by Fact 1 and 2, $\mu_X^C(x) \in [0,1)$. Thus, $\lfloor \mu_X^C(x)\rfloor = 0$ and $\lceil 1 - \mu_X^C(x)\rceil = 1$. Since $x \in FH(X)$, by the definition of $FH(X)$, there exists $y \in X - CL(X)$ such that $x \in \bigcup Md(y)$. Thus, there exists $K_1 \in Md(y)$ such that $K_1 \not\subseteq X$ and $x \in K_1$. So, $\mu_X^C(x) \geq \frac{|K_1 \cap X|}{|K_1|} > 0$. Since $y \in X - CL(X)$, by Fact 1 and 2, $\mu_X^C(y) \in [0,1)$. Thus, $\lceil 1 - \mu_X^C(y)\rceil = 1$. Since $max\{max\{\frac{|K_1 \cap K_2|}{|K_2|} : K_1 \in Md(y), x \in K_2 \in C\} \cdot \lceil 1 - \mu_X^C(y)\rceil : y \in Friends(x) \cap X\} \geq \frac{|K_1 \cap K_1|}{|K_1|} = 1$, by Lemma 2, $\lfloor max\{max\{\frac{|K_1 \cap K_2|}{|K_2|} : K_1 \in Md(y), x \in K_2 \in C\} \cdot \lceil 1 - \mu_X^C(y)\rceil : y \in Friends(x) \cap X\}\rfloor = 1$. Thus, $\mu_X^C(x)_F = \mu_X^C(x) \in (0,1)$. Hence, $x \in \{x \in U : \mu_X^C(x)_F \in (0,1]\}$. So, by arbitrariness of $x, FH(X) \subseteq \{x \in U : \mu_X^C(x)_F \in (0,1]\}$.

We choose any $x \in \{x \in U : \mu_X^C(x)_F \in (0,1]\}$. By Fact 1, $\lfloor \mu_X^C(x)\rfloor = 0$ or 1. If $\lfloor \mu_X^C(x)\rfloor = 1$, by Fact 1 and 2, then $x \in CL(X) \subseteq FH(X)$. If $\lfloor \mu_X^C(x)\rfloor = 0$, by Fact 1, then $\mu_X^C(x) \in [0,1)$. Thus, $\lceil 1 - \mu_X^C(x)\rceil = 1$. Hence, $\mu_X^C(x)_F = \mu_X^C(x) \cdot \lfloor max\{max\{\frac{|K_1 \cap K_2|}{|K_2|} : K_1 \in Md(y), x \in K_2 \in C\} \cdot \lceil 1 - \mu_X^C(y)\rceil : y \in Friends(x) \cap X\}\rfloor \in (0,1]$. By Fact 1 and Lemma 2, $\mu_X^C(x) \in (0,1]$ and $max\{max\{\frac{|K_1 \cap K_2|}{|K_2|} : K_1 \in Md(y), x \in K_2 \in C\} \cdot \lceil 1 - \mu_X^C(y)\rceil : y \in Friends(x) \cap X\} = 1$. So, there exists $y \in Friends(x) \cap X$ such that $max\{\frac{|K_1 \cap K_2|}{|K_2|} : K_1 \in Md(y), x \in K_2 \in C\} \cdot \lceil 1 - \mu_X^C(y)\rceil = 1$. Hence, by Fact 1 and Lemma 1, $\lceil 1 - \mu_X^C(y)\rceil = 1$ and $max\{\frac{|K_1 \cap K_2|}{|K_2|} : K_1 \in Md(y), x \in K_2 \in C\} = 1$. Since $\lceil 1 - \mu_X^C(y)\rceil = 1$, by

Fact 1, $\mu_X^C(y) \in [0,1)$. Since $max\{\frac{|K_1 \cap K_2|}{|K_2|} : K_1 \in Md(y), x \in K_2 \in C\} = 1$, there exist $K_1 \in Md(y)$ and $K_2 \in C, x \in K_2$ such that $\frac{|K_1 \cap K_2|}{|K_2|} = 1$. Since $\mu_X^C(y) \in [0,1)$, by Fact 2, $y \in X - CL(X)$. Since $\frac{|K_1 \cap K_2|}{|K_2|} = 1, |K_1 \cap K_2| = |K_2|$. Thus, owing to the fact that $K_1 \cap K_2 \subseteq K_2$ can imply $|K_1 \cap K_2| \leq |K_2|, K_2 \subseteq K_1$. So, $x \in K_1$. Since $K_1 \in Md(y)$, by the fact that $y \in X - CL(X)$ and the definition of $FH(X), x \in \bigcup Md(y) \subseteq FH(X)$. Hence, by arbitrariness of $x, \{x \in U : \mu_X^C(x)_F \in (0,1]\} \subseteq FH(X)$.

Theorem 3. $\forall X \subseteq U, BN_F(X) = \{x \in U : \mu_X^C(x)_F \in (0,1)\}$.

Proof. Since $BN_F(X) = FH(X) - CL(X)$, by Theorem 1 and 2, $BN_F(X) = \{x \in U : \mu_X^C(x)_F \in (0,1)\}$.

5   Theoretical Backgrounds and Practical Applications of Rough Membership Function on the Covering-Based Rough Set

In this section, we discuss relationship between covering-based probabilistic rough sets and the covering-based rough set first, and which gives the theoretical backgrounds of covering-based rough membership function studied in this paper. Then we employ the example in Sect. 2.4 to illustrate practical applications of this function.

5.1   Theoretical Backgrounds

Definition 9 *(Covering probabilistic approximation space [14]). Let U be the universe of discourse, C a covering of U and P a probability measure on U. We call (U, C, P) a covering probabilistic approximation space. For every $X \subseteq U$ and $0 \leq \beta < \alpha \leq 1$, about the covering probabilistic approximation space (U, C, P), the lower approximation and the upper approximation of X with respect to parameters α and β are defined as follows:*

$$\underline{C}_\alpha(X) = \{x \in U : P(x \in X|C) \geq \alpha\},$$
$$\overline{C}_\beta(X) = \{x \in U : P(x \in X|C) > \beta\},$$

where $P(x \in X|C)$ is the conditional probability that x belongs to X given by C.

The covering-based probabilistic rough sets proposed in this paper can be degenerated into covering-based rough sets as follows.

If the parameters $\alpha = 1, \beta = 0$ and $P(x \in X|C) = \mu_X^C(x)_F$, then the lower approximation $\underline{C}_\alpha(X)$ and the upper approximation $\overline{C}_\beta(X)$ are degenerated into the lower approximation $CL(X)$ and the upper approximation $FH(X)$ respectively in the covering approximation space. That is, for any $X \subseteq U$,

$$\underline{C}_\alpha(X) = \{x \in U : P(x \in X|C) \geq \alpha\} = \{x \in U : \mu_X^C(x)_F = 1\} = CL(X),$$
$$\overline{C}_\beta(X) = \{x \in U : P(x \in X|C) > \beta\} = \{x \in U : \mu_X^C(x)_F > 0\} = FH(X).$$

5.2   Practical Applications

In Sect. 2.4, we point out that we cannot use the Pawlak's rough membership function based on equivalence relation to make the frequent decisions for patients p_{19} and p_{20} in Table 1, because the data of their symptoms of illness is incomplete. In the following, we show that we can solve this problem by using the membership function on covering-based rough set which is proposed in Sect. 4.

Example 2. Denote $U = \{p_i : 1 \le i \le 20, i \ne 17, 18\}$ the set of patients. Let $C = \{$chest pain, short breath, local diffusion, distant metastasis$\}$ be the set of condition attributes and let $D = \{$lung cancer$\}$ be the set of decision attribute. Just like what in Example 1, each row can be seen as information on one specific patient, and 1 denotes yes, 0 denotes no. The patient $p_i (i = 19, 20)$ is waiting for the diagnosis in the hospital, whereas the information of patient $p_i (1 \le i \le 16)$ is from diagnostic database of lung cancer cases in hospital.

For set of condition attributes C, a similarity relation $R_{\widetilde{C}}$ can be defined on U:
$$R_{\widetilde{C}} = \{(x, y) \in U \times U : \forall a \in C, f_a(x) = f_a(y) \text{ or } f_a(x) = * \text{or} *= f_a(y)\},$$
where $f_a(x)$ is the value of a on $x \in U$, and $*$indicates unknown values.

Moreover, for $C = \{$chest pain, short breath, local diffusion, distant metastasis$\}$, we write $[x]_{\widetilde{C}} = \{y \in U : (x, y) \in R_{\widetilde{C}}\}$.

By Table 1, it is easy to verify that

$C_1 = [p_1]_{\widetilde{C}} = [p_2]_{\widetilde{C}} = [p_3]_{\widetilde{C}} = [p_4]_{\widetilde{C}} = [p_{19}]_{\widetilde{C}} = \{p_1, p_2, p_3, p_4, p_{19}\};$

$C_2 = [p_5]_{\widetilde{C}} = [p_7]_{\widetilde{C}} = [p_8]_{\widetilde{C}} = [p_9]_{\widetilde{C}} = [p_{10}]_{\widetilde{C}} = [p_{19}]_{\widetilde{C}} = \{p_5, p_7, p_8, p_9, p_{10}, p_{19}\};$

$C_3 = [p_6]_{\widetilde{C}} = [p_{19}]_{\widetilde{C}} = \{p_6, p_{19}\};$

$C_4 = [p_{11}]_{\widetilde{C}} = [p_{20}]_{\widetilde{C}} = \{p_{11}, p_{20}\};$

$C_5 = [p_{12}]_{\widetilde{C}} = [p_{20}]_{\widetilde{C}} = \{p_{12}, p_{20}\};$

$C_6 = [p_{13}]_{\widetilde{C}} = [p_{14}]_{\widetilde{C}} = [p_{15}]_{\widetilde{C}} = [p_{16}]_{\widetilde{C}} = [p_{20}]_{\widetilde{C}} = \{p_{13}, p_{14}, p_{15}, p_{16}, p_{20}\};$

and $C_i \ne \varnothing, \bigcup C_i = U (1 \le i \le 6)$. Thus, $C' = \{C_i : 1 \le i \le 6\}$ is a covering of U. $\langle U, C' \rangle$ is a covering approximation space.

Let $X_1 = \{p_i : 1 \le i \le 5\}, X_2 = \{p_i : 6 \le i \le 11\}$ and $X_3 = \{p_i : 12 \le i \le 16\}$. By Definition 8, we can obtain:

$$\mu_{X_1}^{C'}(p_{19}) = \frac{4}{5}; \quad \mu_{X_1}^{C'}(p_{20}) = 0;$$

$$\mu_{X_2}^{C'}(p_{19}) = \frac{2}{3}; \quad \mu_{X_2}^{C'}(p_{20}) = \frac{1}{2};$$

$$\mu_{X_3}^{C'}(p_{19}) = 0; \quad \mu_{X_3}^{C'}(p_{20}) = \frac{4}{5}.$$

It is found that the degrees of p_{19} belonging to X_2 and X_3 are only $\frac{2}{3}$, which means that it may not be peripheral lung cancer and thin bronchuses lung cancer with respect to conditional attributes set C, although there are two conditional attributes unknown for p_{19}. The membership degree of p_{19} belonging to X_1 is $\frac{4}{5}$, and it means that p_{19} may well be central lung cancer. Although the accuracy of this decision should be further validated by means of clinical analysis unless central lung cancer has been confirmed, we can make a preliminary judgement which will help the doctors in making their finial decisions. Similarly, according to the membership degrees of p_{20} belonging to $X_i(1 \leq i \leq 3)$, we can make a preliminary decision that p_{20} may well be thin bronchuses lung bubble cancer.

6   Conclusion

The main contribution of this paper is to construct covering-based rough membership function and to discuss its properties and applications in depth. First, by using a practical example in evidence-based medicine, we illustrate applications of the Pawlak's rough membership function in real life and the limitations of it. Then, based on topological structures of the covering-based rough set which is examined by Bonikowski et al. [1], we construct corresponding covering-based rough membership function and present numerical characterizations of the rough sets by this function. Furthermore, the theoretical backgrounds of it are discussed. At the end, we illustrate practical applications of this covering-based rough membership function in medical diagnosis.

There are several issues about covering-based rough membership functions deserving further investigation. For example, for models of covering-based rough set appeared in literature [6,13,24,25,27], how to construct corresponding covering-based rough membership functions on them? Moreover, to find more applications of covering-based rough membership functions in the field of data mining is an exciting area deserved to be explored. We will study these issues in our future research.

Acknowledgment. This work is supported by the National Natural Science Foundation of China (nos. 11301367, 11501404, 61440047, 61562079), Jiangsu Province Natural Science Foundation (no. BK20140583), Natural Science Foundation of Guangxi (no. 2014GXNSFBA118015), Key Laboratory Program of Guangxi University (no. 2016CSOBDP0004), and the Priority Academic Program Development of Jiangsu Higher Education Institutions.

References

1. Bonikowski, Z., Bryniarski, E., Skardowska, U.W.: Extensions and intentions in the rough set theory. Inf. Sci. **107**, 149–167 (1998)
2. Eells, E., Fitelson, B.: Symmetries and asymmetries in evidential support. Philos. Stud. **107**, 129–142 (2002)
3. Greco, S., Matarazzo, B., Slowinski, R.: Parameterized rough set model using rough membership and Bayesian confirmation measures. Int. J. Approx. Reason. **49**, 285–300 (2008)
4. Intan, R., Mukaidono, M.: Generalization of rough membership function based on α-coverings of the universe. In: Pal, N.R., Sugeno, M. (eds.) AFSS 2002. LNCS, vol. 2275, pp. 129–136. Springer, Heidelberg (2002). doi:10.1007/3-540-45631-7_18

5. Lin, G.P., Liang, J.Y., Qian, Y.H.: Multigranulation rough sets: from partition to covering. Inf. Sci. **241**, 101–118 (2013)
6. Ma, L.: On some types of neighborhood-related covering rough sets. Int. J. Approx. Reason. **53**, 901–911 (2012)
7. Miao, D.Q., Li, D.G.: Rough Sets Theory Algorithms and Applications. Tsinghua University Press, Beijing (2008)
8. Pawlak, Z.: Rough sets. Int. J. Comput. Inform. Sci. **11**, 341–356 (1982)
9. Pawlak, Z.: Some issues on rough sets. In: Peters, J.F., Skowron, A., Grzymała-Busse, J.W., Kostek, B., Świniarski, R.W., Szczuka, M.S. (eds.) Transactions on Rough Sets I. LNCS, vol. 3100, pp. 1–58. Springer, Heidelberg (2004). doi:10.1007/978-3-540-27794-1_1
10. Pawlak, Z., Skowron, A.: Rough membership functions. In: Yager, R.R., Fedrizzi, M., Kacprzyk, J. (eds.) Advances in the Dempster-Shafer Theory of Evidence, pp. 251–271. Wiley, New York (1994)
11. Pedrycz, W., Skowron, A., Kreinovich, V.: Handbook of Granular Computing. Wiley, West Sussex (2008)
12. Pomykala, J.A.: Approximation operations in approximation space. Bull. Polish Acad. Sci. Math. **35**, 653–662 (1987)
13. Samanta, P., Chakraborty, M.K.: On extension of dependency and consistency degrees of two knowledges represented by covering. In: Peters, J.F., Skowron, A., Rybiński, H. (eds.) Transactions on Rough Sets IX. LNCS, vol. 5390, pp. 351–364. Springer, Heidelberg (2008). doi:10.1007/978-3-540-89876-4_19
14. Shi, Z.H., Gong, Z.T.: The further investigation of covering-based rough sets: uncertainty characterization, similarity measure and generalized models. Inf. Sci. **180**, 3745–3763 (2010)
15. Wong, S.K.M., Ziarko, W.: Comparison of the probabilistic approximate classification and the fuzzy set model. Fuzzy Sets Syst. **21**, 357–362 (1987)
16. Xu, W.H., Zhang, W.X.: Measuring roughness of generalized rough sets induced by a covering. Fuzzy Sets Syst. **158**, 2443–2455 (2007)
17. Yao, Y.Y.: A comparative study of fuzzy sets and rough sets. Inf. Sci. **109**, 227–242 (1998)
18. Yao, Y.Y.: Probabilistic rough set approximations. Int. J. Approx. Reason. **49**, 255–271 (2008)
19. Yao, Y.Y., Zhang, J.P.: Interpreting fuzzy membership functions in the theory of rough sets. In: Ziarko, W., Yao, Y. (eds.) RSCTC 2000. LNCS, vol. 2005, pp. 82–89. Springer, Heidelberg (2001). doi:10.1007/3-540-45554-X_9
20. Zhang, W.X., Wu, W.Z., Liang, J.Y., Li, D.Y.: Theory and Method of Rough Sets. Science Press, Beijing (2001)
21. Zhang, W.X., Yao, Y.Y., Liang, Y.: Rough Set and Concept Lattice. Xi'an Jiaotong University Press, Xi'an (2006)
22. Zhang, Y.L., Li, J.J., Wu, W.Z.: On axiomatic characterizations of three pairs of covering-based approximation operators. Inf. Sci. **180**, 274–287 (2010)
23. Zhang, Y.L., Luo, M.K.: On minimization of axiom sets characterizing covering-based approximation operators. Inf. Sci. **181**, 3032–3042 (2011)
24. Zhu, P.: Covering rough sets based on neighborhoods: an approach without using neighborhoods. Int. J. Approx. Reason. **52**, 461–472 (2011)
25. Zhu, W.: Topological approaches to covering rough sets. Inf. Sci. **177**, 1499–1508 (2007)
26. Zhu, W., Wang, F.Y.: On three types of covering-based rough sets. IEEE Trans. Knowl. Data Eng. **19**, 1131–1143 (2007)
27. Zhu, W., Wang, F.Y.: The fourth type of covering-based rough sets. Inf. Sci. **201**, 80–92 (2012)

Mereogeometry Based Approach for Behavioral Robotics

Piotr Gnyś[(⊠)]

Department of Computer Science,
Polish-Japanese Academy of Information Technology,
Ul. Koszykowa 86, 02-008 Warsaw, Poland
`pgnys@pja.edu.pl`

Abstract. In this paper we will attempt to create simple behavioral agent with reasoning based in mereogeometry. Main purpose of this research is to check if mereogeometry is viable approach for writing low level behavioral system.

Keywords: Mereology · Mereogeometry · Rough mereology · Behavioral robotics · Flocking

1 Behavioral Robotics

When designing artificial minds we can take one of two approaches. In deliberative approach we would try to write monolithic algorithm that uses sensory fusion to create complex responses from robot. Problem with this approach is that it requires comprehensive knowledge about robot task because we need to create virtual model of it that covers all edge cases. Difficulty of creating such model increases quickly with introduction of new variables into robot environment. So while it is relatively easy to create complete model of manipulator working in especially designed environment the same task for a robot that will work in open, like self driving cars [12], environment may be incredibly complex. And those are just examples of robots that are designed to do one specific task. Creating holistic AI for general purpose robot is literally impossible as sets of rules that describe it tasks and environment are potentially infinite. To deal with this issue we must turn to behavioral robotics that instead of using one monolithic algorithm relay on set of behaviors and arbiters (Figs. 1 and 2).

Following Arkin [1], we require that behaviors display following properties:

1. Parsimony - first level behaviors must be as simple as possible, we consider a behavior to be of the first level if it cannot be redefined as set of smaller behaviors and arbiters.
2. Exploration/speculation - With exception of recharging robot is never stationary, in other words system is never in stable state.
3. Attraction - system will attempt to move towards positive signals.
4. Aversion - system will attempt to move away from negative signals.

© Springer International Publishing AG 2017
L. Polkowski et al. (Eds.): IJCRS 2017, Part II, LNAI 10314, pp. 70–80, 2017.
DOI: 10.1007/978-3-319-60840-2_5

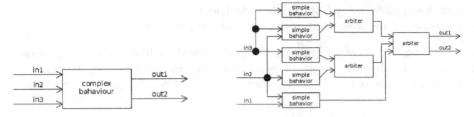

Fig. 1. Monolithic A.I. structure   **Fig. 2.** Behavioral A.I. structure

It should be mentioned that properties of attraction and aversion while very common in behavior design are not universal. behaviors that rely on them are called taxa while those that simply translate set of inputs into predefined set of outputs are called reflexes. Another difference between taxa and reflexes is that reflexes have very short activity time and usually will omit arbiters and directly affect outputs. This distinction between behaviors is based on biology where there are reflexes that very often can be executed without any interaction with central nervous system. In behavioral robotics, complex behaviors do not arise from equally complex algorithm but from interactions between large number of behaviors and arbiters. This allows emergent generation of very complex reactions for previously unknown stimuli and according to some research it is even mechanism lying at the base of conciousness [5]. Very first example of behavioral based robot was W. Grey Walters tortoise created in 1951 and described in his book called The Living Brain [3] (Fig. 3).

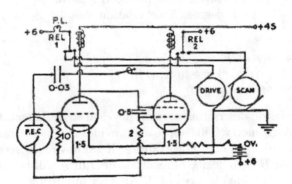

Fig. 3. Circuit of Machina Speculatrix from The Living Brain by W. Grey Walter

All logic of this robot is realized by two vacuum tubes, with third one as a sensor, despite that it displayed rather complex behavioral patterns with following rules as base:

– Sensor will turn around until it detects light source (reflex).
– Robot will head towards dim light (taxa).

– Robot will move away from bright light (taxa).
– If obstacle is hit robot will push on it while turning (reflex).

In case of simple behavioral systems we can analyse them like a dynamic systems. It is especially obvious in case of behavioral engines like Machina Speculatrix because those are realized by electronic circuits whose nature as a dynamic systems is well known [2].

2   Spatial Reasoning with Rough Mereology

Mereology is field of mathematics that focuses on extensional objects [8]. Basics of mereology were developed in early XX century by Leśniewski [4] He used concept of "being part of" as his primitive notion. Another approach to mereology was developed by Whitehead [13] where instead of focusing on "being part of" relation of interconnection was chosen as a primitive notion. choose interconnection relation. In Leśniewski theory being part of is represented as a binary relation $\pi(x, y)$ with means that x is part of y. Such relation fulfils following requirements:

1. Irreflexivility: $\forall x : \neg \pi(x, x)$
2. Transitivity: $\forall(x, y, z) : \pi(x, y) \wedge \pi(y, z) \implies \pi(x, z)$

Another important relation in mereology is called ingredient and can be defined as $ingr(x, y) \iff \pi(x, y) \vee x = y$. In this paper we will use concept of rough inclusion that was first introduced by Polkowski and Skowron [10]. They introduced concept of rough inclusion that provided relation $\mu(x, y, r)$ with means that y is part of x to r degree. This relation can be defined by following postulates:

1. $\mu(x, y, r) \iff ingr(x, y)$
2. $\mu(x, y, r) \implies \forall z[\mu(z, x, r) \implies \mu(z, y, r)]$
3. $\mu(x, y, r) \wedge s < r \implies \mu(x, y, s)$

As our main focus is on description of robot physical environment, that is why we will turn to mereogeometry. This approach provides means to transform euclidean space into mereologic one. For example, if we have two geometric shapes identified as A and B then degree of inclusion of B in A will be area of common part of both figures divided by area of A. Another important relation is mereogeometric distance that can be described as $\kappa(A, B) = max(\mu(A, B), \mu(B, A))$. Based on that definition we can tell that mereogeometric distance displays following properties:

1. $\forall(A, B) : \kappa(A, B) \geq 0 \wedge \kappa(A, B) \leq 1$.
2. In contrast to euclidean notion of distance higher value imply that objects are closer.
3. If objects are disjoint their mereogeometric distance is always 0 even if their euclidean distance changes.

4. If one objects encompasses another their mereogeometric distance is 1 regardless of euclidean distance between their centroids.

Another concept that must be mentioned before we start describing previous work on use of mereology in behavioral robotics is extens. Exntens refers to smallest possible rectangle that will encompass both elements given (Fig. 4).

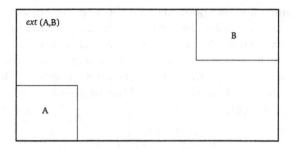

Fig. 4. Extens

3 Previous Works on Application of Mereology in Field of Robotics

Use of mereogeometry in mobile robot control is rather young field of research. Previous approach at tackling this problem was done by Polkowski and Ośmiałowski [7]. Their work was focused on path finding and robot formation. For path finding modified version of potential field algorithm was used [6]. In traditional approach value of potential field in given point is calculated as sum of attraction forces created by robot goals and repulsion originating from obstacles. Algorithm deployed by them instead is based on the concept of rough mereologic inclusion. Potential field is constructed by a discreet construction. Free workspace of a robot is filled with virtual squares in such a way that the density of square field, measured as number of squares intersection the disc of a given radius r centred at the target, increases towards target (Fig. 5).

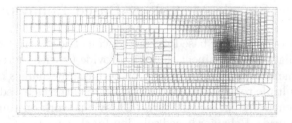

Fig. 5. Obstacles layer together with potential field layer.

After this field is prepared robot will move towards goal by means of following algorithm:

1. If robot is at goal position finish algorithm execution otherwise go to step 2.
2. From the set of square areas that have any common part with previously selected area choose one that have smallest mereological distance to it. Then move robot to centroid of this area and return to step 1.

That algorithm will allow robot to reach the goal, of course as it is a variant of potential field path planning there are configurations that will cause it to fail. Another topic researched by Polkowski and Ośmiałowski was use of mereology in description of robot formations [9]. In their work they focused on use of notion of betweenness and distance to maintain formation of robots. Do define robot formation we define knowledge base that informs robot about their expected relations to each other (Fig. 6).

```
(cross
 (set
  (max−dist 0.25 roomba0 (between roomba0 roomba1 roomba2))
  (max−dist 0.25 roomba0 (between roomba0 roomba3 roomba4))
  (not−between roomba1 roomba3 roomba4)
  (not−between roomba2 roomba3 roomba4)
  (not−between roomba3 roomba1 roomba2)
  (not−between roomba4 roomba1 roomba2)
 )
)
```

Fig. 6. Cross formation definition for four Roomba robots

Basing on this requirements and robots starting position planner will set target positions for all robots. Each robot (except a selected leader) will move towards this generated position. Whenever collision is detected (on the robot bumper device), robot goes back for a while then turns left or right for a while and from this new situation, it tries again to go (Fig 7).

4   Mboids as Simple Mereology Based Behavior Engine

To test concept of behaviors based on mereogeometric description we have to first create simulation environment that will provide us with mereologic sensors. Second requirement of simulation is to provide basic mechanics of motion that will allow for multiple robot to interact an generate patterns based on behaviors. To create such environment we will turn to previous work on simulating movement of flocking birds. Behavior based solution for that problem was proposed in 1987 by Craig Reynolds in form of Boids [11]. Term Boid refers to a single agent in flock that in case of Reynolds work behaves according to following rules.

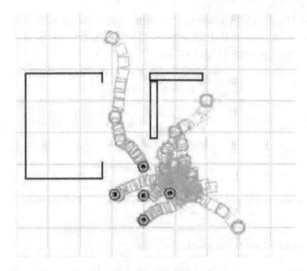

Fig. 7. Roombas in formation, with trials from original positions

1. move away from obstacles
2. move away from local flock mates
3. move towards average position of local flock mates
4. steer towards average heading of local flock mates

From this four basic rules it was possible to create complex flock behaviors (Fig. 8).

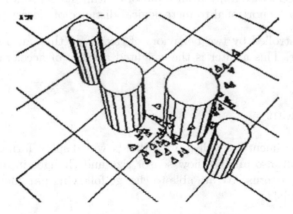

Fig. 8. Example of flock obstacle avoidance [11]

While our approach called Mboids (mereogeometric boids) is directly inspired by Reynolds work there are major differences between two models. Reynold boids used virtual sensor that told them distance towards all other boids within given range and their velocity vector. In our case Mboid will be equipped with four sensors that can only tell mereogeometric distance between area covered by sensor and measured object (Fig. 9).

Fig. 9. Mboid with visualised attractor and sensors

Mboid consists of following parts:

- body (repellent) - black filled square on visualisation, this is element that represents physical body of Mboid
- attractor - small grey square, virtual area visible to sensors of other Mboids
- sensors - represented by four large grey squares, each square represents area covered by single sensor.

Using this elements Mboid displays following behaviors:

1. Mboid will accelerate towards attractors that are within range of its sensors. Acceleration value is reverse proportional to average mereological distance of those attractors.
2. Mboid will accelerate away from repulsors within its sensors range. Acceleration value is proportional to mereological distance of closest repulsor.

So Mboid is controlled by two behaviors of taxa type that means it also must have one arbiter. This arbiter is the weighted average of acceleration forces of both behavior.

5   Experiment

In our first experiment we will see if Mboids will display formation building patterns. We will also analyse how sensor size and changes in arbiter weights influence those patterns. We are able to change following parameters of simulation (Figs. 10 and 11):

- repulsor width,
- repulsor height,
- attractor width,
- attractor height,
- sensor width,
- sensor height,

- mass,
- friction,
- maximum thrust,
- force,
- repulsion force.

Repulsion and attraction forces are respective weights of the arbiter while the maximum thrust, mass and friction refer to physical properties of Mboid. We will only attempt to modify arbiter weights and maximum thrust (Table 1).

Table 1. Experiment parameters

Experiment no.	1	2	3	4
Repulsion	10	10	20	20
Thrust	1	5	1	5

Other parameters remain constants during all experiments and have following values:

- repulsor width = 10,
- repulsor height = 10,
- attractor width = 40,
- attractor height = 40,
- sensor width = 15,
- sensor height = 15,
- mass = 10,
- friction = 0.02,
- attraction force = 10.

We got positive results when running first experiment. Starting from random positions Mboids that are located in vicinity of each other will try to form regular grid. It is worth noting that behaviors do not require four neighbours as evident by empty spaces within the grid. Mboids are not stable as explorative nature of behavioral engines prohibits static states, they are however oscillating around fixed positions with results with pulsating but generally stable formation. This result is fully compatible with our prediction and on it is own proves that it is possible to create simple behavioral agents with use of mereogeometry based spatial reasoning. Another interesting behavior can be observed when a obstacle, represented by grey square, is introduced into formation. It is worth mentioning that while unlike in original boids in our example the obstacle is moving trough stationary flock this do not change avoidance or formation restoration behaviors. As we already know that our algorithm guarantees formation emergence we can check what behaviors of flock will be generated with other settings. If we use settings from experiment number two thrust will be stronger while mass and friction remains same. This should result in more chaotic movement of Mboids

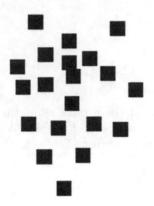

Fig. 10. Mboids initial position

Fig. 11. Mboids after minute of behavior based movement

and make flock formation more difficult. Experiment confirms this expectation as while flock is able to form is much less stable than in experiment one and Mboids must constantly adjust their positions by large margins (Figs. 12, 13 and 14).

Fig. 12. Flock is approached by a obstacle

Fig. 13. Obstacle moves trough flock

Fig. 14. Flock after passing of obstacle

To test if this behavior disappears or only slows down in case of smaller thrust forces we ran simulation with settings from experiment 1 for over 20 min with different starting formations. After running those experiments it became evident that it is not acceleration force that caused formation movement. Instead this behavior appears when asymmetric formation shapes are present (Figs. 15 and 16).

Finally changing repulsion value have no significant effect with current configuration of other parameters.

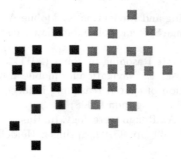

Fig. 15. Formation that starts as black squares moves to position of grey ones without any external motivation in about 5 min.

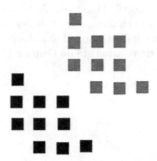

Fig. 16. Example of moving formation with low thrust value

6 Conclusions and Plans for Future Research

After running our experiments we can conclude that mereogeometrical approach is valid for creating simple behavioral systems. We also know from previous work on this topic that it is possible to implement control on higher level of abstraction, like path planning or formation building, with use of rough meregeometry. With that knowledge we can continue our research in design of holistic robot behavioral system based on rough mereogeometric description of environment.

References

1. Arkin, R.C.: Behavioral Based Robotics (2002)
2. Franklin, F., David Powell, J., Emami-Naeini, A.: Feedback control of dynamic systems (1970)
3. Walter, W.G.: The living brain (1953)
4. Leśniewski, S.: On foundation of matemathics (1927)
5. Minsky, M.: The Society of Mind (1986)
6. Osmialowski, P.: On path planning form mobile robots: introducing the mereological potential field method in the framework of mereological spatial reasoning (2008)

7. Osmialowski, P.: Planning and Navigation for Mobile Autonomous Robots Spatial Reasoning in Player/Stage System. Polish Japanese Academy of Computer Science Publisher (2011)
8. Polkowski, L.: Approximate Rasoning by Parts (2011)
9. Osmialowski, P., Polkowski, L.: Navigation for mobile autonomous robots and their formations: an application of spatial reasoning induced from rough mereological geometry. Mobile Robots Navigation (2008)
10. Polkowski, L., Skowron, A.: Rough mereology. In: Raś, Z.W., Zemankova, M. (eds.) ISMIS 1994. LNCS, vol. 869, pp. 85–94. Springer, Heidelberg (1994). doi:10.1007/3-540-58495-1_9
11. Reynolds, C.W.: Flocks, herds and schools: a distributed behavioral model. In: SIGGRAPH 1987 Proceedings of the 14th Annual Conference on Computer Graphics and Interactive Techniques (1987)
12. Urmson, C., Anthal, J., Bagnerll, D., et al.: Autonomous driving in urban environments: boss and the urban challenge. In: Buehler, M., Iagnemma, K., Singh, S. (eds.) The DARPA Urban Challenge, pp. 1–59. Springer, Heidelberg (2009)
13. Whitehead, A.N.: La theorie relationiste de l'espace (1916)

Distinguishing Vagueness from Ambiguity in Dominance-Based Rough Set Approach by Means of a Bipolar Pawlak-Brouwer-Zadeh Lattice

Salvatore Greco[1,2], Benedetto Matarazzo[1], and Roman Słowiński[3,4(✉)]

[1] Department of Economics and Business, University of Catania,
95129 Catania, Italy
{salgreco,matarazz}@unict.it
[2] Portsmouth Business School,
Centre of Operations Research and Logistics (CORL),
University of Portsmouth, Portsmouth PO1 3DE, UK
[3] Institute of Computing Science, Poznań University of Technology,
60-965 Poznań, Poland
roman.slowinski@cs.put.poznan.pl
[4] Institute for Systems Research, Polish Academy of Sciences,
01-447 Warsaw, Poland

Abstract. In this paper, we present a new algebraic model for Dominance-based Rough Set Approach. Extending the Pawlak-Brouwer-Zadeh lattice introduced for indiscernibility-based rough set approach, the new model permits to distinguish between two kinds of imperfect information in case of ordered data: vagueness due to imprecision, and ambiguity due to coarseness typical to rough sets. To build the model we use the bipolar Brouwer-Zadeh lattice to represent a basic vagueness, and to introduce dominance-based rough approximations we define a new operator, called bipolar Pawlak operator. The new model we obtain in this way is called bipolar Pawlak-Brouwer-Zadeh lattice.

Keywords: Dominance-based rough set approach · Algebraic model · Bipolar Pawlak-Brouwer-Zadeh lattice · Vagueness · Ambiguity

1 Introduction

After being introduced as an algebraic structure permitting representation of possibility and necessity in an environment characterized by some form of vagueness, the Brouwer-Zadeh lattice [5] has been considered also as an abstract model for rough set theory [1,2] (for rough set theory see [15,16]; for two extensive surveys on algebraic structures for rough set theory see Chapt. 12 in [17] or [2]). In this case, the elements of the lattice represent the pairs (A, B) where A and B are the lower approximation (interior) and the complement of the upper approximation (exterior) of a given set X, respectively. The bipolar complemented

© Springer International Publishing AG 2017
L. Polkowski et al. (Eds.): IJCRS 2017, Part II, LNAI 10314, pp. 81–93, 2017.
DOI: 10.1007/978-3-319-60840-2_6

de Morgan Brouwer-Zadeh lattice [13] has been recently introduced as an extension of a Brouwer-Zadeh lattice to give an algebraic model for the dominance-based rough set approach (DRSA) [8–12]. [14] proposed another extension of the Brouwer-Zadeh lattice for indiscernibility-based rough set approach, called Pawlak-Brouwer-Zadeh lattice, where the basic vagueness is represented by a pair (A, B), with A being the necessity kernel and B being the non-possibility kernel, and ambiguity due to the coarseness of information is introduced through a new operator, called Pawlak operator. Pawlak operator assigns a pair (C, D) to the pair (A, B), with $A \cap B = \emptyset$, such that C and D represent the lower approximations of A and B, respectively. In this paper, we make a non-trivial synthesis of the ideas that stand behind the bipolar complemented de Morgan Brouwer-Zadeh lattice and the Pawlak-Brouwer-Zadeh lattice in order to get an algebraic model permitting to distinguish vagueness from ambiguity in DRSA.

Let us use an example to explain the intuition that stands behind the bipolar Pawlak-Brouwer-Zadeh lattice. Suppose a financial institution wants to assess the bankruptcy risk of some companies, taking into account the information carried by some financial ratios. With this aim, a committee of experts is asked to consider a certain universe U of companies described by some financial ratios. It will not be surprising, if due to vagueness related to experts' imprecise knowledge, the committee will assign the companies from U to three classes: class A, composed of companies for which for sure there is no risk of bankruptcy; class B, $A \cap B = \emptyset$, composed of companies for which there is a clear risk of bankruptcy, and class $C = U - A - B$, composed of companies for which there is a doubt about their risk of bankruptcy. On the other hand, information about financial ratios permits to define a dominance relation in set U of companies. More precisely, we say that company a (weakly) dominates company b if a is at least as good as b on all the considered financial ratios. Dominance relation is a preorder, that is, a reflexive and transitive binary relation. Using dominance, one can define lower approximation of classes A and B. More precisely, any company dominated only by companies belonging to class A is included in the lower approximation of A, denoted by $\underline{R}^{\geq} A$, as well as any company dominating only companies belonging to class B is included in the lower approximation of B, denoted by $\underline{R}^{\leq} B$. Intuitively, this means that, based on the available data, the financial ratios of companies from $\underline{R}^{\geq} A$ permit to exclude univocally the risk of bankruptcy. Analogously, based on the available data, the financial ratios of companies from $\underline{R}^{\leq} B$ permit to identify univocally the risk of bankruptcy. Using the same data describing the companies in terms of the considered financial ratios, one can also define the upper approximation of classes A and B, denoted by $\overline{R}^{\geq} A$ and $\overline{R}^{\leq} B$, respectively. More precisely, $\overline{R}^{\geq} A$ contains the companies dominating at least one company for which there is no risk of bankruptcy, and $\overline{R}^{\leq} B$ contains the companies dominated by at least one company for which there is the risk of bankruptcy. The difference $\overline{R}^{\geq} A - \underline{R}^{\geq} A$ contains all the companies whose financial ratios do not permit to state with certainty that there is no risk of bankruptcy; analogously, the difference $\overline{R}^{\leq} B - \underline{R}^{\leq} B$ contains the companies whose financial ratios do not permit to state with certainty that there is the risk of bankruptcy.

In this example, we distinguished between two kinds of imperfections of information: on one hand, the vagueness due to imprecise knowledge related to the experts' classification of the companies from U into classes of safe (A), risky (B), and doubtful (C) companies, and, on the other hand, the ambiguity due to coarseness related to granularity of information available in terms of the financial ratios of the companies from U. It is thus meaningful to consider rough (lower and upper) approximations of class A, and class B, in terms of attributes describing the companies (for an interesting real world application of rough set theory to bankruptcy evaluation see [7]).

The paper is organized as follows. In the next section, we recall the Pawlak-Brouwer-Zadeh lattice and its abstract representation of indiscernibility-based rough set theory. In the third section, we introduce the bipolar Pawlak-Brouwer-Zadeh lattice and we show that it is an abstract algebra for dominance-based rough set approach. In the fourth section we present a didactic example illustrating the concepts of Pawlak-Brouwer-Zadeh lattice and bipolar Pawlak-Brouwer-Zadeh lattice. This example suggests a possible application of these concepts in aggregation of multi-expert classifications under vagueness and ambiguity. The last section contains conclusions.

2   The Pawlak-Brouwer-Zadeh Distributive de Morgan Lattice and Indiscernibility-Based Rough Set Theory

In this section, we recall the Pawlak-Brouwer-Zadeh distributive de Morgan lattice introduced in [14], and show how it is an abstract model of the classical rough set approach based on indiscernibility.

A system $\langle \Sigma, \wedge, \vee, ', ^\sim, 0, 1 \rangle$ is a quasi-Brouwer-Zadeh distributive lattice [5] if the following properties (1)–(4) hold:

(1) Σ is a distributive lattice with respect to the join and the meet operations $\vee, \wedge$ whose induced partial order relation is

$$a \leq b \text{ iff } a = a \wedge b \text{ (equivalently } b = a \vee b)$$

Moreover, it is required that Σ is bounded by the least element 0 and the greatest element 1:

$$\forall a \in \Sigma, \quad 0 \leq a \leq 1$$

(2) The unary operation $' : \Sigma \to \Sigma$ is a Kleene (also Zadeh or fuzzy) complementation. In other words, for arbitrary $a, b \in \Sigma$,

(K1) $a'' = a$,
(K2) $(a \vee b)' = a' \wedge b'$,
(K3) $a \wedge a' \leq b \vee b'$.

(3) The unary operation $^\sim : \Sigma \to \Sigma$ is a Brouwer (or intuitionistic) complementation. In other words, for arbitrary $a, b \in \Sigma$,

(B1) $a \wedge a^{\sim\sim} = a$,
(B2) $(a \vee b)^\sim = a^\sim \wedge b^\sim$,
(B3) $a \wedge a^\sim = 0$.

(4) The two complementations are linked by the interconnection rule which must hold for arbitrary $a \in \Sigma$:

(in) $a^\sim \leq a'$.

A structure $\langle \Sigma, \wedge, \vee, ', {}^\sim, 0, 1 \rangle$ is a Brouwer-Zadeh distributive lattice if it is a quasi-Brouwer-Zadeh distributive lattice satisfying the stronger interconnection rule:

(s-in) $a^{\sim\sim} = a^{\sim\prime}$.

A Brouwer-Zadeh distributive lattice satisfying also the $\vee$ de Morgan property

(B2a) $(a \wedge b)^\sim = a^\sim \vee b^\sim$

is called a de Morgan Brouwer-Zadeh distributive lattice.

An approximation operator, called Pawlak operator [14], on a de Morgan Brouwer-Zadeh distributive lattice is an unary operation $^A : \Sigma \to \Sigma$ for which the following properties hold: for $a, b \in \Sigma$

(A1) $a^{A\prime} = a^{\prime A}$;
(A2) $a \leq b$ implies $b^{A\sim} \leq a^{A\sim}$;
(A3) $a^{A\sim} \leq a^\sim$;
(A4) $0^A = 0$;
(A5) $a^\sim = b^\sim$ implies $a^A \wedge b^A = (a \wedge b)^A$;
(A6) $a^A \vee b^A \leq (a \vee b)^A$;
(A7) $a^{AA} = a^A$;
(A8) $a^{A\sim A} = a^{A\sim}$;
(A9) $(a^A \wedge b^A)^A = a^A \wedge b^A$.

2.1 The Pawlak-Brouwer-Zadeh Lattice as an Algebraic Model of Indiscernibility-Based Rough Set Theory

A *knowledge base* $K = (U, R)$ is a relational system where $U \neq \emptyset$ is a finite set called the *universe* and R is an equivalence relation on U. For any $x \in U$, $[x]_R$ is its equivalence class. The quotient set U/R is composed of all the equivalence classes of R on U. Given the knowledge base $K = (U, R)$, one can associate the two subsets $\underline{R}X$ and $\overline{R}X$ to each subset $X \subseteq U$:

$$\underline{R}X = \{x \in U : [x]_R \subseteq X\},$$
$$\overline{R}X = \{x \in U : [x]_R \cap X \neq \emptyset\}.$$

$\underline{R}X$ and $\overline{R}X$ are called the lower and the upper approximation of X, respectively.

Let us consider the set of all pairs $\langle A, B \rangle$ such that $A, B \subseteq U$ and $A \cap B = \emptyset$. We denote by 3^U the set of these pairs, i.e.

$$3^U = \{\langle A, B \rangle : A, B \subseteq U \text{ and } A \cap B = \emptyset\}.$$

Given a knowledge base $K = (U, R)$, we can define an unary operator $^L : 3^U \to 3^U$, as follows: for any $\langle A, B \rangle \in 3^U$

$$\langle A, B \rangle^L = \langle \underline{R}A, \underline{R}B \rangle.$$

Let us consider the following operations on 3^U:

$$\langle A, B \rangle \sqcap \langle C, D \rangle = \langle A \cap C, B \cup D \rangle,$$

$$\langle A, B \rangle \sqcup \langle C, D \rangle = \langle A \cup C, B \cap D \rangle,$$

$$\langle A, B \rangle^- = \langle B, A \rangle,$$

$$\langle A, B \rangle^\approx = \langle B, U - B \rangle.$$

Observe that $\sqcap$ and $\sqcup$ induce the following partial order relation on 3^U: for all $\langle A, B \rangle, \langle C, D \rangle \in 3^U$

$$\langle A, B \rangle \sqsubseteq \langle C, D \rangle \text{ iff } \langle A, B \rangle \sqcap \langle C, D \rangle = \langle A, B \rangle$$
$$\text{(or, equivalently, } \langle A, B \rangle \sqcup \langle C, D \rangle = \langle C, D \rangle)$$

The following results hold [14].

Proposition 1. The structure $\langle 3^U, \sqcap, \sqcup, ^-, ^\approx, ^L, \langle \emptyset, U \rangle, \langle U, \emptyset \rangle \rangle$ is a Pawlak-Brouwer-Zadeh lattice. □

Proposition 2. For every Pawlak-Brouwer-Zadeh lattice $\mathcal{L}_{PBZ} = \langle \Sigma, \wedge, \vee, ', ^\sim, ^A, 0, 1 \rangle$, satisfying the condition

(P) there exists $c \in \Sigma$ for which $c = c'$,

there is a knowledge base $K = (U, R)$ such that the structure

$$RS_{PBZ}(U, R) = \langle 3^U, \sqcap, \sqcup, ^-, ^\approx, ^L, \langle \emptyset, U \rangle, \langle U, \emptyset \rangle \rangle$$

is isomorphic to $\mathcal{L}_{PBZ}$. □

3 The Bipolar Pawlak-Brouwer-Zadeh Distributive de Morgan Lattice and Dominance-Based Rough Set Theory

After giving a formulation of the bipolar de Morgan Brouwer-Zadeh distributive lattice, being a bit simpler and a bit more general than the one given in [13], we propose the bipolar Pawlak-Brouwer-Zadeh distributive de Morgan lattice. It results from a definitely non-trivial synthesis of the basic ideas of [13] and [14]. We show that it constitutes a formal model for dominance-based rough set theory.

A system $\langle \Sigma, \Sigma^+, \wedge, \vee, ', ^\sim, 0, 1 \rangle$ is a bipolar de Morgan Brouwer-Zadeh distributive lattice if

(B1) $\langle \Sigma, \wedge, \vee, ', ^\sim, 0, 1 \rangle$ is a de Morgan Brouwer-Zadeh distributive lattice,
(B2) $\Sigma^+ \subseteq \Sigma$ is a distributive lattice with respect to the join and the meet operations $\vee$ and $\wedge$,
(B3) $a \in \Sigma^+$ implies that $a'^\sim, a^{\sim\prime} \in \Sigma^+$.

Observe that by $(B3)$, $(K1)$ and (s-in), we have that $a \in \Sigma^+$ implies that $a'', a^{\sim\sim} \in \Sigma^+$. Let us consider the set

$$\Sigma^- = \{a \in \Sigma : a = b' \text{ or } a = b^\sim \text{ with } b \in \Sigma^+\}.$$

Σ^- is a distributive lattice with respect to the join and the meet operations $\vee$ and $\wedge$, and $a \in \Sigma^-$ implies that $a'^\sim, a^{\sim\prime}, a^{\sim\sim}, a'' \in \Sigma^-$.

A bipolar approximation operator, called bipolar Pawlak operator, on a bipolar de Morgan Brouwer-Zadeh distributive lattice is a unary operation $^M : \Sigma^+ \to \Sigma^+$ satisfying the following properties $(A2^B)$–$(A9^B)$ (the numbering underlines the correspondence of the properties of bipolar Pawlak operator ^{M} with the analogous properties of Pawlak operator ^{A}):

$(A2^B1)$ $a \leq b$ implies $b^{M\sim} \leq a^{M\sim}$;
$(A2^B2)$ $a \leq b$ implies $a^{M\prime\sim} \leq b^{M\prime\sim}$;
$(A3^B1)$ $a^{M\sim} \leq a^\sim$;
$(A3^B2)$ $a^{M\prime\sim} \leq a'^\sim$;
$(A4^B1)$ $0^M = 0$;
$(A4^B2)$ $1^M = 1$;
$(A5^B1)$ $a^\sim = b^\sim$ implies $a^M \wedge b^M = (a \wedge b)^M$;
$(A5^B2)$ $a'^\sim = b'^\sim$ implies $a^M \vee b^M = (a \vee b)^M$;
$(A6^B1)$ $a^M \vee b^M \leq (a \vee b)^M$;
$(A6^B2)$ $(a \wedge b)^M \leq a^M \wedge b^M$;
$(A7^B)$ $a^{MM} = a^M$;
$(A8^B1)$ $a^{M\sim\prime M} = a^{M\sim\prime}$;
$(A8^B2)$ $a^{M\prime\sim M} = a'^{\sim M}$;
$(A9^B1)$ $(a^M \wedge b^M)^M = a^M \wedge b^M$;
$(A9^B2)$ $(a^M \vee b^M)^M = a^M \vee b^M$;

We define the bipolar Pawlak-Brouwer-Zadeh lattice as system $\langle \Sigma, \Sigma^+, \wedge, \vee, ', ^\sim, ^M, 0, 1 \rangle$, where $\langle \Sigma, \Sigma^+, \wedge, \vee, ', ^\sim, 0, 1 \rangle$ is a bipolar Brouwer-Zadeh distributive de Morgan lattice, and operator ^{M} is a bipolar Pawlak operator.

3.1 The Bipolar Pawlak-Brouwer-Zadeh Lattice as an Algebraic Model of Dominance-Based Rough Set Theory

An *ordered knowledge base* $K = (U, R)$ is a relational system where the universe $U \neq \emptyset$ is a finite set, and R is a preorder on U, that is R is a reflexive and transitive binary relation on U. For any $x \in U$, let us consider its dominating set $[x]_R^\geq = \{y \in U : yRx\}$ and its dominated set $[x]_R^\leq = \{y \in U : xRy\}$. Given the ordered knowledge base $K = (U, R)$, to each subset $X \subseteq U$ one can associate the four subsets $\underline{R}^\geq X$, $\overline{R}^\geq X$, $\underline{R}^\leq X$, $\overline{R}^\leq X$:

$$\underline{R}^\geq X = \{x \in U : [x]_R^\geq \subseteq X\},$$

$$\overline{R}^\geq X = \{x \in U : [x]_R^\leq \cap X \neq \emptyset\},$$

$$\underline{R}^{\leq} X = \{x \in U : [x]_{\overline{R}}^{\leq} \subseteq X\},$$
$$\overline{R}^{\leq} X = \{x \in U : [x]_{\overline{R}}^{\geq} \cap X \neq \emptyset\}.$$

$\underline{R}^{\geq} X$ and $\overline{R}^{\geq} X$ are called the upward lower and upper approximations of X, while $\underline{R}^{\geq} X$ and $\overline{R}^{\geq} X$ are called the downward lower and upper approximations of X.

The preorder R can be identified with the dominance relation which relates two objects a and b (for example companies for which the bankruptcy risk is assessed) evaluated with respect to a set of points of view, technically called criteria (for example, financial ratios), when on all criteria, object a is at least as good as object b.

Given an ordered knowledge base $K = (U, R)$, let us consider $\mathcal{U}^{+} \subseteq 2^{U}$, such that

– $\emptyset, U \in \mathcal{U}^{+}$,
– for all $A, B \subseteq U$, if $A, B \in \mathcal{U}^{+}$ then also $A \cap B, A \cup B \in \mathcal{U}^{+}$,
– for all $A \subseteq U$, if $A \in \mathcal{U}^{+}$ then also $\underline{R}^{\geq} A, \overline{R}^{\geq} A \in \mathcal{U}^{+}$.

The sets $A \subseteq U$, such that $A \in \mathcal{U}^{+}$, are called positive sets. Let us observe that, possibly, $\mathcal{U}^{+} = 2^{U}$, in which case all subsets of U are positive. Having a family $\mathcal{U}^{+}$ of positive sets, it is possible to define a family $\mathcal{U}^{-}$ of negative sets as follows:

$$\mathcal{U}^{-} = \{A \subseteq U : U - A \in \mathcal{U}^{+}\}.$$

On the basis of $\mathcal{U}^{+}$ (and, consequently, of $\mathcal{U}^{-}$) we can define the set $\mathcal{W}(\mathcal{U}^{+})$ of all pairs $\langle A, B \rangle$, such that $A \in \mathcal{U}^{+}$, $B \in \mathcal{U}^{-}$ and $A \cap B = \emptyset$. Let us observe that if $\mathcal{U}^{+} = 2^{U}$, then $\mathcal{W}(\mathcal{U}^{+}) = 3^{U}$.

Given an ordered knowledge base $K = (U, R)$ and a family of positive sets $\mathcal{U}^{+}$ (and, therefore, $\mathcal{W}(\mathcal{U}^{+})$), we can define an unary operator $^{N} : \mathcal{W}(\mathcal{U}^{+}) \to \mathcal{W}(\mathcal{U}^{+})$, as follows: for any $\langle A, B \rangle \in \mathcal{W}(\mathcal{U}^{+})$

$$\langle A, B \rangle^{N} = \langle \underline{R}^{\geq} A, \underline{R}^{\leq} B \rangle.$$

The following result holds.

Proposition 3. The structure $\langle 3^{U}, \mathcal{W}(\mathcal{U}^{+}), \sqcap, \sqcup, ^{-}, ^{\approx}, ^{N}, \langle \emptyset, U \rangle, \langle U, \emptyset \rangle \rangle$ is a bipolar Pawlak-Brouwer-Zadeh lattice.

Sketch of the proof. This can be proved by a relatively straightforward verification. $\langle 3^{U}, \sqcap, \sqcup, ^{-}, ^{\approx}, \langle \emptyset, U \rangle, \langle U, \emptyset \rangle \rangle$ is clearly a de Morgan Brouwer-Zadeh distributive lattice. $\mathcal{W}(\mathcal{U}^{+})$ is a distributive lattice with respect to $\sqcap$ and $\sqcup$ because, by definition, $U \in \mathcal{U}^{+}$ and for all $A, B \subseteq U$, if $A, B \in \mathcal{U}^{+}$ then also $A \cap B, A \cup B \in \mathcal{U}^{+}$. Moreover, ^{N} is a binary operation on $\mathcal{W}(\mathcal{U}^{+})$, because, again by definition, for all $A \subseteq U$, if $A \in \mathcal{U}^{+}$ then also $\underline{R}^{\geq} A, \overline{R}^{\geq} A \in \mathcal{U}^{+}$. Finally, one can prove that ^{N} satisfies all properties $(A2^{B})$–$(A9^{B})$. For example, for all $A, C \in \mathcal{U}^{+}$, $B, D \in \mathcal{U}^{-}$ with $A \cap B = C \cap D = \emptyset$, if $\langle A, B \rangle \sqsubseteq \langle C, D \rangle$, that is $A \subseteq C$ and $B \supseteq D$, we have

$$\langle C, D \rangle^{N\approx} = \langle \underline{R}^{\leq} D, U - \underline{R}^{\leq} D \rangle \sqsubseteq \langle \underline{R}^{\leq} B, U - \underline{R}^{\leq} B \rangle = \langle A, B \rangle^{N\approx}$$

so that property $(A2^{B}1)$ holds. $\qquad\square$

4 Didactic Example

A financial institution wants to assess the bankruptcy risk of a set of six companies. To this end, two experts were contacted. The six companies are evaluated
on three criteria: Debt ratio (Total debt / Total assets), ROA (return on assets,
i.e., Net income / Total assets) an ROS (return on sales, i.e., Net income / Sales
revenue). Using some thresholds on criteria scales, agreed between the experts,
the evaluations were transformed to qualitative ones, as shown in Table 1. Then,
the experts were asked to make their first assessment of the bankruptcy risk,
by assigning the companies to the classes of "safe" and "risky" companies. In
case the experts had doubts with respect to the risk of bankruptcy of some companies, they abstained from the assignment. The financial evaluations and the
classifications of the six companies made by the experts are shown in Table 1,
where the abstentions are marked with "?".

Table 1. Financial data of companies and bankrutcy risk assessment by the two experts

Company	Debt ratio	ROA	ROS	Expert 1	Expert 2
A1	Good	Medium	Medium	Safe	Safe
A2	Medium	Bad	Medium	?	Risky
A3	Medium	Bad	Medium	Risky	?
A4	Medium	Good	Bad	Risky	Safe
A5	Medium	Medium	Bad	?	Risky
A6	Medium	Bad	Good	Safe	?

In this case, the set 3^U is the family of all the pairs of sets $\langle A, B \rangle$ with A
interpreted as the set of safe companies, B as the set of risky companies, and
$U - A - B$ the set of companies for which there is some doubt. The assessment
of each conceivable expert E is therefore represented by one pair $E = \langle A, B \rangle$
from 3^U. For example, the assessment of Expert 1 is represented by the pair
$E_1 = \langle \{A1, A6\}, \{A3, A4\} \rangle$, and the assessment of Expert 2 is represented by
the pair $E_2 = \langle \{A1, A4\}, \{A2, A5\} \rangle$. The operators of the Brouwer-Zadeh lattice
permit to obtain different aggregations of the assessments of the experts.

In particular, the join operator $\sqcup$ gives an optimistic synthesis of the assessments of the two experts, i.e., a company is safe if it is safe for at least one of
the two experts, and a company is risky if it is risky for both the experts. In
case of Expert 1 and Expert 2, we get $E_1 \sqcup E_2 = \langle \{A1, A6, A4\}, \emptyset \rangle$ (Table 2).

On the other hand, the meet operator $\sqcap$ gives a pessimistic synthesis of the
assessments of the two experts, i.e., a company is safe if it is safe for both experts,
and a company is risky if it is risky for at least one of the two experts. In case
of Expert 1 and Expert 2, we get $E_1 \sqcap E_2 = \langle \{A1\}, \{A2, A3, A4, A5\} \rangle$.

The Kleene negation $^-$ represents the assessments of an expert giving inverse
assignments comparing to E, that is an expert E^- for which the companies evaluated safe by expert E are risky, and the companies evaluated risky by expert E

Table 2. Explanation of the meaning of knowledge base $K = (U, R)$ and elements of the Pawlak-Brouwer-Zadeh lattice and bipolar Pawlak-Brouwer-Zadeh lattice in terms of the example.

Element	Meaning
U	Set of companies assessed by the experts wrt risk
R	Indiscernibility relation or dominance relation in the set of companies wrt financial ratios
$\langle A, B \rangle$	Pair of sets of safe companies (A) and risky companies (B) from U
$U - A - B$	Set of doubtful companies wrt risk
3^U	Family of all the pairs of sets $\langle A, B \rangle$
$\mathcal{U}^+$	All possible subsets of companies
$\sqcup$	Join operator on assessment of the experts: gives $\langle A, B \rangle$, where A contains companies safe for at least one expert, and B contains companies risky for all the experts
$\sqcap$	Meet operator on assessment of the experts: gives $\langle A, B \rangle$, where A contains companies safe for all the experts, and B contains companies risky for at least one expert
$-$	Kleen negation: transforms $\langle A, B \rangle$ to $\langle B, A \rangle$, i.e., makes of safe companies risky ones and vice versa
$\approx$	Brouwer negation: transforms $\langle A, B \rangle$ to $\langle B, U - B \rangle$, i.e., makes of risky companies safe ones, and of all the others risky ones
$\approx-$	Conjunction of Brouwer and Kleene negations: transforms $\langle A, B \rangle$ to $\langle U - B, B \rangle$, i.e., adds all doubtful companies to the safe ones
$-\approx$	Conjunction of Kleene and Brouwer negations: transforms $\langle A, B \rangle$ to $\langle A, U - A \rangle$, i.e., adds all doubtful companies to the risky ones
L	Pawlak operator exploiting knowledge about indiscernibility relation in U: transforms $\langle A, B \rangle$ to pair of lower approximations $\langle \underline{R}A, \underline{R}B \rangle$, i.e., eliminates from A and B all companies indiscernible with doubtful ones
N	Pawlak operator exploiting knowledge about dominance relation in U: transforms $\langle A, B \rangle$ to pair of lower approximations $\langle \underline{R}^{\geq}A, \underline{R}^{\leq}B \rangle$, i.e., eliminates from A all companies dominated by risky or doubtful ones, and from B all companies dominating risky or doubtful ones

are safe. For example, for experts E_1 and E_2 we get $E_1^- = \langle \{A3, A4\}, \{A1, A6\} \rangle$ and $E_2^- = \langle \{A2, A5\}, \{A1, A4\} \rangle$.

The Brouwer negation $\approx$ gives back the assessments of an expert $E^{\approx}$ for which the companies evaluated risky by expert E are safe, while all the remaining companies are evaluated risky, so that there is no more space for the doubtful companies. For example, for experts E_1 and E_2 we get $E_1^{\approx} = \langle\{A3, A4\}, \{A1, A2, A5, A6\}\rangle$ and $E_2^{\approx} = \langle\{A1, A6\}, \{A2, A3, A4, A5\}\rangle$.

Of course, one can use multiple operators in conjunction. For example, it is interesting to combine the two negations. Obviously, applying two times the Kleene negation the original pair is obtained, that is $E^{--} = E$. If one applies first the Brouwer negation and after the Kleene negation, one obtains a new pair that can be seen as an optimistic revision of the initial assessment, that is all the companies that were not considered originally as risky are considered as safe. For the two experts E_1 and E_2 we get $E_1^{\approx-} = \langle\{A1, A2, A5, A6\}, \{A3, A4\}\rangle$ and $E_2^{\approx-} = \langle\{A1, A3, A4, A6\}, \{A2, A5\}\rangle$. Instead, if one applies first the Kleene negation and after the Brouwer negation, then one obtains a new pair that can be seen as a pessimistic revision of the initial assessment, that is all the companies that were not considered originally as safe are considered as risky. For the two experts E_1 and E_2 we get $E_1^{-\approx} = \langle\{A3, A4\}, \{A1, A2, A5, A6\}\rangle$ and $E_2^{-\approx} = \langle\{A1, A4\}, \{A2, A3, A5, A6\}\rangle$.

On the logical basis of the Brouwer-Zadeh lattice, taking into account knowledge about the indiscernibility relation in U with respect to financial ratios, one can define the Pawlak rough approximation operator ^{L} which assigns to each pair $E = \langle A, B\rangle$ of safe and risky companies, the pair $E^L = \langle \underline{R}A, \underline{R}B\rangle$ of the rough lower approximations of safe and risky companies. Let us remember that the indiscernibility relation R holds if two companies have equal evaluation with respect to all the considered financial ratios, so that

$$R = \{(A2, A3), (A3, A2)\} \cup \{(Ai, Ai) : i = 1, \ldots, 6\}.$$

Thus, for the two experts E_1 and E_2, we get

$$E_1^L = \langle \underline{R}\{A1, A6\}, \underline{R}\{A3, A4\}\rangle = \langle\{A1, A6\}, \{A4\}\rangle,$$

$$E_2^L = \langle \underline{R}\{A1, A4\}, \underline{R}\{A2, A5\}\rangle = \langle\{A1, A4\}, \{A5\}\rangle.$$

The pairs E_1^L and E_2^L can be interpreted as the assignments to safe and risky companies by experts E_1 and E_2, for which there is no doubt on the basis of the available knowledge. In result of this operation, one can see that according to available knowledge and assessment made by E_1, among the companies considered as certainly risky $A3$ is not present, although it was classified as risky by expert E_1, because it is indiscernible with $A2$ that was not classified as risky. Thus, $A3$ is not present in the lower approximation of the class of risky companies. This fact can also be interpreted such that on the basis of available knowledge, i.e., indiscernibility of $A3$ and $A2$ classified by this expert to different classes, there is some doubt about classifying $A3$ as risky. An analogous argument explains why among the companies considered as certainly risky, according to the available knowledge and assessment made by E_2, company $A2$ is not present.

Of course, the logic structure of the Brouwer-Zadeh lattice can be applied also on the pairs E^L obtained in result of rough approximation using the Pawlak operator. For example, one can consider the optimistic assessment resulting from the application of the Brouwer negation first and then the Kleene negation, that for the two experts E_1 and E_2 gives $E_1^{L \approx -} = \langle \{A1, A2, A3, A5, A6\}, \{A4\} \rangle$ and $E_2^{L \approx -} = \langle \{A1, A2, A3, A4, A6\}, \{A5\} \rangle$. One can also consider the pessimistic assessment resulting from the application of the Kleene negation first and then the Brouwer negation on the rough approximations E_1^L and E_2^L; then, we get $E_1^{L - \approx} = \langle \{A1, A6\}, \{A2, A3, A4, A5\} \rangle$ and $E_2^{L - \approx} = \langle \{A1, A4\}, \{A2, A3, A5, A6\} \rangle$.

Observe now, that the evaluations of the companies on the financial ratios, as well as the assessments given by the two experts E_1 and E_2 are, in fact, ordered. Indeed, with respect to the qualitative evaluations on the financial ratios "Good" is better than "Medium" which, in turn, is better than "Bad", while, with respect to the assessment of the experts, class "Safe" is better than "?" that, in turn, is better than "Risky". Therefore, it seems more appropriate to consider DRSA and its algebraic counterpart, that is the bipolar Brouwer-Zadeh lattice with the bipolar Pawlak operator ^{N}. In this case, any pair $E = \langle A, B \rangle$ has to be approximated using dominance relation R that for two companies is true when the first one is at least as good as the second one with respect to evaluations on all the considered financial ratios. For the six companies $A_1, \ldots, A_6$ evaluated on the three considered financial ratios, shown in Table 1, we have

$$R = \{(A1, A2), (A1, A3), (A1, A5), (A2, A3), (A3, A2), (A4, A5), (A6, A2), (A6, A3)\}$$

$$\cup$$

$$\{(Ai, Ai) : i = 1, \ldots, 6\}.$$

For the assessments of experts E_1 and E_2, the approximated pairs of safe and risky companies obtained by applying the bipolar Pawlak operator ^{N} are the following:

$$E_1^N = \langle \{A1, A6\}, \emptyset \rangle ,$$
$$E_2^N = \langle \{A1, A4\}, \{A5\} \rangle .$$

On these pairs, the operators of the Brouwer-Zadeh lattice can be used again, and based on them, a financial institution can formulate various procedures to aggregate the assessments of the experts taking into account the knowledge supplied by financial ratios. Let us exemplify some of these aggregation procedures:

- aggregation with an optimistic attitude: the join of the rough approximated assessments obtained using the bipolar Pawlak operator, i.e.,

$$E_1^N \sqcup E_2^N = \langle \{A1, A4, A6\}, \emptyset \rangle ;$$

- aggregation with a pessimistic attitude: as in the previous point, replacing the join by the meet, i.e.,

$$E_1^N \sqcap E_2^N = \langle \{A1\}, \{A5\} \rangle ;$$

- aggregation with an extremely optimistic attitude: the join of the optimistic assessments obtained by applying first the Brouwer negation and then the

Kleene negation to the rough approximated assessments obtained using the bipolar Pawlak operator, i.e.,

$$E_1^{N\approx-} \sqcup E_2^{N\approx-} = \langle U, \emptyset \rangle \,;$$

- aggregation with a mildly optimistic attitude: as in the previous point, replacing the join by the meet, i.e.,

$$E_1^{N\approx-} \sqcap E_2^{N\approx-} = \langle \{A1, A2, A3, A4, A6\}, \{A5\} \rangle$$

- aggregation with an extremely pessimistic attitude: the meet of the pessimistic assessment obtained by applying first the Kleene negation and then the Brouwer negation to the rough approximated assessments obtained using the bipolar Pawlak operator, i.e.,

$$E_1^{N-\approx} \sqcap E_2^{N-\approx} = \langle \{A_1\}, \{A2, A3, A4, A5, A6\} \rangle \,;$$

- aggregation with a mildly pessimistic attitude: as in the previous point, replacing the meet by the join, i.e.,

$$E_1^{N-\approx} \sqcup E_2^{N-\approx} = \langle \{A1, A4, A6\}, \{A2, A3, A5\} \rangle$$

5   Conclusions

We extended the Pawlak-Brouwer-Zadeh lattice to the bipolar Pawlak-Brouwer-Zadeh lattice, obtaining a new algebraic model which permits a joint consideration of vagueness due to imprecision typical of fuzzy sets, and ambiguity due to coarseness typical of rough set theory, when reasoning about ordered data using the dominance-based rough set approach (DRSA). In the context of DRSA applied to ordinal classification with monotonicity constraints, vagueness is due to imprecision in object classification - it appears when an expert is hesitant when classifying the objects because her knowledge of the objects is not perfectly precise; ambiguity is due to coarseness or granularity of the description of the objects by the attributes - it appears when some attribute is missing in the description, or when the considered attributes do not have sufficiently fine scales to avoid violation of indiscernibility or dominance principle. Joint consideration of vagueness and ambiguity within DRSA shows once again [6] a complementary character of fuzzy sets and rough sets in dealing with distinct facets of imperfect knowledge.

Using a didactic example, we have shown how the logic structure of the Pawlak-Brouwer-Zadeh lattice can be used to aggregate evaluations of multiple experts taking into account the available information. In the future research, we envisage similar extensions of other algebraic structures for rough set theory, different from Brouwer-Zadeh lattice, such as Nelson algebra, Heyting algebra, Łukasiewicz algebra, Stone algebra, and so on (see, e.g., Chap. 12 in [17] or [2]).

References

1. Cattaneo, G.: Generalized rough sets (preclusivity fuzzy-intuitionistic (BZ) Lattices). Stud. Logica. **58**, 47–77 (1997)
2. Cattaneo, G., Ciucci, D.: Algebraic structures for rough sets. In: Peters, J.F., Skowron, A., Dubois, D., Grzymała-Busse, J.W., Inuiguchi, M., Polkowski, L. (eds.) Transactions on Rough Sets II. LNCS, vol. 3135, pp. 208–252. Springer, Heidelberg (2004). doi:10.1007/978-3-540-27778-1_12
3. Cattaneo, G., Ciucci, D.: Lattices with interior and closure operators and abstract approximation spaces. In: Peters, J.F., Skowron, A., Wolski, M., Chakraborty, M.K., Wu, W.-Z. (eds.) Transactions on Rough Sets X. LNCS, vol. 5656, pp. 67–116. Springer, Heidelberg (2009). doi:10.1007/978-3-642-03281-3_3
4. Cattaneo, G., Ciucci, D., Dubois, D.: Algebraic models of deviant modal operators based on de Morgan and Kleene lattices. Inform. Sci. **181**, 4075–4100 (2011)
5. Cattaneo, G., Nisticò, G.: Brouwer-Zadeh poset and three-valued Łukasiewicz posets. Fuzzy Sets Syst. **33**, 165–190 (1989)
6. Dubois, D., Prade, H., Foreword, In: Pawlak, Z. (ed.) Rough Sets, Kluwer, Dordrecht (1991)
7. Greco, S., Matarazzo, B., Słowiński, R.: A new rough set approach to evaluation of bankruptcy risk. In: Zopounidis, C. (ed.) Operational Tools in the Management of Financial Risks, pp. 121–136. Springer, Berlin (1998)
8. Greco, S., Matarazzo, B., Słowiński, R.: Rough sets theory for multicriteria decision analysis. Eur. J. Oper. Res. **129**, 1–47 (2001)
9. Greco, S., Matarazzo, B., Słowiński, R.: Rough sets methodology for sorting problems in presence of multiple attributes and criteria. Eur. J. Oper. Res. **138**, 247–259 (2002)
10. Greco, S., Matarazzo, B., Słowiński, R.: Rough approximation by dominance relations. Int. J. Intell. Syst. **17**, 153–171 (2002)
11. Greco, S., Matarazzo, B., Slowinski, R.: Decision rule approach. In: Greco, S., Ehrgott, M., Figueira, J.R. (eds.) Multiple Criteria Decision Analysis. ISORMS, vol. 233, pp. 497–552. Springer, New York (2016). doi:10.1007/978-1-4939-3094-4_13
12. Greco, S., Matarazzo, B., Słowiński, R.: Dominance-Based Rough Set Approach as a Proper Way of Handling Graduality in Rough Set Theory. In: Peters, J.F., Skowron, A., Marek, V.W., Orłowska, E., Słowiński, R., Ziarko, W. (eds.) Transactions on Rough Sets VII. LNCS, vol. 4400, pp. 36–52. Springer, Heidelberg (2007). doi:10.1007/978-3-540-71663-1_3
13. Greco, S., Matarazzo, B., Słowiński, R.: The bipolar complemented de Morgan Brouwer-Zadeh Distributive lattice as an algebraic structure for the dominance-based rough set approach. Fundam. Inform. **115**, 25–56 (2012)
14. Greco, S., Matarazzo, B., Słowiński, R.: Distinguishing vagueness from ambiguity by means of Pawlak-Brouwer-Zadeh lattices. In: Greco, S., et al. (eds.) International Conference on Information Processing and Management of Uncertainty in Knowledge-Based Systems - IPMU 2012, CCIS 297, pp. 624–632. Springer, Berlin (2012)
15. Pawlak, Z.: Rough sets. Int. J. Comput. Inf. Sci. **11**, 341–356 (1982)
16. Pawlak, Z.: Rough Sets. Kluwer, Dordrecht (1991)
17. Polkowski, L.: Rough Sets - Mathematical Foundations. Physica-Verlag, Heidelberg (2002)

Similarity Based Rough Sets

Dávid Nagy$^{(\boxtimes)}$, Tamás Mihálydeák, and László Aszalós

Faculty of Informatics, University of Debrecen, Debrecen, Hungary
{nagy.david,mihalydeak.tamas,aszalos.laszlo}@inf.unideb.hu

Abstract. Pawlak's indiscernibility relation (which is an equivalence relation) represents a limit of our knowledge embedded in an information system. In many cases covering approximation spaces rely on tolerance relations instead of equivalence relations. In real practice (for example in data mining) tolerance relations may be generated from the properties of objects. A given tolerance relation represents similarity between objects, but the usage of similarity is very special: it emphasizes the similarity to a given object and not the similarity of objects 'in general'. The authors show that this usage has some problematic consequences. The main goal of the paper is to show that if one uses the method of correlation clustering then there is a way to construct a general (partial) approximation space with disjoint base sets relying on the similarity of objects generated by their properties. At the end a software describing a real life problem is presented.

Keywords: Rough set theory · Correlation clustering · Set approximation

1 Introduction

From the theoretical point of view a Pawlakian approximation space (see in [12–14]) can be characterized by an ordered pair $\langle U, \mathcal{R} \rangle$ where U is a nonempty set of objects and $\mathcal{R}$ is an equivalence relation on U. In order to approximate an arbitrary subset S of U the following tools have to be introduced:

- *the set of base sets*: $\mathfrak{B} = \{B \mid B \subseteq U,$ and $x, y \in B$ if $x\mathcal{R}y\}$, the partition of U generated by the equivalence relation $\mathcal{R}$;
- *the set of definable sets*: $\mathfrak{D}_\mathfrak{B}$ is an extension of $\mathfrak{B}$, and it is given by the following inductive definition:
  1. $\mathfrak{B} \subseteq \mathfrak{D}_\mathfrak{B}$;
  2. $\emptyset \in \mathfrak{D}_\mathfrak{B}$;
  3. if $D_1, D_2 \in \mathfrak{D}_\mathfrak{B}$, then $D_1 \cup D_2 \in \mathfrak{D}_\mathfrak{B}$.
- *the functions* l, u form a Pawlakian approximation pair $\langle \mathsf{l}, \mathsf{u} \rangle$, i.e.
  1. $Dom(\mathsf{l}) = Dom(\mathsf{u}) = 2^U$
  2. $\mathsf{l}(S) = \bigcup\{B \mid B \in \mathfrak{B}$ and $B \subseteq S\}$;
  3. $\mathsf{u}(S) = \bigcup\{B \mid B \in \mathfrak{B}$ and $B \cap S \neq \emptyset\}$.

© Springer International Publishing AG 2017
L. Polkowski et al. (Eds.): IJCRS 2017, Part II, LNAI 10314, pp. 94–107, 2017.
DOI: 10.1007/978-3-319-60840-2_7

$\mathcal{R}$ is called an indiscernibility relation. It represents a sort of limit of our knowledge embedded in an information system (or background knowledge). Indiscernibility has an affect on the membership relation. In some situation it makes our judgment of the membership relation uncertain – making the set vague – because a decision about a given object affects the decision about all other objects which are indiscernible from the given object. Indiscernibility plays a crucial role in approximation process: if we are interested in whether $x \in S$ (where S is the set to be approximated), then

1. the answer 'yes' (i.e. $x \in \mathsf{l}(S)$) means that not only $x \in S$ but all y, such that $x\mathcal{R}y$ are members of S;
2. the answer 'no' (i.e. $x \in \mathsf{l}(\overline{S})$, where $\overline{S}$ is the complement of S) means that not only $x \notin S$ but all y, such that $x\mathcal{R}y$ are not members of S;
3. the answer 'maybe' (i.e. $x \in \mathsf{u}(S) \setminus \mathsf{l}(S)$) means that there are y_1, y_2 such that $x\mathcal{R}y_1$ and $x\mathcal{R}y_2$ for which $y_1 \in S$ and $y_2 \notin S$.

In practical applications indiscernibility relation is too strong: we have to handle indiscernible objects in the same way but in real practice we have to consider them as similar objects. Pawlakian approximation spaces have been generalized using tolerance relations (instead of equivalence ones), which are similarity relations and so they are symmetric and reflexive. Covering-based approximation spaces (see for instance [16]) generalize Pawlakian approximation spaces in two points:

1. $\mathcal{R}$ is (only) a tolerance relation;
2. $\mathfrak{B} = \{[x] \mid [x] \subseteq U, x \in U \text{ and } y \in [x] \text{ if } x\mathcal{R}y\}$, where $[x] = \{y \mid y \in U, x\mathcal{R}y\}$.

These spaces use the definitions of definable sets and approximation pairs of Pawlakian approximation spaces.

Covering approximation spaces use similarity relations instead of equivalence relations, but the usage of similarity relations (which are tolerance relations from the mathematical point of view) is very special. It emphasizes the similarity to a given object and not the similarity of objects 'in general'. We can recognize this feature when we try to understand the precise meaning of the answer coming from an approximation relying on a covering approximation space. If we are interested in whether $x \in S$ (where S is the set to be approximated), then (see Fig. 1)

1. the answer 'yes' (i.e. $x \in \mathsf{l}(S)$) means that there is an object x' such that $x'\mathcal{R}x, x' \in S$ and all y for which $x'\mathcal{R}y$ are members of S;
2. the answer 'no' (i.e. $x \in \mathsf{l}(\overline{S})$) means that there is an object x' such that $x'\mathcal{R}x, x' \notin S$ and all y for which $x'\mathcal{R}y$ are not members of S;
3. otherwise the answer is 'maybe' (informally x is a member of the border of S) means that there is no x' for which $x'\mathcal{R}x, [x'] \subseteq U$, and there is no x'' for which $x''\mathcal{R}x, [x''] \cap U \neq \emptyset$.

Some practical problems of covering approximation spaces:

1. The former answers show, that generally the lower and upper approximations are not close in the following sense (see Fig. 2):

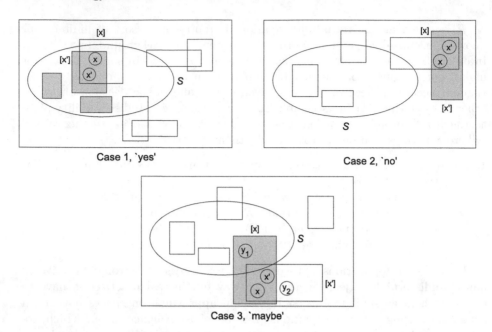

Fig. 1. Some base sets in covering cases

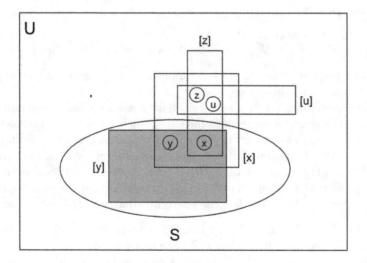

Fig. 2. In covering the lower and upper approximations are not closed

(a) If $x \in l(S)$, then we cannot say that $[x] \subseteq S$.
(b) If $x \in u(S)$, then we cannot say, that $[y] \cap S \neq \emptyset$ for all $y \in [x]$.
2. The number of base sets is not more than the number of members of U, so we have too many base sets for practical applications.

If we want to avoid these problems we can generate a Pawlakian approximation space by constructing a system of disjoint base sets (see in [7]) (see Fig. 3). If we have two base sets B_1, B_2, such that $B_1 \cap B_2 \neq \emptyset$, then we substitute them with the following three sets: $B_1 \setminus B_2, B_2 \setminus B_1, B_1 \cap B_2$. Applying this iteratively we can get the reduction. Although it is not a real solution from the practical point of view. The base sets can become too small for practical applications. The smaller base sets we have, the closer we are to the classical set theory. (If all base sets are singleton, then there is no difference between the approximation space and classical set theory.)

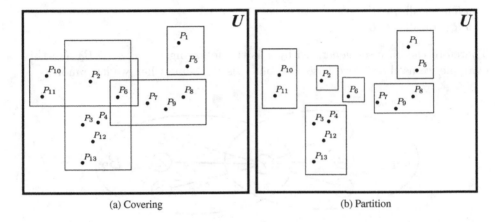

(a) Covering   (b) Partition

Fig. 3. Covering and its reduction to a partition

In rough set theory the members of a given base set share some common properties.

– In Pawlak's original system all members of a given base set have the same attributes (i.e. they have the same properties with respect to the represented knowledge).
– In covering approximation spaces all members of a given base set are similar to a distinguished object (which is used to generate the given base set).

Further generalization is possible (see): General (partial) Pawlakian approximation spaces can be obtained by generalization of the set of base sets:

– let $\mathfrak{B}$ be an arbitrary nonempty set of nonempty subsets of U.

These spaces are Pawlakian in the sense that they use Pawlakian definition of definable sets and approximation pairs. This generalization is very useful because a base set can be taken as a collection of objects with a given property, and we can use very different properties in order to define different base sets. The members of the base set can be handled in the same way relying on their common property. In this case there is no way to give a corresponding relation which is able to generate base sets (similarly to covering approximation spaces), so a general (partial) Pawlakian approximation space can be characterized only by the pair $\langle U, \mathfrak{B} \rangle$, since the lower and upper approximations of a subset of U are determined by the members of $\mathfrak{B}$. However, any system of base sets induces a tolerance relation $\mathcal{R}$ on U: $x\mathcal{R}y$ if there is a base set $B \in \mathfrak{B}$ such that $x, y \in B$. If we use this relation in order to get the system of base sets, the result can be totally different from our original base system (see Fig. 4).

In Fig. 4 x is in the intersection of B_1 and B_2 (B_1 and B_2 are defined by some properties). It means that it has common properties with all y_i and z_i, where $i = 1, 2, 3$. So if some $x \in B_1 \cap B_2$ it means that:

- $x\mathcal{R}y$ for all $y \in B_1$
- $x\mathcal{R}z$ for all $z \in B_2$

Therefore the base set generated by x is the following: $[x] = B_1 \cup B_2$. (In this example we used only two base sets, but it is the same when we have more.)

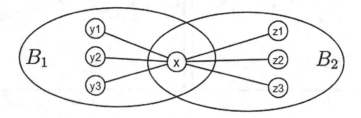

Fig. 4. Base sets by properties of objects

The main goal of the present paper is the following: the authors want to show that there is a way to construct a general (partial) approximation space with disjoint base sets relying on the properties of our objects. These spaces are very useful in data mining. At the very beginning we have a general (partial) approximation space $\langle U, \mathfrak{B} \rangle$. A base set is a collection of objects with the same (practically useful) property. Common properties represent similarity between objects, and the generated tolerance relation can be used to define the system of disjoint base sets with the help of correlation clustering. The final general (partial) Pawlakian approximation space is the core notion of similarity based on rough set theory. This space has the following features:

- the similarity of objects relying on their properties (and not the similarity to a distinguished object) plays a crucial role in the definition of base sets;
- the system of base sets consists of disjoint sets, so the lower and upper approximation are closed;
- only the necessary number of base sets appears (in applications we have to use an acceptable number of base sets);
- the size of base sets is not too small, or too big.

At first the authors overview the most important points of correlation clustering, and then they deal with how to apply correlation clustering in rough set theory. At the end an implementation of similarity based rough set theory is showed.

2   Correlation Clustering

Cluster analysis is a widely used technique in data mining. Our goal is to create groups in which objects are more similar to each other than to those in other groups. Usually the similarity and dissimilarity are based on the attribute values describing the objects. Although there are some cases, when the objects cannot be described by numbers, but we can still say something about their similarity or dissimilarity. Think of the humans for example. It is hard to detail someone's looks by a number, but we still make statements whether two persons are similar to each other or not. Of course these opinions are dependent on the persons. Some can treat two random persons as similar, while others treat them dissimilar. If we want to formulate the similarity and dissimilarity by using mathematics, we need a tolerance relation. If this relation holds for two objects, we can say that they are similar. If this relation does not hold, we say that they are dissimilar. Of course each object is similar to itself, so the relation needs to be reflexive, and it is easy to show, that it also needs to be symmetric. But we cannot go any further, e.g. the transitivity does not hold necessarily.

If we take a human and a mouse, then due to their inner structure they are similar. This is the reason why mice are used in drug experiments. Moreover a human and a Paris doll are similar due to their shape. This is the reason why these dolls are used in show-windows. But there is no similarity between a mouse and a doll except that both are similar to the same object. Correlation clustering is a clustering technique based on a tolerance relation (see in [5, 6, 17]).

Our task is to find an $R \subseteq V \times V$ equivalence relation *closest* to the tolerance relation. A (partial) tolerance relation $\mathcal{R}$ (see in [10, 15]) can be represented by a matrix M. Let matrix $M = (m_{ij})$ be the matrix of the partial relation $\mathcal{R}$ of similarity: $m_{ij} = 1$ whenever objects i and j are similar, $m_{ij} = -1$ whenever objects i and j are dissimilar, and $m_{ij} = 0$ otherwise.

A relation is partial if there exist two elements (i, j) such that $m_{ij} = 0$. It means that if we have an arbitrary relation $R \subseteq V \times V$ we have two sets of pairs. Let R_{true} be the set of those pairs of elements for which the R holds, and R_{false} be the one for which R does not hold. If R is partial then $R_{true} \cup R_{false} \subseteq V \times V$. If R is total then $R_{true} \cup R_{false} = V \times V$.

A partition of a set S is a function $p : S \to \mathbb{N}$. Objects $x, y \in S$ are in the same cluster at partitioning p, if $p(x) = p(y)$.

The cost function counts the negative cases i.e. it gives the number of cases whenever two dissimilar objects are in the same cluster, or two similar objects are in different clusters. The cost function of a partition p and a relation R_M with matrix M is

$$f(p, M) = \frac{1}{2} \sum_{i<j} (m_{ij} + abs(m_{ij})) - \sum_{i<j} \delta_{p(i)p(j)} m_{ij},$$

where δ is the Knockecker delta symbol (see [11]). For a fixed relation the partition with the minimal cost function value is called *optimal*. Solving a correlation clustering problem is equivalent to minimizing its cost function, for the fixed relation. If the value of this optimal cost function is 0, the partition is called *perfect*. Given the $\mathcal{R}$ and R we call the value f the distance of the two relations. The partition given this way, generates an equivalence relation. This relation can be considered as the closest to the tolerance relation.

It is easy to check that the solution cannot be generally perfect for a similarity relation. Take the relation on the left of Fig. 5. The dashed line denotes dissimilarity and the normal line similarity. On the right, Fig. 5 shows all the partition of these objects, where rectangles indicate the clusters. The thick lines denote the pairs which are counted in the cost function. In the upper row the value of the cost function is 1 (in each case), while in the two other cases it is 2 and 3, respectively.

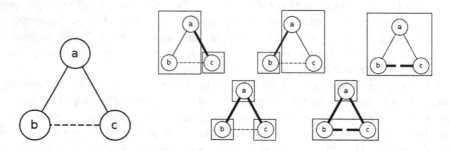

Fig. 5. Minimal frustrated similarity graph and its partitions

The number of partition can be given by the Bell number (see [1]), which grows exponentially. Hence, in general — even in the case of some dozens of objects — the optimal partition cannot be determined in reasonable time, thus a search algorithm which produces a quasi optimal partition would be more useful in practical cases. However in practical examples it gives us the right to handle objects, which are in the same class, the same way.

3   Correlation Clustering in Rough Set Theory

When we would like to define the base sets we use the background knowledge embedded in a given information system. If we have a Pawlakian system then we call two objects indiscernible if all of their known attribute values are the same. In many cases covering systems rely on a similarity (tolerance) relation. As we mentioned earlier some problems can come up using these covering systems. A base set contains members which are similar to a distinguished member.

This means that covering does not consider the similarity relation itself but the similarity with respect to a distinguished object. As a result of the correlation clustering based on the tolerance relation we obtain a partition of the universe [2–4]. The clusters contain elements which are usually similar to each other (not just to a distinguished member). So the partition can be understood as a system of base sets. Singleton base sets represent very little information (its member is only similar to itself). Without increasing the number of conflicts we cannot consider its member similar to any objects. By deleting singleton base sets we get a partial system of base sets.

4 Program

The authors of this article wrote a software, which represents the theory in real life problems. The software can be downloaded from: https://arato.inf.unideb.hu/aszalos.laszlo/covering/.

Fig. 6. Graphical user interface

Figure 6 illustrates the graphical user interface of the program. For giving the input datasets we have two options.

1. Generating random points
2. Reading a predetermined formatted dataset

1. *Random points*
   At first the user gives the number of points, and then the points are generated in a 2 dimensional interval which is also given by the user (These options can be given on the left panel of the user interface). The base of the tolerance relation is the Euclidean distance of the objects (d). We defined a similarity (S) and a dissimilarity threshold (D). The tolerance relation $\mathcal{R}$ can be given this way for any objects A, B:

$$ARB = \begin{cases} +1 & d(A,B) \leq S \\ -1 & d(A,B) > D \\ 0 & \text{otherwise} \end{cases}$$

2. *Predetermined formatted dataset*

The so called ProgCont system (see in [9]), which was developed at the Faculty of Informatics at the University of Debrecen evaluates the programming competitions and midterms. Our software can read and handle data, generated by the ProgCont system. Each record consists of the following attributes: competitor id, problem id, solution id and the id of the programming language. Let A, B be two arbitrary competitors. Let S_A and S_B the sets of the solutions of the problems made by the competitors A and B. So the tolerance relation $\mathcal{R}$ for any competitors A, B is the following:

$$A\mathcal{R}B = \begin{cases} +1 & |S_A \Delta S_B| \leq S \\ -1 & |S_A \Delta S_B| \geq D \\ 0 & \text{otherwise} \end{cases}$$

The similarity and difference are defined by the cardinality of the symmetric difference (Δ) of the given sets.

Algorithm 1. Run method

1: **procedure** RUN(N)
2:      $best\_partition \leftarrow FindBestPartition(N)$
3:      $covering\_base\_sets \leftarrow GetCovering()$
4:      $disjoint\_covering\_base\_sets \leftarrow MakeDisjointSets(covering\_base\_sets)$
5:      print $best\_partition$
6:      print $covering\_base\_sets$
7:      print $disjoint\_covering\_base\_sets$
8: **end procedure**

So in our program two competitors are similar to each other, if among the same solutions there is a difference less than or equal to S, and they are treated as different if this difference is greater than D. They are neutral otherwise. In our algorithm we used 1 as S. We thought that if two persons have only one different solution, then it does not imply that they have different knowledge. The D threshold was set to 3.

After reading/generating the data, the software finds the quasi optimal partition (see Algorithm 1). Whereas numerous algorithms can be used for finding the optimal clustering, we used a genetic search algorithm (see Algorithm 2 in [8]). This algorithm is simple, it can be easily implemented, and it gives a relatively optimal solution for the correlation clustering's problem.

The set to be approximated can also be defined in two ways. The user can select the points of this set manually, or if we have a ProgCont dataset, then we can give IDs of the problems. The algorithm managing the approximation checks which competitors solved the given problems, and adds the points representing them to the set.

Algorithm 2. Genetic algorithm

1: **function** FIND BEST PARTITION(N)
2:     $population \leftarrow random\_population$
3:     **while** $exit\,condition\,false$ **do**
4:         sort(population)
5:         **for** $i \leftarrow 1, N$ **do**
6:             $new\_population.add(population.get(i))$
7:         **end for**
8:         $p_1 \leftarrow select\_parents()$
9:         $p_2 \leftarrow select\_parents()$
10:         $children \leftarrow crossover(p_1, p_2)$
11:         **if** $small\,probability$ **then**
12:             $mutation(children)$
13:         **end if**
14:         $new\_population.add(children)$
15:         $population \leftarrow new\_population$
16:         $max \leftarrow find\_max(population)$
17:     **end while**
18:     **return** max
19: **end function**

As mentioned in the previous sections the singleton base sets hold little information about the similarity. In our software there is an option to throw the singleton base sets away. The base sets, we got this way, are partial because their union does not cover the universe.

5   Results

The execution time of the algorithm managing the set-approximation can be seen in Fig. 7. The axis x represents the number of points, and the axis y represents the execution time in milliseconds.

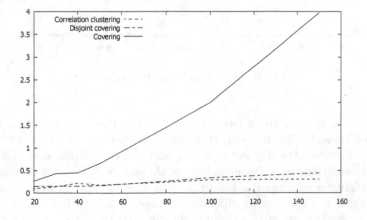

Fig. 7. Execution time

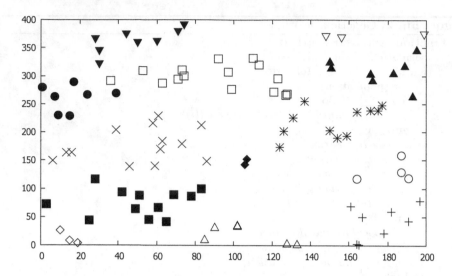

Fig. 8. The clusters

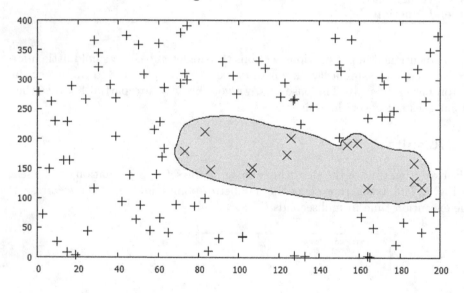

Fig. 9. The set to be approximated

If we take a look at the figure we can see that the approximation by covering is the slowest. This was expected, because there are a lot of base sets to work with. Between the disjoint covering and the correlation clustering there is no significant difference. Nevertheless, as the number of points increases, the correlation clustering gives the fastest way to approximate. It is an interesting fact that there is such a great difference between the covering and its disjoint variant. Despite the fact that a disjoint covering has the largest number of base

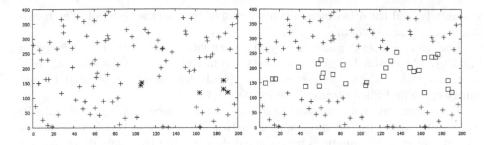

A. The lower (left) and upper (right) approximation by correlation clustering

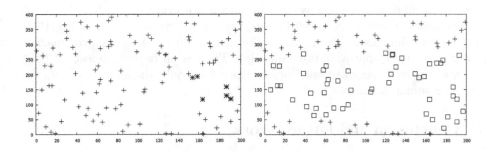

B. The lower (left) and upper (right) approximation by covering

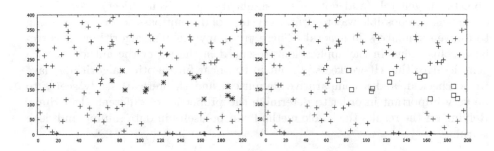

C. The lower (left) and upper (right) approximation by disjoint covering

Fig. 10. The outputs of the approximations by the software

sets, their cardinality is much less (most of them are singleton) than in the case of a regular covering.

The following figures show the output of our software for 100 random points. The similarity threshold S was set to 50, and D was set to 90. Figure 8 represents the clusters (base sets) created by the correlation clustering. The set to be approximated is shown in Fig. 9. The members of this set are denoted by the

× symbols, and the other members are denoted by the cross symbol. The members were chosen randomly.

The approximation generated by the correlation clustering is displayed in Fig. 10A. The cardinality of the base sets is relatively great so the lower approximation consists of only a few members. (Only the members denoted by the empty circle and filled diamond are in the set.)

The approximation generated by the covering is shown in Fig. 10B. Like in correlation clustering the lower approximation consists of only a few members. The two lower approximations have some difference, but they only differ in a set which has two members.

Between the upper approximations we can see a significant difference. The upper approximation defined by covering contains much more objects, almost twice as much as the one defined by correlation clustering.

The approximation generated by the disjoint covering is shown in Fig. 10C. We can see that among the methods this generated the finest approximation (lower and upper approximation coincide). The reason is that almost all base sets are singleton. As mentioned before if we have only singleton base sets we get the common set theory back.

6   Conclusion and Future Work

The authors introduced a new method to define base sets in a general approximation space. The most important novelty of the introduced method is the usage of similarity relation of objects. It emphasizes and so relies on the similarity of objects 'in general' (and not on the similarity to a given object). Correlation clustering is a possible way to define a system of disjoint base sets corresponding to a given similarity 'in general'. There are many different algorithms of correlation clustering. In the application presented in the paper the authors used a genetic algorithm. It worked well, but in the near future other algorithms have to be checked, and a comparative (empirical and theoretical) study seems to be very important in order to determine the properties of different algorithms. Relying on the results the whole method can be useful in data mining and deep learning.

References

1. Aigner, M.: Enumeration via ballot numbers. Discret. Math. **308**(12), 2544–2563 (2008). http://www.sciencedirect.com/science/article/pii/S0012365X07004542
2. Aszalós, L., Mihálydeák, T.: Rough clustering generated by correlation clustering. In: Ciucci, D., Inuiguchi, M., Yao, Y., Ślęzak, D., Wang, G. (eds.) RSFDGrC 2013. LNCS, vol. 8170, pp. 315–324. Springer, Heidelberg (2013). doi:10.1007/978-3-642-41218-9_34. http://dx.doi.org/10.1109/TKDE.2007.1061
3. Aszalós, L., Mihálydeák, T.: Rough classification based on correlation clustering. In: Miao, D., Pedrycz, W., Ślęzak, D., Peters, G., Hu, Q., Wang, R. (eds.) RSKT 2014. LNCS, vol. 8818, pp. 399–410. Springer, Cham (2014). doi:10.1007/978-3-319-11740-9_37

4. Aszalós, L., Mihálydeák, T.: Correlation clustering by contraction. In: 2015 Federated Conference on Computer Science and Information Systems (FedCSIS), pp. 425–434. IEEE (2015)
5. Bansal, N., Blum, A., Chawla, S.: Correlation clustering. Mach. Learn. **56**(1–3), 89–113 (2004)
6. Becker, H.: A survey of correlation clustering. In: Advanced Topics in Computational Learning Theory, pp. 1–10 (2005)
7. Ciucci, D., Mihálydeák, T., Csajbók, Z.E.: On definability and approximations in partial approximation spaces. In: Miao, D., Pedrycz, W., Ślęzak, D., Peters, G., Hu, Q., Wang, R. (eds.) RSKT 2014. LNCS, vol. 8818, pp. 15–26. Springer, Cham (2014). doi:10.1007/978-3-319-11740-9_2
8. Goldberg, D.E., Holland, J.H.: Genetic algorithms and machine learning. Mach. Learn. **3**(2), 95–99 (1988). http://dx.doi.org/10.1023/A:1022602019183
9. Kádek, T., Kósa, M., Pánovics, J.: Experiences of programming competitions supported by the ProgCont system (in Hungarian). In: New Technologies in Science, Research and Education, pp. 152–157 (2012)
10. Mani, A.: Choice inclusive general rough semantics. Inf. Sci. **181**(6), 1097–1115 (2011)
11. Néda, Z., Sumi, R., Ercsey-Ravasz, M., Varga, M., Molnár, B., Cseh, G.: Correlation clustering on networks. J. Phys. A: Math. Theor. **42**(34), 345003 (2009). http://www.journalogy.net/Publication/18892707/correlation-clustering-on-networks
12. Pawlak, Z.: Rough sets. Int. J. Parallel Prog. **11**(5), 341–356 (1982)
13. Pawlak, Z., Skowron, A.: Rudiments of rough sets. Inf. Sci. **177**(1), 3–27 (2007)
14. Pawlak, Z., et al.: Rough Sets: Theoretical Aspects of Reasoning About Data. System Theory Knowledge Engineering and Problem Solving, vol. 9. Kluwer Academic Publishers, Dordrecht (1991)
15. Skowron, A., Stepaniuk, J.: Tolerance approximation spaces. Fundamenta Informaticae **27**(2), 245–253 (1996)
16. Yao, Y., Yao, B.: Covering based rough set approximations. Inf. Sci. **200**, 91–107 (2012). http://www.sciencedirect.com/science/article/pii/S0020025512001934
17. Zimek, A.: Correlation clustering. ACM SIGKDD Explor. Newsl. **11**(1), 53–54 (2009)

On Mereology as a Tool in Problems of Intelligent Control, Granular Computing, Data Analysis and Approximate and Spatial Reasoning

Lech Polkowski[1,2(✉)]

[1] Department of Mathematics and Computer Science,
University of Warmia and Mazury in Olsztyn, Słoneczna str. 54,
10-760 Olsztyn, Poland
[2] Polish-Japanese Academy IT, Koszykowa str. 82, 02-008 Warszawa, Poland
lech.polkowski@pja.edu.pl

Abstract. Mereology is a theory of concepts using the notion of a part as its primitive notion. This notion is well suited for analysis and reasoning about mass concepts like solids, figures, swarms of things. We aim here at highlighting foundations of mereology and its extension, rough mereology in which the notion of a part undergoes a 'fuzzification' to the notion of a part to a degree, along with applications to problems of intelligent control of teams of intelligent agents, granular computing, spatial reasoning, data analysis and approximate reasoning about classification of data into decision classes.

Keywords: Mereology · Rough mereology · Rough set theory · Intelligent control · Granular computing · Data analysis

1 Mereology: First Steps

In this introductory section, we present the two main stems of the mereology tree: the classical mereology due to Leśniewski [8] and the contact mereology whose development ends with Clarke [4]. The primitive notion of mereology due to Leśniewski is that of a *part*. Given a set U of objects, a relation of a part is a binary relation π which should satisfy the followng conditions:

(1) $\pi(u, v) \rightarrow u \neq v$.
(2) $\pi(u, v) \wedge \pi(v, w) \rightarrow \pi(u, w)$.

The relation of *part* induces the relation of an *ingredient, ing*, defined as follows:

(3) $ing(u, v) \leftrightarrow \pi(u, v) \vee u = v$.

The relation of being an ingredient plays some crucial roles in mereology and it is the faithful counterpart of the notion of an element in set theory. First, it is used in definitions of notions parallel to notions of set theory:

L. Polkowski et al. (Eds.): IJCRS 2017, Part II, LNAI 10314, pp. 108–129, 2017.
DOI: 10.1007/978-3-319-60840-2_8

- The Overlap relation: $Ov(u,v) \leftrightarrow \exists z.ing(z,u) \wedge ing(z,v)$.
- The Disconnectedness relation: $Dis(u,v) \leftrightarrow \neg Ov(u,v)$.
- The Subset relation: $Sub(u,v) \leftrightarrow \forall z.[ing(z,u) \rightarrow ing(z,v)]$.

We introduce the Rule of Inference (RI) proved in Leśniewski [8]:

(RI) For each pair u,v of objects, the truth of the formula (4) below for each object t:

(4) $ing(t,u) \rightarrow \exists z.Ov(t,z) \wedge ing(z,v)$

implies that

(5) $ing(u,v)$.

The notion of a mereological class follows; for a non–vacuous property Φ of objects, the *class of* Φ, denoted $Cls\Phi$ is defined by the conditions:

(6) $\Phi(u) \rightarrow ing(u,Cls\Phi)$.
(7) $ing(u,Cls\Phi) \rightarrow \exists z.[\Phi(z) \wedge Ov(u,z)]$.

The class axiom (CL) guarantees the existence of $Cls\Phi$ for each plausible Φ.
(CL) For each non–vacuous property Φ *there exists a class* $Cls\Phi$.
In [8], the uniqueness of the class is secured by an axiom and then (RI) is proved.
The relation $el(u,v)$ of being an element is defined as follows:

(8) $el(u,v) \leftrightarrow \exists \Phi.v = Cls\Phi \wedge \Phi(u)$.

Proposition 1. *The relations of ing, Sub and el are identical.*

For the proof, see [8]. For the property $Ind(u)$, defined by the equivalence

(9) $Ind(u) \leftrightarrow ing(u,u)$,
the class $ClsInd$ is called the *the universe*, in symbols V. It follows that
(10) $\forall u.ing(u,V)$.

The notion of the complement to an object, with respect to another object, is rendered as a ternary relation $comp(u,v,w)$, to be read:'u is the complement to v with respect to w', and it is defined by means of the following requirements:

(11) $ing(v,w)$.
(12) $ing(u,w)$.
(13) $u = Cls\{t : Dis(t,v) \wedge ing(t,w)\}$.

The notion of the complement to u, $-u$ is then rendered as

(14) $-u = Cls\{t : Dis(t,u)\}$,

i.e.,

(15) $comp(-u,u,V)$.

The complement relation $-$ can be a candidate for the boolean complement in a structure of a quasi–Boolean algebra within mereology, constructed in Tarski [44], and anticipated in Tarski [45]. This algebra will be obviously rid of the null element, as the empty object is not allowed in mereology by (9) and the meet of two objects will be possible only when these objects overlap. Under this caveat, the construction of Boolean operators of join and meet proceeds on the following lines:

(16) $ing(u, v + w) \leftrightarrow ing(u, v) \vee ing(u, w)$.
(17) $ing(u, v \cdot w) \leftrightarrow ing(u, v) \wedge ing(v, w)$.

The universe V with operators $-, +, \cdot$ is a complete Boolean algebra with no null element.

1.1   Contact Mereology

The alternate approach to parts, begins with a relation $C(u, v)$ interpreted as '*u and v are connected, in contact, etc.*' The relation C has to satisfy the following conditions:

(18) $C(u, u)$.
(19) $C(u, v) \rightarrow C(v, u)$.
(20) $\forall z.[C(z, x) \leftrightarrow C(z, y)] \rightarrow u = v$.

The relation C induces the relation of C-*ingredient* $C - ing(u, v)$:

(21) $C - ing(u, v) \leftrightarrow \forall z.[C(z, u) \rightarrow C(z, v)]$.

The notion of a C–*part* $C - \pi$ is introduced as follows:

(22) $C - \pi(u, v) \leftrightarrow C - ing(u, v) \wedge u \neq v$.

With $C - ing$ and $C - \pi$, one does introduce C-counterparts of notions of overlap, disconnectedness, complement, meet and join in already standard way. Due to the geometric appeal of the relation C, new relations are introduced:

(23) $EC(u, v) \leftrightarrow C(u, v) \wedge C - Dis(u, v)$.

EC is the *external connectedness* relation, below we define the *tangential ingredient* relation $TC - ing$ and *non–tangential ingredient* $NTC - -ing$

(24) $TC - ing(u, v) \leftrightarrow C - ing(u, v) \wedge \exists z.EC(z, u) \wedge EC(z, v)$,
(25) $NTC - ing(u, v) \leftrightarrow \neg TC - ing(u, v) \wedge C - ing(u, v)$.

1.2   A Model for Mereology

A standard playground for contact mereology, motivated also by practical applications in spatial imagery is the space $RO(E^2)$ of *regular open* sets in the Euclidean plane. We recall that a set X is regular open if and only if the condition is satisfied:

(26) $X = IntClX$,

where Int, Cl are, respectively, the interior and the closure operators in the plane topology. Given two sets A, B in $RO(E^2)$, one lets

(27) $C(A, B) \leftrightarrow ClA \cap ClB \neq \emptyset.$

A straightforward topological computations reveal the meaning of relations $C - ingr, C - Ov, EC, TP, NTP$:

(28) $C - ing(A, B) \leftrightarrow A \subseteq B.$
(29) $C - Ov(A, B) \leftrightarrow A \cap B \neq \emptyset.$
(30) $EC(A, B) \leftrightarrow ClA \cap ClB \neq \emptyset \wedge A \cap B = \emptyset.$
(31) $TP(A, B) \leftrightarrow A \subseteq B \wedge ClA \cap (ClB \setminus B) \neq \emptyset.$
(32) $NTP(A, B) \leftrightarrow ClA \subseteq B.$

Accounts of mereology and contact mereology can be found in Casati and Varzi [3], Calosi and Graziani [2], Simons [40]. An account of applications of mereology is given in Polkowski [18].

2   Rough Mereology

Rough mereology replaces the notion of a part with the notion of a part to a degree called the *rough inclusion* which is a ternary relation $\mu(u, v, r)$ where u, v are *objects* and $r \in [0, 1]$, read '*the object u is a part to degree at least of r to the object v*'. Any rough inclusion is associated with a mereological scheme based on the notion of a part by postulating that $\mu(u, v, 1)$ is equivalent to $ing(u, v)$, where the ingredient relation is defined by the adopted mereological scheme. Our postulates about rough inclusions stem from intuitions about the nature of partial containment; these intuitions can be manifold, a fortiori,postulates about rough inclusions may vary. In our scheme for rough mereology, we begin with some basic postulates which would provide a most general framework. When needed,other postulates, narrowing the variety of possible models, can be introduced.

2.1   Rough Inclusions: General Facts

For a set U of objects, and a given on U part relation π with the associated ingredient relation ing, we have the inference scheme (IR) of mereology at our disposal. The relation $\mu(u, v, r)$, see Polkowski and Skowron [38], [39], is supposed to satisfy the conditions:

(33) $\mu(u, v, 1) \leftrightarrow ing(u, v).$
(34) $\mu(u, v, 1) \rightarrow [\forall z.[\mu(z, u, r) \rightarrow \mu(z, v, r)].$
(35) $\mu(u, v, r) \wedge s < r \rightarrow \mu(u, v, s).$

Proposition 2. *The immediate consequences of postulates (33)–(35) are*

1. $\mu(u, u, 1)$.
2. $\mu(u, v, 1) \wedge \mu(v, z, 1) \to \mu(u, z, 1)$.
3. $\mu(u, v, 1) \wedge \mu(v, u, 1) \leftrightarrow u = v$.
4. $x \neq y \Rightarrow \neg \mu(x, y, 1) \vee \neg \mu(y, x, 1)$.
5. $\forall z. \forall r. [\mu(z, u, r) \leftrightarrow \mu(z, v, r)] \to u = v$.

We now describe some models for rough mereology which at the same time give us methods by which we can define rough inclusions, see Polkowski [17], Chap. 7. An important property of rough inclusions is the transitivity. For a function $f : [0, 1]^2 \to [0, 1]$ such that (i) $f(1, r) = r$ (ii) $f(r, s) = f(s, r)$, we say that a rough inclusion μ is *f–transitive* when the condition

$$\mu(u, v, r) \wedge \mu(v, w, s) \to \mu(u, w, f(r, s))$$

is satisfied.

2.2   Rough Inclusions: Residual Models

We begin with continuous t–norms on the unit interval [0,1]. We recall that it follows from results in Mostert and Shields [10] and Faucett [5], cf., Hájek [7], that the structure of a continuous t–norm T depends on the set $F(T)$ of idempotents of T, i.e., values x such that $T(x, x) = x$; we denote with O_T the countable family of open intervals $A_i \subseteq [0, 1]$ with the property that $\bigcup_i A_i = [0, 1] \setminus F(T)$. Then we have

Proposition 3. $T(x, y)$ *is an isomorph to either* $L(x, y)$ *or* $P(x, y)$ *when* $x, y \in A_i$ *for some* i, *and* $T(x, y) = min\{x, y\}$, *otherwise.*

We recall, that, for a continuous t–norm $T(x, y)$, the *residual implication, residuum,* $x \Rightarrow_T y$ is defined by the condition:

(36) $x \Rightarrow_T y \geq z \Leftrightarrow T(x, z) \leq y$.

It follows that $x \Rightarrow_T y = 1$ if and only if $x \leq y$, as $T(x, x) \leq x$ for each continuous t–norm T. For a continuous t–norm T, we define a relation $\mu_T \subseteq [0, 1]^3$ by means of

(37) $\mu_T(x, y, r) \Leftrightarrow x \Rightarrow_T y \geq r$.

Proposition 4. *The quadruple* $M(T) = ([0, 1], <, \leq, \mu_T)$ *is a model for rough mereology induced by the residuum of the t–norm* T.

Proof. First, let us make positive that μ_T satisfies (33)–(35). For (33), $\mu_T(x, y, 1)$ means that $x \Rightarrow_T y = 1$, hence, $x \leq y$, i.e.,$ingr_M(x, y)$. For (34), assume that $\mu_T(x, y, 1)$ and $\mu_T(z, x, r)$, hence (i) $x \leq y$ (ii) $z \Rightarrow_T x \geq r$, i.e., by (1), (iii) $T(z, r) \leq x$. By (i), (iii), $T(z, r) \leq y$, hence, by (1), $z \Rightarrow_T y \geq r$. (35) follows by (37).

Clearly, the underlying part relation in the above proposition is the strict ordering $<$ and the ingredient relation is $\leq$. In particular important cases, of t–norms L, P, M, one obtains the specific models M_L, M_P, M_M. In each model $M(T)$, $\mu(x, y, 1) \Leftrightarrow x \leq y$, hence, we recall below only the case when $x > y$. In the most important case of the Łukasiewicz t–norm L, the residual implication $\Rightarrow_L$ is the classical Łukasiewicz implication:

(38) $\mu_L(x, y, r) \leftrightarrow min\{1, 1 - x + y\} \geq r$.

From (38), we can extract a transitivity rule.

Proposition 5. *From $\mu_L(x, y, r), \mu_L(y, z, s)$ it follows that $\mu_L(x, z, L(r, s))$.*

Proof. It suffices to consider the case when $x > y$ and $y > z$, by (38), we have $x - y \leq 1 - r$ and $y - z \leq 1 - s$, hence, $x - z \leq 1 - (r + s - 1)$, i.e., $\mu_L(x, y, L(r, s))$.

2.3   Rough Inclusions: Information Models

For an information system $IS = (U, A, V)$ where U is a universe of objects, A is a set of attributes and V is a set of admissible values of attributes, i.e., each attribute $a \in A$ maps the universe U into the set V, we define sets

(39) $DIS(u, v) = \{a \in A; a(u) \neq a(v)\}$

and

(40) $IND(u, v) = \{a \in A : a(u) = a(v)\}$.

Following the idea in (38), we replace the distance $|x - y|$ with the difference set $DIS(u, v)$ and let

(41) $\mu^I(u, v, r) \leftrightarrow \frac{card(DIS(u,v))}{card(A)} \leq 1 - r$.

In virtue of (39) and (40), (41) is equivalent to

(42) $\mu^I(u, v, r) \leftrightarrow \frac{card(IND(u,v))}{card(A)} \geq r$.

The idea of (38) which goes back to Łukasiewicz's idea of partial truth values [9] can be adapted to geometric and set–theoretic contexts.

2.4   Rough Inclusions: Geometric and Set–Theoretic Contexts

Consider a collection of solids in a Euclidean space. For two solids A, B, we let

(43) $\mu^G(A, B, r) \leftrightarrow \frac{area(A \cap B)}{area(A)} \geq r$.

Similarly, for a collection of finite non–empty sets, we let

(44) $\mu^S(X, Y, r) \leftrightarrow \frac{card(X \cap Y)}{card(X)} \geq r$.

Finally, we propose a 3–valued rough inclusion on finite sets.

(45) $\mu^{S,3}(X,Y,1) \leftrightarrow X \subseteq Y$.
(46) $\mu^{S,3}(X,Y,1/2) \leftrightarrow X \triangle Y \neq \emptyset$

and

(47) $\mu^{S,3}(X,Y,0) \leftrightarrow X \cap Y = \emptyset$,

where $X \triangle Y = (X \setminus Y) \cup (Y \setminus X)$.

3   Intelligent Control: An Application of Mereogeometry

We demonstrate in this section usage of rough inclusions in constructing a system for intelligent control of formations of intelligent agents. The system rests on mereogeometry constructed from rough inclusions. Consider a rough inclusion μ^G for the sake of attention, along with a collection of intelligent agents exploring a bounded compact region R of an Euclidean space E. Each agent is perceived as the centre of a regular closed region around it, be it a closed disc, a square or a rectangle, which may be termed the *influence region of an agent*. This region may be determined by the extent of agent's sensors, or a safety region around the agent which is ususal in case of mobile robots. For agents a, b, and their regions of influence $r(a), r(b)$, the value

(48) $argmax_r \mu^G(r(a), r(b), r)$

defines the maximal degree of closeness of the agent a to the agent b whereas

(49) $\mu^G(r(a), r(b), r)$

when true states that the agent a is close to the degree of at least r to the agent b. We define the mereological quasi–distance $\delta(a, b)$ by letting

(50) $\delta(a, b) = min\{r, s\}$,

where $\mu^G(r(a), r(b), r)$ and $\mu^G(r(b), r(a), s)$ hold true.

We observe that $\delta(a, b) = 1$ means $a = b$ whereas $\delta(a, b) = 0$ means that influence regions of a and b do not overlap. We borrow from elementary geometry defined by Alfred Tarski in His Warsaw University lectures in the years 1926–27 as the part of Euclidean geometry which can be described by means of the 1st order logic, the notion of betweenness, see Tarski and Givant [43]. The relation of betweenness in axiomatization of elementary geometry is responsible for affine properties. We will consider the Euclid Axiom relating two principal relations B of betweenness and Eq of equidistance:

(51) $B(x, y, z) \vee B(z, x, y) \vee B(x, z, y) \vee \exists a. Eq(x, a; y, a) \wedge Eq(x, a; z, a)$.

A paraphrase of (51) was proposed in van Benthem [1] in terms of two relations: of *nearness* $N(x,y,z)$ and of *betweenness* $Btw(x,y,z)$.

The relation $N(x, y, z)$ read '*x is nearer to y than z*' becomes formalized in terms of the quasi–distance δ as:

(52) $N(x, y, z) \leftrightarrow \delta(x, y) \geq \delta(y, z)$.

The relation of betweenness $Btw(x, y, z)$ read 'x is between y and z' is then introduced as follows:

(53) $Btw(x, y, z) \leftrightarrow \forall w.[w = x \lor N(x, y, w) \lor N(x, z, w)]$.

Given two robots a, b as discs of same radii, and their safety regions as circumscribed on them regularly positioned rectangles A, B, we search for a proper choice of a region X containing A, and B with the property that a robot C contained in X can be said to be between A and B. For two (possibly but not necessarily) disjoint rectangles A, B, we define the *extent*, $ext(A, B)$ of A and B as the smallest rectangle containing the union $A \cup B$. We can prove.

Proposition 6. *For any two rectangles A, B positioned regularly in the Euclidean plane, the only rectangle between A and B is the extent $ext(A, B)$.*

For details of the exposition which we give now, please consult Ośmiałowski [11–13], Polkowski and Ośmiałowski [31–33], Ośmiałowski and Polkowski [14]. The notion of betweenness along with Proposition 6 permits to define the notion of betweenness for robots. Recall that we represent the disc–shaped Roomba robots by means of safety squares around them, regularly placed, i.e., with sides parallel to coordinate axes. For robots a, b, c, we say that a robot b is *between robots a and c*, in symbols

(54) (between b a c)

in case the rectangle $ext(b)$ is contained in the extent of rectangles $ext(a)$, $ext(c)$, i.e.

(55) $\mu(ext(b), ext(ext(a), ext(c)), 1)$.

This allows as well for a generalization of the notion of betweenness to the notion of *partial betweenness* which models in a more realistic manner spatial relations among a, b, c; we say in this case that robot b is *between robots a and c to a degree of at least r*, in symbols,

(56) (between$-$deg r b a c)

if and only if

(57) $\mu(ext(b), ext[ext(a), ext(c)], r)$.

For a team of robots, $T(r_1, r_2, ..., r_n) = \{r_1, r_2, ..., r_n\}$, an *ideal formation IF* on $T(r_1, r_2, ..., r_n)$ is a betweenness relation (between...) on the set $T(r_1, r_2, ..., r_n)$ of robots. In implementations, ideal formations are represented as lists of expressions of the form

(57) (between a b c)

indicating that the object a is between b, c, for all such triples, along with a list of expressions of the form

(58) (not−between a b c)

indicating triples which are not in the given betweenness relation. To account for dynamic nature of the real world, in which due to sensory perception inadequacies, dynamic nature of the environment etc., we allow for some deviations from ideal formations by allowing that the robot which is between two neighbors can be between them to a degree. This leads to the notion of a real formation. For a team of robots, $T(r_1, r_2, ..., r_n) = \{r_1, r_2, ..., r_n\}$, a *real formation RF* on $T(r_1, r_2, ..., r_n)$ is a betweenness to degree relation (between−deg ...) on the set $T(r_1, r_2, ..., r_n)$ of robots.

In practice, real formations will be given as a list of expressions of the form:

(59) (between−deg η a b c),

indicating that the object a is to degree of η in the extent of b, c, for all triples in the relation (between−deg ...), along with a list of expressions of the form:

(60) (between 0 a b c),

indicating triples which are not in the given betweenness relation. Description of formations, as proposed above, can be a list of relation instances of large cardinality, effectively exponential in size of the formation. The problem can be posed of finding a minimal set of instances sufficient for describing a given formation, i.e., implying the full list of instances of the relation (between...). This problem turns out to be NP–hard, see Ośmiałowski and Polkowski [14].

Proposition 7. *The problem of finding a minimal description of a formation is NP–hard.*

Proof. We construct an *information system Formations* as a triple (U, A, V), where U is a set of objects, A is a set of attributes and V is the set of values of attributes. It will be convenient to add to this description the value assignment, i.e., a mapping $f : A \times U \to V$. For a formation F, with robots $r_1, ..., r_n$ we let $U = T(r_1, ..., r_n)$, a team of robots; $A = \{[r_k, r_l, r_m] : r_k, r_l, r_m$ pairwise distinct robots$\}$. For a given formation F of robots $r_1, ..., r_n$, the value assignment f is defined as follows,

$$f([r_k, r_l, r_m], r_i) = \begin{cases} 1 \text{ in case } r_i = r_l \text{ and (between } r_l\ r_k\ r_l) \\ \frac{1}{2} \text{ in case } r_i = r_l \text{ or } r_i = r_m \text{ and (between } r_l\ r_k\ r_m) \\ 0 \text{ in case } r_i \neq r_l r_k r_m \end{cases} \quad (1)$$

The system *Formations* describes the formation F. Clearly, reducts of the system *Formations* provide a complete description of the formation F and correspond to minimal descriptions of the formation. As shown by Skowron and Rauszer [41] the problem of finding a minimum size reduct of a given information system is NP–hard.

4   Granular Computing: Mereological Granulation of Knowledge

Assume that a rough inclusion μ is given along with the associated ingredient relation ing, on a universe U of objects. The *granule* $g_\mu(u, r)$ of the radius r about the center u is defined as the class of property $\Phi_{u,r}^\mu$:

(62) $\Phi_{u,r}^\mu(v) \Leftrightarrow \mu(v, u, r)$.

The granule $g_\mu(u, r)$ is defined by means of

(63) $g_\mu(u, r) = Cls\Phi_{u,r}^\mu$.

Properties of granules depend, obviously, on the type of rough inclusion used in their definitions. We consider separate cases, as some features revealed by granules differ from a rough inclusion to a rough inclusion. Consult Polkowski [19–28] for details of granule calculi and applications. In case of Archimedean t–norm–induced rough inclusions, or metric–induced rough inclusions, by their transitivity, and symmetry, the important property holds.

Proposition 8. *In case of a symmetric and transitive rough inclusion μ, for each pair u, v of objects, and $r \in [0, 1]$, $ingr(v, g_\mu(u, r))$ if and only if $\mu(v, u, r)$ holds. In effect, the granule $g_\mu(u, r)$ can be represented as the set $\{v : \mu(v, u, r)\}$.*

Proof. Assume that $ingr(v, g_\mu(u, r))$ holds. Thus, there exists z such that $Ov(z, v)$ and $\mu(z, u, r)$. There is x with $ingr(x, v)$, $ingr(x, z)$, hence, by transitivity of μ, also $\mu(x, u, r)$ holds. By symmetry of μ, $ingr(v, x)$, hence, $\mu(v, x, r)$ holds also.

Granules as collective concepts can be objects for rough mereological calculi.

5   Rough Inclusions on Granules

Due to the feature of mereology that it operates (due to the class operator) only on level of individuals, one can extend rough inclusions from objects to granules; the formula for extending a rough inclusion μ to a rough inclusion $\overline{\mu}$ on granules is a modification of the mereological axiom (IR):

(64) $\overline{\mu}(g, h, r) \leftrightarrow \forall z.[ing(z, g) \Rightarrow \exists w.ing(w, h) \wedge \mu(z, w, r)]$.

Proposition 9. *The predicate $\overline{\mu}(g, h, r)$ is a rough inclusion on granules.*

Proof. $\mu(g, h, 1)$ means that for each object z with $ing(z, g)$, there exists an object w with $ing(w, h)$ such that $\mu(z, w, 1)$, i.e., $ing(z, w)$, which, by the inference rule (IR) implies that $ing(g, h)$. This proves (33). For (34), assume that $\mu(g, h, 1)$ and $\mu(k, g, r)$ so for each $ing(x, k)$ there is $ing(y, g)$ with $\mu(x, y, r)$. For y there is z such that $ing(z, h)$ and $\mu(y, z, 1)$, hence, $\mu(x, z, r)$ by property (34) of μ. Thus, $\mu(k, h, r)$. (35) is obviously satisfied.

We now examine rough mereological granules with respect to their properties.

6   General Properties of Rough Mereological Granules

They are collected below in the following proposition:

Proposition 10. *The following constitute a set of basic properties of rough mereological granules*

1. *If $ing(y, x)$ then $ing(y, g_\mu(x, r))$.*
2. *If $ing(y, g_\mu(x, r))$ and $ing(z, y)$ then $ing(z, g_\mu(x, r))$.*
3. *If $\mu(y, x, r)$ then $ing(y, g_\mu(x, r))$.*
4. *If $s < r$ then $ing(g_\mu(x, r), g_\mu(x, s))$.*

which follow straightforwardly from properties (33)–(35) of rough inclusions and the fact that ing is a partial order, in particular it is transitive, regardless of the type of the rough inclusion μ. For transitive rough inclusions, we can be more specific, and prove.

Proposition 11. *For each transitive rough inclusion μ,*

1. *If $ing(y, g_\mu(x, r)$ then $ing(g_\mu(y, s), g_\mu(x, T(r, s)))$.*
2. *If $\mu(y, x, s)$ with $1 > s > r$, then there exists $\alpha < 1$ with the property that $ing(g_\mu(y, \alpha), g_\mu(x, r))$.*

Proof. Property 1 follows by transitivity of μ with the t–norm T. Property 2 results from the fact that the inequality $T(s, \alpha) \geq r$ has a solution in α, e.g., for $T = P$, $\alpha \geq \frac{r}{s}$, and, for $T = L$, $\alpha \geq 1 - s + r$.

It is natural to regard granule system $\{g_r^{\mu_t}(x) : x \in U, r \in (0, 1)\}$ as a neighborhood system for a topology on U that may be called the *granular topology*. In order to make this idea explicit, we define classes of the form

(65) $N^T(x, r) = Cls(\psi_{r,x}^{\mu_T})$,

where

(66) $\psi_{r,x}^{\mu_T}(y) \Leftrightarrow \exists s > r.\mu_T(y, x, s)$.

We declare the system $\{N^T(x, r) : x \in U; r \in (0, 1)\}$ to be a neighborhood basis for a topology θ_μ. This is justified by the following

Proposition 12. *Properties of the system $\{N^T(x, r) : x \in U; r \in (0, 1)\}$ are as follows:*

1. *$ing(y, N^T(x, r)) \rightarrow \exists \delta > 0.ing(N^T(y, \delta), N^T(x, r))$.*
2. *$s > r \rightarrow ing(N^T(x, s), N^T(x, r))$.*
3. *$ing(z, N^T(x, r) \cdot N^T(y, s)) \rightarrow \exists \delta > 0.ing(N^T(z, \delta), N^T(x, r) \cdot N^T(y, s))$.*

Proof. For Property 1, $ing(y, N^t(x, r))$ implies that there exists an $s > r$ such that $\mu_t(y, x, s)$. Let $\delta < 1$ be such that $t(u, s) > r$ whenever $u > \delta$; δ exists by continuity of t and the identity $t(1, s) = s$. Thus, if $ing(z, N^t(y, \delta))$, then $\mu_t(z, y, \eta)$ with $\eta > \delta$ and $\mu_t(z, x, t(\eta, s))$, hence, $ing(z, N^t(x, r))$. Property 2 follows by (35) and Property 3 is a corollary to properties 1 and 2. This concludes the argument.

Granule systems defined above form a basis for applications, where approximate reasoning is a crucial ingredient. We begin with a basic application in which approximate reasoning itself is codified as a many–world (intensional) logic, where granules serve as possible worlds.

7   Reasoning in Information and Decision Systems: Granular Intensional Logics

We assume that a decision system (U, A, V, d) is given, see Pawlak [15,16], where (U, A, V) is an information system, and d is a *decision attribute*, i.e., $d \notin A$, $d : U \to V$, along with a rough inclusion ν, representing either μ^S of (44) or $\mu^{S,3}$ of (45)–(47), on the subsets of the universe U; for a collection of unary predicates Pr, interpreted in the universe U (meaning that for each predicate $\phi \in Pr$ the meaning $[[\phi]]$ is a subset of U), we define the intensional logic GRM_ν by assigning to each predicate ϕ in Pr its intension $I_\nu(\phi)$ defined by the set of extensions $I_\nu^\vee(g)$ at granules g, as

(66) $I_\nu^\vee(g)(\phi) \geq r \;\; \leftrightarrow \nu(g, [[\phi]], r).$

With respect to the rough inclusion μ^S, the formula (61) becomes

(67) $I_{\mu^S}^\vee(g)(\phi) \geq r \;\; \Leftrightarrow \frac{|g \cap [[\phi]]|}{|g|} \geq r.$

The counterpart for $\mu^{S,3}$ is specified by definitions (45)–(47) and it comes down to the following

$$(68)\;\; I_{mu^{S,3}}^\vee(g)(\phi) \geq r \;\; \Leftrightarrow \begin{cases} g \subseteq [[\phi]] \text{ and } r = 1 \\ g \cap [[\phi]] \neq \emptyset \text{ and } r \geq \frac{1}{2} \\ g \cap [[\phi]] = \emptyset \text{ and } r = 0 \end{cases} \tag{2}$$

We say that a formula ϕ interpreted in the universe U of an information system (U, A) is *true* at a granule g with respect to a rough inclusion ν if and only if

(69) $I_\nu^\vee(g)(\phi) = 1.$

We recall that a *decision rule* in a decision system is a formula $\bigwedge_{a \in B}(a, v) \to (d, w)$ where the expression (a, v) is a *descriptor formula* with the meaning defined as $\{u \in U : a(u) = v\}$. Hence, for each of rough inclusions ν, a formula ϕ interpreted in the universe U, with the meaning $[[\phi]] = \{u \in U : u \models \phi\}$, is true at a granule g with respect to ν if and only if

(70) $g \subseteq [[\phi]].$

In particular, for a decision rule $r : p \to q$ in the descriptor logic, the rule r is true at a granule g with respect to a rough inclusion ν if and only if

(71) $g \cap [[p]] \subseteq [[q]].$

We state these facts in the following proposition:

Proposition 13. *For either of rough inclusions ν, a formula ϕ interpreted in the universe U, with the meaning $[[\phi]]$, is true at a granule g with respect to ν if and only if $g \subseteq [[\phi]]$. In particular, for a decision rule $r : p \Rightarrow q$ in the descriptor logic, the rule r is true at a granule g with respect to either of rough inclusions ν if and only if $g \cap [[p]] \subseteq [[q]]$.*

Proof. Indeed, truth of ϕ at g means that $\nu(g, [[\phi]], 1)$ which in turn, by regularity of ν is equivalent to the inclusion $g \subseteq [[\phi]]$.

We will say that a formula ϕ is a *tautology* of our intensional logic if and only if ϕ is true at every world g. The preceding proposition implies that:

Proposition 14. *For either of rough inclusions ν, a formula ϕ is a tautology if and only if $Cls(G) \subseteq [[\phi]]$, where G is the property of being a granule; in the case when granules considered cover the universe U this condition simplifies to $[[\phi]] = U$. This means for a decision rule $p \Rightarrow q$ that it is a tautology if and only if $[[p]] \subseteq [[q]]$.*

Hence, the condition for truth of decision rules in the logic GRM_ν is the same as the truth of an implication in descriptor logic, under caveat that granules considered cover the universe U of objects. Let us observe that results in this section remain true for each *regular* rough inclusion ν, i.e., satisfying the condition that $\nu(X, Y) = 1$ if and only if $X \subseteq Y$.

8   Dependencies and Decision Rules

It is an important feature of rough set theory that it allows for an elegant formulation of the problem of dependency between two sets of attributes, see Pawlak [15, 16], in terms of indiscernibility relations. We recall that in an information system (U, A, V), the indiscernibility relation IND is defined as $\{(u, v) : \forall a \in A : a(u) = a(v)\}$. A relative version $IND(B)$ for $B \subseteq A$ takes into account only attributes in B. We recall that for two sets $C, D \subseteq A$ of attributes, one says that D *depends functionally on* C when $IND(C) \subseteq IND(D)$, symbolically denoted $C \mapsto D$. Functional dependence can be represented locally by means of functional dependency rules of the form:

$$(72) \quad \phi_C(\{v_a : a \in C\}) \Rightarrow \phi_D(\{w_a : a \in D\}),$$

where $\phi_C(\{v_a : a \in C\})$ is the formula $\bigwedge_{a \in C}(a = v_a)$, and $[[\phi_C]] \subseteq [[\phi_D]]$. We assume a regular rough inclusion ν on subsets of the universe U. The proposition holds

Proposition 15. *If $\alpha : \phi_C \Rightarrow \phi_D$ is a functional dependency rule, then α is a tautology of logic induced by ν.*

Proof. For each granule g, we have $g \cap [[\phi_C]] \subseteq [[\phi_D]]$.

Let us observe that the converse statement is also true, i.e., if a formula $\alpha : \phi_C \Rightarrow \phi_D$ is a tautology of logic induced by ν_3, then this formula is a functional dependency rule in the sense of (72). Indeed, assume that α is not any functional dependency rule, i.e., $[[\phi_C]] \setminus [[\phi_D]] \neq \emptyset$. Taking $[[\phi_C]]$ as the witness granule g, we have that g is not any subset of $[[\alpha]]$, i.e., $I^\vee_{\nu_3}(g)(\alpha) \leq \frac{1}{2}$, so α is not true at g, a fortiori it is not any tautology. A more general and also important notion is that of a local proper dependency: a formula $\phi_C \Rightarrow \phi_D$ is a local proper dependency when $[[\phi_C]]cap[[\phi_D]] \neq \emptyset$. We will say that a formula α is *acceptable with respect to a collection M of worlds* when

(73) $I^\vee_{\nu_3}(g)(\alpha) \geq \frac{1}{2}$

for each world $g \in M$, i.e., when α is false at no world $g \in M$. A world g is C–*exact* if $g \subseteq [[\phi_C]]$. Then,

Proposition 16. *If a formula $\alpha : \phi_C \Rightarrow \phi_D$ is a local proper dependency rule, then it is acceptable with respect to all C–exact worlds.*

Proof. Indeed, for a C–exact granule g, the case that $I^\vee_{\nu_3}(g)(\alpha) = 0$ means that $g \subseteq [[\phi_C]]$ and $g \cap [[\phi_D]] = \emptyset$. As g is C–exact and $[[\phi_C]]$ is a C–indiscernibility class, either $[[\phi_C]] \subseteq g$ or $[[\phi_C]] \cap g = \emptyset$. When $[[\phi_C]] \subseteq g$, then $[[\phi_C]] = g$ which makes $g \cap [[\phi_D]] = \emptyset$ impossible. When $[[\phi_C]] \cap g = \emptyset$, then $g \cap [[\phi_D]] = \emptyset$ is impossible. In either case, $I^\vee_\nu(g)(\alpha) = 0$ cannot be satisfied with any C–exact granule g.

Again, the converse is true: when α is not local proper, i.e., $[[\phi_C]] \cap [[\phi_D]] = \emptyset$, then $g = [[\phi_C]]$ does satisfy $I^\vee_\nu(g)(\alpha) = 0$. For a detailed discussion of this topic, the reader may consult Polkowski [20] and Polkowski and Semeniuk–Polkowska [34].

9   Granular Preprocessing in Data Analysis

We assume that we are given a decision system (U, A, V, d) from which a classifier is to be constructed; on the universe U, a rough inclusion μ is given, and a radius $r \in [0, 1]$ is chosen, see Polkowski [21–28]. The detailed study of granular classifiers is conducted in Polkowski and Artiemjew [30]. The granular pre–processing of the system consists in the following steps.

(74) We find granules $g_\mu(u, r)$ for all $u \in U$, and make them into the set $G(\mu, r)$.
(75) From this set, a covering $Cov(\mu, r)$ of the universe U can be selected by means of a chosen strategy $\mathcal{G}$, i.e.,
(76) $Cov(\mu, r) = \mathcal{G}(G(\mu, r))$.

We intend that $Cov(\mu, r)$ becomes a new universe of the decision system whose name will be the *granular reflection* of the original decision system. It remains to define new attributes for this decision system.

r	tst	trn	$rulex$	aex	cex	MI
nil	345	345	5597	0.872	0.994	0.907
0.0	345	1	0	0.0	0.0	0.0
0.0714286	345	1	0	0.0	0.0	0.0
0.142857	345	2	0	0.0	0.0	0.0
0.214286	345	3	7	0.641	1.0	0.762
0.285714	345	4	10	0.812	1.0	0.867
0.357143	345	8	23	0.786	1.0	0.849
0.428571	345	20	96	0.791	1.0	0.850
0.5	345	51	293	0.838	1.0	0.915
0.571429	345	105	933	0.855	1.0	0.896
0.642857	345	205	3157	0.867	1.0	0.904
0.714286	345	309	5271	0.875	1.0	0.891
0.785714	345	340	5563	0.870	1.0	0.890
0.857143	345	340	5574	0.864	1.0	0.902
0.928571	345	342	5595	0.867	1.0	0.904

Fig. 1. Train–and–test; Australian credit; granulation for radii r; RSES exhaustive classifier; r = granule radius, tst = test set size, trn = train set size, rulex = rule number, aex = accuracy, cex = coverage

(77) Each granule g in $Cov(\mu, r)$ is a collection of objects; attributes in the set $A \cup \{d\}$ can be factored through the granule g by means of a chosen strategy $\mathcal{S}$, i.e., for each attribute $q \in A \cup \{d\}$, the new factored attribute $\overline{q}$ is defined by means of the formula:

(78) $\overline{q}(g) = \mathcal{S}(\{a(v) : ingr(v, g_\mu(u, r))\}).$

In effect, a new decision system $(Cov(\mu, r), \{\overline{a} : a \in A\}, \overline{d})$ is defined. The object v with

(79) $Inf(v) = \{(\overline{a} = \overline{a}(g)) : a \in A\}$

is called the *granular reflection of g*. Granular reflections of granules need not be objects found in data set; yet, the results show that they mediate very well between the training and test sets. We begin with a classifier in which granules computed by means of the rough inclusion μ_L form a granular reflection of the data set and then to this new data set the exhaustive classifier, see [37], is applied. In the table of Fig. 1, the results are collected of results obtained after the procedure described above is applied. The classifier applied was exhaustive one; the method was train–and–test. The rough inclusion applied was the Łukasiewicz t–norm induced μ^I and Majority Voting was applied as the averaging strategy. We can compare results expressed in terms of the Michalski index MI as a measure of the trade–off between accuracy and coverage; for template based methods, the best MI is 0.891, for covering or LEM algorithms the best value of MI is 0.804, for exhaustive classifier (r = nil) MI is equal to 0.907 and for granular reflections, the best MI value is 0.915 with few other values exceeding 0.900. What seems worthy of a moment's reflection is the number of rules in the classifier. Whereas for the exhaustive classifier (r = nil) in non–granular case, the number of rules is equal to 5597, in granular case the number of rules can be surprisingly small with a good MI value, e.g., at $r = 0.5$, the number of rules is 293, i.e., 5% of the exhaustive classifier size, with the best MI at all of 0.915. This compression of classifier seems to be the most impressive feature of granular classifiers.

10   Spatial Reasoning: The Boundary Problem

The problem of boundary definition is one of the longest-standing in philosophy, ontology and mereology. It is of the utmost importance for rough set theory as the separator of exact sets from the rough ones. For a mereo–topological analysis of the notion of a boundary see Polkowski and Semeniuk–Polkowska [35,36], Varzi [46], Smith [42]. We prefer here the language of predicates and for a rough inclusion μ assumed to be symmetric and transitive, and $u \in U$, $r \in [0, 1]$, we define a new predicate $N(u, r)(v)$ if there exists an $s \geq r$ such that $\mu(v, u, s)$. $N(u, r)$ is the *neighborhood granular predicate about u of radius r*. Consider a predicate Ψ on U having a non–empty meaning $[[\Psi]]$. The *complement to Ψ* is the predicate $-\Psi$ such that $-\Psi(u)$ if and only if not $\Psi(u)$. We define the *upper extension of Ψ of radius r*, denoted Ψ_r^+ by letting $\Psi_r^+(u)$ if there exists v such that $\Psi(v)$ and $N(u, r)(v)$. Similarly, we define the *lower restriction of Ψ of radius r*, denoted Ψ_r^- by letting $\Psi_r^-(u)$ if and only if not $(-\Psi)_r^+(u)$.

Proposition 17. *1. Predicates Ψ_r^+ and Ψ_r^- are disjoint in the sense that there is no $v \in U$ such that $\Psi_r^+(v)$ and $\Psi_r^-(v)$ hold true. 2. If $\Psi_r^+(u)$ holds true then $\Psi_r^+(v)$ holds true for each v such that $\mu(v, u, 1)$. 3. If $\Psi_r^-(u)$ holds true then $\Psi_r^-(v)$ holds true for each v such that $\mu(v, u, 1)$.*

Proof. Claim 1 follows by definitions of the two predicates. For Claim 2, consider u, v such that $\Psi_r^+(u)$ and $\mu(v, u, 1)$. There exists w such that $\Psi(w)$, $N(u, s)(w)$ hold true with some $s \geq r$ so $\mu(w, u, s)$ holds true. By symmetry of μ, we have $\mu(u, v, 1)$ true and transitivity of μ for an adequate pre–norm f implies that $\mu(w, v, f(1, s))$ holds true, i.e., $\mu(w, v, s)$ holds true which means that $N(v, r)(w)$ holds true and finally $\Psi_r^+(v)$ holds true. For Claim 3, assume that $\Psi_r^-(u)$ and $\mu(v, u, 1)$ hold true, i.e.,

(80) $\neg \exists w, s \geq r.\mu(w, u, s) \wedge \neg \Psi(w)$,

which is equivalent to

(81) $\mu(w, u, s) \rightarrow \Psi(w)$.

As $\mu(v, u, 1)$ is equivalent to $\mu(u, v, 1)$, we have by f–transitivity of μ that

(82) $\mu(w, v, s) \rightarrow \Psi(w)$,

which is equivalent to the thesis $\Psi_r^-(v)$.

We will say that a predicate Ψ is *el–saturated* if and only if true formulas $\Psi(u)$ and $el(v, u)$ imply that $\Psi(v)$. A corollary to Claim 3 in Proposition 17 says that for each $r \in [0, 1]$, predicates Ψ_r^+ and Ψ_r^- are el–saturated.

A Global and Local Definition of the Boundary. For a predicate Ψ, we define the predicate *boundary of Ψ with respect to a rough inclusion μ*, denoted $Bd_\mu\Psi$ as follows:

(84) $Bd_\mu\Psi \leftrightarrow (\neg\Psi_1^+) \wedge (\neg\Psi_1^-)$.

Arguing like in proof of Proposition 17, we prove the following proposition:

Proposition 18. *1. $Bd_\mu\Psi$ is el–saturated 2. For no $w \in U$, $Bd_\mu\Psi(w) \wedge \Psi_1^+(w)$ is true and for no $v \in U$, $Bd_\mu\Psi(v) \wedge \Psi_1^-(v)$ is true.*

Proposition 19. *For each $u \in U$, $Bd_\mu\Psi(u)$ holds true if and only if there exist $w, v \in U$ such that $\Psi(w)$, $-\Psi(v)$, $\mu(w, u, 1)$, $\mu(v, u, 1)$.*

A predicate *Open* is defined on predicates on U and a predicate Φ on U is open, $Open(\Phi)$ in symbols if and only if it is el–saturated.

Corollary 1. *$Open(\Psi_r^+)$ and $Open(\Psi_r^-)$ hold true for each $r \in [0,1]$. Open $(Bd_\mu\Psi)$ holds true.*

Proposition 20. *For a finite collection of predicates $\{\Psi_1, \Psi_2, \dots, \Psi_k\}$ if $Open(\Psi_i)$ holds true for each $i \le k$, then $Open(\bigvee_i \Psi_i)$ holds true.*

A predicate *Closed* holds true for a predicate Ψ if and only if $Open(-\Psi)$ holds true.

Corollary 2. *$Closed(\Psi_r^+)$ and $Closed(\Psi_r^-)$ hold true for each $r \in [0,1]$.* *$Closed(Bd_\mu\Psi)$ holds true.*

10.1   The Pawlak Notion of a Boundary Is a Special Case of the Rough Mereological Notion of a Boundary

We return to an information system (U, A, V). When applying the rough inclusion μ^I we have that the predicate of element $el(v, u)$ holds true if and only if $\mu^I(v, u, 1)$ holds true if and only if $Ind(v, u)$, i.e., v, u are indiscernible. Hence, a predicate is el–saturated if and only if its meaning is the union of a family of indiscernibility classes and rough mereological notions of Ψ_1^+ and Ψ_1^- become, respectively, the notions of the upper and the lower approximations of the meaning of Ψ and the meaning of the boundary predicate $Bd_{\mu^I}\Psi$ is the boundary of the meaning of Ψ.

11   Approximate Assembling

We address the problem of assemblage, important for applications of mereology. The first step in assemblage is *design*. It proceeds with *categories of parts* in a set *Cat*. Categories form an exact ontology and assembling works first on them in a design process. Categories appear as a result of the equivalence relation *sim* on objects, related to a relation of a part π on the universe U of objects:

(85) $u \sim v \leftrightarrow \forall t.[\pi(u,t) \leftrightarrow \pi(v,t)]$.

Categories enter as equivalence classes of *sim*:

(86) $Cat(u) = Cat(v) \leftrightarrow u \sim v$.

Things in the same category Cat are 'universally replaceable'. It is manifest that the part relation π can be factored through categories, to the relation Π of part on categories:

(86) $\Pi(Cat(u), Cat(v)) \leftrightarrow \pi(u,v)$.

In our formalism, design will imitate assembling with things replaced with categories of things and the part relation π replaced with the factorization Π. We need for our treatment of design: the *designer set* D, the *functionality set* F, and the *time set* T. The act of design is expressed by means of a predicate,

$$Des(d, < Cat_1, \cdots, Cat_k >, Cat, f(Cat), t(Cat), T(Cat))$$

which reads: a designer d designs at time t a category of things Cat with functionality $f(Cat)$ according to the design scheme $T(Cat)$ organized by d which is a dag with the out-node Cat, from categories $Cat_1, \cdots, Cat_k$ which are in-nodes of $T(Cat)$. The category Cat_i *enters in the position i* the design process for Cat. The predicate Des is subject to the following requirements.

DES1. If $Des(d, < Cat(v_1(u)), \cdots, Cat(v_k(u)) >, Cat(u), f(u), t(u), T(u))$ and for any i in $\{1, \cdots, k\}$, it holds that

$$Des(p(Cat(v_i(u))), < Cat(v_{i_1}(v_i(u))), \cdots, Cat(v_{i_k}(v_i(u)))) >,$$

$$Cat(v_i(u)), f(v_i(u)), t(v_i(u)), T(v_i(u))),$$

then $t(v_i(u)) < t(u)$, $f(u) \subseteq f(v_i(u))$, $p(v_i(u)) \subseteq p(u)$, and $T(v_i(u))$ attached to $T(u)$ at the leaf $Cat(v_i(u))$ yields a dag, called the *unfolding of $T(u)$ via the design dag for $Cat(v_i(u))$*.

DES2.

$$Des(d, < Cat(v_1(u)), \cdots, Cat(v_k(u)) >, Cat(u), f(u), t(u), T(u)) \Rightarrow$$

$$\Pi(Cat(v_i(u)), Cat(u))$$

for each $v_i(u)$.

Meaning that each object can be designed only from its parts.

We introduce an auxiliary predicate $App(v, i(v), u, t(u))$ meaning: $Cat(v)$ enters in the position i the design process for $Cat(u)$ at time $t(u)$.

DES3. $\Pi(Cat(v), Cat(u)) \Rightarrow \exists Cat(w_1(v,u)), \cdots, Cat(w_k(v,u))$, and,

$$t(w_2(v,u)), \cdots, t(w_k(v,u)), i(w_1(v,u)), \cdots, i(w_{k(v,u)-1}))$$

such that $v = w_1(v,u)$, $t(w_2(v,u)) < \cdots < t(w_k(v,u))$, $w_k(v,u) = u$,

$$App(w_j(v,u)), i(w_j(v,u)), w_{j+1}(v,u), t(w_{j+1}(v,u)))$$

for $j = 1, 2, \cdots, k(v,u) - 1$.

This means that for each object which is a part of the other object, the category of the former will enter the design dag for the category of the latter.

DES4. Values $t(u)$ belong in the set $T = \{0, 1, 2, \cdots\}$ of time moments.

Corollary 3. *The universe of categories is well–founded.*

We define a *design artifact* as a category $Cat(u)$ at an out-node such that $\Pi(Cat(u), Cat(v))$ is true for no v.

11.1   Approximate Assembling Along the Design Scheme

Assembling proceeds along the dag employed in design. The difference is that assembling operates on objects idealistically ordered by the part relation π. In reality, one must take into account the usage of objects which formally regarded as identical to design object factually have a different characteristic, e.g., spare parts for an auto may be not original by manufacturer but substitutes: we are told they will work but for a shorter time etc. To characterize this aspect, we introduce an *endurance factor en*. Let us observe that in a wider ontological sense this may be related to the *endurantism* problem, see Gilmore [6]. Using the factor *en*, each node *node* works in the following way: it establishes a function $Prop_{node}$ which acts on the node incoming objects factors $en(ob_1), en(ob_2), ..., en(ob_k)$ and issues the factor for the node produced object ob_{node}:

(87) $Prop_{node}(en(ob_1), en(ob_2), ..., en(ob_k)) = en(ob_{node})$.

By means of (87), *node*, having a demand $en^*(ob_{node})$ can issue demands to supplying nodes on $en^*(ob_1), en^*(ob_2), ..., en^*(ob_k)$ as to satisfy

(88) $Prop_{node}(en^*(ob_1), en^*(ob_2), ..., en^*(ob_k)) \geq en^*(ob_{node})$.

The requirements for en^* are back–propagated through the design dag from the out-nodes to the in-nodes by means of $Prop$ functions of the nodes. We include the description of the assembling process in analogy to our description of the design process. It does require a category of *operators* P, a category of *functionalities* F, a *linear time* T with the *time origin* 0. The domain of objects is a category *Things(P, F, π)* of objects endowed with a part relation π. The assignment operator S acts as a partial mapping on the Cartesian product $P \times F \times Things(P, F, \pi)$ with values in the category *dag* of dags. The act of assembling is expressed by means of a predicate

$$Art(p(u), < v_1(u), \cdots, v_k(u) >, u, en^*(u), f(u), t(u), T(u)),$$

which reads: *an operator $p(u)$ assembles at time $t(u)$ an object u with endurance factor $en^*(u)$, functionality $f(u)$ according to the assembling scheme $T(u)$ organized by $p(u)$ which is a dag, from things $v_1(u), \cdots, v_k(u)$ which are in–nodes of dag. The thing $v_i(u)$ enters in the position i the assembling process for u.* The predicate ART is subject to the requirements analogous to Des1–Des4 for design. The details of the assembling scheme without the requirements for en^* are to be found in Polkowski [29].

References

1. van Benthem, J.: The Logic of Time. Reidel, Dordrecht (1983)
2. Calosi, C., Graziani, P.: Mereology and the Sciences. Springer Synthese Library, vol. 371. Springer International Publishing, Cham (2014)
3. Casati, R., Varzi, A.C.: Parts and Places. The Structures of Spatial Representations. MIT Press, Cambridge (1999)
4. Clarke, B.L.: A calculus of individuals based on connection. Notre Dame J. Form. Logic **22**(2), 204–218 (1981)
5. Faucett, W.M.: Compact semigroups irreducibly connected between two idempotents. Proc. Am. Math. Soc. **6**, 741–747 (1955)
6. Gilmore, C.: Building enduring objects out of spcetime. In: [2], pp. 5–34
7. Hájek, P.: Metamathematics of Fuzzy Logic. Kluwer, Dordrecht (1998)
8. Leśniewski, S.: Podstawy Ogólnej Teoryi Mnogości, I (Foundations of General Set Theory, I, in Polish). Prace Polskiego Koła Naukowego w Moskwie, Sekcya Matematyczno-przyrodnicza, No. 2, Zaklad Wyd. Poplawski, Moscow (1916)
9. Łukasiewicz, J.: Die Logischen grundlagen der Wahrscheinlichtkeitsrechnung. Krakóow, Spółka Wydawnicza Polska (1913). Translation: Borkowski, L. (ed.): Logical Foundations of Probability Theory, in Selected Works. North-Holland, Amsterdam (1663,1970)
10. Mostert, P.S., Shields, A.L.: On the structure of semigroups on a compact manifold with a boundary. Ann. Math. **65**, 117–143 (1957)
11. Ośmiałowski, P.: On path planning for mobile robots: Introducing the mereological potential field method in the framework of mereological spatial reasoning. J. Autom. Mobile Robot. Intell. Syst. (JAMRIS) **3**(2), 24–33 (2009)
12. Ośmiałowski, P.: A case of planning and programming of a concurrent behavior: planning and navigating with formations of robots. In: Proceedings of CS&P 2009. Concurrency, Specification, Programming, Kraków, September 2009. Warsaw University Press (2009)
13. Ośmiałowski, P.: Spatial reasoning based on rough mereology in planning and navigation problems of autonomous mobile robots. Ph.D. dissertation. Polkowski, L. Polish-Japanese Institute of IT, Warszawa (2010)
14. Osmiaıowski, P., Polkowski, L.: Spatial reasoning based on rough mereology: a notion of a robot formation and path planning problem for formations of mobile autonomous robots. In: Peters, J.F., Skowron, A., Słowiński, R., Lingras, P., Miao, D., Tsumoto, S. (eds.) Transactions on Rough Sets XII. LNCS, vol. 6190, pp. 143–169. Springer, Heidelberg (2010). doi:10.1007/978-3-642-14467-7_8
15. Pawlak, Z.: Rough sets. Int. J. Comput. Inf. Sci. **11**, 341–366 (1982)
16. Pawlak, Z.: Rough Sets: Theoretical Aspects of Reasoning about Data. Kluwer, Dordrecht (1991)
17. Polkowski, L.: Approximate Reasoning by Parts. An Introduction to Rough Mereology. ISRL, vol. 20. Springer, Berlin (2011)
18. Polkowski, L.: Mereology in engneering and computer science. In: [12], pp. 217–292
19. Polkowski, L.: A rough set paradigm for unifying rough set theory and fuzzy set theory. Fundamenta Informaticae **54**, 67–88 (2003). Proceedings RSFDGrC 2003, Chongqing, China. Lecture Notes in Artificial Intelligence, vol. 2639, pp 70–78. Springer, Berlin (2003)
20. Polkowski, L.: A note on 3-valued rough logic accepting decision rules. Fundamenta Informaticae **61**, 37–45 (2004)

21. Polkowski, L.: Formal granular calculi based on rough inclusions. In: Proceedings of IEEE 2005 Conference on Granular Computing, GrC 2005, Beijing, China, pp. 57–62. IEEE Press (2005)
22. Polkowski, L.: Rough-fuzzy-neurocomputing based on rough mereological calculus of granules. Int. J. Hybrid Intell. Syst. **2**, 91–108 (2005)
23. Polkowski, L.: A model of granular computing with applications. In: Proceedings of IEEE 2006 Conference on Granular Computing, GrC 2006, Atlanta, USA, pp 9–16. IEEE Press (2006)
24. Polkowski, L.: Granulation of knowledge in decision systems: the approach based on rough inclusions. The method and its applications. In: Kryszkiewicz, M., Peters, J.F., Rybinski, H., Skowron, A. (eds.) RSEISP 2007. LNCS (LNAI), vol. 4585, pp. 69–79. Springer, Heidelberg (2007). doi:10.1007/978-3-540-73451-2_9
25. Polkowski, L.: The paradigm of granular rough computing. In: Proceedings of the 6th IEEE International Conference on Cognitive Informatics, ICCI 2007, pp 145–163. IEEE Computer Society, Los Alamitos (2007)
26. Polkowski, L.: Rough mereology in analysis of vagueness. In: Wang, G., Li, T., Grzymala-Busse, J.W., Miao, D., Skowron, A., Yao, Y. (eds.) RSKT 2008. LNCS (LNAI), vol. 5009, pp. 197–204. Springer, Heidelberg (2008). doi:10.1007/978-3-540-79721-0_30
27. Polkowski, L.: A unified approach to granulation of knowledge and granular computing based on rough mereology: a survey. In: Pedrycz, W., Skowron, A., Kreinovich, V. (eds.) Handbook of Granular Computing, pp. 375–400. Wiley, Chichester (2008)
28. Polkowski, L.: Granulation of knowledge: similarity based approach in information and decision systems. In: Meyers, R.A. (ed.) Springer Encyclopedia of Complexity and System Sciences. Springer, Berlin (2009). doi:10.1007/978-0-387-30440-3_262. Article 00 788
29. Polkowski, L.: Rough sets, rough mereology and uncertainty. In: Wang, G., et al. (eds.) Thriving Rough Sets. Springer Series in Computational Intelligence. Springer International Publishing, Cham (2017). doi:10.1007/978-3-319-54966-8_4
30. Polkowski, L., Artiemjew, P.: Granular Computing in Decision Approximation. ISRL, vol. 77. Springer International Publishing, Cham (2015)
31. Polkowski, L., Ośmiałowski, P.: Spatial reasoning with applications to mobile robotics. In: Xing-Jian, J. (ed.) Mobile Robots Motion Planning. New Challenges, pp. 433–453. I-Tech, Vienna (2008)
32. Polkowski, L., Ośmiałowski, P.: A framework for multiagent mobile robotics: spatial reasoning based on rough mereology in player/stage system. In: Chan, C.-C., Grzymala-Busse, J.W., Ziarko, W.P. (eds.) RSCTC 2008. LNCS (LNAI), vol. 5306, pp. 142–149. Springer, Heidelberg (2008). doi:10.1007/978-3-540-88425-5_15
33. Polkowski, L., Ośmiałowski, P.: Navigation for mobile autonomous robots and their formations: an application of spatial reasoning induced from rough mereological geometry. In: Barrera, A. (ed.) Mobile Robots Navigation, pp. 329–354. InTech, Zagreb (2010)
34. Polkowski, L., Semeniuk-Polkowska, M.: On rough set logics based on similarity relations. Fundamenta Informaticae **64**, 379–390 (2005)
35. Polkowski, L., Semeniuk-Polkowska, M.: Granular Mereotopology: A First Sketch. http://ceur-ws.org/Vol-1032/paper-28.pdf
36. Polkowski, L., Semeniuk-Polkowska, M.: Boundaries, borders, fences, hedges. Fundamenta Informaticae **129**(1–2), 149–159 (2014). Dedicated to the Memory of Professor Manfred Kudlek

37. RSES. http://mimuw.edu.pl/logic/rses
38. Polkowski, L., Skowron, A.: Rough mereology. In: Raś, Z.W., Zemankova, M. (eds.) ISMIS 1994. LNCS (LNAI), vol. 869, pp. 85–94. Springer, Heidelberg (1994). doi:10.1007/3-540-58495-1_9
39. Polkowski, L., Skowron, A.: Rough mereology: a new paradigm for approximate reasoning. Int. J. Approx. Reason. **15**(4), 333–365 (1997)
40. Simons, P.: Parts. A Study in Ontology. Clarendon Press, Oxford (2003)
41. Skowron, A., Rauszer, C.: The discernibility matrices and functions in decision systems. In: Słowiński, R. (ed.) Intelligent Decision Support. Handbook of Applications and Advances of the Rough Sets Theory, pp. 311–362. Kluwer, Dordrecht (1992)
42. Smith, B.: Boundaries: an essay in mereotopology. In: Hahn, L. (ed.) The Philosophy of Roderick Chisholm (Library of Living Philosophers), pp. 534–561. Open Court, La Salle (1997)
43. Tarski, A., Givant, S.: The Tarski system of geometry. The Bull. Symb. Logic **5**(2), 175–214 (1999)
44. Tarski, A.: Zur Grundlegung der Booleschen Algebra. I. Fundamenta Mathematicae **24**, 177–198 (1935)
45. Tarski, A.: Les fondements de la géométrie des corps. Supplement to Annales de la Société Polonaise de Mathématique **7**, 29–33 (1929)
46. Varzi, A.C.: Boundary. In: Stanford Encyclopedia of Philosophy. http://plato.stanford.edu/entries/boundary/

A Topological Approximation Space Based on Open Sets of Topology Generated by Coverings

Bożena Staruch[(⊠)] and Bogdan Staruch

Faculty of Mathematics and Computer Science,
University of Warmia and Mazury in Olsztyn,
ul. Słoneczna 54, 10-710 Olsztyn, Poland
bostar@matman.uwm.edu.pl

Abstract. In this paper we consider information granules based on coverings. We also present a topological approximation space, where lower and upper approximations are open sets. We show a way of forming neighbourhoods for 'new' (testing) objects. A topological rough fuzzy membership function is defined and then generalized to an extended rough fuzzy membership function of the 'new' objects. Basing on this extended membership function and the least neighbourhood of any 'new' object, we propose a new topological approach to classification problem.

Keywords: Rough sets · Approximation space · Information granules · Topology · Rough fuzzy membership function · Classification

1 Introduction

We consider a topological approach to rough approximation space. Approximation spaces for information systems (see [1,2]) were defined by partitions, whereas these were defined by attributes of a pattern space. Skowron and co-authors [3–5] proposed a more universal approach based on various attribute-dependent coverings, in particular by tolerance and similarity relations defined by attribute values. It also turned out that the problem of existing of missing values (see [6–10]) can be solved by coverings. Some researchers used a topological point of view (see [11–15]) to describe approximation spaces.

An important generalization of an approximation space via the information granulation approach has been proposed by Skowron and Polkowski (see papers like [16–21]). The theoretical results are eventually implemented in machine learning methods for solving practical problems like classification, pattern recognition etc. (see e.g. [22,23]).

In this paper we assume that a covering of the finite set is given. The origin of the covering sets is of two kinds, so the covering set is divided into two parts. The first one is attribute-dependent part where the covering subsets are sets of objects indiscernible under attribute-dependent properties. This part of the

© Springer International Publishing AG 2017
L. Polkowski et al. (Eds.): IJCRS 2017, Part II, LNAI 10314, pp. 130–137, 2017.
DOI: 10.1007/978-3-319-60840-2_9

covering is crucial for recognizing a neighbourhood of any 'new' object via the attribute values of this object (missing values are allowed). The second kind is an expert-dependent part based on available data, domain knowledge as well as subjective decisions of experts.

In Sect. 2 we describe a topology generated by a covering of the set U and we take minimal neighbourhoods of objects of U as the information granules. Such an approach were presented in [14]. Theorem 1 states that the granules are join irreducible elements in the distributive lattice of the topology. This lattice-theoretic fact yields that every open set is a join of granules. Moreover, every open set is a join of maximal granules included in this set, what could be used for minimization of description.

In Sect. 3 we assume that the lower approximation of a set X is given by the topological interior of X and its upper approximation coincides with the least open set that includes X. This latter assumption differs from the usual definition in approximation spaces defined by topological spaces, in which, on the contrary, the upper approximation of a set X is its closure. Our assumption leads to the very natural fact that X is definable if and only if it is open. This extends to arbitrary topological spaces occurring in Pawlak's approximation spaces (in which lower and upper approximations are clopen, that is, closed and open). We also define a rough fuzzy membership function, which could be generalized to a rough inclusion function of open sets into subsets of U.

In Sect. 4 we present an application of our topological approach to the classification problem. The most important issue is to recognize a 'new' object via its attribute values and describe the neighbourhood of this 'new' object i.e. an open set of objects 'indiscernible' (under available information) with the given 'new' object. The value of a rough inclusion function of this neighbourhood to the given decision class is used as an extended rough fuzzy membership function of the 'new' objects to the decision class.

2 Covering Based Granulation

In this paper U is a finite non-empty set of objects. A non-empty family $\mathcal{C}$ of subsets of U is *a covering on U (or covers U)* if and only if $\bigcup \mathcal{C} = U$.

Recall that a family T of subsets of a finite set U is *a topology* on U if and only if $\emptyset, U \in T$ and for any $X, Y \in T$, $X \cap Y \in T$ and $X \cup Y \in T$. Given any family $\mathcal{A}$ of subsets of U there exists the least topology $T(\mathcal{A})$ containing $\mathcal{A}$.

Let $\mathcal{C}$ be a covering of U. For any object $u \in U$ let $\mathcal{N}_{\mathcal{C}}(u) = \{C \in \mathcal{C} : u \in C\}$ denote the family of all its neighbourhoods in $T(\mathcal{C})$. Let $g_{\mathcal{C}}(u) = \bigcap \mathcal{N}_{\mathcal{C}}(u)$. Then $g_{\mathcal{C}}(u)$ is the least neighbourhood of u in $T(\mathcal{C})$. Hence $g_{\mathcal{C}}(u)$ can be treated as the smallest portion of information (*an information granule*) about u in the context of the covering $\mathcal{C}$. The set of all granules $Gran_{\mathcal{C}}(U) = \{g_{\mathcal{C}}(u) : u \in U\}$ will be called *a granulation set* of U determined by $\mathcal{C}$.

It is worth mentioning here that if $\mathcal{C}$ is not a covering of U then there is a $u \in U$ such that $\mathcal{N}_{\mathcal{C}}(u) = \emptyset$. Then taking $\bigcap \emptyset = U$, we get the following equality $Gran_{\mathcal{C}}(U) = Gran_{\mathcal{C} \cup \{U\}}(U) \setminus \{U\}$. From this moment $\mathcal{C}$ denotes a covering on U such that $U \in \mathcal{C}$.

If there is no confusion, we omit the subscript $\mathcal{C}$ writing $\mathcal{N}(u)$, $g(u)$, $Gran(U)$.

Example 1. 1. Let $U = \{u_1, u_2, u_3, u_4, u_5\}$ and let
$\{\{u_1, u_2, u_4\}, \{u_2, u_3, u_4\}, \{u_1, u_2, u_5\}, U\}$ be the given covering of U.
Then $g(u_1) = \{u_1, u_2\}$, $g(u_2) = \{u_2\}$, $g(u_3) = \{u_2, u_3, u_4\}$, $g(u_4) = \{u_2, u_4\}$,
$g(u_5) = \{u_1, u_2, u_5\}$.

2. Consider the granulation: $g(u_1) = \{u_1\}, g(u_2) = \{u_2\}, g(u_3) = \{u_1, u_2, u_3\}, g(u_4) = g(u_5) = \{u_1, u_2, u_4, u_5\}, g(u_6) = U$. This shows that the intersection of two different granules does not necessarily be a granule, two different objects can have equal granules, U is a granule.

Proposition 1. *For any* $u, v \in U$

1. *if* $u \in g(v)$ *then* $g(u) \subseteq g(v)$,
2. $g(u) \subseteq g(v)$ *if and only if* $\mathcal{N}(u) \supseteq \mathcal{N}(v)$,
3. *if* $g(u) \subset g(v)$ *then* $v \notin g(u)$,
4. $g(u) \subset g(v)$ *if and only if* $\mathcal{N}(u) \supset \mathcal{N}(v)$,
5. $(Gran(U), \subseteq)$ *is a partial ordered set dual to* $(\{N_u : u \in U\}, \subseteq)$.

We set $u \, TInd \, v$ if and only if $g(u) = g(v)$ and call $TInd$ a topological indiscernibility relation. Then $[u]_{TInd} = g(u) \setminus \bigcup \{g(v) : v \in g(u), g(v) \subset g(u)\}$.

Notice that every topology $\mathcal{T}$ on a finite set U forms a finite distributive lattice $(\mathcal{T}, \cup, \cap)$. Figure 1 presents the diagrams of the two lattices for topologies obtained by the coverings from Example 1. The granules are labeled.

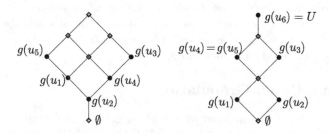

Fig. 1. Lattices of the topologies from Example 1

It is known in lattice theory (see [24]) that join irreducible elements play a crucial role in description of finite distributive lattices. An object $X \in \mathcal{T}$ is *join irreducible* if for any $Y, Z \in \mathcal{T}$, $X = Y \cup Z$ implies $X = Y$ or $X = Z$. Let $J(\mathcal{T})$ be the set of all join irreducible elements in $(\mathcal{T}, \cup, \cap)$ and for any $X \in \mathcal{T}$ let $J(X) = \{Y \subseteq X : Y \in J(\mathcal{T})\}$ and let $J_{max}(X)$ denote all maximal elements in $J(X)$.

For any finite distributive lattice $(\mathcal{T}, \cup, \cap)$ and every $X, Y \in \mathcal{T}$, the following properties of join irreducible elements (see [24]) will be useful in our paper:
$X = \bigcup J(X) = \bigcup J_{max}(X)$, $J(X \cup Y) = J(X) \cup J(Y)$ and $J(X \cap Y) = J(X) \cap J(Y)$.
The next theorem describes all join irreducible elements in $(T(\mathcal{C}), \cup, \cap)$.

Theorem 1. *Let C be any covering of U. Then*

1. *$g(u)$ is join irreducible in $(T(C), \cup, \cap)$ for any $u \in U$,*
2. *$X = \bigcup\{g(x): x \in X\}$ for any non-empty $X \in T(C)$,*
3. *$J(T(C)) \setminus \{\emptyset\} = Gran_C(U)$,*
4. *$T(C) = T(Gran_C(U))$ and $Gran_{Gran_C(U)}(U) = Gran_C(U)$.*

Proof. 1. Let $g(u) = g(v) \cup g(w)$ for some $u, v, w \in U$. Then $g(v), g(w) \subseteq g(u)$ and $u \in g(v)$ or $u \in g(w)$. Hence $g(u) \subseteq g(v)$ or $g(u) \subseteq g(w)$ and thus $g(u) = g(v)$ or $g(u) = g(w)$.
2. Let $X \in T(C) \setminus \{\emptyset\}$ and $x \in X$. Then there is a neighbourhood of x included in X. Hence $g(x) \subseteq X$ as the least neighborhood of x and $X = \bigcup\{g(x): x \in X\}$.
3. Using 1 $Gran_C(U) \subseteq J(T(C))$. By 2, any nonempty $X \in T(C) \setminus Gran_C(U)$ is not join irreducible. Hence $J(T(C)) \setminus \{\emptyset\} = Gran_C(U)$.
4. It is an immediate consequence of 1–3.

The properties of join irreducible elements allow us to choose the unique optimal (in the sense of number of components) granular covering of X consisting of all maximal granules included in X. Also notice that any maximal granule $g(u)$ is obtained by intersection of minimal set $\mathcal{N}(u)$, thus the optimal coverings can be obtained by minimization of sets $\mathcal{N}(.)$. Notice, that all the above properties are true for any topology T on U, because T is a covering of U and $T(T) = T$.

3   Topological Approximation Spaces and Rough Fuzzy Membership Function

Let U be a finite non-empty set of objects and let T be a topology on U. We define a topological approximation space $TAS = (U, T)$ as a topology on U with topological operators of lower and upper approximation of subsets of U as follows (see also [14]):

1. $LOW(X)$ is the greatest open set Y such that $Y \subseteq X$,
2. $UPP(X)$ is the least open set Y such that $X \subseteq Y$.

A subset $X \subseteq U$ is *definable* if $LOW(X) = UPP(X)$. It can be easily observed that $X \subseteq U$ is a definable set in TAS if and only if $X \in T$. Moreover, $LOW(X) = \bigcup\{g(x) : g(x) \subseteq X\}$, $UPP(X) = \bigcup\{g(x) : x \in X\}$, where $g(x)$ denotes a granule of $x \in U$, in the granulation set $Gran_T(U)$.

Let $TAS = (U, T)$ be any topological approximation space. For any $u \in U$, $X \subseteq U$ and $X' = U \setminus X$ we introduce *a rough fuzzy membership function* $\mu(u, X)$ based on TAS as follows:

$$\mu(u, X) = \begin{cases} 0, & \text{for } u \in U \setminus UPP(X) \\ \frac{card(X \cap g(u))}{card(g(u))}, & \text{for } u \in UPP(X) \cap UPP(X') \\ 1, & \text{for } u \in U \setminus UPP(X') \end{cases}$$

Example 2. Let us take the granulation from Example 1.2 and $X = \{u_2, u_3, u_4\}$. Then $UPP(X) = g(u_2) \cup g(u_3) \cup g(u_4) = \{u_1, u_2, u_3, u_4, u_5\}$ and $UPP(X') = g(u_1) \cup g(u_5) \cup g(u_6) = U$. All elements, but u_6, belong to $UPP(X) \cap UPP(X')$.
$g(u_1) = \{u_1\}$ and $X \cap g(u_1) = \emptyset$ and thus $\mu(u_1, X) = 0$
$g(u_2) = \{u_2\}$ and $X \cap g(u_2) = \{u_2\}$ and thus $\mu(u_2, X) = 1$
$g(u_3) = \{u_1, u_2, u_3\}$ and $X \cap g(u_3) = \{u_2, u_3\}$ and thus $\mu(u_3, X) = \frac{2}{3}$
$g(u_4) = g(u_5) = \{u_1, u_2, u_4, u_5\}$ and $X \cap g(u_4) = \{u_2, u_4\}$ and thus
$\mu(u_4, X) = \mu(u_5, X) = \frac{1}{2}$. $u_6 \in UPP(X') \setminus UPP(X)$ and thus $\mu(u_6, X) = 0$.

Notice that $UPP(X) \cap UPP(X')$ would represent an 'uncertainty' region. However, this region cannot be described as $\{u \in U : 0 < \mu(u, X) < 1\}$. In Example 2, $u_1, u_2 \in UPP(X) \cap UPP(X')$ and $\mu(u_1, X) = 0$, $\mu(u_2, X) = 1$.

The next proposition shows that the rough fuzzy membership function determines a two-point probability distribution and preserves topological indiscernibility.

Proposition 2. *For any $u, v \in U$ and $X \subseteq U$*

1. $\mu(u, X) = 1$ *for every $u \in LOW(X)$,*
2. $\mu(u, X) = 0$ *for every $u \in LOW(X')$,*
3. $\mu(u, X') = 1 - \mu(u, X)$,
4. *if $g(u) = g(v)$ then $\mu(u, X) = \mu(v, X)$.*

Proof. We prove only 3. Notice that $U = (U \setminus UPP(X)) \dot{\cup} (U \setminus UPP(X')) \dot{\cup} (UPP(X) \cap UPP(X'))$, where $\dot{\cup}$ denotes the disjoint union of sets. Let $u \in LOW(X')$.

1. If $u \in U \setminus UPP(X)$ then $\mu(u, X) = 0 = 1 - \mu(u, X')$.
2. If $u \in U \setminus UPP(X')$ then $\mu(u, X) = 1 = 1 - \mu(u, X')$.
3. If $u \in UPP(X) \cap UPP(X')$ then $g(u) \subseteq UPP(X) \cap UPP(X')$.
   And $g(u) = g(u) \cap (X \dot{\cup} X') = (g(u) \cap X) \dot{\cup} ((g(u) \cap X')$.
   Hence $1 = \frac{g(u)}{g(u)} = \frac{g(u) \cap X}{g(u)} + \frac{g(u) \cap X'}{g(u)} = \mu(u, X) + \mu(u, X')$.

If $X \subseteq U$ and $V \in \mathcal{T}$ is any open set, we can propose different kinds of rough inclusion measure based on values of the rough fuzzy membership function for objects from V and then we can use this measure to classify new objects. Dependent on the specific application, statistical measures of central tendency can be used as well as some other 'aggregation' methods. Let $\mu(V, X)$ denote any such aggregated measure.

4   Classification Based on TAS

In this section we discuss the application of topological approximation space in building classifiers of new objects to decision classes. We are going to present here the steps to obtain tools for classification. Let U be a finite non-empty set of objects (sample, training set of objects) and let $o \notin U$ be a 'new' object (testing object) that we want to classify into one of the decision classes (categories of objects) $D_1, \ldots, D_k \subseteq U$.

STEP I - Information Table

Start with Pawlak's information system, where missing values are also admitted. Systems with missing values can be obtained, when for example, someone needs to aggregate information from many sources. *An information system* is a pair $IS = (U, A)$, where A is a set of attributes such that for every $a \in A$, a partial function $a : U \to Val_a$ is determined. *An information table* is a table represented by a partial function $IT : U \times A \to \bigcup \{Val_a : a \in A\}$ such that $IT(u, a)$ is defined if and only if $a(u)$ is defined and then $IT(u, a) = a(u)$. If we don't want to use partial functions for some reason, we can add some artificial symbols (like $\star$) for indicating missing values.

We assume that the new object o is described as $\{a(o) : a \in A\}$.

STEP II - Attribute-Dependent Subsets

Let $IS = (U, A)$ be the information system from STEP I. We say that $C \subseteq U$ is *attribute-dependent* if there is a logical condition l based on attribute values (like boolean expression on descriptors), such that $C = C_l$, where C_l is the set of all objects from U satisfying l. For example, if l is a descriptor $a = s$ then $C_l = \{u \in U : a(u) = s\}$ is an attribute dependent set. Let L be the set of logical conditions based on attribute values. Recall that we assumed in Sect. 2 that the covering set contains the set U, so we can add to L a logical formula l_0 which describes a condition like 'an object is of the same category as other objects in U' and then $C_{l_0} = U$. Hence assume that $l_o \in L$. Then $C_L = \{C_l : l \in L\}$ denotes the set of attribute-dependent subsets determined by L. We will say that C_L is *an attribute-dependent part* of the given covering system $(U, \mathcal{C})$ if $C_L \subseteq \mathcal{C}$.

STEP III - Covering and Granulation

We form a covering system $(U, \mathcal{C})$ with $\mathcal{C} = C_L \dot\cup C_+$, where C_L is an attribute-dependent part for some set of logical conditions L and C_+ is a family of subsets which represent the additional information. We will say that C_+ is *the expert-dependent part*. The subsets from the expert-dependent part can be obtained in many ways like expert's indication of similar objects, object properties that cannot be described by attributes, decisions based on hidden premises, hypotheses about the similarity of objects, etc.

Having the covering, we calculate the granulation set $Gran(U)$. This is the moment when reduction of number of covering sets should be done, so we can use some minimal covering sets (like reducts for Pawlak's information systems) with the aim to get the granulation. A reduction of the attribute-dependent part is particularly important, because this part will be used in describing neighbourhoods of new objects (to be classified).

STEP IV - Neighbourhoods of New Objects

In this step we are going to obtain a description of o by the attribute-dependent part C_L. For every $l \in L$ if o 'satisfies' l, then C_l is a neighbourhood of o. Thus $\mathcal{N}(o) = \{C_l : o \text{ satisfies } l, l \in L\}$. Notice that this definition depends on the chosen way of 'satisfaction', especially, when missing values are involved. Different types of satisfaction, were considered in partial algebras theory (see e.g. our papers [25, 26]), and also in partial structures (see [27–30]). In a wider perspective, $\mathcal{N}(o)$ can also contain sets from the expert-dependent part i.e. $\mathcal{N}(o) = \{C_l : o \text{ satisfies } l, l \in L\} \cup \mathcal{C}_0$, where $\mathcal{C}_0 \subseteq \mathcal{C}_+$. The latter holds when at least one of the methods of gaining the additional information is still active during the classification process.

The least neighbourhood of o is the open set $G(o) = \bigcap \mathcal{N}(o)$. Hence $G(o)$ can be interpreted as a reflection of the object o in TAS.

STEP V - Topological Measure of Membership of New Objects and Classification
   Having $G(o)$, we can calculate a value of an extended membership function of the object o to any decision class D_i as $\mu(o, D_i) = \mu(G(o), D_i)$. Finally, we use the calculated value of the extended membership function in the chosen classification method. Certainly, the method of calculating $\mu(G(o), D_i)$ can depend on the method of classification, and vice versa.

References

1. Pawlak, Z., Skowron, A.: Rudiments of rough sets. Inf. Sci. **177**(1), 3–27 (2007)
2. Pawlak, Z., Skowron, A.: Rough sets and boolean reasoning. Inf. Sci. **177**(1), 41–73 (2007)
3. Skowron, A., Stepaniuk, J.: Tolerance approximation spaces. Fundam. Informaticae **27**, 245–253 (1996)
4. Pomykala, J.A.: About tolerance and similarity relations in information systems. In: Alpigini, J.J., Peters, J.F., Skowron, A., Zhong, N. (eds.) RSCTC 2002. LNCS, vol. 2475, pp. 175–182. Springer, Heidelberg (2002). doi:10.1007/3-540-45813-1_22
5. Pawlak, Z., Skowron, A.: Rough sets: some extensions. Inf. Sci. **177**(1), 28–40 (2006)
6. Orłowska, E. (ed.): Incomplete Information: Rough Set Analysis. Physcia-Verlag, Heidelberg (1997)
7. Kryszkiewicz, M., Rybiński, H.: Data mining in incomplete information systems from rough set perspective. In: Polkowski, L., Tsumoto, S., Lin, T.Y. (eds.) Rough Set Methods and Applications. New Developments in Knowledge Discovery in Information Systems. Physica Verlag, pp. 567–580. Physica Verlag, Heidelberg (2000)
8. Grzymala-Busse, J.W., Hu, M.: A comparison of several approaches to missing attribute values in data mining. In: Ziarko, W., Yao, Y. (eds.) RSCTC 2000. LNCS, vol. 2005, pp. 378–385. Springer, Heidelberg (2001). doi:10.1007/3-540-45554-X_46
9. Grzymala-Busse, J.W.: Data with missing attribute values: generalization of indiscernibility relation and rule induction. In: Peters, J.F., Skowron, A., Grzymała-Busse, J.W., Kostek, B., Świniarski, R.W., Szczuka, M.S. (eds.) Transactions on Rough Sets I. LNCS, vol. 3100, pp. 78–95. Springer, Heidelberg (2004). doi:10.1007/978-3-540-27794-1_3
10. Medhat, T.: Missing values via covering rough sets. Int. J. Data Min. Intell. Inf. Technol. Appl. **2**(1), 10–17 (2012)
11. Li, T.-J.: Rough approximation operators in covering approximation spaces. In: Greco, S., Hata, Y., Hirano, S., Inuiguchi, M., Miyamoto, S., Nguyen, H.S., Słowiński, R. (eds.) RSCTC 2006. LNCS, vol. 4259, pp. 174–182. Springer, Heidelberg (2006). doi:10.1007/11908029_20
12. Qin, K., Gao, Y., Pei, Z.: On covering rough sets. In: Yao, J.T., Lingras, P., Wu, W.-Z., Szczuka, M., Cercone, N.J., Ślęzak, D. (eds.) RSKT 2007. LNCS, vol. 4481, pp. 34–41. Springer, Heidelberg (2007). doi:10.1007/978-3-540-72458-2_4

13. Zhu, P.: Covering rough sets based on neighborhoods: an approach without using neighborhoods. Int. J. Approx. Reas. **52**(3), 461–472 (2011)
14. Kumar, A., Banerjee, M.: Definable and rough sets in covering-based approximation spaces. In: Li, T., Nguyen, H.S., Wang, G., Grzymala-Busse, J., Janicki, R., Hassanien, A.E., Yu, H. (eds.) RSKT 2012. LNCS, vol. 7414, pp. 488–495. Springer, Heidelberg (2012). doi:10.1007/978-3-642-31900-6_60
15. Pagliani, P.: Covering rough sets and formal topology. A uniform approach through intensional and extensional constructors. In: Peters, J.F., Skowron, A. (eds.) Transactions on Rough Sets XX, pp. 109–145. Springer, Heidelberg (2016)
16. Skowron, A., Stepaniuk, J.: Information granules and rough-neural computing. In: Pal, S.K., Polkowski, L., Skowron, A. (eds.) Rough Neural Computing. Techniques for Computing with Words, p. 43. Springer, Berlin (2004)
17. Skowron, A., Świniarski, R., Synak, P.: Approximation spaces and information granulation. In: Peters, J.F., Skowron, A. (eds.) Transactions on Rough Sets III. LNCS, vol. 3400, pp. 175–189. Springer, Heidelberg (2005). doi:10.1007/11427834_8
18. Szczuka, M., Jankowski, A., Skowron, A., Ślęzak, D.: Building granular systems - from concepts to applications. In: Yao, Y., Hu, Q., Yu, H., Grzymala-Busse, J.W. (eds.) RSFDGrC 2015. LNCS, vol. 9437, pp. 245–255. Springer, Cham (2015). doi:10.1007/978-3-319-25783-9_22
19. Polkowski, L., Skowron, A.: Rough mereology: a new paradigm for approximate reasoning. Int. J. Approx. Reas. **15**, 333–365 (1996)
20. Polkowski, L., Skowron, A.: Towards adaptive calculus of granules. In: Zadeh, L.A., Kacprzyk, J. (eds.) Computing with Words in Information/Intelligent Systems, pp. 201–227. Physica-Verlag, Heidelberg (1999)
21. Polkowski, L., Artiemjew, P.: Granular Computing in Decision Approximation. An Application of Rough Mereology. Intelligent Systems Reference Library, vol. 77. Springer, Heidelberg (2015)
22. Artiemjew, P.: On classification of data by means of rough mereological granules of objects and rules. In: Wang, G., Li, T., Grzymala-Busse, J.W., Miao, D., Skowron, A., Yao, Y. (eds.) RSKT 2008. LNCS, vol. 5009, pp. 221–228. Springer, Heidelberg (2008). doi:10.1007/978-3-540-79721-0_33
23. Bazan, J.G., Nguyen, H.S., Nguyen, S.H., Synak, P., Wróblewski, J.: Rough set algorithms in classification problems. In: Polkowski, L., Tsumoto, S., Lin, T.Y. (eds.) Rough Set Methods and Applications. New Developments in Knowledge Discovery in Information Systems, pp. 49–88. Physica Verlag, Heidelberg (2000)
24. Grätzer, G.: General Lattice Theory, 2nd edn. Birkhauser Verlag, Basel (1998)
25. Staruch, B., Staruch, B.: Strong regular varieties of partial algebras. Algebra Univers. **31**, 157–176 (1994)
26. Staruch, B.: HSP-type Characterization of Strong Equational Classes of Partial Algebras, pp. 41–65 (2009)
27. Staruch, B., Staruch, B.: Possible sets of equations. Bull. Sect. Logic **32**, 85–95 (2002)
28. Staruch, B.: Derivation from partial knowledge in partial models. Bull. Sect. Logic **32**, 75–84 (2002)
29. Staruch, B.: Extensions of partial structures and their application to modelling of multi-agent systems, Advances in Soft Computing, Monitoring, Security and Rescue Tasks in Multiagent Systems. Springer, Heidelberg (2005)
30. Staruch, B., Staruch, B.: First order theories for partial models. Stud. Logica. **80**, 105–120 (2005)

Actual Existence Predicate in Mereology and Mereotopology (Extended Abstract)

Dimiter Vakarelov$^{(\boxtimes)}$

Department of Mathematical Logic with Applications,
Faculty of Mathematics and Computer Science, Sofia University,
blvd James Bouchier 5, 1126 Sofia, Bulgaria
dvak@fmi.uni-sofia.bg

Abstract. This paper is devoted to an axiomatic characterization of an ontological predicate called "actual existence". We analyze this predicate in the context of some mereological and mereotopological systems. The resulting mereological system is a Boolean algebra with a predicate of actual existence and the resulting system in mereotopology is a Boolean algebra with predicate of actual existence and a binary relation called "actual contact". For both systems we present standard models and prove the corresponding representation theorems.

Keywords: Mereotopology · Contact algebra · Actual existence · Actual contact · Topological representation

1 Introduction

This paper is to be considered as an extended abstract of [16] which was devoted to a formal treatment of the predicate of ontological existence in the context of mereology and mereotopology. We omit in the present text all formal proofs and consider more intuitive explanations and some new motivating examples. We consider [5,9,10] as standard reference books correspondingly for mereology, topology and Boolean algebra.

1.1 Mereology and Mereotopology

"Mereology is a formal theory of part-whole and associated concepts" - Simons [10]. Mereotopology is a combination of mereology with some topological relations between objects. The idea of this combination arose in the first part of 20th century when a number of philosophers, including mainly Whitehead [17–19] and

The author is sponsored by Contract DN02/15/19.12.2016 with Bulgarian NSF. Project title: "Space, Time and Modality: Relational, Algebraic and Topological Models". Thanks are due to the anonymous referees for their valuable remarks and suggestions.

© Springer International Publishing AG 2017
L. Polkowski et al. (Eds.): IJCRS 2017, Part II, LNAI 10314, pp. 138–157, 2017.
DOI: 10.1007/978-3-319-60840-2_10

de Laguna [7], decided to build a new, point-free theory of space based on mere-ology. This was inspired by some criticism to the classical Euclidean approach, based on the primitive notions of point, straight line and plane, which are in a sense some fictions having no separate existence in reality. The aim was to put on the base of the new approach more realistic primitive notions like regions (in Whitehead's terminology) as abstractions of physical bodies and some simple mereological and topological relations between regions, like one region to be a part of another (**part-of** relation), or two regions to have as a common part a third one (**overlap** relation), or two regions to be in a **contact**, which intuitively means to have at least one common point. This idea does not disregard points at all, but requires they to be introduced in the theory later on by appropriate def-initions. Let us note that part-of and overlap relations are typical for mereology, while its language is too weak to express the contact relation, which has some topological nature. That is why the two disciplines - mereology and topology, had to be integrated in "mereotopology". Probably the name "mereotopology" for the new discipline was used for the first time by Simons [10]. Another name, related to the new approach to geometry, is "Region Based Theory of Space" (RBTS). Survey papers on mereotopology and RBTS are, for instance [1,12]. Let us note that due to its simple language for representing spatial knowledge, mereotopology found applications in some applied areas - see, for instance, the survey papers [2,6].

One of the founders of mereology is Leśnewski. In [10] Leśnewski's system is referred to as the system of Classical Extensional Mereology (CEM). Due to Tarski (see [10], p. 25) the algebraic structure of Leśnewski's mereology is that of complete Boolean algebra with zero deleted. However, deleting the zero element from Boolean algebra complicates the existing Boolean theory making the operation of product $x \cdot y$ a partial operation. Probably mereologists do not like the zero 0 because it is in a sense a "nonexisting individual" while ontology is the science of the existent entities. If one wants to use only first-order language for mereology, the first-order theory of Boolean algebras with zero included can be used. So, Boolean algebras in their mereological interpretation can be considered as a first-order version of CEM. We adopt the following signature for Boolean algebra $\underline{B} = (B, \leq, 0, 1, +, \cdot, ^*)$. The elements of B in the intended mereological meaning can be considered as formal analogs of physical (or spatial) bodies and following Whitehead's terminology they will be called regions. The relation $\leq$ is the Boolean ordering which can be considered as representing the part-of relation. The constant 0 (zero) is now interpreted as the only "non-existing" region, and the constant 1 (unit) is the only region "universe", having as its parts all other regions. The Boolean operations $+$ (sum), $\cdot$ (product), and * (complement) can be considered as operations for obtaining new regions from given ones. Let us note that the overlap relation xOy in the language of Boolean algebras has the following equivalent definitions: xOy iff $(\exists z \neq 0)(z \leq x$ and $z \leq y)$ iff $x \cdot y \neq 0$. Note also that the interpretation of 0 as a "non-existing" region makes possible to define a predicate of ontological existence $E(x)$ "x (ontologically) exists" as follows: $E(x) \leftrightarrow_{def} x \neq 0$. The negation of $E(x)$ will be denoted by $\overline{E}(x)$ and will be considered as a non-existence predicate. We will always consider that $1 \neq 0$, which means that the universal region 1 always ontologically exists. Since this paper will deal with some predicates of ontological existence, the above definition of $E(x)$ in Boolean algebras will be discussed later on with more details.

Let us note that part-of and overlap relations can be expressed by the predicate $E(x)$ as follows.

Part-of relation: $x \leq y$ iff $x \cdot y^* = 0$ iff $\overline{E}(x \cdot y^*)$.

Overlap: xOy iff $(\exists z)(z \neq 0$ and $z \leq x$ and $z \leq y)$ iff $(\exists z)(E(z)$ and $z \leq x$ and $z \leq y)$ iff $E(x \cdot y)$.

The representation theory for Boolean algebras as Boolean algebras of subsets gives standard examples for the first-order version of CEM. This representation theory shows the weakness of this language to represent regions as spatial bodies: each set of points is a spatial body which geometrically and ontologically is not satisfactory and it shows that mereology is not capable to distinguish in regions their boundary and internal points. This also shows that some kinds of contact, as for instance, external contact (of having common only boundary points) is not expressible. CEM is criticized in [10] also for his static nature and that it is not capable to express change in time. Let us mention, however, that Boolean algebra considered as a first-order CEM has one good formal property - it is a decidable first-order theory, which is important for some applications.

1.2   Mereotopology and Contact Algebras

Having in mind the fact that mereology can be identified in a certain sense with Boolean algebra, one suitable algebraic formulation of mereotopology is the notion of contact algebra, which is a Boolean algebra $\underline{B}$ extended with the relation C of contact, satisfying a number of simple first-order axioms. Different versions of contact algebras (with different names) were introduced by several authors (see [1,6,12] for their history), but the simplest one was introduced in [3] just with the name "contact algebra" by the following set of axioms for the contact relation:

(C1) If xCy, then $x \neq 0$ and $y \neq 0$,
(C2) If xCy, then yCx,
(C3) If $xCy, x \leq u$ and $y \leq v$, then uCv,
(C4) If $xC(y + z)$, then xCy or xCz,
(C5) If $x.y \neq 0$, then xCy.

The intended meaning of xCy is "the regions x and y share at least one common point" and because the notion of point is not a primitive notion in contact algebras, the contact relation is introduced axiomatically. The point-based definition of contact as sharing a common point is given in the topological models presented below.

Let us note that axioms (C1), (C3) and (C5) can be rephrased as follows:

(C1) If xCy, then $E(x)$ and $E(y)$,

(C3) If xCy, $\overline{E}(x \cdot u^*)$ and $\overline{E}(y \cdot v^*)$, then uCv,

(C5) If $E(x \cdot y)$, then xCy.

Topological Model of Contact Algebra. The following topological model of contact algebra is given in [3]. Let X be a topological space and let $Int(a)$ and $Cl(a)$ be the interior and the closure of a subset a of X. Namely $Int(a)$ is the union of all open sets included in a and $Cl(a)$ is the intersection of all closed sets containing a. A subset $a \subseteq X$ is called a regular closed set (a region) if $a = Cl(Int(a))$ and let $RC(X)$ be the set of all regular closed sets of X. It is a well known fact that $RC(X)$ is a Boolean algebra under the following definitions: $a \le b$ iff $a \subseteq b, 0 = \emptyset, 1 = X, a+b = a \cup b, a \cdot b = Cl(Int(a \cap b)), a^* = Cl(X \setminus a) = Cl(-a)$. If we define the contact as follows: aCb iff $a \cap b \ne \emptyset$, then $RC(X)$ is a contact algebra, called a topological contact algebra over X. It is proved in [3] that each contact algebra can be represented as a topological contact algebra over a certain topological space X (satisfying some additional properties like compactness etc.). On the base of this representation theory topological models can be considered as the main "standard" topological point-based models of contact algebras.

All relations which can be defined by means of C in the signature of contact algebra will be called mereotopological relations. Relations definable by using only the Boolean signature will be called mereological relations. For instance part-of $x \le y$, overlap xOy and existence predicate $E(x)$ are mereological relations. Thus, the Boolean part of the signature of contact algebra can be considered as its *mereological part*, while the contact C represents the topological part. By means of the contact C one can define other interesting mereotopological relations:

- external contact: $aC^{ext}b$ iff aCb and $a\overline{O}b$,
- non-tangential part-of: $a \ll b$ iff $a\overline{C}b^*$,
- tangential part-of: $a \prec b$ iff $a \le b$ and $a \not\ll b$.

The names of these predicates comes from their topological equivalents.

1.3   The Existence Predicate and Time

As we have seen in the above section, the language of contact algebras as an algebraic version of mereotopology considerably extends the expressive power of mereology. Still contact algebras can be considered as a static theory, not incorporating time and change in time, hence mereotopology in this form can be considered as a **static mereotopology**. However, it was shown in [13–15] how to generalize contact algebras in order to obtain their dynamic versions incorporating both space and time in a point-free abstract definition and obtaining in this way the notion of dynamic contact algebra considered as a version of **dynamic mereotopology**. Point-free here means that neither space points, nor time moments are considered as primitives, fulfilling in this way the White-heads program of building an integrated point-free theory of space and time, mentioned for instance in [17], p. 195.

The idea realized in [13–15] can be roughly described as follows. First we define a concrete space-time structure describing an area of changing regions, called the "snapshot model". Second, we define in this structure several spatio-temporal relations between changing regions and study some of their concrete properties, which will be used further as axioms in the abstract definition. Third, we consider the concrete signature of operations and relations as abstract ones satisfying axioms which are facts in the model. Finally, to show that the abstract definition contains the concrete information of the model, we prove a represen-tation theorem, stating that each abstract system is isomorphic to a concrete one. This representation theorem is based on a special canonical construction extracting from the abstract dynamic algebra the time structure, coordinate contact algebras and reconstructing by them the snapshot model.

For the realization of this strategy we start with a notion of time structure, $\underline{T} = (T, \prec)$, where T is a nonempty set of time points (moments of time) and $\prec$ is the standard **before-after** time relation. Then, to each moment of time $i \in T$ we associate a contact algebra (B_i, C_i) (called the coordinate contact algebra corresponding to the moment i) considered as a snapshot of the static configuration of the changing regions at the moment i. Changing regions in this model (called now dynamic regions) are identified with their series of snapshots $a = < a_i >_{i \in T}$, where the coordinate $a_i \in B_i$ is considered as the region a at the moment i.

Dynamic regions form a Boolean algebra defining Boolean operations, con-stants and relations in a coordinate-wise way. This Boolean algebra is then aug-mented with the following important spatio-temporal relations:

- **Space contact** aC^sb iff $(\exists m \in T)(a_m C_m b_m)$.

Intuitively space contact between a and b means that there is a time point in which a and b are in a contact.

- **Time contact** aC^tb iff $(\exists m \in T)(E_m(a_m)$ and $E_m(b_m))$.

Intuitively time contact between a and b means that there exists a time point in which a and b exist simultaneously.

- **Precedence** $a\mathcal{B}b$ iff $(\exists m, n \in T)(m \prec n$ and $E_m(a_m)$ and $E_n(b_n))$

Intuitively a is in a precedence relation with b means that there is a time point in which a exists which is before a time point in which b exists.

Remark 1. (i) The relations time contact C^t and precedence relation $\mathcal{B}$ have a very high expressive power, namely they can define almost all interesting first-order properties of the before-after time relation, studied in temporal logic. For instance consider the density property of $\prec$:

Dens $i \prec j \rightarrow (\exists k)(i \prec k \wedge k \prec j)$ and the formula **dens** $a\mathcal{B}b \rightarrow a\mathcal{B}p$ or $p^*\mathcal{B}b$.

We have the following definability condition:

Dens is true in the time structure iff **dens** is true in the snapshot model.

(ii) The theory of dynamic algebras developed in [15] introduces special constructs expressing **Past**, **Present** and **Future** making possible to express different time situations like, for instance:

(1) "The region a will always be in a contact with the region b and sometimes it will be a part of c".
(2) "The region a does not exist, but it will exist sometimes in the future".

All this shows that dynamic mereotopology is a rich ontological formalism.

(iii) Let us note that the definitions of C^t and $\mathcal{B}$ in the snapshot model are given by using the existence predicate E from the corresponding coordinate contact algebras. In the abstract model the predicates C^t and $\mathcal{B}$ are responsible in the representation theory of dynamic contact algebras for the construction of canonical time structure and the properties of time. This shows the importance of the predicate of ontological existence and its hidden relations to time.

1.4   Actual Existence, Actual Contact and the Aim of the Paper

In Sect. 1.1 we introduced the predicate of ontological existence $E(x) \leftrightarrow_{def} x \neq 0$ and in Sect. 1.3 we discussed its importance in the theory of dynamic contact algebras. However this predicate has some drawbacks which we want to discuss. First its negation $\overline{E}(x) \leftrightarrow x = 0$, the non-existence predicate, is too strong - it shows in fact that all ontologically non-existing regions are equal to the zero region 0. Hence the predicate $E(x)$ is too weak - there are too many existing regions. However, one can consider in reality different modes of existence and nonexistence. One for, instance, is just the predicate $E(x)$ - when x ceases to exist, x disappeares (annihilates) and becomes 0, so $\overline{E}(x) \rightarrow x = 0$ (the converse implication $x = 0 \rightarrow \overline{E}(x)$ is obvious). Example: burning candle - when the candle burns out it nothing remains, the candle ceases to exist and becomes 0. But there are other examples. Consider, for instance, a small lake, which during the summer has no water. So, during the summer the lake actually does not exist and exists only during the other seasons. During the summer time the lake is not equal to 0, because it still is not totally annihilated. So, it is possible for some region a to be different from 0 and at the same time not to exist, but in some other sense. In the natural language this mode of existence and non-existence is captured quite well by the terms "actual existence" and "actual non-existence". Let us denote the new predicate by $AE(x)$ and its negation by $\overline{AE}(x)$. The notation AE comes from "actual existence" but it can also be associated with the "average mode of existence", because average mode of existence is any of the acting modes of existence in reality. Obviously the predicate $AE(x)$ is not definable in Boolean algebra, so it has to be characterized by a set of reasonable postulates. The aim of this paper is just to find these postulates and to study the related notions. First we will do this in the context of Boolean algebra considered as a kind of first-order CEM. By means of $AE(x)$ we define "actual" analogs of the base mereological relations: $x \leq^a y$ - **actual part-of**, $xO^a y$ - **actual overlap**. We will give set theoretical models of Boolean algebras with the predicate $AE(x)$ and prove the corresponding representation theorem. Then we consider the predicate $AE(x)$ together with the contact relation and propose minimal changes in the axioms of contact replacing accordingly the relations part-of, overlap and existence $E(x)$ from the definition of contact algebra by their "actual" versions: $\leq^a, O^a$ and AE. As a result we obtain a generalization of contact relation which is called **actual contact** - notation $xC^a y$. We prove that AE is definable by C^a, which shows that actual existence has a certain spatial meaning. We present relational and topological models for the obtained system and prove related representation theorems. The last section contains some concluding remarks.

2   Boolean Algebras with a Predicate of Actual Existence

Let $\underline{B}$ be a Boolean algebra considered in its mereological interpretation. In Subsect. 1.4 we discussed some properties of the predicate $E(x) \leftrightarrow_{def} x \neq 0$ interpreted as a predicate of ontological existence and concluded that it is too weak and some natural examples show that there are more strong modes of existence for which we adopt the notation $AE(x)$. The problem is what kind of axioms to take for $AE(x)$ preserving the inclusion $AE \subseteq E$ and having E as a natural special case. One way is to find an abstract characterization of the predicate E and then to take a reasonable relaxation.

Proposition 1. *Let $\underline{B}$ be a Boolean algebra and let $E(x) \leftrightarrow_{def} x \neq 0$. Then:*

(i) $E(x)$ satisfies the following firs-order conditions:

    (AE1) $E(1)$ and $\overline{E}(0)$,
    (AE2) If $E(x)$ and $x \leq y$, then $E(y)$,
    (AE3) If $E(x + y)$, then $E(x)$ or $E(y)$.

(ii) $E(x)$ is the maximal (under inclusion) predicate satisfying the axioms (AE1), (AE2) and (AE3).

Proposition 1 suggests to take the first-order conditions (AE1), (AE2), (AE3) as axioms for the predicate of actual existence $AE(x)$. Since it is a one place predicate it can be identified as usual with a subset of B which allows to write both $AE(x)$ or $x \in AE$. Thus we have the following definition.

Definition 1. *Let $\underline{B} = (\underline{B}, AE)$ be a Boolean algebra with an unary predicate $AE(x)$, called a predicate of **actual existence**, which satisfies the axioms (AE1), (AE2), (AE3). The first-order theory of this system is considered as a First-order CEM (Classical Extensional Mereology) with the predicate of actual (ontological) existence. We denote by $\overline{AE}$ the negation of the predicate AE.*

Remark 2. Axiom (AE1) is obvious: 0 is non-existing in any sense and we may consider 0 as a "totally non-existing" region. Axioms (AE2) and (AE3) together can be replaced by one axiom: $AE(x + y)$ iff $AE(x)$ or $AE(y)$. The implication from left to right is obvious and the implication from right to left implies that it is possible for a region to be actually existing and to have parts which are not actually existing which is acceptable. Example: let's assume that John is actually existing. Obviously his appendicitis is a part of John and assume that John is after a surgery of appendicitis. So, after the surgery the appendicitis is not actually existing part of John. Let us note also that the complement of the predicate AE is a proper ideal in B (see [9] for the definition of ideal).

Proposition 2. *The first-order CEM with the predicate of actual existence $AE(x)$ is decidable.*

This proposition follows directly from Rabin's Theorem 2.11 from [8] and the fact that $\overline{AE}$ is an ideal.

2.1   Several Predicates of Existence

A given Boolean algebra may have several non-equivalent existence predicates satisfying the axioms (AE1), (AE2), (AE3). Example: let (B, AE) be a Boolean algebra with a predicate AE of actual existence and assume that there is a $x_0 \neq 0$ such that $x_0 \notin AE$. Define $NAE =_{def} \{x \in B : x \neq 0 \text{ and } x \notin AE\}$. It is easy to see that this new predicate satisfies all axioms (AE1), (AE2), (AE3), so it is an existence predicate such that $NAE(x_0)$. How to interpret it? We may consider it as a predicate of existence but not as the predicate of actual existence. If we have several predicates of existence, considering one of them as the predicate of actual existence we claim that it corresponds to existence statements for the actual state of affairs. Actual existence is a predicate stated only for the actual state of reality, which may have also other, not actual states. Actual state is the state at the moment, now. We may formulate existence statements for things in the past (before "now") or for the things in the future (after "now") and these will be predicates for "past existence" or "future existence", but not for "actual existence". It is possible also a non-temporal but situational meaning for the case of several predicates of existence. Models for Boolean algebras with two predicates of existence with motivation of their names are given in Sect. 2.4.

2.2   Actual Part-of, Actual Overlap

Having in mind that the standard mereological relations part-of and overlap are expressible by the existence predicate $E(x) \leftrightarrow x \neq 0$ (see Sect. 1.1), analogical definitions with the predicate $AE(x)$ can be considered as their "actual" versions.

Actual part-of: $x \leq^a y \leftrightarrow_{def} \overline{AE}(x \cdot y^*)$.

Actual overlap: $xO^a y \leftrightarrow_{def} (\exists z)(AE(z) \text{ and } z \leq^a x \text{ and } z \leq^a y)$.

It is easy to see that for actual overlap the following is true.

Lemma 1. $xO^a y$ iff $AE(x \cdot y)$.

2.3   Set Models of Boolean Algebras with a Predicate of Actual Existence

Definition 2. *By a **discrete space with actual points** we will understand any pair $\underline{X} = (X, X^a)$, where X is a nonempty set and X^a is a nonempty subset of X, called the set of **actual points** of X. Let $\underline{B}(\underline{X})$ be a Boolean algebra of subsets of X and for $\alpha \subseteq X$ define $AE_{\underline{X}}(\alpha) \leftrightarrow_{def} \alpha \cap X^a \neq \emptyset$. Then it is easy to verify that AE satisfies the axioms (EA1), (EA2) and (EA3). If $\underline{B}(\underline{X})$ be the Boolean algebra of all subsets of X, then $(\underline{B}(\underline{X}), AE_{\underline{X}})$ is called full Boolean algebra with the predicate of actual existence over the space $\underline{X}$.*

By this definition of actual existence, a region α actually exists iff it contains at least one actual point. Having in mind the definitions of actual part-of and actual overlap we can easily obtain:

$\alpha \leq^a \beta$ iff all actual points of α are actual points of β,

$\alpha O^a \beta$ iff α and β share at least one actual point.

Now we shall show that set models of Boolean algebras with the predicate of actual existence are typical in the sense of the following representation theorem.

Theorem 1. *Representation theorem for Boolean algebra with a predicate of actual existence. Let $(\underline{B}, AE)$ be a Boolean algebra with the predicate of actual existence. Then there exists a discrete space $\underline{X} = (X, X^a)$ and an isomorphic embedding h into the full Boolean algebra with predicate of actual existence $(\underline{B}(\underline{X}), AE_{\underline{X}})$ over the space $\underline{X}$.*

Let $(\underline{B}, AE)$ be a Boolean algebra with the predicate of actual existence. Remind that U is an ultrafilter in $\underline{B}$ if it is a subset of B satisfying the following conditions:

(Ult 1) $0 \notin U$ and $1 \in U$,

(Ult 2) If $x \in U$ and $x \leq y$, then $y \in U$,

(Ult 3) If $x, y \in U$, then $x \cdot y \in U$,

(Ult 4) If $x + y \in U$, then $x \in U$ or $y \in U$.

We define a canonical discrete space (X, X^a) associated with $(\underline{B}, AE)$ and an isomorphic embedding h over the Boolean algebra with actual contact over (X, X^a) as follows: define X to be the set $ULT(\underline{B})$ of all ultrafilters of $\underline{B}$ and put X^a to be the set of all ultrafilters contained in AE. Let us call such ultrafilters **actual ultrafilters**. Define h to be the Stone embedding: for $x \in B$ put $h(x) = \{U \in X : x \in U\}$. It is clear from the representation theory of Boolean algebras that h is an embedding from B into $B(\underline{X})$. It can be shown also that h preserves the predicate AE which proves the representation theorem.

Remark 3. **Points as properties of regions.** In the representation theorem for Boolean algebras with actual existence ultrafilters play the role of the (definable) points of B. We say that a point U belongs to a region x iff $U \in h(x)$. Since ultrafilters are certain sets of regions, the question arises why these sets have to be considered as spatial points. And a more general question: if spatial points do not have a separate existence in reality, then what is the real ontological nature of spatial points definable as ultrafilters?

To answer the first question, let us start with the algebra of all subsets of the given set X. Let the points of X be called "real points" and for every real point $x \in X$ define the set $Po(x) = \{\alpha \subseteq X : x \in \alpha\}$. The set $Po(x)$ will be called "abstract point associated to the real point x". The first observation is that the collections of subsets of X in the form $Po(x)$ are ultrafilters in the algebra of all subsets of X. Also we have: for all $x \in X$ and $\alpha \subseteq X, x \in \alpha$ iff $\alpha \in Po(x)$. Let us call the subsets of X "real sets" and for each real set α define its abstract analog $H(\alpha) = \{Po(x) : \alpha \in Po(x)\} = \{Po(x) : x \in \alpha\}$ by an analogy with the Stone mapping h and let $\widehat{X} = \{Po(x) : x \in X\}$. It is easy to see that the following holds: $H(\varnothing) = \varnothing, H(X) = \widehat{X}, \alpha \subseteq \beta$ iff $H(\alpha) \subseteq H(\beta), H(X \setminus \alpha) = \widehat{X} \setminus H(\alpha)$, $H(\alpha \cap \beta) = H(\alpha) \cap H(\beta)$ and $H(\alpha \cup \beta) = H(\alpha) \cup H(\beta)$. All this shows that abstract analogs of real points and real sets can replace the real points and the real sets. In the case of the abstract definition of Boolean algebra we imitate the same procedure, which shows that ultrafilters are good for the definition of points and the Stone mapping is a good way to assign points to the members of the algebra.

As for the second question, "what is the real nature of spatial points in Boolean algebra definable as ultrafilters", the answer is more difficult. Many people have an intuition about points which contradicts the fact to treat them as certain sets of regions. One explanation why points are certain sets of regions is to consider these sets as special properties of regions. Since very often we identify a given property of an object by a subset of the universe to which this object belongs, then ultrafilters (as sets of regions) can be treated as certain spatial properties of regions of mereological kind, related to our intuition of a "region to possess a given point" - "point possession", which is formally presented by region x to belong to an ultrafilter U: $x \in U$. Just by the property "point possession" we can obtain an easy description of the basic mereological constants, relations, and operations from the signature of Boolean algebra. For instance, x is a part of y if all points of x are points of y - this corresponds to the following axiom of ultrafilter: if $x \in U$ and $x \leq y$, then $y \in U$ (and similarly for the Boolean operations and constants). The fact that in a Boolean algebra we may define such "properties" of regions as ultrafilters is quite non-trivial and depends of some versions of the axiom of choice. Let us say that "point possession" is not one property - different ultrafilters define different properties of this kind. This is quite similar with properties of the form "color possession" - each different color defines different property. It can be said that the properties of the type "point possession" can be treated as the basic mereological properties of regions. One motivation for this is the following observation. The function h from the representation theorem assigns to a region x the set $h(x)$ of all ultrafilters containing x, namely all "point possesion" properties of x. Having in mind the Leibniz's definition of equality - "two things are equal if they have the same properties", we see that this can be applied also to regions: two regions are "mereologically equal" if they have the same basic mereological properties, formally - $x = y$ iff $h(x) = h(y)$.

The above reasoning shows the real ontological nature of points treating them as certain spatial properties of regions. Then the statement that points have no separate existence in reality, they exists just as properties of regions, stands quite natural. This treatment is just the same for the case of colors: colors do not have separate existence in reality - they just exists as properties of things.

In a similar way actual points considered as actual ultrafilters can be explained as certain **actual properties**, namely actual properties of the type of "point possession". Because actual ultrafilters are, by definition, all ultrafilters contained in the predicate AE, then a region x actually exists - $x \in AE$, iff there exists at least one actual ultrafilter U such that $x \in U$. So x actually exists if it has at least one actual property of the kind "point possession". This interpretation of the predicate of actual existence gives another intuition of this property, reducing them to the property of the kind of "point possession".

2.4 Cartesian Models for Boolean Algebra with a Predicate of Actual Existence

We will give an algebraic construction which also gives models for Boolean algebras with predicate of actual existence.

Let B_1 and B_2 be two non-degenerate Boolean algebras and let $\underline{B} = B_1 \times B_2$ be their Cartesian product. Define $AE = \{(x_1, x_2) : x_2 \neq 0\}$. Then it is easy to verify that AE satisfies the axioms (AE1), (AE2) and (AE3) for actual existence. It can be proved that every Boolean algebra with predicate of actual existence AE such that AE is not the maximal predicate of existence is representable as a subalgebra of such a Cartesian kind, but we will not do this in this paper. This example gives the following intuition. Assume that each element $x = (x_1, x_2)$ represents x at two situations: x_1 is x at situation 1 and x_2 is x at situation 2, and the situation 2 is considered as the actual situation. Then $(x_1, x_2) \in AE$ just states that "x exists in the actual situation", using for "x exists" the definable in B_2 predicate $E(x) \leftrightarrow_{def} x \neq 0$. The predicate $E_1 = \{(x_1, x_2) : x_1 \neq 0\}$ is just the existence predicate for the situation 1. It is definable by AE as follows: $E_1((x_1, x_2))$ iff $(x_1, x_2) \neq (0, 0)$ and $(x_1, x_2) \notin AE$. So $\underline{B}$ has two predicates of existence but we consider only one of them as the predicate of actual existence - the one which corresponds to the actual situation.

3 Boolean Algebras with Predicates of Actual Existence and Actual Contact

3.1 Abstract Definitions

Let $\underline{B} = (B, AE)$ be Boolean algebra with actual existence. We extend its language with a new relation C^a called **actual contact** by "actualizing" the axioms of contact algebra. Namely we obtain the following definition.

Definition 3. *First definition of BA with actual contact.* Axioms of actual contact:

(AC1) If $xC^a y$, then $AE(x)$ and $AE(y)$,
(AC2) If $xC^a y$, then $yC^a x$,
(AC3) If $xC^a y$ and $y \leq^a z$, then $xC^a z$,
(AC4) If $xC^a(y+z)$, then $xC^a y$ or $xC^a z$,
(AC5) If $xO^a y$, then $xC^a y$.

The triple $\underline{B} = (B, AE, C^a)$, where $\underline{B} = (B, AE)$ is Boolean algebra with actual existence and C^a is the relation of actual contact in B, is called Boolean algebra (BA) with actual contact.

Note that $y \leq^a z \leftrightarrow_{def} y \cdot z^* \in \overline{AE}$ and $xO^a y \leftrightarrow_{def} x \cdot y \in AE$ in the above definition are the relations of actual part-of and actual overlap introduced in Sect. 2. The intended meaning of $xC^a y$ in the point topological models (to be introduced later on) is "x and y share an actual point".

Lemma 2. *In BA with actual contact the predicate of actual existence is definable by the following equivalence: $AE(x)$ iff $xC^a x$.*

This fact says, first, that actual existance AE has certain spatial meaning, and second, that the definition of Boolean algebra with actual contact can be simplified without taking the predicate AE as a primitive notion.

Definition 4. *Second definition of Boolean algebra with actual contact.* The pair $\underline{B} = (B, C^a)$ is called a Boolean algebra with actual contact if it satisfies the following list of axioms:

($C^a 1$) $1C^a 1$, $0\overline{C}^a 0$,
($C^a 2$) $xC^a y$, then $yC^a x$,
($C^a 3$) If $xC^a y$, then $xC^a x$,
($C^a 4$) If $xC^a y$ and $y \leq z$, then $xC^a z$,
($C^a 5$) If $xC^a(y+z)$, then $xC^a y$ or $xC^a z$.
$AC(x) \leftrightarrow_{def} xC^a x$.

Lemma 3. *The two definitions of BA with actual contact are equivalent.*

Lemma 4. *Let $\underline{B} = (B, C^a)$ be a Boolean algebra with actual contact according to the second definition and for $x, y \in B$ define $xCy \leftrightarrow_{def} xC^a y$ or $x \cdot y \neq 0$. Then (B, C) is a contact algebra.*

Remark 4. Lemma 4 shows that Boolean algebra with actual contact is a rich system containing also the standard contact relation. This relation can be used in the representation theory of Boolean algebras with actual contact for defining the topological structure in the set of the definable points.

3.2   Actualized Versions of Some Mereotopological Relations

By means of the relation of actual contact we may define "actualized" versions of some important mereotopological relations.

- Actual external contact $xC^{aext}y \leftrightarrow_{def} xC^a y$ and $x\overline{O}^a y$,
- Actual non-tangential part-of $x \ll^a y \leftrightarrow_{def} x\overline{C}^a y^*$,
- Actual tangential part-of $x \prec^a y \leftrightarrow_{def} x \leq^a y$ and $x \not\ll^a y$.

3.3   Topological Models of Boolean Algebras with Actual Contact

Topological model of BA with actual contact is a slight modification of topological models of contact algebra.

Definition 5. *By a topological space with actual points we mean any pair $\underline{X} = (X, X^a)$ such that X is a nonempty topological space and X^a is a nonempty subset of X. Let $RC(\underline{X})$ be the Boolean algebra of regular-closed subsets of X. For $\alpha, \beta \in RC(\underline{X})$ define actual contact $\alpha C_{\underline{X}}^a \beta \leftrightarrow_{def} \alpha \cap \beta \cap X^a \neq \emptyset$. It is easy to see that axioms for C^a from the second definition of BA with actual contact are fulfilled and that $B(\underline{X}) = (RC(\underline{X}), C_{\underline{X}}^a)$ is a Boolean algebra with actual contact.*

We shall show later on that the above model is typical in a sense that each BA with actual contact is representable as a subalgebra of this topological kind.

3.4   Discrete (Relational) Models of BA with Actual Contact

Definition 6. *Let $\underline{X} = (X, R^a)$ be a relational system with a non-empty set X and a binary relation R^a in X. $\underline{X}$ is called adjacency space with actual adjacency relation if R^a satisfies the following conditions:*

(R1) R^a is a nonempty relation,
(R2) R^a is a symmetric relation: $(\forall x, y \in X)(xRy$ implies $yRx)$, and
(R3) R^a is a quasi-reflexive relation: $(\forall x, y \in X)(xRy$ implies $xRx)$.

Let $B(\underline{X})$ be a Boolean algebra of some (or all) subsets of X and for $\alpha, \beta \in B(\underline{X})$ define $\alpha C_R^a \beta \leftrightarrow_{def} (\exists x \in \alpha)(\exists y \in \beta)(xR^a y)$. It is a routine matter to verify that axioms for actual contact from the second definition are fulfilled.

We shall show in the next section that the above kind of models of actual contact are also typical.

If we want to construct from $\underline{X} = (X, R^a)$ the Boolean algebra with actual contact according to the first definition, we need the set X^a of actual points which now is definable: $X^a = \{x \in X : xR^a x\}$ - the set of all reflexive points of X.

Let us note that adjacency spaces for contact algebras are based on reflexive and symmetric R. Note also that the reflexivity of R is equivalent to the axiom (C5) for contact (see [4]). Since quasi-reflexivity does not imply reflexivity (there are easy examples) the above spaces are more general which implies that C^a does not satisfy the axiom (C5).

3.5   Cartesian Models of Boolean Algebras with Actual Contact

The cartesian models of Boolean algebras with actual existence can be easily modified for Boolean algebras with actual contact. Let B_1 be a Boolean algebra and (B_2, C_2) be a contact algebra and let $B = B_1 \times B_2$ be the Cartesian product of the two Boolean algebras. Define actual contact C^a in B as follows: $(x_1, x_2)C^a(y_1, y_2)$ iff $x_2 C_2 y_2$. There is no problem to verify that axioms for actual contact (from the second definition) are fulfilled. It can be proved that each Boolean algebra with actual contact C^a (with some additional assumptions) can be represented as a subalgebra of such Cartesian model. The intuition of this model comes from the suggested intuition for Cartesian model for actual existence: each object $x = (x_1, x_2)$ is presented at two situations 1 and 2 in which 2 is the actual one. Actual contact is just the (standard) contact of x and y at the actual situation 2.

4   Representation Theory of Boolean Algebras with Actual Contact

4.1   Discrete Representation

We assume in this section that $\underline{B} = (B, C^a)$ is a BA with actual contact according to the second definition (Definition 4). Following [4] we will construct a canonical relational system (X, R^a) related to $\underline{B}$ as follows: we put X to be the set $ULT(\underline{B})$ of all ultrafilters of B and for two ultrafilters U, V define $U R^a V \leftrightarrow_{def} (\forall a \in U)(\forall b \in V)(a C^a b)$.

Lemma 5. *The canonical relational system (X, R^a) of $\underline{B}$ is an adjacency space with actual adjacency relation.*

Consider the Boolean algebra with actual contact associated to $\underline{X} = (X, R^a)$ and let h be the Stone mapping - for $x \in B : h(x) = \{U \in X : x \in U\}$. It is known that h is an isomorphic embedding of B into $B(\underline{X})$. It can be proved that h also preserves the actual contact C^a.

This proves the following representation theorem.

Theorem 2. *Let $\underline{B} = (B, C^a)$ be a BA with actual contact. Then there is an adjacency space $\underline{X} = (X, R^a)$ with actual relation R^a and there exists an embedding h from $\underline{B}$ into the BA with actual contact $B(\underline{X}, C_R^a)$ over $\underline{X}$.*

4.2   Topological Representation

We assume in this section that $\underline{B} = (B, C^a)$ is a BA with actual contact according to Definition 4. First we have to extract from $\underline{B}$ a canonical topological space with actual points $\underline{X} = (X, X^a)$ and an embedding h from $\underline{B}$ into the Boolean algebra with actual contact $B(\underline{X}) = (RC(\underline{X}), C_{\underline{X}}^a)$ over $\underline{X}$ (see Sect. 3.3). To this end we will use the fact that $\underline{B}$ has a definable contact relation C which makes possible the adaptation of the topological representation theory for contact algebras developed in [3] to the case of Boolean algebra with actual contact. The abstract points in the representation theory of contact algebras are called **clans** which will be the elements of X. The new thing now is a modification of clan, called **actual clan**, and actual clans will be just the actual points of the set X^a.

Grills, Clans and Actual Clans

Definition 7. *A subset Γ of B is called a grill if the following conditions are fulfilled:*

(Grill 1) $0 \notin \Gamma$,
(Grill 2) If $a \in \Gamma$ and $a \leq b$, then $b \in \Gamma$,
(Grill 3) If $a + b \in \Gamma$, then $a \in \Gamma$ or $b \in \Gamma$.

Grills were introduced by Choquet (see Thron [11]). It follows from this definition that actual existence is a grill containing 1. Note that the complement of a grill is an ideal and all properties for grills can be deduced from this fact. More information about grills can be found, for instance, in [3]. We mention the following lemma.

Lemma 6

(i) **Grill Lemma.** *Let F be a filter in B and G be a grill in B such that $F \subseteq G$. Then there is an ultrafilter U in B such that $F \subseteq U \subseteq G$.*
(ii) *Every grill coincides with the union of all ultrafilters contained in it.*
(iii) *Let G be a grill and $x \in B$. Then $x^* \in G$ iff $(\forall y \in B)(x + y = 1 \rightarrow y \in G)$.*

Remind also the definable contact C in B: $xCy \leftrightarrow_{def} xC^a y$ or $x \cdot y \neq 0$ (see Lemma 4).

Definition 8. *Clan and actual clan. A subset Γ of B is a **clan** if it is a non-empty grill and satisfies the condition*
(Clan) If $x, y \in \Gamma$, then xCy, where C is the defined contact relation in B.
*A subset Γ of B is an **actual clan**, if it is a non-empty grill and satisfies the condition*
(Clan^a) If $x, y \in \Gamma$, then $xC^a y$.
Denote by $CLANS(\underline{B})$ the set of all clans of $\underline{B}$ and by $CLANS^a(\underline{B})$ - the set of all actual clans of $\underline{B}$.

Clans are introduced for the first time by Thron [11] and were used extensively in the theory of contact algebras in [3], actual clans are new.

In order to study clans and actual clans let us remind some facts about ultrafilters in B. For the discrete representation of BA with actual contact (see Sect. 2) we introduced the canonical structure (X, R^a) where X is the set $ULT(\underline{B})$ of all ultrafilters of B with R^a, çalled a canonical relation for C^a is defined in $ULT(\underline{B})$ as follows: UR^aV iff $(\forall x \in U)(\forall y \in V)(xC^a y)$. It follows by Lemma 5 that (X, R^a) is an adjacency space with actual adjacency relation. Define an ultrafilter U to be a **reflexive ultrafilter** if UR^aU. Let us define now the canonical relation R in the set $ULT(\underline{B})$ for the definable contact C:

URV iff $(\forall x \in U)(\forall y \in V)(xCy)$.

The following lemma is true for R.

Lemma 7

(i) URV iff UR^aV or $U = V$.

(ii) R is a reflexive and symmetric relation.

The next lemma describes clans and actual clans.

Lemma 8

(i) Every ultrafilter is a clan.

(ii) Every reflexive ultrafilter is an actual clan.

(iii) Every actual clan is a clan.

(iv) Let Σ be a non-empty set of ultrafilters such that for any $U, V \in \Sigma$ we have URV and let $\Gamma = \bigcup_{U \in \Sigma} U$. Then Γ is a clan and every clan can be obtained in this way.

(v) Let Σ be a non-empty set of ultrafilters such that for any $U, V \in \Sigma$ we have UR^aV and let $\Gamma = \bigcup_{U \in \Sigma} U$. Then Γ is an actual clan and every actual clan can be obtained in this way.

(vi) All ultrafilters contained in an actual clan are reflexive ultrafilters.

(vii) Let Γ be a clan which is not actual clan. Then Γ is an ultrafilter which is not reflexive.

Corollary 1. $CLANS(\underline{B}) = CLANS^a(\underline{B}) \cup \{U \in ULT(\underline{B}) : U\overline{R}^a U\}$.

Lemma 9

(i) [3] xCy iff there exists a clan Γ such that $x, y \in \Gamma$.

(ii) $xC^a y$ iff there exists an actual clan Γ such that $x, y \in \Gamma$.

(iii) [3] $x \leq y$ iff $(\forall \Gamma \in CLANS(\underline{B})(x \in \Gamma \to y \in \Gamma)$.

The Canonical Topological Space. We construct the canonical topological space with actual points $X(\underline{B}) = (X, X^a)$ corresponding to $\underline{B}$ as follows: put X to be the set of all clans of $\underline{B}$ and put X^a to be the set of all actual clans of $\underline{B}$. Note that X^a is a subset of X. To define a topology in X define the mapping h from B into the set of subsets of X as follows: $h(x) = \{\Gamma \in CLANS(\underline{B}) : x \in \Gamma\}$ and consider the set $\mathbf{B}(X) = \{h(x) : x \in B\}$ as a closed sub-basis for a topology in X. Denote by Int and Cl the operations of interior and closure corresponding to the obtained topology.

Lemma 10

(i) $h(1) = X, h(0) = \emptyset$.

(ii) $h(x + y) = h(x) \cup h(y)$.

(iii) $x \leq y$ *iff* $h(x) \subseteq h(y)$.
(iv) $x = y$ *iff* $h(x) = h(y)$, *especially* $x = 1$ *iff* $h(x) = X$.
(v) $h(x^*) = Cl(-h(x))$, *where* $-h(x) = X \setminus h(x)$.
(vi) xCy *iff* $h(x) \cap h(y) \neq \emptyset$.
(vii) $xC^a y$ *iff* $h(x) \cap h(y) \cap X^a \neq \emptyset$.

Lemma 11. $h(x)$ *is a regular-closed subset of* X.

Before formulating the next statement let us remind some topological notions. A topological space X is **semi-regular** if it has a closed base of regular-closed sets. X has the separation property $T0$, if for every two different points there exists an open set containing one of them and not containing the other. X is compact if it satisfies the following condition: let $\{A_i : i \in I\}$ be a non-empty family of closed sets of X such that for every finite subset $J \subseteq I$ the intersection $\bigcap\{A_i : i \in J\} \neq \emptyset$, then $\bigcap\{A_i : i \in I\} \neq \emptyset$.

Lemma 12 [3,13]. *Let* $\underline{X} = (X, X^a)$ *be the canonical space of* $\underline{B}$. *Then the space* X *is semi-regular, $T0$ and compact.*

Theorem 3. *Topological representation theorem for Boolean algebras with actual contact.* *Let* $\underline{B} = (B, C^a)$ *be a BA with actual contact. Then there exists a topological space with actual points* $\underline{X} = (X, X^a)$ *such that X is a compact and $T0$ semiregular space and there exists an embedding h of $\underline{B}$ into the Boolean algebra with actual contact* $B(\underline{X}) = (RC(\underline{X}, C_{\underline{X}}^a)$ *over* $\underline{X} = (X, X^a)$.

Remark 5. **Atomic and molecular points.** In the representation theory of BA with actual existence we used as abstract points ultrafilters (and actual ultrafilters). Now, in the representation theory for BA with actual contact ultrafilters are not enough and we introduce some additional kind of points - clans (and actual clans). By Lemma 8 (iv) and (v) we see that clans and actual clans are unions of ultrafilters connected by the canonical relations R and R^a correspondingly. So in this case we have two sorts of abstract points - of ultrafilter sort and of clan sort and the later are composed in some way by ultrafilters. This gives an intuition to consider **ultrafilters as "atomic points"** and **clans as "molecular points"**. It is interesting to note that in the boundary of a given region $h(x)$ there are no atomic points, so the two kinds of points have different distributions in a given region. Note also that in the classical Euclidean approach to the theory of space, we have only one sort of points and they have no any internal structure.

Remark 6. In Remark 3 we discussed an interpretation of ultrafilters in BA with actual existence as properties of regions of certain kind - "point possession". In BA with actual contact we have other kinds of spatial points - clans and actual clans and the same questions arise: why clans are good for the new spatial points and what is their real ontological meaning. An additional question is why the topology is definable in just the way as proposed in the canonical construction of the associated space of the corresponding BA with actual contact.

Let us start with a given topological space with actual points $\underline{X} = (X, X^a)$ and let $RC(X)$ be the set of regular-closed subsets of X. In general the space X may not be semi-regular, but we may define a new semi-regular topology in X taking the closed base of the new topology to be the set $RC(X)$. Let us note that the new topology defines the same set of regular-closed subsets of X (see [3]), which shows that changing the topology to semi-regular one is inessential, because we will have the same regions. As from Remark 3 we consider points and subsets of X as "real points" and "real sets". For $x \in X$ define the "abstract point" associated to x by $Po(x) = \{\alpha \in RC(X) : x \in \alpha\}$ and for $\alpha \in RC(X)$ define $H(\alpha) = \{Po(x) : x \in \alpha\}$ and let $\widehat{X} = \{Po(x) : x \in X\}$ and $\widehat{X}^a = \{Po(x) : x \in X^a\}$. Define a semi-regulat topology in the set $\widehat{X}$, considering the set $\{H(a) : a \in RC(X)\}$ as a closed base for the topology. The first observation is that $Po(x)$ is a clan, which shows that the definition of a clan is good for the new kind of spatial point for BA with actual contact. More over the following facts are true:

$H(\varnothing) = \varnothing, H(X) = \widehat{X}, \alpha \subseteq \beta$ iff $H(\alpha) \subseteq H(\beta), H(Cl_X(X \setminus \alpha) = Cl_{\widehat{X}}(\widehat{X} \setminus H(\alpha)), H(Cl_X(Int_X(\alpha \cap \beta)) = Cl_{\widehat{X}}(Int_{\widehat{X}}(H(\alpha) \cap H(\beta))$ and $H(\alpha \cup \beta) = \widehat{H}(\alpha) \cup H(\beta)$, and $\alpha \cap \beta \cap X^a \neq \varnothing$ iff $H(\alpha) \cap H(\beta) \cap \widehat{X}^a \neq \varnothing$.

All this shows that abstract analogs of real points and real sets can replace the real points and the real sets. In the case of the abstract definition of Boolean algebra with actual contact we imitate the same procedure, which shows that clans and actual clans are good for the definition of points and actual points and the Stone mapping is a good way to assign points to the members of the algebra. As for the question of the real ontological meaning of clans and actual clans we can consider them as a kind of mereotopological properties of regions of the type of "point possession", repeating the motivations from Remark 3. The new thing is that these properties are now of mereotopological kind and they are similar, but at the same way different from the corresponding mereological properties of the form "point possession", just because clans are different from ultrafilters and have some topological nature on the base of contact relation.

5   Concluding Remarks

We discussed in this paper possible formal explications of the predicate of ontological existence and its importance in dynamic mereotopology. We introduced an extension of Boolean algebra with a one-place predicate AE with intended meaning of "actual (ontological) existence", considering a mereological meaning of the Boolean signature. Then we extend the Boolean algebra with actual existence with a two place relation C^a with the intended meaning of "actual contact", obtaining in this way a generalization of the notion of contact algebra introduced in [3]. We present natural models for actual existence and actual contact and proved the intended representation theorems showing that the formal systems correspond to the given models. We plan to develop the theory of dynamic contact algebras based on the notion of actual existence and actual contact. Another thing which remains to be done is the following. There are extensions of contact algebras with several additional axioms which require special, more good topological models and representation theorems. These are the following axioms:

(Con) If $x \neq 0, 1$, then xCx^* - connectedness axiom.

(Ext) $(\forall z)(xCz \leftrightarrow yCz) \rightarrow x = y$, extensionality axiom.

(I) $x \ll y \rightarrow (\exists z)(x \ll z \ll y)$ - interpolation axiom. Here $x \ll y$ is the definable predicate of non-tangential part-of $x\overline{C}y^*$. This axiom is known also as Efremovič axiom in the following equivalent form

$x\overline{C}y$ implies $(\exists z)(x\overline{C}z \text{ and } z^*\overline{C}y)$.

For instance axiom (Con) is true in contact algebras over connected spaces and contact algebras with (Con) are representable in connected spaces. All results concerning the representation theory of contact algebras extended with some or all of these axioms can be found in [3]. Adding these axioms to BA with actual contact for the definable contact C we may repeat the results from [3] and obtain representation theorems in some T1 and T2 topological spaces (with actual points). In the corresponding representation theorems for T1 and T2 spaces other abstract points are used. In such cases Remarks 3 and 6 have to be stated and rephrased again for the new kinds of abstract points, which shows that mereotopological properties of the form "point possession" depend on the corresponding mereotopology which requires different notion of abstract spatial point.

The above axioms can be formulated also for the actual contact and it will be interesting to see the effect of these axioms for the required models and for the expected representation theory.

References

1. Bennett, B., Düntsch, I.: Axioms, algebras and topology. In: Aiello, M., Pratt, I., van Benthem, J. (eds.) Handbook of Spatial Logics, pp. 99–160. Springer, Dordrecht (2007). doi:10.1007/978-1-4020-5587-4_3
2. Cohn, A., Renz, J.: Qualitative spatial representation and reasoning. In: van Hermelen, F., Lifschitz, V., Porter, B. (eds.) Handbook of Knowledge Representation. Elsevier, Amsterdam (2008)
3. Dimov, G., Vakarelov, D.: Contact algebras and region-based theory of space: a proximity approach I. Fundamenta Informaticae **74**(2–3), 209–249 (2006)
4. Düntsch, I., Vakarelov, D.: Region-based theory of discrete spaces: a proximity approach. In: Nadif, M., Napoli, A., SanJuan, E., Sigayret, A. (eds.) Proceedings of Fourth International Conference Journées de l'informatique Messine, Metz, France, pp. 123–129 (2003). Journal version in: Ann. Math. Artif. Intell. **49**(1–4), 5–14 (2007)
5. Engelking, R.: General Topology. PWN, Warsaw (1977)
6. Hahmann, T., Gröuninger, M.: Region-based theories of space: mereotopology and beyond. In: Hazarika, S. (ed.) Qualitative Spatio-Temporal Representation and Reasoning: Trends and Future Directions, pp. 1–62. IGI Publishing, Hershey (2012)
7. de Laguna, T.: Point, line and surface as sets of solids. J. Philos. **19**, 449–461 (1922)

8. Rabin, M.O.: Decidability of second-order theories and automata on infinite trees. Trans. AMS **141**, 1–35 (1969)
9. Sikorski, R.: Boolean Algebras. Springer, Berlin (1964)
10. Simons, P.: PARTS. A Study in Ontology. Clarendon Press, Oxford (1987)
11. Thron, W.J.: Proximity structures and grills. Math. Ann. **206**, 35–62 (1973)
12. Vakarelov, D.: Region-based theory of space: algebras of regions, representation theory and logics. In: Gabbay, D., et al. (eds.) Mathematical Problems from Applied Logics II. New Logics for the XXIst Century, pp. 267–348. Springer, New York (2007). doi:10.1007/978-0-387-69245-6_6
13. Vakarelov, D., Mereotopology, D.: Dynamic mereotopology: a point-free theory of changing regions. I. Stable and unstable mereotopological relations. Fundamenta Informaticae **100**(1–4), 159–180 (2010)
14. Vakarelov, D.: Dynamic mereotopology II: axiomatizing some Whiteheadian type space-time logics. In: Bolander, T., Braüner, T., Ghilardi, S., Moss, L. (eds.) Advances in Modal Logic, vol. 9, pp. 538–558. King's College, London (2012)
15. Vakarelov, D.: Dynamic mereotopology III. Whiteheadean type of integrated point-free theories of space and time. Part I. Algebra Logic **53**(3), 191–205 (2014). Part II. Algebra Logic **55**(1), 9–197 (2016). Part III. Algebra Logic **55**(3), 181–197 (2016)
16. Vakarelov, D.: Mereotopologies of predicates of actual existence and actual contact, submitted
17. Whitehead, A.N.: The Organization of Thought. William and Norgate, London (1917)
18. Whitehead, A.N.: Science and the Modern World. The MacMillan Company, New York (1925)
19. Whitehead, A.N.: Process and Reality. MacMillan, New York (1929)

Path Planning Based on Potential Fields from Rough Mereology

Lukasz Zmudzinski and Piotr Artiemjew$^{(\boxtimes)}$

Faculty of Mathematics and Computer Science,
University of Warmia and Mazury in Olsztyn, Olsztyn, Poland
contact@zmudzinski.me, artem@matman.uwm.edu.pl

Abstract. This paper focuses on path planning for a remote robotic agent using rough mereology potential field method. We test the proposed path-creation and path-finding algorithms and propose working alternative versions. Furthermore we apply path smoothing with custom collision detection to further optimize the route from the robot initial position to the goal.

Keywords: Robotics · Rough mereology · Path planning · Robot navigation · Mereogeometry

1 Introduction

Rough mereology [1] as a paradigm is successfully used in various fields of computer science: robotics [2–4], medical analysis [5,6], etc. In this work we have tested the path planning algorithm based on mereological potential field, where the path is smoothed and obstacle avoidance procedure is applied. We have performed the real time experiment with exemplary mobile robot, which is controlled via P-controller based on the compass reads and the camera based localization. In the next section, we will describe the process of creating the potential force field using rough mereology.

2 Rough Mereology in Intelligent Agent Control

Rough mereology based reasoning employs the notion of a rough inclusion $\mu(x, y, r)$, which relation needs x is a part of y to a degree of at least r. As our reasoning is concerned with spatial objects, the rough inclusion involved in our reasoning is the one defined as $\mu(X, Y, r)$ if and only if $\frac{|X \cap Y|}{X} >= r$, where X, Y are n-dimensional solids and $|X|$ is the n-volume of X. We consider in this work a planar case of an autonomous mobile robot moving in a 3-dimensional environment, hence, our spatial objects X, Y are figures assumed concept regions and $|X|$ is the area of X. The rough inclusion $\mu(X, Y, r)$ is applied in the construction of the mereological potential field. Elements of this field are square and the distance between them is defined as

$$K(X, Y) = min\{max_r\mu(X, Y, r)\}, max_s\mu(Y, X, s)\}.$$

© Springer International Publishing AG 2017
L. Polkowski et al. (Eds.): IJCRS 2017, Part II, LNAI 10314, pp. 158–168, 2017.
DOI: 10.1007/978-3-319-60840-2_11

The construction of the field is described in Sect. 3. The robot movement through the field to the goal is driven by waypoints defined inductively: the next waypoint is the centroid of the union of set of field squares closest to the square containing the current waypoint with respect to the distance $K(X, Y)$.

3   Square Fill Algorithm

In this paper we are using variations of the **Square Fill Algorithm** as proposed by [2]. The result of the algorithm can be seen on Fig. 1.

1. Define initial values:
   - Set **current distance** to the goal: $d = 0$,
   - Set algorithm **direction** to *clockwise*,
2. Create an empty queue Q:

$$Q = \emptyset \tag{1}$$

3. Add to queue Q the first **potential field** $p(x, y, d)$, where x, y describe the location of the field and d represents the **current distance** to the goal:

$$Q \cup \{p(x, y, d)\} \tag{2}$$

4. Enumerate through Q,
5. If $(\{p_k(x, y, d)\} \cap F) \vee (\{p_k(x, y, d)\} \cap C)$ where $p_k(x, y, d)$ is the current potential field, F is a set of already created potential fields and C is a set of collision objects, then remove the current field $p_k(x, y, d)$ from Q and go back to point **4**,
6. Add the current potential field $p_k(x, y, d)$ to the created potential fields set F:

$$F \cup \{p_k(x, y, d)\} \tag{3}$$

7. Increase the **current distance** to the goal:

$$d = d(p_k) + 0.01 \tag{4}$$

8. Define neighbours depending on the current **direction**:
   - *clockwise* as N:

$$N = \left\{ \begin{array}{l} p_0 = p(x - d, y, d), \\ p_1 = p(x - d, y + d, d), \\ p_2 = p(x, y + d, d), \\ p_3 = p(x + d, y + d, d), \\ p_4 = p(x + d, y, d), \\ p_5 = p(x + d, y - d, d), \\ p_6 = p(x, y - d, d), \\ p_8 = p(x - d, y - d, d) \end{array} \right\} \tag{5}$$

– *anticlockwise* as N':

$$N' = \begin{cases} p_0 = p(x - d, y - d, d), \\ p_1 = p(x, y - d, d), \\ p_2 = p(x + d, y - d, d), \\ p_3 = p(x + d, y, d), \\ p_4 = p(x + d, y + d, d), \\ p_5 = p(x, y + d, d), \\ p_6 = p(x - d, y + d, d), \\ p_8 = p(x - d, y, d) \end{cases} \tag{6}$$

9. Add neighbours to queue Q depending on current direction:
   – If **direction** is *clockwise* then: $Q \cup N$,
   – If **direction** is *anticlockwise* then: $Q \cup N'$,
10. Change the current **direction** to the opposite,
11. Remove the current potential field $p_k(x, y, d)$ from the queue Q,
12. if $Q(p) = \emptyset$ then finish, else go to **4**.

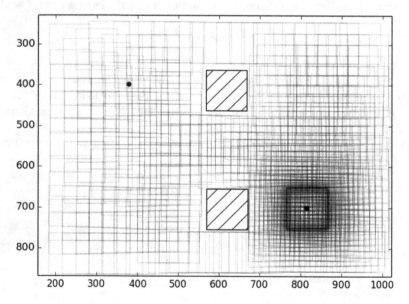

Fig. 1. The potential field created by the Square Fill Algorithm. The white squares represent individual potential cells, hatched squares represent obstacles. The robot initial position and target goal are represented by dots - the left one is the robot initial position

3.1   Path Finding

We are using the **Path Search Algorithm** proposed by [2].

```
IF robot position is equal to goal position
    END
SET the current field to closest to robot
WHILE goal is not found
    ADD field with the smallest mereological
    distance from the current point
    SET the current field to field
END
```

The algorithm can be divided into three steps:

- Checking, if the robot initial position is equal to the goal position,
- Finding the closest field to the robot,
- Moving through potential fields with the smallest mereological distance from the current point until we reach the goal.

4   Extending the Algorithm

After going through tests with the **Square Fill Algorithm** and the generated path, we created a set of changes to the original ideology: neighbouring potential fields creation and path smoothing.

4.1   Type Variation

The default **Square Fill Algorithm** alternates between clockwise and anti-clockwise methods while creating its potential field neighbours. We experimented with possible outcomes:

- Clockwise variation, always using the N set,
- Anticlockwise variation, always using the N' set (Fig. 2).

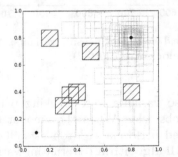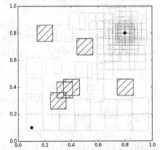

Fig. 2. Potential field on the left was created by the **Clockwise variation**, the one on the right by the **Anticlockwise variation**.

Depending on the complexity of the map and placement of the robot, goal and obstacles different results were produced. For a simple map containing two obstacles (as seen on Fig. 3) the following algorithm time and path length (in pixels) was returned:

- **Alternating**
    - Path creation time: 2234.52 ms
    - Total distance: 557.21 px
- **Clockwise**
    - Path creation time: 2370.07 ms
    - Total distance: 540.86 px
- **Anticlockwise**
    - Path creation time: 2178.11 ms
    - Total distance: 546.27 px

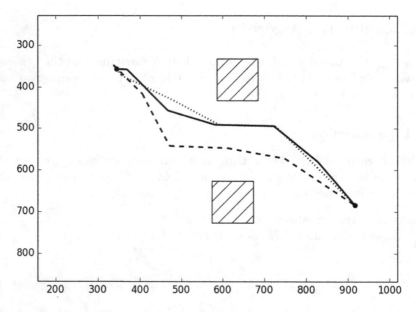

Fig. 3. Comparison of created paths for a real environment using variants: **Alternating** (solid), **Clockwise** (dashed) and **Anticlockwise** (dotted).

The **Clockwise** and **Anticlockwise** variants were working better (and faster) in environments without many obstacles. When the amount of obstacles was increased (10+), we experienced performance drop as well as issues with path-finding. The default **Square fill algorithm** (alternating variant) was working much better in such situations. In order to improve our results, we tried to smooth the created paths, as seen in Sect. 4.2.

4.2   Path Smoothing

After the path from the robot initial position to the goal is created, we are applying a smoothing algorithm, to make the route optimal. We then run the presented algorithm n times, until we get a satisfying result:

1. We apply a chosen **data weight** α and move the position of the point x_k depending on the position of the previous x_{k-1} and next x_{k+1} point on the given path:

$$x_k = x_k + \alpha(x_{k-1} + x_{k+1} - 2x_k) \tag{7}$$

2. Next we are counter balancing the updated position $x + k$ with a chosen **smooth weight** β, so that a straight line isn't created.

$$y_k = y_k + \beta(x_k - y_k) \tag{8}$$

The problem we encountered after going through the smoothing algorithm, is that collisions were ignored, thus creating a path that wasn't usable for the robotic agent as seen on Fig. 4.

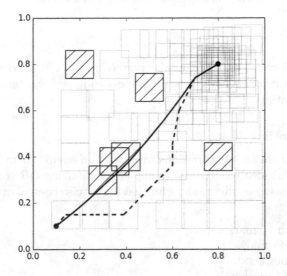

Fig. 4. The figure shows output smoothed path as compared to the original route.

We modified the standard smoothing algorithm, by adding custom conditions, to keep a safe distance from the robot to possible collision fields, as it can be seen on Fig. 5. The final algorithm can be represented as:

```
ITERATE n times
     COMPUTE position applying data weight
     UPDATE position applying smoothing weight
     IF position distance < collision distance
          CONTINUE
     ELSE
          WRITE position
END
```

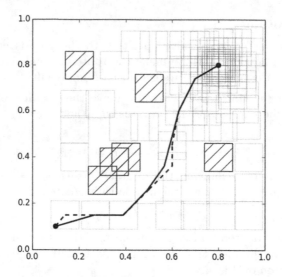

Fig. 5. Custom smoothing algorithm output.

5   Testing

Testing was performed using a top observer (camera, QR marker recognition) and a LEGO Mindstorms NXT robot. The test code was written in python and is available on Github [7].

5.1   Map Creation

To test the algorithm and its variations we needed an environment for the robotic agent (Fig. 6). Our idea was to create map elements using QR code markers, in order to make it easily configurable, while having precise control over key element positions:

- Robot position (1 marker),
- Planned goal (1 marker),
- Obstacles (2 markers),
- Map bounds (4 markers).

To recognize markers, marker ids and their x, y positions through camera output we used **OpenCV**[8] and **Python AR Markers** [9]. Once we got information about all map markers, we used the values as input for our path finding algorithm. All positions were based on the camera image pixel positions (meaning the start point $(0, 0)$ was on the top-left side of the created map).

5.2   Robot Control

We used the **LEGO Mindstorms NXT 2.0** robot for our tests. In order to be able to run the agent through the desired path we used the **NXT Python** library [10].

Fig. 6. Test environment based on Augmented Reality - see the video [11].

Each **Robot** object, had the following properties:

- Motor access (Port B and C),
- Compass sensor access (Port 4),
- NXT Brick reference,
- Current position (relative to map),
- Desired goal (next point on path to goal),
- Robot North (relative to map top).

The first step after connecting to the robot, was setting the **Robot North** property, in order to set a relative point to the map (to allow easier path-following). Each time the Robot marker was found, the robot was establishing movement based on the **P-Controller**.

5.3 P-Controller

The robot we used in experimental part is equipped with the compass sensor, which allows tracking the fixed direction. After the path is created and smoothed with obstacle avoidance mode, we obtain the set of coordinates, which we can use to reach the goal. The robot is localised in real time based on the camera view with use of robot's marker detection. The goal position can vary, but in each run of experimentations is chosen as a static point.

With assumption that (x, y) is the current robot position and (x', y') is the next point on the route to the goal. And that the $(0, 0)$ position is on the left top side of map. To obtain the proper direction in range $[0, ..., 359]$, where 0 is the North, 90 is the East, 180 is South, and 270 is West, for path tracking we use the estimation of direction based on these points considering the following options.

```
IF  x == x' and  y < y':
    direction = 180
IF  x == x' and  y > y'
    direction = 0
IF  y == y' and  x < x'
    direction = 90
IF  y == y' and  x > x'
    direction = 270
```

Assuming that $c = \sqrt{a^2 + b^2}$, $alpha = arccos(\frac{a}{c}) * (\frac{180.}{\pi})$,

```
IF  x < x' and  y < y'
    a = x' - x,  b = y' - y,  direction = 90 + alpha
IF  x > x' and  y < y'
    a = y' - y,  b = x - x',  direction = 180 + alpha
IF  x > x' and  y > y'
    a = y - y',  b = x - x',  direction = 360 - alpha
IF  x < x' and  y > y'
    a = y - y',  b = x' - x,  direction = alpha
```

Considering the new north direction of the map, we have to convert direction as follows,

$$direction = (direction + (360 - north\_direction\_of\_map))\%360 \qquad (9)$$

After goal direction estimation, we use P-controller to drive to the next points. Our version of controller use the conversion of compass readings according to the current goal direction. Conversion consists of the following mapping:

```
values  [direction, direction +1,..., direction +180]
are  converted  into  [0,1,...,180]
values  [direction, direction −1,..., direction −179]
are  converted  into  [−1,−2,...,−179]
```

The conversion can be obtain based on the following steps,

```
current_compass_reading −= direction,
orient=current_compass_reading;
IF  orient > 180:
    orient −= 360
IF  orient < −180
    orient += 360
```

and the P controller works as follows,

```
speed_wheel_1 = speed
speed_wheel_2 = speed
cte = orient
  IF  cte <= 0:
    IF  |cte| > precision:
        speed_wheel_1 = −speed_wheel_2
    ELSE:
        speed_wheel_1 = speed_wheel_2 + (ksi * cte)
  IF  cte > 0:
    IF  cte > precision:
        speed_wheel_2 = −speed_wheel_1
    ELSE:
        speed_wheel_2 = speed_wheel_1 − (ksi * cte)
  self.motor_b.run(speed_wheel_1, False)
  self.motor_c.run(speed_wheel_2, False)
```

where *cte* is the cross track error, and *ksi* is the steering scalar, *orient* is the current compass reading.

6 Conclusion

In this work we have developed three variants of an algorithm for the problem of path planning based on the mereological potential field. An additional problem was to smooth the path and use the obstacle avoidance mode during smoothing. The path algorithm was tested in the robotic laboratory - see [11]. To achieve our goal we have used a mobile robot equipped with electronic compass sensor and a camera used for robot localisation. Our tests demonstrate the effectiveness of path planning, the optimal path is generated in a fast way, robot can effectively reach the goal position tracking the points of path. We have tested variants where the potential field is generated clockwise, anticlockwise and alternately. The experiments show that the two first variants are more effective for simple maps, with small number of obstacles, but in case of complex maps the alternating variant wins in most cases. In our future work, we plan to apply the various types of potential field generation algorithms and to apply it to the other robots including Nao humanoidal robot. The other direction of further research is to apply the idea of path planning to three dimensions with applications to drones in mind.

Acknowledgements. This research has been supported by a grant 23.610.007-300 from the Ministry of Science and Higher Education of the Republic of Poland, and grant 23.620.0010-300 for young scientists from Department of Mathematics and Computer Sciences of University of Warmia and Mazury in Olsztyn.

References

1. Polkowski, L.: Rough mereology: a new paradigm for approximate reasoning. Int. J. Approx. Reason. **15**(4), 333–365 (1996)
2. Osmialowski, P.: Planning and Navigation for Mobile Autonomous Robots Spatial Reasoning in Player/Stage System (2011)
3. O'smiaɪowski, P., Polkowski, L.: Spatial reasoning based on rough mereology: a notion of a robot formation and path planning problem for formations of mobile autonomous robots. In: Peters, J.F., Skowron, A., Słowiński, R., Lingras, P., Miao, D., Tsumoto, S. (eds.) Transactions on Rough Sets XII. LNCS, vol. 6190, pp. 143–169. Springer, Heidelberg (2010). doi:10.1007/978-3-642-14467-7_8
4. Szmigielski, A., Polkowski, L.: Computing from words via rough mereology in mobile robot navigation. In: Proceedings of the 2003 IEEE/RSJ International Conference on Intelligent Robots and Systems, (IROS 2003) (2003)
5. Artiemjew, P.: Rough mereology classifier vs simple DNA microarray gene extraction methods. Int. J. Data Min. Model. Manag. Spec. Issue: Pattern Recogn. **6**(2), 110–126 (2014)
6. Klinov, P., Mazlack, J.L.: On possible applications of rough mereology to handling granularity in ontological knowledge. In: Proceedings of the Twenty-Second AAAI Conference on Artificial Intelligence, 22–26 July 2007, Vancouver, British Columbia, Canada (2007)
7. Mereology Camera Navigation. https://github.com/lukzmu/mereology-camera-navigation

168   L. Zmudzinski and P. Artiemjew

8. OpenCV. http://opencv.org
9. Python AR Markers. https://github.com/DebVortex/python-ar-markers
10. NXT Python. https://github.com/Eelviny/nxt-python
11. The result of tests in the video. https://youtu.be/UrGvUoj_yeI

Three-Way Decisions, Uncertainty, Granular Computing

Three-Way Dicision Community Detection Algorithm Based on Local Group Information

Jie Chen[1,2], Liandi Fang[1,2], Yanping Zhang[1,2(✉)], Shu Zhao[1,2], Ling Zhang[1,2], Fulan Qian[1,2], Feng Liu[1,2], Xiangyang Wang[3], and Xuegang Hu[4]

[1] Key Laboratory of Intelligent Computing and Signal Processing of Ministry of Education, Hefei 230601, Anhui, People's Republic of China
zhangyp2@gmail.com
[2] School of Computer Science and Technology, Anhui University,
Hefei 230601, Anhui, People's Republic of China
[3] Anhui Electrical Engineering Professional Technique College,
Hefei 230051, Anhui, People's Republic of China
[4] School of Computer and Information, Hefei University of Technology,
Hefei 230009, Anhui, People's Republic of China
http://ailab.ahu.edu.cn

Abstract. In network, nodes are joined together in tightly knit groups. Local group information is used to search the natural community. It can be crucial to help us to understand the functional properties of the networks and detect the true community structure. In this paper, we propose an algorithm called Three-way Decision Community Detection Algorithm based on Local Group Information(LGI-TWD) to detect community structure by using local group information. Firstly, we define sub-communities of each node v. Node v and v's neighbors which are reachable to each other construct one sub-communities of node v. Then, each sub-communities is regarded as a granular, and then hierarchical structure is constructed based on granulation coefficient. Finally, a further classification for boundary region's nodes can be done according to belonging degree. Compared with other community detection algorithms (N-TWD, CACDA, GN, NFA, LPA), the experimental results on six real world social networks show that LGI-TWD gets higher modularity value Q and more accurate communities.

Keywords: Communities · Three-way decision · Local group information · Sub-community

1 Introduction

Many complex networks in society, nature, and technology display a common feature, called community structure [1]. Communities are groups of vertices, many links connect vertices of the same group and comparatively few links join vertices of different groups [1,2].Various complex network examples include

© Springer International Publishing AG 2017
L. Polkowski et al. (Eds.): IJCRS 2017, Part II, LNAI 10314, pp. 171–182, 2017.
DOI: 10.1007/978-3-319-60840-2_12

social networks in the Internet, interpersonal networks in social systems, neuronal networks and protein interaction networks in ecosystems. Therefore, many algorithms have been proposed to detect communities. With a further study, overlapping problem of community has attracted much research attention. Overlapping nodes play a special role in complex network system. How to divide the overlapping nodes into a single community to achieve non-overlapping community is crucial to reveal abundant hidden information and help us to understand the functional properties of the networks [3, 4].

In recent years, a great number of algorithms have been proposed to detect nonoverlapping community. Two of most classical algorithms are GN algorithm and Newman Fast Algorithm (NFA). GN algorithm [5]measures the importance of each edge by betweenness. Newman Fast Algorithm (NFA)[6] obtains the optimization depending on modularity. Zhao et al. [7] proposed Tolerance Granulation based Community Detection Algorithm (TGCDA), which uses tolerance relation (namely tolerance granulation) to granulate a network hierarchically. Generally, these methods are suitable for various networks and most of them can perform well. However, these algorithms only use the traditional two-way decisions which takes the decision simply according to present information for acceptance and rejection, regardless of whether information is lacking. This approach may result in wrong decisions when the information is insufficient. So the three-way decision theory is introduced into non-overlapping community detection to deal with overlapping problem.

Three-way decision theory has been proposed by Professor Yao [8], which can solve the uncertainty problem effectively. The main idea of three way decision theory [9, 10] is to divide the whole region of discourse into three parts: positive region (POS), negative region (NEG) and boundary region (BND). Different parts were adopted different ways to solve respectively. The positive decision rules generated by positive region make decision of acceptance. The negative decision rules generated by negative region make decision of rejection. With the difference between the two-way decisions of acceptance or rejection, the boundary region leads to a third way of decision, namely noncommitment or defrement [11], and the problem in the boundary region will be further handled to make the right judgement to achieve final two-way decision. Three-way decision has been widely used in many applications of uncertain information [12–17].

In our previous work, three-way decision was introduced into non-overlapping community division and an algorithm of three-Way Decisions Based on Nonoverlapping Community Division was proposed, shorted by N-TWD. N-TWD can get communities by initial granulation operation. And then hierarchical granulation is used to acquire final communities. The granules are regarded as communities so that the granulation for a network is actually the community partition of the network. N-TWD algorithm is based on hierarchical granulation. An original granular contains n nodes and its all neighborhood nodes. However, it get communities which consist of nodes loosely connected. How to get the small, tightly connected overlapping communities are valuable to further study.

As we all know, the property of community structure, in which network nodes are joined together in tightly knit groups, between which there are only looser connections [1]. Therefore, local group nodes information can be used to search for the natural community of each node. For example, in a social network, separate sub-communities may represent the groups of the individual's friends from college, friends from senior, acquaintances from work, and so on. When we consider the subgraph immediately around node v, those of v's neighbors that know one another from the same community are likely to be better connected to one another than to those of v's neighbors that v knows from a different group (e.g., v's friends from college likely know each other, but are less likely to know v's co-workers).

Therefore, we further improve the initial granulation method of N-TWD's and propose Three-way Decision Community Detection Algorithm based on Local Group Information (LGI-TWD)in this paper. Firstly, sub-communities are constructed by the node v and v's neighbors which are reachable to each other. Secondly, these sub-communities which satisfy granulation coefficient are hierarchically merged to construct hierarchical structure. Finally, a further partition for boundary region's nodes can be done according to the belonging degree.

The rest of the paper is organized as follows: The related work was briefly reviewed in Sect. 2; In Sect. 3, local group information algorithm which can identify sub-communities in network G, and we combine a community partition algorithm which based on three way decision theory to form the final non-overlapping community. In Sect. 4, we display and analyze the experimental results; Finally, the paper presents the summary in Sect. 5.

2 Related Basic Concepts

In this section, hierarchical granulation process and three region of community detection representation were reviewed. And index of community evaluation also was given.

2.1 Hierarchical Granulation

In our previous work, N-TWD got overlapping communities by initial granulation operation. Each node in the network was regarded as an original granule $Gr_i = Granule\,(v_i)$ which formed by the neighbor nodes of v_i. And then the granule set $Gr = \{Gr_i \,|\, \forall\, v_i \in V, Gr_i = Granule\,(v_i)\}$ was obtained by initial granulation operation $Gran\,(G, Gr)$. To get hierarchical overlapping communities structure Gr_i^{m+1}, two granules Gr_i^m and Gr_j^m from m-th layer comply granulation operations. The process was finished until the granulation coefficient was not satisfied granulation coefficient condition and hierarchical granulation structure of $Gr^1, Gr^2, \ldots Gr^m$ were formed, a granule set Gr^l with maximum Q which existed overlapping community was selected to achieve the final non-overlapping community.

Definition 1. Granulation Coefficient [18]: $f(Gr_i^m, Gr_j^m)$:

$$f(Gr_i^m, Gr_j^m) = \frac{\|\, Gr_i^m \cap Gr_j^m \,\|}{\|\, Gr_i^m \cup Gr_j^m \,\|}, Gr_i^m, Gr_j^m \in Gr^m \tag{1}$$

Definition 2. Granulation Operations: $GO(Gr_i^m, Gr_j^m)$:

$$Gr_i^{m+1} \leftarrow Gr_i^m \cup Gr_j^m$$
$$Gr^{m+1} \leftarrow Gr^m + Gr_i^{m+1} - Gr_i^m - Gr_j^m \qquad (2)$$

2.2   Three Region of Community Detection

Based on the three-way decision theory, the result of overlapping communities structure can be defined as positive region, negative region and boundary region.

1. Boundary region (BND(Gr_i, Gr_j)): the overlapping nodes between Gr_i and Gr_j, $BND = Gr_i \cap Gr_j$
2. Positive region (POS(Gr_i, Gr_j)): the non-overlapping nodes of left community Gr_i, $POS = Gr_i - BND$
3. Negative region (NEG(Gr_i, Gr_j)): the non-overlapping nodes of right community Gr_j, $NEG = Gr_j - BND$.

So, three regions of overlapping communities are given as:

$$BND = \bigcup(BND(Gr_i, Gr_j));$$
$$POS = \bigcup(POS(Gr_i, Gr_j)); \qquad (3)$$
$$NEG = \bigcup(NEG(Gr_i, Gr_j));$$

Therefore, granulation coefficient can be represented as follows:

Granulation Coefficient Based on Three Way Decision Theory:

$$GC = \frac{||BND||}{||POS + NEG + BND||}. \qquad (4)$$

2.3   Modularity Q

The most widely used and accepted metric designed specifically for the purpose of measuring quality of a network division into communities is modularity (Q)[19], calculated as follows.

$$Q = \frac{1}{2m} \sum_{ij} (A_{ij} - \frac{k_i k_j}{2m})\delta(C_i, C_j) \qquad (5)$$

Where i, j are two arbitrary vertices, m are the total number of the networks, ($A_{i,j}$) is the element of adjacency matrix. The value ranges from $Q = 0$, when the within-community edges are no better than random, to $Q = 1$. Generally speaking, the value of Q typically range from about 0.3 to 0.7 real-world networks.

3 Three-Way Decision Community Detection Algorithm Based on Local Group Information

In this section, we firstly define sub-communities of each node v (shorted by $SubC(v)$) as a original granular based on Local Group Information which truly produce overlapping community's structure. Then final non-overlapping community structure is obtained by using the three-way decision community detection algorithm.

3.1 Sub-communities of Each Node v Based on Local Group Information

Local Group Information can predict the change rule of network and grasp potential function better, thus it can help us to understand the common preference and group behaviors of the networks.

To get communities which consist of nodes tightly connected, each node v in network is iterated, and one or more sub-communities $SubC(v)$ which contain node v and node v's partial neighbors can be created. Nodes in one sub-community are reachable to each other. The same sub-community may be created multiple times, and we allow multiple copies of the same sub-community, but one may consider only one copy.

Given an undirected network $G(V, E)$, where V is the set of vertices and E is the set of edges. For $\forall v \in V$, Let $L(v)$ notes the neighbor notes set of node v. For each $v \in V$, we can get sub-communities $SubC(v) = \{C^i(v) = (V^i(v), E^i(v))\}$.

Where $SubC(v)$ means the node v and sub-communities around v. An example of sub-community is shown in Fig. 1. Assume node A is regarded as the center $L(A) = \{B, C, D, E, F\}$. Therefore, sub-community $SubC(A) = \{SubC1 = \{A, B, C, D\}, SubC2 = \{A, F, E\}\}$.

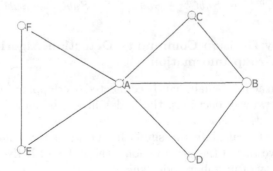

Fig. 1. The network with 6 vertices and 8 edges.

Along with different node as center, same sub-community may be created repeatedly. For example, $SubC(E) = SubC(F) = \{A, E, F\}$. The detail of sub-communities detection algorithm is described as follows.

Algorithm 1. $SubC(v)$ Detection Algorithm

Input: $G = (V, E)$.
Output: $SubC(V)$.
Initialize $i = 0, V^i(v) = \{v\}, E^i(v) = \emptyset$.
for each $v_m \in L(v)$ and $L(v) \neq \emptyset$ **do**
$\quad V^i(v) = V^i(v) + v_m$
$\quad E^i(v) = E^i(v) + (v_m, v)$
$\quad L(V) = L(V) - \{v_m\}$
while $\forall v_n \in L(v), \forall v_m \in V^i(v), (v_m, v_n) \in E$ **do**
$\quad V^i(v) = V^i(v) + v_m$
$\quad E^i(v) = E^i(v) + (v_m, v_n)$
$\quad L(V) = L(V) - \{v_n\}$
end while
$\quad i = i + 1$
end for
Output $SubC(v) = \left\{ C^i(v) = \left(V^i(v), E^i(v) \right) \right\}$

$SubC$ are the original granule sets acquired by Algorithm 1, which can be merged to form hierarchical structure after granulation operations. Assume that $SubCi, SubCj \in SubC$. The redefinition of three region are given as:

$$\begin{aligned} POS &= SubC_i - BND; \\ NEG &= SubC_j - BND; \\ BND &= SubC_i \cap SubC_j; \end{aligned} \tag{6}$$

Therefore, sub-communities are hierarchically merged as follows according to Granulation Operations $SGO\left(Sub_i^m, Sub_j^m\right)$:

$$\begin{aligned} SubC_i^{m+1} &\leftarrow SubC_i^m \cup SubC_j^m \\ SubC^{m+1} &\leftarrow SubC^m + SubC_i^{m+1} - SubC_i^m - SubC_j^m \end{aligned} \tag{7}$$

3.2 Three-Way Decision Community Detection Algorithm Based on Local Group Information

In Sect. 3.1, we can acquire small, tightly connected overlapping sub-communities. To achieve final two-way decisions, the nodes in the boundary can be further divided through further observations.

Here, in order to calculate the similarity between the nodes in boundary region and positive region (negative region), the index of LHN-I [20] is used to define the similarity of neighbor nodes svv.

$$svv(v_i, v_j) = \frac{|\Gamma(v_i) \cap \Gamma(v_j)|}{k(v_i) \times k(v_j)} \tag{8}$$

In addition, the belonging degree B_P, B_N is defined in formula (9) of. It is denotes as:

for $\forall v \in BND\left(SubC^l\right)$,

$$B_P = \frac{\sum\limits_{i}^{N_P} svv(v_i, v_j)}{N_P} * N_{LP}$$

$$B_N = \frac{\sum\limits_{i}^{N_N} svv(v_i, v_j)}{N_N} * N_{LN}$$

(9)

Where $v_i \in BND, v_j \in POS(NEG)$, N_{LP} denotes number of neighbors between $BND\left(v\right)$ and $POS\left(SubC^l\right)$. N_{LN} denotes number of neighbors between $BND\left(v\right)$ and $NEG\left(SubC^l\right)$. N_P is the number of nodes in positive region, N_N is the number of nodes in negative region.

The differences of belonging degree $|d_{PN}|$ can be calculated as follows:

$$|d_{PN}| = \frac{|B_P - B_N|}{|B_P - B_N|_{\max}}$$

(10)

where $|X|$ denotes the absolute value of X.

Based on Algorithm 1 and the index of further division in definition(10), the detail of Three-way Decision Community Detection Algorithm based on Local Group Information $(LGI - TWD)$ is described as follows.

According to the definition of $|d_{PN}|$, the nodes in boundary regions are divided into positive region or negative region when $|d_{PN}| > \gamma$. However, there may be a few nodes which are still in the boundary regions that satisfied $|d_{PN}| < \gamma$. Therefore, these nodes in the boundary region will finally be determined by voting according to link number.

4   Experiment and Analysis

In order to verify the performance of LGI-TWD, we have carried out a number of experiments on five data sets with six compared algorithms, such as N-TWD,CACDA [18], GN [1], NFA [6] and LPA [21]. Our experiments were performed on six data sets from http://www-personal.umich.edu/~mejn/netdata/ and http://arnetminer.org/lab-datasets/soinf/. The detail of data sets is shown in Table 1.

In LGI-TWD algorithm, two parameters are granulation parameter λ and boundary parameter γ. The parameter of $\lambda \in (0,1)$ is regarded as a granulation criterion which can determine the process of granulation operation and control the granularity of the initial sub-communities. The merger processing of sub-communities is stop when the value of granulation coefficient $GC\left(SubC_i, SubC_j\right) < \lambda$.

The parameter of $\gamma \in (0,1)$ is defined as boundary parameter, its value have great influence on the boundary region division. If $\gamma = 1$, the nodes in the boundary domain are all divided by neighbor voting; If $\gamma = 0$, the nodes in the boundary domain are all divided according to belonging degree. Besides, the nodes in the boundary domain are divided by both methods.

Algorithm 2. LGI-TWD Algorithm

Input: $G = (V, E)$
Output: Non-overlapping community structure $POS\left(SubC^l\right), NEG\left(SubC^l\right)$.
1. Generate Sub-Communities of $POS\left(SubC\right), NEG\left(SubC\right), BND\left(SubC\right)$ by Algorithm 1;
2. Build hierarchical structure $POS\left(SubC^m\right), NEG\left(SubC^m\right), BND\left(SubC^m\right)$
    for $\forall SubC_i, SubC_j \in SubC$
    $m = 1, Q_{\max} = 0$
    Calculate $GC\left(SubC_i, SubC_j\right)$
    end for
    if $\exists GC\left(SubC_i^m, SubC_j^m\right)$ is maximum
    $SGO\left(SubC_i^m, SubC_j^m\right)$
    Calculate value of $Q, Q = Q^{m+1}$
    if $Q^{m+1} > Q_{\max}$
    then $Q_{\max} = Q^{m+1}, l = m + 1$
    $m \leftarrow m + 1$
    until $SubC^m$ include one granule
    end if
3. Select a granule set $SubC^l$ with maximum $Q_{\max}$, l is the layer of maximum. And three regions $POS\left(SubC^l\right), NEG\left(SubC^l\right), BND\left(SubC^l\right)$ are formed.
For $v \in BND\left(SubC^l\right)$ **do**
4. According to the formula (8),calculate the belonging degree (B_P, B_N)
    While $\exists v \in BND, |d_{PN}| > \gamma$ **do**
        if $d_{PN} > \gamma$ **then**
            $POS = POS \cup v, BND = BND - v;$
        else
            $NEG = NEG \cup v, BND = BND - v;$
    End while
    While $\exists v \in BND, |d_{PN}| < \gamma$ **do**
        if edges between v and POS is maximum;
        $POS = POS \cup v$
        else
        $NEG = NEG \cup v$
    End while
end for
Return $POS\left(SubC^l\right), NEG\left(SubC^l\right)$
end

Table 1. The information of data sets

Data set	Number of vertices	Number of edges
Karate	34	78
Football	115	613
Dolphin	62	159
Les misrables	77	254
Book US politics	105	441
Topic16	679	1687

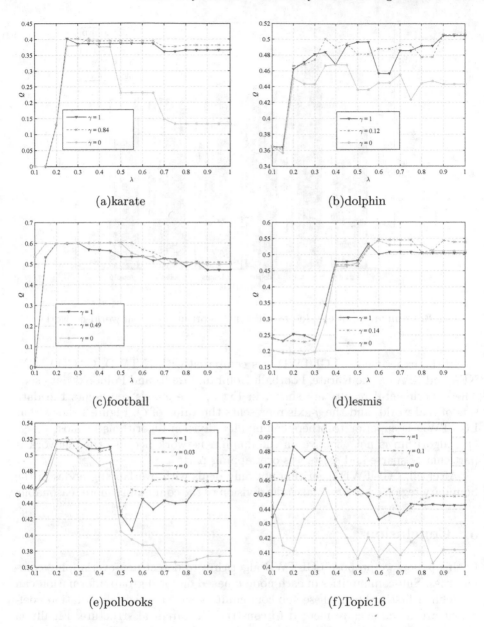

Fig. 2. The connection between λ and Q in different value of γ

In Fig. 2, nineteen groups of experimental thresholds were listed. According to Fig. 2 (a,c,d,e), we can find that with the increasing of granulation parameter λ, the value of Q is clear better than $\gamma = 0$ or $\gamma = 1$. In Fig. 2(b), the division result is not obvious because the dolphin data set is particularly sparse and have less overlapping nodes.

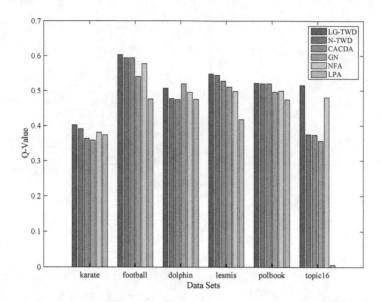

Fig. 3. Comparison of Q-value by different algorithms on real world networks.

In the experiments, LGI-TWD was compared with N-TWD, CACDA, GN, NFA and LPA on the Karate, Football, Dolphin, Lesmis and Polbooks data sets. The experimental results are shown in Fig. 3. The x-axis represents the data sets of real world, and the y-axis represents the value of Q. Figure 3 shows that LGI-TWD is superior to others community division algorithms in most cases. Our algorithm is not effective on the dolphin network because this network is particularly sparse and exists less overlapping parts.

After all, LGI-TWD algorithm not only deals with overlapping nodes in the boundary regions, but also makes the division of the community more reasonable.

5   Conclusion

In this paper, we propose LGI-TWD algorithm to detect non-overlapping communities. Sub-communities of each node v based on local group information can be defined firstly. Then, these sub-communities which satisfy granulation coefficient are hierarchically merged to construct hierarchical structure. Finally, a further division for boundary region's nodes can be done according to belonging degree. Compared with others community division algorithm (N-TWD, CACDA, GN, NFA, LPA), the experimental results on five real world social networks show that LGI-TWD algorithm get a higher modularity value Q and can get a quite reasonable division results.

Acknowledgments. This work was supported by the National Natural Science Foundation of China (Nos. 61602003, 61673020, 61402006), supported by the Provincial Natural Science Foundation of Anhui Province (Nos. 1508085MF113, 1708085QF156, 1708085QF143) supported by Provincial Natural Science Research Program of Higher Education Institutions of Anhui Province (Nos. KJ2013A016, KJ2016A016), supported by MOE (Ministry of Education in China) Project of Humanities, supported by Social Sciences (No.14YJC860020) and supported by the Scientific Research Foundation for the Returned Overseas Chinese Scholars, State Education Ministry (49th).

References

1. Girvan, M., Newman, M.E.J.: Community structure in social and biological networks. Proc. Natl. Acad. Sci. **99**(12), 7821–7826 (2002)
2. Newman, M.E.J.: Detecting community structure in networks. Eur. Phys. J. B-Condens. Matter Complex Syst. **38**(2), 321–330 (2004)
3. Lancichinetti, A., Fortunato, S., Radicchi, F.: Benchmark graphs for testing community detection algorithms. Phys. Rev. E **78**(4), 046110 (2008)
4. Fortunato, S.: Community detection in graphs. Phys. Rep. **486**(3), 75–174 (2010)
5. Kleinberg, J.M.: Authoritative sources in a hyperlinked environment. J. ACM (JACM) **46**(5), 604–632 (1999)
6. Newman, M.E.J.: Fast algorithm for detecting community structure in networks. Phys. Rev. E **69**(6 Pt 2), 066133 (2004)
7. Zhao, S., Ke, W., Chen, J., et al.: Tolerance granulation based community detection algorithm. Tsinghua Sci. Technol. **20**(6), 620–626 (2015)
8. Yao, Y.: An outline of a theory of three-way decisions. In: Yao, J.T., Yang, Y., Słowiński, R., Greco, S., Li, H., Mitra, S., Polkowski, L. (eds.) RSCTC 2012. LNCS, vol. 7413, pp. 1–17. Springer, Heidelberg (2012). doi:10.1007/978-3-642-32115-3_1
9. Yao, Y.: Three-way decisions and cognitive computing. Cogn. Comput. **8**(4), 543–554 (2016)
10. Yao, Y.: Two semantic issues in a probabilistic rough set model. Fundamenta Inform. **108**(3–4), 249–265 (2011)
11. Liu, D., Liang, D., Wang, C.: A novel three-way decision model based on incomplete information system. Knowl.-Based Syst. **91**, 32–45 (2016)
12. Li, F., Miao, D., Zhang, W.: Three-way decisions based multi-label learning algorithm with label dependency. In: Flores, V., Gomide, F., Janusz, A., Meneses, C., Miao, D., Peters, G., Ślęzak, D., Wang, G., Weber, R., Yao, Y. (eds.) IJCRS 2016. LNCS, vol. 9920, pp. 240–249. Springer, Cham (2016). doi:10.1007/978-3-319-47160-0_22
13. Yu, H., Zhang, H.: A three-way decision clustering approach for high dimensional data. In: Flores, V., Gomide, F., Janusz, A., Meneses, C., Miao, D., Peters, G., Ślęzak, D., Wang, G., Weber, R., Yao, Y. (eds.) IJCRS 2016. LNCS, vol. 9920, pp. 229–239. Springer, Cham (2016). doi:10.1007/978-3-319-47160-0_21
14. Chen, J., Zhang, Y., Zhao, S.: Multi-granular mining for boundary regions in three-way decision theory. Knowl.-Based Syst. **91**, 287–292 (2016)
15. Yu, H., Wang, Y., Jiao, P.: A three-way decisions approach to density-based overlapping clustering. In: Peters, J.F., Skowron, A., Li, T., Yang, Y., Yao, J.T., Nguyen, H.S. (eds.) Transactions Rough Sets XVIII, pp. 92–109. Springer, Heidelberg (2014)
16. Yu, H., Wang, G.Y., Li, T.R., et al.: Three Way Decisions Methods and Practices for Complex Problem Solving. Science Press, Beijing (2015)

17. Yao, Y.Y., Wong, S.K.M.: A decision theoretic framework for approximating concepts. Int. J. Man-Mach. Stud. **37**(6), 793–809 (1992)
18. Zhao, S., Ke, W., Chen, J., et al.: Community detection algorithm based on clustering granulation. J. Comput. Appl. **34**(10), 2812–2815 (2014)
19. Steinhaeuser, K., Chawla, N.V.: Identifying and evaluating community structure in complex networks. Pattern Recogn. Lett. **31**(5), 413–421 (2010)
20. Leicht, E.A., Holme, P., Newman, M.E.: Vertex similarity in networks. Phys. Rev. E Stat. Nonlinear. Soft Matter Phys. **73**(2), 026120 (2006)
21. Raghavan, U.N., Albert, R., Kumara, S.: Near linear time algorithm to detect community structures in large-scale networks. Phys. Rev. E **76**(2), 036106 (2007)

Actionable Strategies in Three-Way Decisions with Rough Sets

Cong Gao[✉] and Yiyu Yao

Department of Computer Science, University of Regina,
Regina, SK S4S 0A2, Canada
{gao266,yyao}@cs.uregina.ca

Abstract. Rough set theory uses three pair-wise disjoint regions to approximate a concept. This paper adopts actionable strategies in three-way decision with rough sets. We suggest actionable rules for transferring objects from one region to another and propose a model of optimal actions based on cost-benefit analysis. Actionable strategies allow us to transfer objects from less favourable regions to a favourable region, so that we can reduce the boundary region and the negative region. We design and analyze an algorithm for searching for an optimal solution. The experimental results on a real dataset show that the algorithm has promising outcomes and objects can be effectively moved between regions.

Keywords: Rough sets · Three-way decisions · Actionable strategies · Actionable rules · Actions

1 Introduction

The theory of rough sets may be interpreted in terms of three-way decisions [26–28]. Given a set of objects X representing the instances of a concept, based on their descriptions, we divide a universal set of objects OB into three pair-wise disjoint regions. The positive region $\text{POS}(X)$ consists of objects, based on their descriptions, belonging to X and the negative region $\text{NEG}(X)$ consists of objects not belonging to X. For an object in the boundary region $\text{BND}(X)$, based on its description we cannot determine if it is in X or not. Probabilistic rough sets [27] use a pair of thresholds to divide OB into three regions according to the conditional probability of an object belonging to X given its description. Many approaches have been proposed to find an optimal pair of thresholds according to certain criteria in different applications. Examples of criteria include cost [31], information entropy [5], Gini index [33], chi-square statistic [8], variance [2], and other statistical measures [30].

There are two steps in the trisecting-and-acting model of three-way decisions. The first step trisects the universal set into three pair-wise disjoint regions and the second step adopts actions to process objects in these regions. In this paper, we introduce the notion of actionable strategies based on actionable rules [23] and

© Springer International Publishing AG 2017
L. Polkowski et al. (Eds.): IJCRS 2017, Part II, LNAI 10314, pp. 183–199, 2017.
DOI: 10.1007/978-3-319-60840-2_13

action rules [19] in data mining into the second step of three-way decisions with rough sets. Specifically, by analyzing descriptions of objects in the three probabilistic regions, we propose to design actionable rules for transferring objects from one region to another. For example, if a suspected patient is determined having a disease, that is, he or she is classified into the positive region, we will take an action of treatment, in order to transfer the patient into the negative region NEG(X).

Silberschatz and Tuzhilin [21] introduced the concept of actionability that a user can react to realize his or her advantage. Ras and Wieczorkowska [19] adopted action rules to mine profitable pattern for banks. Yang et al. [25] introduced a postprocessing decision tree method to find actions for benefit. Su et al. [22] searched actionable behavioral rules with a high utility. Many studies on actionable rules and action rules cover topics in data mining and machine learning, such as association rule mining [14,20], classfication [4,6,18,19,23–25], clustering [1,12,15,32], and outlier detecting [3,11,13]. These studies on actionable rules and action rules provide a basis of actionable strategies in three-way decisions.

The rest of the paper is organized as follows. Section 2 reviews the basic concept of probabilistic rough sets and actionable rules. Section 3 proposes a model to improve the quality of three regions. Section 4 designs and analyzes an algorithm. Section 5 presents experimental results.

2   Three-Way Decisions with Rough Sets

This section reviews the basic idea of probabilistic rough sets in the context of three-way decisions.

The trisecting-and-acting three-way decision model [29] suggests two steps, i.e., trisecting and acting. The trisecting step divides a universal set into three pair-wise disjoint regions and the acting step takes actions to process objects in the three regions. The ideas of trisecting and acting are often used in our daily works. Let us consider the example of election. Based on an opinion poll, one typically divides a set of voters into three groups: voters who support the candidate, voters who oppose the candidate, and voters who are undecided or not willing to tell their decisions. According to the poll result, the candidate may take actions to sustain the group of supporters, to persuade the undecided voters, and to change the non-supporters.

2.1   Trisecting

In probabilistic rough sets, we assume that we can divide a universal set of objects into equivalence classes based on their descriptions [10,27,31]. Let $[x]$ denote the equivalence class of objects that have the same description as x. Let $Pr(X|[x])$ denote the conditional probability that an object is in X given that the object is in $[x]$, which may be computed by

$$Pr(X|[x]) = \frac{|[x] \cap X|}{|[x]|}, \tag{1}$$

where $|\cdot|$ is the cardinality of a set. Let us consider a class $X \subseteq OB$ representing a concept. Given a pair of thresholds (α, β) with $0 \leq \beta < \alpha \leq 1$, we divide a universal set of objects OB into positive, boundary, and negative regions, denoted by $\text{POS}_{(\alpha,\beta)}(X)$, $\text{BND}_{(\alpha,\beta)}(X)$, and $\text{NEG}_{(\alpha,\beta)}(X)$, respectively:

$$\text{POS}_{(\alpha,\beta)}(X) = \{x \in OB \mid Pr(X|[x]) \geq \alpha\},$$
$$\text{BND}_{(\alpha,\beta)}(X) = \{x \in OB \mid \beta < Pr(X|[x]) < \alpha\},$$
$$\text{NEG}_{(\alpha,\beta)}(X) = \{x \in OB \mid Pr(X|[x]) \leq \beta\}. \tag{2}$$

The pair of thresholds can be computed by using different criteria. In the Pawlak rough sets [16], we have $\alpha = 1$ and $\beta = 0$.

To get an optimal trisection $\pi = (\text{POS}_{(\alpha,\beta)}(X), \text{BND}_{(\alpha,\beta)}(X), \text{NEG}_{(\alpha,\beta)}(X))$, we construct an objective function to measure the quality or effectiveness of three regions as follows [8,26]:

$$Q(\pi) = w_P Q(\text{POS}_{(\alpha,\beta)}(X)) + w_B Q(\text{BND}_{(\alpha,\beta)}(X)) + w_N Q(\text{NEG}_{(\alpha,\beta)}(X)), \tag{3}$$

where $Q(\text{POS}_{(\alpha,\beta)}(X))$, $Q(\text{BND}_{(\alpha,\beta)}(X))$, and $Q(\text{NEG}_{(\alpha,\beta)}(X))$ are goodness (quality, cost, or other measure) of the positive, boundary, and negative regions, respectively, and w_P, w_B, and w_N represent the relative importances of three regions. The overall measure of the trisection is determined by the weighted sum of the corresponding measure of each region. An optimal trisection is the one that maximizes or minimizes Eq. (3). Depending on particular applications, we may have different meaningful objective functions. The objective functions based on cost [31], information entropy [5], and Gini index [33] should be minimized and those based on chi-square statistic [8] and variance [2] should be maximized. Without loss of generality, we minimize the objective function in Eq. (3) in the rest of this paper.

2.2 Acting

In the acting step, strategies and actions for processing each region take a decision maker's advantage. Different strategies and actions may be used in different applications, such as description of concept, prediction of the classes of objects, and transferring objects between different regions. In rough set theory, the actions for three regions are accepting objects to be in X, rejecting objects to be in X, and making non-commitment decisions, respectively.

In this paper, we consider actionable strategies that lead to movement of objects between different regions. Given the original trisection $\pi = (\text{POS}_{(\alpha,\beta)}(X)$, $\text{BND}_{(\alpha,\beta)}(X)$, $\text{NEG}_{(\alpha,\beta)}(X))$, we can design strategies to promote movement of objects from less preferred regions to preferred regions. Specifically, strategies enable us to obtain a new trisection, denoted by $\pi' = (\text{POS}_{(\alpha,\beta)}(X')$, $\text{BND}_{(\alpha,\beta)}(X')$, $\text{NEG}_{(\alpha,\beta)}(X'))$, where X' is a new set of objects obtained by movement of objects on X and represents the same concept as X. According to the objective function, we can search for optimal strategies by minimizing $Q(\pi')$:

$$\min \ Q(\pi').$$

Fundamental question in such a framework is to define the class of possible strategies and to construct an algorithm to minimize the objective function $Q(\pi')$.

3   Actionable Strategies for Transferring Objects

In this section, we introduce the concept of actionable rules for transferring objects, analyze benefit and cost of actions, and provide an example to illustrate the main idea.

3.1   Actionable Rules

We formulate actionable strategies based on the notion of a decision table.

Definition 1. *A **decision table** is the following tuple:*

$$S = (OB, \ AT = A_s \cup A_f \cup \{d\}, \ \{V_a \mid a \in AT\}, \ \{I_a \mid a \in AT\})$$

*where OB is a nonempty finite set of objects, AT is a finite nonempty set consisting of attributes composed by three subsets, in which A_s stands for **stable attributes**, A_f **flexible attributes** and d a **decision attribute**, V_a is a nonempty set of values for every attribute $a \in AT$, and $I_a : OB \longrightarrow V_a$ is a mapping. For every $x \in OB$, an attribute $a \in AT$, and a value $v \in V_a$, $I_a(x) = v$ means that the object x has the value v on attribute a.*

In Definition 1, the set of stable attributes A_s consists of attributes that their values cannot be modified, such as age, flexible attributes are attributes that their values can be modified by actions, such as cholesterol level and blood pressure.

Given an object $x \in OB$, $[x]$ is the equivalence class of x based on values on attributes $A_s \cup A_f$:

$$[x] = \{y \in OB \mid I_a(y) = I_a(x), \forall a \in A_s \cup A_f\}.$$

Classification rules in rough set theory have $X \Rightarrow Y$ form that indicates if X then Y. Given two objects with equivalence classes $[x]$ and $[y]$, we can get two classification rules:

$$r_{[x]} : \left[\bigwedge_{s \in A_s} s = I_s(x) \right] \wedge \left[\bigwedge_{f \in A_f} f = I_f(x) \right] \Rightarrow d = I_d(x),$$

$$r_{[y]} : \left[\bigwedge_{s \in A_s} s = I_s(y) \right] \wedge \left[\bigwedge_{f \in A_f} f = I_f(y) \right] \Rightarrow d = I_d(y).$$

The left hand side of the rule, X, is a conjunction of all stable and flexible attribute-value pairs and the right hand side of the rule, Y, is the decision attribute-value pair. Let $ST(r_{[x]})$ be the stable attributes part in the left hand side of the rule $r_{[x]}$, $FL(r_{[x]})$ be the flexible attributes part in the left hand side of the rule $r_{[x]}$, i.e.,

$$ST(r_{[x]}) = \left[\bigwedge_{s \in A_s} s = I_s(x) \right],$$

$$FL(r_{[x]}) = \left[\bigwedge_{f \in A_f} f = I_f(x) \right]. \tag{4}$$

We use $ST(r_{[y]}) = ST(r_{[x]})$ to denote that $[x]$ and $[y]$ have the same values on each stable attribute. If $ST(r_{[y]}) = ST(r_{[x]})$, then $[x]$ and $[y]$ can be changed to each other by changing the flexible attributes values via actions. If a user wants to change $[x]$ into $[y]$, the action is to execute the following actionable rule:

$$r_{[x]} \rightsquigarrow r_{[y]} : \overset{\rightsquigarrow}{\bigwedge_{f \in A_f}} I_f(x) \rightsquigarrow I_f(y), \quad subject\ to \bigwedge_{s \in A_s} I_s(x) = I_s(y) \qquad (5)$$

where $I_f(x) \rightsquigarrow I_f(y)$ means that the value of attribute f is changed from $I_f(x)$ to $I_f(y)$ and the symbol $\overset{\rightsquigarrow}{\bigwedge}$ means all the flexible attributes' values have to be changed.

We define some concepts of actionable rule as follows.

Definition 2. *An equivalence class* $[x] \subseteq OB$ *is called* ***actionable*** *if* $\exists [y] \subseteq OB, [y] \neq [x]$, *such that* $ST(r_{[x]}) = ST(r_{[y]})$. *The notation* $r_{[x]} \rightsquigarrow r_{[y]}$ *given in Eq. (5) is called an* ***actionable rule*** *that changes* $[x]$ *into* $[y]$ *and each clause* $I_f(x) \rightsquigarrow I_f(y)$ *for* $f \in A_f$ *is called a* ***sub-actionable rule***. $[x]$ *is called* ***non-actionable*** *if* $\nexists [y] \subseteq OB$ *satisfying* $ST(r_{[x]}) = ST(r_{[y]})$

In Definition 2, equivalence classes may be from different regions or the same region. If $[x]$ is non-actionable, then we cannot find any actionable rule for transferring $[x]$ to a different region.

The actionable rules can be used to design actions to transfer objects between regions. The action process does not change the classification rules generated in trisecting step. In this paper, we analyze benefit and cost from actionable rules. We also call actionable rule as **action** and sub-actionable rule as **sub-action**.

3.2   Cost-Benefit Analysis of Actions

Each action incurs cost and brings benefit. The motivation of taking actions is to minimize the objective function by least cost. Therefore, we can define the benefit as follows:

$$B = Q(\pi) - Q(\pi'), \qquad (6)$$

where π' is a new trisection after taking some actions on π.

We use misclassification cost matrix in Table 1, in which $\lambda_{PP}, \lambda_{BP}, \lambda_{NP}$ indicate the costs of classifying an object in X to the positive, boundary, and negative regions, respectively. Others are explained similarly. Therefore, the qualities of three regions can be computed by:

$$Q(\text{POS}_{(\alpha,\beta)}(X)) = |X \cap \text{POS}_{(\alpha,\beta)}(X)|\lambda_{PP} + |X^C \cap \text{POS}_{(\alpha,\beta)}(X)|\lambda_{PN},$$
$$Q(\text{BND}_{(\alpha,\beta)}(X)) = |X \cap \text{BND}_{(\alpha,\beta)}(X)|\lambda_{BP} + |X^C \cap \text{BND}_{(\alpha,\beta)}(X)|\lambda_{BN},$$
$$Q(\text{NEG}_{(\alpha,\beta)}(X)) = |X \cap \text{NEG}_{(\alpha,\beta)}(X)|\lambda_{NP} + |X^C \cap \text{NEG}_{(\alpha,\beta)}(X)|\lambda_{NN}. (7)$$

Table 1. Misclassification cost matrix.

	POS	BND	NEG
X	λ_{PP}	λ_{BP}	λ_{NP}
X^C	λ_{PN}	λ_{BN}	λ_{NN}

We now analyze the benefit of one actionable rule $r_{[x]} \rightsquigarrow r_{[y]}$. Let a denote the number of objects in $[x]$ belonging to class X and b the number of objects in changed $[x]$ belonging to class X':

$$a = |X \cap [x]|,$$
$$b = |X' \cap [x]|, \tag{8}$$

where X' is a new set of objects obtained by changing $[x]$ into $[y]$, representing the same concept as X. We use Eq. (1) to compute a and use an assumption to compute b:

(A1) After taking an action $r_{[x]} \rightsquigarrow r_{[y]}$, the changed equivalence class $[x]$ will have the same probability with $[y]$'s, i.e., $Pr(X'|[x]) = Pr(X|[y])$.

The idea of this assumption can be explained by an example. Some people in Canada will change all season tires to winter tires for their cars in winter due to safety. This assumption suggests that replacing to winter tires will improve the safety level to the level of those cars using winter tires. Therefore, after taking action $r_{[x]} \rightsquigarrow r_{[y]}$, b can be computed by:

$$b = |X' \cap [x]| = |[x]|Pr(X'|[x]) = |[x]|Pr(X|[y]) = |[x]||X \cap [y]|/|[y]|. \tag{9}$$

Further, we have the following proposition:

Proposition 1. *Taking any action $r_{[x]} \rightsquigarrow r_{[y]}$ to transfer objects from region V to W, the benefit is computed by:*

$$B_{r_{[x]} \rightsquigarrow r_{[y]}} = w_W \big[- b\lambda_{WP} - (|[x]| - b)\lambda_{WN} \big] + w_V \big[a\lambda_{VP} + (|[x]| - a)\lambda_{VN} \big], \tag{10}$$

where $V, W \in \{P, B, N\}$, in which P, B, and N represent positive, boundary, and negative regions, respectively.

The notation $B_{r_{[x]} \rightsquigarrow r_{[y]}}$ indicates the benefit of action $r_{[x]} \rightsquigarrow r_{[y]}$.

There are many types of cost involved with changing attribute values, such as money, time, and other resources. We suppose that all kinds of cost associated with a sub-action $I_f(x) \rightsquigarrow I_f(y)$ can be synthesized as one cost defined by a function C_f:

$$C_f : V_f \times V_f \longrightarrow \Re, \ \forall f \in A_f.$$

For each $f \in A_f$, $C_f(v_1, v_2)$ denotes the cost of changing the value of attribute f from v_1 to v_2 and $C_f(v_1, v_2)$ does not have to be equal to $C_f(v_2, v_1)$. Generally, the cost functions $\{C_f \mid f \in A_f\}$ are given by domain experts and they have no impact on the misclassification cost.

Further, we use two assumptions:

(A2) Value changings among different attributes are independent, which means the value changing of one attribute will not affect others.

(A3) All actions are independent, which means any action will only affect two equivalence classes, all other equivalence classes will not be affected.

Assumption (A2) allows us to calculate the cost of transferring one object by simply summing all sub-action costs up. For example, the cost of transferring an object from $[x]$ to $[y]$ is:

$$\sum_{f \in A_f} C_f(I_f(x), I_f(y)). \tag{11}$$

Let $C_{r_{[x]} \leadsto r_{[y]}}$ denote the cost of action $r_{[x]} \leadsto r_{[y]}$ and it can be computed by:

$$C_{r_{[x]} \leadsto r_{[y]}} = |[x]| \sum_{f \in A_f} C_f(I_f(x), I_f(y)). \tag{12}$$

Assumption (A3) allows us to calculate and analyze the benefit and cost of any action independently. Based on this assumption, given any two actions $r_{[x]} \leadsto r_{[y]}$ and $r_{[p]} \leadsto r_{[q]}$, whether or not we take action $r_{[p]} \leadsto r_{[q]}$, the $B_{r_{[x]} \leadsto r_{[y]}}$ and $C_{r_{[x]} \leadsto r_{[y]}}$ will not be changed.

3.3 An Illustrative Example

Table 2 is an example decision table describing the relation between a heart disease and some symptoms. The table consists of 9 people (rows), 3 symptoms or attributes (columns), and a diagnosis. Chol and Bp stand for cholesterol level and blood pressure, respectively. The first three attributes are symptoms and the last column is the diagnosis result of the heart disease. Symbols $+$ and $-$ denote that a suspected patient does not have heart disease and has the heart disease, respectively.

Table 2. A decision table for medicine.

#	Gender	Chol	Bp	Result
o_1	Female	Medium	Normal	+
o_2	Female	Medium	Normal	−
o_3	Female	Low	Normal	+
o_4	Female	Low	Normal	−
o_5	Female	Low	Normal	−
o_6	Female	Medium	Low	+
o_7	Female	High	High	−
o_8	Male	High	Low	−
o_9	Male	Low	Normal	+

Table 3. Cost matrix.

	POS	BND	NEG
X	2	4	8
X^C	11	9	8

According to this table, $A_s = \{Gender\}$, $A_f = \{Chol, Bp\}$, and $d = Result$, $V_d = \{+, -\}$, and $OB = \{o_1, o_2, \cdots, o_9\}$. We can get following equivalence classes: $[o_1] = \{o_1, o_2\}$, $[o_3] = \{o_3, o_4, o_5\}$, $[o_6] = \{o_6\}$, $[o_7] = \{o_7\}$, $[o_8] = \{o_8\}$, and $[o_9] = \{o_9\}$. Their conditional probabilities are 0.5, 0.3, 1.0, 0.0, 0.0, and 1.0, respectively with regard to $X = \{o_i \in OB \mid I_d(o_i) = +\} = \{o_1, o_3, o_6, o_9\}$. Given cost matrix in Table 3, we can compute $(\alpha, \beta) = (0.5, 0.2)$ that minimizes the objective function and three regions are constructed:

$$\text{POS}_{(0.5,0.2)}(X) = \{x \in OB \mid Pr(X|[x]) \geq 0.5\} = \{o_1, o_2, o_6, o_9\},$$
$$\text{BND}_{(0.5,0.2)}(X) = \{x \in OB \mid 0.2 < Pr(X|[x]) < 0.5\} = \{o_3, o_4, o_5\},$$
$$\text{NEG}_{(0.5,0.2)}(X) = \{x \in OB \mid Pr(X|[x]) \leq 0.2\} = \{o_7, o_8\}.$$

Now, we consider to transfer $[o_7] \subseteq \text{NEG}(X)$ to $\text{POS}(X)$. There are two actions that can transfer it: $r_{[o_7]} \rightsquigarrow r_{[o_1]}$ and $r_{[o_7]} \rightsquigarrow r_{[o_6]}$. The cost functions C_{Chol} and C_{Bp} are given in Table 4 and Table 5, respectively.

Table 4. Cost function C_{Chol}.

	Low	Medium	High
Low	0	1	3
Medium	2	0	1
High	4	1	0

Table 5. Cost function C_{Bp}.

	Low	Normal	High
Low	0	1	2
Normal	1	0	1
High	2	1	0

Then the costs of these two actions can be computed as follows according to Eq. (12):

$$C_{r_{[o_7]} \rightsquigarrow r_{[o_1]}} = |[o_7]|(C_{Chol}(high, medium) + C_{Bp}(high, normal)) = 2,$$
$$C_{r_{[o_7]} \rightsquigarrow r_{[o_6]}} = |[o_7]|(C_{Chol}(high, medium) + C_{Bp}(high, low)) = 3.$$

Now, we compute the benefits of two actions. According to Eq. (10) and using $w_P = w_B = w_N = 1$, we can get:

$$\begin{aligned}
B_{r_{[o_7]} \rightsquigarrow r_{[o_1]}} &= w_P\big[-b\lambda_{PP} - (|[o_7]| - b)\lambda_{PN}\big] + w_N\big[a\lambda_{NP} + (|[o_7]| - a)\lambda_{NN}\big] \\
&= -0.5 * 2 - (1 - 0.5) * 11 + 0 * 8 + (1 - 0) * 8 = 1.5,
\end{aligned}$$
$$\begin{aligned}
B_{r_{[o_7]} \rightsquigarrow r_{[o_6]}} &= w_P\big[-b\lambda_{PP} - (|[o_7]| - b)\lambda_{PN}\big] + w_N\big[a\lambda_{NP} + (|[o_7]| - a)\lambda_{NN}\big] \\
&= -1 * 2 - (1 - 1) * 11 + 0 * 8 + (1 - 0) * 8 = 6.
\end{aligned}$$

Obviously, action $r_{[o_7]} \rightsquigarrow r_{[o_1]}$ has less cost but less benefit and $r_{[o_7]} \rightsquigarrow r_{[o_6]}$ has both larger cost and benefit.

4   An Optimization-Based Solution

There are different criteria in different applications. For example, one may want to enlarge positive region, one may want to reduce boundary region, and one may want to simultaneously enlarge one region and reduce another. In this paper, we consider to enlarge positive region.

4.1   The Optimal Solution

Given any actionable equivalence class $[x_i] \subseteq OB$, $i = 1, \cdots, n$, there may exist many equivalence classes $[y_1], \cdots, [y_{n_i}]$ satisfying $ST(r_{[x_i]}) = ST(r_{[y_j]})$, $j = 1, \cdots, n_i$. Therefore, we may have many action options to transfer $[x_i]$ and they have different benefits and costs. We use c_{ij} and b_{ij} to denote the cost and benefit of action $r_{[x_i]} \rightsquigarrow r_{[y_j]}, j = 1, \cdots, n_i$, respectively and use $a_{ij} \in \{0, 1\}$ to indicate taking or not taking the $[x_i]$'s j^{th} action. For example, c_{23} denotes the cost of $[x_2]$'s 3rd action, b_{35} denotes the benefit of $[x_3]$'s 5th action, $a_{24} = 1$ indicates that $[x_2]$'s 4th action is taken, and $a_{21} = 0$ indicates that $[x_2]$'s 1st action is not taken. For all actions transferring $[x_i]$, we may take none or one of them. In other words, given $[x_i]$, all a_{ij} satisfy $\sum_{j=1}^{n_i} a_{ij} \leq 1$, $a_{ij} \in \{0, 1\}$.

We want to find a solution that maximizes the benefit when we have limited cost. Based on these notations, we define the optimal solution as follows:

Definition 3. *Given a trisection π, actionable equivalence class $[x_i]$ has n_i actions, and the cost and benefit of $[x_i]$'s j^{th} action are denoted as c_{ij} and b_{ij}, respectively, $j = 1, \cdots, n_i$. The optimal solution with maximum benefit under limited action cost c_a is to find a set of a_{ij} that*

$$\max \sum_{i=1}^{n} \sum_{j=1}^{n_i} a_{ij} b_{ij}, \quad \text{subject to} \sum_{i=1}^{n} \sum_{j=1}^{n_i} a_{ij} c_{ij} \leq c_a,$$

where $\sum_{j=1}^{n_i} a_{ij} \leq 1$, $a_{ij} \in \{0, 1\}$, $i = 1, \cdots, n$.

Definition 3 formulates a wide range of constrained optimization problems in real applications. For example, a company may have limited budget to make maximum profit from a product and a government may have limited resources to improve a social problem.

The problem defined in Definition 3 is similar to the multiple-choice knapsack problem (MCKP) [17], where the constraint of a_{ij} in our problem is looser (MCKP requires $\sum_{j=1}^{n_i} a_{ij} = 1$, $a_{ij} \in \{0, 1\}$, $i = 1, \cdots, n$). Suppose there are n actionable equivalence classes and each has m actions, then the exhaustive search for the solution has to check m^n combinations. Due to the similarity to the MCKP, it is also NP-hard to find the optimal solution of the problem in Definition 3.

4.2 Algorithm

To efficiently search for an approximate optimal solution of Definition 3, a dynamic programming based strategy can be adopted. Suppose we have n actionable equivalence classes given in an order, denoted as $[x_1], \cdots, [x_n]$. Any order can be used and will not affect the result of algorithm. Let $f(i, k)$ denote the maximum benefit for the first i actionable equivalence classes (i.e., $[x_1], \cdots, [x_i]$, $i \leq n$) and k is the limited action cost ($k \leq c_a$). Therefore, $f(n, c_a)$ is the maximum benefit under limited cost c_a. Suppose we know all the values of $f(i - 1, k'), k' = 0, \cdots, k$ (i.e., the maximum benefit when we have the first $i - 1$ equivalence classes under different limited action costs from 0 to k). To calculate the maximum benefit when we take the ith equivalence class $[x_i]$ into account, we have to consider all $[x_i]$'s actions and the $f(i, k)$ will be computed as the maximum one from the following $n_i + 1$ cases:

(0) $f(i, k) = f(i - 1, k)$, if none of $[x_i]$'s action is taken;
(1) $f(i, k) = f(i - 1, k - c_{i1}) + b_{i1}$, if $[x_i]$'s first action is taken;
(2) $f(i, k) = f(i - 1, k - c_{i2}) + b_{i2}$, if $[x_i]$'s second action is taken;
$\cdots$
(n_i) $f(i, k) = f(i - 1, k - c_{in_i}) + b_{in_i}$, if $[x_i]$'s last action is taken.

We define $c_{i0} = 0$ and $b_{i0} = 0$, $i = 0, \cdots, n$, i.e., there are no benefit and cost if we do not take any $[x_i]$'s action. Thus, the first case (0) can be rewritten in the same form as others, i.e., $f(i, k) = f(i - 1, k - c_{i0}) + b_{i0}$. By synthesising all cases, $f(i, k)$ is computed by:

$$f(i, k) = \max\{f(i - 1, k - c_{ij}) + b_{ij} \mid c_{ij} \leq k\}, j = 0, \cdots, n_i.$$

The number j that maximizes $f(i, k)$ is chosen, which means $[x_i]$'s j^{th} action is taken:

$$a_{ij} = \begin{cases} 1, & j = \arg \max_{l=0, \cdots, n_i} \{f(i - 1, k - c_{il}) + b_{il} \mid c_{il} \leq k\}; \\ 0 & \text{otherwise.} \end{cases} \tag{13}$$

This is an iterative strategy gradually reducing the size of problem (i.e., the number of equivalence classes). That is, to compute $f(i, k)$, we have to know $f(i - 1, 0), \cdots$, and $f(i - 1, k)$, and to compute $f(i - 1, k)$, we have to know $f(i - 2, 0), \cdots$, and $f(i - 2, k)$. Finally, the base conditions $f(0, 0), \cdots, f(0, k)$ will be reached. We define $f(0, k) = 0, k = 0, \cdots, c_a$, because there is no benefit when no equivalence class can be transferred. Thus, a complete iterative formula for computing $f(i, k)$ can be formulated as follows:

$$f(i, k) = \begin{cases} 0 & \text{if } i = 0; \\ \max\{f(i - 1, k - c_{ij}) + b_{ij} \mid c_{ij} \leq k\}, j = 0, \cdots, n_i & \text{otherwise.} \end{cases} \tag{14}$$

We continue to use previous example to show how the strategy works.

Table 6. A list of all actionable equivalence classes with costs and benefits from Table 2.

$[o_3]$	b_{ij}	c_{ij}
$r_{[o_3]} \leadsto r_{[o_1]}$	2.5	3
$r_{[o_3]} \leadsto r_{[o_6]}$	16	6

$[o_7]$	b_{ij}	c_{ij}
$r_{[o_7]} \leadsto r_{[o_1]}$	1.5	2
$r_{[o_7]} \leadsto r_{[o_6]}$	6	3

$[o_8]$	b_{ij}	c_{ij}
$r_{[o_8]} \leadsto r_{[o_9]}$	6	5

Example 1. We consider enlarging positive region by transferring objects from $NEG(X)$ and $BND(X)$ to $POS(X)$. Based on Table 2, we list all benefits and costs with regard to actionable equivalence classes in Table 6.

Suppose the limited cost $c_a = 10$, therefore the task is to find $f(3, 10)$. We compute all values of $f(i, k)$ in a table by considering equivalence classes one by one. Without losing generality, we use order: $[o_3], [o_7], [o_8]$ and notations $[x_1] = [o_3]$, $[x_2] = [o_7]$, and $[x_3] = [o_8]$. In the beginning, $i = 0$. According to Eq. (14), we have Table 7, in which column $[x_i]$ shows equivalence classes, column c_{ij} and b_{ij} are action costs and benefits, respectively, and columns from $k = 1$ to 10 stand for different action cost k from 1 to c_a. The $[x_0]$ does not exist, we use it as a symbol to compute $f(i, k)$. The first row is the base condition computed by $f(0, k) = 0, k = 1, \cdots, 10$ according to Eq. (14).

Table 7. A maximum benefit computing table when $i = 0$.

$[x_i]$	c_{ij}	b_{ij}	$k = 1$	2	3	4	5	6	7	8	9	10
$[x_0]$	0	0	0		0	0	0	0	0	0	0	0

Next, we take $[x_1]$ into account and get Table 8 according to Eq. (14). We provide the computations of cell $f(1, 1)$ and $f(1, 10)$ here, other cells are similar. To compute $f(1, 1)$, the current limited action cost is $k = 1$, there is no $[x_1]$'s action has cost less than 1. Therefore, $0(0)$ is written into the cell $(1, 1)$, the row of $[x_0]$ is not counted here, which means the first row is the row of $[x_1]$. The first number 0 denotes benefit, the second number 0 in the parenthesis denotes the sequence number of action that is taken to get such benefit, i.e., j, 0 means that no action is taken. Similarly, when $k = 10$, we have three options for $f(i - 1, k - c_{ij}) + b_{ij}$, where $i = 1$ and $j = 0, \cdots, 2$. The values are $0(0)$, $2.5(1)$, and $16(2)$, respectively. Therefore, $f(1, 10) = \max\{0, 2.5, 16\} = 16$ and $16(2)$ is written into the cell $(1, 10)$.

Table 8. A maximum benefit computing table when $i = 1$.

$[x_i]$	c_{ij}	b_{ij}	$k = 1$	2	3	4	5	6	7	8	9	10
$[x_0]$	0	0	0		0	0	0	0	0	0	0	0
$[x_1]$	3, 6	2.5, 16	0(0)		0(0)	2.5(1)	2.5(1)	2.5(1)	16(2)	16(2)	16(2)	16(2)	16(2)

By repeating the procedure for $[x_2]$ and $[x_3]$, we get Table 9. The maximum benefit is in the bottom right cell of the table, i.e., $f(3,10) = 22$. It is worth mentioning that the optimal solution may be not unique.

Table 9. The complete maximum benefit computing table.

$[x_i]$	c_{ij}	b_{ij}	$k=1$	2	3	4	5	6	7	8	9	10
$[x_0]$	0	0	0	0	0	0	0	0	0	0	0	0
$[x_1]$	3,6	2.5,16	0(0)	0(0)	2.5(1)	2.5(1)	2.5(1)	16(2)	**16(2)**	16(2)	16(2)	16(2)
$[x_2]$	2,3	1.5,6	0(0)	1.5(1)	6(2)	6(2)	6(2)	16(0)	16(0)	17.5(1)	22(2)	**22(2)**
$[x_3]$	5	6	0(0)	1.5(0)	6(0)	6(0)	6(0)	16(0)	16(0)	17.5(0)	22(0)	**22(0)**

Once the maximum benefit is found, the associated set of actions to obtain this benefit, i.e., the set of a_{ij}, can be inferred reversely. According to Table 9, the maximum benefit 22 is reached by taking none of $[x_3]$'s action. Thus, we consider $f(3 - 1, 10) = f(2, 10)$. We get 22(2) in cell $(2, 10)$ and it indicates $[x_2]$'s 2nd action is taken. Then we get rest cost 7 by subtracting cost 3 (the taken action's cost $c_{22} = 3$) from 10. Next, we check the cell of $f(2 - 1, 10 - 3) = f(1, 7)$ and we get 16(2), it shows that $[x_1]$'s 2nd action is taken. Finally, by checking $f(1-1, 7-6) = f(0, 1) = 0$, we reach the top row, inferring procedure completes. We get $a_{22} = 1$ and $a_{12} = 1$ and all other a_{ij} are 0. In other words, the optimal solution with maximum benefit 22 under limited cost 10 is realized by taking following actions:

$$r_{[o7]} \rightsquigarrow r_{[o6]} \ and \ r_{[o3]} \rightsquigarrow r_{[o6]}.$$

The inferring procedure is indicated by arrows in Table 9.

According to the strategies analyzed above, an algorithm is designed and shown in Algorithm 1. The algorithm consists of three parts. Part one is from line 1 to line 4, it computes all action costs and benefits for each actionable equivalence class. The second part is from line 6 to line 22, it is the main part of the algorithm computing the complete maximum benefit table (i.e., $f(i, k)$). The last part is from line 24 to line 33, it infers actions (i.e., a_{ij}) which are taken to obtain the maximum benefit. $h(i, k)$ is an action table associated with $f(i, k)$ by simply collecting all numbers in parentheses of Table 9. For example, $h(2, 4) = 3$ means that $[x_2]$'s 3rd action maximizes the benefit when action cost is limited at 4. Thus, the last part of the algorithm is accomplished by $h(i, k)$ table.

The function $floor(a)$ offers the largest integer less than a. It is used to ensure that the column index $floor(k - c_{ij})$ is always an integer. Because the action cost c_{ij} may be a decimal number in real applications. Thus, $k - c_{ij}$ as a column index might be a decimal number, this makes an incorrect reference to a cell $(i - 1, k - c_{ij})$. By using $floor(\cdot)$, each reference to a cell gets an equal or less benefit than the maximum benefit that can be obtained. Therefore, the computed maximum benefit from the algorithm is an approximate value that is equal to or less than the real maximum benefit. Suppose B' is the real maximum

---

Algorithm 1. Compute maximum benefit under limited action cost.

---

input : Trisection π, cost matrix, cost functions, and limited action cost c_a.
output: B, a_{ij}.   //B is the approximate maximum benefit.

1 **foreach** $[x_i] \subseteq \mathrm{BND}(X) \cup \mathrm{NEG}(X)$ **do**
2   $\quad$ Find all $[y_1], \cdots, [y_{n_i}] \in \mathrm{POS}(X)$, where $ST(r_{[x_i]}) = ST(r_{[y_j]})$, $j = 1, \cdots, n_i$;
3   $\quad$ let $c_{ij} = C_{r_{[x_i]} \rightsquigarrow r_{[y_j]}}$, $b_{ij} = B_{r_{[x_i]} \rightsquigarrow r_{[y_j]}}$;
4 **end**
5 let $f(0, k) = 0$, $h(0, k) = 0$, where $k = 0, \cdots, c_a$;   //f and h are benefit table and action
   table, respectively.
6 **for** $i = 1$ to n **do**
7   $\quad$ **for** $k = 1$ to c_a **do**
8   $\quad\quad$ let $b = 0$, $t = f(i - 1, k)$, $p = 0$;   //temporary variables;
9   $\quad\quad$ **for** $j = 1$ to n_i **do**
10 $\quad\quad\quad$ **if** $c_{ij} \leq k$ **then**
11 $\quad\quad\quad\quad$ $b = f(i - 1, floor(k - c_{ij})) + b_{ij}$;
12 $\quad\quad\quad$ **else**
13 $\quad\quad\quad\quad$ $b = 0$;
14 $\quad\quad\quad$ **endif**
15 $\quad\quad\quad$ **if** $b > t$ **then**
16 $\quad\quad\quad\quad$ $t = b$;
17 $\quad\quad\quad\quad$ $p = j$;
18 $\quad\quad\quad$ **endif**
19 $\quad\quad$ **end**
20 $\quad\quad$ let $f(i, k) = t$, $h(i, k) = p$;
21 $\quad$ **end**
22 **end**
23 let $B = f(n, c_a)$, $k = c_a$, all $a_{ij} = 0$;
24 **for** $i = n$ to 0 **do**
25 $\quad$ **if** $k \leq 0$ **then**
26 $\quad\quad$ break;
27 $\quad$ **endif**
28 $\quad$ let $t = h(i, k)$;
29 $\quad$ **if** $t > 0$ **then**
30 $\quad\quad$ let $a_{it} = 1$;
31 $\quad\quad$ let $k = floor(k - c_{it})$;   //c_{it} is the ith equivalence class' t^{th} action's action cost.
32 $\quad$ **endif**
33 **end**
34 Output B and a_{ij}.

---

benefit, B is the benefit obtained by Algorithm 1, they satisfy $(B' - c_a) < B \leq B'$. Specifically, we have $B = B'$ when all c_{ij} are integers.

The time complexity analysis of Algorithm 1 is straightforward. In the first part of the this algorithm, each equivalence class in $\mathrm{BND}(X) \cup \mathrm{NEG}(X)$ has to check all equivalence classes in $\mathrm{POS}(X)$ by comparing all attributes' values. Therefore, the maximum computation of this part is $|\mathrm{POS}(X)||\mathrm{BND}(X) \cup \mathrm{NEG}(X)||A_s \cup A_f|$, or simply denoted as $|OB|^2|AT|$. The second part has three nested loops, the computation is $nc_a m$, where m is the average of all n_i, i.e., $m = 1/n \sum_{i=1}^{n} n_i$. The last part has one loop and its computation is n. Overall, the algorithm reduces the time complexity from NP-hard to polynomial by searching for an approximate optimal solution.

5   Experimental Results

We use heart disease Cleveland data set [9], which has 303 people, 13 symptoms, and one diagnosis. Three attributes, age, sex, and ca (i.e., number of major vessels) are recognized as stable attributes, others are flexible. The values of some attributes are grouped and reassigned as follows. Age is categorized into 5 groups, i.e., 0–20, 21–39, 40–59, 60–79, and 80+, they are reassigned to values 1 to 5 respectively. Cholesterol is categorized into 3 groups: 0–199, 200–239, and 240+, they are reassigned to values 1 to 3 respectively. Blood pressure is categorized into 3 groups: 0–89, 90–139, and 140+, they are reassigned to 1 to 3 as well. Maximum heart rate is categorized into 3 groups: 0–149, 150–209, and 210+, they are reassigned to 1, 3, and 5, respectively. All missing values are filled with most often appeared values. The decision attribute has 5 categories, valued from 0 to 4, in which only the value 0 means healthy. Therefore, we construct three regions to approximate the concept of healthy people $X = \{x \in OB \mid I_d(x) = 0\}$. Table 10 is used to compute the quality of three regions. We use cost functions $C_f(v_1, v_2) = |v_1 - v_2|$ for all flexible attributes.

Table 10. Cost matrix for experiments.

	POS	BND	NEG
X	1	10	25
X^C	100	60	40

Two experiments are studied based on this setting, one is to compare the performances of our algorithm and random-action-select method, the other is to show the relation between cost and the number of transferred objects. The experimental results are shown in Fig. 1. All lines in Fig. 1(a) and (b) are drawn by connecting the points that have step of 10 on x-axis, i.e., limited cost.

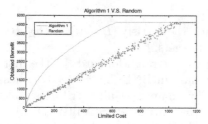

(a) The performance of Algorithm 1.

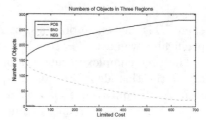

(b) Numbers of objects in regions.

Fig. 1. Results of two experiments. (Color figure online)

In Fig. 1(a), the solid line shows the result of Algorithm 1 and every dot shows the obtained benefit by randomly choosing actions under a limited cost. Obviously, our algorithm has overwhelming outcomes. The algorithm reaches the maximum benefit when cost is about 630, the random method needs almost twice cost to obtain it. In Fig. 1(b), the black solid line, red dashed line, and blue solid line indicate the numbers of objects in $POS(X')$, $NEG(X')$, and $BND(X')$, respectively. By increasing the cost, objects are gradually transferred from negative region and boundary region to positive region. When the cost reaches about 630, three regions get to a stable status, no object will be transferred. This is because the rest equivalence classes of objects in negative region are non-actionable. In this status, the $POS(X')$, $BND(X')$, and $NEG(X')$ regions have about 280, 0, and 20 objects, respectively. Most objects in less favourable regions are transferred into favourable region.

6   Conclusion

The transitional probabilistic rough sets focus on searching for an optimal trisection of the universal set of objects based on an objective function. In this paper, we adopt actions to facilitate movement of objects between regions. The movement of objects reflects a change of the original set of objects representing a concept to a new set of objects. Such movement leads to a new trisection and can improve the qualities of three regions.

By cost-benefit analysis of actions, a dynamic programming based algorithm is designed to search for optimal actions. Such optimal actions can produce maximum benefit under limited cost. The algorithm has polynomial time complexity. The experimental results on a real dataset show that the algorithm has promising outcomes and objects can be effectively moved between regions.

In the future, we will study more constrained optimization problems and movement patterns in real applications. The action cost is strongly related to attributes and we prefer to find a reduct with low cost attributes. Therefore, an addition strategy based reduct construction method [7] may be used to minimize action costs.

Acknowledgements. This work is partially supported by a Discovery Grant (NSERC, Canada), Mitacs, Saskatchewan Innovation and Opportunity Graduate Scholarship, Gerhard Herzberg Fellowship, and Sampson J. Goodfellow Scholarship. The authors thank Professor Howard Hamilton and Dr. Mehdi Sadeqi for their constructive suggestions and comments.

References

1. Abidi, S.S.R., Hoe, K.M., Goh, A.: Analyzing data clusters: a rough sets approach to extract cluster-defining symbolic rules. In: Hoffmann, F., Hand, D.J., Adams, N., Fisher, D., Guimaraes, G. (eds.) IDA 2001. LNCS, vol. 2189, pp. 248–257. Springer, Heidelberg (2001). doi:10.1007/3-540-44816-0_25
2. Azam, N., Yao, J.T.: Variance based determination of three-way decisions using probabilistic rough sets. In: Flores, V., et al. (eds.) IJCRS 2016. LNCS, vol. 9920, pp. 209–218. Springer, Cham (2016). doi:10.1007/978-3-319-47160-0_19
3. Chen, Z., Tang, J., Fu, A.W.-C.: Modeling and efficient mining of intentional knowledge of outliers. In: 7th International Database Engineering and Applications Symposium (IDEAS), pp. 44–53 (2003)

4. Dardzinska, A.: Action Rules Mining. Springer, Heidelberg (2013)
5. Deng, X.F., Yao, Y.Y.: A multifaceted analysis of probabilistic three-way decisions. Fundam. Informaticae **132**(3), 291–313 (2014)
6. Elovici, Y., Braha, D.: A decition-theoretic approach to data mining. IEEE Trans. Syst. Man Cybern. Part A **33**(1), 42–51 (2003)
7. Gao, C., Yao, Y.Y.: An addition strategy for reduct construction. In: Miao, D., Pedrycz, W., Ślęzak, D., Peters, G., Hu, Q., Wang, R. (eds.) RSKT 2014. LNCS, vol. 8818, pp. 535–546. Springer, Cham (2014). doi:10.1007/978-3-319-11740-9_49
8. Gao, C., Yao, Y.Y.: Determining thresholds in three-way decisions with chi-square statistic. In: Flores, V., et al. (eds.) IJCRS 2016. LNCS, vol. 9920, pp. 272–281. Springer, Cham (2016). doi:10.1007/978-3-319-47160-0_25
9. Gennari, J.H., Langley, P., Fisher, D.: Models of incremental concept formation. Artif. Intell. **40**, 11–61 (1989)
10. Grzymala-Busse, J.W., Clark, P.G., Kuehnhausen, M.: Generalized probabilistic approximations of incomplete data. Int. J. Approx. Reason. **55**, 180–196 (2014)
11. He, Z., Xu, X., Huang, J.Z., Deng, S.: Mining class outlier: concepts, algorithms and applications in CRM. Expert Syst. Appl. **27**(11), 681–697 (2004)
12. Jonker, J.-J., Piersma, N., Van den Poel, D.: Joint optimization of customer segmentation and marketing policy to maximize long-term profitability. Expert Syst. Appl. **27**(2), 159–168 (2004)
13. Knorr, E.M., Ng, R.T.: Finding intentional knowledge of distance-based outliers. In: VLDB 1999, pp. 211–222 (1999)
14. Liu, B., Hsu, W., Ma, Y.: Identifying non-actionable association rules. In: Proceedings of the 7th ACM SIGKDD International Conference on Knowledge Discovery and Data Mining (KDD), pp. 329–334 (2001)
15. Mishra, N., Ron, D., Swaminathan, R.: A new conceptual clustering framework. Mach. Learn. **56**, 115–151 (2004)
16. Pawlak, Z.: Rough Sets: Theoretical Aspects of Reasoning About Data. Kluwer Academic Publishers, Dordrecht (1991)
17. Pisinger, D.: Algorithms for Knapsack Problems. Ph.D. thesis, University of Copenhagen, Department of Computer Science (1995)
18. Ras, Z.W., Tsay, L.S.: Discovering extended action-rules (System DEAR). In: Kłopotek, M.A., Wierzchoń, S.T., Trojanowski, K. (eds.) Intelligent Information Processing and Web Mining. AINSC, vol. 22, pp. 293–300. Springer, Heidelberg (2003). doi:10.1007/978-3-540-36562-4_31
19. Ras, Z.W., Wieczorkowska, A.: Action-rules: how to increase profit of a company. In: Zighed, D.A., Komorowski, J., Żytkow, J. (eds.) PKDD 2000. LNCS, vol. 1910, pp. 587–592. Springer, Heidelberg (2000). doi:10.1007/3-540-45372-5_70
20. Shen, Y.-D., Yang, Q., Zhang, Z.: Objective-oriented utility-based association mining. In: IEEE International Conference on Data Mining (ICDM) (2002)
21. Silberschatz, A., Tuzihilin, A.: On subjective measures of interestingness in knowledge discovery. In: Proceedings of the 1st International Conference on Knowledge Discovery and Data Mining (KDD), pp. 275–281 (1995)
22. Su, P., Mao, W., Zeng, D., Zhao, H.: Mining actionable behavioral rules. Decis. Support Syst. **54**(1), 142–152 (2012)
23. Tsay, L.-S.: Interestingness measures for actionable patterns. In: Kryszkiewicz, M., Cornelis, C., Ciucci, D., Medina-Moreno, J., Motoda, H., Raś, Z.W. (eds.) RSEISP 2014. LNCS, vol. 8537, pp. 277–284. Springer, Cham (2014). doi:10.1007/978-3-319-08729-0_27
24. Yang, Q., Cheng, H.: Mining case bases for action recommendation. In: IEEE International Conference on Data Mining (ICDM), pp. 522–529 (2002)

25. Yang, Q., Yin, J., Ling, C.X., Chen, T.: Postprocessing decision trees to extract actionable knowledge. In: IEEE International Conference on Data Mining (ICDM) (2003)

26. Yao, Y.Y.: An outline of a theory of three-way decisions. In: Yao, J.T., Yang, Y., Słowiński, R., Greco, S., Li, H., Mitra, S., Polkowski, L. (eds.) RSCTC 2012. LNCS, vol. 7413, pp. 1–17. Springer, Heidelberg (2012). doi:10.1007/978-3-642-32115-3_1

27. Yao, Y.Y.: Probabilistic rough set approximations. Int. J. Approx. Reason. **49**(2), 255–271 (2008)

28. Yao, Y.Y.: Rough sets and three-way decisions. In: Ciucci, D., Wang, G., Mitra, S., Wu, W.-Z. (eds.) RSKT 2015. LNCS, vol. 9436, pp. 62–73. Springer, Cham (2015). doi:10.1007/978-3-319-25754-9_6

29. Yao, Y.Y.: Three-way decisions and cognitive computing. Cogn. Comput. **8**(4), 543–554 (2016)

30. Yao, Y.Y., Gao, C.: Statistical interpretations of three-way decisions. In: Ciucci, D., Wang, G., Mitra, S., Wu, W.-Z. (eds.) RSKT 2015. LNCS, vol. 9436, pp. 309–320. Springer, Cham (2015). doi:10.1007/978-3-319-25754-9_28

31. Yao, Y.Y., Wong, S.K.M.: A decision theoretic framework for approximating concepts. Int. J. Man-Mach. Stud. **37**(6), 793–809 (1992)

32. Zhang, H., Padmanabhan, B., Tuzhilin, A.: On the discovery of significant statistical quantitative rules. In: KDD 2004, pp. 374–383 (2004)

33. Zhang, Y., Yao, J.T.: Gini objective functions for three-way classifications. Int. J. Approx. Reason. **81**, 103–114 (2017)

Rough Set Approximations in an Incomplete Information Table

Mengjun J. Hu[(✉)] and Yiyu Y. Yao

Department of Computer Science, University of Regina,
Regina, SK S4S 0A2, Canada
{hu258,yyao}@cs.uregina.ca

Abstract. We present a new method for constructing and interpreting rough set approximations in an incomplete information table in four steps. Step 1: we introduce the notion of conjunctively definable concepts in a complete table. Step 2: we suggest a slightly different version of Pawlak rough set approximations in a complete table by using the family of conjunctively definable concepts. Step 3: we adapt a possible-world semantics that interprets an incomplete table as a family of complete tables. Correspondingly to conjunctively definable concepts in a complete table, we introduce the notion of conjunctively definable interval concepts in an incomplete table. Step 4: we study rough set approximations in an incomplete table by using the family of conjunctively definable interval concepts. Our method focuses on a conceptual understanding of rough set approximations for the purpose of rule induction. It avoids difficulties with existing approaches with respect to semantical interpretations.

1 Introduction

Analyzing an incomplete information table for rule induction is an important topic in rough set theory. Following Pawlak's formulations of rough set approximations using equivalence relations in a complete table [18,19], the majority of commonly used approaches is to construct a similarity or tolerance relation on a set of objects and to define generalized rough set approximations by using similarity classes. A fundamental difficulty with this type of approaches is that a partially defined similarity relation does not truthfully and fully reflect the available partial knowledge given in an incomplete table. For this reason, many authors have proposed and studied different definitions of similarity relations [3,7,9–12,17,21,22]. However, those solutions are not entirely satisfactory. It is necessary to study the family of all possible similarity relations in an incomplete table [13].

Yao [24] argued that there are two sides of rough set theory. The conceptual formulation focuses on the meanings of various concepts and notions of rough set theory. The computational formulation focuses on methods for constructing

---

Y.Y. Yao—This work is partially supported by a Discovery Grant from NSERC, Canada.

L. Polkowski et al. (Eds.): IJCRS 2017, Part II, LNAI 10314, pp. 200–215, 2017.
DOI: 10.1007/978-3-319-60840-2_14

these concepts and notions. Pawlak's formulation based on an equivalence relation in a complete table is an example of computational formulations. A conceptual formulation of rough sets uses a description language and explains rough set approximations in terms of the definability of sets under the description language [3,4,15,24]. To obtain a semantically sound and superior interpretation of rough set approximations in an incomplete table, we adopt the notion of a possible-world semantics of an incomplete table, that is, we truthfully represent an incomplete table by using a family of all its possible complete tables. The possible-world semantics of an incomplete table was used in interpreting incomplete databases by Lipski [14]. Several authors, for example, Li and Yao [13], Sakai et al. [16,20] and Hu and Yao [8], have adopted this semantics to study rough sets. By representing an incomplete table as a family of complete tables, we have an advantage of simply using any existing approaches to analyze an incomplete table, without the need to introduce new approaches. With the possible-world semantics of an incomplete table, we have shown earlier that, correspondingly to definable sets, one has the notion of definable interval sets [8]. Continuing with our study, in this paper we investigate rough set approximations by using definable interval concepts.

There are two formulations of rough sets. One uses a pair of lower and upper approximations. The other uses three pair-wise disjoint positive, boundary and negative regions. The latter has led to the introduction of three-way decisions with rough sets [25,26]. The positive and negative regions can be used to learn acceptance and rejection (i.e., rule-out) rules, respectively. However, we cannot learn such acceptance or rejection rules from the boundary region. Therefore, it is sufficient and meaningful to investigate, in this paper, only the positive and negative regions.

For simplicity, we only consider conjunctive rules in which the left-hand-side of a rule contains only logic conjunctions. We only study conjunctively definable concepts in a complete table and conjunctively definable interval concepts in an incomplete table. This enables us to arrive at the main results of this paper: rough set approximations are families of conjunctively definable concepts in a complete table and are families of conjunctively definable interval concepts in an incomplete table.

2 Conjunctively Definable Concepts and Rule Induction

An important task in rough set theory is to construct decision rules to classify objects. The left-hand-side of a conjunctive decision rule is a conjunction of conditions. For such a purpose, we introduced the notion of structured rough set approximations in a complete information table by using conjunctively definable concepts [28]. Compared with Pawlak rough set approximations [18,19], the structured approximations not only give the same definable part of a given set but also reveal their internal structure in terms of conjunctively definable concepts. This facilities the learning process of decision rules.

2.1 Conjunctively Definable Concepts in a Complete Information Table

An information table provides the context for concept analysis with rough sets [23]. According to whether the information is complete or not, there are two types of information tables, namely, complete and incomplete information tables. Formally, a complete information table T is represented by a tuple:

$$T = (OB, AT, \{V_a \mid a \in AT\}, \{I_a : OB \to V_a \mid a \in AT\}), \tag{1}$$

where OB is a finite nonempty set of objects as rows, AT is a finite nonempty set of attributes as columns, V_a is the domain of an attribute $a \in AT$ and I_a is an information function mapping each object to a unique value in the domain of the attribute a.

A description language is commonly used to describe the objects in an information table. In this paper, we consider a description language DL_0 that contains only logic conjunctions and is a sublanguage of the commonly used one in rough set analysis [3,4,14,15,18,24]:

(1)   Atomic formulas : $\forall a \in AT, v \in V_a, (a = v) \in \mathrm{DL}_0$;
(2)   If $p, q \in \mathrm{DL}_0$, and p and q do not share any attribute, then $p \wedge q \in \mathrm{DL}_0$.

By demanding that p and q do not share any attribute, we actually consider a subset of conjunctive formulas in which each attribute appears at most once.

Given a formula in DL_0, an object satisfies the formula if it takes values on the corresponding attributes as specified by the formula. Formally, for an object $x \in OB$, an attribute $a \in AT$, a value $v \in V_a$ and two formulas $p, q \in \mathrm{DL}_0$, the satisfiability $\models$ is defined as:

(1) $x \models (a = v)$ iff $I_a(x) = v$;
(2) $x \models p \wedge q$ iff $x \models p$ and $x \models q$. \tag{2}

The set of objects satisfying a formula describes the semantics or meaning of the formula.

Definition 1. *Given a formula $p \in \mathrm{DL}_0$, the following set of objects:*

$$m(p) = \{x \in OB \mid x \models p\}, \tag{3}$$

is called the meaning set of p.

Finding the meaning set of a formula is an easy task. However, given an arbitrary set of objects, there might not be a formula in the description language whose meaning set contains exactly these given objects. In other words, such a set cannot be described or defined with respect to the description language. In this sense, we may divide all sets of objects into two categories by their definability, that is, definable and undefinable sets. According to the school of Port-Royal Logic [1,2], a concept is represented by a pair of its intension and extension, where the intension describes the properties of the concept and the extension is the set of instances of the concept. Based on the ideas from formal concept analysis, Yao [23] represented a conjunctively definable concept as a pair of a conjunctive formula and the corresponding conjunctively definable set, which makes the meaning of the set explicit for the purpose of rule induction. D'eer et al. [3,4] adopted the conjunctively definable concepts and presented a semantically sound approach to Pawlak rough set and covering-based rough set models, which focuses on the conceptual understanding of those models.

Definition 2. *A pair of a formula and a set of objects (p, X) is a conjunctively definable concept if $p \in DL_0$ and $X = m(p)$. The set $m(p)$ is called a conjunctively definable set.*

The family of all conjunctively definable concepts is denoted by $\mathrm{CDEF}(OB) = \{(p, m(p)) \mid p \in DL_0\}$. It should be noted that a conjunctively definable set may be defined by more than one formula.

2.2 Approximating a Set by Structured Positive and Negative Regions

Suppose that a subset of objects $X \subseteq OB$ consists of instances of a concept, that is, X is the extension of the concept. A fundamental issue of rough set theory is to describe the concept or its extension X by using definable concepts or sets. With respect to the family of conjunctively definable concepts $\mathrm{CDEF}(OB)$, we use a pair of positive and negative regions to approximate X. Instead of using the standard definition, we adopt the definition of structured approximations [28].

Definition 3. *Given a set of objects $X \subseteq OB$, the following families of conjunctively definable concepts:*

$$\mathrm{SPOS}(X) = \{(p, m(p)) \in \mathrm{CDEF}(OB) \mid m(p) \subseteq X, m(p) \neq \emptyset\},$$
$$\mathrm{SNEG}(X) = \{(p, m(p)) \in \mathrm{CDEF}(OB) \mid m(p) \subseteq X^c, m(p) \neq \emptyset\}, \qquad (4)$$

are called the structured positive and negative regions of X, respectively.

Figure 1 demonstrates the relationships between a conjunctively definable set $m(p)$ in the structured positive and negative regions and the set of objects X, respectively. To construct the structured positive region, we collect all conjunctively definable concepts whose extensions are included in the given set of objects. In this way, we explicitly indicate the composition of the family of conjunctively definable concepts used to approximate the given set. Similarly, to construct the structured negative region, we collect all conjunctively definable concepts whose extensions are included in the complement set of the given set of objects. There might be two conjunctively definable concepts with the same conjunctively definable set but different formulas. We include all the possible formulas for a conjunctively definable set in defining a region. There might be redundant conjunctively definable concepts in each of the two regions.

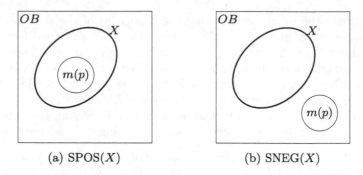

(a) SPOS(X)   (b) SNEG(X)

Fig. 1. Relationships between X and $m(p)$ in the two regions

The structured positive and negative regions cover the same sets of objects as defined by the lower approximation of X and X^c, respectively, in Pawlak's framework [18,19], that is:

$$\underline{apr}(X) = \bigcup \{m(p) \mid (p, m(p)) \in \text{SPOS}(X)\},$$
$$\underline{apr}(X^c) = \bigcup \{m(p) \mid (p, m(p)) \in \text{SNEG}(X)\}. \tag{5}$$

They also cover the same sets of objects in the standard unstructured positive and negative regions of X, that is, POS(X) and NEG(X), respectively [25]:

$$\text{POS}(X) = \bigcup \{m(p) \mid (p, m(p)) \in \text{SPOS}(X)\},$$
$$\text{NEG}(X) = \bigcup \{m(p) \mid (p, m(p)) \in \text{SNEG}(X)\}. \tag{6}$$

The two sets of objects POS(X) and NEG(X) may not contain all objects in OB. The set
$$\text{BND}(X) = (\text{POS}(X) \cup \text{NEG}(X))^c \tag{7}$$
is the boundary region of X. We define the structured boundary region as follows:

$$\text{SBND}(X) = \{(p, m(p)) \in \text{CDEF}(U) \mid m(p) \subseteq \text{BND}(X), m(p) \neq \emptyset\}. \tag{8}$$

If we want to define the structured boundary region of X by using X directly, we need to consider conjunctively definable concepts with specific properties. The details are omitted in this paper.

2.3   Acceptance and Rejection Rules

According to the three regions, we can construct a three-way decision model for rough set theory [25]. From the positive region, we build rules of acceptance for accepting an object to be an instance of the concept represented by X by examining the descriptions of the object. In the same way, we can build rules of rejection for rejecting an object to be an instance of the concept represented by X. For the boundary region, we cannot make such a definite decision. For this reason, in this paper, we are not interested in building rules from the boundary region.

Given a set of objects $X \subseteq OB$, we can build two sets of acceptance and rejection rules from the structured positive and negative regions, respectively. The explicit representation of the intension of a conjunctively definable concept in the structured regions makes this task much simpler. From a conjunctively definable concept $(p, m(p))$ in the structured positive region $\text{SPOS}(X)$, one may immediately get an acceptance rule by taking the formula p as the left-hand-side, that is:

$$\text{If an object } x \text{ satisfies } p, \text{ then accept } x \in X, \text{ denoted by } p \rightarrow X. \qquad (9)$$

Similarly, from a conjunctively definable concept $(q, m(q))$ in the structured negative region $\text{SNEG}(X)$, one may immediately get a rejection rule by taking the formula q as the left-hand-side, that is:

$$\text{If an object } x \text{ satisfies } q, \text{ then reject } x \in X, \text{ denoted by } q \rightarrow \neg X. \qquad (10)$$

Since there might be redundancy in the two regions, redundant rules may exist in the derived sets of acceptance and rejection rules. Removing redundant rules, that is, finding a rule redundant, is a future research topic.

3   Approximations in an Incomplete Information Table

The notion of definable interval sets was presented to investigate the definability in an incomplete information table [8]. By considering the conjunctive formulas, we present the notion of conjunctively definable interval concepts and use it to define two types of structured positive and negative regions to approximate a set of objects in an incomplete information table. Our approach focuses on a conceptual understanding of the approximations with incomplete information.

3.1   Conjunctively Definable Interval Concepts

An interval set is typically defined by a lower bound and an upper bound [27]. The interval set contains the family of all sets between the two bounds.

Definition 4. *Suppose OB is a universe of objects. An interval set is defined by:*

$$\mathcal{A} = [A_l, A_u] = \{A \subseteq OB \mid A_l \subseteq A \subseteq A_u\}. \qquad (11)$$

A_l and A_u are the lower and upper bounds, respectively, and they satisfy the condition $A_l \subseteq A_u$.

The value of an object on an attribute is unique. However, due to incomplete information, we may not know this unique value. Instead, a set of values is known to be possible. Let 2^{V_a} denote the power set of a set of values V_a, that is, the family of all subsets of V_a. An incomplete information table is represented by the following tuple:

$$\widetilde{T} = (OB, AT, \{V_a \mid a \in AT\}, \{\widetilde{I_a} : OB \to 2^{V_a} - \{\emptyset\} \mid a \in AT\}), \qquad (12)$$

where OB is a finite nonempty set of objects as rows, AT is a finite nonempty set of attributes as columns, V_a is the domain of an attribute a and $\widetilde{I_a}$ is the information function mapping one object to a nonempty subset of values in the domain of a. We assume that all attributes are applicable to all objects, and demand a nonempty subset of values for every object on every attribute.

Lipski [14] presented a possible-world semantics that interprets an incomplete table as a collection of complete tables. It provides a method to study an incomplete table through a family of complete tables.

Definition 5. *For an incomplete table* $\widetilde{T} = (OB, AT, \{V_a \mid a \in AT\}, \{\widetilde{I_a} : OB \to 2^{V_a} - \{\emptyset\} \mid a \in AT\})$, *a complete table* $T = (OB, AT, \{V_a \mid a \in AT\}, \{I_a : OB \to V_a \mid a \in AT\})$ *is called a completion of* $\widetilde{T}$ *if and only if it satisfies the following condition:*

$$\forall x \in OB, a \in AT, I_a(x) \in \widetilde{I_a}(x). \qquad (13)$$

That is, a completion takes exactly one value from the incomplete table for every object on every attribute. The family of all completions of $\widetilde{T}$ is denoted by $\mathrm{COMP}(\widetilde{T}) = \{T \mid T \text{ is a completion of } \widetilde{T}\}$. Since in the incomplete table $\widetilde{T}$, $\widetilde{I_a}(x)$ represents all possibilities of the actual value of x on a, the family $\mathrm{COMP}(\widetilde{T})$ is the collection of all possibilities of the actual table. In other words, once the information becomes complete, we will get a completion in $\mathrm{COMP}(\widetilde{T})$.

For a formula $p \in \mathrm{DL}_0$, we can get a meaning set $m(p|T)$ in each completion $T \in \mathrm{COMP}(\widetilde{T})$. By collecting all the meaning sets of p in the family $\mathrm{COMP}(\widetilde{T})$, we get a family of sets that interprets p in the incomplete table $\widetilde{T}$.

Definition 6. *For a formula* $p \in \mathrm{DL}_0$ *in an incomplete table* $\widetilde{T}$, *its meaning set is defined as:*

$$\widetilde{m}(p) = \{m(p|T) \mid T \in \mathrm{COMP}(\widetilde{T})\}, \qquad (14)$$

where $m(p|T)$ *is the meaning set of* p *in a completion* T.

Our definition of the meaning set of a formula is related to the formulation proposed by Grzymala-Busse et al. [5,6]. In particular, they called an atomic formula an attribute-value pair, and a conjunctive formula a complex. However, they defined the meaning set as a set of objects; we define it as a family of sets of objects.

The meaning set of a formula in an incomplete table is actually an interval set, which is formally stated in the following theorem whose proof is given in Appendix A.

Theorem 1. *For a formula $p \in \mathrm{DL_0}$ in an incomplete table $\widetilde{T}$, its meaning set $\widetilde{m}(p)$ is an interval set with $\cap\widetilde{m}(p)$ as the lower bound and $\cup\widetilde{m}(p)$ as the upper bound:*

$$\widetilde{m}(p) = [\cap\widetilde{m}(p), \cup\widetilde{m}(p)]. \tag{15}$$

By Definition 6, the interval set $\widetilde{m}(p)$ is actually the family of all possibilities of the actual meaning set of p. In this sense, the sets $\cap\widetilde{m}(p)$ and $\cup\widetilde{m}(p)$ are the lower and upper bounds of the actual meaning set of p. Thus, we denote the sets $\cap\widetilde{m}(p)$ and $\cup\widetilde{m}(p)$ as $m_*(p)$ and $m^*(p)$, respectively. Accordingly, Eq. (15) can be written as $\widetilde{m}(p) = [m_*(p), m^*(p)]$. The two bounds can be interpreted in terms of the family $\mathrm{COMP}(\widetilde{T})$ as follows:

$$m_*(p) = \bigcap_{T \in \mathrm{COMP}(\widetilde{T})} m(p|T) = \{x \in OB \mid \forall T \in \mathrm{COMP}(\widetilde{T}), x \in m(p|T)\},$$

$$m^*(p) = \bigcup_{T \in \mathrm{COMP}(\widetilde{T})} m(p|T) = \{x \in OB \mid \exists T \in \mathrm{COMP}(\widetilde{T}), x \in m(p|T)\}. \tag{16}$$

By Theorem 1, the meaning set of a conjunctive formula in $\mathrm{DL_0}$ in an incomplete table is an interval set. Such an interval set is considered to be conjunctively definable. By explicitly giving the conjunctive formulas, we define a conjunctively definable interval concept as a pair of a formula and its meaning set in an incomplete table.

Definition 7. *A pair of a formula and an interval set $(p, \mathcal{A})$ is a conjunctively definable interval concept if $p \in \mathrm{DL_0}$ and $\mathcal{A} = \widetilde{m}(p)$. The interval set $\widetilde{m}(p)$ is called a conjunctively definable interval set.*

The family of all conjunctively definable interval concepts is denoted as $\mathrm{CDEFI}(OB) = \{(p, \widetilde{m}(p)) \mid p \in \mathrm{DL_0}\} = \{(p, [m_*(p), m^*(p)]) \mid p \in \mathrm{DL_0}\}$.

3.2 Two Types of Structured Positive and Negative Regions in an Incomplete Table

By using the family $\mathrm{CDEFI}(OB)$ instead of the family $\mathrm{CDEF}(OB)$, we generalize the structured positive and negative regions in a complete table into two types of structured positive and negative regions in an incomplete table.

Given a set of objects X in a complete table, its structured positive and negative regions are defined by considering the set-theoretic inclusion relationships between a conjunctively definable set, that is, the meaning set of a conjunctive formula, and X and X^c, respectively. With respect to an incomplete table, the meaning set of a formula becomes a conjunctively definable interval set. The family $\mathrm{CDEFI}(OB)$ is consequently used to define the structured positive and negative regions. We consider the component-wise inclusion relationships between a conjunctively definable interval set and X and X^c, that is, the set-theoretic inclusion between a set in the interval set and X and X^c. This leads to two types of structured positive and negative regions.

Definition 8. *For a set of objects X in an incomplete table $\widetilde{T}$, we define two types of structured positive and negative regions of X as follows:*

(1) $\text{SPOS}_*(X) = \{(p, \widetilde{m}(p)) \in \text{CDEFI}(OB) \mid \widetilde{m}(p) \neq [\emptyset, \emptyset], \forall S \in \widetilde{m}(p), S \subseteq X\},$

$\quad\;\; \text{SNEG}_*(X) = \{(p, \widetilde{m}(p)) \in \text{CDEFI}(OB) \mid \widetilde{m}(p) \neq [\emptyset, \emptyset], \forall S \in \widetilde{m}(p), S \subseteq X^c\};$

(2) $\text{SPOS}^*(X) = \{(p, \widetilde{m}(p)) \in \text{CDEFI}(OB) \mid \exists S \in \widetilde{m}(p), S \neq \emptyset, S \subseteq X\},$

$\quad\;\; \text{SNEG}^*(X) = \{(p, \widetilde{m}(p)) \in \text{CDEFI}(OB) \mid \exists S \in \widetilde{m}(p), S \neq \emptyset, S \subseteq X^c\}. \qquad (17)$

It should be noted that the intersection of the two regions $\text{SPOS}^*(X)$ and $\text{SNEG}^*(X)$ may not be empty since we use the existence of the set S to define these two regions. Suppose $(p, [\emptyset, m^*(p)])$ is a conjunctively definable interval concept where $m^*(p) \cap X = S_1 \neq \emptyset$ and $m^*(p) \cap X^c = S_2 \neq \emptyset$. Since $S_1, S_2 \subseteq m^*(p)$, we have $S_1, S_2 \in [\emptyset, m^*(p)]$. By Definition 8 and the fact that $S_1 \subseteq X$ and $S_2 \subseteq X^c$, the concept $(p, [\emptyset, m^*(p)])$ will be included in both $\text{SPOS}^*(X)$ and $\text{SNEG}^*(X)$.

By Definition 6, the meaning set $\widetilde{m}(p)$ is actually the collection of the meaning sets of p in all the completions. Thus, we can re-write Definition 8 as given in the following theorem.

Theorem 2. *For a set of objects X in an incomplete table $\widetilde{T}$, its two types of structured positive and negative regions can be equivalently expressed as:*

(1) $\text{SPOS}_*(X) = \{(p, \widetilde{m}(p)) \in \text{CDEFI}(OB) \mid \widetilde{m}(p) \neq [\emptyset, \emptyset], \forall T \in \text{COMP}(\widetilde{T}),$
$\qquad\qquad\qquad m(p|T) \subseteq X\},$

$\quad\;\; \text{SNEG}_*(X) = \{(p, \widetilde{m}(p)) \in \text{CDEFI}(OB) \mid \widetilde{m}(p) \neq [\emptyset, \emptyset], \forall T \in \text{COMP}(\widetilde{T}),$
$\qquad\qquad\qquad m(p|T) \subseteq X^c\};$

(2) $\text{SPOS}^*(X) = \{(p, \widetilde{m}(p)) \in \text{CDEFI}(OB) \mid \exists T \in \text{COMP}(\widetilde{T}), m(p|T) \neq \emptyset,$
$\qquad\qquad\qquad m(p|T) \subseteq X\},$

$\quad\;\; \text{SNEG}^*(X) = \{(p, \widetilde{m}(p)) \in \text{CDEFI}(OB) \mid \exists T \in \text{COMP}(\widetilde{T}), m(p|T) \neq \emptyset,$
$\qquad\qquad\qquad m(p|T) \subseteq X^c\}. \qquad (18)$

By the fact that $m_*(p) \subseteq m^*(p)$, the two types of structured regions could be computed in terms of the two bounds of the interval sets, which is given in the following theorem.

Theorem 3. *For a set of objects X in an incomplete table $\widetilde{T}$, its two types of structured positive and negative regions can be computed as:*

(1) $\text{SPOS}_*(X) = \{(p, [m_*(p), m^*(p)]) \in \text{CDEFI}(OB) \mid m^*(p) \neq \emptyset, m^*(p) \subseteq X\},$

$\quad\;\; \text{SNEG}_*(X) = \{(p, [m_*(p), m^*(p)]) \in \text{CDEFI}(OB) \mid m^*(p) \neq \emptyset, m^*(p) \subseteq X^c\};$

(2) $\text{SPOS}^*(X) = \{(p, [m_*(p), m^*(p)]) \in \text{CDEFI}(OB) \mid (m_*(p) \neq \emptyset \wedge m_*(p) \subseteq X)$
$\qquad\qquad\qquad \vee(m_*(p) = \emptyset \wedge m^*(p) \cap X \neq \emptyset)\},$

$\quad\;\; \text{SNEG}^*(X) = \{(p, [m_*(p), m^*(p)]) \in \text{CDEFI}(OB) \mid (m_*(p) \neq \emptyset \wedge m_*(p) \subseteq X^c)$
$\qquad\qquad\qquad \vee(m_*(p) = \emptyset \wedge m^*(p) \cap X^c \neq \emptyset)\}. \qquad (19)$

By Theorem 3, we call $SPOS_*(X)$ and $SNEG_*(X)$ the upper-bound structured positive and negative regions, respectively; and $SPOS^*(X)$ and $SNEG^*(X)$ the lower-bound structured positive and negative regions, respectively. The relationships between the set of objects X and a conjunctively definable interval set $\widetilde{m}(p)$ in the four regions can be depicted by Fig. 2. We use two concentric circles to represent $\widetilde{m}(p)$, one with solid line to represent the lower bound and the other with dashed line to represent the upper bound. There are other possibilities of the relationships in Fig. 2. We only focus on the upper bound for $SPOS_*(X)$ and $SNEG_*(X)$, and the lower bound for $SPOS^*(X)$ and $SNEG^*(X)$.

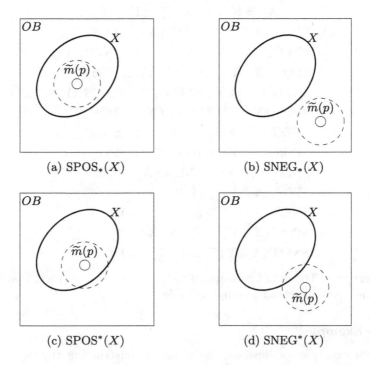

(a) $SPOS_*(X)$ (b) $SNEG_*(X)$

(c) $SPOS^*(X)$ (d) $SNEG^*(X)$

Fig. 2. Relationships between X and $\widetilde{m}(p)$ in the four regions

We have discussed three equivalent forms for the four regions. Definition 8 provides a direct generalization of the structured positive and negative regions in a complete table. Theorem 2 clarifies the semantical meanings of the four regions in terms of the family of completions. Theorem 3 offers a computational formalization by using the bounds of the interval sets. Theorem 2 could be viewed as a conceptual model of the regions and Theorem 3 as a computational model [24].

One may easily verify the properties of the four regions stated in the following theorem by using any of the three forms.

Theorem 4. *For two sets of objects $X, Y \subseteq OB$, the following properties are satisfied:*

(1) $\text{SPOS}_*(X) \cap \text{SNEG}_*(X) = \emptyset$;

(2) $\text{SPOS}_*(X) \subseteq \text{SPOS}^*(X)$,
    $\text{SNEG}_*(X) \subseteq \text{SNEG}^*(X)$;

(3) $X \subseteq Y \Longrightarrow \text{SPOS}_*(X) \subseteq \text{SPOS}_*(Y)$,
    $X \subseteq Y \Longrightarrow \text{SNEG}_*(X) \supseteq \text{SNEG}_*(Y)$,
    $X \subseteq Y \Longrightarrow \text{SPOS}^*(X) \subseteq \text{SPOS}^*(Y)$,
    $X \subseteq Y \Longrightarrow \text{SNEG}^*(X) \supseteq \text{SNEG}^*(Y)$;

(4) $\text{SPOS}_*(X \cap Y) = \text{SPOS}_*(X) \cap \text{SPOS}_*(Y)$,
    $\text{SNEG}_*(X \cap Y) \supseteq \text{SNEG}_*(X) \cap \text{SNEG}_*(Y)$,
    $\text{SPOS}^*(X \cap Y) = \text{SPOS}^*(X) \cap \text{SPOS}^*(Y)$,
    $\text{SNEG}^*(X \cap Y) \supseteq \text{SNEG}^*(X) \cap \text{SNEG}^*(Y)$;

(5) $\text{SPOS}_*(X \cup Y) \supseteq \text{SPOS}_*(X) \cup \text{SPOS}_*(Y)$,
    $\text{SNEG}_*(X \cup Y) = \text{SNEG}_*(X) \cap \text{SNEG}_*(Y)$,
    $\text{SPOS}^*(X \cup Y) \supseteq \text{SPOS}^*(X) \cup \text{SPOS}^*(Y)$,
    $\text{SNEG}^*(X \cup Y) = \text{SNEG}^*(X) \cap \text{SNEG}^*(Y)$;

(6) $\text{SPOS}_*(X \cap Y) \subseteq \text{SPOS}_*(X \cup Y)$,
    $\text{SNEG}_*(X \cap Y) \supseteq \text{SNEG}_*(X \cup Y)$,
    $\text{SPOS}^*(X \cap Y) \subseteq \text{SPOS}^*(X \cup Y)$,
    $\text{SNEG}^*(X \cap Y) \supseteq \text{SNEG}^*(X \cup Y)$.   (20)

The properties in Theorem 4 correspond to the properties of positive and negative regions of rough sets in a complete table.

3.3   An Example

We give an example to illustrate the ideas of constructing the two types of structured positive and negative regions in an incomplete table. Suppose we have an incomplete table given in Table 1.

Table 1. An incomplete table $\widetilde{T}$

	a	b	c
o_1	$\{1\}$	$\{3\}$	$\{6\}$
o_2	$\{1\}$	$\{4\}$	$\{6\}$
o_3	$\{1, 2\}$	$\{5\}$	$\{6\}$
o_4	$\{1\}$	$\{4, 5\}$	$\{6\}$
o_5	$\{2\}$	$\{5\}$	$\{7\}$
o_6	$\{2\}$	$\{5\}$	$\{7\}$

The table $\widetilde{T}$ could be equivalently represented by the family of its completions given in Table 2.

Table 2. The family of completions COMP($\widetilde{T}$)

	a	b	c
o_1	{1}	{3}	{6}
o_2	{1}	{4}	{6}
o_3	**{1}**	{5}	{6}
o_4	{1}	**{4}**	{6}
o_5	{2}	{5}	{7}
o_6	{2}	{5}	{7}

(a) A completion T_1

	a	b	c
o_1	{1}	{3}	{6}
o_2	{1}	{4}	{6}
o_3	**{1}**	{5}	{6}
o_4	{1}	**{5}**	{6}
o_5	{2}	{5}	{7}
o_6	{2}	{5}	{7}

(b) A completion T_2

	a	b	c
o_1	{1}	{3}	{6}
o_2	{1}	{4}	{6}
o_3	**{2}**	{5}	{6}
o_4	{1}	**{4}**	{6}
o_5	{2}	{5}	{7}
o_6	{2}	{5}	{7}

(c) A completion T_3

	a	b	c
o_1	{1}	{3}	{6}
o_2	{1}	{4}	{6}
o_3	**{2}**	{5}	{6}
o_4	{1}	**{5}**	{6}
o_5	{2}	{5}	{7}
o_6	{2}	{5}	{7}

(d) A completion T_4

The formulas in DL_0 and the family CDEFI(OB) are given by Tables 3 and 4, respectively. We take $p_1 = (a = 1)$ as an example. The meaning sets of p_1 in the four completions are:

$$m(p_1|T_1) = \{o_1, o_2, o_3, o_4\},$$
$$m(p_1|T_2) = \{o_1, o_2, o_3, o_4\},$$
$$m(p_1|T_3) = \{o_1, o_2, o_4\},$$
$$m(p_1|T_4) = \{o_1, o_2, o_4\}. \tag{21}$$

By Definition 6, the meaning set of p_1 in $\widetilde{T}$ is:

$$\widetilde{m}(p_1) = \{m(p_1|T), m(p_2|T), m(p_3|T), m(p_4|T)\}$$
$$= \{\{o_1, o_2, o_4\}, \{o_1, o_2, o_3, o_4\}\}. \tag{22}$$

By Theorem 1, $\tilde{m}(p_1)$ is an interval set:

$$\tilde{m}(p_1) = [\{o_1, o_2, o_4\}, \{o_1, o_2, o_3, o_4\}], \tag{23}$$

which is a conjunctively definable interval set. The corresponding conjunctively definable interval concept is:

$$\begin{aligned}
\mathcal{C}_1 &= (p_1, [\{o_1, o_2, o_4\}, \{o_1, o_2, o_3, o_4\}]) \\
&= (a = 1, [\{o_1, o_2, o_4\}, \{o_1, o_2, o_3, o_4\}]). \tag{24}
\end{aligned}$$

Table 3. The formulas in DL_0 in the example

Label	Formula	Label	Formula
p_1	$a = 1$	p_{19}	$(b = 3) \wedge (c = 7)$
p_2	$a = 2$	p_{20}	$(b = 4) \wedge (c = 6)$
p_3	$b = 3$	p_{21}	$(b = 4) \wedge (c = 7)$
p_4	$b = 4$	p_{22}	$(b = 5) \wedge (c = 6)$
p_5	$b = 5$	p_{23}	$(b = 5) \wedge (c = 7)$
p_6	$c = 6$	p_{24}	$(a = 1) \wedge (b = 3) \wedge (c = 6)$
p_7	$c = 7$	p_{25}	$(a = 1) \wedge (b = 3) \wedge (c = 7)$
p_8	$(a = 1) \wedge (b = 3)$	p_{26}	$(a = 1) \wedge (b = 4) \wedge (c = 6)$
p_9	$(a = 1) \wedge (b = 4)$	p_{27}	$(a = 1) \wedge (b = 4) \wedge (c = 7)$
p_{10}	$(a = 1) \wedge (b = 5)$	p_{28}	$(a = 1) \wedge (b = 5) \wedge (c = 6)$
p_{11}	$(a = 2) \wedge (b = 3)$	p_{29}	$(a = 1) \wedge (b = 5) \wedge (c = 7)$
p_{12}	$(a = 2) \wedge (b = 4)$	p_{30}	$(a = 2) \wedge (b = 3) \wedge (c = 6)$
p_{13}	$(a = 2) \wedge (b = 5)$	p_{31}	$(a = 2) \wedge (b = 3) \wedge (c = 7)$
p_{14}	$(a = 1) \wedge (c = 6)$	p_{32}	$(a = 2) \wedge (b = 4) \wedge (c = 6)$
p_{15}	$(a = 1) \wedge (c = 7)$	p_{33}	$(a = 2) \wedge (b = 4) \wedge (c = 7)$
p_{16}	$(a = 2) \wedge (c = 6)$	p_{34}	$(a = 2) \wedge (b = 5) \wedge (c = 6)$
p_{17}	$(a = 2) \wedge (c = 7)$	p_{35}	$(a = 2) \wedge (b = 5) \wedge (c = 7)$
p_{18}	$(b = 3) \wedge (c = 6)$		

Given a set of objects $X = \{o_1, o_3, o_5\}$ and its complement set $X^c = \{o_2, o_4, o_6\}$, the four regions of X are as follows:

(1) $\text{SPOS}_*(X) = \{\mathcal{C}_3, \mathcal{C}_8, \mathcal{C}_{16}, \mathcal{C}_{18}, \mathcal{C}_{24}, \mathcal{C}_{34}\},$
   $\text{SNEG}_*(X) = \{\mathcal{C}_4, \mathcal{C}_9, \mathcal{C}_{20}, \mathcal{C}_{26}\};$

(2) $\text{SPOS}^*(X) = \{\mathcal{C}_3, \mathcal{C}_8, \mathcal{C}_{10}, \mathcal{C}_{16}, \mathcal{C}_{18}, \mathcal{C}_{22}, \mathcal{C}_{24}, \mathcal{C}_{28}, \mathcal{C}_{34}\},$
   $\text{SNEG}^*(X) = \{\mathcal{C}_4, \mathcal{C}_9, \mathcal{C}_{10}, \mathcal{C}_{20}, \mathcal{C}_{26}, \mathcal{C}_{28}\}. \tag{25}$

There is redundancy in these four regions. For example, the two concepts $\mathcal{C}_4$ and $\mathcal{C}_{26}$ have the same extension but different intensions. Accordingly, the regions including both $\mathcal{C}_4$ and $\mathcal{C}_{26}$, that is, $\text{SNEG}_*(X)$ and $\text{SNEG}^*(X)$, have redundancy in them.

Table 4. The family CDEFI(OB) in the example

Label	Intension	Extension	Label	Intension	Extension
C_1	p_1	$[\{o_1, o_2, o_4\}, \{o_1, o_2, o_3, o_4\}]$	C_{19}	p_{19}	$[\emptyset, \emptyset]$
C_2	p_2	$[\{o_5, o_6\}, \{o_3, o_5, o_6\}]$	C_{20}	p_{20}	$[\{o_2\}, \{o_2, o_4\}]$
C_3	p_3	$[\{o_1\}, \{o_1\}]$	C_{21}	p_{21}	$[\emptyset, \emptyset]$
C_4	p_4	$[\{o_2\}, \{o_2, o_4\}]$	C_{22}	p_{22}	$[\{o_3\}, \{o_3, o_4\}]$
C_5	p_5	$[\{o_3, o_5, o_6\}, \{o_3, o_4, o_5, o_6\}]$	C_{23}	p_{23}	$[\{o_5, o_6\}, \{o_5, o_6\}]$
C_6	p_6	$[\{o_1, o_2, o_3, o_4\}, \{o_1, o_2, o_3, o_4\}]$	C_{24}	p_{24}	$[\{o_1\}, \{o_1\}]$
C_7	p_7	$[\{o_5, o_6\}, \{o_5, o_6\}]$	C_{25}	p_{25}	$[\emptyset, \emptyset]$
C_8	p_8	$[\{o_1\}, \{o_1\}]$	C_{26}	p_{26}	$[\{o_2\}, \{o_2, o_4\}]$
C_9	p_9	$[\{o_2\}, \{o_2, o_4\}]$	C_{27}	p_{27}	$[\emptyset, \emptyset]$
C_{10}	p_{10}	$[\emptyset, \{o_3, o_4\}]$	C_{28}	p_{28}	$[\emptyset, \{o_3, o_4\}]$
C_{11}	p_{11}	$[\emptyset, \emptyset]$	C_{29}	p_{29}	$[\emptyset, \emptyset]$
C_{12}	p_{12}	$[\emptyset, \emptyset]$	C_{30}	p_{30}	$[\emptyset, \emptyset]$
C_{13}	p_{13}	$[\{o_5, o_6\}, \{o_3, o_5, o_6\}]$	C_{31}	p_{31}	$[\emptyset, \emptyset]$
C_{14}	p_{14}	$[\{o_1, o_2, o_4\}, \{o_1, o_2, o_3, o_4\}]$	C_{32}	p_{32}	$[\emptyset, \emptyset]$
C_{15}	p_{15}	$[\emptyset, \emptyset]$	C_{33}	p_{33}	$[\emptyset, \emptyset]$
C_{16}	p_{16}	$[\emptyset, \{o_3\}]$	C_{34}	p_{34}	$[\emptyset, \{o_3\}]$
C_{17}	p_{17}	$[\{o_5, o_6\}, \{o_5, o_6\}]$	C_{35}	p_{35}	$[\{o_5, o_6\}, \{o_5, o_6\}]$
C_{18}	p_{18}	$[\{o_1\}, \{o_1\}]$			

4   Conclusions

We have proposed a new semantically sound framework to study rough set approximations in an incomplete table. In a complete table, we use the family of conjunctively definable concepts to define a pair of structured positive and negative regions in order to approximate a set of objects. These two structured regions correspond to Pawlak rough set approximations and the standard positive and negative regions. Following the same argument, in an incomplete table we introduced the notion of conjunctively definable interval concepts. By using the family of conjunctively definable interval concepts, we construct two types of structured positive and negative regions. These regions are semantically meaningful in the sense that the possible-world semantics fully and truthfully reflects all partial information of an incomplete table. By adopting possible-world semantics of an incomplete table, we transform the study of an incomplete table into a study of a family of complete tables. By using concepts instead of sets to construct the regions, we explicitly include the intensions, that is, the formulas, which makes the rule induction much simpler. As future work, we will investigate rule induction in an incomplete table based on the structured regions introduced in this paper.

A   Appendix: Proof of Theorem 1

We prove Theorem 1 by verifying $\tilde{m}(p) \subseteq [\cap\tilde{m}(p), \cup\tilde{m}(p)]$ and $[\cap\tilde{m}(p), \cup\tilde{m}(p)] \subseteq \tilde{m}(p)$.

(1) $\tilde{m}(p) \subseteq [\cap\tilde{m}(p), \cup\tilde{m}(p)]$.

For any set $S \in \tilde{m}(p)$, it is evident that $\cap\tilde{m}(p) \subseteq S \subseteq \cup\tilde{m}(p)$, which means $S \in [\cap\tilde{m}(p), \cup\tilde{m}(p)]$. Thus, $\tilde{m}(p) \subseteq [\cap\tilde{m}(p), \cup\tilde{m}(p)]$.

(2) $[\cap\tilde{m}(p), \cup\tilde{m}(p)] \subseteq \tilde{m}(p)$.

By Definition 6, for any set $S \in [\cap\tilde{m}(p), \cup\tilde{m}(p)]$, we prove that $S \in \tilde{m}(p)$ by constructing a completion $T \in \text{COMP}(\tilde{T})$ in which $S = m(p|T)$. Suppose $p = (a_1 = v_1) \wedge (a_2 = v_2) \wedge \cdots \wedge (a_m = v_m)$ and $A_p = \{a_1, a_2 \ldots, a_m\}$. The completion T is constructed as given in Table 5. One can easily verify that in Table 5, the objects in S satisfy p and the objects in $OB - S$ do not satisfy p. That is, $S = m(p|T)$. Thus, $[\cap\tilde{m}(p), \cup\tilde{m}(p)] \subseteq \tilde{m}(p)$.

Table 5. A completion T in which $S = m(p|T)$

Objects	Attributes	
	A_p	$AT - A_p$
S	$\forall a_i \in A_p, I_{a_i}(x) = v_i$	$\forall a \in AT - A_p, I_a(x) \in \tilde{I}_a(x)$
$OB - S$	$\exists a_i \in A_p, I_{a_i}(x) \in \tilde{I}_{a_i}(x) - \{v_i\}$	

References

1. Arnauld, A., Nicole, P.: Logic or the Art of Thinking. Trans. Jill Vance Buroker. Cambridge University Press, Cambridge (1996)
2. Buroker, J.: Port Royal Logic. Stanford Encyclopedia of Philosophy. http://plato. stanford.edu/entries/port-royal-logic/. Accessed 13 Mar 2017
3. D'eer, L.: A semantical and computational approach to covering-based rough sets. Ph.D. thesis, Universiteit Gent (2017)
4. D'eer, L., Cornelis, C., Yao, Y.Y.: A semantically sound approach to Pawlak rough sets and covering-based rough sets. Int. J. Approx. Reason. **78**, 62–72 (2016)
5. Grzymała-Busse, J.W., Clark, P.G., Kuehnhausen, M.: Generalized probabilistic approximations of incomplete data. Int. J. Approx. Reason. **55**, 180–196 (2014)
6. Grzymała-Busse, J.W., Rzasa, W.: Local and global approximations for incomplete data. In: Peters, J.F., Skowron, A. (eds.) Transactions on Rough Sets VIII. LNCS, vol. 5084, pp. 21–34. Springer, Heidelberg (2008). doi:10.1007/978-3-540-85064-9_2
7. Guan, Y.Y., Wang, H.K.: Set-valued information systems. Inf. Sci. **176**, 2507–2525 (2006)
8. Hu, M.J., Yao, Y.Y.: Definability in incomplete information tables. In: Flores, V., et al. (eds.) IJCRS 2016. LNCS, vol. 9920, pp. 177–186. Springer, Cham (2016). doi:10.1007/978-3-319-47160-0_16
9. Jaworski, W.: Generalized indiscernibility relations: applications for missing values and analysis of structural objects. In: Peters, J.F., Skowron, A. (eds.) Transactions on Rough Sets VIII. LNCS, vol. 5084, pp. 116–145. Springer, Heidelberg (2008). doi:10.1007/978-3-540-85064-9_7

10. Kryszkiewicz, M.: Rules in incomplete information systems. Inf. Sci. **113**, 271–292 (1999)
11. Kryszkiewicz, M.: Rough set approach to incomplete information systems. Inf. Sci. **112**, 39–49 (1998)
12. Leung, Y., Li, D.: Maximal consistent block technique for rule acquisition in incomplete information systems. Inf. Sci. **153**, 85–106 (2003)
13. Li, R.P., Yao, Y.Y.: Indiscernibility and similarity in an incomplete information table. In: Yu, J., Greco, S., Lingras, P., Wang, G.Y., Skowron, A. (eds.) RSKT 2010. LNCS, vol. 6401, pp. 110–117. Springer, Heidelberg (2010). doi:10.1007/978-3-642-16248-0_20
14. Lipski, W.: On semantics issues connected with incomplete information table. ACM Trans. Database Syst. **4**, 262–296 (1979)
15. Marek, W., Pawlak, Z.: Information storage and retrieval systems: mathematical foundations. Theoret. Comput. Sci. **1**, 331–354 (1976)
16. Nakata, M., Sakai, H.: Twofold rough approximations under incomplete information. Int. J. Gen. Syst. **42**, 546–571 (2013)
17. Orlowska, E.: Incomplete Information: Rough Set Analysis, vol. 13. Physica, Heidelberg (1998)
18. Pawlak, Z.: Rough Sets: Theoretical Aspects of Reasoning About Data. Kluwer Academic Publishers, Boston (1991)
19. Pawlak, Z.: Rough sets. Int. J. Comput. Inf. Sci. **11**, 341–356 (1982)
20. Sakai, H., Nakata, M., Ślęzak, D.: Rule generation in Lipski's incomplete information databases. In: Szczuka, M., Kryszkiewicz, M., Ramanna, S., Jensen, R., Hu, Q.H. (eds.) RSCTC 2010. LNCS, vol. 6086, pp. 376–385. Springer, Heidelberg (2010). doi:10.1007/978-3-642-13529-3_40
21. Stefanowski, J., Tsoukiàs, A.: On the extension of rough sets under incomplete information. In: Zhong, N., Skowron, A., Ohsuga, S. (eds.) RSFDGrC 1999. LNCS, vol. 1711, pp. 73–81. Springer, Heidelberg (1999). doi:10.1007/978-3-540-48061-7_11
22. Wang, G.Y.: Extension of rough set under incomplete information systems. J. Comput. Res. Dev. **39**, 1238–1243 (2002)
23. Yao, Y.Y.: Rough-set concept analysis: interpreting RS-definable concepts based on ideas from formal concept analysis. Inf. Sci. **346–347**, 442–462 (2016)
24. Yao, Y.Y.: The two sides of the theory of rough sets. Knowl.-Based Syst. **80**, 67–77 (2015)
25. Yao, Y.Y.: Rough sets and three-way decisions. In: Ciucci, D., Wang, G.Y., Mitra, S., Wu, W.Z. (eds.) RSKT 2015. LNCS, vol. 9436, pp. 62–73. Springer, Cham (2015). doi:10.1007/978-3-319-25754-9_6
26. Yao, Y.Y.: An outline of a theory of three-way decisions. In: Yao, J.T., Yang, Y., Słowiński, R., Greco, S., Li, H., Mitra, S., Polkowski, L. (eds.) RSCTC 2012. LNCS, vol. 7413, pp. 1–17. Springer, Heidelberg (2012). doi:10.1007/978-3-642-32115-3_1
27. Yao, Y.Y.: Interval-set algebra for qualitative knowledge representation. In: Proceedings of the Fifth International Conference on Computing and Information, pp. 370–374 (1993)
28. Yao, Y.Y., Hu, M.J.: A definition of structured rough set approximations. In: Kryszkiewicz, M., Cornelis, C., Ciucci, D., Medina-Moreno, J., Motoda, H., Raś, Z.W. (eds.) RSEISP 2014. LNCS, vol. 8537, pp. 111–122. Springer, Cham (2014). doi:10.1007/978-3-319-08729-0_10

Two Novel Decomposition Approaches for Knowledge Acquisition Model

Na Jiao$^{(\boxtimes)}$

Department of Information Science and Technology,
East China University of Political Science and Law,
Shanghai 201620, People's Republic of China
zdx.jn@163.com

Abstract. Knowledge acquisition, one of essential issues for data mining, has always been a hot topic due to the explosive growth of information. However, when handling large-scale data, many current knowledge acquisition algorithms based on rough set theory are inefficient. In this paper, novel decomposition approaches for knowledge acquisition are put forward. The principal of decomposition is to split a complex problem in several problems. Those problems are composed of a master-problem and several sub-problems which are simpler, more manageable and more solvable by using existing induction methods, then joining them together in order to solve the original problem. Compared with some traditional algorithms, the efficiency of the proposed approaches can be illustrated by experiments with standard datasets from UCI database.

Keywords: Knowledge acquisition · Decomposition · Master-problem · Sub-problem · Rough sets

1 Introduction

Knowledge acquisition can be viewed as one of the most fundamental problems in the field of data mining. It is defined as a process of eliminating superfluous attributes and selecting relevant attributes out of the larger set of candidate attributes. Rough sets is a powerful mathematical tool proposed by Pawlak [1–4,10–13], for dealing with imprecise, uncertain, and vague information. One limitation of rough set theory is the lack of effective algorithms for processing a relative large number of attributes. We may gain worse performance even get no result when dealing with large-scale data with traditional knowledge acquisition algorithms based on rough set theory.

The main motivation of this study is to design a approach that can deal with massive and complicated real-world problems. We apply a decomposition idea to solve complex problems. The principal of decomposition [5,6] is to split a large and complex task in several simpler and more manageable subtasks that can be solved by using existing induction algorithms. Their results will be jointed together in the sequel in order to solve the original problem.

© Springer International Publishing AG 2017
L. Polkowski et al. (Eds.): IJCRS 2017, Part II, LNAI 10314, pp. 216–225, 2017.
DOI: 10.1007/978-3-319-60840-2_15

The decomposition method can make the original task easier and less time consuming. However, some decomposition approaches may result in the loss of information or distortion of original data and knowledge, and can even lead to the original data mining system unusable.

We should choose the appropriate decomposition approach in order to avoid these disadvantages of decomposition in data mining. Jiawei Han introduces multirelational data mining [7] using keys to link multiple tables, furthermore, there is the same expression in database. When we convert a single table into multirelational tables, there is no any loss of information or distortion of original data and knowledge. Therefore, we split a large-scale information system in a master-information system and several sub-information systems. This approach may greatly improve computational efficiency.

2   Preliminaries

In this section, we briefly introduce the basic concepts of rough sets and describe two reduct construction algorithms and computing core algorithm.

2.1   Rough Set Theory

We assume that knowledge discussed in this paper is represented by information system (also called information table).

Definition 1. Information system: An information system is defined as $S = \langle U, A, V, f \rangle$, where U is a non-empty finite set of objects; A is a non-empty finite set of featutes; $V = \bigcup_{a \in A} V_a$, V_a is a set of attribute values of attribute a; and $f : U \times A \to V$ is an information function.

For any $B \subseteq A$, an equivalence(indiscernibility) relation induced B by on U is defined as Definition 2.

Definition 2. Equivalence relation:

$$IND(B) = \{(x, y) \in U \times U | \forall b \in B, b(x) = b(y)\}. \tag{1}$$

The family of all equivalence classes of $IND(B)$, i.e., the partition induced by B, is given in Definition 3.

Definition 3. Partition:

$$U/IND(B) = \{[x]_B | x \in U\}, \tag{2}$$

where $[x]_B$ is the equivalence class containing x. All the elements in $[x]_B$ are equivalent (indiscernible) with respect to B. Equivalence classes are elementary sets in rough set theory.

For any $B \subseteq A$, B is called a reduct of A, if B satisfies the two conditions.

Definition 4. Reduct:

- $U/IND(B) = U/IND(A)$;
- for any $a \in B$, $U/IND(B - \{a\}) \neq U/IND(A)$.

Core is defined as Definition 5.

Definition 5. Core:

$$Core = \cap_{j \leq r} W_j. \tag{3}$$

$\{W_j | j \leq r\}$ is the set of reducts.

Finding all reducts is NP-hard. However, it is usually enough for most practical applications to find one of the reducts. The knowledge reduction methods of this paper are to find a reduct.

2.2   Knowledge Reduction Algorithms and Computing Core Algorithm

General knowledge reduction algorithm (GKR) starts with the entire attribute set and consecutively deletes one attribure at a time until we obtain a reduct. The algorithm can check every attribute and eliminate the attributes that are superfluous.

Computing core algorithm (CC) can check all attributes in information system. If the attribute is indispensable, it is a core attribute, or else continues the next loop. At last, we get all the core attributes.

According to CC algorithm, core is computed. Core knowledge reduction algorithm (CKR) starts with core, checks the remainder and deletes one attribute at a time until we obtain a reduct.

GKR and CKR algorithms are very brief and comprehensible. And they are efficient when the number of attributes is small. However, a large number of attributes in information system will decrease the performance greatly because GKR and CKR algorithms have to check every attribute.

In order to solve the problem we employ a decomposition method for knowledge reduction. The idea of decomposition is to break a large and complex table down into several simpler and more manageable sub-tables that can be solved by using existing induction methods. Their results will be jointed together in the sequel in order to solve the original table. The decomposition approach can make the original task easier and less time consuming. In this paper, we propose a decomposition based method to perform knowledge reduction. The proposed knowledge reduction algorithms based on decomposition can be described as detailed below.

3   Proposed Algorithms

In this section, we introduce some definitions and properties at first. Then the knowledge reduction and computing core algorithms based on decomposition are proposed.

3.1 Basic Definitions

We break an information table down into a master-table and several sub-tables. The master-table consists of several joint attributes which are the keywords in sub-tables. The sub-table is composed of a subset of attributes.

Definition 6. Sub-table, master-table and mid-table. Given an information system $S =< U, A, V, f >$.

- A sub-table is defined as $S^{B_i} =< U^{B_i}, B_i \cup \{b_i\}, V^{B_i}, f^{B_i} >$, $i = 1, 2, \cdots, m$, where U is a non-empty finite set of objects, called universe; $B_i \subseteq A, i = 1, 2, \cdots, m$, $A = \cup_{i=1}^{m} B_i$ and $B_i \cap B_j = \emptyset, i \neq j$. b_i is a joint attribute which join the sub-table to the master-table and it is a keyword in S^{B_i}; $V^{B_i} = \bigcup_{a \in B_i} V_a^{B_i}$, $V_a^{B_i}$ is a set of attribute values of attribute a; and $f^{B_i} : U^{B_i} \times B_i \to V^{B_i}$ is an information function.
- A master-table is defined as $S^Q =< U, Q, V^Q, f^Q >$, where U is a non-empty finite set of objects, called universe; $Q = \cup_{i=1}^{m} \{b_i\}$ is a set of all joint attributes; $V^Q = \bigcup_{a \in Q} V_a^Q$, V_a^Q is a set of attribute values of attribute a; and $f^Q : U \times Q \to V^Q$ is an information function.
- A mid-table is defined as $S^{M_i} =< U, M_i, V^{M_i}, f^{M_i} >$, $i = 1, 2, \cdots, m$, where U is a non-empty finite set of objects, called universe; $M_i = (Q - \{b_i\}) \cup B_i$; $V^{M_i} = \bigcup_{a \in M_i} V_a^{M_i}$, $V_a^{M_i}$ is a set of attribute values of attribute a; and $f^{M_i} : U \times M_i \to V^{M_i}$ is an information function.

Example 1. Table 1 is a information table, we decompose it into one master-table (Table 2) and two sub-tables (Tables 3 and 4). Combine Tables 2 and 3 to compose a mid-table Table 5. Similarly, Table 6 comes from Tables 2 and 4.

Table 1. An information table

U	a_1	a_2	a_3	a_4
1	1	1	1	0
2	1	0	1	1
3	0	0	0	1
4	1	0	1	0

Table 2. A master-table

U	b_1	b_2
1	b_1^1	b_2^1
2	b_1^2	b_2^2
3	b_1^3	b_2^3
4	b_1^2	b_2^1

Table 3. The first sub-table

b_1	a_1	a_2
b_1^1	1	1
b_1^2	1	0
b_1^3	0	0

Table 4. The second sub-table

b_2	a_3	a_4
b_2^1	1	0
b_2^2	1	1
b_2^3	0	1

Table 5. The first mid-table

U	a_1	a_2	b_2
1	1	1	b_2^1
2	1	0	b_2^2
3	0	0	b_2^3
4	1	0	b_2^1

Table 6. The second mid-table

U	b_1	a_3	a_4
1	b_1^1	1	0
2	b_1^2	1	1
3	b_1^3	0	1
4	b_1^2	1	0

3.2 Basic Properties

The following are some properties according to the above definition. Assume an information system $S = < U, A, V, f >$, sub-tables $S^{B_i} = < U^{B_i}, B_i \cup \{b_i\}, V^{B_i}, f^{B_i} >$, $i = 1, 2, \cdots, m$, a master-table $S^Q = < U, Q, V^Q, f^Q >$, mid-tables $S^{M_i} = < U, M_i, V^{M_i}, f^{M_i} >$, $i = 1, 2, \cdots, m$. Some properties are described as follows.

Property 1. The attribute a in the original information table S is indispensable, that is $U/IND\,(A - \{a\}) \neq U/IND\,(A)$, iff the attribute a in S belongs to $Core$, that is $a \in Core$.

Property 2. The partition induced by Q in the master-table S^Q is equivalent to the partition induced by A in the original information table S, that is $U/IND\,(Q) = U/IND\,(A)$.

Corollary 1. The partition induced by M_i in the mid-table S^{M_i} is equivalent to the partition induced by A in the original information table S, that is $U/IND\,(M_i) = U/IND\,(A)$.

Property 3. The joint attribute b_i in the master-table S^Q is dispensable, that is $U/IND\,(Q - \{b_i\}) = U/IND\,(Q)$, iff the attribute set B_i in the original information table S corresponding to the joint attribute b_i is dispensable, that is $U/IND\,(A - B_i) = U/IND\,(A)$.

Corollary 2. The attribute a in the mid-table S^{M_i} is dispensable, that is $a \in B_i, U/IND\,(M_i - \{a\}) = U/IND\,(M_i)$, iff the attribute a in the original information table S is dispensable, that is $U/IND\,(A - \{a\}) = U/IND\,(A)$.

Corollary 3. If the joint attribute b_i in the master-table S^Q is indispensable, that is $U/IND\,(Q - \{b_i\}) \neq U/IND\,(Q)$, then a subset E included in the attribute set B_i corresponding to the joint attribute b_i is indispensable in the original information table S, that is $E \subseteq B_i, U/IND\,(A - E) \neq U/IND\,(A)$.

Corollary 4. If the attribute a in the mid-table S^{M_i} is indispensable (a core attribute), that is $U/IND\,(M_i - \{a\}) \neq U/IND\,(M_i)$, then the attribute a in the original information table S is indispensable (a core attribute), that is $U/IND\,(A - \{a\}) \neq U/IND\,(A)$.

These properties will be applied in following methods.

3.3 General Knowledge Reduction Based on Decomposition

According to the above definitions and properties, we employ decomposition principle and modify GKR algorithm. Suppose that the number of sub-tables is k. First, we break the original information table down into one master-table and k sub-tables. The attributes of the original information table are divided equally among k sub-tables. The joint attribute and a subset of attributes compose a sub-table. The master-table is made up of k joint attributes that are the key words in sub-tables.

Then if the joint attribute in master-table is dispensable, we can delete the joint attribute in master-table and combine the same objects (Properties 2, 3). Judge the next joint attribute. Otherwise, we combine a sub-table with the master-table to compose a mid-table, if the attribute in the mid-table is dispensable, we can delete the attribute in the mid-table and combine the same objects (Corollaries 1, 2), or else continue the next loop. Finally, a reduction can be found.

Algorithm 1. General knowledge reduction method based on decomposition (GKRD)

  Input: An information system $S = \langle U, A, V, f \rangle$. The number of sub-tables is k.

  Output: A reduct P.

  (1) Break S down into one master-table $S^Q =< U, Q, V^Q, f^Q >$ and sub-
      tables $S^{B_i} =< U^{B_i}, B_i \cup \{b_i\}, V^{B_i}, f^{B_i} >$, $i = 1, \cdots, k$. Set $P = A$.

  (2) **While** every joint attribute $b_i \in Q$ **do**

  (3)   **If** $U/IND\,(Q - \{b_i\}) = U/IND\,(Q)$, **then**

  (4) b_i is dispensable and delete it from S^Q, i.e., $Q = Q - \{b_i\}$.

  (5) $P = P - B_i$.

  (6)   Combine the same objects.

  (7)   **Else**

  (8)   Compose a mid-table$S^{M_i}$with a sub-table$S^{B_i}$and the master-tableS^Q.

  (9)   **While** every attribute $a \in B_i$ **do**

  (10)   **If** $U/IND\,(M_i - \{a\}) = U/IND\,(M_i)$, **then**

  (11) a is dispensable and delete it from S^{M_i}, i.e., $B_i = B_i - \{a\}$.

  (12) $P = P - \{a\}$.

  (13)   Combine the same objects.

  (14) Output P.

The attributes of an information table are divided into several parts. We process every part instead of every attribute. Every part is substituted by a joint attribute. In other words, $|A|$ attributes are compressed to k joint attributes. If the joint attribute is dispensable, the attribute set corresponding to the joint attribute is dispensable and can be deleted all at once. Each attribute in this attribute set needn't to be checked again. Even though the joint attribute is indispensable, the scale of the mid-table is compressed a lot.

3.4   Computing Core Based on Decomposition

Core knowledge reduction method is to construct a reduct from the core, and consequently delete one attribute from the remainder until a reduct is obtained. Hence we firstly modify computing core algorithm according to the proposed decomposition principle.

We assume that the number of sub-tables is k. We decompose the original information table into one master-table and k sub-tables.

Algorithm 2. The method of computing core based on decomposition (CCD)

    Input: An information system $S = \langle U, A, V, f \rangle$. The number of sub-tables is k.

    Output: Core denoted by $CORE$.

(1) Break S down into one master-table $S^Q = <U, Q, V^Q, f^Q>$ and sub-tables $S^{B_i} = <U^{B_i}, B_i \cup \{b_i\}, V^{B_i}, f^{B_i}>$, $i = 1, \cdots, k$. Set $CORE = \emptyset$.

(2) **While** every joint attribute $b_i \in Q$ **do**

(3)   **If** $U/IND\,(Q - \{b_i\}) \neq U/IND\,(Q)$, **then**

(4)   Compose a mid-table S^{M_i} with a sub-table S^{B_i} and the master-table S^Q.

(5)   **While** every attribute $a \in B_i$ **do**

(6)   **If** $U/IND\,(M_i - \{a\}) \neq U/IND\,(M_i)$, **then**

(7) a is indispensable, i.e., $CORE = CORE \cup \{a\}$.

(8) Output $CORE$.

3.5   Core Knowledge Reduction Based on Decomposition

According to the above computing core method, core is put into the first sub-table and others are decomposed equally into $k - 1$ sub-tables. Initial condition starts at the second joint attribute. Repeating the same procedure as GKRD algorithm, all selected attributes consist of a reduct.

Algorithm 3. Core knowledge reduction method based on decomposition (CKRD)

    Input: An information system $S = \langle U, A, V, f \rangle$. The number of sub-tables is k.

    Output: A reduct P.

(1) According to CCD algorithm, calculate the core $CORE$ in S.

(2) **If** $U/IND\,(CORE) = U/IND\,(A)$, **then** $P = CORE$, **stop**

(3) Set $P = A$.

(4) Break S down into one master-table $S^Q = <U, Q, V^Q, f^Q>$ and sub-tables $S^{B_i} = <U^{B_i}, B_i \cup \{b_i\}, V^{B_i}, f^{B_i}>$, $i = 1, \cdots, k$. (core $CORE$ is put

        into the first sub-table and others are decomposed equally into $k - 1$ sub-tables)

(5) **While** every joint attribute $b_i \in Q$ ($i = 2, \cdots, k$) **do**

(6)   **If** $U/IND\,(Q - \{b_i\}) = U/IND\,(Q)$, **then**

(7) b_i is dispensable and delete it from S^Q, i.e., $Q = Q - \{b_i\}$.

(8) $P = P - B_i$.

(9)   Combine the same objects.

(10)   **Else**

(11)   Compose a mid-table S^{M_i} with a sub-table S^{B_i} and the master-table S^Q.

(12)   **While** every attribute $a \in B_i$ **do**

(13)   **If** $U/IND\,(M_i - \{a\}) = U/IND\,(M_i)$, **then**

(14) a is dispensable and delete it from S^{M_i}, i.e., $B_i = B_i - \{a\}$.

(15) $P = P - \{a\}$.

(16)   Combine the same objects.

(17) Output P.

Clearly, the chance of deleting joint attributes of CKRD algorithm all at once is higher than GKRD algorithm, the procedure of computing core will increase the computation time. The time complexity of CKRD involves two parts which are the time complexity of CCD and time complexity of rest procedures.

4 Experiments

In this section, we show that our knowledge reduction methods based on decomposition can reduce the computation complexity significantly.

4.1 A Comparative Experiment on Six Datasets

In order to test the validity of the algorithm, we compare the proposed methods with general knowledge reduction algorithm (GKR), computing core algorithm (CC) and core knowledge reduction algorithm (CKR). According to GKRD, CCD and CKRD algorithms of this paper, we suppose the number of sub-tables is four. We perform the experiments on publicly available datasets from UCI database (These datasets can be downloaded at http://www.ics.uci.edu). The experiment results are shown in Table 7. The results is average of repeating 10 times experiments.

When there are missing values in datasets, these values are filled with mean values for continuous attributes and majority values for nominal attributes [8]. If the datasets are numerical, all continuous attributes are discretized using Equal Frequency per Interval [9].

Table 7. Comparison of efficiencies of different knowledge reduction algorithms

Dataset	Objects	Attributes	GKR	**GKRD**	CKR	**CKRD**
Breast	699	10	1S	**1S**	2S	**1S**
Chess	3196	37	52S	**18S**	102S	**32S**
Insurance	9822	86	190S	**44S**	1706S	**64S**
Mushroom	8124	23	112S	**31S**	596S	**57S**
Optical	1796	65	15S	**4S**	44S	**10S**
SPECT	267	45	6S	**1S**	15S	**3S**

As listed in Table 7, the performance of GKRD algorithm outperforms that of GKR algorithm. CKRD method is less time consuming than CKR method. GKRD and CKRD have been shown to be superior to GKR and CKR.

4.2 An Experiment on Optical Dataset with Different Attributes

The second experiment is performed on Optical dataset which has 65 attributes and 1796 objects. We select bottom 10, 20, 30, 40, 50, 60 and 65 attributes from this dataset respectively. According to our proposed two methods we break the datasets down into one master-table and four sub-tables.

From Fig. 1, we can see the comparison of efficiencies of various methods as attributes increasing gradually. As depicted in Fig. 1, the running time of our methods increases slightly as attributes increasing gradually. However, other methods consume much more time. GKRD and CKRD outperform other two methods.

4.3 An Experiment on Mushroom Dataset with Different Objects

We do another experiment on Mushroom dataset which has 23 attributes and 8124 objects. We select top 2000, 4000, 6000 and 8124 objects from this dataset. The number of sub-tables is the same as the above experiments.

Figure 2 shows the comparison of efficiencies of various algorithms based on different size of objects. As depicted in Fig. 2, GKRD and CKRD can achieve better performance than GKR and CKR.

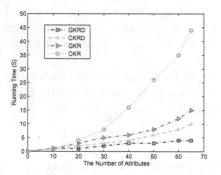
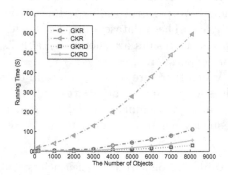

The comparison of performances of different attributes on Optical dataset

The comparison of performances of different objects on Mushroom dataset

Fig. 1. The comparison of performances of different attributes on optical dataset

Fig. 2. The comparison of performances of different objects on Mushroom dataset

5   Conclusions

Knowledge reduction is a key task in the research on rough set theory. Existing traditional methods do not perform very well on large datasets. In this paper, we introduce some efficient decomposition methods for rough set knowledge reduction and core calculation. We decompose a complex information table into a master-table and several sub-tables, which can be dealt with simply, more manageable and solvable with existing induction methods. Then after joining the results of decomposition together, the original table can be easily handed. Extensive experiments conducted on UCI database are to test validity of the proposed algorithms. Experimental results demonstrate that our methods are efficient for various datasets.

Acknowledgements. This paper is supported by the National Social Science Fund (Granted No. 13CFX049), Shanghai University Young Teacher Training Program (Granted No. hdzf10008) and the Research Fund for East China University of Political science and Law (Granted No. 11H2K034).

References

1. Pawlak, Z.: Rough sets. Int. J. Inf. Comput. Sci. **11**(5), 341–356 (1982)
2. Yao, Y.Y., Zhao, Y.: Discernibility matrix simplification for constructing attribute reducts. Inform. Sci. **179**, 867–882 (2009)
3. Miao, D.Q., Wang, J.: Information-based algorithm for reduction of knowledge. In: IEEE International Conference on Intelligent Processing Systems, pp. 1155–1158 (1997)
4. Wang, G.Y.: Rough Set Theory and Knowledge Acquisition, Xi'an Jiaotong University Press, Xi'an (2001) (in Chinese)
5. Rokach, L.: Decomposition methodology for classification tasks: a meta decomposer framework. Pattern Anal. Appl. **9**, 257–271 (2006)
6. Cheng, C.B., Wang, K.P.: Solving a vehicle routing problem with time windows by a decomposition technique and a genetic algorithm. Expert Syst. Appl. **36**, 7758–7763 (2009)
7. Han, J.W., Kamber, M., Mining, D.: Concepts and Techniques, 2nd edn. Morgan Kaufmann, Burlington (2006)
8. Grzymala-Busse, J.W., Grzymala-Busse, W.J.: Handling missing attribute values. In: Maimon, O., Rokach, L. (eds.) Handbook of Data Mining and Knowledge Discovery, pp. 37–57. Springer US, New York (2005). doi:10.1007/0-387-25465-X_3
9. Grzymala-Busse, J.W.: Discretization of numerical attributes. In: Klsgen, W., Zytkow, J. (eds.) Handbook of Data Mining and Knowledge Discovery, pp. 218–225. Oxford University Press, Oxford (2002)
10. Muhammad, S.R., Usman, Q.: An incremental dependency calculation technique for feature selection using rough sets. Inf. Sci. **343–344**(20), 41–65 (2016)
11. Meng, Z.Q., Shi, Z.Z.: On quick attribute reduction in decision-theoretic rough set models. Inf. Sci. **330**(10), 226–244 (2016)
12. Zhang, X.H., Miao, D.Q., Liu, C.H., Le, M.L.: Constructive methods of rough approximation operators and multigranulation rough sets. Knowl.-Based Syst. **91**(1), 114–125 (2016)
13. Yao, Y.Y., She, Y.H.: Rough set models in multigranulation spaces. Inf. Sci. **327**(10), 40–56 (2016)

Three-Way Decisions with DEA Approach

Dun Liu[1,2(✉)] and Decui Liang[3]

[1] School of Economics and Management, Southwest Jiaotong University,
Chengdu 610031, People's Republic of China
newton83@163.com
[2] Institute for Software Research, Carnegie Mellon University,
Pittsburgh, PA 15213, USA
[3] School of Management and Economics,
University of Electronic Science and Technology of China,
Chengdu 610054, People's Republic of China
decuiliang@126.com

Abstract. In this paper, we set up a data envelopment analysis (DEA) based three-way decision approach to solve the "multi-input and multi-output" problem when the decision attributes are "more than one" in rough sets. The estimation of production frontiers of DEA, is used to generate the three regions by three-way decisions: DEA efficiency region, weak DEA efficiency region and DEA inefficiency region, respectively. An empirical study of company efficiency evaluation is employed to validate the reasonability and effectiveness of the proposed method.

Keywords: Three-way decisions · Data envelopment analysis · Rough sets · Multiple decision-making

1 Introduction

Three-way decisions (3WD), a "trisecting-and-acting" cognitive model proposed by Yao [19], have drawn more and more attentions in nearly seven years. The basic idea of three-way decisions is to divide a universal set into three pairwise disjoint regions, and then the decision makers utilize appropriate strategies to generate decision rules from the different regions. Yao presented some basic models of three-way decisions in [18], *e.g.*, interval sets and three-valued logic, three-valued approximations and fuzzy sets, shadowed sets, Pawlak approximations and rough sets, etc. These perspectives provided some new ideas to help people to easily understand the intension and extension of three-way decisions.

As a fundamental uncertainty mathematical theory on soft computing, rough set theory (RST) uses lower and upper approximations to describe the uncertainties on decision problems. Three regions (positive region, boundary region and negative region), form a trisection or a tri-partition of an universal set. If we further consider the linearly ordered relation of three regions, *e.g.*, positive region ≻ boundary region ≻ negative region in rough sets, three different types of decision rules are created after decision procedure. The rules generated by the

© Springer International Publishing AG 2017
L. Polkowski et al. (Eds.): IJCRS 2017, Part II, LNAI 10314, pp. 226–237, 2017.
DOI: 10.1007/978-3-319-60840-2_16

positive region are used for making a decision of acceptance, the rules generated by the negative region are used for making a decision of rejection, the rules generated by the boundary region are used for making a decision of noncommitment [16,17]. In general, rough sets can be seemed as a special cognitive model of three-way decisions.

In many decision problems, we usually consider a decision table has "multiple conditional attributes but one decision attribute", which is called a "single decision systems" in rough sets. However, decision tables with many-valued decisions arise often in various applications. Pawlak gave a decision table with two decision attributions in [15]. Chikalov and Zielosko [3] investigated decision rules for decision tables with many-valued decisions. Moshkov and Zielosko [13] constructed an α-decision trees for tables with many-valued decisions. Azad et. al [1] proposed a greedy algorithm for the construction of approximate decision rules with many-valued decisions. Yu et. al [20] presented a rough sets based knowledge acquisition methods for multi-label decision system. Liu et. al [8] gave their ideas for a DEA evaluation model of transportation manufacturing based on rough sets. In summary, there are two routes to solve the "many-valued decision" problems. One is simply converting this "many-valued system" to several "single decision systems", then utilize classical rough set method to deal with these single systems, respectively [12]. The other is extending the definitions of classical rough sets, and redefine the rough approximations to achieve the goal [20]. In this paper, we introduce the model of "data envelopment analysis (DEA)" into rough sets with economics perspective. The multiple conditional attributes are treated as the "input features", and the multiple decision attributes are labeled as "output features". As well, we treat the objects in decision table as the decision making units (DMUs) in DEA, and the productive efficiency of DEA are used to determine the DEA efficiency for DMUs. At last, a three-way decision model with DEA is constructed.

The remainder of this paper is organized as follows: Sect. 2 provides the basic concepts of three-way decisions, DEA model and their extensions. A DEA based three-way decision model with "multi-input, multi-output" production functions is proposed in Sect. 3. Then, a case study of company efficiency evaluation is used to elucidate our model in Sect. 4. Section 5 concludes the paper and outlines the future work.

2   Preliminaries

Basic concepts, notations and results of three-way decisions and DEA model are briefly reviewed in this section [5–7,9–11,14,21,22]. In [18,19], Yao gave some generalized descriptions of three-way decisions.

Definition 1. *Suppose U denotes a universal set. The triplet $\{R_1, R_2, R_3\}$ is called a tri-partition of U and satisfies the following two properties:*
  (1). $U = R_1 \cup R_2 \cup R_3$;
  (2). $R_1 \cap R_2 = \varnothing$, $R_1 \cap R_3 = \varnothing$, $R_2 \cap R_3 = \varnothing$.

For three regions R_i, one can develop three different strategies, *e.g.*, Strategy 1, Strategy 2 and Strategy 3, respectively. Specially, if there exists one region $R_l = \varnothing$ ($l = 1$, 2, or 3), the three-way decision problem converts to two-way decision problem. Intuitively, the basic ideas of the three-way decision model can be simply outlined in Fig. 1.

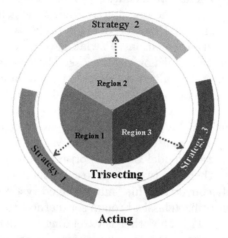

Fig. 1. The basic ideas of three-way decision model

In [19], Yao named the cognitive process in Fig. 1 as "trisecting-and-acting" model. As Yao stated in [18], many generalizations of sets have been proposed and studied with three-way decisions, including interval sets and three-valued logic, Pawlak rough sets, decision-theoretic rough sets (DTRS), three-valued approximations in many-valued logic, fuzzy sets and shadowed sets, etc. Obviously, rough set theory is one kind of typical model of three-way decisions when we treat R_1, R_2 and R_3 as positive region, boundary region and negative region, respectively.

Data envelopment analysis (DEA) is a nonparametric method in operations research and decision making for the estimation of production frontiers. It is used to empirically measure productive efficiency of decision making units (DMUs). The basic DEA model (called CCR model), which was proposed by Charnes, Cooper and Rhodes [4], is defined as Definition 2.

Definition 2. *Supposed there are p decision units with the same varieties, and we denote the kth unit as DMU_k, $k = 1, 2, \cdots, p$. To each decision unit, there are m kinds of input indicators and n kinds of output indicators, and we denote the ith input indicator as X_i, $i = 1, 2, \cdots, m$; and the jth output indicator as Y_j, $j = 1, 2, \cdots, n$. The total efficiency respected with the k_0th decision unit is:*

$$\theta^* = min\ \theta$$

$$s.t. \begin{cases} \sum_{k=1}^{p} \lambda_k X_k \leq \theta X_{k_0} \\ \sum_{k=1}^{p} \lambda_k Y_k \geq Y_{k_0} \\ \lambda_k \geq 0, \quad k = 1, 2, \cdots, p. \end{cases} \tag{1}$$

where DMU_{k_0} represents one of the k DMUs, X_{k_0} and Y_{k_0} are the input and output for DMU_{k_0}, respectively. λ_k is the weight given to DMU_k in its efforts to dominate DMU_{k_0} and θ is the efficiency of DMU_{k_0}. Since DMU_{k_0} appears on the left hand side of the equations as well, the optimal θ cannot possibly be more than 1. In [5], Cooper et al. gave the definitions of "DEA efficiency" and "DEA relative efficiency", respectively.

Definition 3 (Efficiency). *Full efficiency is attained by any DMU iff none of it's inputs or outputs can be improved without worsening some of its other inputs or outputs.*

Definition 4 (Relative Efficiency). *A DMU is to be rated as fully efficient on the basis of available evidence iff the performances of other DMUs does not show that some of its inputs or outputs can be improved without worsening some of its other inputs or outputs.*

Based on the CCR model, Banker, Charnes and Cooper [2] further adjoined the constrain of $\sum_{k=1}^{p} \lambda_k = 1$ to CCR model, and propose the BCC model. If we further consider the input slacks $s_i^{\theta-}$ and output slacks $s_j^{\theta+}$ for BCC model, we can build the linear programming model to determine the possible non-zero slacks as follows.

$$max \ \sum_{i=1}^{m} s_i^{\theta-} + \sum_{j=1}^{n} s_i^{\theta+}$$

$$s.t. \begin{cases} \sum_{k=1}^{p} \lambda_k x_{ik} + s_i^{\theta-} = \theta^* x_{ik_0} & i = 1, 2, \cdots, m \\ \sum_{k=1}^{p} \lambda_k y_{jk} - s_j^{\theta+} = y_{jk_0} & j = 1, 2, \cdots, n \\ \lambda_k \geq 0, \quad k = 1, 2, \cdots, p \\ \sum_{k=1}^{p} \lambda_k = 1 \end{cases} \quad (2)$$

where, θ^* is calculated by the minimizing θ in (1), it's a two stages process to compute the θ^* and the $s_i^{\theta-}, s_j^{\theta+}$ represent input and output slacks, respectively.

In fact, the models (1) and (2) represent a two-stage DEA process involved in the following DEA model.

$$min \ [\theta - \varepsilon(\sum_{i=1}^{m} s_i^{\theta-} + \sum_{j=1}^{n} s_j^{\theta+})]$$

$$s.t. \begin{cases} \sum_{k=1}^{p} \lambda_k x_{ik} + s_i^{\theta-} = \theta x_{ik_0} & i = 1, 2, \cdots, m \\ \sum_{k=1}^{p} \lambda_k y_{jk} - s_j^{\theta+} = y_{jk_0} & j = 1, 2, \cdots, n \\ \lambda_k \geq 0, \quad k = 1, 2, \cdots, p \\ \sum_{k=1}^{p} \lambda_k = 1 \end{cases} \quad (3)$$

where, the non-Archimedean ε of the objective function of (3) effectively allows the minimization over θ to preempt the optimization involving the slacks, $s_i^{\theta-}$ and $s_j^{\theta+}$. Note that the frontier determined by model (3) exhibits variable returns to scale (VRS). Model (3) is called input-oriented DEA model. DMU_{k_0} is efficient to DEA if and only if $\theta^* = 1$ and $s_i^{\theta-} = s_i^{\theta+} = 0$ for all i and j. DMU_{k_0} is weak efficient if $\theta^* = 1$ and $s_i^{\theta-} \neq 0$ and (or) $s_j^{\theta+} \neq 0$ for some i and j.

Analogously, we can define the output-oriented DEA model, which can be expressed as:

$$max\ [\phi + \varepsilon(\sum_{i=1}^{m} s_i^{\phi-} + \sum_{j=1}^{n} s_j^{\phi+})]$$

$$s.t. \begin{cases} \sum_{k=1}^{p} \lambda_k x_{ik} + s_i^{\phi-} = x_{ik_0} & i = 1, 2, \cdots, m \\ \sum_{k=1}^{p} \lambda_k y_{jk} - s_j^{\phi+} = \phi y_{jk_0} & j = 1, 2, \cdots, n \\ \lambda_k \geq 0, \quad k = 1, 2, \cdots, p \\ \sum_{k=1}^{p} \lambda_k = 1 \end{cases} \quad (4)$$

DMU_{k_0} is efficient to DEA if and only if $\phi^* = 1$ and $s_i^{\phi-} = s_j^{\phi+} = 0$ for all i and j. DMU_{k_0} is weak efficient if $\phi^* = 1$ and $s_i^{\phi-} \neq 0$ and (or) $s_j^{\phi+} \neq 0$ for some i and j.

Ozcan [14] gave some semantic interpretations for (3) and (4). He pointed out the efficiency and effectiveness evaluations are two important measures in DEA. The efficiency in input-oriented DEA model generally refers to using the minimum number of inputs for a given number of outputs. As well, the effectiveness in output-oriented DEA model encourages us to ask if the necessary inputs are being used in order to produce the vest possible outcomes.

3   A DEA Based Three-Way Decision Model

In rough set theory, an information system is utilized to store the related information of decision units. An information system is a quadruple $S = (U, A, V, f)$. U is a finite set of reference actions, called the domain; A is a finite set of attributes, $A = C \cup D$ and $C \cap D = \emptyset$, where C denotes the condition attributes and D denotes the decision attributes. $V = \underset{a \in A}{\cup} V_a$, V_a is a domain of the attribute a. $f: U \times A \rightarrow V$ is an information function such that $f(x, a) \in V_a$ for every $x \in U$, $a \in A$. Specially, if $D = \{d\}$ and the system have only one decision attribute, we call the information system as a decision table.

In our following discussions, we assume there are p decision units $U = \{DMU_1, DMU_2, \cdots, DMU_p\}$ in a DEA decision system. $X = \{x_1, x_2, \cdots, x_m\}$ denotes m input indicators, which can be treated as C in S. Similarly, $Y = \{y_1, y_2, \cdots, y_n\}$ denotes n output indicators, which can be dealt with D in S. Obviously, the DEA model is a "multiple conditional attributes and multiple decision attributes" model. In our proposed model, we combine the input and output indicators together to generate the new condition attribute set $\mathcal{C}$, and further integrate the parameters θ, ϕ, as well as the slack variables vector $\mathcal{S} = \{s_i^{\theta-}, s_j^{\theta+}; s_i^{\phi-}, s_j^{\phi+}\}$ to construct the new decision attribute set $\mathcal{D}$, then utilize $\mathcal{D}$ to evaluate the efficiency of the decision unit DMU_k $(k = 1, 2, \cdots, p)$ in U. An integrated matrix can clearly illuminate the key ideas of this method.

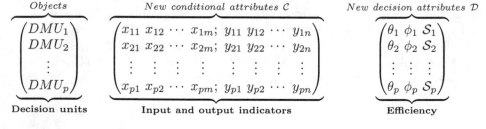

On basis of the above matrix and the definitions (3) and (4), we generate the DEA based three-way decisions. The three-way decision rules for DEA, namely, efficiency, weak efficiency and inefficiency can be described as follows:

- **Efficiency decision region:** If $\theta_k^* = \phi_k^* = 1$ and $s_i^{\theta-} = s_j^{\theta+} = 0$; $s_i^{\phi-} = s_j^{\phi+} = 0$ for all i and j, the decision union DMU_k is DEA efficiency;
- **Weak efficiency decision region:** If $\theta_k^* = \phi_k^* = 1$, and at least one slack parameter $s_i^{\theta-}$, $s_j^{\theta+}$, $s_i^{\phi-}$, $s_j^{\phi+}$ not equal to zero for i and j, the decision union DMU_k is DEA weak efficiency;
- **Inefficiency decision region:** If $\theta_k^* \neq 1$ and $\phi_k^* \neq 1$, the decision union DMU_k is DEA inefficiency.

With the above discussions, we summarize four key steps to construct the DEA based three-way decision approach, and the framework of our study is displayed in Fig. 2.

Step I: Selecting the decision unions and determining the input and output indicators in a decision problem.

Step II: Using BCC model to calculate the efficiency of each decision unit with input-oriented and output-oriented viewpoints, respectively.

Step III: Generating three-way decision regions/rules followed by the three criteria with DEA based three-way decisions.

Step IV: Providing some improvement strategies for the no efficient decision units after three-way decisions in DEA.

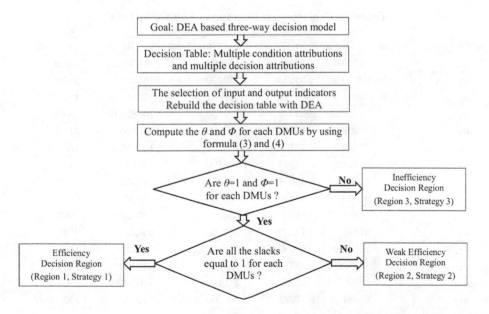

Fig. 2. The framework of DEA based three-way decisions

4   An Illustration

In this section, we utilize a didactic example of company efficiency evaluation to illustrate the proposed model. Table 1 presents 15 companies from the top Fortune Global 500 list in 1995 (Data can available from [22]). We denote the 15 companies $U = \{u_1, u_2, \cdots, u_{15}\}$ as 15 decision unions in our following discussions, where u_1: Mitsubishi; u_2: Mitsui; u_3: Itochu; u_4: General Motors; u_5: Sumitomo; u_6: Marubeni; u_7: Ford Motor; u_8: Toyota Motor; u_9: Exxon; u_{10}: Royal Dutch/Shell Group; u_{11}: WalMart; u_{12}: Hitachi; u_{13}: Nippon Life Insurance; u_{14}: Nippon Telegraph & Telephone; u_{15}: AT&T. In addition, there are three input indicators: x_1 assets ($ millions), x_2 equity ($ millions), x_3 number of employees; and two output indicators: y_1 revenue ($ millions), y_2 profit ($ millions).

Followed by Table 1, we firstly compute the efficiency of each decision union with the input-oriented and output-oriented DEA model, respectively. The scores on x-axis stand for the DEA efficiency evaluations; the companies on y-axis stand for the 15 DMUs in Table 1. The calculating results are outlined in Figs. 3 and 4.

According to the above two figures, $\{u_7, u_8, u_{12}, u_{14}, u_{15}\}$ are DEA inefficiency. Although the scores of $\{u_1, u_2, u_3, u_4, u_5, u_6, u_9, u_{10}, u_{11}, u_{13}\}$ are equal to 1 on both input-oriented and output-oriented models, we need to do further investigations to distinguish the DEA efficiency DMUs and weak efficiency DMUs.

Then, we check the slack variables by solving the programming (3) and (4), the calculating results are outlined in Table 2. Here, the θ^* in the second column

Table 1. 15 companies from fortune global 500 list

Company (DMUs)	x_1 (Assets)	x_2 (Equity)	x_3 (Employees)	y_1 (Revenue)	y_2 (Profit)
u_1	91920.6	10950	36000	184365.2	346.2
u_2	68770.9	5553.9	80000	181518.7	314.8
u_3	65708.9	4271.1	7182	169164.6	121.2
u_4	217123.4	23345.5	709000	168828.6	6880.7
u_5	50268.9	6681	6193	167530.7	210.5
u_6	71439.3	5239.1	6702	161057.4	156.6
u_7	243283	24547	346990	137137	4139
u_8	106004.2	49691.6	146855	111052	2662.4
u_9	91296	40436	82000	110009	6470
u_{10}	118011.6	58986.4	104000	109833.7	6904.6
u_{11}	37871	14762	675000	93627	2740
u_{12}	91620.9	29907.2	331852	84167.1	1468.8
u_{13}	364762.5	2241.9	89690	83206.7	2426.6
u_{14}	127077.3	42240.1	231400	81937.2	2209.1
u_{15}	88884	17274	299300	79609	139

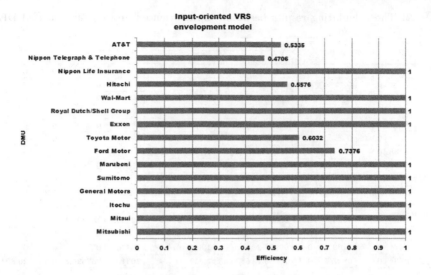

Fig. 3. The efficiency of companies with input-oriented DEA model

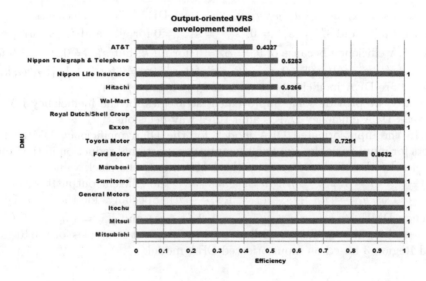

Fig. 4. The efficiency of companies with output-oriented DEA model

are equivalent to the score in Fig. 3; and the ϕ^* in the eighth column are equivalent to the 1/score in Fig. 4.

In Table 2, we can easily generate three decision regions for the 15 companies followed by the decision criteria in Sect. 3.

Region 1: (DEA Efficiency): $\{u_1, u_2, u_3, u_4, u_5, u_9, u_{11}, u_{13}\}$.

Region 2: (Weak DEA Efficiency): $\{u_6, u_{10}\}$.

Region 3: (DEA Inefficiency): $\{u_7, u_8, u_{12}, u_{14}, u_{15}\}$.

Table 2. The calculating results based on input-oriented and output-oriented DEA models

DMU	θ^*	$s_1^{\theta-}$	$s_2^{\theta-}$	$s_3^{\theta-}$	$s_1^{\theta+}$	$s_2^{\theta+}$	ϕ^*	$s_1^{\phi-}$	$s_2^{\phi-}$	$s_3^{\phi-}$	$s_1^{\phi+}$	$s_2^{\phi+}$
u_1	1	0	0	0	0	0	1	0	0	0	0	0
u_2	1	0	0	0	0	0	1	0	0	0	0	0
u_3	1	0	0	0	0	0	1	0	0	0	0	0
u_4	1	0	0	0	0	0	1	0	0	0	0	0
u_5	1	0	0	0	0	0	1	0	0	0	0	0
u_6	1	2.946	0	0	0	0	1	8.201	0	0	0	0
u_7	0.738	0	0	0	457.489	0	1.159	94925.9	0	0	0	0
u_8	0.603	0	10532.1	0	29761.7	0	1.372	0	25810.6	0	0	0
u_9	1	0	0	0	0	0	1	0	0	0	0	0
u_{10}	1	0.278	0.965	0	1.126	0	1	0.083	0.287	0	0.335	0
u_{11}	1	0	0	0	0	0	1	0	0	0	0	0
u_{12}	0.558	0	4634.8	0	58811.5	0	1.898	0	12485.2	181494.1	0	0
u_{13}	1	0	0	0	0	0	1	0	0	0	0	0
u_{14}	0.471	0	3103.8	0	60994.2	0	1.892	0	16476.4	0	0	0
u_{15}	0.534	0	680.77	0	70958.7	652.033	2.311	0	7031.92	257526.3	0	20.824

Obviously, $\{u_1, u_2, u_3, u_4, u_5, u_9, u_{11}, u_{13}\}$ are DEA efficiency because of $\theta_k^* = \phi_k^* = 1$ for all k and $s_i^{\theta-} = s_j^{\theta+} = 0$; $s_i^{\phi-} = s_j^{\phi+} = 0$ for all i and j. $\{u_6, u_{10}\}$ are weak DEA efficiency because of $\theta_k^* = \phi_k^* = 1$ for all k, but $s_1^{\theta-} \neq 0$, $s_1^{\phi-} \neq 0$ for $\{u_6\}$; $s_1^{\theta-} \neq 0$, $s_2^{\theta-} \neq 0$, $s_1^{\theta+} \neq 0$, $s_1^{\phi-} \neq 0$, $s_2^{\phi-} \neq 0$, $s_1^{+*}(\phi) \neq 0$ for $\{u_{10}\}$. $\{u_7, u_8, u_{12}, u_{14}, u_{15}\}$ are DEA inefficiency because of $\theta_k^* \neq 1$ and $\phi_k^* \neq 1$.

Finally, we provide some improvement strategies for the inefficiency DMUs and weak DEA efficiency DMUs after three-way decisions.

• In the input-oriented DEA model, for the DEA inefficiency DMUs, the targets for input variables (x_{ik}) will comprise proportional reduction in the input variables by the efficiency score of the DMU minus the slack value as: $\widehat{x_{ik}} = \theta^* x_{ik} - s_i^{\theta-}$ ($i = 1, 2, \cdots, m$). In the same way, the efficient output targets are calculated as $\widehat{y_{jk}} = y_{jk} + s_j^{\theta+}$ ($j = 1, 2, \cdots, n$). Specially, for the weak DEA efficiency DMUs, $\widehat{x_{ik}} = x_{ik} - s_i^{\theta-}$ ($i = 1, 2, \cdots, m$) and $\widehat{y_{jk}} = y_{jk} + s_j^{\theta+}$ ($j = 1, 2, \cdots, n$) for $\theta^* = 1$. Table 3 outlines the improvement strategies for the Region 2 and Region 3 based on input-oriented DEA model.

Table 3. Improvement strategies of input-oriented DEA model

u_k	Efficiency	x_{1k}	$\widehat{x_{1k}}$	x_{2k}	$\widehat{x_{2k}}$	x_{3k}	$\widehat{x_{3k}}$	y_{1k}	$\widehat{y_{1k}}$	y_{2k}	$\widehat{y_{2k}}$
u_6	Weak	71439.3	71435.9↓	5239.1	5239.1	6702	6702	161057.4	161057.4	156.6	156.6
u_7	Non	243283	179434.4↓	24547	18104.7↓	346990	255924↓	137137	137594.5↑	4139	4139
u_8	Non	106004.2	63946.1↓	49691.6	19443.9↓	146855	88589↓	111052	140813.7↑	2662.4	2662.4
u_{10}	Weak	118011.6	118008.5↓	58986.4	58984.1↓	104000	104000	109833.7	109834.8↑	6904.6	6904.6
u_{12}	Non	91620.9	51087↓	29907.2	12041.2↓	331852	185038↓	84167.1	142978.6↑	1468.8	1468.8
u_{14}	Non	127077.3	59803.5↓	42240.1	16774.7↓	231400	108899↓	81937.2	142931.4↑	2209.1	2209.1
u_{15}	Non	88884	47423↓	17274	8535.6↓	299300	159688↓	79609	150567.7↑	139	791↑

From Table 3, u_6 and u_{10} are weak DEA efficiency DMUs, these companies are closer to an efficiency frontier and only need a little change for their inputs and outputs. Take u_{10} for an example, we just reduce a little bit resources (Assets: 118011.6 to 118008.5; Equity: 104000 to 103998) and increase a little bit achievements (Profit: 58986.4 to 58986.1). Furthermore, companies $\{u_7, u_8, u_{12}, u_{14}, u_{15}\}$ are identified as inefficient in the input-oriented model. These companies can improve their efficiency, or reduce their inefficiencies proportionately, by reducing their inputs. For example, u_8 can improve its efficiency by reducing inputs (Assets: 106004.2 to 63946.1; Equity: 49691.6 to 19443.9; Employees: 146855 to 88589), and increasing it's outputs (Revenue: 111052 to 140813.7).

• In the outnput-oriented DEA model, for the DEA inefficiency DMUs, the targets for output variables (y_{jk}) will comprise proportional increment in the output variables by the efficiency score of the DMU add the slack value as: $\widehat{y_{jk}} = \phi^* y_{jk} + s_j^{\phi-}$ $(j = 1, 2, \cdots, n)$. In the same way, the efficient input targets are calculated as: $\widehat{x_{ik}} = x_{ik} - s_i^{\phi-}$ $(i = 1, 2, \cdots, m)$. Specially, for the weak DEA efficiency DMUs, $\widehat{y_{jk}} = y_{jk} + s_j^{\phi+}$ $(j = 1, 2, \cdots, n)$ and $\widehat{x_{ik}} = x_{ik} - s_i^{\phi-}$ $(i = 1, 2, \cdots, m)$ for $\phi^* = 1$. Table 4 outlines the improvement strategies for the Region 2 and Region 3 based on output-oriented DEA model.

Table 4. Improvement strategies of output-oriented DEA model

u_k	Efficiency	x_{1k}	$\widehat{x_{1k}}$	x_{2k}	$\widehat{x_{2k}}$	x_{3k}	$\widehat{x_{3k}}$	y_{1k}	$\widehat{y_{1k}}$	y_{2k}	$\widehat{y_{2k}}$
u_6	Weak	71439.3	71431.1↓	5239.1	5239.1	6702	6702	161057.4	161057.4	156.6	156.6
u_7	Non	243283	148357.2↓	24547	24547	346990	346990	137137	158862.8↑	4139	4794.7↑
u_8	Non	106004.2	106004.2	49691.6	23881↓	146855	146855	111052	152318.9↑	2662.4	3651.7↑
u_{10}	Weak	118011.6	118011.5↓	58986.4	58986.1↓	104000	104000	109833.7	109834.8↑	6904.6	6904.6
u_{12}	Non	91620.9	91620.9	29907.2	17422↓	331852	150358↓	84167.1	159829.4↑	1468.8	2789.2↑
u_{14}	Non	127077.3	127077.3	42240.1	25763.7↓	231400	231400↓	81937.2	155101.6↑	2209.1	4181.7↑
u_{15}	Non	88884	88884	17274	10242.1↓	299300	41773.7↓	79609	183993.5↑	139	342.1↑

From Table 4, we also do some small changes for the weak DEA efficiency DMUs u_6 and u_{10}. Take u_{10} for an example, we just reduce a little bit resources (Assets: 118011.6 to 118008.5; Equity: 58986.4 to 58986.1) and increase a little bit achievements (Profit: 109833.7 to 109834.8). In addition, companies $\{u_7, u_8, u_{12}, u_{14}, u_{15}\}$ have scores greater than 1; thus they are identified as inefficient in the output-oriented model. These companies can improve their efficiency, or reduce their inefficiencies proportionately, by augmenting their outputs. For example, u_8 can improve its efficiency by increasing outputs (Revenue: 111052 to 152318.9; Profit: 2662.4 to 3651.7), and reducing it's inputs (Equity: 49691.6 to 23881).

Overall, with the insightful gains from Tables 3 and 4, we can use the above two methods to improve the DEA efficiency for these weak DEA efficiency DMUs (in Region 2) and DEA inefficiency DMUs (in Region 3) with input-oriented and output-oriented viewpoints. Compared with the existing rough set methods, DEA based three-way decisions provides a useful way to improve the DMUSs in boundary region (Region 2) and negative region (Region 3), to positive region (Region 1). In a short, we can provide three different strategies for their corresponding regions as follows.

Strategy 1: Keep unchanged for the DMUs $\{u_1, u_2, u_3, u_4, u_5, u_9, u_{11}, u_{13}\}$ in Region 1.

Strategy 2: Do small changes for the DMUs $\{u_6, u_{10}\}$ in Region 2 to improve their efficiencies.

Strategy 3: Do some significant changes for the DMUs $\{u_7, u_8, u_{12}, u_{14}, u_{15}\}$ in Region 3 to improve their efficiencies.

5   Conclusions

Decision tables with multiple conditional attributes and multiple decision attributes are frequently used in real decision procedure. In order to solve this problem, an DEA based three-way decision method is proposed in this paper. The conditional and decision attributes (also viewed as the input and output indicators in DEA) are treated as the new conditional attributes on DEA based three-way decisions. The two parameters θ and ϕ, as well as the slacks are utilized to construct new decision attributions. Three decision regions: efficiency decision region, weak efficiency decision region and inefficiency decision region, can be automatically generated by the decision criteria of DEA. We also use an empirical study to validate our model, and give some improvement strategies for these weak DEA efficiency and DEA inefficiency DMUs. Our method provides an interesting semantic interpretations and a new perspective to better understand three-way decisions. In the future, we will focus on the attribute reduction on DEA based three-way decisions, and the rule generation of DEA based three-way decision.

Acknowledgements. This work is partially supported by the National Science Foundation of China (Nos. 71571148, 71201133, 71401026), the Applied Basic Research Project of Science & Technology Department of Sichuan Province (2017JY0220), the Social Science Planning Project of Sichuan Province (Nos. SC16B097, SC15C009) and the Young Eagle Scholar Plan of SWJTU.

References

1. Azad, M., Moshkov, M., Zielosko, B.: Greedy algorithm for the construction of approximate decision rules for decision tables with many-valued decisions. Trans. Rough Sets **20**, 24–50 (2016)
2. Banker, R.D., Charnes, A., Cooper, W.W.: Some models for estimating technical and scale inefficiencies in data envelopment analysis. Manage. Sci. **30**, 1078–1092 (1984)
3. Chikalov, I., Zielosko, B.: Decision rules for decision tables with many-valued decisions. In: Yao, J.T., Ramanna, S., Wang, G., Suraj, Z. (eds.) RSKT 2011. LNCS, vol. 6954, pp. 763–768. Springer, Heidelberg (2011). doi:10.1007/978-3-642-24425-4_95

4. Charnes, A., Cooper, W.W., Rhodes, E.L.: Measuring the efficiency of decision making units. Eur. J. Oper. Res. **2**, 429–444 (1978)
5. Cooper, W.W., Seiford, L.M., Zhu, J.: Data envelopment analysis history, models, and interpretations. In: Cooper, W.W., Seiford, L.M., Zhu, J. (eds.) Handbook on Data Envelopment Analysis, International Series in Operations Research & Management Science, pp. 1–39. Springer, Heidelberg (2011)
6. Li, H.X., Zhou, X.Z.: Risk decision making based on decision-theoretic rough set: a three-way view decision model. Int. J. Comput. Intell. Syst. **4**, 1–11 (2011)
7. Liang, D.C., Liu, D., Kobina, A.: Three-way group decisions with decision-theoretic rough sets. Inf. Sci. **345**, 46–64 (2016)
8. Liu, D., Hu, P., Li, G.Q., Chen, L.: The DEA evaluation model of transportation manufacturing based on rough set theory. In: Proceeding of 8th International Conference of Chinese Logistics and Transportation Professionals, pp. 3029–3037 (2008)
9. Liu, D., Li, T.R., Ruan, D.: Probabilistic model criteria with decision-theoretic rough sets. Inf. Sci. **181**, 3709–3722 (2011)
10. Liu, D., Liang, D.C., Wang, C.C.: A novel three-way decision model based on incomplete information system. Knowl.-Based Syst. **91**, 16–31 (2016)
11. Min, F., He, H.P., Qian, Y.H., Zhu, W.: Test-cost-sensitive attribute reduction. Inf. Sci. **181**, 4928–4942 (2011)
12. Meng, Z.Q., Shi, Z.Z.: Extended rough set-based attribute reduction in inconsistent incomplete decision systems. Inf. Sci. **204**, 44–69 (2012)
13. Moshkov, M., Zielosko, B.: Construction of α-decision trees for tables with many-valued decisions. In: Yao, J.T., Ramanna, S., Wang, G., Suraj, Z. (eds.) RSKT 2011. LNCS, vol. 6954, pp. 486–494. Springer, Heidelberg (2011). doi:10.1007/978-3-642-24425-4_63
14. Ozcan, Y.A.: Health care benchmarking and performance evaluation: an assessment using data envelopment analysis. Int. Ser. Oper. Res. Manag. Sci. **120**, 3–14 (2008)
15. Pawlak, Z.: Rough sets and decision tables. Comput. Theory, 187–196 (1985)
16. Yao, Y.Y.: Three-way decisions with probabilistic rough sets. Inf. Sci. **180**, 341–353 (2010)
17. Yao, Y.Y.: The superiority of three-way decision in probabilistic rough set models. Inf. Sci. **181**, 1080–1096 (2011)
18. Yao, Y.: An outline of a theory of three-way decisions. In: Yao, J.T., Yang, Y., Słowiński, R., Greco, S., Li, H., Mitra, S., Polkowski, L. (eds.) RSCTC 2012. LNCS, vol. 7413, pp. 1–17. Springer, Heidelberg (2012). doi:10.1007/978-3-642-32115-3_1
19. Yao, Y.Y.: Three-way decisions and cognitive computing. Cogn. Comput. **8**(4), 543–554 (2016)
20. Yu, Y., Miao, D.Q., Zhao, C.R., et al.: Knowledge acquisition methods for multi-label decision system based on rough sets. J. Front. Comput. Sci. Technol. **9**, 94–104 (2015)
21. Zhou, B.: Multi-class decision-theoretic rough sets. Int. J. Approx. Reas. **55**, 211–224 (2014)
22. Zhu, J.: Quantitative models for performance evaluation and benchmarking. Int. Ser. Oper. Res. Manag. Sci. **213**, 11–20 (2014)

Covering-Based Optimistic Multigranulation Decision-Theoretic Rough Sets Based on Maximal Descriptors

Caihui Liu[1]([✉]), Meizhi Wang[2], and Nan Zhang[3]

[1] Department of Mathematics and Computer Science, Gannan Normal University,
Ganzhou 341000, Jiangxi, China
liu_caihui@163.com
[2] Department of Physical Education, Gannan Normal University,
Ganzhou 341000, China
dei2002@163.com
[3] School of Computer and Control Engineering, Yantai University,
Yantai 264005, Shandong, China
zhangnan0851@163.com

Abstract. This paper investigates decision-theoretic rough set approach in the frameworks of multi-covering approximation space. We mainly discuss optimistic multigranulation decision-theoretic rough sets by employing maximal descriptors of elements. First, we present the definitions of covering-based optimistic multigranulation decision-theoretic rough sets on the basis of Bayesian decision procedure. Then, we disclose some important and interesting properties of the model. Finally, we investigate the relationships between the proposed model and other related rough set models.

Keywords: Multigranulation · Decision-theoretic rough sets · Optimistic · Maximal descriptor

1 Introduction

A three-way decision model is an extension of the commonly used two-way, binary-decision model with an added third option. With respect to the probabilistic positive, negative and boundary regions, one can build rules for making a decision of acceptance,rejection and non-commitment, respectively. This interpretation provides insights in to a deeper understanding of rough set theory and its applicability in granular computing. Since Yao and Wong [1] proposed the notion of decision-theoretic rough sets (DTRS), many researchers have been working on the theory. For example, Herbert and Yao [2] explored the game-theoretic rough set by combining game theory with DTRS. Liu et al. [3] discussed a multiple-category classification approach with decision-theoretic rough sets, which can effectively reduce misclassification rate. Yu et al. [4] studied an

L. Polkowski et al. (Eds.): IJCRS 2017, Part II, LNAI 10314, pp. 238–248, 2017.
DOI: 10.1007/978-3-319-60840-2_17

automatic method of clustering analysis with the decision-theoretic rough set theory. Li et al. [5] studied an axiomatic characterization of decision-theoretic rough sets. Jia et al. [6] proposed an optimization representation of decision-theoretic rough set model and developed a heuristic approach and a particle swarm optimization approach for searching an attribute reduction with a minimum cost. Based on the DTRS, Yao [7,8] presented a new decision-making method known as three-way decisions, where a universe is divided into three pairwise disjoint regions, positive, negative and boundary regions by using an evaluation function and a pair of thresholds. Three-way decisions have been applied to many domains, such as email filtering [9], cost-sensitive face recognition [10], recommender system design [11], and so on.

The study on decision-theoretic rough set in a multigranulation environment is a new and interesting topic. Qian et al. [12] developed the multigranulation decision-theoretic rough set and proved that it is a general framework of many existing multigranulation rough set models. To tackle the problem of computational cost in calculating the approximation of a target set with larger scale data, Qian et al. [13] proposed the combination of local rough sets with multigranulation decision-theoretic rough sets to obtain local multigranulation decision-theoretic rough sets (LMG-DTRSs) as a semi-unsupervised learning method. It is proved to be an excellent solution for dealing with data that have limited labels. However, those two models have their own limitations: (1) All granular structures in those models are based on equivalence relations, hence they are not suitable for coverings or neighborhoods based environments. (2) The models evaluate the multigranulation approximations in a quantitative way, so they are not suitable for the situations where general binary relations are considered. To tackle the above problems, Liu et al. [14] have proposed optimistic multigranulation decision-theoretic rough set model by employing the minimal descriptors of elements in a multi-covering space. The model may help to build a more reasonable and suitable decision environment for solving real world problems. The maximal descriptor of x contains all objects in the approximation space that are related to x, and the maximal descriptor may provide a detailed and comprehensive description for x when we discuss the issue of set approximations. As Yao et al. [15] have pointed out that the utilization of the maximal descriptors of objects is equally reasonable as the utilization of the minimal ones in a covering approximation space. Therefore, in this paper, we discuss the optimistic multigranulation decision-theoretic rough set model by using the maximal descriptors of elements.

The remainder of the paper is organized as follows. Section 2 reviews some basic notions and notations. Section 3 proposes the optimistic multigranulation decision-theoretic rough set model and discusses the interrelationships with the other generalized rough sets. Section 4 concludes the paper.

2   Preliminaries

In this section, some basic notions and notations will be reviewed.

2.1   Covering-Based Rough Sets

In this subsection, we will review some concepts related to the covering-based rough sets.

Definition 1 [16]. Let U be a universe of discourse and C a family of nonempty subsets of U. If $\cup C = U$, then C is called a covering of U. The ordered pair $\langle U, C \rangle$ is called a covering approximation space.

Definition 2 [19]. Let $\langle U, C \rangle$ be a covering approximation space, $x \in U$, then $MD_C(x) = \{K \in C_x | \forall S \in C_x(S \supseteq K \Rightarrow K = S)\}$ is called the maximal descriptor of x, where $C_x = \{K \in C | x \in K\}$.

2.2   Qian's MGRS

In this subsection, we will briefly outline the definition of optimistic multi-granulation rough sets.

Definition 3. Let $K = (U, \mathbf{R})$ be a knowledge base, where $\mathbf{R}$ is a family of equivalence relations on the universe U. Let $A_1, A_2, \ldots, A_m \in \mathbf{R}$, where m is a natural number. For any $X \subseteq U$, its optimistic lower and upper approximations with respect to $A_1, A_2 \ldots, A_m$ are defined as follows.

$$\overline{\sum_{i=1}^{m} A_i(X)} = \{x \in U | [x]_{A_1} \subseteq X \text{ or } [x]_{A_2} \subseteq X \text{ or } \cdots \text{ or } [x]_{A_m} \subseteq X\}$$

$$\overline{\sum_{i=1}^{m} A_i(X)} = \sim \overline{\sum_{i=1}^{m} A_i(\sim X)}$$

where $\sim X$ denotes the complement set of X. $(\underline{\sum_{i=1}^{m} A_i(X)}, \overline{\sum_{i=1}^{m} A_i(X)})$ is called the optimistic multi-granulation rough sets of X. Here, the word "optimistic" means that only a single granular structure is needed to satisfy the inclusion condition between an equivalence class and a target concept when multiple independent granular structures are available in the problem.

2.3   Decision-Theoretic Rough Sets

In [8], Yao proposed the theory of three-way decisions. Compared with two-way decisions, three-way decisions exhibit a third option, that is, non-commitment in addition to acceptance and rejection. The theory of three-way decisions can be described as follows.

Within the frame of three-way decisions, the set of states is given by $\Omega = \{X, \neg X\}$ (where $\neg X$ denotes the complement of X), the set of actions is given by $A = \{a_P, a_B, a_N\}$, where a_P, a_B and a_N represent the three actions in classifying an object x, namely, deciding $x \in POS(X)$, deciding x should be further investigated $x \in BND(X)$, and deciding $x \in NEG(X)$. $\lambda_{PP}, \lambda_{BP}$ and λ_{NP} denote the loss incurred for taking actions of a_P, a_B and a_N, respectively, when an object belongs to X. Similarly, $\lambda_{PN}, \lambda_{BN}$ and λ_{NN} denote the loss incurred for taking the correspondence actions when the object belongs to $\neg X$. By Bayesian decision procedure, for an object x, the expected loss $R(a_\bullet|[x])$ associated with taking the individual actions can be expressed as

$$R(a_P|[x]) = \lambda_{PP}P(X|[x]) + \lambda_{PN}P(\neg X|[x]),$$
$$R(a_N|[x]) = \lambda_{NP}P(X|[x]) + \lambda_{NN}P(\neg X|[x]),$$
$$R(a_B|[x]) = \lambda_{BP}P(X|[x]) + \lambda_{BN}P(\neg X|[x]).$$

Then the Bayesian decision procedure suggests the following three minimum-risk decision rules.

(P1) If $R(a_P|[x]) \leq R(a_B|[x])$ and $R(a_P|[x]) \leq R(a_N|[x])$, decide $x \in POS(X)$,
(N1) If $R(a_N|[x]) \leq R(a_P|[x])$ and $R(a_N|[x]) \leq R(a_B|[x])$, decide $x \in NEG(X)$,
(B1) If $R(a_B|[x]) \leq R(a_P|[x])$ and $R(a_B|[x]) \leq R(a_N|[x])$, decide $x \in BND(X)$.

By considering $0 \leq \lambda_{PP} \leq \lambda_{BP} < \lambda_{NP}$ and $0 \leq \lambda_{NN} \leq \lambda_{BN} < \lambda_{PN}$, (P1)–(B1) can be expressed concisely as:
(P2) If $P(X|[x]) \geq \alpha$ and $P(X|[x]) \geq \gamma$, decide $x \in POS(X)$,
(N2) If $P(X|[x]) \leq \gamma$ and $P(X|[x]) \leq \beta$, decide $x \in NEG(X)$,
(B2) If $P(X|[x]) \leq \alpha$ and $P(X|[x]) \geq \beta$, decide $x \in BND(X)$,

where:
$$\alpha = \frac{\lambda_{PN}-\lambda_{BN}}{(\lambda_{PN}-\lambda_{BN})+(\lambda_{BP}-\lambda_{PP})},$$
$$\beta = \frac{\lambda_{BN}-\lambda_{NN}}{(\lambda_{BN}-\lambda_{NN})+(\lambda_{NP}-\lambda_{BP})},$$
$$\gamma = \frac{\lambda_{PN}-\lambda_{NN}}{(\lambda_{PN}-\lambda_{NN})+(\lambda_{NP}-\lambda_{PP})}.$$

If $0 \leq \beta < \gamma < \alpha \leq 1$, (P2)–(B2) can be rewritten as follows:

(P3) If $P(X|[x]) \geq \alpha$, decide $x \in POS(X)$,
(N3) If $P(X|[x]) \leq \beta$, decide $x \in NEG(X)$,
(B3) If $\beta < P(X|[x]) < \alpha$, decide $x \in BND(X)$.

Based on the decision rules above, we obtain lower and upper approximations of the decision-theoretic rough sets as follows.
$$\underline{PR}(X) = \{x \in U \mid P(X|[x]) \geq \alpha\} \text{ and } \overline{PR}(X) = \{x \in U \mid P(X|[x]) > \beta\}.$$

3   Optimistic Multigranulation Decision-Theoretic Rough Sets Based on Maximal Descriptors

In this paper, we define $\langle U, \mathbf{C} \rangle$ as a multi-covering approximation space, where U is a universe of discourse and $\mathbf{C}$ is a family of coverings on the universe U. $C_1, C_2 \in \mathbf{C}$ are two granular structures of U. The set $\Omega_i = \{X, \neg X\}$ of two states for i-th granular structure ($i = 1, 2$) indicates that an element is in X or not. $A = \{a_P, a_B, a_N\}$ denotes the set of actions, where a_P means deciding $x \in POS(X)$, a_B means deciding $x \in BND(X)$ and a_N deciding $x \in NEG(X)$. $\lambda_{PP}^i, \lambda_{BP}^i$ and λ_{NP}^i denote the loss, or cost, for a_P, a_B and a_N, respectively, when an object x belongs to X under i-th granular structure. Analogously, $\lambda_{PN}^i, \lambda_{BN}^i$ and λ_{NN}^i denote the loss, or cost, for taking the corresponding actions when x belongs to $\neg X$.

For each $x \in U$, $\cup MD_{C_i}(x)$ is adopted as its description. For the i-th granular structure, the expected losses of taking different actions for x are as follows.

$$R(a_P| \cup MD_{C_i}(x)) = \lambda_{PP}^i P(X| \cup MD_{C_i}(x)) + \lambda_{PN}^i P(\neg X| \cup MD_{C_i}(x)),$$
$$R(a_B| \cup MD_{C_i}(x)) = \lambda_{BP}^i P(X| \cup MD_{C_i}(x)) + \lambda_{BN}^i P(\neg X| \cup MD_{C_i}(x)),$$
$$R(a_N| \cup MD_{C_i}(x)) = \lambda_{NP}^i P(X| \cup MD_{C_i}(x)) + \lambda_{NN}^i P(\neg X| \cup MD_{C_i}(x)).$$

If we suppose $\lambda_{PP}^1 = \cdots \lambda_{PP}^i$, $\lambda_{PN}^1 = \cdots \lambda_{PN}^i$, $\lambda_{BP}^1 = \cdots \lambda_{BP}^i$, $\lambda_{BN}^1 = \cdots \lambda_{BN}^i$, $\lambda_{NP}^1 = \cdots \lambda_{NP}^i$, $\lambda_{NN}^1 = \cdots \lambda_{NN}^i$, then considering the strategy "seeking commonality while preserving difference", the expected overall loss of taking actions a_P, a_B and a_N for x can be computed as follows.

$$R(a_P|(\cup MD_{C_1}(x), \cup MD_{C_2}(x)))$$
$$= \lambda_{PP} \bigwedge_{i=1}^{2} P(X| \cup MD_{C_i}(x)) + \lambda_{PN} \bigwedge_{i=1}^{2} P(\neg X| \cup MD_{C_i}(x)),$$
$$R(a_B|(\cup MD_{C_1}(x), \cup MD_{C_2}(x)))$$
$$= \lambda_{BP} \bigwedge_{i=1}^{2} P(X| \cup MD_{C_i}(x)) + \lambda_{BN} \bigwedge_{i=1}^{2} P(\neg X| \cup MD_{C_i}(x)),$$
$$R(a_N|(\cup MD_{C_1}(x), \cup MD_{C_2}(x)))$$
$$= \lambda_{NP} \bigwedge_{i=1}^{2} P(X| \cup MD_{C_i}(x)) + \lambda_{NN} \bigwedge_{i=1}^{2} P(\neg X| \cup MD_{C_i}(x)).$$

where "$\bigwedge$" denotes the operation "minimum".

Then the Bayesian decision procedure is suggested to use the following three minimum-risk decision rules.

(OMP1) If $R(a_P|(\cup MD_{C_1}(x), \cup MD_{C_2}(x))) R(a_B|(\cup MD_{C_1}(x), \cup MD_{C_2}(x)))$ and $R(a_P|(\cup MD_{C_1}(x), \cup MD_{C_2}(x))) \leq R(a_N|(\cup MD_{C_1}(x), \cup MD_{C_2}(x)))$, decide $x \in POS_{C_1+C_2}^{OM}(X)$;

(OMN1) If $R(a_N|(\cup MD_{C_1}(x), \cup MD_{C_2}(x))) R(a_P|(\cup MD_{C_1}(x), \cup MD_{C_2}(x)))$ and $R(a_N|(\cup MD_{C_1}(x), \cup MD_{C_2}(x))) \leq R(a_B|(\cup MD_{C_1}(x), \cup MD_{C_2}(x)))$, decide $x \in NEG_{C_1+C_2}^{OM}(X)$;

(OMB1) If $R(a_B|(\cup MD_{C_1}(x), \cup MD_{C_2}(x))) R(a_P|(\cup MD_{C_1}(x), \cup MD_{C_2}(x)))$ and $R(a_B|(\cup MD_{C_1}(x), \cup MD_{C_2}(x))) \leq R(a_N|(\cup MD_{C_1}(x), \cup MD_{C_2}(x)))$, decide $x \in BND_{C_1+C_2}^{OM}(X)$.

Consider a special kind of loss function satisfies $0 \leq \lambda_{PP} \leq \lambda_{BP} < \lambda_{NP}$ and $0 \leq \lambda_{NN} \leq \lambda_{BN} < \lambda_{PN}$, that is, the loss of classifying an object x in state X into the positive region X is less than or equal to the loss of classifying x into the boundary region X, and both of these losses are less than the of classifying x into the negative region X. Then use $P(X|\cup MD_{C_i}(x)) + P(\neg X|\cup MD_{C_i}(x)) = 1$, we have:

(1) For rule (OMP1):

$$R(a_P|(\cup MD_{C_1}(x), \cup MD_{C_2}(x))) \leq R(a_B|(\cup MD_{C_1}(x), \cup MD_{C_2}(x)))$$

$$\Longleftrightarrow \frac{\bigwedge_{i=1}^{2} P(X|\cup MD_{C_i}(x))}{1+\bigwedge_{i=1}^{2} P(X|\cup MD_{C_i}(x))-\bigvee_{i=1}^{2} P(X|\cup MD_{C_i}(x))} \geq \frac{\lambda_{PN}-\lambda_{BN}}{(\lambda_{PN}-\lambda_{BN})+(\lambda_{BP}-\lambda_{PP})}$$

and

$$R(a_P|(\cup MD_{C_1}(x), \cup MD_{C_2}(x))) \leq R(a_N|(\cup MD_{C_1}(x), \cup MD_{C_2}(x)))$$

$$\Longleftrightarrow \frac{\bigwedge_{i=1}^{2} P(X|\cup MD_{C_i}(x))}{1+\bigwedge_{i=1}^{2} P(X|\cup MD_{C_i}(x))-\bigvee_{i=1}^{2} P(X|\cup MD_{C_i}(x))} \geq \frac{\lambda_{PN}-\lambda_{NN}}{(\lambda_{PN}-\lambda_{NN})+(\lambda_{NP}-\lambda_{PP})}.$$

where "$\bigvee$" denotes the operation "maximum".

(2) For rule (OMN1):

$$R(a_N|(\cup MD_{C_1}(x), \cup MD_{C_2}(x))) \leq R(a_P|(\cup MD_{C_1}(x), \cup MD_{C_2}(x)))$$

$$\Longleftrightarrow \frac{\bigwedge_{i=1}^{2} P(X|\cup MD_{C_i}(x))}{1+\bigwedge_{i=1}^{2} P(X|\cup MD_{C_i}(x))-\bigvee_{i=1}^{2} P(X|\cup MD_{C_i}(x))} \leq \frac{\lambda_{PN}-\lambda_{NN}}{(\lambda_{PN}-\lambda_{NN})+(\lambda_{NP}-\lambda_{PP})}$$

and

$$R(a_N|(\cup MD_{C_1}(x), \cup MD_{C_2}(x))) \leq R(a_B|(\cup MD_{C_1}(x), \cup MD_{C_2}(x)))$$

$$\Longleftrightarrow \frac{\bigwedge_{i=1}^{2} P(X|\cup MD_{C_i}(x))}{1+\bigwedge_{i=1}^{2} P(X|\cup MD_{C_i}(x))-\bigvee_{i=1}^{2} P(X|\cup MD_{C_i}(x))} \leq \frac{\lambda_{BN}-\lambda_{NN}}{(\lambda_{BN}-\lambda_{NN})+(\lambda_{NP}-\lambda_{BP})}.$$

(3) For rule (OMB1):

$$R(a_B|(\cup MD_{C_1}(x), \cup MD_{C_m}(x))) \leq R(a_P|(\cup MD_{C_1}(x), \cup MD_{C_2}(x)))$$

$$\Longleftrightarrow \frac{\bigwedge_{i=1}^{2} P(X|\cup MD_{C_i}(x)}{1+\bigwedge_{i=1}^{2} P(X|\cup MD_{C_i}(x))-\bigvee_{i=1}^{2} P(X|\cup MD_{C_i}(x))} \leq \frac{\lambda_{PN}-\lambda_{BN}}{(\lambda_{PN}-\lambda_{BN})+(\lambda_{BP}-\lambda_{PP})}$$

and

$$R(a_B|(\cup MD_{C_1}(x), \cup MD_{C_2}(x))) \leq R(a_N|(\cup MD_{C_1}(x), \cup MD_{C_2}(x)))$$

$$\Longleftrightarrow \frac{\bigwedge_{i=1}^{2} P(X|\cup MD_{C_i}(x))}{1+\bigwedge_{i=1}^{2} P(X|\cup MD_{C_i}(x))-\bigvee_{i=1}^{2} P(X|\cup MD_{C_i}(x))} \geq \frac{\lambda_{BN}-\lambda_{NN}}{(\lambda_{BN}-\lambda_{NN})+(\lambda_{NP}-\lambda_{BP})}.$$

Therefore, the rules (OMP1)–(OMB1) can be rewritten as:

(OMP2) If $\dfrac{\bigwedge_{i=1}^{2} P(X|\cup MD_{C_i}(x))}{1+\bigwedge_{i=1}^{2} P(X|\cup MD_{C_i}(x))-\bigvee_{i=1}^{2} P(X|\cup MD_{C_i}(x))} \geq \alpha$ and

$$\frac{\bigwedge_{i=1}^{2} P(X|\cup MD_{C_i}(x))}{1+\bigwedge_{i=1}^{2} P(X|\cup MD_{C_i}(x))-\bigvee_{i=1}^{2} P(X|\cup MD_{C_i}(x))} \geq \gamma$$

decide $x \in POS_{C_1+C_2}{}^{O}(X)$;

(OMN2) If $\dfrac{\bigwedge_{i=1}^{2} P(X|\cup MD_{C_i}(x))}{1+\bigwedge_{i=1}^{2} P(X|\cup MD_{C_i}(x))-\bigvee_{i=1}^{2} P(X|\cup MD_{C_i}(x))} \leq \gamma$ and

$$\frac{\bigwedge_{i=1}^{2} P(X|\cup MD_{C_i}(x))}{1+\bigwedge_{i=1}^{2} P(X|\cup MD_{C_i}(x))-\bigvee_{i=1}^{2} P(X|\cup MD_{C_i}(x))} \leq \beta$$

decide $x \in NEG_{C_1+C_2}{}^{O}(X)$;

(OMB2) If $\dfrac{\bigwedge_{i=1}^{2} P(X|\cup MD_{C_i}(x))}{1+\bigwedge_{i=1}^{2} P(X|\cup MD_{C_i}(x))-\bigvee_{i=1}^{2} P(X|\cup MD_{C_i}(x))} \leq \alpha$ and

$$\frac{\bigwedge_{i=1}^{2} P(X|\cup MD_{C_i}(x))}{1+\bigwedge_{i=1}^{2} P(X|\cup MD_{C_i}(x))-\bigvee_{i=1}^{2} P(X|\cup MD_{C_i}(x))} \geq \beta$$

decide $x \in BND_{C_1+C_2}{}^O(X)$.

Where $\alpha = \frac{\lambda_{PN}-\lambda_{BN}}{(\lambda_{PN}-\lambda_{BN})+(\lambda_{BP}-\lambda_{PP})}$, $\beta = \frac{\lambda_{BN}-\lambda_{NN}}{(\lambda_{BN}-\lambda_{NN})+(\lambda_{NP}-\lambda_{BP})}$,

$\gamma = \frac{\lambda_{PN}-\lambda_{NN}}{(\lambda_{PN}-\lambda_{NN})+(\lambda_{NP}-\lambda_{PP})}$.

Consider an additional condition on the loss function with $(\lambda_{PN} - \lambda_{BN})(\lambda_{NP} - \lambda_{BP}) > (\lambda_{BN} - \lambda_{NN})(\lambda_{BP} - \lambda_{PP})$. It follows that $0 \leq \beta < \gamma < \alpha \leq 1$. Thus the following simplified rules are obtained.

(OMP3) If $\frac{\bigwedge_{i=1}^{2} P(X|\cup MD_{C_i}(x))}{1+\bigwedge_{i=1}^{2} P(X|\cup MD_{C_i}(x))-\bigvee_{i=1}^{2} P(X|\cup MD_{C_i}(x))} \geq \alpha$,

decide $x \in POS_{C_1+C_2}{}^O(X)$;

(OMN3) If $\frac{\bigwedge_{i=1}^{2} P(X|\cup MD_{C_i}(x))}{1+\bigwedge_{i=1}^{2} P(X|\cup MD_{C_i}(x))-\bigvee_{i=1}^{2} P(X|\cup MD_{C_i}(x))} \leq \beta$,

decide $x \in NEG_{C_1+C_2}{}^O(X)$;

(OMB3) If $\beta < \frac{\bigwedge_{i=1}^{2} P(X|\cup MD_{C_i}(x))}{1+\bigwedge_{i=1}^{2} P(X|\cup MD_{C_i}(x))-\bigvee_{i=1}^{2} P(X|\cup MD_{C_i}(x))} < \alpha$,

decide $x \in BND_{C_1+C_2}{}^O(X)$.

By rules (OMP3)–(OMB3), we therefore obtain the optimistic multigranulation positive, negative, and boundary regions for X, as follows.

Definition 4. Let $\langle U, \mathbf{C} \rangle$ be a covering approximation space, $C_1, C_2 \in \mathbf{C}$, and $P : 2^U \longrightarrow [0,1]$ is a probability function defined on the power set 2^U. For any $X \subseteq U$, the positive, negative, and boundary regions of X of covering-based optimistic multigranulation decision-theoretic rough set are defined as:

$$POS_{C_1+C_2}{}^{OM}(X) = \{x \in U \mid \frac{\bigwedge_{i=1}^{2} P(X| \cup MD_{C_i}(x))}{1 + \bigwedge_{i=1}^{2} P(X| \cup MD_{C_i}(x)) - \bigvee_{i=1}^{2} P(X| \cup MD_{C_i}(x))} \geq \alpha\}$$

$$NEG_{C_1+C_2}{}^{OM}(X) = \{x \in U \mid \frac{\bigwedge_{i=1}^{2} P(X| \cup MD_{C_i}(x))}{1 + \bigwedge_{i=1}^{2} P(X| \cup MD_{C_i}(x)) - \bigvee_{i=1}^{2} P(X| \cup MD_{C_i}(x))} \leq \beta\}$$

$$BND_{C_1+C_2}{}^{OM}(X) = \{x \in U \mid \beta < \frac{\bigwedge_{i=1}^{2} P(X| \cup MD_{C_i}(x))}{1 + \bigwedge_{i=1}^{2} P(X| \cup MD_{C_i}(x)) - \bigvee_{i=1}^{2} P(X| \cup MD_{C_i}(x))} < \alpha\}.$$

The corresponding lower and upper approximations of X of optimistic multigranulation decision-theoretic rough sets can be defined as follows.

Definition 5. Let $\langle U, \mathbf{C} \rangle$ be a covering approximation space, $C_1, C_2 \in \mathbf{C}$, and $P : 2^U \longrightarrow [0,1]$ is a probability function defined on the power set 2^U. For any $X \subseteq U$, the lower and upper approximations of X are defined as follows.

$$\underline{C_1 + C_2}^{OM,\alpha}(X) = \{x \in U \mid \frac{\bigwedge_{i=1}^{2} P(X|\cup MD_{C_i}(x))}{1+\bigwedge_{i=1}^{2} P(X|\cup MD_{C_i}(x))-\bigvee_{i=1}^{2} P(X|\cup MD_{C_i}(x))} \geq \alpha\}$$

$$\overline{C_1 + C_2}^{OM,\beta}(X) = \{x \in U \mid \frac{\bigwedge_{i=1}^{2} P(X|\cup MD_{C_i}(x))}{1+\bigwedge_{i=1}^{2} P(X|\cup MD_{C_i}(x))-\bigvee_{i=1}^{2} P(X|\cup MD_{C_i}(x))} > \beta\}$$

The pair $(\underline{C_1 + C_2}^{OM,\alpha}(X), \overline{C_1 + C_2}^{OM,\beta}(X))$ is called an optimistic multigranulation decision-theoretic rough set.

By the definition of optimistic multigranulation decision-theoretic lower and upper approximations, we have the following properties.

Proposition 1. Let $\langle U, \mathbf{C} \rangle$ be a covering approximation space, $C_1, C_2 \in \mathbf{C}$, and $P : 2^U \longrightarrow [0,1]$ is a probability function defined on the power set 2^U. For any $0 \leq \beta < \alpha \leq 1$, and $X, Y \subseteq U$, we have

(1) $\underline{C_1 + C_2}^{OM,\alpha}(\emptyset) = \overline{C_1 + C_2}^{OM,\beta}(\emptyset) = \emptyset$,

$\underline{C_1 + C_2}^{OM,\alpha}(U) = \overline{C_1 + C_2}^{OM,\beta}(U) = U$;

(2) $\underline{C_1 + C_2}^{OM,\alpha}(X) \subseteq X \subseteq \overline{C_1 + C_2}^{OM,\beta}(X)$;

(3) If $X \subseteq Y$, we have $\underline{C_1 + C_2}^{OM,\alpha}(X) \subseteq \underline{C_1 + C_2}^{OM,\alpha}(Y)$ and

$\overline{C_1 + C_2}^{OM,\beta}(X) \subseteq \overline{C_1 + C_2}^{OM,\beta}(Y)$;

(4) If $\alpha > 0.5$, we have $\underline{C_1 + C_2}^{OM,\alpha}(X) = \neg\overline{C_1 + C_2}^{OM,1-\alpha}(\neg X)$;

If $\beta < 0.5$, we have $\overline{C_1 + C_2}^{OM,\beta}(X) = \neg\underline{C_1 + C_2}^{OM,1-\beta}(\neg X)$.

Proof. We only offer the proofs of (4) here, others can be easily proved according to Definition 5.
For given $\alpha > 0.5$,

$$\neg\overline{C_1 + C_2}^{OM,1-\alpha}(\neg X)$$

$$= \neg\{x \in U \mid \frac{\bigwedge_{i=1}^{2} P(\neg X \mid \cup MD_{C_i}(x))}{1 + \bigwedge_{i=1}^{2} P(\neg X \mid \cup MD_{C_i}(x)) - \bigvee_{i=1}^{2} P(\neg X \mid \cup MD_{C_i}(x))} > 1 - \alpha\}$$

$$= \{x \in U \mid \frac{1 - \bigvee_{i=1}^{2} P(X \mid \cup MD_{C_i}(x))}{1 - \bigvee_{i=1}^{2} P(X \mid \cup MD_{C_i}(x)) + \bigwedge_{i=1}^{2} P(X \mid \cup MD_{C_i}(x))} \leq 1 - \alpha\}$$

$$= \{x \in U \mid \frac{\bigwedge_{i=1}^{2} P(X \mid \cup MD_{C_i}(x))}{1 + \bigwedge_{i=1}^{2} P(X \mid \cup MD_{C_i}(x)) - \bigvee_{i=1}^{2} P(X \mid \cup MD_{C_i}(x))} \geq \alpha\}$$

$$= \underline{C_1 + C_2}^{OM,\alpha}(X).$$

Other part of (4) can be proved in a similar way.

Theorem 1. Let $\langle U, \mathbf{C} \rangle$ be a covering approximation space, $C_1, C_2 \in \mathbf{C}$, for any $0 \leq \beta < \alpha \leq 1$, and $X \subseteq U$, we have

(1) $\underline{C_1 + C_2}^{OM,\alpha}(\underline{C_1 + C_2}^{OM,\alpha}(X)) \subseteq \overline{C_1 + C_2}^{OM,\beta}(\underline{C_1 + C_2}^{OM,\alpha}(X))$;

(2) $\overline{C_1 + C_2}^{OM,\beta}(\overline{C_1 + C_2}^{OM,\beta}(X)) \supseteq \underline{C_1 + C_2}^{OM,\alpha}(\overline{C_1 + C_2}^{OM,\beta}(X))$.

Theorem 2. Let $\langle U, \mathbf{C} \rangle$ be a covering approximation space, $C_1, C_2 \in \mathbf{C}$, for any $0 \leq \beta_2 \leq \beta_1 \leq \alpha_1 \leq \alpha_2 \leq 1$, and $X \subseteq U$, we have

$$\underline{C_1 + C_2}^{OM,\alpha_2}(X) \quad \subseteq \quad \underline{C_1 + C_2}^{OM,\alpha_1}(X) \quad \subseteq \quad \overline{C_1 + C_2}^{OM,\beta_1}(X) \quad \subseteq$$
$$\overline{C_1 + C_2}^{OM,\beta_2}(X)$$

Theorem 3. Let $\langle U, \mathbf{C} \rangle$ be a covering approximation space, $C_1, C_2 \in \mathbf{C}$, for any $0 \leq \beta < \alpha \leq 1$, and $X \subseteq U$, we have

(1) $\underline{C_1 + C_2}^{OM,\alpha}(X) \subseteq \underline{C_1 + C_2}^{O,\alpha}(X)$;

(2) $\overline{C_1 + C_2}^{O,\beta}(X) \subseteq \overline{C_1 + C_2}^{OM,\beta}(X)$.

Where $\underline{C_1 + C_2}^{O,\alpha}(X)$ and $\overline{C_1 + C_2}^{O,\beta}(X)$ are defined by Liu et al. in [14].

Theorem 4. Let $\langle U, \mathbf{C} \rangle$ be a covering approximation space, $C_1, C_2 \in \mathbf{C}$, for any $0 \leq \beta < \alpha \leq 1$, and $X \subseteq U$, we have

(1) If $\alpha = 1$, $\underline{C_1 + C_2}^{O,\alpha}(X) = \underline{S_{C_1 + C_2}}(X)$

(2) If $\beta = 0$, $\overline{C_1 + C_2}^{O,\alpha}(X) = \overline{S_{C_1 + C_2}}(X)$

Where $\underline{S_{C_1 + C_2}}(X)$ and $\overline{S_{C_1 + C_2}}(X)$ are defined by Liu et al. in [17].

Proof. If $\alpha = 1$, noting that $P(X| \cup MD_{C_i}(x)) = \frac{|X \cup (\cup MD_{C_i}(x))|}{|\cup MD_{C_i}(x)|}$, then

$$\underline{C_1 + C_2}^{O,1}(X) = \{x \in U \mid \frac{\bigwedge_{i=1}^{2} P(X| \cup MD_{C_i}(x))}{1 + \bigwedge_{i=1}^{2} P(X| \cup MD_{C_i}(x)) - \bigvee_{i=1}^{2} P(X| \cup MD_{C_i}(x))} \geq 1\}$$

$$= \{x \in U \mid \bigvee_{i=1}^{2} P(X| \cup MD_{C_i}(x)) \geq 1\}$$

$$= \{x \in U \mid P(X| \cup MD_{C_1}(x)) = 1 \text{ or } P(X| \cup MD_{C_2}(x)) = 1\}$$

$$= \{x \in U \mid \cup MD_{C_1}(x) \subseteq X \text{ or } \cup MD_{C_2}(x) \subseteq X\}$$

$$= \underline{S_{C_1 + C_2}}(X);$$

If $\beta = 0$, we have that

$$\overline{C_1 + C_2}^{O,0}(X) = \{x \in U \mid \frac{\bigwedge_{i=1}^{2} P(X| \cup MD_{C_i}(x))}{1 + \bigwedge_{i=1}^{2} P(X| \cup MD_{C_i}(x)) - \bigvee_{i=1}^{2} P(X| \cap MD_{C_i}(x))} > 0\}$$

$$= \{x \in U \mid \bigwedge_{i=1}^{2} P(X| \cap MD_{C_i}(x)) > 0\}$$

$$= \{x \in U \mid P(X| \cup MD_{C_1}(x)) > 0 \text{ and } P(X| \cup MD_{C_2}(x)) > 0\}$$

$$= \{x \in U \mid \cup MD_{C_1}(x) \cap X \neq \emptyset \text{ and } \cup MD_{C_2}(x) \cap X \neq \emptyset\}$$

$$= \overline{S_{C_1 + C_2}}(X).$$

Theorem 4 implies that, in this case, the optimistic multigranulation decision-theoretic rough set model will degenerate to the covering-based multigranulation rough set model in [17].

Remark 1. If $\mathbf{C}$ is a set of partitions of U, the optimistic multigranulation decision-theoretic rough set model in multi-covering space will degenerate to the optimistic multigranulation decision-theoretic rough set model in [12].

For the readers' convenience, the relationships of the lower and upper operators between the proposed model and the models in [17,18] are shown as Fig. 1.

In Fig. 1, each node denotes an approximation or a concept. Each line connects two approximations, where the lower element is a subset of the upper element. Each arrow means that when the corresponding condition is given, the head element in the arrow will degenerate to the rear one.

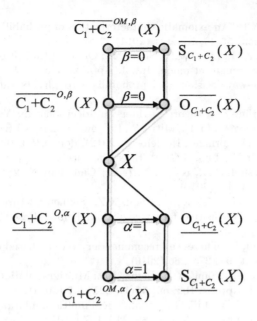

Fig. 1. Relationships of multigranution DTRSs

4   Conclusion

In the present paper, we mainly discussed a kind of multigranulation decision-theoretic rough set model in the multi-covering space by employing the maximal descriptions of elements. We gave the properties of the proposed model. And we also found some interrelationships between the proposed model and other existing models.

Acknowledgements. This work was supported by the China National Natural Science Foundation of Science Foundation under Grant Nos.: 61663002, 61403329, 61305052 and Jiangxi Province Natural Science Foundation of China under Grant No.: 20171BAB202034.

References

1. Yao, Y.Y., Wong, S.K.M.: A decision theoretic framework for approximating concepts. Int. J. Man-Mach. Stud. **37**, 793–809 (1992)
2. Herbert, J.P., Yao, J.T.: Game-theoretic rough sets. Fundam. Inform. **108**(3–4), 267–286 (2011)
3. Liu, D., Li, T.R., Li, H.X.: A multiple-category classification approach with decision-theoretic rough sets. Fundam. Inform. **115**(2–3), 173–188 (2012)
4. Yu, H., Liu, Z.G., Wang, G.Y.: An automatic method to determine the number of clusters using decision-theoretic rough set. Int. J. Approx. Reason. **55**(1), 101–115 (2014)

5. Li, T.J., Yang, X.P.: An axiomatic characterization of probabilistic rough sets. Int. J. Approx. Reason. **55**(1), 130–141 (2014)
6. Jia, X.Y., Tang, Z.M., Liao, W.H., Shang, L.: On an optimization representation of decision-theoretic rough set model. Int. J. Approx. Reason. **55**(1), 156–166 (2014)
7. Yao, Y.Y.: Three-way decisions with probabilistic rough sets. Inf. Sci. **180**, 341–353 (2010)
8. Yao, Y.: An outline of a theory of three-way decisions. In: Yao, J.T., Yang, Y., Słowiński, R., Greco, S., Li, H., Mitra, S., Polkowski, L. (eds.) RSCTC 2012. LNCS, vol. 7413, pp. 1–17. Springer, Heidelberg (2012). doi:10.1007/978-3-642-32115-3_1
9. Zhou, B., Yao, Y.Y., Luo, J.G.: A three-way decision approach to email spam filtering. In: Farzindar, A., Keselj, V. (eds.) Canadian AI 2010, LNAI 6085, pp. 28–39. Springer, Berlin (2010)
10. Li, H.X., Zhang, L.B., Huang, B., Zhou, X.Z.: Sequential three-way decision and granulation for cost-sensitive face recognition. Knowl.-Based Syst. **91**, 241–251 (2016)
11. Zhang, H.R., Min, F.: Three-way recommender systems based on random forests. Knowl.-Based Syst. **91**, 275–286 (2016)
12. Qian, Y.H., Zhang, H., Sang, Y.L., Liang, J.L.: Multigranulation decision-theoretic rough sets. Int. J. Approx. Reason. **55**(1), 225–237 (2014)
13. Qian, Y.H., Liang, X.Y., Lin, G.P., et al.: Local multigranulation decision-theoretic rough sets. Int. J. Approx. Reason. **82**, 119–137 (2017)
14. Liu, C., Wang, M.: Optimistic decision-theoretic rough sets in multi-covering space. In: Flores, V., Gomide, F., Janusz, A., Meneses, C., Miao, D., Peters, G., Ślęzak, D., Wang, G., Weber, R., Yao, Y. (eds.) IJCRS 2016. LNCS, vol. 9920, pp. 282–293. Springer, Cham (2016). doi:10.1007/978-3-319-47160-0_26
15. Yao, Y.Y., Yao, B.: Covering based rough set approximations. Inf. Sci. **200**, 91–107 (2012)
16. Zakowski, W.: Approximations in the space (U, Π). Demonstr. Math. **16**, 761–769 (1983)
17. Liu, C.H.: Covering-based multi-granulation rough set model based on maximal description of elements. Comput. Sci. **40**(12), 64–67 (2013). (In Chinese)
18. Liu, C.H., Cai, K.C.: Multi-granulation covering rough sets based on the union of minimal descriptions of elements. CAAI Trans. Intell. Syst. **11**(4), 534–538 (2016). (in Chinese)
19. Zhu, W., Wang, F.Y.: On three types of covering rough sets. IEEE Trans. Knowl. Data Eng. **19**, 1131–1144 (2007)

A Three-Way Decision Model Based on Intuitionistic Fuzzy Decision Systems

Jiubing Liu[1], Xianzhong Zhou[1,2(✉)], Bing Huang[3], and Huaxiong Li[1]

[1] School of Management and Engineering, Nanjing University,
Nanjing 210093, People's Republic of China
zhouxz@nju.edu.cn
[2] Research Center for Novel Technology of Intelligent Equipment,
Nanjing University, Nanjing 210093, People's Republic of China
[3] School of Technology, Nanjing Audit University,
Nanjing 211815, People's Republic of China

Abstract. The similarity degree and divergence degree between intuitionistic fuzzy objects are defined respectively, and the related properties are presented in this paper. Then, we define the (α, β)-level cut-sets based on intuitionistic fuzzy similarity relation under decision objective circumstances. Moreover, the upper and lower approximation sets of objective sets are derived by utilizing the defined rough membership function. Some properties of the derived upper and lower approximations are discussed, and a ranking method for intuitionistic fuzzy numbers is proposed. According to Bayesian decisions, an intuitionistic fuzzy three-way decision-theoretic model and a rule induction algorithm based on intuitionistic fuzzy decision systems are constructed. Finally, a numerical example is given to illustrate the effectiveness of the proposed method.

Keywords: Similarity degree · Divergence degree · Intuitionistic fuzzy decision systems · Three-way decisions

1 Introduction

The model of three-way decisions is usually encountered in handling cost-sensitive decision issues [1–3], e.g., text classification [4], risk decision [5], clustering analysis [6], etc. Since it was initially proposed by Yao based on rough set, it has received much attention and has widely applied in many fields, such as spam filtering [7], face recognition [8], granularity computing [9–11] and fuzzy information systems [12,13].

As a generalization of rough set, the decision-theoretic rough set (DTRS) was proposed by Yao and vastly pushed the development of three-way decisions [14]. According to Bayesian decision theory, considering the minimum of overall risk, Yao [14] proposed the model for deriving three-way decisions with DTRS. So far, the researches on three-way decisions with DTRS have made many theoretical and applied achievements. For example, Liu et al. [15] concluded four-level choosing criteria for probabilistic rules. Qian et al. [16] developed a multi-granulation

© Springer International Publishing AG 2017
L. Polkowski et al. (Eds.): IJCRS 2017, Part II, LNAI 10314, pp. 249–263, 2017.
DOI: 10.1007/978-3-319-60840-2_18

decision-theoretic rough set with the help of DTRS and multi-granular structures. For multiple sets of decision preferences, Yang and Yao [17] studied some aggregations of loss functions under the multi-agent DTRS model. With respect to the reduction problem, Zhang and Miao [18] constructed a reduction framework on two-category decision-theoretic rough sets. Besides, Liang et al. [19], Liu et al. [20,21], Liang and Liu [22] evaluated the loss function by the form of triangular fuzzy numbers, intervals, hesitant fuzzy set, and linguistic value effectively. With the previous literature, the determination of loss function is a key issue [25], and nowadays the uncertain evaluation scenarios are a novel research direction for three-way decisions with DTRS, which can further extend the applications of three-way decisions [26].

Intuitionistic fuzzy set (IFS) is served as a new form of the uncertain evaluation scenarios. The IFS, proposed by Atanassov [23], can better describe the uncertainty or vagueness by the membership degree and non-membership degree than the fuzzy set [24]. By introducing the new evaluation form of loss function with the IFS, Liang and Liu [25] proposed a method to derive three-way decisions in multi-period decision making under intuitionistic fuzzy environment. Liang et al. [26] discussed the decision principles of three-way decision rules based on the variation of loss functions with IFS.

From the existing literature, there are few researches on discussing the internal relationship between IFS and DTRS in the frame of three-way decisions. Soothly, the IFS and DTRS are consistent but limited. For one thing, they can all characterize the fuzziness or uncertainty, the IFS describes the uncertainty by the hesitation index between the membership and non-membership degree, while the DTRS by adding boundary decisions between positive and negative decisions. Moreover, the elements between them exist one to one corresponding relationship. For another thing, the IFS determines its membership, non-membership and hesitation degree through mankind's subjective judgement, but the positive, negative and boundary decisions in DTRS model are determined by Bayesian theory, which is objective when the loss function is given by decision makers as IFS. If both combination, we can integrate the advantages of two theories, respectively. Hence, there is a need to be intensive research. In this paper, we propose a novel three-way decision-theoretic model based on both combination.

2   Preliminaries

The basic concepts of an intuitionistic fuzzy set and an intuitionistic fuzzy information system are briefly reviewed in this section.

Definition 1 [23]. *Let U be a finite non-empty universe set, an intuitionistic fuzzy set(IFS) in U is defined as $\widetilde{A} = \{\langle x, u_{\widetilde{A}}(x), v_{\widetilde{A}}(x)\rangle | x \in U\}$, which is described by the membership function $u_{\widetilde{A}} : U \mapsto [0,1]$ and non-membership function $v_{\widetilde{A}} : U \mapsto [0,1]$ with $u_{\widetilde{A}}(x) + v_{\widetilde{A}}(x) \in [0,1]$ for $\forall x \in U$. Furthermore, $\pi_{\widetilde{A}}(x) = 1 - u_{\widetilde{A}}(x) - v_{\widetilde{A}}(x)$ is called the hesitation degree or hesitation margin of the element x to the set $\widetilde{A}$. Especially when $\pi_{\widetilde{A}}(x) = 0$, an IFS $\widetilde{A}$ is degraded to the fuzzy set.*

The complement of an IFS $\widetilde{A}$ can be denoted by $\widetilde{A}^c = \{\langle x, v_{\widetilde{A}}(x), u_{\widetilde{A}}(x)\rangle | x \in U\}$. We call $\langle u_{\widetilde{A}}(x), v_{\widetilde{A}}(x)\rangle$ an intuitionistic fuzzy number (IFN) [27].

Let $\langle L, \geq_L \rangle$ be a complete bounded lattice with $L = \{\langle x, y \rangle \in [0,1] \times [0,1] | 0 \leq x + y \leq 1\}$. Suppose $\widetilde{a}_i = \langle u_i, v_i \rangle (i = 1, 2)$ are two IFNs, the operations for IFNs are given as follows [27]:

$$
\begin{aligned}
&(1)\ \widetilde{a}_1 \oplus \widetilde{a}_2 = \langle 1 - (1 - u_1)(1 - u_2), v_1 v_2 \rangle; \\
&(2)\ k\widetilde{a}_1 = \langle 1 - (1 - u_1)^k, v_1^k \rangle\ where\ k > 0; \\
&(3)\ The\ complement\ set\widetilde{a}_1^c = \langle v_1, u_1 \rangle; \\
&(4)\ \widetilde{a}_1 \geq_L \widetilde{a}_2\ if\ and\ only\ if\ u_1 \geq u_2\ and\ v_1 \leq v_2.
\end{aligned}
\tag{1}
$$

In addition, Li [28] and Xu [29] presented the definition of the normalized hamming distance $d(\widetilde{a}_1, \widetilde{a}_2)$ and the intuitionistic fuzzy divergence $e(\widetilde{a}_1, \widetilde{a}_2)$ between $\widetilde{a}_1$ and $\widetilde{a}_2$, respectively.

$$
\begin{aligned}
d(\widetilde{a}_1, \widetilde{a}_2) &= \frac{1}{2}(|u_1 - u_2| + |v_1 - v_2| + |\pi_1 - \pi_2|), \\
e(\widetilde{a}_1, \widetilde{a}_2) &= \frac{1}{2}(|u_1 - u_2| + |v_1 - v_2|).
\end{aligned}
\tag{2}
$$

Definition 2 [30]. *An intuitionistic fuzzy information system(IFIS) is defined as a 4-tuple $S = (U, A = C \cup D, V, f)$, where U is a non-empty finite object set. A represents a non-empty finite set of attributes, including the conditional attribute set C and decision attribute set D. $V = \cup_{c \in C} V_c$ and V_c is a domain of the attribute c, and $f : U \times A \mapsto V$ is an information function such that $f(x, c) = \langle u, v \rangle \in V_c$ for $\forall x \in U$. Especially, if $C \cap D \neq \emptyset$, IFIS is called an intuitionistic fuzzy decision system(IFDS).*

Definition 3 [31]. *Let U be a given domain, a binary intuitionistic fuzzy relation R is defined as follows:*

$$
R = \{\langle (x, y), u_R(x, y), v_R(x, y) \rangle | (x, y) \in U \times U\},
\tag{3}
$$

where $u_R : U \times U \mapsto [0,1]$ and $v_R : U \times U \mapsto [0,1]$ denote, respectively, the membership function and non-membership degree with the relation R between x and y satisfying the condition: $0 \leq u_R(x, y) + v_R(x, y) \leq 1$ for every $(x, y) \in U \times U$. Besides, we say that R is a binary intuitionistic fuzzy similarity relation(BIFSR) in $U \times U$, the following condition is required.

(1) R is reflexive, if $u_R(x, x) = 1$ and $v_R(x, x) = 0$ for any $x \in U$.
(2) R is symmetric, if $u_R(x, y) = u_R(y, x)$ and $v_R(x, y) = v_R(y, x)$ for $x, y \in U$.

3   Intuitionistic Fuzzy Rough Approximation

In order to construct a binary intuitionistic fuzzy similarity relation, which is used to characterize the similarity degree between two objects with respect to the attributes in intuitionistic fuzzy information systems. We first propose a new general definition on the similarity degree between IFNs based on the normalized hamming distance, as presented in Definition 4.

Definition 4. *Let* $a_i = \langle u_i, v_i \rangle (i = 1, 2)$ *be two IFNs. The IFN similarity degree* $s(a_1, a_2)$ *between* a_1 *and* a_2 *is defined as follows:*

$$s(a_1, a_2) = 1 - \frac{1}{2}(|u_1 - u_2| + |v_1 - v_2| + |\pi_1 - \pi_2|), \tag{4}$$

where $\pi_i = 1 - u_i - v_i$ *for* $i = 1, 2$.

It is obviously required that $s(a_1, a_2) \leq 1$. If $a_1 = a_2$, then $s(a_1, a_2) = 1$. Especially when a_1 and a_2 are taken as two extreme cases respectively, that is $a_1 = \langle 1, 0 \rangle$ and $a_2 = \langle 0, 1 \rangle$. $s(a_1, a_2)$ is equal to 0 which is consistent with practical implication. Here we mainly prove the conclusion of $s(a_1, a_2) \geq 0$.

Proof. (1) When $\pi_1 = \pi_2$, clearly, $s(a_1, a_2) \geq 0$; (2) when $\pi_1 \neq \pi_2$, (a) if $u_1 = u_2$ and $v_1 = v_2$, $s(a_1, a_2) \geq 0$ holds; (b) if $u_1 = u_2$ and $v_1 \neq v_2$, $s(a_1, a_2) \geq 0$ holds; (c) if $u_1 \neq u_2$ and $v_1 = v_2$, $s(a_1, a_2) \geq 0$ also holds; (d) if $u_1 \neq u_2$ and $v_1 \neq v_2$, i.e., there are four cases as follows: $u_1 < u_2$ and $v_1 > v_2$; $u_1 < u_2$ and $v_1 < v_2$; $u_1 > u_2$ and $v_1 < v_2$; $u_1 > u_2$ and $v_1 > v_2$. we prove that $s(a_1, a_2) \geq 0$ with the aid of the geometrical representation of IFNs. Without loss of generality, we only prove that $0 \leq s(a_1, a_2) \leq 1$ under the case of $u_1 < u_2$ and $v_1 > v_2$, and the same with the others. For convenience, let $h = |u_1 - u_2|, l_1 = |v_1 - v_2|, l_2 = |\pi_1 - \pi_2|$ and S be the area of the right trapezoid $CHDG$ (See the Fig. 1). According to the geometrical representation of IFNs, we require $|GC| = h, |GD| = l_1, |CH| = l_2$. Thus, we can get $S = \frac{1}{2}(l_2 + l_1)h$ by the formula of trapezoid area, and $l_1 = h + l_2$ with $l_1, l_2, h \in [0, 1]$. We further require $l_2 + l_1 = \frac{2S}{h}$. Since $S = S_1 + S_2 = \frac{1}{2}h^2 + hl_2$, so we get $\frac{2S}{h} = h + 2l_2$. It is easy to obtain $s(a_1, a_2) = 1 - \frac{1}{2}(h + l_1 + l_2) = 1 - \frac{1}{2}(h + \frac{2S}{h}) = 1 - \frac{1}{2}(2h + 2l_2) = 1 - l_1 > 0$. Hence, $0 \leq s(a_1, a_2) \leq 1$.

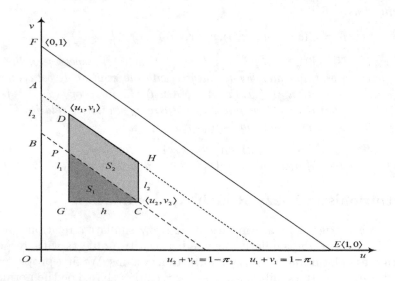

Fig. 1. The geometrical representation of IFNs

In view of Definition 4, we try to introduce the similarity degree and divergence degree of IFNs into IFIS. The similarity degree $u_R(x, y)$ and divergence degree $v_R(x, y)$ between two objects on the attributes are defined below.

Definition 5. *Let* $S = (U, A = C \cup D, V, f)$ *be an IFDS and R be a BIFSR,* $B \subseteq C$ *is a subset of attributes. Suppose that* $f(x, c) = \langle u_c(x), v_c(x) \rangle$ *is an intuitionistic fuzzy attribute value of an object* $x \in U$ *under the attribute* $c \in B$. *The similarity degree* $u_R(x, y)$ *and divergence degree* $v_R(x, y)$ *with respect to the attribute set B between x and y are respectively defined as follows:*

$$
\begin{aligned}
u_R(x, y) &= \min_{c \in B}\{s(f(x, c), f(y, c))\} \\
v_R(x, y) &= \max_{c \in B}\{e(f(x, c), f(y, c))\},
\end{aligned}
\tag{5}
$$

where $s(f(x, c), f(y, c))$ *and* $e(f(x, c), f(y, c))$ *represent the similarity degree and divergence degree of the IFNs* $f(x, c)$ *and* $f(y, c)$, *respectively.*

Theorem 1. *Let* $S = (U, C \cup D, V, f)$ *be an IFDS and R be a BIFSR.* $x, y \in U$, $c \in B \subseteq C$. *The similarity degree* $u_R(x, y)$ *and divergence degree* $v_R(x, y)$ *for the attribute set B between x and y have the following properties:*

(1) $0 \leq u_R(x, y) \leq 1, 0 \leq v_R(x, y) \leq 1$ *and* $0 \leq u_R(x, y) + v_R(x, y) \leq 1$;
(2) $u_R(x, y) = u_R(y, x)$ *and* $v_R(x, y) = v_R(y, x)$;
(3) *If* $u_R(x, y) = 1$, *then* $v_R(x, y) = 0$ *and vice versa*;
(4) $f(x, c) = f(y, c)$ *for any* $c \in B$ *if and only if* $u_R(x, y) = 1$ *and* $v_R(x, y) = 0$;
(5) *If* $f(x, c) = \langle 1, 0 \rangle$ *and* $f(y, c) = \langle 0, 1 \rangle$ *for any* $c \in B$, *then* $u_R(x, y) = 0$ *and* $v_R(x, y) = 1$;
(6) *If* $f(x, c) = \langle 1, 0 \rangle$ *and* $f(y, c) = \langle 0.5, 0.5 \rangle$ *for any* $c \in B$, *then* $u_R(x, y) = 0.5$ *and* $v_R(x, y) = 0.5$;
(7) *If* $f(x, c) = \langle 0.5, 0.5 \rangle$ *and* $f(y, c) = \langle 0, 1 \rangle$ *for any* $c \in B$, *then* $u_R(x, y) = 0.5$ *and* $v_R(x, y) = 0.5$.

Proof. It is straightforward to prove Theorem 1 by use of Definition 5.

Definition 6. *Let* $S = (U, C \cup D, V, f)$ *be an IFDS and R be a BIFSR. For any* $\alpha, \beta \in [0, 1]$ *with* $0 \leq \alpha + \beta \leq 1$. $u_R(x, y)$ *and* $v_R(x, y)$ *denote the similarity degree and divergence degree of* $x, y \in U$ *with respect to the attribute set* $B \subseteq C$. *We define* (α, β)*-level cut-sets* R_α^β *based on a binary intuitionistic fuzzy similarity relation as follow:*

$$
\begin{aligned}
R_\alpha^\beta &= \{(x, y) \in U \times U | u_R(x, y) \geq \alpha \text{ and } v_R(x, y) \leq \beta\}, i.e., \\
R_\alpha^\beta(x) &= \{y \in U | (x, y) \in R_\alpha^\beta\}.
\end{aligned}
\tag{6}
$$

Furthermore, $R_\alpha = \{(x, y) \in U \times U | u_R(x, y) \geq \alpha\}$ *is called* α*-level cut-sets which consist of two tuples whose the membership degree between them belonging to R is no less than* α, *while* $R^\beta = \{(x, y) \in U \times U | v_R(x, y) \leq \beta\}$ *is defined as* β*-level cut-sets which consist of two tuples whose non-membership degree between them belonging to R is less than* β.

Obviously, R_α^β is a classical binary relation where $\alpha \in [0,1]$ is regarded as a given least threshold on membership values and $\beta \in [0,1]$ is considered as a given largest threshold on non-membership values. For real decision process in practice, the threshold α and β is usually given by decision makers according to actual requirements on "membership levels" and "non-membership levels" respectively.

Theorem 2. *Let R be a $BIFSR$, then (α, β)-level cut-sets R_α^β is a binary intuitionistic fuzzy similarity relation in $U \times U$.*

Proof. $\forall \alpha \in [0,1]$, notice that $u_R(x,x) = 1 \geq \alpha, v_R(x,x) = 0 \leq \beta$, thus $(x,x) \in R_\alpha^\beta$. Namely, R_α^β satisfies reflexivity. Besides, if $(x,y) \in R_\alpha^\beta$, then $u_R(x,y) \geq \alpha$ and $v_R(x,y) \leq \beta$. Considering that $R \in BIFSR$, so $u_R(y,x) = u_R(x,y) \geq \alpha$ and $v_R(y,x) = v_R(x,y) \leq \beta$. Therefore, $(y,x) \in R_\alpha^\beta$. Namely, R_α^β satisfies symmetry. Nevertheless, R_α^β is not generally transitive. As have discussed above, R_α^β is a binary intuitionistic fuzzy similarity relation.

Definition 7. *Let $S = (U, C \cup D, V, f)$ be an $IFDS$ and $\langle L, \geq_L \rangle$ be a complete bounded lattice with $L = \{\langle x, y \rangle \in [0,1] \times [0,1] | 0 \leq x + y \leq 1\}$. A given threshold pair (α, β) satisfying $\alpha, \beta \in [0,1]$ and $\alpha + \beta \leq 1$. The (α, β)-level cut-sets X_α^β under intuitionistic fuzzy decision objects is defined as*

$$X_\alpha^\beta = \{y \in U | f(y,c) \geq_L \langle \alpha, \beta \rangle, \forall c \in D\}, \tag{7}$$

where $\langle \alpha, \beta \rangle$ is an constant IFN which consists both of the threshold α and β.

Definition 8. *Let X_α^β be a non-empty finite set in U and $R_\alpha^\beta(x)$ be a similarity class under intuitionistic fuzzy (α, β)-level cut-sets. The threshold $\tilde\alpha, \tilde\beta \in [0,1]$ satisfying: $0 \leq \tilde\beta \leq \tilde\alpha \leq 1$ and $\tilde\alpha + \tilde\beta \leq 1$. We define the $(\tilde\alpha, \tilde\beta)$-probabilistic lower and upper approximations of X_α^β regarding R_α^β as follows, respectively.*

$$\begin{aligned} \underline{apr}^{(\tilde\alpha, \tilde\beta)}(X_\alpha^\beta) &= \{x \in U | Pr(X_\alpha^\beta | R_\alpha^\beta(x)) \geq \tilde\alpha\}, \\ \overline{apr}^{(\tilde\alpha, \tilde\beta)}(X_\alpha^\beta) &= \{x \in U | Pr(X_\alpha^\beta | R_\alpha^\beta(x)) > \tilde\beta\}, \end{aligned} \tag{8}$$

where $Pr(X_\alpha^\beta | R_\alpha^\beta(x))$ represents the conditional probability of X_α^β given the description $R_\alpha^\beta(x)$, i.e., $Pr(X_\alpha^\beta | R_\alpha^\beta(x)) = \frac{|R_\alpha^\beta(x) \cap X_\alpha^\beta|}{|R_\alpha^\beta(x)|}$, and $|\cdot|$ denotes the cardinality or element numbers of a given set.

We further call the pair $(\underline{apr}^{(\tilde\alpha, \tilde\beta)}(X_\alpha^\beta), \overline{apr}^{(\tilde\alpha, \tilde\beta)}(X_\alpha^\beta))$ an intuitionistic fuzzy rough set based on the relation R_α^β. Moreover, the positive region $POS_{R_\alpha^\beta}^{(\tilde\alpha, \tilde\beta)}(X_\alpha^\beta)$, negative region $NEG_{R_\alpha^\beta}^{(\tilde\alpha, \tilde\beta)}(X_\alpha^\beta)$ and boundary region $BND_{R_\alpha^\beta}^{(\tilde\alpha, \tilde\beta)}(X_\alpha^\beta)$ are given as follows:

$$POS_{R_\alpha^\beta}^{(\tilde\alpha, \tilde\beta)}(X_\alpha^\beta) = \underline{apr}^{(\tilde\alpha, \tilde\beta)}(X_\alpha^\beta) = \{x \in U | Pr(X_\alpha^\beta | R_\alpha^\beta(x)) \geq \tilde\alpha\},$$

$$BND_{R_\alpha^\beta}^{(\tilde\alpha, \tilde\beta)}(X_\alpha^\beta) = \overline{apr}^{(\tilde\alpha, \tilde\beta)}(X_\alpha^\beta) - \underline{apr}^{(\tilde\alpha, \tilde\beta)}(X_\alpha^\beta) = \{x \in U | \tilde\beta < Pr(X_\alpha^\beta | R_\alpha^\beta(x)) < \tilde\alpha\},$$

$$NEG_{R_\alpha^\beta}^{(\tilde\alpha, \tilde\beta)}(X_\alpha^\beta) = U - \overline{apr}^{(\tilde\alpha, \tilde\beta)}(X_\alpha^\beta) = \{x \in U | Pr(X_\alpha^\beta | R_\alpha^\beta(x)) \leq \tilde\beta\}.$$

Theorem 3. *Let $S = (U, C \cup D, V, f)$ be an IFDS. $X_{\alpha_1}^{\beta_1}, X_{\alpha_2}^{\beta_2} \subseteq U$ where $0 \leq \alpha_1, \beta_1, \alpha_2, \beta_2 \leq 1$. Then the $(\tilde{\alpha}, \tilde{\beta})$-probabilistic lower and upper approximations of $X_{\alpha_1}^{\beta_1}$ and $X_{\alpha_2}^{\beta_2}$ have the following properties:*

(1) $\underline{apr}^{(\tilde{\alpha}, \tilde{\beta})}(X_{\alpha_1}^{\beta_1}) \subseteq X_{\alpha_1}^{\beta_1} \subseteq \overline{apr}^{(\tilde{\alpha}, \tilde{\beta})}(X_{\alpha_1}^{\beta_1})$; (2) $\underline{apr}^{(\tilde{\alpha}, \tilde{\beta})}(U) = \overline{apr}^{(\tilde{\alpha}, \tilde{\beta})}(U) = U$;

(3) $\underline{apr}^{(\tilde{\alpha}, \tilde{\beta})}(\emptyset) = \overline{apr}^{(\tilde{\alpha}, \tilde{\beta})}(\emptyset) = \emptyset$; (4) $If X_{\alpha_1}^{\beta_1} \subseteq X_{\alpha_2}^{\beta_2}, then \underline{apr}^{(\tilde{\alpha}, \tilde{\beta})}(X_{\alpha_1}^{\beta_1}) \subseteq$

$\underline{apr}^{(\tilde{\alpha}, \tilde{\beta})}(X_{\alpha_2}^{\beta_2}), \overline{apr}^{(\tilde{\alpha}, \tilde{\beta})}(X_{\alpha_1}^{\beta_1}) \subseteq \overline{apr}^{(\tilde{\alpha}, \tilde{\beta})}(X_{\alpha_2}^{\beta_2})$;

(5) $\underline{apr}^{(\tilde{\alpha}, \tilde{\beta})}(X_{\alpha_1}^{\beta_1} \cap X_{\alpha_2}^{\beta_2}) = \underline{apr}^{(\tilde{\alpha}, \tilde{\beta})}(X_{\alpha_1}^{\beta_1}) \cap \underline{apr}^{(\tilde{\alpha}, \tilde{\beta})}(X_{\alpha_2}^{\beta_2})$,

$\overline{apr}^{(\tilde{\alpha}, \tilde{\beta})}(X_{\alpha_1}^{\beta_1} \cup X_{\alpha_2}^{\beta_2}) = \overline{apr}^{(\tilde{\alpha}, \tilde{\beta})}(X_{\alpha_1}^{\beta_1}) \cup \overline{apr}^{(\tilde{\alpha}, \tilde{\beta})}(X_{\alpha_2}^{\beta_2})$;

(6) $\underline{apr}^{(\tilde{\alpha}, \tilde{\beta})}(X_{\alpha_1}^{\beta_1} \cup X_{\alpha_2}^{\beta_2}) \supseteq \underline{apr}^{(\tilde{\alpha}, \tilde{\beta})}(X_{\alpha_1}^{\beta_1}) \cup \underline{apr}^{(\tilde{\alpha}, \tilde{\beta})}(X_{\alpha_2}^{\beta_2})$,

$\overline{apr}^{(\tilde{\alpha}, \tilde{\beta})}(X_{\alpha_1}^{\beta_1} \cap X_{\alpha_2}^{\beta_2}) \subseteq \overline{apr}^{(\tilde{\alpha}, \tilde{\beta})}(X_{\alpha_1}^{\beta_1}) \cap \overline{apr}^{(\tilde{\alpha}, \tilde{\beta})}(X_{\alpha_2}^{\beta_2})$;

(7) $\underline{apr}^{(\tilde{\alpha}, \tilde{\beta})}(X_{\alpha_1}^{\beta_1}) = \sim \overline{apr}^{(\tilde{\alpha}, \tilde{\beta})}(\sim X_{\alpha_1}^{\beta_1}), \overline{apr}^{(\tilde{\alpha}, \tilde{\beta})}(X_{\alpha_1}^{\beta_1}) = \sim \underline{apr}^{(\tilde{\alpha}, \tilde{\beta})}(\sim X_{\alpha_1}^{\beta_1})$.

Proof. The proofs are straightforward from Definition 8.

In order to rank IFNs $a_i = \langle u_i, v_i \rangle (i = 1, 2)$, a novel method to rank IFNs is proposed in [32]. For two IFNs $a_1 = \langle 0.6, 0.1 \rangle$ and $a_2 = \langle 0.7, 0.3 \rangle$, we get $\tau(a_1) = \frac{1-0.1}{1+0.3} = 0.6923$ and $\tau(a_2) = \frac{1-0.3}{1+0} = 0.7$ by the method in [32], that is $a_1 \prec a_2$. However, we have $a_1 \succ a_2$ via adopting the ranking method based on score function and accurate function [27], which is extremely classical rankings of IFNs and widely applied in practice. Thereby the rankings of two IFNs in [32] are worthy of further research.

Let $a = \langle u, v \rangle$ be an intuitionistic fuzzy number, it is clearly acknowledged that $a^+ = \langle 1, 0 \rangle$ and $a^- = \langle 0, 1 \rangle$ are the positive and negative ideal point of a, respectively. According to (4), we get

$$s(a, a^+) = 1 - \frac{1}{2}(|u - 1| + |v - 0| + |\pi - 0|) = u, \tag{9}$$

$$s(a, a^-) = 1 - \frac{1}{2}(|u - 0| + |v - 1| + |\pi - 0|) = v, \tag{10}$$

where $\pi = 1 - u - v$.

The longer the similarity degree between a and a^+ while the smaller the similarity degree between a and a^-, the better the a by TOPSIS. Hence, the closeness degree of the a is defined as follows:

Definition 9. *Let $a = \langle u, v \rangle$ be an intuitionistic fuzzy number. The closeness degree $\tau(a)$ of a is calculated as:*

$$\tau(a) = \frac{s(a, a^+)}{s(a, a^+) + s(a, a^-)} = \frac{u}{1 - \pi}, \tag{11}$$

where $s(a, a^+)$ denotes the degree of similarity between a and a^+ as (9) and $s(a, a^-)$ stands for the similarity degree between a and a^- as (10).

In addition, Wan et al. proposed to employ $\varphi(a) = 1 - \frac{1}{2}\pi^2$ to measure information reliability, which has apparent geomet-ric meaning by geometrical representation of IFNs [32]. Thus, a more reasonable ranking is developed to deal with the above problem.

Definition 10. *Let $a_1 = \langle u_1, v_1 \rangle$ and $a_2 = \langle u_2, v_2 \rangle$ be two IFNs. Then the ranking of them can be given as follows:*

(1) *If $\tau(a_1) > \tau(a_2)$, then a_1 is better than a_2, denoted as: $a_1 \succ a_2$;*
(2) *If $\tau(a_1) = \tau(a_2)$, then a) if $\varphi(a_1) > \varphi(a_2)$, then a_1 is better than a_2, denoted as: $a_1 \succ a_2$; b) if $\varphi(a_1) = \varphi(a_2)$, then a_1 is indifferent to a_2, denoted as: $a_1 \sim a_2$; c) if $\varphi(a_1) < \varphi(a_2)$, then a_1 is worse than a_2, denoted as: $a_1 \prec a_2$.*

For the above IFNs $a_1 = \langle 0.6, 0.1 \rangle$ and $a_2 = \langle 0.7, 0.3 \rangle$, according to Definition 9, we can recover $\tau(a_1) = \frac{0.6}{1-0.3} = 0.8571$ and $\tau(a_2) = \frac{0.7}{1-0} = 0.7$. Then $a_1 \succ a_2$, which conforms to the ranking with score function and accurate function widely applied to rank IFNs.

Suppose $a_i = \langle u_i, v_i \rangle (i = 1, 2)$ are two IFNs. $a^+ = \langle 1, 0 \rangle, \bar{a} = \langle 0.5, 0.5 \rangle$ and $a^- = \langle 0, 1 \rangle$ are the positive ideal point, intermediate point and negative ideal point of IFNs respectively. Some practical results on the rankings of IFNs with the closeness degree are given as follows:

(1) $\tau(a^+) = 1, \tau(\bar{a}) = 0.5$ *and* $\tau(a^-) = 0$.
(2) *If $a_1 \geq_L a_2$, that is to say that $u_1 \geq u_2$ and $v_1 \leq v_2$, then $\tau(a_1) \succeq \tau(a_2)$.*
(3) $\tau(a_1) + \tau(a_1^c) = 1$, *especially, if $u_1 > v_1$, then $a_1 \succ a_1^c$.*

4   Intuitionistic Fuzzy Three-Way Decision Model

In this section, we introduce an intuitionistic fuzzy three-way decision model based on three-way decision theory. There are two states $\Omega = \{X_\alpha^\beta, \neg X_\alpha^\beta\} \triangleq \{P, N\}$ and three actions $A = \{a_P, a_B, a_N\}$ (positive decision, delayed decision and negative decision). The state set Ω denotes an element in X_α^β and not in $\neg X_\alpha^\beta$, respectively; the action a_P, a_B and a_N represent three decision actions that an object is in positive region, boundary region and negative region respectively. Suppose that the losts of taking different actions under two states take the form of the IFN $\widetilde{A}(\lambda_{ij}) = \langle u_{\widetilde{A}}(\lambda_{ij}), v_{\widetilde{A}}(\lambda_{ij}) \rangle (i = P, B, N; j = P, N)$. That is, when an object belongs to X_α^β, $\widetilde{A}(\lambda_{PP}), \widetilde{A}(\lambda_{BP})$ and $\widetilde{A}(\lambda_{NP})$ represent the costs of adopting actions P, B and N respectively while when an object does not belong to X_α^β, $\widetilde{A}(\lambda_{PN}), \widetilde{A}(\lambda_{BN})$ and $\widetilde{A}(\lambda_{NN})$ represent the costs of adopting the same three actions, respectively. The loss functions with regard to two states X_α^β and $\neg X_\alpha^\beta$ can be expressed by a 3×2 matrix, as shown in Table 1.

Suppose that $S = (U, A, V, f)$ is an $IFDS$, we have $Pr(X_\alpha^\beta | R_\alpha^\beta(x)) = \frac{|R_\alpha^\beta(x) \cap X_\alpha^\beta|}{|R_\alpha^\beta(x)|}$ and $Pr(\neg X_\alpha^\beta | R_\alpha^\beta(x)) = 1 - Pr(X_\alpha^\beta | R_\alpha^\beta(x))$ by Definition 8. Based on Bayesian

Table 1. The cost matrix of intuitionistic fuzzy decision

	$X_\alpha^\beta(P)$	$\neg X_\alpha^\beta(N)$
a_P	$\widetilde{A}(\lambda_{PP}) = \langle u_{\widetilde{A}}(\lambda_{PP}), v_{\widetilde{A}}(\lambda_{PP}) \rangle$	$\widetilde{A}(\lambda_{PN}) = \langle u_{\widetilde{A}}(\lambda_{PN}), v_{\widetilde{A}}(\lambda_{PN}) \rangle$
a_B	$\widetilde{A}(\lambda_{BP}) = \langle u_{\widetilde{A}}(\lambda_{BP}), v_{\widetilde{A}}(\lambda_{BP}) \rangle$	$\widetilde{A}(\lambda_{BN}) = \langle u_{\widetilde{A}}(\lambda_{BN}), v_{\widetilde{A}}(\lambda_{BN}) \rangle$
a_N	$\widetilde{A}(\lambda_{NP}) = \langle u_{\widetilde{A}}(\lambda_{NP}), v_{\widetilde{A}}(\lambda_{NP}) \rangle$	$\widetilde{A}(\lambda_{NN}) = \langle u_{\widetilde{A}}(\lambda_{NN}), v_{\widetilde{A}}(\lambda_{NN}) \rangle$

decision theory, the decision costs $f_{ix} = \widetilde{R}(a_i | R_\alpha^\beta(x))(i = P, B, N)$ can be computed as follows:

$$f_{Px} = \widetilde{R}(a_P | R_\alpha^\beta(x)) = \widetilde{A}(\lambda_{PP})Pr(X_\alpha^\beta | R_\alpha^\beta(x)) \oplus \widetilde{A}(\lambda_{PN})Pr(\neg X_\alpha^\beta | R_\alpha^\beta(x))$$
$$f_{Bx} = \widetilde{R}(a_B | R_\alpha^\beta(x)) = \widetilde{A}(\lambda_{BP})Pr(X_\alpha^\beta | R_\alpha^\beta(x)) \oplus \widetilde{A}(\lambda_{BN})Pr(\neg X_\alpha^\beta | R_\alpha^\beta(x))$$
$$f_{Nx} = \widetilde{R}(a_N | R_\alpha^\beta(x)) = \widetilde{A}(\lambda_{NP})Pr(X_\alpha^\beta | R_\alpha^\beta(x)) \oplus \widetilde{A}(\lambda_{NN})Pr(\neg X_\alpha^\beta | R_\alpha^\beta(x))$$

For simplification, we introduce several symbols, denote $\eta = Pr(X_\alpha^\beta | R_\alpha^\beta(x))$ and $\gamma = Pr(\neg X_\alpha^\beta | R_\alpha^\beta(x))$ with $\eta + \gamma = 1$, where the conditional probabilities η and γ are the respective possibilities of elements in $R_\alpha^\beta(x)$ divided into X_α^β and $\neg X_\alpha^\beta$. Then the $f_{ix}(i = P, B, N)$ above can be further presented with the aid of (1) as follows:

$$f_{Px} = \langle 1 - (1 - u_{\widetilde{A}}(\lambda_{PP}))^\eta (1 - u_{\widetilde{A}}(\lambda_{PN}))^\gamma, (v_{\widetilde{A}}(\lambda_{PP}))^\eta (v_{\widetilde{A}}(\lambda_{PN}))^\gamma \rangle \triangleq \langle u_P, v_P \rangle$$
$$f_{Bx} = \langle 1 - (1 - u_{\widetilde{A}}(\lambda_{BP}))^\eta (1 - u_{\widetilde{A}}(\lambda_{BN}))^\gamma, (v_{\widetilde{A}}(\lambda_{BP}))^\eta (v_{\widetilde{A}}(\lambda_{BN}))^\gamma \rangle \triangleq \langle u_B, v_B \rangle$$
$$f_{Nx} = \langle 1 - (1 - u_{\widetilde{A}}(\lambda_{NP}))^\eta (1 - u_{\widetilde{A}}(\lambda_{NN}))^\gamma, (v_{\widetilde{A}}(\lambda_{NP}))^\eta (v_{\widetilde{A}}(\lambda_{NN}))^\gamma \rangle \triangleq \langle u_N, v_N \rangle$$

In light of Definition 9, the closeness degree $\tau(f_{ix})$ and $\varphi(f_{ix})$ of $f_{ix}(i = P, B, N)$ can be computed as

$$\tau(f_{Px}) = \frac{u_P}{1 - \pi_P}, \tau(f_{Bx}) = \frac{u_B}{1 - \pi_B}, \tau(f_{Nx}) = \frac{u_N}{1 - \pi_N};$$
$$\varphi(f_{Px}) = 1 - \frac{1}{2}(\pi_P)^2, \varphi(f_{Bx}) = 1 - \frac{1}{2}(\pi_B)^2, \varphi(f_{Nx}) = 1 - \frac{1}{2}(\pi_N)^2.$$

where $\pi_i = 1 - u_i - v_i$ for any $i = P, B, N$.

According to Definition 10, we can further rank f_{Px}, f_{Bx} and f_{Nx}. Therefore, some prerequisites $(C1) - (C12)$ on intuitionistic fuzzy three-way decision are established as follows:

$$(C1): \tau(f_{Px}) < \tau(f_{Bx}); (C2): \tau(f_{Px}) = \tau(f_{Bx}) \wedge \varphi(f_{Px}) \leq \varphi(f_{Bx});$$
$$(C3): \tau(f_{Px}) < \tau(f_{Nx}); (C4): \tau(f_{Px}) = \tau(f_{Nx}) \wedge \varphi(f_{Px}) \leq \varphi(f_{Nx});$$
$$(C5): \tau(f_{Bx}) < \tau(f_{Px}); (C6): \tau(f_{Bx}) = \tau(f_{Px}) \wedge \varphi(f_{Bx}) \leq \varphi(f_{Px});$$
$$(C7): \tau(f_{Bx}) < \tau(f_{Nx}); (C8): \tau(f_{Bx}) = \tau(f_{Nx}) \wedge \varphi(f_{Bx}) \leq \varphi(f_{Nx});$$
$$(C9): \tau(f_{Nx}) < \tau(f_{Px}); (C10): \tau(f_{Nx}) = \tau(f_{Px}) \wedge \varphi(f_{Nx}) \leq \varphi(f_{Px});$$
$$(C11): \tau(f_{Nx}) < \tau(f_{Bx}); (C12): \tau(f_{Nx}) = \tau(f_{Bx}) \wedge \varphi(f_{Nx}) \leq \varphi(f_{Bx}).$$

Hence, a three-way decision rule with intuitionistic fuzzy risk preference can be constructed based on the above prerequisites as follows:

$$(P): If\ (C1 \lor C2) \land (C3 \lor C4), then\ \ decide: x \in POS_{R_\alpha^\beta}^{(\widetilde{\alpha},\widetilde{\beta})}(X_\alpha^\beta);$$

$$(B): If\ (C5 \lor C6) \land (C7 \lor C8), then\ \ decide: x \in BND_{R_\alpha^\beta}^{(\widetilde{\alpha},\widetilde{\beta})}(X_\alpha^\beta);$$

$$(N): If\ (C9 \lor C10) \land (C11 \lor C12), then\ \ decide: x \in NEG_{R_\alpha^\beta}^{(\widetilde{\alpha},\widetilde{\beta})}(X_\alpha^\beta).$$

Especially when $\forall\ \pi_i = 1 - u_i - v_i = 0(i = P, B, N)$, namely, $u_i + v_i = 1(i = P, B, N)$, then the above three-way decision rules $(P) - (N)$ are reduced to decision rules $(P') - (N')$ or $(P'') - (N'')$ as follows:

$$(P'): If\ u_P \leq u_B\ and\ u_P \leq u_N, then\ \ decide: x \in POS_{R_\alpha^\beta}^{(\widetilde{\alpha},\widetilde{\beta})}(X_\alpha^\beta);$$

$$(B'): If\ u_B \leq u_P\ and\ u_B \leq u_N, then\ \ decide: x \in BND_{R_\alpha^\beta}^{(\widetilde{\alpha},\widetilde{\beta})}(X_\alpha^\beta);$$

$$(N'): If\ u_N \leq u_P\ and\ u_N \leq u_B, then\ \ decide: x \in NEG_{R_\alpha^\beta}^{(\widetilde{\alpha},\widetilde{\beta})}(X_\alpha^\beta).$$

or

$$(P''): If\ v_P \geq v_B\ and\ v_P \geq v_N, then\ \ decide: x \in POS_{R_\alpha^\beta}^{(\widetilde{\alpha},\widetilde{\beta})}(X_\alpha^\beta);$$

$$(B''): If\ v_B \geq v_P\ and\ v_B \geq u_N, then\ \ decide: x \in BND_{R_\alpha^\beta}^{(\widetilde{\alpha},\widetilde{\beta})}(X_\alpha^\beta);$$

$$(N''): If\ v_N \geq v_P\ and\ v_N \geq v_B, then\ \ decide: x \in NEG_{R_\alpha^\beta}^{(\widetilde{\alpha},\widetilde{\beta})}(X_\alpha^\beta).$$

5   Rule Induction Algorithm to Derive 3WD from IFDS

This section summarizes four steps to derive three-way decision (3WD) rules from intuitionistic fuzzy decision systems (IFDS) based on the proposed method. These steps focus on the combination of IFDS and loss function with IFSs in DTRS model together, and the rule induction algorithm is outlined in Algorithm 1 in detail.

Step 1: Given an $IFDS = (U, A = C \cup D, V, f)$, we use (5) to calculate the similarity degree $u_R(x, y)$ and divergence degree $v_R(x, y)$ for the attribute set $B \subseteq C$ between x and y in U.

Step 2: Given a certain α and β, for any $x \in U$, we can compute the similarity class $R_\alpha^\beta(x)$ via (6) and (α, β)-level cut-sets X_α^β by (7) as well as rough membership degree $\eta = Pr(X_\alpha^\beta | R_\alpha^\beta(x))$, respectively.

Step 3: We further compute the risk costs $f_{ix}(i = P, B, N)$ of $x \in U$ under three decision actions a_i respectively and then calculate $\tau(f_{ix})$, $\varphi(f_{ix})$.

Step 4: According to the prerequisites $(C1) - (C12)$ and three-way decision rules $(P) - (N)$ to acquire the corresponding three-way decision rules.

Algorithm 1. Rule induction algorithm to derive 3WD from IFDS

Input: $IFDS = (U, A = C \cup D, V, f)$, two parameters α and β, a concept $B \subseteq U$.
Output: The three-way decision rules for any $x \in U$.
 1: **begin**: Suppose $G = \{P, B, N\}$, given a concept $B \subseteq U$, α and β.
 2: **for** $x \in U$ **do**
 3:      **for** $y \in U$ **do**
 4:          Compute $u_R(x, y)$ and $v_R(x, y)$ via (5) respectively.
 5:      **end for**
 6:      Compute $R_\alpha^\beta(x) = \{y \in U | (x, y) \in R_\alpha^\beta\}$ using (6); we then take (7) to calculate
          X_α^β and $\eta = Pr(X_\alpha^\beta | R_\alpha^\beta(x))$ respectively.
 7:      **for** $i \in G$ **do**
 8:          Compute the corresponding $f_{ix}, \tau(f_{ix})$ and $\varphi(f_{ix})$.
 9:      **end for**
10:      Calculate $t_k = min\{\tau(f_{Px}), \tau(f_{Bx}), \tau(f_{Nx})\}, k = P, B$ or N and then assume
          $\{g_1, g_2\} = G - \{k\}$.
11:      **if** $(k == P) \wedge (C1 \vee C2) \wedge (C3 \vee C4)$ **then** decide $x \in POS_{R_\alpha^\beta}^{(\tilde{\alpha}, \tilde{\beta})}(X_\alpha^\beta)$.
12:      **end if**
13:      **if** $(k == B) \wedge (C5 \vee C6) \wedge (C7 \vee C8)$ **then** decide $x \in BND_{R_\alpha^\beta}^{(\tilde{\alpha}, \tilde{\beta})}(X_\alpha^\beta)$.
14:      **end if**
15:      **if** $(k == N) \wedge (C9 \vee C10) \wedge (C11 \vee C12)$ **then** decide $x \in NEG_{R_\alpha^\beta}^{(\tilde{\alpha}, \tilde{\beta})}(X_\alpha^\beta)$.
16:      **end if**
17: **end for**
18: **end**

---

6 A Numerical Example

This section presents a numerical example [33] to illustrate the effectiveness of the proposed intuitionistic fuzzy three-way decision method. An intuitionistic fuzzy decision system on the security audit assessment is given in Table 2 whose the object set of audit is $x = \{x_1, x_2, x_3, x_4\}$. The set of the conditional attributes is $C = \{c_1, c_2, c_3, c_4, c_5\}$, where c_1, c_2, c_3, c_4 and c_5 stand for eminent system environment, preferable system control, reliably financial data, credible auditing software and standard operation, respectively; the decision attribute is c_6 which denotes acceptable safety audit risk. The value of any conditional attribute is comprehensively given by many auditing experts based on auditing results and their professional quality, e.g. $f(x_4, c_4) = \langle 0.7, 0.1 \rangle$ representing the value of the attribute c_4 with regard to x_4, which means that 70% of experts on audit consider the auditing software of the object x_4 creditable while 10% believe it not creditable. In addition, 20% failed to make a decision. Similarly, for the decision attribute c_6, $f(x_2, c_6) = \langle 0.6, 0.4 \rangle$ can be understood that 60% of the experts believe security audit risk acceptable while 40% believe it not acceptable. The risk costs of taking different actions under two states(acceptable and not acceptable for audit risk) take form of IFNs, as shown in Table 3.

Suppose the threshold $\alpha = 0.7$ and $\beta = 0.3$ are given in advance by experts. In this paper, we adopt the proposed method to acquire the related decision rules, in which the detailed steps are as follows:

Table 2. Intuitionistic fuzzy decision systems on the security audit assessment

	c_1	c_2	c_3	c_4	c_5	c_6
x_1	$\langle 0.8, 0.2 \rangle$	$\langle 0.7, 0.3 \rangle$	$\langle 0.6, 0.3 \rangle$	$\langle 0.5, 0.5 \rangle$	$\langle 0.7, 0.2 \rangle$	$\langle 0.7, 0.3 \rangle$
x_2	$\langle 0.7, 0.2 \rangle$	$\langle 0.6, 0.4 \rangle$	$\langle 0.8, 0.2 \rangle$	$\langle 0.7, 0.3 \rangle$	$\langle 0.5, 0.5 \rangle$	$\langle 0.6, 0.4 \rangle$
x_3	$\langle 0.6, 0.4 \rangle$	$\langle 0.9, 0.1 \rangle$	$\langle 0.8, 0.2 \rangle$	$\langle 0.4, 0.6 \rangle$	$\langle 0.7, 0.3 \rangle$	$\langle 0.7, 0.3 \rangle$
x_4	$\langle 0.9, 0.1 \rangle$	$\langle 0.5, 0.4 \rangle$	$\langle 0.6, 0.3 \rangle$	$\langle 0.7, 0.1 \rangle$	$\langle 0.6, 0.4 \rangle$	$\langle 0.8, 0.2 \rangle$

Table 3. Risk cost matrix of intuitionistic fuzzy decision

	$X_\alpha^\beta (accept)$	$\neg X_\alpha^\beta (not\ accept)$
a_P	$\langle 0.1, 0.8 \rangle$	$\langle 0.8, 0.2 \rangle$
a_B	$\langle 0.5, 0.5 \rangle$	$\langle 0.6, 0.4 \rangle$
a_N	$\langle 0.8, 0.2 \rangle$	$\langle 0.1, 0.8 \rangle$

Step 1: Calculate the similarity degree $u_R(x_j, x_k)$ and divergence degree $v_R(x_j, x_k)$ between x_j and $x_k (j, k = 1, 2, 3, 4; j \neq k)$ below.

$$u_R(x_1, x_2) = 0.7, v_R(x_1, x_2) = 0.25; u_R(x_1, x_3) = 0.8, v_R(x_1, x_3) = 0.2;$$
$$u_R(x_1, x_4) = 0.6, v_R(x_1, x_4) = 0.3; u_R(x_2, x_3) = 0.7, v_R(x_2, x_3) = 0.3;$$
$$u_R(x_2, x_4) = 0.8, v_R(x_2, x_4) = 0.15; u_R(x_3, x_4) = 0.5, v_R(x_3, x_4) = 0.4.$$

Step 2: Compute the similarity class $R_\alpha^\beta(x_j)(j = 1, 2, 3, 4)$ and the (α, β)-level cut-sets X_α^β as well as rough membership degree η_j as follows:

$$R_\alpha^\beta(x_1) = \{x_1, x_2, x_3\}, R_\alpha^\beta(x_2) = \{x_1, x_2, x_3, x_4\}, R_\alpha^\beta(x_3) = \{x_1, x_2, x_3, x_4\},$$
$$R_\alpha^\beta(x_4) = \{x_2, x_4\}, X_\alpha^\beta = \{x_1, x_3, x_4\}, \neg X_\alpha^\beta = \{x_2\}, \eta_1 = \frac{2}{3}, \eta_2 = \eta_3 = \frac{3}{4}, \eta_4 = \frac{1}{2}.$$

Step 3: We can further compute the risk costs f_{ix_j} of x_j, $\tau(f_{ix_j})$ and $\varphi(f_{ix_j})(i = P, B, N; j = 1, 2, 3, 4)$.

$$f_{Px_1} = \langle 0.4549, 0.5040 \rangle, f_{Bx_1} = \langle 0.5358, 0.4642 \rangle, f_{Nx_1} = \langle 0.6698, 0.3175 \rangle,$$
$$f_{Px_2} = \langle 0.3821, 0.5657 \rangle, f_{Bx_2} = \langle 0.5271, 0.4729 \rangle, f_{Nx_2} = \langle 0.7087, 0.2828 \rangle,$$
$$f_{Px_3} = \langle 0.3821, 0.5657 \rangle, f_{Bx_3} = \langle 0.5271, 0.4729 \rangle, f_{Nx_3} = \langle 0.7087, 0.2828 \rangle,$$
$$f_{Px_4} = \langle 0.5757, 0.4000 \rangle, f_{Bx_4} = \langle 0.5528, 0.4472 \rangle, f_{Nx_4} = \langle 0.5757, 0.4000 \rangle.$$

the corresponding $\tau(f_{ix_j})$ of f_{ix_j} can be computed as follows:

$$\tau(f_{Px_1}) = 0.4744, \tau(f_{Bx_1}) = 0.5358, \tau(f_{Nx_1}) = 0.6784, \tau(f_{Px_2}) = 0.4031,$$
$$\tau(f_{Bx_2}) = 0.5271, \tau(f_{Nx_2}) = 0.7148, \tau(f_{Px_3}) = 0.4031, \tau(f_{Bx_3}) = 0.5271,$$
$$\tau(f_{Nx_3}) = 0.7148, \tau(f_{Px_4}) = 0.5900, \tau(f_{Bx_4}) = 0.5528, \tau(f_{Nx_4}) = 0.5900.$$

Step 4: According to the prerequisites $(C1) - (C12)$ and three-way decision rules $(P) - (N)$ to require rules as follows:

$$x_1 \in POS_{R_\alpha^\beta}^{(\widetilde{\alpha},\widetilde{\beta})}(X_\alpha^\beta), x_2 \in POS_{R_\alpha^\beta}^{(\widetilde{\alpha},\widetilde{\beta})}(X_\alpha^\beta), x_3 \in POS_{R_\alpha^\beta}^{(\widetilde{\alpha},\widetilde{\beta})}(X_\alpha^\beta), x_4 \in BND_{R_\alpha^\beta}^{(\widetilde{\alpha},\widetilde{\beta})}(X_\alpha^\beta).$$

That is, the auditing risk is deemed to be safe for the object x_1, x_2 and x_3 under a confidence level $\alpha = 0.7$ and $\beta = 0.3$ while the risk of x_4 is further discussed.

As we can see from this example, the proposed model in this paper can well deal with three-way decision problems whose the loss function is IFNs, and it is also an extension to the classical three-way decision model. Besides, deriving three-way decision rules may different for taking different threshold α and β. Hence, we focus on the research of the threshold α and β in follow-up work.

7   Conclusion

In this paper, we propose an intuitionistic fuzzy three-way decision-theoretic model with intuitionistic fuzzy decision systems to obtain three-way decision rules, and then a novel rule induction algorithm is developed. Whereafter, a numerical example is presented to illustrate the effectiveness of the proposed method. In the future, we will further explore the intuitionistic fuzzy three-way decision theory based on intuitionistic fuzzy decision systems.

Acknowledgments. This research is supported by the National Natural Science Foundation of China under grant No. 71671086, 61473157, 61403200, 71201076 and 71171107.

References

1. Yao, Y.Y., Wong, S.K.M., Lingras, P.: A decision-theoretic rough set model. In: Methodologies for Intelligent Systems, vol. 5, pp. 17–24. North-Holland, New York (1990)
2. Ju, H.R., Li, H.X., Yang, X.B., Zhou, X.Z., Huang, B.: Cost-sensitive rough set: a multi-granulation approach. Knowl.-Based Syst. **123**, 137–153 (2017)
3. Li, H.X., Zhang, L.B., Zhou, X.Z., Huang, B.: Cost-sensitive sequential three-way decision modeling using a deep neural network. Int. J. Approx. Reason. **85**, 68–78 (2017)
4. Li, W., Miao, D.Q., Wang, W.L., Zhang, N.: Hierarchical rough decision theoretic framework for text classification. In: Proceedings of the 9th IEEE International Conference on Cognitive Informatics, pp. 484–489 (2010)
5. Li, H.X., Zhou, X.Z.: Risk decision making based on decision-theoretic rough set: a three-way view decision model. Int. J. Comput. Intell. Syst. **4**, 1–11 (2011)
6. Yu, H., Liu, Z.G., Wang, G.Y.: An automatic method to determine the number of clusters using decision-theoretic rough set. Int. J. Approx. Reason. **55**, 142–155 (2014)

7. Jia, X., Zheng, K., Li, W., Liu, T., Shang, L.: Three-way decisions solution to filter spam email: an empirical study. In: Yao, J.T., Yang, Y., Słowiński, R., Greco, S., Li, H., Mitra, S., Polkowski, L. (eds.) RSCTC 2012. LNCS (LNAI), vol. 7413, pp. 287–296. Springer, Heidelberg (2012). doi:10.1007/978-3-642-32115-3_34

8. Li, H.X., Zhang, L.B., Huang, B.: Sequential three-way decision and granulation for cost-sensitive face recognition. Knowl.-Based Syst. **91**(1), 241–251 (2016)

9. Li, J.H., Huang, C.C., Qi, J.J.: Three-way cognitive concept learning via multi-granularity. Inf. Sci. **378**, 244–263 (2017)

10. She, Y.H., He, X.L., Shi, H.X., Quan, Y.: A multiple-valued logic approach for multigranulation rough set model. Int. J. Approx. Reason. **82**, 270–284 (2017)

11. Qian, Y.H., Liang, X.Y., Lin, G.P., Guo, Q., Liang, J.Y.: Local multigranulation decision-theoretic rough sets. Int. J. Approx. Reason. **82**, 119–137 (2017)

12. Li, H.X., Wang, M.H., Zhou, X.Z., Zhao, J.B.: An interval set model for learning rules from incomplete information table. Int. J. Approx. Reason. **53**(1), 24–37 (2012)

13. Liu, D., Liang, D.C., Wang, C.C.: A novel three-way decision model based on incomplete information system. Knowl.-Based Syst. **91**, 32–45 (2016)

14. Yao, Y.Y.: The superiority of three-way decisions in probabilistic rough set models. Inf. Sci. **180**, 1080–1096 (2011)

15. Liu, D., Li, T.R., Ruan, D.: Probabilistic model criteria with decision-theoretic rough sets. Informance Sci. **181**, 3709–3722 (2011)

16. Qian, Y.H., Zhang, H., Sang, Y.L., Liang, J.Y.: Multigranulation decision-theoretic rough sets. Int. J. Approx. Reason. **55**, 225–237 (2014)

17. Yang, X.P., Yao, J.T.: Modelling multi-agen three-way decisions with decision theoretic rough sets. Fundam. Informaticae **115**(2–3), 157–171 (2012)

18. Zhang, X.Y., Miao, D.Q.: Reduction target structure-based hierarchical attribute reduction for two-category decision-theoretic rough sets. Informance Sci. **277**, 755–776 (2014)

19. Liang, D.C., Liu, D., Pedrycz, W., Hu, P.: Triangular fuzzy decision theoretic rough sets. Int. J. Approx. Reason. **54**(8), 1087–1106 (2013)

20. Liang, D.C., Liu, D.: Systematic studies on three-way decisions with interval-valued decision-theoretic rough sets. Informance Sci. **276**, 186–203 (2014)

21. Liang, D.C., Liu, D.: A novel risk decision-making based on decision-theoretic rough sets under hesitant fuzzy information. IEEE Trans. Fuzzy Syst. **23**(2), 237–247 (2015)

22. Liang, D.C., Pedrycz, W., Liu, D., Hu, P.: Three-way decisions based on decision-theoretic rough sets under linguistic assessment with the aid of group decision making. Appl. Soft Comput. **29**, 256–269 (2015)

23. Atanassov, K.T.: Intuitionistic fuzzy sets. Fuzzy Sets Syst. **20**, 87–96 (1986)

24. Deng, X.F., Yao, Y.Y.: Decision-theoretic three-way approximations of fuzzy sets. Informance Sci. **279**, 702–715 (2014)

25. Liang, D.C., Liu, D.: Deriving three-way decisions from intuitionistic fuzzy decision-theoretic rough sets. Inf. Sci. **300**, 28–48 (2015)

26. Liang, D.C., Xu, Z.S., Liu, D.: Three-way decisions with intuitionistic fuzzy decision-theoretic rough sets based on point operators. Inf. Sci. **375**, 183–201 (2017)

27. Xu, Z.S., Yager, R.R.: Some geometric aggregation operators based on intuitionistic fuzzy sets. Int. J. Gen. Syst. **35**, 417–433 (2006)

28. Li, D.F.: Some measures of dissimilarity in intuitionistic fuzzy structures. J. Comput. Syst. Sci. **68**, 115–122 (2004)

29. Xu, Z.S., Yager, R.R.: Intuitionistic and interval-valued intuitionistic fuzzy preference relations and their measures of similarity for the evaluation of agreement within a group. Fuzzy Optim. Decis. Making **8**(2), 123–139 (2009)
30. Zhang, X.X., Chen, D.G., Tsang, E.C.C.: Generalized dominance rough set models for the dominance intuitionistic fuzzy information systems. Inf. Sci. **378**, 1–25 (2017)
31. Bustince, H., Burillo, P.: Structures on intuitionistic fuzzy relations. Fuzzy Sets Syst. **78**, 293–303 (1996)
32. Wan, S.P., Wang, F., Dong, J.Y.: A novel risk attitudinal ranking method for intuitionistic fuzzy values and application to MADM. Appl. Soft Comput. **40**, 98–112 (2016)
33. Huang, B., Wei, D.K.: Distance-based rough set model in intuitionistic fuzzy information systems and its application. Systems Engineering Theory &. Practice **336**, 1356–1362 (2011)

Sequential Three-Way Decisions in Efficient Classification of Piecewise Stationary Speech Signals

Andrey V. Savchenko[(✉)]

Laboratory of Algorithms and Technologies for Network Analysis,
National Research University Higher School of Economics,
Nizhny Novgorod, Russian Federation
avsavchenko@hse.ru

Abstract. In this paper it is proposed to improve performance of the automatic speech recognition by using sequential three-way decisions. At first, the largest piecewise quasi-stationary segments are detected in the speech signal. Every segment is classified using the maximum a-posteriori (MAP) method implemented with the Kullback-Leibler minimum information discrimination principle. The three-way decisions are taken for each segment using the multiple comparisons and asymptotical properties of the Kullback-Leibler divergence. If the non-commitment option is chosen for any segment, it is divided into small subparts, and the decision-making is sequentially repeated by fusing the classification results for each subpart until accept or reject options are chosen or the size of each subpart becomes relatively low. Thus, each segment is associated with a hierarchy of variable-scale subparts (granules in rough set theory). In the experimental study the proposed procedure is used in speech recognition with Russian language. It was shown that our approach makes it possible to achieve high efficiency even in the presence of high level of noise in the observed utterance.

Keywords: Signal processing · Speech recognition · Three-way decisions · Sequential analysis · Granular computing · Kullback-Leibler divergence

1 Introduction

The mathematical model of the piecewise stationary stochastic (random) process [1,2] is widely used in many practical pattern recognition tasks including signal classification [3,4], computer vision [5] and speech processing [6]. One of the most popular approach to classify its realization (sample function) is based on the hidden Markov model (HMM), specially developed for recognition of the piecewise stationary signals [6]. In these methods an observed realization of stochastic process [7] is divided into stationary parts using a fixed scale time window (typically 20–30 ms) [1]. Next, the corresponding parts (segments) of

© Springer International Publishing AG 2017
L. Polkowski et al. (Eds.): IJCRS 2017, Part II, LNAI 10314, pp. 264–277, 2017.
DOI: 10.1007/978-3-319-60840-2_19

the observation and all instances in the database are matched using such models of these segments, as the GMM (Gaussian Mixture Model), and the total similarity is estimated. The recent research has moved focus from GMMs to more complex classifiers based on the deep neural networks (DNN), which have established the state-of-the-art results for several multimedia recognition tasks [8,9]. The most impressive modern results are achieved with acoustic models based on long-short term memory (LSTM) recurrent neural networks trained with connectionist temporal classification [10]. Unfortunately, the run-time complexity of all these approaches is rather high, especially for large utterances, which contain many phones [6,11]. In practice the situation is even worse, because the segments are usually aligned using dynamic programming to deal with inaccurate segmentation.

It is known [1], that the speech signals are multi-scale in nature (vowel phones last for 40–400 ms while stops last for 3–250 ms). Hence, to improve classification performance, this paper explores the potential of sequential three-way decisions (TWD) [12], which has been recently used to speed-up the face recognition algorithms [13,14]. The TWD theory [15,16] have grown from the ideas of the rough set theory [17] to divide the universal set into positive, negative and boundary regions. Unlike the traditional two-way decision, the TWD incorporates the delay decision as an optional one. It is selected, if the cost of such delay is minimal [15]. It is of great importance in practice, besides taking a hard decision, to allow such "I do not know" option. There are several industrial applications of TWD in such data mining tasks, as visual feature extractions using deep neural networks [18], frequent item sets mining [19], attribute reduction [20], medical decision support systems [21], recommender systems [22] and software defect prediction [23]. However, the research of TWD in the classification problems for complex data has just begun [13]. Thus, in this paper we propose to examine the hierarchical representation of each segment using the methodology of granular computing [24,25]. The more detailed representation is explored only if the non-commitment option of TWD was chosen for the current representation.

The rest of the paper is organized as follows. In Sect. 2 we describe statistical speech recognition using an autoregression (AR) model [6,26]. In Sect. 3 we introduce the proposed classification algorithm based on sequential TWD. Section 4 contains experimental study of our approach in speech recognition for Russian language. Concluding comments are given in Sect. 5.

2 Conventional Classification of Piecewise-Stationary Speech Signals Using Statistical Approach

In this section we explore the task of isolated word recognition, which typically appears in, e.g., the voice control intelligent systems [27]. Let a vocabulary of $D > 1$ words/phrases be given. The dth word is usually specified by a sequence of phones $\{c_{d,1}, \ldots, c_{d,S_d}\}$. Here $c_{d,j} \in \{1, \ldots, C\}$ are the the class (phone) labels, and $S_d \geq 1$ is the transcription length of the dth word. It is required to assign the new utterance X to the closest word/phrase from the vocabulary. We focus on the speaker-dependent mode [6], i.e. the phonetic database of $R \geq C$ reference signals $\{\mathbf{x}_r\}, r \in \{1, \ldots, R\}$ with labels $c(r) \in \{1, \ldots, C\}$ of all phones of the current speaker should be available.

We use the typical assumption that the speech signal X can be represented as a piecewise stationary time-varying AR ergodic Gaussian process with zero mean [1,7,26]. To apply this model, the input utterance is divided into T fixed-size (20–30 ms) partially overlapped quasi-stationary frames $\{\mathbf{x}(t)\}, t \in \{1, \ldots, T\}$, where $\{\mathbf{x}(t)\}$ is a feature vector with the fixed dimension size. Next, each frame is assigned to one of C reference phones. It is known [28,29] that the maximal likelihood (ML) solution for testing hypothesis $W_c, c \in \{1, \ldots, C\}$ about covariance matrix of the Gaussian signal $\mathbf{x}(t)$ is achieved with the Kullback-Leibler (KL) minimum information discrimination principle [30]

$$c^*(\mathbf{x}(t)) = \underset{c(r), r \in \{1, \ldots, R\}}{\operatorname{argmin}} \rho_{KL}(\mathbf{x}(t), \mathbf{x}_r), \tag{1}$$

where the KL divergence between the zero-mean Gaussian distributions is computed as follows

$$\rho_{KL}(\mathbf{x}(t), \mathbf{x}_r) = \frac{1}{2} \ln \frac{\det(\Sigma_r)}{\det(\Sigma(t))} + \frac{1}{2} \operatorname{tr}(\Sigma(t)(\Sigma_r)^{-1}) - \frac{p}{2}.$$

Here $\Sigma(t)$ and Σ_r are the estimates of the covariance matrices of signals $\mathbf{x}(t)$ and $\mathbf{x}_r$, respectively, $\det(\Sigma)$ and $\operatorname{tr}(\Sigma)$ stand for the determinant and trace of the matrix Σ. This KL discrimination for the Gaussian model of the quasi-stationary speech signals can be computed as the Itakura-Saito distance [26,28] between power spectral densities (PSD) $G_{\mathbf{x}(t)}(f)$ and $G_r(f)$ of the input frame $\mathbf{x}(t)$ and $\mathbf{x}_r$:

$$\rho_{KL}(\mathbf{x}(t), \mathbf{x}_r) = \frac{2}{F} \sum_{f=1}^{F/2} \left(\frac{G_{\mathbf{x}(t)}(f)}{G_r(f)} - \ln \frac{G_{\mathbf{x}(t)}(f)}{G_r(f)} - 1 \right). \tag{2}$$

Here $f \in \{1, \ldots, F\}$, is the discrete frequency, and F is the sample rate (Hz). The PSDs in (2) can be estimated using the Levinson-Durbin algorithm and the Burg method [31]. The Itakura-Saito divergence between PSDs (2) is well known in speech processing due to its strong correlation with the subjective MOS (mean opinion score) estimate of speech closeness [6].

Finally, the obtained transcription $\{c^*(\mathbf{x}(1)), c^*(\mathbf{x}(2)), \ldots, c^*(\mathbf{x}(T))\}$ of the utterance X is dynamically aligned with the transcription of each word from the vocabulary to establish the temporary compliance between the sounds. Such alignment is implemented with the dynamic programming techniques, e.g., Dynamic Time Warping or the Viterbi algorithm in the HMM [6]. The decision can be made in favor to the closest word from the vocabulary in terms of the total conditional probability or, equivalently, the sum of distances (2).

The typical implementation of the described procedure includes the estimation of AR coefficients and the PSDs for each frame, matching with all phones (1), (2) and dynamic alignment with transcriptions of all words in the vocabulary. Thus, the runtime complexity of this algorithm is equal to

$O(F \cdot p \cdot T + R \cdot F \cdot T + T \cdot \sum_{d=1}^{D} S_d)$, where p is the order of AR model. The more is the count of frames T, the less is the recognition performance. Unfortunately, as it is written in introduction, the duration of every phone varies significantly even for the same speaker. Hence, the frame is usually chosen to be very small in order to contain only one quasi-stationary part of the speech signal. In the next section we propose to apply the TWD theory to speed-up the recognition procedure by using multi-scale representation of the speech segments.

3   Sequential Three-Way Decisions in Speech Recognition

3.1   Three-Way Decisions

Though speech recognition on the phonetic level at the present time is comparable in quality with the phoneme recognition by human [6], the variability sources (the noisy environment, children speech, foreign accents, speech rate, voice disease, etc.) usually lead to the misclassification errors [32]. Hence, in this paper we apply the TWD to represent each cth phone with three pair-wise disjoint regions (positive POS, negative NEG and boundary BND). These regions can be defined using the known asymptotic chi-squared distribution of the KL divergence between feature vectors of the same class [29,30]:

$$POS_{(\alpha,\beta)}(c) = \{\mathbf{x} \in \mathbf{X} | 2(n(\mathbf{x}) - p)\rho(\mathbf{x}, c) < \chi^2_{1-\alpha,p(p+1)/2}\}, \tag{3}$$

$$NEG_{(\alpha,\beta)}(c) = \{\mathbf{x} \in \mathbf{X} | 2(n(\mathbf{x}) - p)\rho(\mathbf{x}, c) \geq \chi^2_{1-\beta,p(p+1)/2}\}, \tag{4}$$

$$BND_{(\alpha,\beta)}(c) = \mathbf{X} - (POS_{(\alpha,\beta)}(c) \cup NEG_{(\alpha,\beta)}(c)), \tag{5}$$

where

$$\rho(\mathbf{x}, c) = \min_{r \in \{1,\dots,R\}, c(r)=c} \rho_{KL}(\mathbf{x}, \mathbf{x}_r). \tag{6}$$

Here $\mathbf{X}$ is the universal set of the stationary speech signals, $n(\mathbf{x})$ is the count of samples in the signal $\mathbf{x}$, $\chi^2_{\alpha,p(p+1)/2}$ is the α-quantile of the chi-squared distribution with $p(p+1)/2$ degrees of freedom, $0 < \beta < \alpha < 1$ is the pair of thresholds, which define the type II and type I errors of the given utterance representing the cth phone. In this case the type I error is detected if the cth phoneme is not assigned to the positive region (3). The type II error takes place when the utterance from any other phoneme is not rejected (4).

3.2   Multi-class Three-Way Decisions

Though the described approach (3)-(5) can provide an additional robustness of speech recognition, it does not deal with the multi-scale nature of the speech signals [1]. To solve the issues with performance of traditional approach, we will use the multi-granulation approach [24,35] and describe the stationary utterance as a hierarchy of fragments. Namely, we obtain the largest piecewise quasi-stationary speech segments $X(s), s \in \{1,\dots,S\}$

with the borders $(t_1(s), t_2(s)), 1 \leq t_1(s) < t_2(s) \leq T$ in observed utterance using an appropriate speech segmentation technique [1,11]. Here S is the count of extracted segments. Then, l speech parts of the same size are extracted at the lth granularity level, where the kth part $\mathbf{x}_k^{(l)}(s) = \left[\mathbf{x}\left(t_1(s) + \left\lfloor \frac{(k-1)\cdot(t_2(s)-t_1(s)+1)}{l} \right\rfloor \right), \ldots, \mathbf{x}\left(t_1(s) + \left\lceil \frac{k\cdot(t_2(s)-t_1(s)+1)}{l} \right\rceil \right) \right]$. Hence, only one part $\mathbf{x}_1^{(1)}(s) = X(s)$ of the sth segment is examined at the coarsest granularity level $l = 1$, and all $L = (t_2(s) - t_1(s) + 1)$ frames are processed at the finest granularity level.

According to the idea of sequential TWD [12], it is necessary to assign three decision regions at each granularity level. Though the concept of a phoneme is naturally mapped into TWD theory (3)-(5), speech recognition involves the choice of only one phoneme for each segment (1). Three basic options of acceptance, rejection and non-commitment are best interpreted in the binary classification task $(C = 2)$ [15]. It includes three decision types: positive (accept the first class), negative (reject the first class and accept the second class), and boundary (delay the final decision and do not accept either first or second class). It cannot directly deal with *multi-class* problems $(C > 2)$. This problem has been studied earlier in the context of multiple-category classification using decision-theoretic rough sets [34]. Lingras et al. [33] discussed the Bayesian decision procedure with C classes and specially constructed $2^C - 1$ cost functions. Liu et al. [37] proposed a two stages algorithm, in which, at first, the positive region is defined to make a decision of acceptance of any class, and the best candidate classification is chosen at the second stage using Bayesian discriminant analysis. Deng and Jia [36] derived positive, negative and boundary regions of each class from the cost matrix in classical cost-sensitive learning task.

However, in this paper we examine another enhancement of the idea of TWD for multi-class recognition, namely, $(C+1)$-way decisions, i.e., acceptance of any of C classes or delaying the decision process, in case of an unreliable recognition result [13]. In this case, it is necessary to define C positive regions $POS_{(\alpha,\beta)}^{(l)}(c)$ for each cth phone and one boundary region $BND_{(\alpha,\beta)}^{(l)}$ for delay option.

3.3   Proposed Approach

Let us aggregate the three regions of each phoneme (3)–(5) into such $(C+1)$-way decisions. The most obvious way is to assign an utterance $\mathbf{x}$ to the cth phone if this utterance is included into the positive region (3) of only this class:

$$POS_{(\alpha,\beta)}^{(l)}(c) = POS_{(\alpha,\beta)}(c) - \bigcup_{i \in \{1,\ldots,c-1,c+1,\ldots,C\}} POS_{(\alpha,\beta)}(i), \qquad (7)$$

$$BND_{(\alpha,\beta)}^{(l)} = \mathbf{X} - \bigcup_{c=1}^{C} POS_{(\alpha,\beta)}^{(l)}(c). \qquad (8)$$

It is not difficult to show, that the signal $\mathbf{x}$ is included into the positive region (7) of the nearest class $c^*(\mathbf{x})$ (1), only if

$$\begin{cases} 2(n(\mathbf{x}) - p)\rho(\mathbf{x}, c^*(\mathbf{x})) < \chi^2_{1-\alpha, p(p+1)/2} \\ 2(n(\mathbf{x}) - p)\rho(\mathbf{x}, c_2^*(\mathbf{x})) \geq \chi^2_{1-\alpha, p(p+1)/2} \end{cases} . \tag{9}$$

Here the second nearest neighbor class for the utterance $\mathbf{x}$ is denoted as

$$c_2^*(\mathbf{x}) = \underset{c \in \{1, \ldots, C\}, c \neq c^*(\mathbf{x})}{\operatorname{argmin}} \rho(\mathbf{x}, c). \tag{10}$$

However, in such definition of the positive regions the parameter α does not stand for the type I error anymore. As a matter of fact, the multiple-testing problem occurs in the multi-class classification, so appropriate correction should be used in the thresholds (9) [38]. If we would like to control the false discovery rate and accept the cth phone if only one hypothesis is accepted, the Benjamini-Hochberg test [39] with $(C-1)/C$ correction of type I error of the second hypothesis can be applied:

$$\begin{cases} 2(n(\mathbf{x}) - p)\rho(\mathbf{x}, c^*(\mathbf{x})) < \rho_1(\alpha) \\ 2(n(\mathbf{x}) - p)\rho(\mathbf{x}, c_2^*(\mathbf{x})) \geq \rho_2(\alpha) \end{cases} , \tag{11}$$

where the thresholds are defined as follows: $\rho_1(\alpha) = \chi^2_{1-\alpha, p(p+1)/2}$, $\rho_2(\alpha) = \chi^2_{1-\alpha(C-1)/C, p(p+1)/2}$. If condition (11) holds for all l parts at the lth granularity level, then the closest phones $c^*(\mathbf{x}_k^{(l)}(s))$ (1) are accepted as the final decisions. Otherwise, the delayed decision is chosen and the phoneme recognition problem is examined at a finer granulation level $l+1$ with more detailed information [12].

Unfortunately, the proposed procedure (11) can be hardly used in practice, because the distance between real utterances of the same phoneme is rather large and does not satisfy the theoretical chi-squared distribution with $p(p+1)/2$ degrees of freedom [29]. Hence, the first condition in (11) does not hold anymore. Thus, it is necessary to tune the thresholds ρ_1, ρ_2. However, in this paper we explore an alternative solution. Namely, the search termination condition (10) is modified by using the known probability distribution of the KL divergence between different hypothesis [30]. If the utterance $\mathbf{x}$ corresponds to the nearest neighbor phoneme $c^*(\mathbf{x})$, then the $2(n(\mathbf{x}) - p)$-times distance $\rho(\mathbf{x}, c_2^*(\mathbf{x}))$ is distributed as the non-central chi-squared distribution with $p(p+1)/2$ degrees of freedom and the non-centrality parameter proportional to the distance between phonemes $\rho(c^*(\mathbf{x}), c_2^*(\mathbf{x}))$ [27,40]. Thus, the ratio of the distances between the input signal and its second and first nearest neighbor has the non-central F-distribution $F(p(p+1)/2, p(p+1)/2; 2(n(\mathbf{x}) - p))\rho(c^*(\mathbf{x}), c_2^*(\mathbf{x}))$. Hence, in this paper we will use the following positive region for acceptance of class c:

$$POS_{(\alpha, \beta)}^{(l)}(c) = \{\mathbf{x} \in \mathbf{X} | c = c^*(\mathbf{x}) \& \frac{\rho(\mathbf{x}, c_2^*(\mathbf{x}))}{\rho(\mathbf{x}, c^*(\mathbf{x}))} > \rho_{2/1}(\alpha)\}, \tag{12}$$

where a threshold $\rho_{2/1}(\alpha)$ is chosen from the α-quantile of the non-central F-distribution described above.

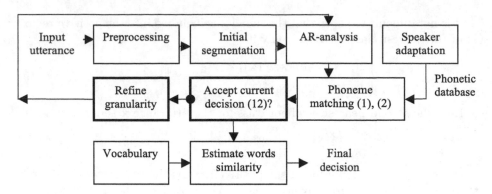

Fig. 1. Complete data flow of speech recognition using sequential three-way decisions and granular computing.

The complete data flow of the proposed recognition procedure using sequential TWD is shown in Fig. 1. At first, the input signal is preprocessed in order to decrease its variability, detect voice activity regions, etc. [6]. Next, the largest piecewise quasi-stationary speech segments are detected, and the coarsest approximation of the observed signal is analyzed. After that, each extracted segment is processed alternately. As we assume, that the scale of each part of the large segment $X(s)$ is identical, so the sequential analysis is terminated only when decisions are accepted for any speech part $\mathbf{x}_k^{(l)}(s)$. This procedure can be also implemented with the Benjamini-Hochberg correction of the type I error in (12). If it is possible to obtain a reliable solution $\mathbf{x}(s) \in POS_{(\alpha,\beta)}^{(l)}(c)(12)$, the phoneme matching process (1), (2) is terminated and, as a result, the $c^*(\mathbf{x}(s))$ class label is assigned to this segment. Otherwise, its scale is refined, and the process is repeated for each part, until any of these parts are accepted (12). If the absence of acceptance decisions at all L levels for individual frames $\mathbf{x}(t)$, we can obtain the least unreliable level [13]. Finally, the estimated transcription of the refined segments can be processed using the dynamic programming techniques [6] in order to obtain the final decision of the speech recognition problem.

Let us demonstrate how the proposed procedure works in practice. In this example we consider rather simple task of Russian vowel recognition in a syllable "tro"(/t/ /r/ /oo/). Table 1 contains the KL distances (2) between $R = 6$ vowel phonemes and all segments in $L = 2$ hierarchical levels. The closest distance in each row is marked by bold. Here the vowel /aa/ is the nearest neighbor (1) of the signal $\mathbf{x}_1^{(1)}$ (see the first row in Table 1). Hence, the whole syllable ($l = 1$) is incorrectly classified. However, this decision cannot be accepted (12), because the distance to the second nearest neighbor /oo/ is quite close to the distance between $\mathbf{x}_1^{(1)}$ and the first nearest neighbor ($45.38/38.4 = 1.18$). Thus, according to sequential TWD scheme (Fig. 1) the granularity level should be refined, and the whole syllable is divided into $l = 2$ parts. Though the first part is still misclassified (second row in Table 1), this decision is still unacceptable as the distance ration in (12) is rather low (57.94/38.40 = 1.6). At the same time, the second part of the utterance is correctly recognized as the phone /oo/. This decision can be accepted (12), because the distance to the second nearest neighbor is rather large (46.02/5.83 = 7.89). As we know, that a syllable contains only one vowel, we can accept /oo/ phone as the final decision for the whole syllable. Thus, the proposed approach can be use to increase the recognition accuracy. In the next section we experimentally demonstrate that an additional refinement of the granularity level makes it possible to significantly decrease the decision making time.

Table 1. Computed distances (2) in the vowel recognition in the syllable /t/ /r/ /oo/

Level	/aa/	/ee/	/ii/	/oo/	/uu/	/y/
$l = 1$	**38.40**	85.38	270.80	45.38	113.33	99.28
$l = 2$	**36.17**	77.26	277.83	57.94	129.84	93.16
	333.39	303.94	198.47	**5.83**	46.02	460.33

4   Experimental Results

In this section the proposed approach (Fig. 1) in used in the isolated words recognition for Russian language. All tests are performed at a 4 core i7 laptop with 6 Gb RAM. Two vocabularies are used, namely, (1) the list of 1832 Russian cities with corresponding regions; and (2) the list of 1913 drugs. All speakers pronounced every word from all vocabularies twice in isolated syllable mode to simplify the recognition procedure [27,40]. In such mode every vowel in the syllable is made stressed, thus, it is recognized quite stably. The part of speech data suitable to reproduce our experiments is available for free download[1]. In the configuration mode, each speaker clearly spoke ten vowels of the Russian language (/aa/, /ja/, /ee/, /je/, /oo/, /jo/, /ii/, /y/, /uu/, /ju/) in isolated mode [41]. The following parameters are chosen: sampling frequency $F = 8$ kHz, AR-model order $p = 20$. The sampling rate was set on telephone level, because we carried out this experiment with our special software [27,42], which was mainly developed for application in remote voice control systems.

The closed sounds /aa/, /ja/, /ee/, /je/, /oo/, /jo/, /ii/, /y/, /uu/, /ju/ are united into $C = 5$ clusters [6]. Observed utterances are divided into 30 ms frames with 10 ms overlap. The syllables in the test signals are extracted with the amplitude detector and the vowels are recognized in each syllable by the simple voting [40] based on the results obtained using vowel recognition. The latter is implemented using either proposed sequential TWD procedure with termination condition (12), or traditional techniques: (1) recognition (1), (2) of low-scale frames with identical size; (2) distance thresholding (11); and (2) the

---

[1] https://sites.google.com/site/andreyvsavchenko/SpeechDataIsolatedSyllables.zip.

state-of-the-art recognition of vowels in each syllable using the DNN from the Kaldi framework [43] trained with the Voxforge corpus. We added an artificially generated white noise to each test utterance using the following procedure. At first, the signal-to-noise ratio (SNR) is fixed. Next, the pauses are detected in each utterance using simple energy thresholding, and the standard deviation of the remaining part with high energy is estimated. Finally, these standard deviation was corrected using given SNR, and uncorrelated normal random numbers with zero mean and the resulted standard deviation was added to each value of the speech signal.

Except the KL divergence (2), its symmetric version (COSH distance [2, 28]) is implemented:

$$\rho_{COSH}(\mathbf{x}(t), \mathbf{x}_r) = \frac{1}{F} \sum_{f=1}^{F/2} \frac{(G_{\mathbf{x}(t)}(f) - G_r(f))^2}{G_{\mathbf{x}(t)}(f) G_r(f)}. \tag{13}$$

The thresholds in (11), (12) for each discrimination type are tuned experimentally using the small validation set of 5 vowels per phone class[2]. Namely, we compute the pairwise distances between all utterances from this validation set $\mathbf{X}_{val}$. If type I error rate is fixed $\alpha = const$, then $\rho_{2/1}(\alpha)$ is evaluated as a $(1 - \alpha)$-quantile of the ratio of these distances

$$\left\{ \frac{\min\limits_{\mathbf{x}_r \in \mathbf{X}_{val}, c(\mathbf{x}_r) \neq c(\mathbf{x})} \rho(\mathbf{x}, \mathbf{x}_r)}{\min\limits_{\mathbf{x}_r \in \mathbf{X}_{val}, \mathbf{x}_r \neq \mathbf{x}} \rho(\mathbf{x}, \mathbf{x}_r)} \middle| \mathbf{x} \in \mathbf{X}_{val} \right\}.$$

Similar procedure is applied to estimate thresholds in (11) [5]. The dependence of the words recognition accuracy on the SNR is shown in Tables 2 and 3 for cities and drugs vocabularies, respectively. The average time to recognize one testing phrase is shown in Figs. 2 and 3.

Table 2. Dependence of error rate (%) on SNR (dB), cities vocabulary

Distance	Method	25 dB	20 dB	15 dB	10 dB	5 dB	0 dB
	DNN	6.3	7.9	10.2	18.9	30.6	34.1
	Conventional approach (1)	7	7.9	8.8	14.5	31.6	38.2
KL divergence	Distance thresholding (11)	7.5	8.8	10.5	18.9	30.1	36.1
	Proposed approach (12)	6.3	7.3	9.6	17.3	31.1	37.1
	Conventional approach (1)	3.9	4.2	4.1	9.8	23.7	28.1
COSH distance	Distance thresholding (11)	3.1	3.9	4.7	10.8	26	32.7
	Proposed approach (12)	3.9	4.7	5.3	11.8	26.9	33.9

Though the state-of-the-art DNN does not use speaker adaptation, its accuracy of vowel recognition is comparable to the nearest neighbor search (1), which

---

[2] https://sites.google.com/site/andreyvsavchenko/ValidationDataVowels.zip.

Table 3. Dependence of error rate (%) on SNR (dB), drugs vocabulary

Distance	Method	25 dB	20 dB	15 dB	10 dB	5 dB	0 dB
	DNN	9.9	10.6	11.4	13.9	18.4	23.2
	Conventional approach (1)	3.1	5.4	8.1	8.3	15.9	20.4
KL divergence	Distance thresholding (11)	4.1	6.6	8.7	8.7	17	20.3
	Proposed approach (12)	3.9	6.6	8.3	8.6	15.9	19.9
	Conventional approach (1)	5.6	6.6	6.8	6.8	14.3	17.4
COSH distance	Distance thresholding (11)	3.5	4.3	7.5	7.9	14.1	18.6
	Proposed approach (12)	2.9	3.7	7.5	8.1	14.1	17.4

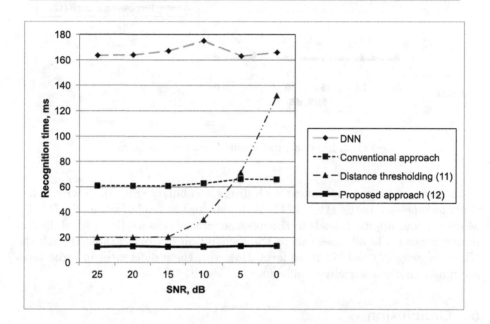

Fig. 2. Experimental results, cities vocabulary.

is implemented in other examined techniques. However, the DNN's performance is inappropriate: it is 2–10 times slower than all other methods. McNemar's test [44] with 0.95 confidence verified that the COSH distance is more accurate in most cases, than the KL divergence. This result supports our statement about superiority of the distances based on the homogeneity testing in audio and visual recognition tasks [2]. The obvious implementation of sequential TWD (11) is inefficient in the case of high noise levels, because the thresholds in (11) cannot be reliably estimated for huge variations in speech signals. Finally, the proposed approach (Fig. 1) allows to increasing the recognition performance. Our implementation of sequential TWD is 12–14 times faster that the DNN and 4–5 times faster than the conventional approach with matching of the fine-grained frames (1). McNemar's test verified that this improvement of performance is significant

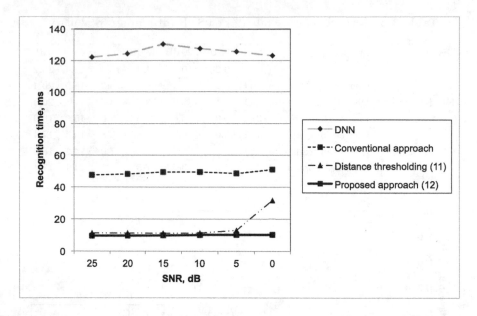

Fig. 3. Experimental results, drugs vocabulary.

in all cases except the experiment with drugs vocabulary (Fig. 3), in which classification speed of both (11) and (12) is similar for low level of noise ($SNR > 5$). Moreover, our approach leads to the most accurate decisions (for a fixed dissimilarity measure) in all cases except the recognition of drugs (Table 3) with the KL-divergence (2) and low noise level. However, these differences in error rates are mostly not statistically significant.

5   Conclusion

To sum it up, this article introduced an efficient implementation (1), (6), (10), (12) of sequential three-way decisions in multi-class recognition of piecewise stationary signals. It was demonstrated how to define the granularity levels in quasi-stationary parts of the signal, so that the count of the coarse-grained granules is usually rather low. As a result, the new observation can be classified very fast. The acceptance region (12) was defined using the theory of multiple comparisons and contains only computing the KL divergence. Hence, our method can be applied with an arbitrary distance by tuning the threshold $\rho_{2/1}$. The experimental study demonstrated the potential of our procedure (Fig. 1) to significantly speed-up speech recognition when compared with conventional algorithms (Figs. 2 and 3). Thus, it is possible to conclude that the proposed technique makes it possible to build a reliable speech recognition module, which is suitable for implementing, e.g., a voice control intelligent system with fast speaker adaptation [27].

As a matter of fact, our experiments are reported on own speech data with requirement of isolated syllable pronunciation. Thus, our results are not directly comparable with other ASR methods. Hence, the further research of the proposed method can be continued in the following directions. First, it should be applied in continuous speech recognition, in which only the last granularity level is analyzed with the computationally expensive state-of-the-art procedures (HMMs with GMMs/DNNs or LSTMs) [6,9,10]. Second possible direction is the application of our method with non-stationary signal classification tasks [4].

Acknowledgements.. The work was prepared within the framework of the Academic Fund Program at the National Research University Higher School of Economics (HSE) in 2017 (grant No 17-05-0007) and is supported by the Russian Academic Excellence Project "5–100" and Russian Federation President grant no. MD-306.2017.9.

References

1. Tyagi, V., Bourlard, H., Wellekens, C.: On variable-scale piecewise stationary spectral analysis of speech signals for ASR. Speech Commun. **48**, 1182–1191 (2006)
2. Savchenko, A.V., Belova, N.S.: Statistical testing of segment homogeneity in classification of piecewise-regular objects. Int. J. Appl. Math. Comput. Sci. **25**, 915–925 (2015)
3. Huang, K., Aviyente, S.: Sparse representation for signal classification. In: Advances of Neural Information Processing Systems (NIPS), pp. 609–616. MIT Press (2006)
4. Khan, M.R., Padhi, S.K., Sahu, B.N., Behera, S.: Non stationary signal analysis and classification using FTT transform and naive bayes classifier. In: IEEE Power, Communication and Information Technology Conference (PCITC), pp. 967–972. IEEE Press (2015)
5. Savchenko, A.V.: Search Techniques in Intelligent Classification Systems. Springer International Publishing, New York (2016)
6. Benesty, J., Sondhi, M.M., Huang, Y.: Springer Handbook of Speech Processing. Springer, Berlin (2008)
7. Peebles, P.Z., Read, J., Read, P.: Probability, Random Variables, and Random Signal Principles. McGraw-Hill, New York (2001)
8. Goodfellow, I., Bengio, Y., Courville, A.: Deep Learning. The MIT Press, Cambridge (2016)
9. Yu, D., Deng, L.: Automatic Speech Recognition: A Deep Learning Approach. Springer, New York (2014)
10. Sak, H., Senior, A.W., Beaufays, F.: Long short-term memory recurrent neural network architectures for large scale acoustic modeling. In: Interspeech, pp. 338–342 (2014)
11. Stan, A., Mamiya, Y., Yamagishi, J., Bell, P., Watts, O., Clark, R.A., King, S.: ALISA: an automatic lightly supervised speech segmentation and alignment tool. Comput. Speech Lang. **35**, 116–133 (2016)
12. Yao, Y.Y.: Granular computing and sequential three-way decisions. In: Lingras, P., Wolski, M., Cornelis, C., Mitra, S., Wasilewski, P. (eds.) RSKT 2013. LNCS (LNAI), vol. 8171, pp. 16–27. Springer, Heidelberg (2013)

13. Savchenko, A.V.: Fast multi-class recognition of piecewise regular objects based on sequential three-way decisions and granular computing. Knowl.-Based Syst. **91**, 252–262 (2016)
14. Li, H., Zhang, L., Huang, B., Zhou, X.: Sequential three-way decision and granulation for cost-sensitive face recognition. Knowl.-Based Syst. **91**, 241–251 (2016)
15. Yao, Y.: Three-way decisions with probabilistic rough sets. Inf. Sci. **180**, 341–353 (2010)
16. Yao, Y.: Interval sets and three-way concept analysis in incomplete contexts. Int. J. Mach. Learn. Cybern. **8**(1), 1–18 (2017)
17. Pawlak, Z.: Rough Sets: Theoretical Aspects of Reasoning About Data. Kluwer Academic Publishers, Norwell, MA, USA (1992)
18. Li, H., Zhang, L., Zhou, X., Huang, B.: Cost-sensitive sequential three-way decision modeling using a deep neural network. Int. J. Approx. Reason. **85**, 68–78 (2017)
19. Li, Y., Zhang, Z.H., Chen, W.B., Min, F.: TDUP: an approach to incremental mining of frequent itemsets with three-way-decision pattern updating. Int. J. Mach. Learn. Cybern. **8**(2), 441–453 (2017)
20. Ren, R., Wei, L.: The attribute reductions of three-way concept lattices. Knowl.-Based Syst. **99**, 92–102 (2016)
21. Yao, J., Azam, N.: Web-based medical decision support systems for three-way medical decision making with game-theoretic rough sets. IEEE Trans. Fuzzy Syst. **23**(1), 3–15 (2015)
22. Zhang, H.R., Min, F., Shi, B.: Regression-based three-way recommendation. Inf. Sci. **378**, 444–461 (2017)
23. Li, W., Huang, Z., Li, Q.: Three-way decisions based software defect prediction. Knowl.-Based Syst. **91**, 263–274 (2016)
24. Pedrycz, W.: Granular Computing: Analysis and Design of Intelligent Systems. CRC Press, Boca Raton (2013)
25. Wang, X., Pedrycz, W., Gacek, A., Liu, X.: From numeric data to information granules: a design through clustering and the principle of justifiable granularity. Knowl.-Based Syst. **101**, 100–113 (2016)
26. Itakura, F.: Minimum prediction residual principle applied to speech recognition. IEEE Trans. Acoust. Speech Signal Process. **23**, 67–72 (1975)
27. Savchenko, A.V., Savchenko, L.V.: Towards the creation of reliable voice control system based on a fuzzy approach. Pattern Recognit. Lett. **65**, 145–151 (2015)
28. Gray, R.M., Buzo, A., Gray, J.A., Matsuyama, Y.: Distortion Measures for Speech Processing. IEEE Trans. Acoust. Speech Signal Process. **28**, 367–376 (1980)
29. Savchenko, V.V., Savchenko, A.V.: Information-theoretic analysis of efficiency of the phonetic encoding-decoding method in automatic speech recognition. J. Commun. Technol. Electron. **61**, 430–435 (2016)
30. Kullback, S.: Information Theory and Statistics. Dover Publications, New York (1997)
31. Marple, S.L.: Digital Spectral Analysis: With Applications. Prentice Hall, Upper Saddle River (1987)
32. Benzeghiba, M., De Mori, R., Deroo, O., Dupont, S., Erbes, T., Jouvet, D., Fissore, L., Laface, P., Mertins, A., Ris, C., Rose, R., Tyagi, V., Wellekens, C.: Automatic speech recognition and speech variability: a review. Speech Commun. **49**, 763–786 (2007)
33. Lingras, P., Chen, M., Miao, D.: Rough multi-category decision theoretic framework. In: Wang, G., Li, T., Grzymala-Busse, J.W., Miao, D., Skowron, A., Yao, Y. (eds.) RSKT 2008. LNCS, vol. 5009, pp. 676–683. Springer, Heidelberg (2008). doi:10.1007/978-3-540-79721-0_90

34. Zhou, B.: Multi-class decision-theoretic rough sets. Int. J. Approx. Reason. **55**(1), 211–224 (2014)
35. Ju, H.R., Li, H.X., Yang, X.B., Zhou, X.Z.: Cost-sensitive rough set: a multi-granulation approach. Knowl.-Based Syst. **123**, 137–153 (2017)
36. Deng, G., Jia, X.: A decision-theoretic rough set approach to multi-class cost-sensitive classification. In: Flores, V., et al. (eds.) IJCRS 2016. LNCS, vol. 9920, pp. 250–260. Springer, Cham (2016). doi:10.1007/978-3-319-47160-0_23
37. Liu, D., Li, T., Li, H.: A multiple-category classification approach with decision-theoretic rough sets. Fundam. Inform. **115**(2–3), 173–188 (2012)
38. Hochberg, Y., Tamhane, A.C.: Multiple Comparison Procedures. Wiley, Hoboken (2009)
39. Benjamini, Y., Hochberg, Y.: Controlling the false discovery rate: a practical and powerful approach to multiple testing. J. Royal Stat. Soc. Series B (Methodol.) **57**(1), 289–300 (1995)
40. Savchenko, A.V., Savchenko, L.V.: Classification of a sequence of objects with the fuzzy decoding method. In: Cornelis, C., Kryszkiewicz, M., Ślęzak, D., Ruiz, E.M., Bello, R., Shang, L. (eds.) RSCTC 2014. LNCS, vol. 8536, pp. 309–318. Springer, Cham (2014). doi:10.1007/978-3-319-08644-6_32
41. Savchenko, A.V.: Semi-automated speaker adaptation: how to control the quality of adaptation? In: Elmoataz, A., Lezoray, O., Nouboud, F., Mammass, D. (eds.) ICISP 2014. LNCS, vol. 8509, pp. 638–646. Springer, Cham (2014). doi:10.1007/978-3-319-07998-1_73
42. Savchenko, A.V.: Phonetic words decoding software in the problem of Russian speech recognition. Autom. Remote Control **74**(7), 1225–1232 (2013)
43. Povey, D., Ghoshal, A., Boulianne, G., Burget, L., Glembek, O., Goel, N., Hannemann, M., Motlicek, P., Qian, Y., Schwarz, P., Silovsky, J.: The kaldi speech recognition toolkit. In: IEEE 2011 Workshop on Automatic Speech Recognition and Understanding. IEEE Signal Processing Society (2011)
44. Gillick, L., Cox, S.: Some statistical issues in the comparison of speech recognition algorithms. In: Proceedings of the IEEE International Conference on Acoustics, Speech and Signal Processing (ICASSP), pp. 532–535 (1989)

A Three-Way Recommender System for Popularity-Based Costs

Yuan-Yuan Xu, Heng-Ru Zhang, and Fan Min[✉]

School of Computer Science, Southwest Petroleum University,
Chengdu 610500, China
yuanyuanxu.cn@gmail.com, zhanghrswpu@163.com, minfanphd@163.com

Abstract. Recommender systems help e-commerce corporations to make profit among a large amount of customers. Three-way recommender systems handle this issue through considering misclassification and promotion costs. The setting of costs in existing approaches is the same for items with different popularity. However, success recommendation of unpopular items is more profitable. In this paper, we define a new cost-sensitive recommendation problem. The new problem is more general than existing ones in that the cost function is variable w.r.t the popularity of the item. First, we adopt a three-way approach with three kinds of actions: recommending, not recommending and promoting. For any item, a threshold pair is calculated from its cost matrix. Second, we employ the M-distance to obtain the probability which measures how much a user likes an item. Consequently, the action to any item for any user is determined. Experiments are undertaken on the well-known Movielens dataset. Compared with the existing three-way recommendation algorithm, our algorithm results in less average cost through recommending more unpopular items.

Keywords: Cost-sensitive learning · Popularity · Recommender system · Three-way decision

1 Introduction

Shopping online has become a part of our daily life, and e-commerce corporations have gained much success in the last decade. Amazon.com is the first website attracting more than 30 million customers. At the end of 2014, Taobao.com has nearly 500 million registered members, including 120 million active users. Its turnover is around 120 billion yuan on November 11th (double eleven), 2016. These websites usually provide some hyper-links including "find similar", "find relevant", and "guess you like" to improve user satisfaction and promote the sale. The software in charge of these issues is called a recommender system (RS). Naturally, the performance of an RS has an essential impact to the success of the corporation.

A number of measures have been designed for different scenarios to evaluate the quality of an RS. For top-N recommendation, recall [2,18] refers to

© Springer International Publishing AG 2017
L. Polkowski et al. (Eds.): IJCRS 2017, Part II, LNAI 10314, pp. 278–289, 2017.
DOI: 10.1007/978-3-319-60840-2_20

the proportion of successful recommended items. For numeric rating prediction, MAE [1] refers the mean absolute error across all ratings of users to items. For "find all good items" task, coverage refers to percentage of items the RS can form predictions for [7,8]. For classification recommendation [8], accuracy refers to the proportion of correct behavior (recommend or not). For cost-sensitive recommendation [14,24], average cost is more general than accuracy through considering different costs for different behaviors. An appropriate measure helps attracting customers or maximizing the profit of the corporation.

Three-way recommender systems (3RSs) [24,25] aim at minimizing the average cost considering both misclassification and promotion costs. Misclassification indicates that an item belongs to class X when its real class is Y, while promotion through coupon distribution is widely adopted by corporations. The misclassification and promotion costs are expressed as a 3×2 cost matrix. The rows correspond to three actions, namely recommending, not recommending, and promotion; while the columns are users' two actual preferences, namely like or dislike. For simplicity, we let the costs of correct behaviors be 0s. This approach coincides with the three-way theory [9,13,22]. However, the cost matrix of existing 3RS is fixed for any item. Since success recommendation of unpopular items is more profitable, this setting is not reasonable.

In this paper, we define a new cost-sensitive recommendation problem. It is more general than existing ones in that the cost function is variable w.r.t the popularity of the item. The input includes the rating information and the cost function. Let the situation of recommending an item that a user dislike be PN, and not recommending an item that a user like be NP. For items with smaller popularity, the cost of NP is bigger, while the cost of PN is smaller. The purpose is to encourage the recommendation of unpopular items. The output is the action to each user-item pair. Naturally, the optimization objective is to minimize the average cost.

First, we adopt a three-way approach with three kinds of actions mentioned above. For each item, the popularity is determined by the number of rating times without considering the rating values. With the popularity, the cost matrix is computed from the cost function. Then a threshold pair (α, β) is calculated from the cost matrix according to the three-way theory [22]. α determines the probability necessary to recommend an item, and β determines that necessary not to recommend an item. The cost function is designed in the way that for items with lower popularity, the cost of PN are smaller, and the cost of NP are bigger. Consequently, both α and β values for items with lower popularity are smaller such that they are more likely to be recommended or promoted.

Second, we employ the M-distance [26] to compute the liking probability P of a user on an item. Similar to [26], we obtain the neighbors of the predicted object through setting a certain radius. Different from [26], we count the rating distribution, rather than compute the prediction. Using the like threshold, we obtain the probability of a user liking an item.

Finally, we determine the recommender's behavior based on α, β and P. If P is greater than α, the item is recommended. If P is less than β, the item is not recommended. Otherwise, we pay a promotion cost to learn his/her preference.

Experiments on the well-known MovieLens dataset show that (1) our algorithm results in less average cost and (2) recommends more unpopular items than the existing three-way recommendation algorithm [24].

This paper is organized as follows. Section 2 gives the related works, including the data model, the cost-sensitive learning and the theory of three-way decision. 3RS for popularity-based costs (3RSPC) is described in detail in Sect. 3. Section 4 shows extensive experiments to validate the effectiveness of our algorithm. Section 5 concludes the paper.

2   Related Works

In this section, we review some related works. First, we revisit the data model for RSs. It includes the demographic, the content, and the rating tables. Second, we revisit the existing 3RSs. There is only one cost matrix for the problem.

2.1   Data Model

Generally, there are a set of users, a set of items, and a table of ratings from different users rating to different items.

Definition 1. *Let U_A to be the matrix of users and their attributes. $U = \{u_1, u_2, \ldots, u_n\}$ is the set of users as the column of matrix U_A, and $A = \{a_1, a_2, \ldots, a_m\}$ is the set of attributes as the row of matrix U_A.*

Definition 2. *Let M_A to be the matrix of items and their attributes. Its rows and columns are a set of identifications of movies $M = \{m_1, m_2, \ldots, m_k\}$ and a set of release years genres of movies respectively. For example, a movie m_3 is an action movie and the value of attribute Action is equal to 1.*

Definition 3. *Let R to be a rating matrix of every movie from different users, shown in Table 1. R contains the identifications of users and the ratings for some movies. We set $\{1, 2, 3, 4, 5\}$ as the range of scores, and set 3 as the threshold. If the score is over 3, the user likes the movie. Conversely, if the score is below or equal to 3, the user dislikes the movie. The rating function is defined as (1):*

$$U_A \times M_A \rightarrow R \tag{1}$$

We can conclude from Table 1 that the user u_1 likes m_2, dislikes m_1 and m_4 and does not watch the m_3 and m_5.

Table 1. Users rating for movies

UID \ MID	m_1	m_2	m_3	m_4	m_5
u_1	3	4	0	1	0
u_2	2	0	1	3	0
u_3	0	2	1	0	5
u_4	1	4	5	4	3
u_5	4	1	2	0	1

2.2   Cost-Sensitive Learning

Cost-sensitive learning has extended machine learning methods [5,10,11], where classification plays an essential role. Minimizing the cost of misclassification and avoiding the shortcomings of traditional classifiers have become the aims of cost-sensitive learning [20]. Min et al. [14,15] aimed to decrease the test cost and improve the classification accuracy.

Fan [6] proposed a misclassification cost-sensitive boosting method. Pendharkar [17] designed a two-stage solution approach for solving misclassification cost minimizing feature selection problem. In our case, misclassification cost is paid for wrong recommender behaviors. For example, the RS recommends a movie to a costumer who dislikes, or do not recommend it when the type of the song is just her favourite [24]. We also consider the promotion cost.

The contribution of promotion cost is to obtain the feedback of customers' preference. Active learning algorithms can actively query the user for labels and guide the acquisition of new knowledge suitable to update related information [19,24]. Promotion cost in this paper is produced by sending coupons and discounts to users.

2.3   Existing 3RS Problem

The existing three-way recommendation problem is stated as follows [24].

Problem 1. Existing three-way recommendation problem.
Input: U_A, M_A, R, $\mathbf{C}_{3\times 2}$,
Output: T,
Optimization objective: minimizing the average cost.

U_A, M_A and R have been mentioned in Sect. 2.1. $\mathbf{C}_{3\times 2}$ is a cost matrix with fixed values. T is possible actions of a user-item pair according to three-way decision. The detail is as follows.

Using Pawlak rough-set model [16], we define a subset $X \subset U$ and obtain a pair of concept lower and upper approximations:

$$\underline{apr}(X) = \{x \in U | [x] \subseteq X\}, \tag{2}$$

$$\overline{apr}(X) = \{x \in U | [x] \cap X = \emptyset\}. \tag{3}$$

Yao proposed the rules of three-way decision [22]. It divided the universe into three disjoint regions: the positive region, the negative region and the boundary region. They are expressed as *POS(X)*, *NEG(X)* and *BND(X)* respectively:

$$POS(X) = \underline{apr}(X), \tag{4}$$

$$NEG(X) = U - \overline{apr}(X), \tag{5}$$

$$BND(X) = \overline{apr}(X) - \underline{apr}(X). \tag{6}$$

Yao et al. have been developing the Decision-theoretic rough set models [4,12,23]. The expected cost associated with different actions is

$$R(a_j|x) = \sum_{i=1}^{m} \lambda(a_j|\omega_i)P(\omega_i|x). \tag{7}$$

a_j expresses one kind of n possible actions in the set $T = \{a_1, a_2, \ldots, a_n\}$, and $a_j|x$ means we have taken action a_j to object x. Let $\lambda(a_j|\omega_i)$ denote the loss of taking action a_j under the state ω_i. Let the set $\Omega = \{\omega_1, \omega_2, \ldots, \omega_m\}$ be the set of all kinds of states. Let $P(\omega_i|x)$ be the conditional probability of classification. For the Bayesian decision procedure, we define the set $\Omega = \{X, \overline{X}\}$ to indicate that the customers like or dislike the item recommended. Explicitly, we define the set of actions $T = \{a_P, a_B, a_N\}$. a_P denotes that we classify an item into $POS(X)$ (recommend), a_B denotes that we classify an item into $BND(X)$ (promote) and a_N denotes that we classify an item into $NEG(X)$ (not recommend). So the cost matrix $\mathbf{C}_{3\times2}$ is given by Table 2.

Table 2. Cost matrix

Action\Preference	X	$\overline{X}$
a_P	λ_{PP}	λ_{PN}
a_B	λ_{BP}	λ_{BN}
a_N	λ_{NP}	λ_{NN}

The expected cost $R(a_j|x)$ associated with taking the individual actions can be expressed as:

$$R_P = \lambda_{PP}P(X|[x]) + \lambda_{PN}P(\overline{X}|[x]), \tag{8}$$
$$R_B = \lambda_{BP}P(X|[x]) + \lambda_{BN}P(\overline{X}|[x]), \tag{9}$$
$$R_N = \lambda_{NP}P(X|[x]) + \lambda_{NN}P(\overline{X}|[x]). \tag{10}$$

The Bayesian decision procedure suggests the following minimum-risk decision rules [21,23]:

(P) If $R_P \leq R_N$ and $R_P \leq R_B$, then decide $x \in POS(X)$;
(B) If $R_B \leq R_P$ and $R_B \leq R_N$, then decide $x \in BND(X)$;
(N) If $R_N \leq R_P$ and $R_B \leq R_B$, then decide $x \in NEG(X)$.

There should be some constraints added. Let us first set the rule that each item can be classified into only one region:

$$P(X|[x]) + P(\overline{X}|[x]) = 1. \tag{11}$$

Second, we limit the vales of different kinds of loss:

$$\lambda_{PP} \leq \lambda_{BP} < \lambda_{NP}, \tag{12}$$
$$\lambda_{NN} \leq \lambda_{BN} < \lambda_{PN}. \tag{13}$$

The inequality (12) describes that if RS recommends an item that user likes, the cost is less than or equal to the cost produced by the situation that RS promotes an item that user likes. Both of the two kinds of loss must be less than the cost of not recommending an item that user likes. According to (11) and (12), we can derive and simplify our decision rules from$(P)$to(N) as follows:

(P1) If $P(X|[x]) \geq \alpha$ and $P(X|[x]) \geq \gamma$, then decide $x \in POS(X)$;
(B1) If $P(X|[x]) \leq \alpha$ and $P(X|[x]) \geq \beta$, then decide $x \in BND(X)$;
(N1) If $P(X|[x]) \leq \beta$ and $P(X|[x]) \leq \gamma$, then decide $x \in NEG(X)$.

Here, α, β and γ are expressed as:

$$\alpha = \frac{\lambda_{PN} - \lambda_{BN}}{(\lambda_{PN} - \lambda_{BN}) + (\lambda_{BP} - \lambda_{PP})}, \tag{14}$$

$$\beta = \frac{\lambda_{BN} - \lambda_{NN}}{(\lambda_{BN} - \lambda_{NN}) + (\lambda_{NP} - \lambda_{BP})}, \tag{15}$$

$$\gamma = \frac{\lambda_{PN} - \lambda_{NN}}{(\lambda_{PN} - \lambda_{NN}) + (\lambda_{NP} - \lambda_{PP})}. \tag{16}$$

Additionally, the condition of rule (B1) should be $\alpha \geq \beta$. So we have

$$\frac{\lambda_{NP} - \lambda_{BP}}{\lambda_{BN} - \lambda_{NN}} > \frac{\lambda_{BP} - \lambda_{PP}}{\lambda_{PN} - \lambda_{BN}}. \tag{17}$$

We also have $0 \leq \beta < \alpha \leq 1$. After tie-breaking, we can rewrite and simplify our decision rules again:

(P2) If $P(X|[x]) > \alpha$, then decide $x \in POS(X)$;
(B2) If $\beta < P(X|[x]) < \alpha$, then decide $x \in BND(X)$;
(N2) If $P(X|[x]) \leq \beta$, then decide $x \in NEG(X)$.

Then the existing recommendation approach employ the random tree to predict the probability P of a user-item pair. P determines the three possibilities of T. It has proven that the three-way decision model has lowest average cost not only on the training set but also on the testing set. So the threshold pair (α, β) is optimal.

3 The Proposed Approach

In this section, we first introduce a new problem with a cost function. We propose three kinds of cost functions for different scenarios. We also discuss the parameter settings for cost functions to satisfy our requirements, namely, unpopular items are more desired. For items with different popularity, the cost matrix is different. Third, we propose an algorithm to the new problem.

3.1　Problem Statement

Our new problem is stated as follows.

Problem 2. **Three-way recommendation with a cost function.**
Input: U_A, M_A, R, c_{PRM}, c_{NP}, c_{PN},
Output: T,
Optimization objective: Minimizing the average cost.

As discussed in Sect. 3.1, U_A is the demographic information, M_A is the content information, and R is the rating information. For simplicity, the promotion cost c_{PRM} is set to be fixed rather than variable. c_{NP}, c_{PN} are the misclassification functions where the argument of functions is the item popularity. c_{NP} and c_{PN} are the misclassification cost for false positive and false negative, respectively.

3.2　The Cost Function Design and Threshold Pairs

Our 3RSPC aims at promoting more unpopular items. Not every cost function is fit for our 3RSPC, some of which would suitable for promoting the popular ones. So some constraints should be added. In Sect. 1, we have mentioned that the penalty of *NP* are more than that of *PN* at lower popularity. Based on the three-way decision rules, it is conductive for promoting the unpopular that a threshold pair (α, β) should keep a certain interval.

We sample the popularity to express the popularity as a vector conveniently. We choose eleven points on the popularity, and averagely divide this range $[0, 1]$ into ten intervals. So the popularity is expressed as 0 through 10. 0 and 10 indicate the lowest and highest popularity respectively. We have a linear cost of *PN* between 60 and 80, and the common difference is equal to $(80 - 60)/10 = 2$. The cost of *NP* are from 100 down to 60, and the common difference is equal to $(60 - 100)/10 = -4$. The c_{PN} and c_{NP} are shown in Fig. 1.

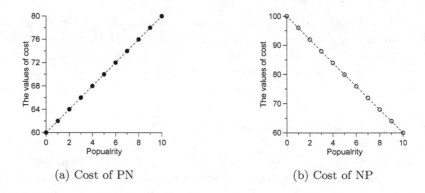

(a) Cost of PN　　　　　　　　　(b) Cost of NP

Fig. 1. Cost of PN and NP

Naturally, the optimal setting of thresholds α and β are dependent on the misclassification costs. Therefore there are essentially two threshold functions $f_\alpha, f_\beta : (0, 1) \to \mathbb{R}$. Let us assume initially that c_{PRM} is equal to 20. Equations (14) and (15) are re-expressed as

$$f_\alpha = 1 - \frac{20}{c_{PN}}, \tag{18}$$

and

$$f_\beta = \frac{20}{c_{NP}}. \tag{19}$$

Figure 2 shows that both α and β are increasing with the popularity.

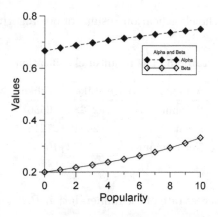

Fig. 2. α and β in 3RSPC

3.3 Favorite Probability Prediction

We employ the M-distance [26] to solve the problem of the favorite probability. The detail is stated as follows.

Problem 3. **Favorite probability prediction.**
Input: R, *Radius*,
Output: P.

R is the rating information of dataset, and *Radius* is a parameter to determine a range of neighbours. P describes a probability that a user likes a movie. We employ leave-one-out approach to predict the favorite probability. The content of the approach is as follows [3, 26]. Suppose n is the rating times of users for the same item. We remove one of the n training samples, and test the resulting hypothesis on the training example that was left out.

Then we compute the average score of the $n - 1$ samples, and set a radius to obtain a range. For example, we predict the probability of the user-item pair (u_1, m_1). First, we compute the average score 3.2 except the score 4 at (u_1, m_1). Second, we set a radius 0.3 to obtain a range $[2.9, 3.5]$. In this range, there are 23 ratings but only 10 records above the threshold. So the favourite probability is $10/23 = 0.435$.

There is a special case that only one user rates for a movie before computation. In leave-one-out algorithm, the denominator will be 0. So we consider the average score is equal to 3.

4   Experiments

Table 3 has shown us the classification results of our algorithm.

Table 3. The result of classification

Action\Preference	Like	Dislike
Recommend	27284	6556
Promote	26219	27212
Not recommend	1872	10857

We compute the success rate of recommendation R_{rec} and success rate of not recommendation R_{nrec}:

$$R_{rec} = \frac{PP}{PP + PN} = \frac{27284}{27284 + 6556} = 81\%, \tag{20}$$

$$R_{nrec} = \frac{NN}{NP + NN} = \frac{10857}{1872 + 10857} = 85\%. \tag{21}$$

Figure 3 demonstrates the distributions of instances in each class. It shows the classified instances change when the popularity changes with a interval of 1. The items with lower popularity (less than 4) in Fig. 3(a) and (c) have account for 71% and 78% ($19498/27284 = 0.71$, $20563/26219 = 0.78$). So, we can conclude that the unpopular items are recommended well in our 3RSPC.

Compared with [24], even if our costs of PN and NP are more than that of [24], we still obtain the lower average cost than that of [24] (Table 4).

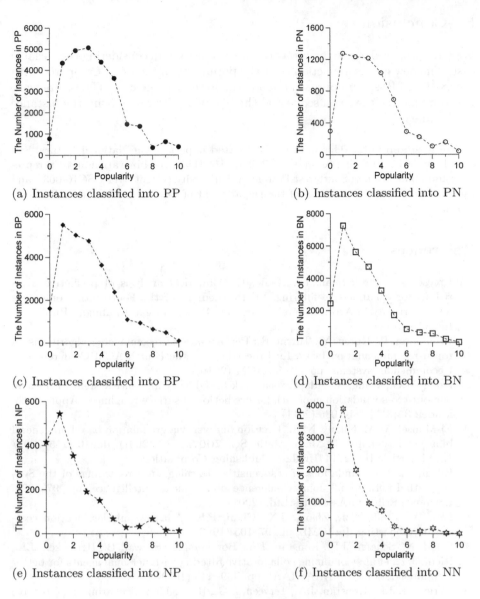

Fig. 3. Instances classified into six classes

Table 4. Comparing the results of [24] and 3RSPC

	[24]	3RSPC
Cost of PN	50	60–80
Cost of NP	40	100–60
Average cost	17.25(testing set)	16.75

5   Conclusion

We have proposed a new three-way recommender system considering the variable cost. The new cost is a function w.r.t the popularity of the item. Compared with the existing 3RSs, our approach obtains the lower average cost. The future work will combine the theory of sequential three-way decision to classify the instance in boundary.

Acknowledgements. This work was supported in part by the National Natural Science Foundation of China (Grants 61379089, 41604114), the Innovation and Entrepreneurship Foundation of Southwest Petroleum University (Grant SWPUSC16-003), and the Natural Science Foundation of the Department of Education of Sichuan Province (Grant 16ZA0060).

References

1. Breese, J.S., Heckerman, D., Kadie, C.: Empirical analysis of predictive algorithms for collaborative filtering. In: Proceedings of the Fourteenth Conference on Uncertainty in Artificial Intelligence, pp. 43–52. Morgan Kaufmann Publishers Inc. (1998)
2. Cremonesi, P., Koren, Y., Turrin, R.: Performance of recommender algorithms on top-n recommendation tasks. In: Proceedings of the Fourth ACM Conference on Recommender systems, pp. 39–46. ACM (2010)
3. Dong, M.G., Wang, N.: Adaptive network-based fuzzy inference system with leave-one-out-cross validation approach for prediction of surface roughness. Appl. Math. Model. **35**(3), 1024–1035 (2011)
4. El-Monsef, M.A., Kilany, N.M.: Decision analysis via granulation based on general binary relation. Int. J. Math. Math. Sci. **2007**, 1–13 (2007). doi:10.1155/2007/12714. Article ID 12714. Hindawi Publishing Corporation
5. Elkan, C.: The foundations of cost-sensitive learning. In: Proceedings of the Seventeenth International Joint Conference on Artificial Intelligence, pp. 973–978. Lawrence Erlbaum Associates Ltd. (2001)
6. Fan, W., Stolfo, S.J., Zhang, J.X., Chan, P.K.: Adacost: misclassification cost-sensitive boosting. In: ICML, pp. 97–105 (1999)
7. Good, N., Schafer, J.B., Konstan, J.A., Borchers, A., Sarwar, B., Herlocker, J.L., Riedl, J.T., et al.: Combining collaborative filtering with personal agents for better recommendations. In: AAAI/IAAI, pp. 439–446 (1999)
8. Herlocker, J.L., Konstan, J.A., Terveen, L.G., Riedl, J.T.: Evaluating collaborative filtering recommender systems. ACM Trans. Inf. Syst. (TOIS) **22**(1), 5–53 (2004)
9. Jia, X., Zheng, K., Li, W., Liu, T., Shang, L.: Three-way decisions solution to filter spam email: an empirical study. In: Yao, J.T., Yang, Y., Słowiński, R., Greco, S., Li, H., Mitra, S., Polkowski, L. (eds.) RSCTC 2012. LNCS, vol. 7413, pp. 287–296. Springer, Heidelberg (2012). doi:10.1007/978-3-642-32115-3_34
10. Kukar, M., Kononenko, I.: Cost-sensitive learning with neural networks. In: ECAI, pp. 445–449 (1998)
11. Li, X.J., Zhao, H., Zhu, W.: A cost sensitive decision tree algorithm with two adaptive mechanisms. Knowl.-Based Syst. **88**, 24–33 (2015)

12. Liu, D., Li, T., Hu, P., Li, H.: Multiple-category classification with decision-theoretic rough sets. In: Yu, J., Greco, S., Lingras, P., Wang, G., Skowron, A. (eds.) RSKT 2010. LNCS, vol. 6401, pp. 703–710. Springer, Heidelberg (2010). doi:10.1007/978-3-642-16248-0_95
13. Liu, D., Li, T.R., Ruan, D.: Probabilistic model criteria with decision-theoretic rough sets. Inf. Sci. **181**(17), 3709–3722 (2011)
14. Min, F., He, H.P., Qian, Y.H., Zhu, W.: Test-cost-sensitive attribute reduction. Inf. Sci. **181**(22), 4928–4942 (2011)
15. Min, F., Hu, Q.H., Zhu, W.: Feature selection with test cost constraint. Int. J. Approx. Reas. **55**(1), 167–179 (2014)
16. Pawlak, Z.: Rough Sets: Theoretical Aspects of Reasoning About Data. Theory and Decision Library D. Springer Science & Business Media, Heidelberg (2012)
17. Pendharkar, P.C.: A misclassification cost risk bound based on hybrid particle swarm optimization heuristic. Expert Syst. Appl. **41**(4), 1483–1491 (2014)
18. Powers, D.M.: Evaluation: from precision, recall and f-measure to ROC, informedness, markedness and correlation. J. Mach. Learn. Technol. **2**(1), 37–63 (2011)
19. Settles, B.: Active learning literature survey. Computer Sciences Technical report 1648. University of Wisconsin-Madison (2009)
20. Tapkan, P., Özbakır, L., Kulluk, S., Baykasoğlu, A.: A cost-sensitive classification algorithm: BEE-miner. Knowl.-Based Syst. **95**, 99–113 (2016)
21. Yao, Y.Y.: Probabilistic approaches to rough sets. Expert Syst. **20**(5), 287–297 (2003)
22. Yao, Y.Y.: Three-way decisions with probabilistic rough sets. Inf. Sci. **180**(3), 341–353 (2010)
23. Yao, Y.Y., Wong, S.K.M.: A decision theoretic framework for approximating concepts. Int. J. Man Mach. Stud. **37**(6), 793–809 (1992)
24. Zhang, H.R., Min, F.: Three-way recommender systems based on random forests. Knowl.-Based Syst. **91**, 275–286 (2016)
25. Zhang, H.R., Min, F., Shi, B.: Regression-based three-way recommendation. Inf. Sci. **378**, 444–461 (2017)
26. Zheng, M., Min, F., Zhang, H.R., Chen, W.B.: Fast recommendations with the m-distance. IEEE Access **4**, 1464–1468 (2016)

Three-Way Decisions Based on Intuitionistic Fuzzy Sets

Xiaoping Yang[1,2(✉)] and Anhui Tan[1,2]

[1] School of Mathematics, Physics and Information Science,
Zhejiang Ocean University, Zhoushan 316022, Zhejiang, People's Republic of China
yxpzyp@sina.com, tananhui86@163.com
[2] Key Laboratory of Oceanographic Big Data Mining and Application of Zhejiang
Province, Zhoushan 316022, Zhejiang, People's Republic of China

Abstract. The intuitionistic fuzzy set is introduced to incomplete information systems, in which the membership and non-membership degrees that an object belongs to a concept are constructed by the rough set approximations based on similarity relation. Then, by combining the intuitionistic fuzzy set and three-way decisions, we proposed two evaluation functions to generate decision rules and make three-way decisions in incomplete information systems.

Keywords: Intuitionistic fuzzy sets · Incomplete information systems · Three-way decisions · Rough sets

1 Introduction

In 1982, Pawlak [14] originally proposed rough set theory to deal with uncertain knowledge in information systems. In this theory, the notions of lower and upper approximations are introduced, by which a universe is divided into three nonempty and disjoint regions: positive, negative and boundary regions. By this means, knowledge hidden in information systems may be unravelled and expressed in the form of decision rules. Concretely, an object is contained in the positive region of a set if and only if its equivalence class is fully contained in the set. This results in the rigidness of partition and makes positive region small. To resolve this problem, decision-theoretic rough sets have been proposed and studied as generalizations of Pawlak rough sets [16,17,20–23,31,32]. Many methods were used to research decision-theoretic rough sets. To get the theory frame, three-way decisions are further used in the interpretation of the rough set by three regions [24–26]. Many studies further investigated extensions and applications of three-way decisions [2,4,5,7,10–13,18,19,28].

In 1965, Zadeh [29] proposed the concept of fuzzy set in which the membership degree specified as a real number in the unit interval was used to describe the clingingness of objects to a set. Fuzzy set theory is widely used in many fields nowadays. Nevertheless, it is difficult for a fuzzy set to express both the positive and negative information of knowledge. For this reason, Atanassov [1]

© Springer International Publishing AG 2017
L. Polkowski et al. (Eds.): IJCRS 2017, Part II, LNAI 10314, pp. 290–299, 2017.
DOI: 10.1007/978-3-319-60840-2_21

proposed the concept of intuitionistic fuzzy set, in which both membership and non-membership degrees are used to deal with uncertain information, and their sum does not exceed 1. Thus, an intuitionistic fuzzy set expresses the positive and the negative information more flexibly than a fuzzy set.

There have been many studies in combining fuzzy sets or intuitionistic fuzzy sets with rough sets [3,6,15,30]. As we know, the membership, non-membership and hesitancy degrees in intuitionistic fuzzy sets correspond to the positive, negative and boundary regions in three-way decisions, respectively. This means, the intuitionistic fuzzy sets and three-way decisions may be combined for improving their individual performance in decision making. In decision-theoretic rough set, the evaluation functions are usually related to condition probabilities and a pair of thresholds (α, β) need to be chosen. In this paper, we use membership degrees in evaluation functions instead of condition probabilities. Further more, we try to omit the pair of thresholds by comparing the membership degrees in some cases. We apply intuitionistic fuzzy sets to deal with the data in incomplete information systems and propose three-way decisions for the incomplete information systems.

2   Incomplete Information Systems and Intuitionistic Fuzzy Sets

We will briefly introduce the basic notions of incomplete information systems and intuitionistic fuzzy sets which will be used throughout the paper.

2.1   Incomplete Information Systems

A pair $S = (U, AT)$ is referred to as an information system, where U is a non-empty finite set of objects called the universe of discourse, AT is a non-empty finite set of attributes such that $a : U \to V_a$ for any $a \in AT$, where V_a is called the value set of a. It may happen that some attribute values of objects are missing. We will denote the missing value by "$*$". A system $S = (U, AT)$ with missing values is called an incomplete information system [8,9].

Let $S = (U, AT)$ be an incomplete information system, and $A \subseteq AT$, a similarity relation on U is defined as follows [8]:

$SIM(A) = \{(x, y) \in U \times U | \forall a \in A, a(x) = a(y) \text{ or } a(x) = * \text{ or } a(y) = *\}$.

$S_A(x) = \{y \in U | (x, y) \in SIM(A)\}$ denotes the set of all objects similar to x with respective to A.

Example 2.1. Table 1 [8] depicts an incomplete information system $S = (U, AT)$, where $U = \{x_1, x_2, x_3, x_4, x_5, x_6\}$, $AT = \{P, M, S, X\}$, and P, M, S, X stand for Price, Mileage, Size, Max-Speed, respectively.

Let $A = \{P, S, X\}$, we have $S_A(x_1) = \{x_1\}$, $S_A(x_2) = \{x_2, x_6\}$, $S_A(x_3) = \{x_3\}$, $S_A(x_4) = \{x_4, x_5\}$, $S_A(x_5) = \{x_4, x_5, x_6\}$, $S_A(x_6) = \{x_2, x_5, x_6\}$. These similarity sets constitute a cover of U.

Table 1. An incomplete information system

Car	Price	Mileage	Size	Max-Speed
x_1	High	High	Full	Low
x_2	Low	*	Full	Low
x_3	*	*	Compact	High
x_4	High	*	Full	High
x_5	*	*	Full	High
x_6	Low	High	Full	*

A decision table (DT) is an information system $S = (U, AT \cup \{d\})$, where $d \notin AT$ and $* \notin V_d$, d is a distinguished attribute called the decision, and the elements of AT are called conditions. If $S = (U, AT \cup \{d\})$ is an incomplete information system, then the DT is called an incomplete decision table.

Example 2.2. Table 2 [8] depicts an incomplete decision table $S = (U, AT \cup \{d\})$.

Table 2. An incomplete decision table

Car	Price	Mileage	Size	Max-Speed	d
x_1	High	High	Full	Low	Good
x_2	Low	*	Full	Low	Good
x_3	*	*	Compact	High	Poor
x_4	High	*	Full	High	Good
x_5	*	*	Full	High	Excel
x_6	Low	High	Full	*	Good

For $X \subseteq U$ and $A \subseteq AT$, the lower and upper approximations of X are defined by similarity relation as follows [8]:

$$\underline{A}X = \{x \in U | S_A(x) \subseteq X\} = \{x \in X | S_A(x) \subseteq X\},$$
$$\overline{A}X = \{x \in U | S_A(x) \cap X \neq \emptyset\} = \bigcup \{S_A(x) | x \in X\}.$$

Obviously, $\underline{A}X$ is the set of objects that belong to X with certainty, $\overline{A}X$ is the set of objects that possibly belong to X, $\sim \overline{A}X$ is a set of objects that impossibly belong to X. Denote $BN_A X = \overline{A}X - \underline{A}X$, which is called the boundary set, and objects in $BN_A X$ may or may not belong to X.

2.2 Intuitionistic Fuzzy Sets

Let U be a non-empty finite set of objects called the universe of discourse, an intuitionistic fuzzy set X on U is defined as follows [1]:

$$X = \{\langle x, \mu_X(x), \gamma_X(x) \rangle | x \in U\},$$

where $\mu_X(x) \in [0,1]$ is called the degree of membership of x in X and $\gamma_X(x) \in [0,1]$ is the degree of non-membership of x in X, and $0 \le \mu_X(x) + \gamma_X(x) \le 1$. Denote $\pi_X(x) = 1 - \mu_X(x) - \gamma_X(x)$, which is called the hesitancy degree of the element x in X.

2.3   Intuitionistic Fuzzy Sets in Incomplete Information Systems

Now we try to introduce the intuitionistic fuzzy sets to incomplete information system. We present the definition of intuitionistic fuzzy sets in incomplete information system.

Let $S = (U, AT)$ be an incomplete information system, $X \subseteq U$ and $A \subseteq AT$. Denote $|X|$ as the cardinality of set X. Define

$$X^* = \{\langle x, A\mu_X(x), A\gamma_X(x)\rangle | x \in U\},$$

where $A\mu_X(x) = \frac{|S_A(x) \cap \underline{A}X|}{|S_A(x)|}$, $A\gamma_X(x) = \frac{|S_A(x) \cap \sim \overline{A}X|}{|S_A(x)|}$.

According to the definition, $A\mu_X : U \to [0,1]$, $A\gamma_X : U \to [0,1]$, and for all $x \in U$, $A\mu_X(x) + A\gamma_X(x) \le 1$. So X^* is an intuitionistic fuzzy set on U. We denote

$$A\pi_X(x) = 1 - A\mu_X(x) - A\gamma_X(x) = 1 - \frac{|S_A(x) \cap \underline{A}X|}{|S_A(x)|} - \frac{|S_A(x) \cap \sim \overline{A}X|}{|S_A(x)|} = \frac{|S_A(x) \cap BN_AX|}{|S_A(x)|}.$$

Obviously, $A\mu_X(x)$, $A\gamma_X(x)$ and $A\pi_X(x)$ indicate the degrees of membership, non-membership and hesitancy, respectively.

3   Three-Way Decisions Based on Intuitionistic Fuzzy Sets

In this section, we study the three-way decisions. A basic idea of three-way decisions is to classify a universe into three regions, called the positive, negative and boundary regions, respectively, by using an evaluation function and a pair of thresholds [27].

3.1   Evaluation Functions for Three-Way Decisions

There are three degrees in intuitionistic fuzzy sets. If the membership degree of x belonging to X is large and the non-membership degree of x belonging to X is small, we decide x belongs to the positive region. If the membership degree of x belonging to X is small and the non-membership degree of x belong to X is large, we decide x belongs to the negative region. If both of the membership and non-membership degrees of x belonging to X are small, the hesitancy degree must be large, we decide x belongs to the boundary region. Thus, we give out evaluation function and decision Rule I as follows:

Rule I

(P) If $A\mu_X(x) - A\gamma_X(x) > \alpha$,   decide $x \in POS(X)$;

(N) If $A\mu_X(x) - A\gamma_X(x) < \beta$,   decide $x \in NEG(X)$;

(B) If $\beta \le A\mu_X(x) - A\gamma_X(x) \le \alpha$, decide $x \in BND(X)$

The pair of thresholds (α, β) $(0 < \alpha < 1, -1 < \beta < 0)$ need to be chosen according to the practical background. We usually suggest that $\alpha = 0.5$, $\beta = -0.5$ for convenience.

Since the three degrees in intuitionistic fuzzy sets describe the extent of x belonging to the three regions, it is reasonable to make decision by comparing the three degrees. We give out Rule II as follows:

Rule II

(P) If $A\mu_X(x) > A\gamma_X(x)$, $A\mu_X(x) > A\pi_X(x)$, decide $x \in POS(X)$;

(N) If $A\gamma_X(x) > A\mu_X(x)$, $A\gamma_X(x) > A\pi_X(x)$, decide $x \in NEG(X)$;

(B) Otherwise,   decide $x \in BND(X)$.

In Rule II, α and β are unnecessary.

3.2 Application of the Intuitionistic Fuzzy Sets in Incomplete Information Systems

Obviously, $A\mu_X(x)$ describes the membership degree of $x \in \underline{A}X$. $A\gamma_X(x)$ describes the non-membership degree of $x \notin \overline{A}X$. $A\pi_X(x)$ describes the membership degree of $x \in BN_AX$ which implies that x may or may not be in X. Thus, given an object x, we can figure out all its degrees of membership, non-membership and hesitancy, and get the intuitionistic fuzzy sets. By these three degrees we decide which class it might belong to.

Example 3.1. Let us consider Table 2 which depicts an incomplete decision table $S = (U, AT \cup \{d\})$, where $U = \{x_1, x_2, x_3, x_4, x_5, x_6\}$, $AT = \{P, M, S, X\}$, $\{d\} = \{\text{Good, Poor, Excel}\}$. The decision classes classified by decision attribute are D_1, D_2 and D_3, namely, $D_1 = \{x_i | d(x_i) = \text{Good}\} = \{x_1, x_2, x_4, x_6\}$, $D_2 = \{x_i | d(x_i) = \text{Poor}\} = \{x_3\}$, $D_3 = \{x_i | d(x_i) = \text{Excel}\} = \{x_5\}$ which mean good, poor and excellent car sets, respectively. They constitute a partition of U. From the incomplete decision table, we decide which class a car might belong to by its condition attribute values.

First, we classify U with similarity relation according to the chosen subset of attributes. Let $A = AT$, $U/SIM(A) = \{S_A(x_1), S_A(x_2), S_A(x_3), S_A(x_4), S_A(x_5), S_A(x_6)\}$, where $S_A(x_1) = \{x_1\}$, $S_A(x_2) = \{x_2, x_6\}$, $S_A(x_3) = \{x_3\}$, $S_A(x_4) = \{x_4, x_5\}$, $S_A(x_5) = \{x_4, x_5, x_6\}$, $S_A(x_6) = \{x_2, x_5, x_6\}$. These similar sets constitute a cover of U. We calculate the lower and upper approximations, the negative and boundary of D_i and list these results in Table 3.

All kinds of the degrees of membership and non-membership belonging to each D_i are listed in Table 4.

For x_1, from Table 4 we see the degree of membership of $x_1 \in D_1$ is 1 and that of non-membership is 0; Let $\alpha = 0.5$, $\beta = -0.5$, $A\mu_X(x_1) - A\gamma_X(x_1) = 1 > \alpha$, according to Rule I, decide $x_1 \in POS(D_1)$.

For x_2, $A\mu_X(x_2) - A\gamma_X(x_2) = 0.5$, decide $x_2 \in BND(D_1)$.

Table 3. The approximations, the negative and boundary sets

D_i	$\underline{A}D_i$	$\overline{A}D_i$	$\sim \overline{A}D_i$	$BN_A D_i$
$\{x_1, x_2, x_4, x_6\}$	$\{x_1, x_2\}$	$\{x_1, x_2, x_4, x_5, x_6\}$	$\{x_3\}$	$\{x_4, x_5, x_6\}$
$\{x_3\}$	$\{x_3\}$	$\{x_3\}$	$\{x_1, x_2, x_4, x_5, x_6\}$	$\emptyset$
$\{x_5\}$	$\emptyset$	$\{x_4, x_5, x_6\}$	$\{x_1, x_2, x_3\}$	$\{x_4, x_5, x_6\}$

Table 4. The degrees of membership and non-membership

x_i	$A\mu_{D_1}(x_i)$	$A\gamma_{D_1}(x_i)$	$A\mu_{D_2}(x_i)$	$A\gamma_{D_2}(x_i)$	$A\mu_{D_3}(x_i)$	$A\gamma_{D_3}(x_i)$
x_1	1	0	0	1	0	1
x_2	1/2	0	0	1	0	1/2
x_3	0	1	1	0	0	1
x_4	0	0	0	1	0	0
x_5	0	0	0	1	0	0
x_6	1/3	0	0	1	0	1/3

For x_3, $A\mu_X(x_3) - A\gamma_X(x_3) = 0 - 1 = -1$, decide $x_3 \in NEG(D_1)$.
For x_4, $-0.5 \leq A\mu_X(x_4) - A\gamma_X(x_4) \leq 0.5$, decide $x_4 \in BND(D_1)$.
For x_5, $-0.5 \leq A\mu_X(x_5) - A\gamma_X(x_5) \leq 0.5$, decide $x_5 \in BND(D_1)$.
For x_6, $-0.5 \leq A\mu_X(x_6) - A\gamma_X(x_6) \leq 0.5$, decide $x_6 \in BND(D_1)$.
So, $POS(D_1) = \{x_1\}$; $NEG(D_1) = \{x_3\}$; $BND(D_1) = \{x_2, x_4, x_5, x_6\}$.
In the same way, we have
$POS(D_2) = \{x_3\}$; $NEG(D_2) = \{x_1, x_2, x_4, x_5, x_6\}$; $BND(D_2) = \emptyset$
$POS(D_3) = \emptyset$; $NEG(D_3) = \{x_1, x_3\}$; $BND(D_3) = \{x_2, x_4, x_5, x_6\}$
The regions above are listed as Table 5.

Table 5. The regions got by Rule I

D_i	$POS(D_i)$	$NEG(D_i)$	$BND(D_i)$
$\{x_1, x_2, x_4, x_6\}$	$\{x_1\}$	$\{x_3\}$	$\{x_2, x_4, x_5, x_6\}$
$\{x_3\}$	$\{x_3\}$	$\{x_1, x_2, x_4, x_5, x_6\}$	$\emptyset$
$\{x_5\}$	$\emptyset$	$\{x_1, x_3\}$	$\{x_2, x_4, x_5, x_6\}$

We also make three-way decisions with Rule II.
For x_1, $A\mu_{D_1}(x_1) > A\gamma_{D_1}(x_1)$, $A\mu_{D_1}(x_1) > A\pi_{D_1}(x_1)$, decide $x_1 \in POS(D_1)$.
In the same way, we decide $x_3 \in NEG(D_1)$, $x_2, x_4, x_5, x_6 \in BND(D_1)$.
We list all three regions in Table 6
The three regions in Table 5 and 6 happened to be the same.
We make decisions according to Table 5.

Table 6. The regions got by Rule II

D_i	$POS(D_i)$	$NEG(D_i)$	$BND(D_i)$
$\{x_1, x_2, x_4, x_6\}$	$\{x_1\}$	$\{x_3\}$	$\{x_2, x_4, x_5, x_6\}$
$\{x_3\}$	$\{x_3\}$	$\{x_1, x_2, x_4, x_5, x_6\}$	$\emptyset$
$\{x_5\}$	$\emptyset$	$\{x_1, x_3\}$	$\{x_2, x_4, x_5, x_6\}$

For x_1, we see the $x_1 \in POS(D_1)$; $x_1 \in NEG(D_2)$; $x_1 \in NEG(D_3)$. So we decide x_1 is a good car, not a poor car, not an excellent car.

For x_2, we see $x_2 \in BND(D_1)$, $x_2 \in NEG(D_2)$ and $x_2 \in BND(D_3)$; It is not certain x_2 is a good car; It is not certain x_2 is an excellent car, but it is certain x_2 is not a poor car.

For x_3, we see $x_3 \in NEG(D_1)$, $x_3 \in POS(D_2)$ and $x_3 \in NEG(D_3)$. So it is certain x_3 is not a good car; it is certain x_3 is a poor car, it is certain x_3 is not an excellent car.

For x_4, x_5 and x_6, similar to x_2, we see they are in $BND(D_1)$, $NEG(D_2)$ and $BND(D_3)$; So it is not certain they are good cars or excellent cars, but it is certain they are not poor cars.

4   Making Three-Way Decision in Incomplete Information Systems

The main purpose of three-way decision is to make decisions by knowledge discovered in training sample database. There is no equivalence relation in incomplete information systems, so we use similarity relation instead of equivalence relation to make decision with uncertainty. We take the incomplete decision table as a training sample table and make decision according to the acquired knowledge. For an object y with same attribute values in training sample table, we make decision as in above section. For the object y with different attribute values from the training sample table, if y is compatible with objects in training sample table, we also use similarity relation to deal with y. In incomplete information system, some attribute values are unknown, these unknown values mean all possible values. Given an object y outside the incomplete decision table, similarity set of the object $S(y)$ might be found, objects in similarity set from the table may be used for making decision. The more missing data there are in incomplete decision table, the more objects outside the table will be compatible with the objects in the training table and may be made decision but with less accuracy. The more missing attribute values are in an object y, the larger its similarity set $S(y)$ is. This results in larger boundary region and uncertainty.

Now we make decisions. For a car which has the same attribute values as one of the cars in U, we can use the way as in above section to discuss the car. For a car y which has the different attribute values from anyone in U, we first find the similar set of y in training sample table. Then, we find intuitionistic fuzzy set $\{\langle y, A\mu_{D_i}(y), A\gamma_{D_i}(y)\rangle\}$. At last, we make three way decisions. We discuss it by illustration in Example 4.1.

Example 4.1. Take Table 2 as a training sample table. Given cars y_1, y_2 and y_3 with attribute values listed in Table 7. We discuss which class each car might belong to.

Table 7. The attribute values of the cars

Car	Price	Mileage	Size	Max-Speed
y_1	*	High	Full	Low
y_2	*	*	Full	Low
y_3	*	*	*	High

We first calculate the similar set of y_i according to Table 1, that is, $S_{AT}(y_1) = \{x_1, x_2, x_6\}$, $S_{AT}(y_2) = \{x_1, x_2, x_6\}$, $S_{AT}(y_3) = \{x_3, x_4, x_5, x_6\}$. Then we get all the degrees of membership and non-membership listed in Table 8.

Table 8. The degrees of membership and non-membership of the car y_1

y_i	$A\mu_{D_1}(y_i)$	$A\gamma_{D_1}(y_i)$	$A\mu_{D_2}(y_i)$	$A\gamma_{D_2}(y_i)$	$A\mu_{D_3}(y_i)$	$A\gamma_{D_3}(y_i)$
y_1	2/3	0	0	1	0	2/3
y_2	2/3	0	0	1	0	2/3
y_3	0	1/4	1/4	3/4	0	1/4

For y_1, from Table 8, we see the degree of membership of $y_1 \in D_1$ is 2/3, and that of non-membership is 0; Let $\alpha = 0.5$, $\beta = -0.5$, according to Rule I,
$$A\mu_{D_1}(y_1) - A\gamma_{D_1}(y_1) = 2/3, \quad \text{decide} \quad y_1 \in POS(D_1);$$
$$A\mu_{D_2}(y_1) - A\gamma_{D_2}(y_1) = -1, \quad \text{decide} \quad y_1 \in NEG(D_2);$$
$$A\mu_{D_3}(y_1) - A\gamma_{D_3}(y_1) = -2/3, \quad \text{decide} \quad y_1 \in NEG(D_3).$$
Thus, we decide y_1 is a good car, y_1 is not a poor car, y_1 is not an excellent car.

For y_2 has the same degrees of membership and non-membership as y_1 in Table 8, we decide y_2 is good car, not a poor car and not an excellent car.

For y_3,
$$A\mu_{D_1}(y_3) - A\gamma_{D_1}(y_3) = -1/4, \quad \text{decide} \quad y_3 \in BND(D_1);$$
$$A\mu_{D_2}(y_3) - A\gamma_{D_2}(y_3) = -2/4, \quad \text{decide} \quad y_3 \in BND(D_2);$$
$$A\mu_{D_3}(y_3) - A\gamma_{D_3}(y_3) = -1/4, \quad \text{decide} \quad y_3 \in BND(D_3).$$
So, we can not decide whether y_3 is a good car or not, y_3 is a poor car or not, y_3 is an excellent car or not.

We also use Rule II to make decisions.
$$A\mu_{D_1}(y_1) = 2/3 > A\gamma_{D_1}(y_1), A\mu_{D_1}(y_1) > A\pi_{D_1}(y_1), \text{ decide } y_1 \in POS(D_1);$$
$$A\gamma_{D_2}(y_1) = 1 > A\mu_{D_2}(y_1), A\gamma_{D_2}(y_1) > A\pi_{D_2}(y_1), \text{ decide } y_1 \in NEG(D_2);$$
$$A\gamma_{D_3}(y_1) = 2/3 > A\mu_{D_3}(y_1), A\gamma_{D_3}(y_1) > A\pi_{D_3}(y_1), \text{ decide } y_1 \in NEG(D_3).$$
According to Rule II, y_1 is a good car, y_1 is not a poor car, y_1 is not an excellent car.

For y_2, we decide y_2 is a good car, not a poor car and not an excellent car for the same reason.

For y_3,

$A\pi_{D_1}(y_3) = 3/4 > A\mu_{D_1}(y_3), A\pi_{D_1}(y_3) > A\gamma_{D_1}(y_3)$, decide $y_3 \in BND(D_1)$;
$A\gamma_{D_2}(y_3) = 3/4 > A\mu_{D_2}(y_3), A\gamma_{D_2}(y_3) > A\pi_{D_2}(y_3)$, decide $y_3 \in NEG(D_2)$;
$A\pi_{D_3}(y_3) = 3/4 > A\mu_{D_3}(y_3), A\pi_{D_3}(y_3) > A\gamma_{D_3}(y_3)$, decide $y_3 \in BND(D_3)$.

So, it is not certain y_3 is a good car. It is certain y_3 is not a poor car.
It is not certain y_3 is an excellent car.

5   Conclusion

Three-way decision has been applied to many fields. It is a useful method to deal with uncertainty. Owing to the rampant existence of incomplete information systems in real life, it is significant to find a suitable way to make a reasonable decision from incomplete information systems. In this paper, intuitionistic fuzzy sets have been introduced in incomplete information systems, in which membership, non-membership and hesitancy degrees of an object belonging to a concept have been defined. Using the three degrees in the intuitionistic fuzzy sets, we have proposed evaluation functions to make three-way decisions. The study in this paper has put forward three-way decisions in incomplete information systems based on intuitionistic fuzzy sets.

Acknowledgement. This work was supported by a grant from the National Natural Science Foundation of China (No. 61602415).

References

1. Atanassov, K.: Intuitionistic fuzzy sets. Fuzzy Sets Syst. **20**, 87–96 (1986)
2. Azam, N., Yao, J.T.: Multiple criteria decision analysis with game-theoretic rough sets. In: Li, T., Nguyen, H.S., Wang, G., Grzymala-Busse, J., Janicki, R., Hassanien, A.E., Yu, H. (eds.) RSKT 2012. LNCS (LNAI), vol. 7414, pp. 399–408. Springer, Heidelberg (2012). doi:10.1007/978-3-642-31900-6_49
3. Cornelis, C., Cock, M.D., Kerre, E.E.: Intuitionistic fuzzy rough sets: at the crossroads of imperfect knowledge. Expert Syst. **20**, 260–270 (2003)
4. Grzymala-Busse, J.W., Yao, Y.Y.: Probabilistic rule induction with the LERS data mining system. Int. J. Intell. Syst. **26**, 518–539 (2011)
5. Herbert, J.P., Yao, J.T.: Game-theoretic rough sets. Fundamenta Informaticae **108**, 267–286 (2011)
6. Jena, S.P., Ghosh, S.K.: Intuitionistic fuzzy rough sets. Notes Intuitionistic Fuzzy Sets **8**, 1–18 (2002)
7. Jia, X., Zheng, K., Li, W., Liu, T., Shang, L.: Three-way decisions solution to filter spam email: an empirical study. In: Yao, J.T., Yang, Y., Słowiński, R., Greco, S., Li, H., Mitra, S., Polkowski, L. (eds.) RSCTC 2012. LNCS (LNAI), vol. 7413, pp. 287–296. Springer, Heidelberg (2012). doi:10.1007/978-3-642-32115-3_34
8. Kryszkiewicz, M.: Rough set approach to incomplete information systems. Inf. Sci. **112**, 39–49 (1998)
9. Kryszkiewicz, M.: Rules in incomplete information systems. Inf. Sci. **113**, 271–292 (1999)

10. Li, H.X., Zhou, X.Z.: Risk decision making based on decision-theoretic rough set: a three-way view decision model. Int. J. Comput. Intell. Syst. **4**, 1–11 (2011)
11. Li, W., Miao, D.Q., Wang, W.L., Zhang, N.: Hierarchical rough decision theoretic framework for text classification. In: Proceedings of the 9th IEEE International Conference on Cognitive Informatics, pp. 484–489 (2009)
12. Liu, D., Li, T.R., Li, H.X.: A multiple-category classification approach with decision-theoretic rough sets. Fundamenta Informaticae **115**, 173–188 (2012)
13. Liu, D., Liang, D., Wang, C.: A novel three-way decision model based on incomplete information system. Knowl.-Based Syst. **91**, 32–45 (2016)
14. Pawlak, Z.: Rough sets. Int. J. Comput. Inf. Sci. **11**, 341–356 (1982)
15. Radzikowska, A.M.: Rough approximation operations based on IF sets. In: Rutkowski, L., Tadeusiewicz, R., Zadeh, L.A., Żurada, J.M. (eds.) ICAISC 2006. LNCS (LNAI), vol. 4029, pp. 528–537. Springer, Heidelberg (2006). doi:10.1007/11785231_56
16. Wong, S.K.M., Ziarko, W.: A probabilistic model of approximate classification and decision rules with uncertainty in inductive learning, Technical report CS-85-23. University of Regina, Department of Computer Science (1985)
17. Wong, S.K.M., Ziarko, W.: Comparison of the probabilistic approximate classification and the fuzzy set model. Fuzzy Sets Syst. **21**, 357–362 (1987)
18. Yang, X.P., Yao, J.T.: Modelling multi-agent three-way decisions with decision-theoretic rough sets. Fundamenta Informaticae **115**, 157–171 (2012)
19. Yang, X.P., Lu, Z.J., Li, T.J.: Decision-theoretic rough sets in incomplete information system. Fundamenta Informaticae **126**, 353–375 (2013)
20. Yao, Y.Y., Wong, S.K.M.: A decision theoretic framework for approximating concepts. Int. J. Man-Mach. Stud. **37**, 793–809 (1992)
21. Yao, Y.: Decision-theoretic rough set models. In: Yao, J.T., Lingras, P., Wu, W.-Z., Szczuka, M., Cercone, N.J., Ślęzak, D. (eds.) RSKT 2007. LNCS (LNAI), vol. 4481, pp. 1–12. Springer, Heidelberg (2007). doi:10.1007/978-3-540-72458-2_1
22. Yao, Y.Y.: Probabilistic approaches to rough sets. Expert Syst. **20**, 287–297 (2003)
23. Yao, Y.Y.: Probabilistic rough set approximations. Int. J. Approx. Reason. **49**, 255–271 (2008)
24. Yao, Y.: Three-way decision: an interpretation of rules in rough set theory. In: Wen, P., Li, Y., Polkowski, L., Yao, Y., Tsumoto, S., Wang, G. (eds.) RSKT 2009. LNCS (LNAI), vol. 5589, pp. 642–649. Springer, Heidelberg (2009). doi:10.1007/978-3-642-02962-2_81
25. Yao, Y.: Three-way decisions with probabilistic rough sets. Inf. Sci. **180**, 341–353 (2010)
26. Yao, Y.: The superiority of three-way decisions in probabilistic rough set models. Inf. Sci. **181**, 1080–1096 (2011)
27. Yao, Y.: An outline of a theory of three-way decisions. In: Yao, J.T., Yang, Y., Słowiński, R., Greco, S., Li, H., Mitra, S., Polkowski, L. (eds.) RSCTC 2012. LNCS (LNAI), vol. 7413, pp. 1–17. Springer, Heidelberg (2012). doi:10.1007/978-3-642-32115-3_1
28. Yu, H., Chu, S.S., Yang, D.C.: Autonomous knowledge-oriented clustering using decision-theoretic rough set theory. Fundamenta Informaticae **115**, 141–156 (2012)
29. Zadeh, L.A.: Fuzzy sets. Inf. Control **8**, 338–353 (1965)
30. Zhou, L., Wu, W.-Z.: On generalized intuitionistic fuzzy rough approximation operators. Inf. Sci. **178**, 2448–2465 (2008)
31. Ziarko, W.: Variable precision rough set model. J. Comput. Syst. Sci. **46**, 39–50 (1993)
32. Ziarko, W.: Probabilistic approach to rough sets. Int. J. Approx. Reason. **49**, 272–284 (2008)

A Framework of Three-Way Cluster Analysis

Hong Yu[✉]

Chongqing Key Laboratory of Computational Intelligence,
Chongqing University of Posts and Telecommunications,
Chongqing 400065, China
yuhong@cqupt.edu.cn

Abstract. A new framework of clustering is proposed inspired by the theory of three-way decisions, which is an alternative formulation different from the ones used in the existing studies. The novel three-way representation intuitively shows which objects are fringe to the cluster and it is proposed for dealing with uncertainty clustering. Instead of using two regions to represent a cluster by a single set, a cluster is represented using three regions through a pair of sets, and there are three regions such as the core region, fringe region and trivial region. A cluster is therefore more realistically characterized by a set of core objects and a set of boundary objects. In this paper, we also illustrate an algorithm for incomplete data by using the proposed evaluation-based three-way cluster model. The preliminary experimental results show that the proposed method is effective for clustering incomplete data which is one kind of uncertainty data. Furthermore, this paper reviews some three-way clustering approaches and discusses some future perspectives and potential research topics based on the three-way cluster analysis.

Keywords: Clustering · Three-way decision theory · Uncertainty · Three-way clustering

1 Introduction

Clustering is a method that uses unsupervised learning and it has been widely applied to many areas such as information retrieval, image analysis, bioinformatics, networks structure analysis and a number of other applications [16]. Often, there is uncertainty in the real world. To take the social networks services as an example, the user's interests are changing and the interest community is also varied. The study of artificial intelligence and cognitive science had observed a well recognized feature of human intelligence, that is, in the cognition and treatment of real world problems, human often observe and analyze the same problem from different levels or different granularity. The process of clustering just reflects the process of making decision in different levels. That is, clustering is a process of deciding whether an object belongs to a cluster or not on a certain granularity level.

© Springer International Publishing AG 2017
L. Polkowski et al. (Eds.): IJCRS 2017, Part II, LNAI 10314, pp. 300–312, 2017.
DOI: 10.1007/978-3-319-60840-2_22

Let us take the objects in Fig. 1 as a universe. For the finest granularity clustering result, each object is taken as a single cluster. For a coarser granularity clustering result, the objects may be clustered in two classes. For the coarsest granularity clustering result, all objects are included in a large cluster. In the process of clustering, if the known information is enough, a certain clustering result corresponding to a granularity will be obtained; if the known information is not sufficient to judge whether an object belongs to a cluster, it needs further information to make decision.

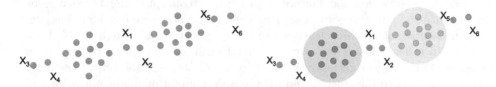

Fig. 1. Schematic diagram of a data set

Fig. 2. Schematic diagram of clustering (Color figure online)

Let us observe Fig. 1 again. When we observe the universe in view of a granularity level, we see that there are two distinct clusters, the red one and the yellow one shown in Fig. 2. Then, let us observe x_1 and x_2, they might belong to the red cluster, but it is also possible that they belong to the yellow cluster. One of the solving strategies is that an object "determinately" belongs to different clusters. In view of this strategy, it is often referred to some terminologies such as soft clustering, fuzzy clustering, or an overlapping clustering; in other words, an object can belong to different clusters. We continue to observe x_3 and x_4. It is absolutely reasonable that we assign them into the red cluster. It is the same to x_5 and x_6. The results are shown in Fig. 3 and it is a typical two-way result of overlapping (soft) clustering. Actually, this kind of clustering strategy is a two-way decision result, namely, it decides that an object belongs to a certain cluster or not belongs to this certain cluster. At present, researches are basically based on the two-way decisions. However, the two-way result can not intuitively reveal the fact that x_3 and x_4 are the fringe objects of the red cluster, the same to x_5 and x_6. By contrast, Fig. 4 depicts a three-way clustering result, where x_1, x_2, x_3 and x_4 are assigned into the fringe regions of the red cluster.

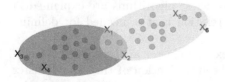

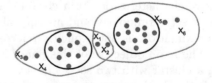

Fig. 3. The two-way clustering result (Color figure online)

Fig. 4. The three-way clustering result

One usually makes a decision based on available information and evidence. However, the information acquisition is usually a dynamic process. Since the current information is not sufficient, we can produce another solution to the uncertain clustering problem. For those objects which are difficult to make decision at present, we can put forward a two-way decisions result after game playing under the existing knowledge system; we can also produce a three-way decisions result, which makes decisions exactly for these objects which have enough information and waits for new information to make further decisions for those objects whose information is not sufficient. This is a typical idea of three-way decisions.

The three-way decision method represents a concept using three regions instead of two. This three-way decisions scheme has not been considered explicitly in theories of machine learning and rule induction, although it has been studied in other fields. There are three relationships between an object and a cluster: (1) the object certainly belongs to the cluster, (2) the object certainly does not belong to the cluster, and (3) the object might or might not belong to the cluster. It is a typical three-way decision processing to decide the relationship between an object and a cluster. Such relationships will inspire us to introduce the three-way decisions into the cluster analysis problem in this paper.

2   Related Work

A common assumption underlying many cluster analysis methods is that a cluster can be represented by a single set, where the boundary of the cluster is crisp. The crisp boundary leads to easy analytical results but may be too restrictive for some practical applications. Several proposals have been made to reduce such a stringent assumption.

In the fuzzy cluster analysis, it is assumed that a cluster is represented by a fuzzy set that models a gradually changing boundary [6]. However, a fuzzy clustering provides a quantitative characterization of the unclear cluster boundary at the expense of losing the qualitative characterization that better shows the structures provided by a clustering. To resolve this problem, Lingras and his associates [12,13] studied rough clustering and interval set clustering. Yao et al. [20] represented each cluster by an interval set instead of a single set as the representation of a cluster. Chen and Miao [3] described a clustering method by incorporating interval sets in the rough k-means. The basic idea of these work is to derive and describe a cluster by a pair of lower and upper bounds. By describing a cluster in terms of a pair of crisp sets, one recovers the qualitative characterization of a cluster. Most of these algorithms are explained in rough set terminology and an equivalence relation that is needed for defining approximations is not explicitly referred to.

The main objective of this paper is to extend cluster analysis by representing a cluster with two sets. This leads to the introduction of three-way cluster analysis. Furthermore, the strategy of three-way cluster analysis does not require an equivalence relation. Objects in the core region are typical elements of the cluster and objects in the fringe region are fringe elements of the cluster. That is, a cluster is more realistically characterized by a set of core objects and a set of fringe objects.

The essential ideas of three-way decisions are commonly used in everyday life and widely applied in many fields and disciplines including medical decision-making, social judgement theory, hypothesis testing in statistics, management sciences and peer review process. Therefore, Yao [17,18] introduced and studied the notion of three-way decisions, consisting of the positive, boundary and negative rules. Three-way decisions construct from three regions which are associated with different actions and decisions.

Recently, the three-way decisions approach has been achieved in some areas such as decision making [1,8–11], email spam filtering [31], clustering analysis [21, 22], and so on [2,7,19,26–28,30]. We also proposed some clustering approaches based on the three-way decisions [23–25]. In this paper, we first formalize the representation of a cluster with two sets, then we illustrate a clustering approach for incomplete data based on the proposed framework.

3 Framework of Three-Way Clustering

3.1 Representation of Three-Way Clustering

Let $U = \{x_1, \cdots, x_n, \cdots, x_N\}$ be a finite set, called the universe or the reference set. x_n is an object which has D attributes, namely, $x_n = (x_n^1, \cdots, x_n^d, \cdots, x_n^D)$. x_n^d denotes the value of the d-th attribute of the object x_n, where $n \in \{1, \cdots, N\}$, and $d \in \{1, \cdots, D\}$. The result of clustering scheme $\mathbf{C} = \{C^1, \cdots, C^k, \cdots, C^K\}$ is a family of clusters of the universe, in which K means this universe is composed of K clusters.

According to Vladimir Estivill-Castro, the notion of a "cluster" cannot be precisely defined, which is one of the reasons why there are so many clustering algorithms [4]. There is a common denominator: a group of data objects. Cluster analysis or clustering is the task of grouping a set of objects in such a way that objects in the same group (called a cluster) are more similar (in some sense or another) to each other than to those in other groups (clusters).

In the existing works, a cluster is usually represented by a single set, namely, $C^k = \{x_1^k, \cdots, x_i^k, \cdots, x_{|C^k|}^k\}$, abbreviated as C without ambiguous. From the view of making decisions, the representation of a single set means that, the objects in the set belong to this cluster definitely, the objects not in the set do not belong to this cluster definitely. This is a typical result of two-way decisions. For hard clustering, one object just belong to one cluster; for soft clustering, one object might belong to more than one cluster. However, this representation cannot show which objects might belong to this cluster, and it cannot show the degree of the object influence on the form of the cluster intuitively. As discussed before, the use of three regions to represent a cluster is more appropriate than the use of a crisp set, which also directly leads to three-way decisions based interpretation of clustering.

In contrast to the general crisp representation of a cluster, we represent a three-way cluster C as a pair of sets:

$$C = \{Co(C), Fr(C)\}. \tag{1}$$

Here, $Co(C) \subseteq U$ and $Fr(C) \subseteq U$. Let $Tr(C) = U - Co(C) - Fr(C)$. Then, $Co(C)$, $Fr(C)$ and $Tr(C)$ naturally form the three regions of a cluster as Core Region, Fringe Region and Trivial Region respectively. That is:

$$\begin{aligned} CoreRegion(C) &= Co(C), \\ FringeRegion(C) &= Fr(C), \\ TrivialRegion(C) &= U - Co(C) - Fr(C). \end{aligned} \tag{2}$$

If $\mathbf{x} \in CoreRegion(C)$, the object $\mathbf{x}$ belongs to the cluster C definitely; if $\mathbf{x} \in FringeRegion(C)$, the object $\mathbf{x}$ might belong to C; if $\mathbf{x} \in TrivialRegion(C)$, the object $\mathbf{x}$ does not belong to C definitely.

These subsets have the following properties.

$$\begin{aligned} U &= Co(C) \cup Fr(C) \cup Tr(C), \\ Co(C) &\cap Fr(C) = \emptyset, \\ Fr(C) &\cap Tr(C) = \emptyset, \\ Tr(C) &\cap Co(C) = \emptyset. \end{aligned} \tag{3}$$

If $Fr(C) = \emptyset$, the representation of C in Eq. (1) turns into $C = Co(C)$; it is a single set and $Tr(C) = U - Co(C)$. This is a representation of two-way decisions. In other words, the representation of a single set is a special case of the representation of three-way cluster.

Furthermore, according to Formula (3), we know that it is enough to represent expediently a cluster by the core region and the fringe region.

In another way, we can define a cluster scheme by the following properties:

$$\begin{aligned} &(i) \; Co(C^k) \neq \emptyset, 1 \leq k \leq K; \\ &(ii) \; \bigcup Co(C^k) \bigcup Fr(C^k) = U, 1 \leq k \leq K. \end{aligned} \tag{4}$$

Property (i) implies that a cluster cannot be empty. This makes sure that a cluster is physically meaningful. Property (ii) states that any object of U must definitely belong to or might belong to a cluster, which ensures that every object is properly clustered.

With respect to the family of clusters, $\mathbf{C}$, we have the following family of clusters formulated by three-way representation as:

$$\mathbf{C} = \{\{Co(C^1), Fr(C^1)\}, \cdots, \{Co(C^k), Fr(C^k)\}, \cdots, \{Co(C^K), Fr(C^K)\}\}. \tag{5}$$

Obviously, we have the following family of clusters formulated by two-way decisions as:

$$\mathbf{C} = \{Co(C^1), \cdots, Co(C^k), \cdots, Co(C^K)\}. \tag{6}$$

3.2 An Evaluation-Based Three-Way Cluster Model

In this subsection, we will introduce an evaluation-based three-way cluster model, which produces three regions by using an evaluation function and a pair of thresholds on the values of the evaluation function. The model partially addresses the issue of trisecting a universal set into three regions.

Suppose there are a pair of thresholds (α, β) and $\alpha \geq \beta$. Although evaluations based on a total order are restrictive, they have a computational advantage. One can obtain the three regions by simply comparing the evaluation value with a pair of thresholds. Based on the evaluation function $v(\mathbf{x})$, we get the following three-way decision rules:

$$
\begin{aligned}
Co(C^k) &= \{x \in U | v(\mathbf{x}) > \alpha\}, \\
Fr(C^k) &= \{x \in U | \beta \leq v(\mathbf{x}) \leq \alpha\}, \\
Tr(C^k) &= \{x \in U | v(\mathbf{x}) < \beta\}.
\end{aligned}
\tag{7}
$$

In fact, the evaluation function $v(\mathbf{x})$ can be a risk decision function, a similarity function and so on. In other words, the evaluation function will be specified accordingly when an algorithm is devised. We will give an algorithm as an example in Sect. 4 for clustering incomplete data, since incomplete data is a typical kind of uncertain data.

Objects in $Co(C^k)$ definitely belong to the cluster C^k, objects in $Tr(C^k)$ definitely do not belong to the cluster C^k, and objects in the region $Fr(C^k)$ might or might not belong to the cluster. For the objects in $Fr(C^k) \neq \emptyset$, we need more information to make decisions.

Under the representation, we can formulate the soft clustering and hard clustering as follows. For a clustering, if there exists $k \neq t$, such that

$$
\begin{aligned}
&(1)\ Co(C^k) \cap Co(C^t) \neq \emptyset, \ or \\
&(2)\ Fr(C^k) \cap Fr(C^t) \neq \emptyset, \ or \\
&(3)\ Co(C^k) \cap Fr(C^t) \neq \emptyset, \ or \\
&(4)\ Fr(C^k) \cap Co(C^t) \neq \emptyset,
\end{aligned}
\tag{8}
$$

we call it is a soft clustering; otherwise, it is a hard clustering.

As long as one condition from Eq. (8) is satisfied, there must exist at least one object belonging to more than one cluster.

4 An Algorithm for Incomplete Data Using the Three-Way Cluster Model

4.1 To Measure Distance Between Incomplete Objects

In this paper, we suppose we have the attribute significance degrees in advance. Of course, it is another interesting research issue, which is not discussed here for sake of space. Thus, we set the descending order of attribute importance degree to be $A = \{a_1, \cdots, a_D\}$, D is the number of attributes. Set $W = \{w_1, w_2, \cdots, w_d, \cdots, w_D\}$ be the set of attribute weights, and $w_1 \geq w_2 \geq \cdots \geq w_k \geq \cdots \geq w_D$.

Cluster analysis or clustering is the task of grouping a set of objects in such a way that objects in the same group are more similar to each other than to those in other groups. So how to measure the distance or similarity between objects is a key problem in cluster analysis. However, some common methods for computing similarity could not be used to calculate the similarity between incomplete data directly because of the missing values. The partial Euclidean distance formula [5, 14, 29] is used to measure the distance between the two incomplete data. But the formula only considers non-missing attributes and ignores the impact of missing values on similarity. Besides, Euclidean distance is not conducive to find the spherical structure.

Therefore, we proposed a new similarity measurement between incomplete data by improving the existing partial Euclidean distance formula. The proposed method considers the influence on similarity from the attribute importance as well as the missing rate. Let us consider the following situation, there are two incomplete data in far away distance in fact. The attribute values are similar on non-important attributes but different on important attributes. When the two objects miss a great deal of important attributes, the distance computed by the previous formula will be much less than the actually distance because the result might come from some non-important attributes. The inaccurate distance could seriously affect the effect of the clustering algorithm. In order to avoid this situation, the missing rate and the sum of missing attribute weight are added to the weighted partial Euclidean distance formula. Thus, the improved formula will drastically enlarge the distance when missing lots of important values. Similarly, the improved formula just increases the distance slightly when missing a small account of non-important values. Then, the improved partial Euclidean distance formula is given as follows:

$$Dist(\mathbf{x}_i, \mathbf{x}_j) = \frac{1}{\sum_{d=1}^{D} I_d w_d} \frac{\left(\sum_{d=1}^{D}(x_i^d - x_j^d)^2 I_d w_d^2\right)^{1/2}}{\left(\sum_{d=1}^{D}(x_i^d I_d w_d)^2\right)^{1/2} + \left(\sum_{d=1}^{D}(x_j^d I_d w_d)^2\right)^{1/2}} \quad (9)$$
$$+ W_{miss} \times MR,$$

where $I_d = \begin{cases} 1, x_d \neq * \wedge x_j^d \neq * \\ 0, else \end{cases}$, $*$ means the value is missing, and W_{miss} is the sum of attribute weights which are missing on $\mathbf{x}_i$ or $\mathbf{x}_j$, the formula is as follows:

$$W_{miss} = \sum_{x_i^d = * \vee x_j^d = *} w_d. \quad (10)$$

MR is the joint miss rate of object $\mathbf{x}_i$ and $\mathbf{x}_j$. It is the proportion of the number of missing attributes on the total number of attributes as follows: $MR = \frac{\sum_{d=1}^{D} MI_d}{D}$, where $MI_d = \begin{cases} 1, x_i^d = * \vee x_j^d = * \\ 0, else \end{cases}$.

If there is no missing value on the two objects, the proposed formula is the tradition Euclidean distance formula.

4.2   The Algorithm Based on Three-Way Cluster Framework

So far, Formula 9 can be used as the evaluation function in applications. However, we find that the property of clustering is not good enough as required. Thus, we proposed to divide the incomplete data into four types such as sufficient data, valuable data, inadequate data and invalid data according to the concept of complete degree in [23]. In this paper, we continue the sort thought except further working on the measurement of similarity as described in the last subsection.

The proposed three-way clustering algorithm for incomplete data is depicted in Algorithm 1: the three-way clustering algorithm for incomplete data, shorted by TWD-ID. We first divide the data set to four subset, i.e., sufficient data, valuable data, inadequate data and invalid data. Generally speaking, sufficient data have more information. Thus, we find the center of K clusters in the sufficient data set. In fact, there are a bunch of clustering approaches to determine the center. In our experiments, we adopt the outstanding density peaks clustering method in the reference [15]. So, the left work is to decide the left objects where to go. Step 4 describes how to decide the left objects in sufficient data, and Step 5 describes how to decide the other types data.

Algorithm 1. the three-way clustering algorithm for incomplete data

---

Input: U, $W = \{w_1, w_2, \cdots, w_D\}$, K, α, β, R_{th1};
Output: $\mathbf{C} = \{\{Co(C^1), Fr(C^1)\}, \cdots, \{Co(C^K), Fr(C^K)\}\}$.
Step 1: divide the incomplete data set into four subsets according to the concept of complete degree in [25];
Step 2: compute the distance matrix between objects using Eq. (9);
Step 3: obtain the K center of clusters using the method [17] in the sufficient data subset;
Step 4: compute the local density for each remaining sufficient data point and sort the local densities in descending order; and assign the remaining sufficient data to the core region of the cluster which is its nearest neighbor of highest density;
Step 5: decide the rest of objects to the core region or fringe region of the corresponding cluster according to the three-way decision rules [112].

There could be many missing values in important attributes in the valuable data, inadequate data and invalid data, it is often that the common strategy of filling values may cause new uncertainty. Thus, it is more reasonable that we assign the incomplete data to the fringe regions of clusters waiting more information to help further decision than assign them arbitrarily to the core region or trivial region, when decision information is insufficient or the object just meet the divided condition to the fringe region.

In order to make decisions on these data, we find the neighbors $X_{i-Neighbor}$ within the neighbor radius R_{th} of the object $\mathbf{x}_i$ first, where $X_{i-Neighbor} = \{\mathbf{x}_j | Dist(\mathbf{x}_i, \mathbf{x}_j) \leqslant R_{th}\}$. Then, the object $\mathbf{x}_i$ is assigned to the core region or fringe region of the corresponding clusters according to the proportion of each cluster in the neighbor objects set $X_{i-Neighbor}$. That is, the proportion is defined as follows:

$$P(X_{i-Neighbor}|C^k) = \frac{\left|\{\mathbf{x}_j|\mathbf{x}_j \in X_{i-Neighbor} \wedge \mathbf{x}_j \in C^k\}\right|}{|X_{i-Neighbor}|} \qquad (11)$$

According to the above formula, the three-way decision rules are given as follows:

$$\begin{aligned}
&if \ P(X_{i-Neighbor}|C^k) \geq \alpha, \ the \ object \ is \ decided \ to \ Co(C^k);\\
&if \ \beta < P(X_{i-Neighbor}|C^k) < \alpha, \ the \ object \ is \ decided \ to \ Fr(C^k); \qquad (12)\\
&if \ P(X_{i-Neighbor}|C^k) \leqslant \beta, \ the \ objecis \ decided \ to \ Tr(C^k).
\end{aligned}$$

How to decide the threshold α and β automatically is still an unsolved problem. We can decide the thresholds by experience or through active learning method.

4.3 Experimental Results

In this subsection, we validate the proposed method TWD-ID on three UCI repository [32] data sets with some classical clustering strategies for incomplete data such as WDS-FCM, PDS-FCM, OCS-FCM, NPS-FCM [5] and NNI-FCM [29]. All the experiments are performed on a 3.2 GHz computer with 4 GB memory, and all algorithms are programmed in C++. The quality of the final clustering is evaluated by the traditional indices such as the Accuracy and F-measure, where the objects in fringe regions are deemed to be core regions to fit these common formulae.

In order to reflect the effect of the missing rate on the performance of algorithms, the incomplete data set is constructed randomly according to the 10%, 15% and 20% missing rate. To avoid the effect by the distribution of missing data, we test 10 times by generating different incomplete data sets randomly for each UCI data set. The mean and standard deviation of the results for 10 times under each missing rate are recorded in the following tables, where $\alpha = 0.7$ and $\beta = 0.45$ (Tables 1, 2 and 3).

Table 1. Experimental results on the iris data set

Algorithm	Miss rate					
	10%		15%		20%	
	Accuracy	F-measure	Accuracy	F-measure	Accuracy	F-measure
TWD-ID	$\mathbf{0.914 \pm 0.031}$	$\mathbf{0.913 \pm 0.035}$	$\mathbf{0.917 \pm 0.038}$	$\mathbf{0.915 \pm 0.041}$	$\mathbf{0.893 \pm 0.019}$	$\mathbf{0.888 \pm 0.020}$
WDS-FCM	0.583 ± 0.020	0.586 ± 0.022	0.468 ± 0.036	0.476 ± 0.036	0.464 ± 0.069	0.447 ± 0.092
PDS-FCM	0.898 ± 0.006	0.897 ± 0.006	0.892 ± 0.012	0.891 ± 0.012	0.889 ± 0.008	0.888 ± 0.007
OCS-FCM	0.883 ± 0.015	0.882 ± 0.014	0.858 ± 0.073	0.846 ± 0.108	0.867 ± 0.026	0.866 ± 0.027
NPS-FCM	0.869 ± 0.020	0.868 ± 0.021	0.845 ± 0.024	0.844 ± 0.024	0.807 ± 0.067	0.800 ± 0.076
NNI-FCM	0.900 ± 0.014	0.899 ± 0.014	0.889 ± 0.020	0.889 ± 0.019	0.811 ± 0.073	0.802 ± 0.083

Table 2. Experimental results on the page blocks data set

Algorithm	Miss rate					
	10%		15%		20%	
	Accuracy	F-measure	Accuracy	F-measure	Accuracy	F-measure
TWD-ID	**0.825 ± 0.064**	**0.827 ± 0.033**	**0.802 ± 0.063**	**0.811 ± 0.037**	**0.810 ± 0.069**	**0.810 ± 0.069**
WDS-FCM	0.607 ± 0.006	0.688 ± 0.004	0.710 ± 0.051	0.755 ± 0.032	0.772 ± 0.061	0.790 ± 0.036
PDS-FCM	0.690 ± 0.013	0.743 ± 0.007	0.689 ± 0.006	0.743 ± 0.004	0.691 ± 0.014	0.744 ± 0.008
OCS-FCM	0.652 ± 0.020	0.720 ± 0.013	0.613 ± 0.017	0.693 ± 0.012	0.583 ± 0.023	0.671 ± 0.018
NPS-FCM	0.668 ± 0.028	0.729 ± 0.017	0.656 ± 0.045	0.721 ± 0.029	0.648 ± 0.048	0.716 ± 0.031
NNI-FCM	0.717 ± 0.005	0.758 ± 0.003	0.697 ± 0.033	0.746 ± 0.021	0.692 ± 0.024	0.743 ± 0.014

Table 3. Experimental results on the pendigits data set

Algorithm	Miss rate					
	10%		15%		20%	
	Accuracy	F-measure	Accuracy	F-measure	Accuracy	F-measure
TWD-ID	**0.753 ± 0.035**	**0.731 ± 0.043**	**0.746 ± 0.033**	**0.727 ± 0.041**	**0.737 ± 0.037**	**0.717 ± 0.048**
WDS-FCM	0.331 ± 0.023	0.280 ± 0.024	0.323 ± 0.021	0.242 ± 0.023	0.319 ± 0.030	0.242 ± 0.026
PDS-FCM	0.663 ± 0.031	0.623 ± 0.033	0.689 ± 0.025	0.660 ± 0.036	0.676 ± 0.028	0.641 ± 0.041
OCS-FCM	0.539 ± 0.081	0.465 ± 0.099	0.464 ± 0.050	0.385 ± 0.061	0.369 ± 0.050	0.268 ± 0.055
NPS-FCM	0.630 ± 0.024	0.575 ± 0.028	0.581 ± 0.034	0.518 ± 0.044	0.530 ± 0.056	0.465 ± 0.066
NNI-FCM	0.489 ± 0.046	0.412 ± 0.051	0.481 ± 0.043	0.408 ± 0.051	0.421 ± 0.050	0.324 ± 0.064

The experiment results show that the proposed method is appropriate for clustering uncertainty data such as incomplete data. Besides, the accuracy and F-measure of the proposed algorithm are higher than the compared algorithms in the experiments.

5   Discussions

This paper aims at presenting an interpretation of three-way clustering for uncertainty clustering. The existing work usually represents a cluster with a single set and it is a typical result of two-way decisions. That is, objects in the set belong to the cluster definitely and objects not in the set do not belong to the cluster definitely. There are two regions to describe a cluster. In the proposed framework, we use three regions to represent a cluster inspired by the theory of three-way decisions. Objects in the core region belong to the cluster definitely, objects in the trivial region do not belong to the cluster definitely and objects in fringe region are the boundary elements of the cluster. The representation not only shows which objects just belong to this cluster but also shows which objects might belong to the cluster intuitively.

Through the further work on the fringe region, we can know the degree of an object influences on the form of the cluster intuitively, which is very helpful in some practical applications. Furthermore, an evaluation-based three-way cluster model and an algorithm for clustering incomplete data based on the proposed model are introduced.

In the following paper, I will summarize and conclude the paper with listing some important issues and research trends about the three-way clustering.

- Representation of three-way clustering. There are some work had been proposed in view of interval sets, decision-theoretic rough sets [22]. We can also represent the model of three-way clustering by using fuzzy set, shadow set and other models. Different interpretations of three-way clustering could give different solutions to different kinds of clustering problems.
- How to get the three-way clustering. It is a good way to extend from the classical two-way decision clustering approaches. The following properties are important to the efficiency and effectiveness of a novel algorithm: how to decide the thresholds, how to know the truth number of clusters.
- Developing new clustering approaches for more uncertainty situations such as dynamic, incomplete data or multi-source data. For example, we had done some preliminary work [23, 25].
- Application of three regions. We can put forward the three-way clustering strategy to the application fields such as social network services, cyber marketing, E-commerce, recommendation service and other fields.

Acknowledgments. I am grateful to Professor Yiyu Yao for his suggestions, and I would like to thank Ms. Ting Su for her help to complete the experimental work. In addition, this work was supported in part by the National Natural Science Foundation of China under grant No. 61379114 and No. 61533020.

References

1. Azam, N., Yao, J.T.: Analyzing uncertainties of probabilistic rough set regions with game-theoretic rough sets. Int. J. Approx. Reason. **55**(1), 142–155 (2014)
2. Chen, H.M., Li, T.R., Luo, C., Horng, S., Wang, G.Y.: A decision-theoretic rough set approach for dynamic data mining. IEEE Trans. Fuzzy Syst. **99**(1) (2015). doi:10.1109/TFUZZ.2014.2387877
3. Chen, M., Miao, D.Q.: Interval set clustering. Expert Syst. Appl. **38**(4), 2923–2932 (2011)
4. Estivill-Castro, V.: Why so many clustering algorithms: a position paper. ACM SIGKDD Explor. Newsl. **4**(1), 65–75 (2002)
5. Hathaway, R.J., Bezdek, J.C.: Fuzzy C-means clustering of incomplete data. IEEE Trans. Syst. Man Cybern. Part B (Cybern.) **31**(5), 735–744 (2001)
6. Höppner, F., Klawonn, F., Kruse, R., Runkler, T.: Fuzzy Cluster Analysis: Methods for Classification, Data Analysis and Image Recognition. Wiley, Chichester (1999)
7. Li, H.X., Zhou, X.Z.: Risk decision making based on decision-theoretic rough set: a three-way view decision model. Int. J. Comput. Intell. Syst. **4**(1), 1–11 (2011)
8. Li, Y., Zhang, Z., Chen, W.B., Min, F.: TDUP: an approach to incremental mining of frequent itemsets with three-way-decision pattern updating. Int. J. Mach. Learn. Cybern. **8**(1), 441–453 (2015)
9. Liang, D.C., Xu, Z.S., Liu, D.: Three-way decisions with intuitionistic fuzzy decision-theoretic rough sets based on point operators. Inf. Sci. **375**, 183–201 (2017)
10. Liang, D.C., Liu, D.: A novel risk decision-making based on decision-theoretic rough sets under hesitant fuzzy information. J. IEEE Trans. Fuzzy Syst. **23**(2), 237–247 (2015)

11. Liu, D., Liang, D.C., Wang, C.C.: A novel three-way decision model based on incomplete information system. Knowl. Based Syst. **91**, 32–45 (2016)
12. Lingras, P., Yan, R.: Interval clustering using fuzzy and rough set theory. In: Proceedings of the 2004 IEEE Annual Meeting of the Fuzzy Information, Banff, Alberta, pp. 780–784 (2004)
13. Lingras, P., West, C.: Interval set clustering of web users with rough K-means. J. Intell. Inf. Syst. **23**(1), 5–16 (2004)
14. Lu, C., Song, S., Wu, C.: K-nearest neighbor intervals based AP clustering algorithm for large incomplete data. Math. Probl. Eng. **2015** (2015). http://dx.doi.org/10.1155/2015/535932
15. Rodriguez, A., Laio, A.: Clustering by fast search and find of density peaks. Science **344**(6191), 1492–1496 (2014)
16. Xu, R., Wunsch, D.: Survey of clustering algorithms. IEEE Trans. Neural Netw. **16**(3), 645–678 (2005)
17. Yao, Y.: An outline of a theory of three-way decisions. In: Yao, J.T., Yang, Y., Słowiński, R., Greco, S., Li, H., Mitra, S., Polkowski, L. (eds.) RSCTC 2012. LNCS, vol. 7413, pp. 1–17. Springer, Heidelberg (2012). doi:10.1007/978-3-642-32115-3_1
18. Yao, Y.: Three-way decisions and cognitive computing. Cogn. Comput. (2016). doi:10.1007/s12559-016-9397-5
19. Yao, Y.: Interval sets and three-way concept analysis in incomplete contexts. Int. J. Mach. Learn. Cybern. **8**(1), 3–20 (2017)
20. Yao, Y.Y., Lingras, P., Wang, R.Z., Miao, D.Q.: Interval set cluster analysis: a reformulation. Rough Sets. Fuzzy Sets, Data Mining and Granular Computing, pp. 398–405. Springer, Berlin Heidelberg (2009). doi:10.1007/978-3-642-10646-0_48
21. Yu, H., Jiao, P., Yao, Y.Y., Wang, G.Y.: Detecting and refining overlapping regions in complex networks with three-way decisions. Inf. Sci. **373**, 21–41 (2016)
22. Yu, H., Liu, Z.G., Wang, G.Y.: An automatic method to determine the number of clusters using decision-theoretic rough set. Int. J. Approx. Reason. **55**, 101–115 (2014)
23. Yu, H., Su, T., Zeng, X.: A three-way decisions clustering algorithm for incomplete data. In: Miao, D., Pedrycz, W., Ślęzak, D., Peters, G., Hu, Q., Wang, R. (eds.) RSKT 2014. LNCS, vol. 8818, pp. 765–776. Springer, Cham (2014). doi:10.1007/978-3-319-11740-9_70
24. Yu, H., Wang, Y.: Three-way decisions method for overlapping clustering. In: Yao, J.T., Yang, Y., Słowiński, R., Greco, S., Li, H., Mitra, S., Polkowski, L. (eds.) RSCTC 2012. LNCS, vol. 7413, pp. 277–286. Springer, Heidelberg (2012). doi:10.1007/978-3-642-32115-3_33
25. Yu, H., Zhang, C., Wang, G.Y.: A tree-based incremental overlapping clustering method using the three-way decision theory. Knowl.-Based Syst. **91**, 189–203 (2016)
26. Yu, H., Wang, G.Y., Li, T.R., Liang, J.Y., Miao, D.Q., Yao, Y.Y.: Three-way Decisions: Methods and Practices for Complex Problem Solving. Science Press, Beijing (2015). (in Chinese)
27. Zhang, H.R., Min, F., Shi, B.: Regression-based three-way recommendation. Inf. Sci. **378**, 444–461 (2017)
28. Zhang, Y., Zou, H., Chen, X., Wang, X., Tang, X., Zhao, S.: Cost-sensitive three-way decisions model based on CCA. In: Cornelis, C., Kryszkiewicz, M., Ślęzak, D., Ruiz, E.M., Bello, R., Shang, L. (eds.) RSCTC 2014. LNCS, vol. 8536, pp. 172–180. Springer, Cham (2014). doi:10.1007/978-3-319-08644-6_18

29. Zhang, L., Li, B., Zhang, L., Li, D.: Fuzzy clustering of incomplete data based on missing attribute interval size. In: 2015 IEEE 9th International Conference on Anticounterfeiting, Security, and Identification (ASID), pp. 101–104. IEEE (2015)
30. Zhang, Y., Yao, J.T.: Gini objective functions for three-way classifications. Int. J. Approx. Reason. **81**, 103–114 (2017)
31. Zhou, B., Yao, Y., Luo, J.G.: Cost-sensitive three-way email spam filtering. J. Intell. Inf. Syst. **42**, 19–45 (2013)
32. UCI Machine Learning Repository. http://archive.ics.uci.edu/ml

A Semi-supervised Three-Way Clustering Framework for Multi-view Data

Hong Yu$^{(\boxtimes)}$, Xincheng Wang, and Guoyin Wang

Chongqing Key Laboratory of Computational Intelligence,
Chongqing University of Posts and Telecommunications,
Chongqing 400065, People's Republic of China
yuhong@cqupt.edu.cn

Abstract. A new semi-supervised clustering framework for uncertain multi-view data is proposed inspired by the theory of three-way decisions, which is an alternative formulation different from the ones used in the existing studies. A cluster is represented by three regions such as the core region, fringe region and trivial region. The three-way representation intuitively shows which objects are fringe to the cluster. The proposed method is an iterative processing which includes two parts: (1) the three-way spectral clustering algorithm which is devised to obtain the three-way representation result; and (2) the active learning strategy which is designed to obtain the prior supervision information from the fringe regions, and the pairwise constraints information is used to adjust the similarity matrix between objects. Experimental results show that the proposed method can cluster multi-view data effectively and is better in performances than the compared single-view clusterings and other semi-supervised clustering approaches.

Keywords: Multi-view data · Three-way decisions · Semi-supervised clustering · Spectral clustering · Active learning

1 Introduction

In some applications such as computer video, social computing, and multimedia area, objects are usually represented in several different ways. This kind of data is termed as the multi-view data. Multi-view clustering, which is also one kind of multi-view learning, has attracted more and more attentions [1–3,12,19]. In the existing methods, spectral clustering [4,13] is a popular one for multi-view data because it represents multi-view data via graph structure and makes it possible to handle complex data such as high-dimensional and heterogeneous as well as it can easily use the pairwise constraint information provided by users. Therefore, some scholars research on spectral clustering for multi-view data [5,8,17].

Generally speaking, there are two types of typical prior supervised information, namely, class labels and pairwise constraints [5,6,16]. In practice, it is difficult to obtain the independent class labels, yet it could be relatively easy to ensure correlated or uncorrelated information among data objects. Therefore,

© Springer International Publishing AG 2017
L. Polkowski et al. (Eds.): IJCRS 2017, Part II, LNAI 10314, pp. 313–325, 2017.
DOI: 10.1007/978-3-319-60840-2_23

pairwise constraints describe two objects whether they should be assigned to the same class or the different classes. However, choosing the supervised information is random in most of existing methods, and it does not produce positive effect on improving the clustering result when the algorithm itself can find the prior information or there are amounts of noises in the prior information. Therefore, the active learning method is introduced to optimize the selection of the constraints for semi-supervised clustering [15, 18, 28].

Most of the existing researches on the topic has focused on selecting an initial set of pairwise constraints before performing semi-supervised clustering. This is not suitable if we wish to iteratively improve the clustering model by actively querying users. In fact, many clustering approaches are based on iterative framework. Obviously, it is much better in each iteration that we determine objects with the most important information toward improving the current clustering result and form queries accordingly than just choosing the information randomly. The responses to the queries (i.e., constraints) are then used to update the clustering. This process repeats until we reach the stop conditions. Such an iterative framework is widely used in active learning for semi-supervised clustering.

In this paper, we focus on how to improve the quality of clustering for multi-view data with the aid of pairwise constraints. Therefore, we propose a semi-supervised clustering framework based on active learning by using three-way decisions. In order to further choosing the supervision information during the iterative processing, we introduce the idea of three-way decisions into this work, inspired by the three-way decisions theory as suggested by Yao [21, 22]. Three-way decisions extend binary-decisions in order to overcome some drawbacks of binary-decisions. The basic ideas of three-way decisions have been widely used in real-world decision-making problems, such as decision making [23], email spam filtering [29], three-way investment decisions [9] and many others [25]. Interval sets provide an ideal mechanism to represent soft clustering. Lingras and Yan [10] introduced interval sets to represent clusters. Lingras and West [11] proposed an interval set clustering method with rough k-means for mining clusters of web visitors. Yao et al. [20] represented each cluster by an interval set instead of a single set as the representation of a cluster. Inspired by these results, we have introduced a framework of three-way cluster analysis [26, 27].

In our work, a three-way representation for a cluster is presented, where a cluster is represented by three regions, i.e., the core region, fringe region and trivial region, instead of two regions as the other existing methods. Objects in the core region are typical elements of the cluster, objects in the fringe region are fringe elements of the cluster, and objects in the trivial region do not belong to the cluster definitely. A cluster is therefore more realistically characterized by a set of core objects and a set of boundary objects. The three-way representation intuitively shows which objects are fringe to the cluster. Thus, we can reduce the search space to the fringe regions when selecting the pairwise constraints. The basic idea of the work is to propose an iterative processing, in which a three-way clustering algorithm is devised to obtain the three-way clustering result and an active learning strategy is designed to obtain the prior supervision information from the fringe regions.

The remainder of this paper is organized as follows. Section 2 introduces some basic concepts. Section 3 describes the proposed framework, the three-way spectral clustering algorithm and the active learning strategy. Section 4 reports the results of comparative experiments and conclusions are provided in Sect. 5.

2 Preliminaries

In this section, some basic concepts of multi-view and semi-supervised clustering are introduced.

2.1 Multi-view Data

In the multi-view setting, an object (data point) $\mathbf{x}$ is described with several different disjoint sets of features. Let $X = \{\mathbf{x}_1, \cdots, \mathbf{x}_i, \cdots, \mathbf{x}_N\}$ be a universe with N objects. There are H numbers of views to describe the objects, and $X^{(1)}, X^{(2)}, \cdots, X^{(h)}, \cdots, X^{(H)}$ be the data matrix of each view respectively.

For h-th view, $X^{(h)} \in \mathbb{R}^{N \times d^{(h)}}$, and $d^{(h)}$ is the feature dimension of the h-th view. $X^{(h)} = \{\mathbf{x}_1^{(h)}, \mathbf{x}_2^{(h)}, \cdots, \mathbf{x}_i^{(h)}, \cdots, \mathbf{x}_N^{(h)}\}$, where $\mathbf{x}_i^{(h)} = (x_{i,h}^1, x_{i,h}^2, \cdots, x_{i,h}^j, \cdots, x_{i,h}^{d^{(h)}})$ is its i-th object, and $x_{i,h}^j$ is the j-th feature of i-th object in the h-th view.

2.2 Pairwise Constraints

Pairwise constraints is one kind of typical prior information for semi-supervised clustering. Wagstaff and Cardie [14] introduce must-link (positive association) and cannot-link (negative association) to reflect the constraint relations between the data points.

For the universe $X = \{\mathbf{x}_1, \cdots, \mathbf{x}_i, \cdots, \mathbf{x}_N\}$, let $Y = \{y_1, \cdots, y_i, \cdots, y_N\}$ be the class labels of objects respectively. Must-link constraint requires that the two points must belong to the same cluster, and this relation is denoted by $ML = \{(\mathbf{x}_i, \mathbf{x}_j) \mid y_i = y_j, \; for \; i \neq j, \mathbf{x}_i, \mathbf{x}_j \in X, y_i, y_j \in Y\}$. Cannot-link constraint requires that the two points must belong to different clusters, and this relation is denoted by $CL = \{(\mathbf{x}_p, \mathbf{x}_q) \mid y_p \neq y_q, \; for \; p \neq q, \; \mathbf{x}_p, \mathbf{x}_q \in X, y_p, y_q \in Y\}$. Klein et al. [7] found that must-link constraint has the transitivity properties on objects, namely, for $\mathbf{x}_i, \mathbf{x}_j, \mathbf{x}_k \in X$,

$$
\begin{aligned}
(\mathbf{x}_i, \mathbf{x}_j) \in ML \; \& \; (\mathbf{x}_j, \mathbf{x}_k) \in ML \Rightarrow (\mathbf{x}_i, \mathbf{x}_k) \in ML, \\
(\mathbf{x}_i, \mathbf{x}_j) \in ML \; \& \; (\mathbf{x}_j, \mathbf{x}_k) \in CL \Rightarrow (\mathbf{x}_i, \mathbf{x}_k) \in CL.
\end{aligned}
\tag{1}
$$

In fact, simply using the constraint information in the algorithm may cause a deflection problem of the singular points during the clustering process. The so-called deflection of singular points is that the points belonging to ML are assigned to CL or the points belonging to CL are assigned to ML. Therefore, it is not always true that there are more pairwise constraints the better the clustering result is. We hope to obtain the best possible result with fewer constraints which is just the purpose of active learning.

2.3   Representation of Three-Way Clustering

The purpose of clustering is to divide the N objects of a universe X into some clusters. If there are K clusters, the family of clusters, $\mathbf{C}$, is represented as $\mathbf{C} = \{C_1, \cdots, C_k, \cdots, C_K\}$. A cluster is usually represented by a single set in the existing works, namely, $C_k = \{\mathbf{x}_1, \cdots, \mathbf{x}_i, \cdots, \mathbf{x}_{|C_k|}\}$, and it is abbreviated as C by removing the subscript when there is no ambiguity. From the view of making decisions, the representation of a single set means that, the objects in the set belong to this cluster definitely, the objects not in the set do not belong to this cluster definitely. This is a typical result of two-way decisions. For hard clustering, one object just belong to one cluster; for soft clustering, one object might belong to more than one cluster. However, this representation cannot show which objects might belong to this cluster, and it cannot show the degree of the object influence on the form of the cluster intuitively. Thus, the use of three regions to represent a cluster is more appropriate than the use of a crisp set, which also directly leads to three-way decisions based interpretation of clustering.

In contrast to the general crisp representation of a cluster, we represent a three-way cluster C as a pair of sets:

$$C = (Co(C), Fr(C)). \tag{2}$$

Here, $Co(C) \subseteq X$ and $Fr(C) \subseteq X$. Let $Tr(C) = X - Co(C) - Fr(C)$. Then, $Co(C)$, $Fr(C)$ and $Tr(C)$ naturally form the three regions of a cluster as Core Region, Fringe Region and Trivial Region respectively. That is:

$$\begin{aligned}
CoreRegion(C) &= Co(C), \\
FringeRegion(C) &= Fr(C), \\
TrivialRegion(C) &= X - Co(C) - Fr(C).
\end{aligned} \tag{3}$$

If $\mathbf{x} \in CoreRegion(C)$, the object $\mathbf{x}$ belongs to the cluster C definitely; if $\mathbf{x} \in FringeRegion(C)$, the object $\mathbf{x}$ might belong to C; if $\mathbf{x} \in TrivialRegion(C)$, the object $\mathbf{x}$ does not belong to C definitely.

These subsets have the following properties.

$$\begin{aligned}
X &= Co(C) \cup Fr(C) \cup Tr(C), \\
Co(C) &\cap Fr(C) = \emptyset, \\
Fr(C) &\cap Tr(C) = \emptyset, \\
Tr(C) &\cap Co(C) = \emptyset.
\end{aligned} \tag{4}$$

If $Fr(C) = \emptyset$, the representation of C in Eq. (2) turns into $C = Co(C)$; it is a single set and $Tr(C) = X - Co(C)$. This is a representation of two-way decisions. In other words, the representation of a single set is a special case of the representation of three-way cluster.

Furthermore, according to Eq. (4), we know that it is enough to represent a cluster expediently by the core region and the fringe region.

In another way, we can define a cluster by the following properties:

$$\begin{aligned}
&(i) \ Co(C_k) \neq \emptyset, 1 \leq k \leq K; \\
&(ii) \ \bigcup Co(C_k) \bigcup Fr(C_k) = X, 1 \leq k \leq K.
\end{aligned} \tag{5}$$

Property (i) implies that a cluster cannot be empty. This makes sure that a cluster is physically meaningful. Property (ii) states that any object of X must definitely belong to or might belong to a cluster, which ensures that every object is properly clustered.

With respect to the family of clusters, $\mathbf{C}$, we have the following family of clusters formulated by three-way decisions as:

$$\mathbf{C} = \{(Co(C_1), Fr(C_1)), \cdots, (Co(C_k), Fr(C_k)), \cdots, (Co(C_K), Fr(C_K))\}. \quad (6)$$

Obviously, we have the following family of clusters formulated by two-way decisions as:

$$\mathbf{C} = \{Co(C_1), \cdots, Co(C_k), \cdots, Co(C_K)\}. \quad (7)$$

3 The Proposed Semi-supervised Clustering Method

In this section, a semi-supervised three-way clustering framework for multi-view data is proposed. The three-way spectral clustering algorithm and the active learning strategy are described.

3.1 The Framework

The proposed semi-supervised three-way clustering framework for multi-view data (or SS-TWC, for short) is shown in Fig. 1, which is an iterative processing. In short, the framework consists of two parts, i.e., the three-way clustering and the active learning. The main goal of Part 1 is to produce the clustering result in three-way representation. In other words, the other clustering algorithm also works as long as we alter it to adopt to the three-way representation. The task of Part 2 is to choose some objects (points) to query experts. The responses to the queries (i.e., constraints) are then used to update the clustering in Part 1.

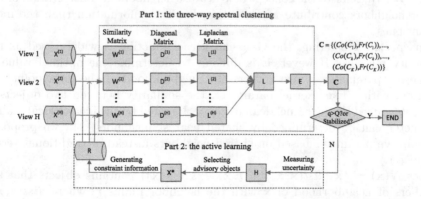

Fig. 1. SS-TWC: semi-supervised three-way clustering framework for multi-view data

In this paper, the spectral clustering approach is used to produce the three-way clustering in Part 1. The framework of three-way spectral clustering algorithm is described in Algorithm 1 in Subsect. 3.2. The algorithm computes on the multiple views $X^{(1)}, X^{(2)}, \cdots, X^{(H)}$, to find a low-dimensional feature space E of original data points by calculating eigenvectors of fused Laplacian matrix L. In order to obtain more accurate partitions, uncertain objects are assigned to the fringe region of corresponding cluster. For these uncertain objects, they can get further decision when information is sufficient.

In Part 2, the SS-TWC uses the active learning method to learn dynamically objects with most important information toward improving the current clustering result. The framework of active learning algorithm is described in Algorithm 2 in Subsect. 3.3. In each iteration, the active learning measures uncertain objects in fringe regions with a certain strategy. The produced pairwise constraints information is applied to adjust the similarity matrix between data points in Algorithm 1, which makes objects being more compact in one cluster and more discrete in different clusters.

We need to note that the final result of clustering can be expressed by two-way or three-way representation according to the user demands. In the framework, the result of the first iteration is in three-way representation, and the fringe regions reduce after processing iterations. In each iteration, we query experts to acquire the prior information by choosing the objects from fringe regions. The algorithm obtains the two-way clustering result finally when the iteration is going on until the fringe regions are empty, which is the results in our experiments. The algorithm also can obtain the three-way clustering result finally, if it stops when the clustering result is stable or the iterative times q reaches the maximum number Q.

3.2   The Three-Way Spectral Clustering

First, we need to map the data set $X = \{\mathbf{x}_1, \cdots, \mathbf{x}_i, \cdots, \mathbf{x}_N\}$ to a similarity matrix W. We refer to the concept of k-nearest neighbors in consideration of the nearer neighbors contribute more to the classified information than the more distant ones.

In spectral clustering, the Gaussian kernel function is widely used as the similarity measure. However, it is difficult to determine the optimal value of the kernel parameter, which reflects the neighborhood of the data points. In addition, with a fixed kernel parameter, the similarity between two objects is only determined by their Euclidean distance. Inspired by the idea of local scaling parameter can be determined by shared nearest neighbors [24], we proposed an adaptive parameter based on shared neighbors instead of traditional kernel parameter.

Let $N(\mathbf{x}) = \{\mathbf{x}_s | dist(\mathbf{x}, \mathbf{x}_s) \leq r, \mathbf{x}_s \in kNN(\mathbf{x})\}$ contains objects that are members of neighborhood of $\mathbf{x}$ with the neighbor radius r, where $dist(\mathbf{x}, \mathbf{x}_s)$ describes the Euclidean distance between $\mathbf{x}$ and $\mathbf{x}_s$, $kNN(\mathbf{x})$ denotes k neighbor points of $\mathbf{x}$. The neighbor radius r of object $\mathbf{x}$ is defined as $r = \frac{1}{k} \sum_{s=1}^{k}$

$dist(\mathbf{x}, \mathbf{x}_s)$, such that $\mathbf{x}_s \in kNN(\mathbf{x})$. Neighbor radius of each object can be confirmed by its k neighbor points. In addition, the number of points in the join neighborhood of two objects indicates their closeness. Therefore, a similarity function that considers global distribution and local consistency is given by:

$$
w_{ij} = \begin{cases} exp(-\dfrac{\|\mathbf{x}_i - \mathbf{x}_j\|^2}{r_i^2 r_j^2 |N(\mathbf{x}_i) \bigcap N(\mathbf{x}_i)| + 1}), \mathbf{x}_i \in kNN(\mathbf{x}_j) \ or \ \mathbf{x}_j \in kNN(\mathbf{x}_i), \\ 0, \ others. \end{cases}
$$

$$(8)$$

where r_i and r_j are the neighbor radius of $\mathbf{x}_i$ and $\mathbf{x}_j$ respectively, $|N(\mathbf{x}_i) \bigcap N(\mathbf{x}_j)|$ is the number of objects in the join neighborhood of $\mathbf{x}_i$ and $\mathbf{x}_j$.

We adopt graphs $G^{(1)}, \cdots, G^{(H)}$ to describe the multiple views $X^{(1)}, \cdots, X^{(H)}$ respectively. $G^{(h)} = (V^{(h)}, E^{(h)}, W^{(h)})$, where $W^{(h)}$ represents the similarity relationship among data points of h-th view. $L^{(h)}$ denotes the normalized graph Laplacian matrix of $G^{(h)}$ and is defined as:

$$
L^{(h)} = I - (D^{(h)})^{-1/2} W^{(h)} (D^{(h)})^{-1/2},
$$

$$(9)$$

where $D^{(h)} \in \mathbb{R}^{N \times N}$ denotes the degree matrix of graph $G^{(h)}$ whose i-th diagonal element is $d_i^{(h)} = \sum_{j=1}^{N} w_{ij}^{(h)}$.

The objective function of the normalized spectral clustering is defined as:

$$
\min_{G \in \mathbb{R}^{N \times K}} \sum_{h=1}^{H} tr(G^T (L^h) G), \quad s.t. \ G^T G = I
$$

$$(10)$$

Due to G is the identical matrix of all views, Eq. 10 can be converted to:

$$
\min_{G \in \mathbb{R}^{N \times K}} tr(G^T (\sum_{h=1}^{H} L^h) G), \quad s.t. \ G^T G = I
$$

$$(11)$$

In fact, the three-way spectral clustering algorithm (see Algorithm 1) implements the initial clustering and the iterative clustering. In the initial processing, i.e. the iteration times be 1, the constraint set $R = \emptyset$. That means there is no prior information and the spectral clustering is a unsupervised learning for multi-view data. In the iterative clustering processing, i.e. the iteration times more than 1, pairwise constraints information produced by the active learning algorithm (see Algorithm 2) are added to the constraint set R. The similarity matrixes of spectral clustering are adjusted by the following formula:

$$
if \ (\mathbf{x}_i, \mathbf{x}_j) \in ML, \ then \ w_{ij}^{(h)} = w_{ji}^{(h)} = 1;
$$
$$
if \ (\mathbf{x}_i, \mathbf{x}_j) \in CL, \ then \ w_{ij}^{(h)} = w_{ji}^{(h)} = 0.
$$

$$(12)$$

Based on the idea of three-way decisions, the proposed framework assigns the current uncertain objects to the corresponding fringe region. First, for the objects need to be divided, the proposed algorithm finds the neighborhood $N(\mathbf{x}_i)$ with neighbor radius r_i. Then, it calculates the proportion of the objects in $N(\mathbf{x}_i)$

Algorithm 1. The three-way spectral clustering algorithm

Input: the multi-view data $\{X^{(1)}, X^{(2)}, \cdots, X^{(H)}\}$, the number of clusters K,
the constraint set R, the threshold values α and β.
Output: $\mathbf{C} = \{(Co(C_1), Fr(C_1)), \cdots, (Co(C_K), Fr(C_K))\}$.
for *each view* $X^{(h)}$ **do**
    if $R \neq \emptyset$ **then**
        └ to adjust similarity matrix $W^{(h)}$ according to Eq. 12;
    else
        └ to compute similarity w_{ij} according to Eq. 8;
    └ to construct the normalized graph Laplacian matrix $L^{(h)}$ according to Eq. 9;
to compute the fused normalized Laplacian matrix L according to Eq. 11; to
compute the K smallest eigenvectors of L and construct eigenvector matrix E;
to normalize the rows of E to have unit norm; to cluster E by using k-means
algorithms, to assign objects to core regions, fringe regions and trivial regions,
by using the three-way rules Eq. 14.

---

belong to each cluster; and it assigns $\mathbf{x}_i$ to the corresponding core region or
fringe region. The proportion that objects in $N(\mathbf{x}_i)$ belong to C_k is given by:

$$P(N(\mathbf{x}_i)|C_k) = \frac{|\mathbf{x}_j|\mathbf{x}_j \in N(\mathbf{x}_i) \wedge \mathbf{x}_j \in C_k|}{|N(\mathbf{x}_i)|} \tag{13}$$

Naturally, we have the three-way decision rules as follows.

$$
\begin{aligned}
&\textit{if } P(N(\mathbf{x}_i)|C_k) \geqslant \alpha, \textit{ then } \mathbf{x}_i \textit{ is assigned to } Co(C_k);\\
&\textit{if } \beta < P(N(\mathbf{x}_i)|C_k) < \alpha, \textit{ then } \mathbf{x}_i \textit{ is assigned to } Fr(C_k);\\
&\textit{if } P(N(\mathbf{x}_i)|C_k) \leqslant \beta, \textit{ then } \mathbf{x}_i \textit{ is assigned to } Tr(C_k);
\end{aligned}
\tag{14}
$$

where α and β are the three-way decision thresholds.

3.3   The Active Learning to Acquire Pairwise Constraints

In this work, we consider active learning of constraints in the iterative framework.
The search space is reduced to the fringe regions in the proposed method. In the
current iteration, we need to decide which objects have the most important
information toward improving the current clustering result and form queries
accordingly. The responses to the queries (i.e., constraints) are then used to
update the similarity matrix by using Eq. 12.

Specifically, we define the uncertainty in terms of the concept of entropy,
which is a classic measure of uncertainty. In the h-th view, $w_{ij}^{(h)}$ denotes similarity
between points $\mathbf{x}_i^{(h)}$ and $\mathbf{x}_j^{(h)}$, the probability of $\mathbf{x}^{(h)}$ belongs to different core
regions $Co(C_k)(1 \leqslant k \leqslant K)$ is defined as:

$$p^{(h)}(\mathbf{x} \mid Co(C_k)) = \frac{\frac{1}{|Co(C_k)|}\sum_{\mathbf{x}_j \in Co(C_k)} w_{\cdot j}^{(h)}}{\sum_{p=1}^{K}\left(\frac{1}{|Co(C_p)|}\sum_{\mathbf{x}_j \in Co(C_p)} w_{\cdot j}^{(h)}\right)}, \tag{15}$$

where $|Co(C_k)|$ is the cardinality of $Co(C_k)$.

Then, the maximum entropy of $\mathbf{x}$ among H views is calculated by the following formula.

$$H_{Max}(\mathbf{x}) = arg\max_{h=1}^{H}(-\frac{1}{K}\sum_{k=1}^{K}(p^{(h)}(\mathbf{x} \mid Co(C_k))\ log_2 p^{(h)}(\mathbf{x} \mid Co(C_k)))). \quad (16)$$

An object with the bigger entropy will have more classification information to help decision-making. Thus, the object with most important information is selected by the following formula.

$$\mathbf{x}^* = arg\max_{\mathbf{x} \in U} H_{Max}(\mathbf{x}), \quad (17)$$

where U denotes the set of unlabeled data.

In order to reduce the cost of queries, we first sort the K probabilities, $p^{(h)}(\mathbf{x}^* \mid Co(C_k))$ for $1 \leq k \leq K$, in descending order. Then, we begin query the core of the cluster from the higher one until a must-link constraint satisfied.

Algorithm 2. The strategy of active learning

Input: the clustering result $\mathbf{C}$
Output: the constraint set R
for *each view $X^{(h)}$* **do**
   for $k = 1$ *to K* **do**
      for $\mathbf{x} \in Fr(C_k)$, to compute $p^{(h)}(\mathbf{x} \mid Co(C_k))$ according to Eq. 15;

to compute $H_{Max}(\mathbf{x})$ according to Eq. 16;
to select the most information object $\mathbf{x}^*$ according to Eq. 17;
to sort probabilities $p(\mathbf{x}^* \mid Co(C_k))$ in descending order;
for $k = 1$ *to K* **do**
   to query whether $\mathbf{x}^*$ belongs to $Co(C_k)$);
   if *the response is True* **then**
      to select a point $\mathbf{x}$ from $Co(C_k)$ randomly, set $(\mathbf{x}^*, \mathbf{x}) \in ML$, and $Co(C_k) = Co(C_k) \bigcup \{\mathbf{x}^*\}$;
      to update the constraint set R according to Eq. 12; break;
   else
      to construct pairwise constraint information $(\mathbf{x}^*, \mathbf{x}_i) \in CL$;

---

4 Experimental Results

In this section, we validate the proposed method on some real-world datasets. Table 1 gives the summary information about the datasets. SensIT[1] uses two sensors to classify three types of vehicle. We randomly sample 100 data for each class, and then conduct experiments on 2 views and 3 classes. Reuters[2]

---

[1] https://www.csie.ntu.edu.tw/~cjlin/libsvmtools/datasets/multiclass.html.
[2] https://archive.ics.uci.edu/ml/datasets.html.

contains feature characteristics of documents originally written in five different languages, and their translations over a common set of 6 categories. We use documents originally in English as the first view and their French and German translations as the second and the third view respectively. We randomly sample 1200 documents from this text collection, with each of the 6 clusters having 200 documents. Cora[3] and CiteSeer[4] collect kinds of scientific publications, with the first view being the textual content of documents and the second view being citation links between documents.

Table 1. Information about the datasets

Datasets	Size	#View	#Cluster
SensIT	300	2	3
Reuters	1200	3	6
Cora	2708	2	7
CiteSeer	3312	2	6

We compare the proposed SS-TWC method with some representative multi-view clustering strategies.

- Best Single View(BSV): running the proposed semi-supervised spectral clustering on each input view, and then reporting the results of the view that achieves the best performance.
- Feature Concatenation(FeatCon): concatenating the features of all views to form a single representation, and then applying the proposed semi-supervised spectral clustering on the concatenated view.
- AMVNMF: the adaptive multi-view semi-supervised nonnegative matrix factorization, it is an iterative multi-view semi-supervised clustering algorithm from the reference [16].
- SS-TWC(R): the method is similar with the SS-TWC except it obtains equivalent constraint information by using the random strategy instead of the active learning strategy in Algorithm 2.

The quality of the final clustering is evaluated by the traditional indices such as the accuracy (AC) and normalized mutual information (NMI). To ensure the objectivity of the experimental results, the results of AMVNMF are from the reference [16] and the other methods are programmed in C++. Each test runs 10 times, the average values of AC and the NMI are recorded in Table 2. The k, the number of neighbors, is set to be the 5% of the universe in the tests.

Obviously, the SS-TWC outperforms the other compared methods on the four datasets. Unlike the BSV and FeatCon, the SS-TWC profits from the correlative and complementary information among multiple views. Compared to the

---

[3] http://linqs.umiacs.umd.edu/projects//projects/lbc/index.html.
[4] http://linqs.umiacs.umd.edu/projects//projects/lbc/index.html.

Table 2. Comparison of experimental results

Indices	Datasets	BSV	FeatCon	AMVNMF	SS-TWC(R)	SS-TWC
AC	SensIT	68.73	76.39	71.33	67.71	**77.67**
	Reuters	54.67	58.43	59.88	57.20	**66.22**
	Cora	42.70	46.27	48.71	40.67	**51.88**
	Citeseer	46.16	53.36	53.14	45.39	**56.04**
NMI	SensIT	34.58	38.02	31.73	24.87	**41.16**
	Reuters	44.35	45.62	42.75	32.13	**47.88**
	Cora	30.71	34.41	34.59	20.19	**36.72**
	Citeseer	21.49	23.38	26.13	18.27	**30.26**

AMVNMF, the proposed SS-TWC has the benefit of processing the uncertainty in multi-view data by using the three-way decisions. In addition, the compared results between the SS-TWC and the SS-TWC(R) show that the proposed strategy of selecting pairwise constraints dynamically is much effective. In short, the proposed method work well in dealing with multi-view data.

5   Conclusions

In many scenarios, more than one view can be provided to describe the data due to the fact that data may be collected from different sources or be represented by different kind of feature sets for different tasks. Clustering multi-view data is an important problem. In this paper, we proposed a semi-supervised three-way clustering framework for multi-view data. The framework is an iterative processing, which consists of two parts, i.e., the three-way clustering and the active learning. The main goal of three-way clustering is to produce the clustering result in three-way representation, in which the objects in fringe regions intuitively gives the clue to query. Thus, the task of the active learning is to choose some objects (points) from fringe regions to query experts, and the responses to the queries (i.e., constraints) are then used to update the clustering result in iterations. The spectral clustering and the active learning strategies are used to implement the framework. The experimental results show that the proposed method achieves better performance in both the accuracy and the NMI than the compared methods. However, we need further work to improve the time complexity though the cost for computing has reduced little by constructing kNN graph. To consider the different contribution of different view is another direction for future research.

Acknowledgments. This work was supported in part by the National Natural Science Foundation of China under Grant Nos. 61379114 & 61533020.

References

1. Blum, A., Mitchell, T.: Combining labeled and unlabeled data with co-training. In: Proceeding of the Eleventh Annual Conference on Computational Learning Theory, pp. 92–100. ACM (1998)
2. Bickel, S., Scheffer, T.: Multi-view clustering. In: ICDM, vol. 4, pp. 19–26 (2004)
3. Chaudhuri, K., Kakade, S.M., Livescu, K., Sridharan, K.: Multi-view clustering via canonical correlation analysis. In: Proceedings of the 26th Annual International Conference on Machine Learning, pp. 129–136. ACM (2009)
4. Chen, W., Feng, G.: Spectral clustering: a semi-supervised approach. Neurocomputing **77**(1), 229–242 (2012)
5. Ding, S., Jia, H., Zhang, L., Jin, F.: Research of semi-supervised spectral clustering algorithm based on pairwise constraints. Neural Comput. Appl. **24**(1), 211–219 (2014)
6. Grira, N., Crucianu, M., Boujemaa, N.: Unsupervised and semi-supervised clustering: a brief survey (2005)
7. Klein, D., Kamvar, S.D., Manning, C.D.: From instrance-level constraints to space-level constraints: making the most of prior knowledge in data clustering. Stanford (2002)
8. Li, Y., Nie, F., Huang, H., Huang, J.: Large-scale multi-view spectral clustering via bipartite graph. In: AAAI, pp. 2750–2756 (2015)
9. Liang, D., Liu, D.: Systematic studies on three-way decisions with interval-valued decision-theoretic rough sets. Inf. Sci. **276**, 186–203 (2014)
10. Lingras, P., Yan, R.: Interval clustering using fuzzy and rough set theory. In: Proceedings 2004 IEEE Annual Meeting, Fuzzy Information, Banff, Alberta, pp. 780–784 (2004)
11. Lingras, P., West, C.: Interval set clustering of web users with rough k-means. J. Intell. Inf. Syst. **23**(1), 5–16 (2004)
12. Liu, J., Wang, C., Guo, J., Han, J.: Multi-view clustering via joint nonnegative matrix factorization. In: Proceeding of the 2013 SIAM International Conference on Data Mining, pp. 252–260. Society for Industrial and Applied Mathematics (2013)
13. Luxburg, U.: A tutorial on spectral clustering. Stat. Comput. **17**(4), 395–416 (2007)
14. Wagstaff, K., Cardie, C.: Clustering with instance-level constraints. In: AAAI/IAAI, vol. 1097 (2000)
15. Wang, W., Zhou, Z.H.: On multi-view active learning and the combination with semi-supervised learning. In: Proceedings of the 25th International Conference on Machine Learning, pp. 1152–1159. ACM (2008)
16. Wang, J., Wang, X., Tian, F., Liu, C.H., Yu, H., Liu, Y.: Adaptive multi-view semi-supervised nonnegative matrix factorization. In: Hirose, A., Ozawa, S., Doya, K., Ikeda, K., Lee, M., Liu, D. (eds.) ICONIP 2016. LNCS, vol. 9948, pp. 435–444. Springer, Cham (2016). doi:10.1007/978-3-319-46672-9_49
17. Xia, T., Tao, D., Mei, T., Zhang, Y.: Multiview spectral embedding. IEEE Trans. Syst. Man Cybern. Part B (Cybern.) **40**(6), 1438–1446 (2010)
18. Xiong, S., Azimi, J., Fern, X.Z.: Active learning of constraints for semi-supervised clustering. IEEE Trans. Knowl. Data Eng. **26**(1), 43–54 (2014)
19. Xu, C., Tao, D., Xu, C.: A survey on multi-view learning. arXiv preprint arXiv:1304.5634 (2013)

20. Yao, Y., Lingras, P., Wang, R., Miao, D.: Interval set cluster analysis: a reformulation. In: Sakai, H., Chakraborty, M.K., Hassanien, A.E., Ślęzak, D., Zhu, W. (eds.) RSFDGrC 2009. LNCS, vol. 5908, pp. 398–405. Springer, Heidelberg (2009). doi:10.1007/978-3-642-10646-0_48

21. Yao, Y.: An outline of a theory of three-way decisions. In: Yao, J.T., Yang, Y., Słowiński, R., Greco, S., Li, H., Mitra, S., Polkowski, L. (eds.) RSCTC 2012. LNCS, vol. 7413, pp. 1–17. Springer, Heidelberg (2012). doi:10.1007/978-3-642-32115-3_1

22. Yao, Y.: Three-way decisions and cognitive computing. Cogn. Comput. **8**(4), 543–554 (2016)

23. Yao, J., Azam, N.: Web-based medical decision support systems for three-way medical decision making with game-theoretic rough sets. IEEE Trans. Fuzzy Syst. **23**(1), 3–15 (2015)

24. Ye, X., Sakurai, T.: Robust similairty measure for spectral clustering based on shared neighbors. ETRI J. **38**(3), 540–550 (2016)

25. Yu, H., Wang, G.Y., Li, T.R., Liang, J.Y., Miao, D.Q., Yao, Y.Y.: Three-Way Decisions: Methods and Practices for Complex Problem Solving. Science Press, Beijing (2015). (in Chinese)

26. Yu, H., Zhang, C., Wang, G.: A tree-based incremental overlapping clustering method using the three-way decision theory. Knowl.-Based Syst. **91**, 189–203 (2016)

27. Yu, H., et al.: Methods and practices of three-way decisions for complex problem solving. In: Ciucci, D., Wang, G., Mitra, S., Wu, W.-Z. (eds.) RSKT 2015. LNCS, vol. 9436, pp. 255–265. Springer, Cham (2015). doi:10.1007/978-3-319-25754-9_23

28. Zhang, X., Zhao, D.Y., Wei, S., Xiao, W.X.: Active semi-supervised clustering based on multi-view learning. In: WRI Global Congress on Intelligent Systems, GCIS 2009, vol. 3, pp. 495–499. IEEE (2009)

29. Zhou, B., Yao, Y., Luo, J.: Cost-sensitive three-way email spam fitering. J. Intell. Inf. Syst. **42**(1), 19–45 (2014)

Determining Thresholds in Three-Way Decisions: A Multi-object Optimization View

Yuanjian Zhang[1,2], Duoqian Miao[1,2(✉)], Jianfeng Xu[1,2], and Zhifei Zhang[1,3]

[1] Department of Computer Science and Technology, Tongji University,
Shanghai 201804, China
zhangyj901029@gmail.com, dqmiao@tongji.edu.cn
[2] Key Laboratory of Embedded System and Service Computing
Ministry of Education, Tongji University, Shanghai 201804, China
[3] Big Data and Network Security Research Center, Tongji University,
Shanghai 200092, China

Abstract. Determination of thresholds is recognized as a fundamental problem in decision-theoretic rough sets. Traditionally, thresholds are determined by observing Bayesian decision theory. Although the semantic seems to be enriched as compared to probabilistic rough sets, the functionality of risk is not comprehensively explored. In allusion to this situation, we develop a multi-object optimization view based model on determining thresholds. By generalizing the expected loss function to target function, this model claims that thresholds in three-way are radically constructed by pair-wise region-based target functions. By transferring the principle of pair-wise region-based target functions on multi-quantitative scenario, we present a finer-grained formulation for thresholds solving. Furthermore, we investigate the multi-layer of presented model. Finally, the optimistic and pessimistic multi-quantitative decision-theoretic rough set is defined to illustrate the value of presented model.

Keywords: Three-way decisions · Decision-theoretic rough sets · Multi-object optimization · Multi-quantitative

1 Introduction

Three-way decisions (TWD) [1], originated from rough set theory [2], has demonstrated the superiority in performing decision-making with uncertainty. Roughly speaking, three-way decisions managed to divide the universe into three non-overlapped regions and take actions of acceptance, rejection or non-commitment respectively. A rational explanation for taking different strategies is that the committed decision, whether acceptance or rejection, corresponds to the information with satisfied discernibility, whereas the non-commitment decision implies the information with flawed discrimination. By incorporating with three-way decisions, an increasing number of successful cases have been reported in different

© Springer International Publishing AG 2017
L. Polkowski et al. (Eds.): IJCRS 2017, Part II, LNAI 10314, pp. 326–339, 2017.
DOI: 10.1007/978-3-319-60840-2_24

applications, including e-mail spam filtering [3], text semantic analysis [4,5] image recognition [6], and cognitive computing [7].

Thresholds play a pivot role in determining the region boundary, and the selections reflect the degree that concepts can be approximately defined by certain granular structure. In *decision-theoretic rough sets* (DTRS) [8], different combinations of thresholds correspond to different risk, and the minimization of risk is the decision principle. Studies on threshold solving can be categorized into two groups. In the first case, all loss coefficients are given but may uncertain. As suggested by [9], an analytical solution is invariantly expected. In the second case, however, only part of them are roughly known, while no specific expressions of the remaining are given. In this case, only numerical solutions can be expected [10,11]. Although both solutions can be interpreted from optimization view, it is not explicitly declared in terms of region construction. Consequently, the semantics of α, β, and γ are merely enriched by introducing more loss coefficients $\lambda_{\bullet\bullet}$. The problem thus becomes more obvious in the discussion of generalized double-quantitative rough sets [12], where the approximation operators are merely generated on the basis of parameters.

In this paper, we take a multi-object optimization (MOP) view for thresholds solving. By generalizing expected loss coefficients of DTRS to target functions, this paper provides a revisit to decision-theoretic rough sets. The confrontation within regions are thoroughly embodied in threshold solving. Accordingly, the semantics of thresholds in DTRS are more intuitive, and the construction of three-way structure is enriched simultaneously. By investigating the combinations of pair-wise region-based target functions, we present a finer-grained view for construction of thresholds. We further declare that under multi-quantitative scenario, more combinations of thresholds can be generated by considering diversity fusions of homogeneous region-based target function meanwhile. The formalized representation is constructive in flourishing approximate knowledge representation of multi-quantitative based rough sets.

The rest of the paper is organized as follows. Section 2 briefly reviews the basic concepts with regard to decision-theoretic rough sets. In Sect. 3, a multi-object optimization based model is investigated to solve the thresholds. By extending the syntax of optimizing principal presented in Sect. 3, proposed model is competent for thresholds solving for multi-quantitative scenario, as illustrated in Sect. 4. Finally, it is concluded in Sect. 5.

2   Preliminary

In this section, we present a review of some basic concepts with regard to decision-theoretic rough sets.

Definition 1 [2]. *$IS = \{U, A, V, f\}$ is an information system with quadruple, where U denotes a non-empty finite universe, $A = C \cup D$ be a set of attributes, V be the values of all attributes and is determined by the mapping function $f : U \times A \rightarrow V$.*

Under the equivalence relation R, a corresponding partition of U (U/R) can be generated.

Elements in the identical equivalence class constitute a basic information granule $[x]$. The affiliation of information granular $[x]$ to certain decision class X can be measured by conditional probability $P(X|[x])$. Although this measure can reflect the decision quality, the semantic of thresholds that support the three-way structure is vagueness. To address this issue, Yao [13] introduced loss coefficients $\lambda_{\bullet\bullet}$ to evaluate the effects of three-way decisions. Taking two classes classification problem as an example, there are totally six loss coefficients, as illustrated in Table 1.

Table 1. Loss coefficient matrix for two class classification problem

	X	$\neg X$
acceptance (a)	λ_{ap}	λ_{an}
non-commitment (n)	λ_{np}	λ_{nn}
rejection (r)	λ_{rp}	λ_{rn}

Consequently, the risk of all equivalence class $[x]$ in the process of decision making can be calculated as:

$$R = \sum_{[x]} R(a|[x]) + R(n|[x]) + R(r|[x]) \tag{1}$$

where $R(a|[x]), R(r|[x])$ and $R(n|[x])$ are defined as:

$$R(a|[x]) = \lambda_{ap} \times P(X|[x]) + \lambda_{an} \times P(\neg X|[x]);$$
$$R(n|[x]) = \lambda_{np} \times P(X|[x]) + \lambda_{nn} \times P(\neg X|[x]);$$
$$R(r|[x]) = \lambda_{rp} \times P(X|[x]) + \lambda_{rn} \times P(\neg X|[x]).$$

The risk minimization principle indicates that the affiliation of information granular $[x]$ with regard to class X is reasonable if the following three inequality are satisfied simultaneously.

$$R(a|[x]) \le R(n|[x]) \wedge R(a|[x]) \le R(r|[x]) \Rightarrow decide\ [x] \subseteq POS(X);$$
$$R(n|[x]) \le R(a|[x]) \wedge R(n|[x]) \le R(r|[x]) \Rightarrow decide\ [x] \subseteq BND(X);$$
$$R(r|[x]) \le R(a|[x]) \wedge R(r|[x]) \le R(n|[x]) \Rightarrow decide\ [x] \subseteq NEG(X).$$

Hence, we can make three-way decisions on the risk level. The DTRS model is thus defined as follows:

Definition 2 [13]. *Given relationship of loss coefficients $\lambda_{ap} \le \lambda_{np} \le \lambda_{rp}$ and $\lambda_{rn} \le \lambda_{nn} \le \lambda_{an}$ and condition $(\lambda_{rp} - \lambda_{np})(\lambda_{an} - \lambda_{nn}) \ge (\lambda_{np} - \lambda_{ap})(\lambda_{nn} - \lambda_{rn})$, three-way region with regard to X is defined as*

$$POS(X) = \{[x]|P(X|[x]) \ge \alpha\};$$
$$BND(X) = \{[x]|\beta < P(X|[x]) < \alpha\};$$
$$NEG(X) = \{[x]|P(X|[x]) \le \beta\}.$$

where parameters α and β are defined as:

$$\alpha = \frac{\lambda_{an} - \lambda_{nn}}{(\lambda_{an} - \lambda_{nn}) + (\lambda_{np} - \lambda_{ap})}; \quad \beta = \frac{\lambda_{nn} - \lambda_{rn}}{(\lambda_{nn} - \lambda_{rn}) + (\lambda_{rp} - \lambda_{np})};$$

3 Multi-object Optimization View for Threshold Solving with Single Quantification

For a given information system, decision risks of positive region, negative region and defer region fluctuate as the selection of thresholds changes. It is reasonable to assume that each threshold is determined by pair-wise region-based target function, thus a multi-object optimization problem is formulated. To elaborate the solving mechanism, this section will limit the scope of target function on single granular structure.

3.1 Problem Formulation

Suppose the conditional probability $P(X|[x])$ is considered as evaluation criterion, we term target functions as:

Definition 3. *Target function T is an assemble of functions with T_P, T_B and T_N which describes the decision cost of positive region, boundary region and negative region induced by $P(X|[x])$ respectively.*

$$T_P = (\lambda_{ap} - \lambda_{an}) P(X|[x]) + \lambda_{an};$$
$$T_B = (\lambda_{np} - \lambda_{nn}) P(X|[x]) + \lambda_{nn};$$
$$T_N = (\lambda_{rp} - \lambda_{rn}) P(X|[x]) + \lambda_{rn}.$$

All target functions suggest that region-based decision cost is linearly related to the conditional probability. Since three-way can be described by at most two parameters, we can formulate the thresholds solving problem as follows:

$$\underset{(\alpha^*,\beta^*)}{\arg\min} T|(\alpha,\beta,\gamma) = \{T_P|(\alpha,\beta,\gamma), T_B|(\alpha,\beta,\gamma), T_N|(\alpha,\beta,\gamma)\} \qquad (2)$$

where $\alpha^* \geq \beta^*$, $\alpha^*, \beta^* \in \{\alpha, \beta, \gamma\}$ and $T|(\alpha,\beta,\gamma)$ denotes the target value given α, β, γ. α, β, and γ are three conditional probabilities that are to be optimized. The selection of α implies the relative boundary between positive region and boundary region, while β and γ suggest the relative boundary of negative region and boundary region, positive region and negative region respectively. To solve the problem formulated in Eq. (2), we define the following optimization model.

Definition 4. *Let $T_\alpha, T_\beta, T_\gamma$ be the decision cost induced merely by α, β and γ respectively, parameters α, β, γ can be solved by three pair-wise object optimization.*

$$\underset{(\alpha)}{\arg\min} T_\alpha = \begin{cases} T_P = (\lambda_{ap} - \lambda_{an}) \times \alpha + \lambda_{an} \\ T_B = (\lambda_{np} - \lambda_{nn}) \times \alpha + \lambda_{nn} \end{cases};$$

$$\underset{(\beta)}{\arg\min} T_\beta = \begin{cases} T_B = (\lambda_{np} - \lambda_{nn}) \times \beta + \lambda_{nn} \\ T_N = (\lambda_{rp} - \lambda_{rn}) \times \beta + \lambda_{rn} \end{cases};$$

$$\underset{(\gamma)}{\arg\min} T_\gamma = \begin{cases} T_P = (\lambda_{ap} - \lambda_{an}) \times \gamma + \lambda_{an} \\ T_N = (\lambda_{rp} - \lambda_{rn}) \times \gamma + \lambda_{rn} \end{cases}.$$

$$s.t. \quad 0 < \alpha < 1, 0 < \beta < 1, 0 < \gamma < 1$$

3.2   Problem Solving

It can be deduced from Definition 4 that solving for any parameter is similar. Without losing generality, we investigate the solving process for parameter α.

Let $T_P = T_B$, we have $P(X|[x]) = \frac{\lambda_{an}-\lambda_{nn}}{(\lambda_{an}-\lambda_{nn})+(\lambda_{np}-\lambda_{ap})}$. Then we have the following Theorem.

Theorem 1. T_α achieves the minimum value if $\alpha = \frac{\lambda_{an}-\lambda_{nn}}{(\lambda_{an}-\lambda_{nn})+(\lambda_{np}-\lambda_{ap})}$.

Proof. Given $\lambda_{ap} - \lambda_{an} > \lambda_{np} - \lambda_{nn}$, the slope of T_P is larger than that of T_B. If α is smaller than intersection of two target functions (see α_1 and α_0 in Fig. 1(a)), then the equivalence class with conditional probability in interval (α_1, α_0) will be determined to boundary region, which will have larger cost. If α is bigger than intersection of two target functions (see α_2 and α_0 in Fig. 1(a)), then the equivalence class with conditional probability in interval (α_0, α_2) will be determined to positive region, which will also have larger cost. Analogously, intersection α_0 corresponds to minimum cost given $\lambda_{ap} - \lambda_{an} < \lambda_{np} - \lambda_{nn}$, as illustrated in Fig. 1(b).

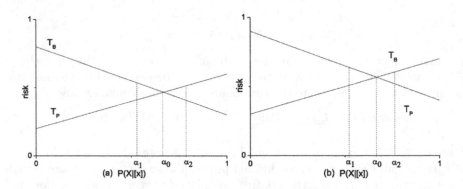

Fig. 1. Determination of parameter α given target function T_P and T_B

Based on Theorem 1, we have the following corollary holds.

Corollary 1. Let $\alpha = \frac{\lambda_{an}-\lambda_{nn}}{(\lambda_{an}-\lambda_{nn})+(\lambda_{np}-\lambda_{ap})}$, we have:

$$((\lambda_{ap} - \lambda_{an}) > (\lambda_{np} - \lambda_{nn})) \wedge (1 > P(X|[x]) > \alpha > 0) \Rightarrow T_P > T_B;$$
$$((\lambda_{ap} - \lambda_{an}) > (\lambda_{np} - \lambda_{nn})) \wedge (0 < P(X|[x]) < \alpha < 1) \Rightarrow T_P < T_B;$$
$$((\lambda_{ap} - \lambda_{an}) < (\lambda_{np} - \lambda_{nn})) \wedge (1 > P(X|[x]) > \alpha > 0) \Rightarrow T_P < T_B;$$
$$((\lambda_{ap} - \lambda_{an}) < (\lambda_{np} - \lambda_{nn})) \wedge (0 < P(X|[x]) < \alpha < 1) \Rightarrow T_P > T_B.$$

Proof. It is straightforward as Theorem 1 implies.

Analogously, we have the property with regard to β and γ according to Definition 4. For β, let $T_B = T_N$, we have $P(X|[x]) = \frac{\lambda_{nn}-\lambda_{rn}}{(\lambda_{nn}-\lambda_{rn})+(\lambda_{rp}-\lambda_{np})}$. Then we have Theorem 2 and Corollary 2 as follows:

Theorem 2. T_β *achieves the minimum value if* $\beta = \frac{\lambda_{nn}-\lambda_{rn}}{(\lambda_{nn}-\lambda_{rn})+(\lambda_{rp}-\lambda_{np})}$

Proof. It is similar to that of Theorem 1.

Corollary 2. Let $\beta = \frac{\lambda_{nn}-\lambda_{rn}}{(\lambda_{nn}-\lambda_{rn})+(\lambda_{rp}-\lambda_{np})}$, we have:

$$((\lambda_{rp} - \lambda_{rn}) > (\lambda_{np} - \lambda_{nn})) \wedge (1 > P(X\,||[x]) > \beta > 0) \Rightarrow T_N > T_B;$$
$$((\lambda_{rp} - \lambda_{rn}) > (\lambda_{np} - \lambda_{nn})) \wedge (0 < P(X\,||[x]) < \beta < 1) \Rightarrow T_N < T_B;$$
$$((\lambda_{rp} - \lambda_{rn}) < (\lambda_{np} - \lambda_{nn})) \wedge (1 > P(X\,||[x]) > \beta > 0) \Rightarrow T_N < T_B;$$
$$((\lambda_{rp} - \lambda_{rn}) < (\lambda_{np} - \lambda_{nn})) \wedge (0 < P(X\,||[x]) < \beta < 1) \Rightarrow T_N > T_B.$$

Proof. It is straightforward as Theorem 2 implies.

For γ, let $T_P = T_N$, we have $P(X\,||[x]) = \frac{\lambda_{an}-\lambda_{rn}}{(\lambda_{an}-\lambda_{rn})+(\lambda_{rp}-\lambda_{ap})}$, then we have Theorem 3 and Corollary 3.

Theorem 3. T_γ *achieves the minimum value if* $\gamma = \frac{\lambda_{an}-\lambda_{rn}}{(\lambda_{an}-\lambda_{rn})+(\lambda_{rp}-\lambda_{ap})}$.

Proof. It is similar to that of Theorem 1.

Corollary 3. Let $\gamma = \frac{\lambda_{an}-\lambda_{rn}}{(\lambda_{an}-\lambda_{rn})+(\lambda_{rp}-\lambda_{ap})}$, we have:

$$((\lambda_{ap} - \lambda_{an}) > (\lambda_{rp} - \lambda_{rn})) \wedge (1 > P(X\,||[x]) > \gamma > 0) \Rightarrow T_P > T_N;$$
$$((\lambda_{ap} - \lambda_{an}) > (\lambda_{rp} - \lambda_{rn})) \wedge (0 < P(X\,||[x]) < \gamma < 1) \Rightarrow T_P < T_N;$$
$$((\lambda_{ap} - \lambda_{an}) < (\lambda_{rp} - \lambda_{rn})) \wedge (1 > P(X\,||[x]) > \gamma > 0) \Rightarrow T_P < T_N;$$
$$((\lambda_{ap} - \lambda_{an}) < (\lambda_{rp} - \lambda_{rn})) \wedge (0 < P(X\,||[x]) < \gamma < 1) \Rightarrow T_P > T_N.$$

Proof. It is straightforward as Theorem 3 implies.

By simultaneously considering the relations of relative parameters and slope of target functions, we can determine the three-way structure as following theorems:

Theorem 4. *If* $(\lambda_{rp} - \lambda_{rn}) > (\lambda_{np} - \lambda_{nn}) > (\lambda_{ap} - \lambda_{an})$ *and* $\beta \leq \gamma \leq \alpha$, *then the following decision rules hold: (P)* $P(X||[x]) \geq \alpha$, *decide* $x \in POS(X)$; *(B)* $\beta < P(X||[x]) < \alpha$, *decide* $x \in BND(X)$; *(N)* $P(X||[x]) \leq \beta$, *decide* $x \in NEG(X)$.

Proof. Since the condition $(\lambda_{rp} - \lambda_{rn}) > (\lambda_{np} - \lambda_{nn}) > (\lambda_{ap} - \lambda_{an})$ is satisfied, we have $(\lambda_{rp} - \lambda_{rn}) > (\lambda_{np} - \lambda_{nn})$, $(\lambda_{np} - \lambda_{nn}) > (\lambda_{ap} - \lambda_{an})$, and $(\lambda_{rp} - \lambda_{rn}) > (\lambda_{ap} - \lambda_{an})$. Similarly, $\alpha \leq \gamma \leq \beta$ is equivalent to $\alpha \leq \gamma, \gamma \leq \beta$ and $\alpha \leq \beta$. According to Corollaries 1 and 3, if additional condition $P(X||[x]) \geq \alpha$ holds, decide $x \in POS(X)$. According to Corollaries 1 and 2, if additional condition $\beta < P(X||[x]) < \alpha$ holds, decide $x \in BND(X)$. According to Corollaries 2 and 3, if additional condition $P(X||[x]) \leq \beta$ holds, decide $x \in NEG(X)$.

Theorem 5. *If* $(\lambda_{rp} - \lambda_{rn}) > (\lambda_{np} - \lambda_{nn}) > (\lambda_{ap} - \lambda_{an})$ *and* $\alpha \leq \gamma \leq \beta$, *then the following decision rules hold: (P)* $P(X||[x]) \leq \gamma$, *decide* $x \in NEG(X)$; *(N)* $P(X||[x]) \geq \gamma$, *decide* $x \in POS(X)$.

Proof. It is similar to that of Theorem 4.

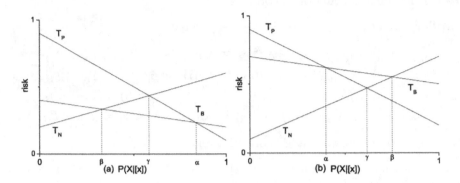

Fig. 2. Three-way structure for X given conditional probability $P(X|[x])$

Theorems 4 and 5 illustrate that three-way structure can be different given the relative relation of slope, as shown in Fig. 2. It reflects that the introduction of target function T_B do not necessarily give rise to three non-empty regions.

The three-way structure with regard to $\neg X$ is derivable from the conditional probability $P(X|[x])$. Since X and $\neg X$ is complementary with regard to 1, the slope of T_P, T_B and T_N is opposite. Consequently, the condition $(\lambda_{rp} - \lambda_{rn}) < (\lambda_{np} - \lambda_{nn}) < (\lambda_{ap} - \lambda_{an})$ is satisfied. Based on it, we investigate the relative relation of parameter α, β and γ.

Theorem 6. *If* $(\lambda_{rp} - \lambda_{rn}) < (\lambda_{np} - \lambda_{nn}) < (\lambda_{ap} - \lambda_{an})$ *and* $\alpha \leq \gamma \leq \beta$, *then the following decision rules hold: (P)* $P(X|[x]) \leq \alpha$, *decide* $x \in POS(X)$; *(B)* $\alpha < P(X|[x]) < \beta$, *decide* $x \in BND(X)$; *(N)* $P(X|[x]) \geq \beta$, *decide* $x \in NEG(X)$.

Proof. It is similar to that of Theorem 4, as illustrated in Fig. 3(a).

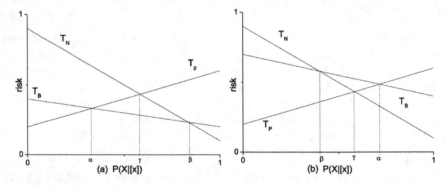

Fig. 3. Three-way structure for $\neg X$ given conditional probability $P(X|[x])$

Theorem 7. *If $(\lambda_{rp} - \lambda_{rn}) < (\lambda_{np} - \lambda_{nn}) < (\lambda_{ap} - \lambda_{an})$ and $\beta \leq \gamma \leq \alpha$, then the following decision rules hold: (P) $P(X|[x]) \leq \gamma$, decide $x \in POS(X)$; (N) $P(X|[x]) \geq \gamma$, decide $x \in NEG(X)$.*

Proof. It is similar to that of Theorem 4, as illustrated in Fig. 3(b).

4 Multi-object Optimization View for Threshold Solving with Multiple Quantification

The multi-view of target function is quite ubiquitous in complicated applications such as group decision-making and double-quantification. It signifies that for a specific object x, we may observe from different views, resulting in the appearance of x in at least two different granular structures. Although double-quantitative can define concepts with multi-view to some degree, some complicated concepts still cannot be defined. For example, consider the following requirements:

- To accept concept X, precision weighs more than grade, and precision should be at least 80%;
- The relative differences between precision and grade are limited to 10%, and percentages for cardinality of equivalent class in information system should be at least 5%;
- Both precision and grade contribute to the three-way decisions, but the evaluation metrics for different regions are different.

The aforementioned requirements cannot be resolved in existing double-quantitative rough set model since thresholds are not determined by target functions from homogeneous quantification. Regarding every target function as an atomic quantitative metric, this section intends to further examine the thresholds construction on multiple granulation.

4.1 Problem Formulation

Compared to single quantification, major difference is that the three regions with regard to concept X are implicitly determined by granular structures. We introduce three region integration functions f_P, f_B and f_N to induce the integrated region-based target function T_P, T_B, and T_N. Therefore, Eq. 2 is rewritten as:

$$\underset{(\alpha^*,\beta^*)}{\arg\min} T|(\alpha,\beta,\gamma) = \{f_P|(\alpha,\beta,\gamma), f_B|(\alpha,\beta,\gamma), f_N|(\alpha,\beta,\gamma)\} \qquad (3)$$

Suppose there are two groups of target functions $(T^i, T^j$, with $T^i = \{T_P^i, T_B^i, T_N^i\}$, $T^j = \{T_P^j, T_B^j, T_N^j\}$), then parameters α, β and γ can be solved by transferring the principle of region confrontation, defined as:

Definition 5. *Let* (T_P^i, T_B^i, T_N^i) *and* (T_P^j, T_B^j, T_N^j) *represent two different groups of target functions that are determined by Definition 4 respectively, then* (α, β, γ) *can be computed as:*

$$\arg\min_{(\alpha)} T_\alpha = \begin{cases} f_P(T_P^i, T_P^j) \\ f_B(T_B^i, T_B^j) \end{cases};$$

$$\arg\min_{(\beta)} T_\beta = \begin{cases} f_B(T_B^i, T_B^j) \\ f_N(T_N^i, T_N^j) \end{cases};$$

$$\arg\min_{(\gamma)} T_\gamma = \begin{cases} f_P(T_P^i, T_P^j) \\ f_N(T_N^i, T_N^j) \end{cases}.$$

$$s.t. 0 < \alpha < 1, 0 < \beta < 1, 0 < \gamma < 1$$

where

$$T_P^i = \left(\lambda_{ap}^i - \lambda_{an}^i\right) \times \alpha + \lambda_{an}^i, \quad T_P^j = \left(\lambda_{ap}^j - \lambda_{an}^j\right) \times \alpha + \lambda_{an}^j$$

$$T_B^i = \left(\lambda_{np}^i - \lambda_{nn}^i\right) \times \beta + \lambda_{nn}^i, \quad T_B^j = \left(\lambda_{np}^j - \lambda_{nn}^j\right) \times \beta + \lambda_{nn}^j$$

$$T_N^i = \left(\lambda_{rp}^i - \lambda_{rn}^i\right) \times \gamma + \lambda_{rn}^i, \quad T_N^j = \left(\lambda_{rp}^j - \lambda_{rn}^j\right) \times \gamma + \lambda_{rn}^j$$

To elaborate the structure of integrated region, we consider the trivial case, namely, the output of region integration function is one of the integrated target functions:

$$f_P(T_P^i, T_P^j) \in \{T_P^i, T_P^j\}; \quad f_B(T_B^i, T_B^j) \in \{T_B^i, T_B^j\}; \quad f_N(T_N^i, T_N^j) \in \{T_N^i, T_N^j\}.$$

It can be inferred from Definition 5 that for each parameter α, β, γ, there are four candidate combinations. Figure 4 illustrates the candidate α and β in multi-quantification space for trivial cases, and combinations of the three-way structure in this scenario can be at most sixteen cases.

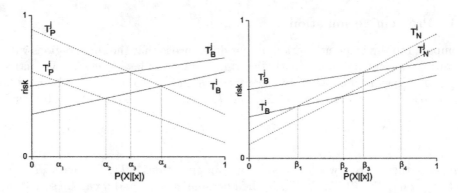

Fig. 4. Thresholds solving in multi-quantification: α (left) and β (right)

By allowing integrations on two different region integration functions, the multi-objective optimization based model can be further generalized as:

Definition 6. *Let* (f_P^i, f_B^i, f_N^i) *and* (f_P^j, f_B^j, f_N^j) *represent two different groups of integrated target functions, then* (α, β, γ) *can be computed as:*

$$\underset{(\alpha)}{\arg\min} T_\alpha = \begin{cases} f_P(f_P^i, f_P^j) \\ f_B(f_B^i, f_B^j) \end{cases};$$

$$\underset{(\beta)}{\arg\min} T_\beta = \begin{cases} f_B(f_B^i, f_B^j) \\ f_N(f_N^i, f_N^j) \end{cases};$$

$$\underset{(\gamma)}{\arg\min} T_\gamma = \begin{cases} f_P(f_P^i, f_P^j) \\ f_N(f_N^i, f_N^j) \end{cases}.$$

$$s.t. \quad 0 < \alpha < 1, 0 < \beta < 1, 0 < \gamma < 1$$

4.2   Problem Solving

Definitions 5 and 6 are applicable in explaining thresholds construction of double-quantitative rough sets [14]. Although the incorporation of decision-theoretic has been discussed, it still deserves to be improved. For example, in GMDq-DTRS [12], thresholds are approximated by performing operations on pair-wise three-way thresholds. The results can be regarded as adding additional requirements on Definition 5 that $i = j$ holds for both α and β but with heterogeneous trivial selections, whereas the remaining cases are not covered. Indeed, the trivial cases correspond to the semantic that certain thresholds are completely determined by certain target functions, whereas the non-trivial cases reflect the relevant degree to target functions for certain thresholds. For example, one may define that an equivalent class with 90% precision but with 10 objects should be deferred, whereas an equivalent class with 80% precision but with 50 objects should be accepted. The reason is that the acceptance of the latter may yield to a more robust decision than acceptance of the former.

Figure 5 systematically illustrates the multi-object optimization perspective for solving thresholds (α^*, β^*) of three-way decisions in granulation space. From finest to coarsest, there are three levels. In the first level (Sq-TWD), only pair-wise region confrontation is required to generate region boundary. The three-way structure is totally determined by the very group of target function, which means the three-way can not be further optimized given the target function T. Thresholds solving for single-quantitative three-way decisions is completed in this level. However, given another group of target function, the level is upgraded to the second (Dq-TWD), where the three-way is determined by both target functions (T^i, T^j) and integrated target functions (f_P, f_B, f_N). The result of integrated target functions can be either trivial or non-trivial, and how to define the integrated target function is an open issue. Take α for example, the f_P can generate trivial or non-trivial results, and similarly for f_B and f_N. Consequently, the number of solution structure for each parameter is four. As an example, we enumerate the cases for α as follows:

$$(trivial_P, trivial_B), (trivial_P, non - trivial_B),$$
$$(non - trivial_P, trivial_B), (non - trivial_P, non - trivial_B).$$

where $trivial_P \in \{T_P^i, T_P^j\}, trivial_B \in \{T_B^i, T_B^j\}$.

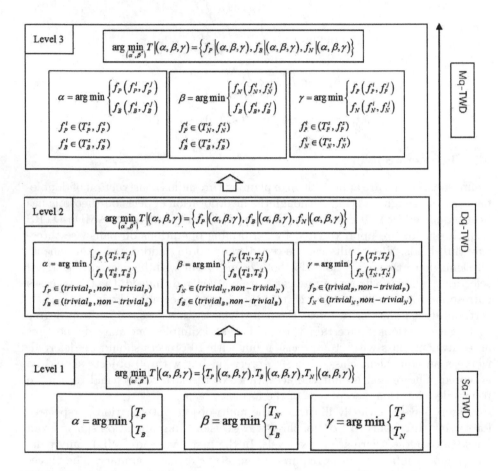

Fig. 5. Levels for threshold solving of three-way decisions from multi-objective optimization view

Thresholds of double-quantitative rough set with decision-theoretic rough set are solved in this level. In the third level (Mq-TWD), there are more than two groups of target functions, which indicates that integrated target functions may be iteratively used. The trivial output is defined as the result which is identical to either input. In terms of input type, there are also four cases for f_P^i as follows:

$$(T_P^s, T_P^t), (T_P^s, f_P^t), (f_P^s, T_P^t), (f_P^s, f_P^t).$$

It corresponds the general case for multi-granulation rough sets. For thresholds with uncertainty like [16,17], we argue that they are the extensions of the exact solution, and thus are not particularly treated as a level.

4.3   Examples

Three-way structure of multi-quantitative rough set is not as intuitive as single-quantitative because of uncertainty in the selection of integrated target functions f_P, f_B, and f_N. Suppose the solutions for all integrated target functions are trivial, by introducing the idea of optimistic and pessimistic defined in [15], we can define optimistic multi-quantitative decision-theoretic rough set and pessimistic multi-quantitative decision-theoretic rough set respectively as:

Definition 7. *Given information system* $IS = (U, A, V, f)$, *if* $(\lambda_{rp} - \lambda_{rn}) < (\lambda_{np} - \lambda_{nn}) < (\lambda_{ap} - \lambda_{an})$ *and* $\alpha \geq \gamma \geq \beta$, *then optimistic multi-quantitative rough set with regard to concept* X *are defined as:*

$$\underline{X} = \{x | P(X | [x]) \geq \alpha\}$$
$$\overline{X} = \{x | P(X | [x]) \geq \beta\}$$

where $\alpha = \underset{(\alpha)}{\arg\min}(f_P(T_P^i, T_P^j) = f_B(T_B^i, T_B^j)), \forall i, j$

$\beta = \underset{(\beta)}{\arg\max}(f_N(T_N^i, T_N^j) = f_B(T_B^i, T_B^j)), \forall i, j.$

The boundary region of optimistic multi-quantification rough set is the smallest. Specifically, $\alpha = \alpha_1, \beta = \beta_4$ if target functions T_i and T_j are as shown in Fig. 4.

Definition 8. *Given information system* $IS = (U, A, V, f)$, *if* $(\lambda_{rp} - \lambda_{rn}) < (\lambda_{np} - \lambda_{nn}) < (\lambda_{ap} - \lambda_{an})$ *and* $\alpha \geq \gamma \geq \beta$, *then pessimistic multi-quantitative rough sets with regard to concept* X *are defined as:*

$$\underline{X} = \{x | P(X | [x]) \geq \alpha\}$$
$$\overline{X} = \{x | P(X | [x]) \geq \beta\}$$

where $\alpha = \underset{(\alpha)}{\arg\max}(f_P(T_P^i, T_P^j) = f_B(T_B^i, T_B^j)), \forall i, j$

$\beta = \underset{(\beta)}{\arg\min}(f_N(T_N^i, T_N^j) = f_B(T_B^i, T_B^j)), \forall i, j.$

The boundary region of pessimistic multi-quantitative rough set is the smallest. Specifically, $\alpha = \alpha_4, \beta = \beta_1$ if target functions T_i and T_j are as shown in Fig. 4.

For other concept descriptions, there are varying methods to develop three-way structure. One feasible solution is to interpret the problem as learning the weights among pair-wise target functions, and for this part we intend to elaborate the details in our future work. Hence, we argue that our work present a finer-grained threshold construction, since we can not only enrich the meaning of three-way in single quantification but also applicable in describing complicated concept.

5 Conclusion

This paper presents a novel threshold solving model from the perspective of multi-object optimization for three-way decisions. From the view of region-based target function, theories on determining three-way thresholds are significantly enriched. Multi-object optimization on target function is demonstrated to generate finer-grained thresholds as compared to discussions on double-quantitative decision-theoretic rough set. In the next step, we will not only theoretically examine the properties of multi-quantitative rough set, but also practically investigate efficient algorithms for knowledge reduction.

Acknowledgements. The authors would like to thank the anonymous reviewers for their constructive comments that help improve the manuscript. This research was supported by the National Natural Science Foundation of China (No. 61273304, 61673301, 61573255, 61573259), the Specialized Research Fund for the Doctoral Program of Higher Education of China (No. 20130072130004), and Natural Science Foundation of Shanghai (No. 14ZR1442600).

References

1. Yao, Y.: Three-way decision: an interpretation of rules in rough set theory. In: Wen, P., Li, Y., Polkowski, L., Yao, Y., Tsumoto, S., Wang, G. (eds.) RSKT 2009. LNCS, vol. 5589, pp. 642–649. Springer, Heidelberg (2009). doi:10.1007/978-3-642-02962-2_81
2. Pawlak, Z.: Rough Sets: Theoretical Aspects of Reasoning About Data. Kluwer Academic Publishers, Dordrecht (1991)
3. Zhou, B., Yao, Y.Y., Luo, J.G.: Cost-sensitive three-way email spam filtering. J. Intell. Inf. Syst. **42**(1), 19–45 (2014)
4. Zhang, Z.F., Miao, D.Q., Nie, J.Y., Yue, X.D.: Sentiment uncertainty measure and classification of negative sentences. J. Comput. Res. Dev. (in Chinese) **52**(8), 1806–1816 (2015)
5. Khan, M.T., Azam, N., Khalid, S., Yao, J.T.: A three-way approach for learning rules in automatic knowledge-based topic models. Int. J. Approx. Reason. **82**, 210–226 (2017)
6. Savchenko, A.V.: Fast multi-class recognition of piecewise regular objects based on sequential three-way decisions and granular computing. Knowl. Based Syst. **91**, 252–262 (2016)
7. Shivhare, R., Cherukuri, A.K.: Three-way conceptual approach for cognitive memory functionalities. Int. J. Mach. Learn. Cybern. **8**(1), 21–34 (2017)
8. Yao, Y.Y.: The superiority of three-way decisions in probabilistic rough set models. Inf. Sci. **181**, 1080–1096 (2011)
9. Liu, D., Liang, D.: An overview of function based three-way decisions. In: Miao, D., Pedrycz, W., Ślęzak, D., Peters, G., Hu, Q., Wang, R. (eds.) RSKT 2014. LNCS, vol. 8818, pp. 812–823. Springer, Cham (2014). doi:10.1007/978-3-319-11740-9_74
10. Jia, X.Y., Tang, Z.M., Liao, W.H., Shang, L.: On an optimization representation of decision-theoretic rough set model. Int. J. Approx. Reason. **55**, 156–166 (2014)
11. Pan, R.L., Zhang, Z.C., Fan, Y.L., Cao, J.H., Lu, K., Yang, T.S.: Multi-objective optimization method for learning thresholds in a decision-theoretic rough set model. Int. J. Approx. Reason. **71**, 34–49 (2016)

12. Xu, W.H., Guo, Y.T.: Generalized multigranulation double-quantitative decision-theoretic rough set. Knowl. Based Syst. **105**, 190–225 (2016)
13. Yao, Y.Y., Wong, S.K.M.: A decision theoretic framework for approximating concepts. Int. J. Man Mach. Stud. **37**(6), 793–809 (1992)
14. Zhang, X.Y., Miao, D.Q.: Two basic double-quantitative rough set models of precision and grade and their investigation using granular computing. Int. J. Approx. Reason. **54**, 1130–1148 (2013)
15. Qian, Y.H., Liang, J.Y., Yao, Y.Y., Dang, C.Y.: MGRS: a multi-granulation rough set. Inf. Sci. **180**, 949–970 (2010)
16. Sun, B.Z., Ma, W.M., Xiao, X.: Three-way group decision making based on multi-granulation fuzzy decision-theoretic rough set over two universes. Int. J. Approx. Reason. **81**, 87–102 (2017)
17. Fan, B.J., Tsang, E.C.C., Xu, W.H., Yu, J.H.: Double-quantitative rough fuzzy set based decisions: a logical operations method. Inf. Sci. **378**, 264–281 (2017)

Three-Way Decisions Cost Model Based on Continuous Domain

Tao Zhang[1], Qinghua Zhang[1(✉)], and Chenchen Yang[2]

[1] The Chongqing Key Laboratory of Computational Intelligence,
Chongqing University of Posts and Telecommunications,
Chongqing 400065, China
zhangqh@cqupt.edu.cn
[2] School of Science, Chongqing University of Posts and Telecommunications,
Chongqing 400065, China

Abstract. Three-way decisions theory is an intelligent strategy to deal with the uncertain information. The cost of three-way decisions could be reduced by selecting a pair of appropriate thresholds. The complexity of obtaining a pair of optimal thresholds will increase when processing the large datasets. In this paper, firstly, a new concept on number of equal probability object is defined in continuous domain. Secondly, the three-way decisions cost model based on continuous domain is established. Finally, an efficient algorithm for searching optimal thresholds of three-way decisions model is proposed for continuous domain. The experimental results demonstrate that the proposed model is better in the efficiency, robustness and generalization ability than that of the model based on discrete domain for large datasets. These results further enrich the theory of three-way decisions model.

Keywords: Three-way decisions · Optimal thresholds · Continuous domain · Cost · Number of equal probability object

1 Introduction

More and more imprecise, inconsistent or uncertain information has been flooded into people's life from the middle of the 20th century [1], and many researchers make great efforts to find some workable methods for dealing with the uncertain information. Fuzzy set theory, which describes imprecise features by a membership function, is proposed by Zadeh in 1965 [2]. D-S evidence theory is proposed by Dempster and Shafer [8] in 1976. However, D-S evidence theory needs to depend on prior knowledge and it also has very high computational complexity. Hence, rough set theory is proposed by Pawlak to solve the defect of D-S evidence theory in 1982 [4]. Nowadays, rough set model has successfully been applied to many fields, such as data mining, machine learning, cloud computing, network security and so on [5–9, 30–34]. Some scholars propose other practicable extended models [10–12]. Probabilistic rough set is proposed by Yao and it could describe the uncertain information [13]. In 1993, variable precision rough set model is put forward by Ziarko [14]. Then, Yao brings a pair of thresholds α and $\beta(0 \leq \beta < \alpha \leq 1)$ into Pawlak's rough set theory and establishes

© Springer International Publishing AG 2017
L. Polkowski et al. (Eds.): IJCRS 2017, Part II, LNAI 10314, pp. 340–358, 2017.
DOI: 10.1007/978-3-319-60840-2_25

probabilistic rough set model in 90's [15]. Probabilistic rough set model has been widely used in many fields and disciplines now, including decision-theoretic rough set model [16], Bayesian rough set model [17], information-theoretic analysis [18, 19], attribute reduction [20], three-way decisions rough set model [21–23] and game-theoretic rough set model [24]. Yao proposes three-way decisions rough set model [21–23], and provides reasonable semantic interpretations for three regions of rough set. Nowadays, the three-way decisions rough set model is widely used in daily life, such as management sciences [25], peering review process [26], medical decision-making [27, 28] and e-mail filtering [29].

To some extent, the three-way decisions rough set model can satisfy the demands in real life. But some aspects should be further studied and improved. Firstly, there are only four types of decision errors: Rejecting an object x which belongs to X (where X is a target set), accepting an object x which does not belong to X, making a deferred decisions for an object x which can't be determined whether belongs or not belongs to X. Secondly, in the case of large datasets, the problem how to calculate decisions cost in the continuous domain could be solved, and continuous domain means the values of conditional probability of classification is continuous. Finally, the question how to obtain the optimal thresholds α and $\beta(0 \le \beta < \alpha \le 1)$ from the perspective of global optimal is also worth considering.

Hence, according to the three-way decisions cost model containing four types of decision errors, the new concept on the number of equal probability object is defined at first. Secondly, the three-way decisions cost model based on continuous domain is put forward consequently. Finally, an efficient algorithm for searching optimal thresholds of three-way decisions model is proposed for the continuous domain. The experimental results show that the efficiency, robustness and generalization ability of the proposed model are better than those based on discrete domain for large datasets. In specific situations, the thresholds α and β can be calculated without prior knowledge, and it is convenient to make decisions. Therefore, the proposed three-way decisions cost model based on continuous domain may further develop three-way decisions theory.

The rest of this paper is organized as follows. First, some preliminary concepts about rough set and three-way decisions theory are reviewed in Sect. 2. Then, the number of equal probability object, three-way decisions cost model based on continuous domain, and an efficient algorithm for searching optimal thresholds are proposed in Sect. 3. Next, the experimental analysis is discussed in Sect. 4. Finally, the paper is concluded in Sect. 5.

2 Preliminaries

The Pawlak's rough set model is a mathematical tool to analyze uncertain information [4]. Many scholars constantly extend this model to some new extensions, such as, probabilistic rough set model and decision-theoretic rough set model, variable precision rough set model. What's more, according to granular computing, multi-granulation rough set model was presented by Qian [36]. Yao [21–23] put forward the concept of three-way decisions. In order to improve readability, many basic concepts on rough set and three-way decisions are reviewed briefly in this section.

Definition 1 (Indiscernible relation [3]). Given an information system $S = (U, R)$, U is a nonempty finite set and A is an attribute set. For any subset of attributes $R \subseteq A$, an indiscernible relation (or equivalence relation) $IND(R)$ is defined as follows,

$$IND(R) = \{(x, y) | (x, y) \in U^2, \forall_{b \in R}(b(x) = b(y))\}.$$

Definition 2 (Rough sets [3]). Given an information system $S = (U, R)$, attribute subset $R \subseteq A$. For any target subset $X \subseteq U$, its lower and upper approximation sets are defined, respectively, as follows,

$$\underline{R}(X) = \{x \in U | [x] \in X\} \text{ and } \bar{R}(X) = \{x \in U | [x] \cap X \neq \emptyset\}.$$

Where $[x]$ denotes the equivalence class of x. If and only if $\underline{R}(X) \neq \bar{R}(X)$, X is called a rough set with respect to R.

Definition 3 (Probabilistic rough set model [15]). Given an information system $S = (U, R)$ with a pair of thresholds α and $\beta (0 \leq \beta < \alpha \leq 1)$, where $R \subseteq A$ is a subset of the attributes. For any $X \subseteq U$, the lower and upper approximation sets of X on universe U are defined as follows,

$$\underline{R}^{(\alpha,\beta)}(X) = \{x \in U | P(X | [x]) \geq \alpha\} \quad \text{and} \quad \bar{R}^{(\alpha,\beta)}(X) = \{x \in U | P(X | [x]) > \beta\}.$$

Where $P(X | [x]) = |[x] \cap X| / |[x]|$ denotes conditional probability of classification. $|\bullet|$ is the cardinality of a set. And the domain is divided into three disjoint regions as follows,

$$POS_R^{(\alpha,\beta)}(X) = \{x \in U | P(X | [x] \geq \alpha\} = \underline{R}^{(\alpha,\beta)}(X),$$
$$NEG_R^{(\alpha,\beta)}(X) = \{x \in U | P(X | [x] \leq \beta\} = U - \bar{R}^{(\alpha,\beta)}(X),$$
$$BND_R^{(\alpha,\beta)}(X) = \{x \in U | \beta < P(X | [x] < \alpha\} = \bar{R}^{(\alpha,\beta)}(X) - \underline{R}^{(\alpha,\beta)}(X).$$

Definition 4 (Three-way decisions rough set model [21–23]). Let $\Omega = \{C, C^c\}$ be the set of states. $A = \{\alpha_P, \alpha_N, \alpha_B\}$ be the set of actions, where α_P, α_N and α_B represent the three actions in classifying an object x, Namely, deciding $x \in POS(X)$, deciding $x \in NEG(X)$, and deciding $x \in BND(X)$, respectively. The positive region $POS(X)$ and the negative region $NEG(X)$, still correspond to the decisions of acceptance and rejection, respectively. The third region $BND(X)$ corresponds to the decision of deferment.

If $P(C | [x]) \geq \alpha$ and $P(C | [x]) \geq \gamma$, decide $x \in POS(X)$;
If $P(C | [x]) < \beta$ and $P(C | [x]) < \gamma$, decide $x \in NEG(X)$;
If $P(C | [x]) < \alpha$ and $P(C | [x]) > \beta$, decide $x \in BND(X)$.

When an object belongs to X, λ_{PP}, λ_{NP} and λ_{BP} denote the cost for taking actions α_P, α_N and α_B, respectively, while λ_{PN}, λ_{NN} and λ_{BN} denote the cost of taking the same actions when the object does not belong to X. Where the three thresholds α, β and γ are calculated from the cost function as follows:

$$\alpha = \frac{(\lambda_{PN} - \lambda_{BN})}{(\lambda_{PN} - \lambda_{BN}) + (\lambda_{BP} - \lambda_{PP})}, \quad \beta = \frac{(\lambda_{BN} - \lambda_{NN})}{(\lambda_{BN} - \lambda_{NN}) + (\lambda_{NP} - \lambda_{BP})} \text{ and } \gamma$$

$$= \frac{(\lambda_{PN} - \lambda_{NN})}{(\lambda_{PN} - \lambda_{BN}) + (\lambda_{NP} - \lambda_{PP})}.$$

With the introduction of the third action, the cost function is now given by the 3×2 matrix:

	C : positive	C^c : negative
α_P : accept	λ_{PP}	λ_{PN}
α_N : reject	λ_{NP}	λ_{NN}
α_B : defer	λ_{BP}	λ_{BN}

In Yao's three-way decisions model [21–23], the values of α and β are obtained with minimum decisions cost based on discrete domain. However, when facing to big datasets in the continuous domain this model need to be improved. In this paper, the three-way decisions cost model based on continuous domain is presented, and an efficient algorithm for searching optimal thresholds of three-way decisions model is established from thought of global optimum. Accordingly, in this paper, some tentative researches on three-way decisions based on continuous domain have been studied.

3 Three-Way Decisions Cost Model

At present many scholars usually discuss three-way decisions theory in the nonempty finite set, which greatly limits the development of three-way decisions theory based on continuous domain. In this section, firstly, according to three-way decisions cost model based on discrete domain, a new concept on number of equal probability object is defined for indicating three-way decisions in the continuous domain. Secondly, three-way decisions cost model based on continuous domain is proposed. Finally, an efficient algorithm is proposed to obtain the optimal thresholds α and β of this model.

3.1 Three-Way Decisions Cost Model Based on Discrete Domain

The domain U will be divided into positive region $POS_R(X)$, negative region $NEG_R(X)$ and boundary region $BND_R(X)$ by an equivalence relation R and a target set $X \subseteq U$. However, in this process, it is inevitable to make wrong decisions. So, four types of decision errors are defined to calculate the cost of three-way decisions model.

Definition 5 (Four types of decisions errors). Given an information system $S = (U, R)$, $X(X \subseteq U)$ is a target set, R is an equivalence relation on U.

The first type of decision error (Error-1): If $x \in X$, but x is classified into $NEG_R(X)$, and the cost coefficient is denoted as $\lambda_1(\lambda_1 > 0)$.

The second type of decision error (Error-2): If $x \notin X$, but x is classified into $POS_R(X)$, and the cost coefficient is denoted as $\lambda_2(\lambda_2 > 0)$.

The third type of decision error (Error-3): If $x \in X$, but x is classified into $BND_R(X)$, and the cost coefficient is denoted as $u_1(u_1 > 0)$.

The fourth type of decision error (Error-4): If $x \notin X$, but x is classified into $BND_R(X)$, and the cost coefficient is denoted as $u_2(u_2 > 0)$.

In the probabilistic rough set model, an equivalence class $[x]$ may be classified into different regions based on its conditional probability $P(X|[x]) = |[x] \cap X|/|[x]|$, and the decision rules are shown as follows $(0 \leq \beta < \alpha \leq 1)$,

$$\begin{cases} [x] \subseteq POS_R(X), \alpha \leq P(X|[x]) \leq 1, \\ [x] \subseteq NEG_R(X), 0 \leq P(X|[x]) \leq \beta, \\ [x] \subseteq BND_R(X), \beta < P(X|[x]) < \alpha. \end{cases}$$

Figure 1 shows the relationship between probabilistic rough set model and three-way decisions model.

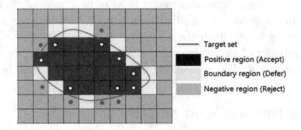

Fig. 1. Relationship between probabilistic rough set model and three-way decisions model.

Let $C([x])$ denote the decisions cost function of the equivalence class $[x]$ as follows,

$$C([x]) = \begin{cases} \lambda_2 \times (1 - P(X|[x])) \times |[x]|, & \alpha \leq P(X|[x]) \leq 1, \\ \lambda_1 \times P(X|[x]) \times |[x]|, & 0 \leq P(X|[x]) \leq \beta, \\ u_1 \times P(X|[x]) \times |[x]| + u_2 \times (1 - P(X|[x])) \times |[x]|, & \beta < P(X|[x]) < \alpha. \end{cases}$$

Namely, $C([x]) = \begin{cases} \lambda_2 \times (|[x]| - |[x] \cap X|), & \alpha \leq P(X|[x]) \leq 1, \\ \lambda_1 \times |[x] \cap X|, & 0 \leq P(X|[x]) \leq \beta, \\ u_1 \times |[x] \cap X| + u_2 \times (|[x]| - |[x] \cap X|), & \beta < P(X|[x]) < \alpha. \end{cases}$

For convenience, let $C(P) = \sum\limits_{[x] \subseteq POS} C([x])$, $C(N) = \sum\limits_{[x] \subseteq NEG} C([x])$ and $C(B) = \sum\limits_{[x] \subseteq BND} C([x])$. The calculation methods of decisions cost for different equivalent classes are explained respectively.

(1) When $P(X|[x]) \geq \alpha$, $C([x])$ indicates that the cost of the equivalence class $[x]$ which is classified into positive region, and it can be calculated as following formula,

$$C([x]) = \lambda_2 \times (1 - P(X|[x])) \times |[x]| = \lambda_2 \times (|[x]| - |[x] \cap X|);$$

(2) When $P(X|[x]) \leq \beta$, $C([x])$ indicates that cost of the equivalence class $[x]$ which is classified into negative region, and it can be calculated as following formula,

$$C([x]) = \lambda_1 \times P(X|[x]) \times |[x]| = \lambda_1 \times (|[x] \cap X|);$$

(3) When $\beta < P(X|[x]) < \alpha$, namely equivalent class $[x]$ is divided into boundary region), $C([x])$ indicates that cost of the equivalence $[x]$ which is classified into boundary region, and it can be calculated as following formula,

$$C([x]) = u_1 \times P(X|[x]) \times |[x]| + u_2 \times (1 - P(X|[x])) \times |[x]|$$
$$= u_1 \times |[x] \cap X| + u_2 \times (|[x]| - |[x] \cap X|).$$

Obviously, in Pawlak's rough set, $[x] \subseteq POS_R(X)$ only when $P(X|[x]) = 1$, so $C(P) = 0$, similarly, $[x] \subseteq NEG_R(X)$ only when $P(X|[x]) = 0$, so $C(N) = 0$. From the above analysis, we can know that the decisions cost of Pawlak's rough set only comes from the boundary domain, namely, $C(U) = C(B)$.

Three-way decisions cost model based on discrete domain can be established by the four types of decisions errors and the decisions cost function.

Definition 6 (Three-way decisions cost model based on discrete domain). The three-way decisions cost model based on discrete domain can be established as follows:

$$C(U) = C(P) + C(N) + C(B)$$
$$= \sum_{\alpha \leq P(X|[x]) \leq 1} C([x]) + \sum_{0 \leq P(X|[x]) \leq \beta} C([x]) + \sum_{\beta < P(X|[x]) < \alpha} C([x])$$
$$= \sum_{\alpha \leq P(X|[x]) \leq 1} \lambda_2 \times (|[x]| - |[x] \cap X|) + \sum_{0 \leq P(X|[x]) \leq \beta} \lambda_1 \times |[x] \cap X|$$
$$+ \sum_{\beta < P(X|[x]) < \alpha} u_1 \times |[x] \cap X| + u_2 \times (|[x]| - |[x] \cap X|).$$

The cost coefficient of four types of decisions errors are λ_1, λ_2, u_1 and u_2 (see Definition 5). The decision rules are shown as follows:

$$\begin{cases} x \in POS_R(X), \alpha \leq P(X|[x]) \leq 1, \\ x \in NEG_R(X), 0 \leq P(X|[x]) \leq \beta, \\ x \in BND_R(X), \beta < P(X|[x]) < \alpha. \end{cases}$$

Next, an example of the proposed model is presented in the following Example 1.

Example 1. An information system is constructed by using the Adult [35] dataset in UCI (see Table 1), for convenience, we only select 27 samples in the Adults data set (namely, the domain $U = \{x_1, x_2, \cdots, x_{27}\}$ in S_1). The four condition attributes are "Workclass", "Education", "Sex" and "Race" respectively, and the decision attribute is "Salary". The cost coefficient of four types of decision errors are denoted as λ_1, λ_2, u_1 and u_2 respectively.

Table 1. Information system S_1.

id	Workclass	Education	Sex	Race	Salary
X_1	Federal-gov	10th	Female	Amer-Indian-Eskimo	$\leq 50K$
X_2	Federal-gov	10th	Female	White	$\leq 50K$
X_3	Local-gov	10th	Female	Black	$\leq 50K$
X_4	Never-worked	10th	Male	White	$\leq 50K$
X_5	Private	10th	Female	Amer-Indian-Eskimo	$\leq 50K$
X_6	Private	Assoc-acdm	Female	Amer-Indian-Eskimo	$\leq 50K$
X_7	Local-gov	Bachelors	Male	Asian-Pac-Islander	$\leq 50K$
X_8	Local-gov	Bachelors	Male	Black	$\leq 50K$
X_9	Federal-gov	Some-college	Male	White	$\leq 50K$
X_{10}	Local-gov	Some-college	Male	White	$\leq 50K$
X_{11}	Never-worked	Some-college	Male	White	$\leq 50K$
X_{12}	Private	Some-college	Female	White	$\leq 50K$
X_{13}	Local-gov	Assoc-acdm	Female	White	>50K
X_{14}	Private	Assoc-acdm	Male	Asian-Pac-Islander	>50K
X_{15}	Federal-gov	Bachelors	Male	White	>50K
X_{16}	Federal-gov	Doctorate	Female	Amer-Indian-Eskimo	>50K
X_{17}	Local-gov	Doctorate	Male	White	>50K
X_{18}	Federal-gov	Doctorate	Female	Black	>50K
X_{19}	Federal-gov	Doctorate	Female	White	>50K
X_{20}	Federal-gov	Doctorate	Male	Asian-Pac-Islander	>50K
X_{21}	Federal-gov	Doctorate	Male	White	>50K
X_{22}	Federal-gov	Masters	Female	White	>50K
X_{23}	Private	Masters	Male	Asian-Pac-Islander	>50K
X_{24}	Private	Prof-school	Female	Asian-Pac-Islander	>50K
X_{25}	Private	Prof-school	Female	White	>50K
X_{26}	Private	Prof-school	Male	White	>50K
X_{27}	Federal-gov	Some-college	Male	Asian-Pac-Islander	>50K

Supposing the target set is $X = \{x_{13}, x_{14}, \cdots, x_{27}\}$ in S_1, then all objects in S_1 will be divided into 7 equivalent classes by attribute "Education", namely $R = \{10^{th}, ASSoc\text{-}acdm, Bachelors, Some\text{-}college, Doctorate, Prof\text{-}school, Masters\}$, they are shown as follows,

$$U/R = \{\{x_1, x_2, x_3, x_4, x_5\}, \{x_6, x_{13}, x_{14}\}, \{x_7, x_8\},$$
$$\{x_9, x_{10}, x_{11}, x_{12}, x_{15}\}, \{x_{24}, x_{25}, x_{26}\}, \{x_{22}, x_{23}\}\}$$
$$= \{X_1, X_2, X_3, X_4, X_5, X_6, X_7\}.$$

Therefore, the conditional probabilities of each equivalent class will be calculated as follows,

$$P(X|X_1) = |X_1 \cap X|/|X_1| = 0, \quad P(X|X_2) = |X_2 \cap X|/|X_2| = \frac{2}{3},$$

$$P(X|X_3) = |X_3 \cap X|/|X_3| = 0, \quad P(X|X_4) = |X_4 \cap X|/|X_4| = \frac{1}{5},$$

$$P(X|X_5) = |X_5 \cap X|/|X_5| = 1, \quad P(X|X_6) = |X_6 \cap X|/|X_6| = 1 \quad \text{and}$$

$$P(X|X_7) = |X_7 \cap X|/|X_7| = 1.$$

(1) In Pawlak's rough set, the decisions cost for information system S_1 can be computed as follows,

$$C(U) = C(B)$$
$$= \sum_{\beta < P(X|[x]) < \alpha} \{u_1 \times |[x] \cap X| + u_2 \times (|[x]| - |[x] \cap X|)\}$$
$$= 2u_1 + u_2 + u_1 + 4u_2$$
$$= 3u_1 + 5u_2.$$

(2) In the probabilistic rough set, the decisions cost for information system S_1 will change with the thresholds α and β $(0 \leq \beta < \alpha \leq 1)$, and they are shown in Table 2.

Table 2. Decisions cost in the probabilistic rough set.

Thresholds α, β	Decisions cost
$0 \leq \beta < \alpha \leq \frac{1}{5}$	$5\lambda_2$
$\frac{1}{5} < \beta < \alpha < \frac{2}{3}$	$\lambda_1 + \lambda_2$
$\frac{2}{3} < \beta < \alpha \leq \frac{1}{5}$	$3\lambda_1$
$0 \leq \beta < \frac{1}{5} < \alpha < \frac{2}{3}$	$\lambda_2 + \mu_1 + 4\mu_2$
$\frac{1}{5} < \beta < \frac{2}{3} < \alpha \leq 1$	$\lambda_1 + 2\mu_1 + \mu_2$
$0 \leq \beta < \frac{1}{5} < \frac{2}{3} < \alpha \leq 1$	$3\mu_1 + 5\mu_2$

In real life, the optimal thresholds α and β can be obtained by solving the cost minimization problem in Pawlak's rough set model or probabilistic rough set model. Table 3 shows the relationship among the cost coefficients of four types of decisions errors, optimal thresholds (α and β) and decisions cost in Example 1.

The above analysis is the process of obtaining the minimum decisions cost and the optimal thresholds in the discrete domain. But there are two difficulties. One is very high time complexity. That is to say, the more values the conditional probability is, the

Table 3. Relationship among the cost coefficients, the optimal thresholds and decisions cost.

Cost coefficients	Minimum decisions cost	Optimal thresholds	Cost coefficients	Minimum decisions cost	Optimal thresholds
$\begin{cases} \lambda_1 > \mu_1 + \frac{5}{3}\mu_2 \\ \lambda_2 > \frac{5}{3}\mu_1 + \mu_2 \end{cases}$	$3\mu_1 + 5\mu_2$	$0 \le \beta < \frac{1}{3} < \frac{2}{3} < \alpha \le 1$	$\begin{cases} \lambda_1 < \frac{1}{2}\lambda_2 \\ \lambda_1 < \mu_1 + \frac{1}{2}\mu_2 \\ \lambda_1 < \frac{1}{3}\lambda_2 + \frac{1}{3}\mu_1 + \frac{4}{3} \end{cases}$	$3\lambda_1$	$\frac{2}{3} < \beta < \alpha \le 1$
$\begin{cases} \lambda_2 < \frac{1}{4}\lambda_1 \\ \lambda_2 < \frac{1}{4}\mu_1 + \mu_2 \\ \lambda_2 < \frac{1}{3}\lambda_1 + \frac{2}{3}\mu_1 + \frac{1}{3}\mu_2 \end{cases}$	$5\lambda_2$	$0 \le \beta < \alpha \le \frac{1}{3}$	$\begin{cases} \lambda_1 > \mu_1 + 4\mu_2 \\ \frac{1}{4}\mu_1 + \mu_2 < \lambda_2 < 2\mu_1 \end{cases}$	$\lambda_2 + \mu_1 + 4\mu_2$	$0 \le \beta < \frac{1}{3} < \alpha < \frac{2}{3}$
$\begin{cases} \lambda_1 < \mu_1 + 4\mu_2 \\ \lambda_2 < 2\mu_1 + \mu_2 \end{cases}$	$\lambda_1 + \lambda_2$	$\frac{1}{3} < \beta < \alpha < \frac{2}{3}$	$\begin{cases} \lambda_2 > 2\mu_1 + \mu_2 \\ \lambda_1 > \mu_1 + \frac{1}{2}\mu_2 \end{cases}$	$\lambda_1 + 2\mu_1 + \mu_2$	$\frac{1}{3} < \beta < \frac{2}{3} < \alpha \le 1$

higher the time complexity of solving the optimal thresholds. The other is that the optimal thresholds is an interval value in the discrete domain, so the accuracy, robustness and generalization ability of this model are relatively low.

In order to solve above two problems, in this paper, the equal number of objects is defined, and a three-way decisions cost model based on continuous domain is proposed from a new viewpoint.

3.2   Three-Way Decisions Cost Model Based on Continuous Domain

In this section, the number of equal probability object is defined, then, the way of obtaining the optimal thresholds is presented in the three-way decisions cost model based on continuous domain.

Definition 7 (The number of equal probability object). Given an information system $S=(U,R)$, $\forall x, y(x,y \in U)$, $\exists P(X|[x])=P(X|[y])=p(p \in [0,1])$, x and y be called equal probability. $f(p) = |\{x|x \in U \wedge P(X|[x]) = p\}|$ is called the number of equal probability object.

In the Example 1, the number of equal probability object for each equivalent class are calculated as follows.

$$P(X|X_1) = P(X|X_3) = 0, \text{ so } f(0) = |X_1| + |X_3| = 7;$$
$$P(X|X_5) = P(X|X_6) = P(X|X_7) = 1, \text{ so } f(1) = |X_5| + |X_6| + |X_7| = 11;$$
$$P(X|X_2) = \frac{2}{3}, \text{ so } f(\frac{2}{3}) = |X_2| = 3; \quad P(X|X_4) = \frac{1}{5}, \text{ so } f(\frac{1}{5}) = |X_4| = 5.$$

Therefore, there is a new method to calculate the three-way decisions cost by the number of equal probability object. Then, the process of the decision cost in the information system S_1 is shown as follows.

(1) The total decisions cost can be calculated as following formula when $0 \le \beta < \alpha < \frac{1}{5}$.

$$C(U) = C(P) + C(N) + C(B)$$
$$= \lambda_2 \sum_{\alpha \le q < 1} (1-p)f(p) + 0 + 0 = 5\lambda_2.$$

(2) The total decision cost can be calculated as following formula when $\frac{1}{5} < \beta < \alpha < \frac{2}{3}$.

$$C(U) = C(P) + C(N) + C(B)$$
$$= \lambda_2 \sum_{\alpha \leq p < 1} (1 - p)f(p) + \lambda_1 \sum_{0 < p \leq \beta} pf(p) + 0 = \lambda_1 + \lambda_2.$$

(3) The total decision cost can be calculated as following formula when $\frac{2}{3} < \beta < \alpha \leq 1$.

$$C(U) = C(P) + C(N) + C(B)$$
$$= 0 + \lambda_1 \sum_{0 < p \leq \beta} pf(p) + 0 = 3\lambda_1.$$

(4) The total decision cost can be calculated as following formula when $0 \leq \beta < \frac{1}{5} < \alpha < \frac{2}{3}$.

$$C(U) = C(P) + C(N) + C(B)$$
$$= \lambda_2 \sum_{\alpha \leq p < 1} (1 - p)f(p) + 0 + u_1 \sum_{\beta < p < \alpha} pf(p) + u_2 \sum_{\beta < p < \alpha} (1 - p)f(p)$$
$$= \lambda_2 + u_1 + 4u_2.$$

(5) The total decision cost can be calculated as following formula when $\frac{1}{5} < \beta < \frac{2}{3} < \alpha \leq 1$.

$$C(U) = C(P) + C(N) + C(B)$$
$$= 0 + \lambda_1 \sum_{0 < p \leq \beta} pf(p) + u_1 \sum_{\beta < p < \alpha} pf(p) + u_2 \sum_{\beta < p < \alpha} (1 - p)f(p)$$
$$= \lambda_1 + 2u_1 + u_2.$$

(6) The total decision cost can be calculated as following formula when $0 \leq \beta < \frac{1}{5} < \frac{2}{3} < \alpha \leq 1$.

$$C(U) = C(P) + C(N) + C(B)$$
$$= 0 + 0 + u_1 \sum_{\beta < p < \alpha} pf(p) + u_2 \sum_{\beta < p < \alpha} (1 - p)f(p)$$
$$= 3u_1 + 5u_2.$$

It is easy to calculate the three-way decisions cost based on discrete domain by the number of equal probability object. In this paper, the discrete domain is extended to the continuous domain for solving mass and high-dimensional data. At the same time, the optimal thresholds can be obtained by new method, and it can improve the precision and generalization ability of three-way decisions cost model.

It is difficult to accurately calculate each number of equal probability object when the domain is too large. So, in this paper, the number of equal probability object with different conditions probability $p(p \in [0,1])$ will be obtained by sampling fitting, and supposing that $f(p) \in (0, +\infty)$. The three-way decisions cost model based on continuous domain is defined as follows.

Definition 8 (The three-way decisions cost model based on continuous domain). Given an information system $S=(U,R)$, Let $p(p \in [0,1])$ be the conditional probability, and the number of equal probability object $f(p)$ is continuous differential. Then the function of three-way decisions cost model based on continuous domain is $C_U(\alpha, \beta)$ can be defined as follows:

$$C_U(\alpha, \beta) = C(P) + C(N) + C(B)$$
$$= \lambda_2 \int_{\alpha}^{1} (1-p)f(p)dp + \lambda_1 \int_{0}^{\beta} pf(p)dp$$
$$+ u_1 \int_{\beta}^{\alpha} pf(p)dp + u_2 \int_{\beta}^{\alpha} (1-p)f(p)dp.$$

Where α and $\beta (0 \leq \beta < \alpha \leq 1)$ is the thresholds of this model, and the cost coefficient of four types of decisions errors are $\lambda_1, \lambda_2, \mu_1$ and μ_2 ($\lambda_1 \geq 0, \lambda_2 \geq 0, u_1 \geq 0$ and $u_2 \geq 0$).

The meaning of three parts of this model can be explained as follows.

(1) All the equivalent classes whose conditional probability is $p(\alpha \leq p \leq 1)$ will be classified into positive region, and $(1-p)f(p)$ indicates the number of objects that are classified into positive region but they do not belong to the target set, and λ_2 is the cost coefficient of Error-1. So the first part $\lambda_2 \int_{\alpha}^{1} (1-p)f(p)dp$ is the decision cost of positive region.

(2) All the equivalent classes whose conditional probability is $p(0 \leq p \leq \beta)$ will be classified into negative region, and $pf(p)$ indicates the number of objects that are classified into negative region but they belong to the target set, and λ_1 is the cost coefficient of Error-2. So the second part $\lambda_1 \int_{0}^{\beta} pf(p)dp$ is the decision cost of negative region.

(3) All the equivalent classes whose conditional probability is $p(\alpha < p < \beta)$ will be classified into boundary region, and $pf(p)$ indicates the number of objects that are divided into boundary region but they belong to the target set, and $(1-p)f(p)$ indicates the number of objects that are classified into boundary region but they do not belong to the target set. u_1 and u_2 are the cost coefficients of Error-3 and Error-4 respectively. So the third part $u_1 \int_{\beta}^{\alpha} pf(p)dp + u_2 \int_{\beta}^{\alpha} (1-p)f(p)dp$ is the decision cost of boundary region.

In conclusion, $C_U(\alpha, \beta)$ can represent the three-way decisions cost in the whole domain.

Theorem 1. In the three-way decisions cost model based on continuous domain, let $\lambda_1, \lambda_2, u_1$ and u_2 be the cost coefficient of four types of decisions errors respectively

$(\lambda_1 \geq 0,\ \lambda_2 \geq 0,\ u_1 \geq 0$ and $u_2 \geq 0)$. If $\lambda_1 > u_1 - u_2$ and $\lambda_2 > u_1 + u_2$, the optimal thresholds α_0 and $\beta_0 (0 \leq \beta_0 < \alpha_0 \leq 1)$ will be easily calculated as follows:

$$\alpha_0 = \frac{\lambda_2 - u_2}{\lambda_2 + u_1 - u_2},\ \beta_0 = \frac{u_2}{\lambda_1 - u_1 + u_2}.$$

Proof. The first derivatives of $C_U(\alpha, \beta)$ are $\frac{\partial C_U(\alpha,\beta)}{\partial \alpha}$ and $\frac{\partial C_U(\alpha,\beta)}{\partial \beta}$.

$$\frac{\partial C_U(\alpha, \beta)}{\partial \alpha} = -\lambda_2(1 - \alpha)f(\alpha) + u_1 \alpha f(\alpha) + u_2(1 - \alpha)f(\alpha)$$

$$= f(\alpha)[(\lambda_2 + u_1 - u_2)\alpha - \lambda_2 + u_2];$$

$$\frac{\partial C_U(\alpha, \beta)}{\partial \beta} = \lambda_1 \beta f(\beta) - u_1 \beta f(\beta) - u_2(1 - \beta)f(\beta)$$

$$= -f(\beta)[(u_1 - u_2 - \lambda_1)\beta + u_2].$$

Because $f(\alpha)$ and $f(\beta)$ are constants, (α_0, β_0) is the stationary point as follows.

$$\alpha_0 = \frac{\lambda_2 - u_2}{\lambda_2 + u_1 - u_2},\ \beta_0 = \frac{u_2}{\lambda_1 - u_1 + u_2}.$$

The second derivatives of $C_U(\alpha, \beta)$ are $\frac{\partial^2 C_U(\alpha,\beta)}{(\partial \alpha)^2}$ and $\frac{\partial^2 C_U(\alpha,\beta)}{(\partial \beta)^2}$.

$$\frac{\partial^2 C_U(\alpha, \beta)}{(\partial \alpha)^2} = f'(\alpha)[(\lambda_2 + u_1 - u_2)\alpha - \lambda_2 + u_2] + f(\alpha)(\lambda_2 + u_1 - u_2)$$

$$= A_1 + A_2 = A;$$

$$\frac{\partial^2 C_U(\alpha, \beta)}{(\partial \beta)^2} = -f'(\beta)[(u_1 - u_2 - \lambda_1)\beta + u_2] - f(\beta)(u_1 - u_2 - \lambda_1)$$

$$= C_1 + C_2 = C;$$

$$\frac{\partial^2 C_U(\alpha, \beta)}{\partial \alpha \partial \beta} = 0 = B.$$

The function of three-way decisions cost model based on continuous domain $C_U(\alpha, \beta)$ can be minimized when the stationary point (α_0, β_0) satisfies $A > 0$ and $AC - B^2 > 0$. Namely, the three-way decisions cost will reach minimum when $\lambda_1 > u_1 - u_2$, $\lambda_2 > u_1 + u_2$ and the thresholds is α_0 and β_0 (where $\alpha_0 = \lambda_2 - u_2/\lambda_2 + u_1 - u_2$ and $\beta_0 = u_2/\lambda_1 - u_1 + u_2$).

In summary, the proof is completed.

According to Theorem 1, the optimal thresholds are $\alpha_0 = \lambda_2 - u_2/\lambda_2 + u_1 - u_2$ and $\beta_0 = u_2/\lambda_1 - u_1 + u_2$ when $\lambda_1 > u_1 - u_2$ and $\lambda_2 > u_1 + u_2$ (namely, the cost coefficient of Error-2 more than the sum of Error-3 and Error-4, and the cost coefficient of

Error-1 more than the difference of Error-3 and Error-4). But in practice, the conditions $\lambda_1 > u_1 - u_2$ and $\lambda_2 > u_1 + u_2$ are hard to satisfy. So it is not easy to find the optimal thresholds, and the minimum value of cost function is in the endpoint.

In the process of dealing with mass data, it is difficult to obtain the optimal thresholds in the time and space by the three-way decisions cost model based on discrete domain. So, the total cost of three-way decisions cost on the whole domain will be fitted by the randomly sampling data. Then, Algorithm 1 is proposed to obtain the optimal thresholds and the minimal decision cost based on continuous domain.

Algorithm 1. An efficient algorithm for searching optimal thresholds of three-way decisions model based on continuous (**EASOT**).

Input:　　An information system (S) and the cost coefficients of four types of decisions errors ($\lambda_1 \geq 0$, $\lambda_2 \geq 0$, $u_1 \geq 0$ and $u_2 \geq 0$).

Output:　The thresholds of three-way decisions α_0 and $\beta_0 (0 \leq \beta_0 < \alpha_0 \leq 1)$ and the minimal decision cost.

Step 1.　The cost coefficients of the four types of decisions errors will be judged whether satisfies the conditions $\lambda_1 > u_1 - u_2$ and $\lambda_2 > u_1 + u_2$.

Step 2.　If the cost coefficients satisfy the above conditions, the optimal thresholds will be $\alpha_0 = \lambda_2 - u_2 / \lambda_2 + u_1 - u_2$ and $\beta_0 = u_2 / \lambda_1 - u_1 + u_2$, then go to **step 6**.

Step 3.　If the cost coefficients do not satisfy the above conditions, the number of equal probability object function $f(p)$ will be fitted by randomly sampling some objects in the domain.

Step 4.　According to the three-way decisions cost model based on continuous domain, $C_U(\alpha, \beta)$ will be established by the number of equal probability object function in **Step 3**.

Step 5.　The optimal thresholds (α_0, β_0) will be calculated by $C_U(\alpha, \beta)$.

Step 6.　Return (α_0, β_0) and $C_U(\alpha, \beta)$.

The algorithm flowchart is shown in Fig. 2.

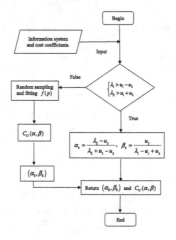

Fig. 2. Flowchart of EASOT.

4 Experiments and Analysis

In the first experiment, the correctness of the proposed model is verified with artificial datasets. In the second experiment, the performance of the three-way decisions cost model based on continuous domain will be compared with the model based on discrete domain with actual data. Experimental environment is 8 G RAM, 3.0 GHz CPU, and WIN 8.1 operating system, and the programming languages are MATLAB and Python.

4.1 Experiment Analysis with Artificial Datasets

In this experiment, the cost coefficient of four types of decisions errors ($\lambda_1 \geq 0$, $\lambda_2 \geq 0$, $u_1 \geq 0$ and $u_2 \geq 0$) meet the conditions $\lambda_1 > u_1 - u_2$ and $\lambda_2 > u_1 + u_2$. And then there are four functions of equal probabilistic object $f_i(p)(i = 1, 2, 3, 4; p \in [0, 1])$, which are $f_1 = 100 + (p - 0.5)^2$, $f_2 = 100 + (p - 0.5)^2$, $f_3 = 100 + \log_{0.5}^p$ and $f_4 = 100 + e^p$. The function images are shown in Figs. 3, 4, 5, 6, and the datasets are 5×10^5 (namely, every domain collects 5×10^5 points from $f(p)$).

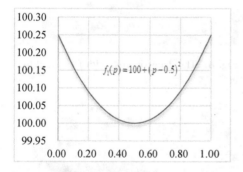

Fig. 3. The function picture of $f_1(p)$.

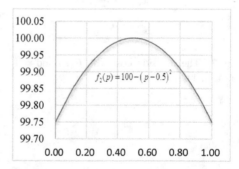

Fig. 4. The function picture of $f_2(p)$.

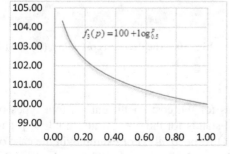

Fig. 5. The function picture of $f_3(p)$.

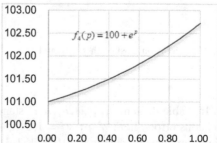

Fig. 6. The function picture of $f_4(p)$.

Table 4. The results of experimental 1.

$(\lambda_1, \lambda_2, u_1, u_2)$	$f_1(p)$	$f_2(p)$	$f_3(p)$	$f_4(p)$
(3, 5, 1, 2)	(0.75, 0.5, 87.59)	(0.75, 0.5, 87.46)	(0.75, 0.5, 86.25)	(0.75, 0.5, 89.03)
(4, 6, 2, 3)	(0.6, 0.6, 120.05)	(0.6, 0.6, 119.95)	(0.6, 0.6, 122.77)	(0.6, 0.6, 122.09)
(5, 4, 2, 1)	(0.6, 0.25, 97.55)	(0.6, 0.25, 97.45)	(0.6, 0.25, 95.99)	(0.6, 0.25, 99.13)

Experimental results shown in Table 4 indicate the relationship among the cost coefficients of four types of decisions errors, the four functions $f_i(p)(i = 1, 2, 3, 4; p \in [0, 1])$, the minimum cost value and the optimal thresholds α and β. The partial images of decision cost are shown in Figs. 7, 8, 9, 10.

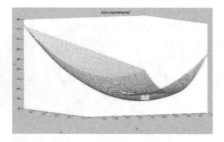

Fig. 7. The decision cost with $f_1(p)$ and (5, 4, 2, 1).

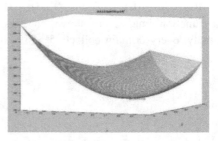

Fig. 8. The decision cost with $f_2(p)$ and (4, 6, 2, 3).

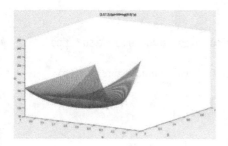

Fig. 9. The decision cost with $f_3(p)$ and (3, 5, 1, 2).

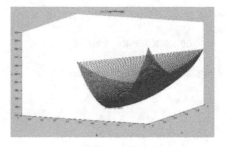

Fig. 10. The decision cost with $f_4(p)$ and (4, 6, 2, 3).

In Table 4, item "$(\lambda_1, \lambda_2, u_1, u_2)$" stands for the cost coefficients of four types of decisions errors. Item "$f_i(p)$" ($i = 1, 2, 3, 4$) stands for the optimal thresholds α, β and minimum decision cost in $f_i(p)(i = 1, 2, 3, 4)$ respectively. For example, in the case of $f_1(p)$, (0.6,0.25,97.55) shows that the minimum decision cost is 97.55, when $\alpha = 0.6$ and $\beta = 0.25$. From the results of experimental 1, it is known that the optimal thresholds are $\alpha = \lambda_2 - u_2/\lambda_2 + u_1 - u_2$ and $\beta = u_2/\lambda_1 - u_1 + u_2$, when the cost coefficient of four types of decisions errors meet $\lambda_1 > u_1 - u_2$ and $\lambda_2 > u_1 + u_2$ ($\lambda_1 \geq 0$, $\lambda_2 \geq 0$, $u_1 \geq 0$ and $u_2 \geq 0$). Namely, in the case of the three-way decisions domain described by the number of equal probability object, the optimal thresholds and minimum cost have no relevance with the cost coefficients of four types of decision errors. This result presents a new perspective to calculate the optimal thresholds and total cost of three-way decisions model.

4.2   Comparative Analysis Experiment

In UCI datasets, there is a large dataset Hepmass [35], which has 3.5×10^6 objects and 28 attributes, and it can be divided into 984497 equivalent classes. The above two models are established by randomly sampling 1% objects of this big dataset. In the three-way decisions cost model based on continuous domain, the minimum decision cost and the optimal thresholds can be calculated by EASOT. In the three-way decisions cost model based on discrete domain, the minimum decision cost and the optimal thresholds can be calculated by traversing model. And the experimental results are shown in Table 5.

Table 5. Comparative analysis

$(\lambda_1, \lambda_2, u_1, u_2)$	Thresholds (continuous)	Thresholds (discrete)	Run time(s)		Decision cost	
			Continuous	Discrete	Continuous	Discrete
(1, 2, 3, 4)	(1, 1)	(0.654, 0.673)	0.0008	0.0869	1749125	3245843
(2, 4, 3, 1)	(1, 1)	(0.994, 1)	0.0009	0.0875	3610459	3498251
(3, 2, 4, 1)	(0, 0)	(0.389, 0.418)	0.0008	0.0702	3501500	3418449
(4, 1, 3, 2)	(0, 0)	(0, 0.329)	0.0009	0.0678	1750750	1762310
(2, 3, 1, 4)	(1, 1)	(0.439, 0.617)	0.0009	0.0678	3498251	3846888
(2, 1, 4, 3)	(0, 0)	(0.329, 0.339)	0.0006	0.0692	1750750	2145036

From Table 5, we can see that the continuous model (three-way decisions cost model based on continuous domain) performs better than the discrete model (three-way decisions cost model based on discrete domain). In terms of time, the continuous model only accounts for 1% of discrete model. In terms of cost, the continuous model is less 11% than discrete model, and in the optimal situation, the cost of continuous model is even less 46%. There are two main reasons as follows.

(1) One is that the thought of calculating the optimal thresholds are different between the two models. That is to say, the continuous model searches the optimal thresholds based on the idea of global optimum, while the discrete model is based on the thought of local optimum. So the accuracy, robustness and generalization of the continuous model are stronger than the discrete model.

(2) The other is that the method of calculating the optimal thresholds are different between the two models. In the continuous model, cost function is established by equal probabilistic objects, and the optimal thresholds are obtained by searching

the minimum value of the cost function. While in the discrete model, the only way of calculating the optimal thresholds is that all the conditional probabilities of equivalence classes should be traversed. So the time complexity of the continuous model is significantly less than discrete model. Surely, the bigger the domain is, the more advantages continuous model has.

5 Conclusions

In this paper, initially, a new concept on number of equal probability is defined for indicating three-way decisions in the continuous domain. After that, the three-way decisions cost based on continuous domain is established, and Theorem 1 is proposed and proved successful. Finally, the algorithm of EASOT is presented to search the optimal thresholds. And the experimental results show that the efficiency, robustness and generalization ability of the proposed model are better than the model based on discrete domain for large datasets. In our future research, we will focus on applying the proposed model to the practical engineering projects and others. We hope these researches can promote the development of three-way decisions theory and further enrich the decisions models from different viewpoints.

Acknowledgments. This work is supported by the National Natural Science Foundation of China (No. 61472056).

References

1. Li, D., Liu, C., Du, Y., et al.: Artificial intelligence with uncertainty. J. Soft. **15**(11), 1583–1594 (2004)
2. Zadeh, L.: Fuzzy sets. Inf. Control **8**(3), 338–353 (1965)
3. Pawlak, Z.: Rough sets international journal of information and computer sciences. Inf. Sci. **11**(5), 341–356 (1982)
4. Shafer, G.: A Mathematical Theory of Evidence. Princeton University Press, Princeton (1976)
5. Zhang, Z., Miao, D., Zhang, H.: Multi-label emotion classification based on decision-theoretic rough set. Moshi Shibie Yu Rengong Zhineng/Pattern Recogn. Artif. Intell. **28**(8), 680–685 (2015)
6. Li, Y., Zhang, Z., Chen, W., et al.: TDUP: an approach to incremental mining of frequent item sets with three-way-decision pattern updating. Int. J. Mach. Learn. Cybern. **8**(2), 1–13 (2015)
7. Zhang, Q., Wang, G., Xiao, Y.: Approximation sets of rough sets. J. Softw. **23**(7), 1745–1759 (2012)
8. Feng, T., Mi, J.: Variable precision multigranulation decision-theoretic fuzzy rough sets. Knowl.-Based Syst. **91**, 93–101 (2016)
9. Liang, D., Pedrycz, W., Liu, D., et al.: Three-way decisions based on decision-theoretic rough sets under linguistic assessment with the aid of group decision making. Appl. Soft Comput. **29**(C), 256–269 (2015)

10. Wang, G., Yao, Y., Yu, H.: A survey on rough set theory and applications. Chin. J. Comput. **32**(7), 1229–1246 (2009)
11. Liu, D., Liang, D., Wang, C.: A novel three-way decision model based on incomplete information system. Knowl.-Based Syst. **91**(C), 32–45 (2015)
12. Yao, Y.: Decision-theoretic rough set models. In: Yao, J., Lingras, P., Wu, W.-Z., Szczuka, M., Cercone, Nick J., Ślęzak, D. (eds.) RSKT 2007. LNCS, vol. 4481, pp. 1–12. Springer, Heidelberg (2007). doi:10.1007/978-3-540-72458-2_1
13. Yao, Y.: Two views of the theory of rough sets in finite universes. Int. J. Approx. Reason. **15**(4), 291–317 (1996)
14. Li, H., Zhang, L., Huang, B., et al.: Sequential three-way decision and granulation for cost-sensitive face recognition. Knowl.-Based Syst. **91**(C), 241–251 (2015)
15. Yao, Y., Wong, S.: Generalized probabilistic rough set models. In: Proceedings of the Fuzzy Systems Symposium, Soft Computing in Intelligent Systems and Information Processing, pp. 158–163. IEEE Xplore (1997)
16. Yao, Y.: Probabilistic rough set approximations. Int. J. Approx. Reason. **49**(2), 255–271 (2008)
17. Yao, Y., Wong, S.: A decision theoretic framework for approximating concepts. Int. J. Man Mach. Stud. **37**(6), 793–809 (1992)
18. Xu, F., Miao, D., Wei, L., Feng, Q., Bi, Y.: Mutual information-based algorithm for fuzzy-rough attribute reduction. J. Electron. Inf. Technol. **30**(6), 1372–1375 (2008)
19. Liang, D., Liu, D.: Systematic studies on three-way decisions with interval-valued decision-theoretic rough sets. Inf. Sci. **276**(C), 186–203 (2014)
20. Min, F., Zhu, W.: Attribute reduction of data with error ranges and test costs. Inf. Sci. **211**(211), 48–67 (2012)
21. Yao, Y.: Three-way decisions with probabilistic rough sets. Inf. Sci. **180**(3), 341–353 (2010)
22. Yao, Y.: The superiority of three-way decisions in probabilistic rough set models. Inf. Sci. **181**(6), 1080–1096 (2011)
23. Yao, Y.: Three-way decision: an interpretation of rules in rough set theory. In: Wen, P., Li, Y., Polkowski, L., Yao, Y., Tsumoto, S., Wang, G. (eds.) RSKT 2009. LNCS, vol. 5589, pp. 642–649. Springer, Heidelberg (2009). doi:10.1007/978-3-642-02962-2_81
24. Herbert, J., Yao, J.: Game-theoretic rough sets. Fundam. Informaticae **108**(3–4), 267–286 (2011)
25. Liu, J., Liao, X., Yang, J.: A group decision-making approach based on evidential reasoning for multiple criteria sorting problem with uncertainty. Eur. J. Oper. Res. **246**(3), 858–873 (2015)
26. Line, M.: Editorial peer review: its strengths and weaknesses. Libr. Manag. **23**(8/9), 449–450 (2002)
27. Chen, J., Zhang, Y., Zhao, S.: Multi-granular mining for boundary regions in three-way decision theory. Knowl.-Based Syst. **91**, 287–292 (2015)
28. Lurie, J., Sox, H.: Principles of medical decision making. Spine **24**(24), 493–498 (1999)
29. Basto-fernandes, V., Yevseyeva, I., Mendez, J., et al.: A spam filtering multi-objective optimization study covering parsimony maximization and three-way classification. Appl. Soft Comput. **48**, 111–123 (2016)
30. Zhang, Q., Xing, Y., Zhou, Y.: The incremental knowledge acquisition algorithm based on granular computing. J. Electron. Inf. Technol. **33**(2), 435–441 (2011)
31. Yu, H., Wang, G., Yao, Y.: Curret research and future perspectives on decision-theoretic rough sets. Chin. J. Comput. **8**, 435–441 (2015)
32. Jia, X., Li, W., Shang, L., et al.: An adaptive learning parameters algorithm in three-way decision-theoretic rough set model. Acta Electronica Sin. **39**(11), 2520–2525 (2011)

33. Yu, H., Wang, Y.: Three-way decisions method for overlapping clustering. In: Yao, J., Yang, Y., Słowiński, R., Greco, S., Li, H., Mitra, S., Polkowski, L. (eds.) RSCTC 2012. LNCS, vol. 7413, pp. 277–286. Springer, Heidelberg (2012). doi:10.1007/978-3-642-32115-3_33

34. Yu, H., Zhang, C., Wang, G.: A tree-based incremental overlapping clustering method using the three-way decision theory. Knowl.-Based Syst. **91**(C), 189–203 (2015)

35. UCI Machine Learning Repository (Adult Data Set).http://archive.ics.uci.edu/ml/datasets/Adult. (Hepmass Data Set). http://archive.ics.uci.edu/ml/datasets/HEPMASS

36. Qian, Y., Liang, J., Yao, Y., et al.: MGRS: A multi-granulation rough set ✩. Inf. Sci. **180**(6), 949–970 (2010)

Conflict Analysis for Pythagorean Fuzzy Information Systems

Guangming Lang[1,2], Duoqian Miao[2(✉)], Zhifei Zhang[3], and Ning Yao[2]

[1] School of Mathematics and Statistics,
Changsha University of Science and Technology,
Changsha 410114, Hunan, People's Republic of China
langguangming1984@126.com
[2] Department of Computer Science and Technology, Tongji University,
Shanghai 201804, People's Republic of China
dqmiao@tongji.edu.cn, xinhuperfect@163.com
[3] Big Data and Network Security Research Center, Tongji University,
Shanghai 200092, People's Republic of China
zhifeizhang@tongji.edu.cn

Abstract. Pythagorean fuzzy sets as generalizations of intuitionistic fuzzy sets are effective for dealing with uncertainty information, but little effort has been paid to conflict analysis of Pythagorean fuzzy information systems. In this paper, we present the concepts of the maximum positive alliance, central alliance, and negative alliance with the two thresholds α and β. Then we show how to compute the thresholds α and β for conflict analysis based on decision-theoretic rough set theory. Finally, we employ several examples to illustrate how to compute the maximum positive alliance, central alliance, and negative alliance from the view of matrix.

Keywords: Pythagorean fuzzy sets · Pythagorean fuzzy information systems · Three-way decision · Decision-theoretic rough sets

1 Introduction

Pythagorean fuzzy sets (PFSs), as generalizations of intuitionistic fuzzy sets (IFSs), are characterized by a membership degree and a non-membership degree satisfying the condition that the square sum of its membership degree and non-membership degree is equal to or less than 1, and they have more powerful ability than IFSs satisfying the condition that the sum of its membership degree and non-membership degree is equal to or less than 1 to model the uncertain information in decision making problems. So far, much effort [1,2,15,19] has been paid to Pythagorean fuzzy sets. For example, Beliakov et al. [1] provided the averaging aggregation functions for preferences expressed as Pythagorean membership grades and fuzzy orthopairs. Bustince et al. [2] investigated a historical account of types of fuzzy sets and discussed their relationships. Reformat et al. [15] proposed a novel collaborative-based recommender system that provides a

© Springer International Publishing AG 2017
L. Polkowski et al. (Eds.): IJCRS 2017, Part II, LNAI 10314, pp. 359–367, 2017.
DOI: 10.1007/978-3-319-60840-2_26

user with the ability to control a process of constructing a list of suggested items. Yager [19] introduced a variety of aggregation operations for Pythagorean fuzzy subsets.

Many scholars [3,9,11–14,16,17] focused on conflict analysis of information systems, and improved the relationship between the two sides of a conflict by finding the essence of the conflict issue. For example, Deja [3] examined nature of conflicts as we are formally defining the conflict situation model. Pawlak [12] initially considered the auxiliary functions and distance functions and offered deeper insight into the structure of conflicts and enables the analysis of relationships between parties and the issues being debated. Silva et al. [13] presented a multicriteria approach for analysis of conflicts in evidence theory. Sun et al. [16] subsequently proposed a conflict analysis decision model and developed a matrix approach for conflict analysis based on rough set theory over two universes. Skowron et al. [17] explained the nature of conflict and defined the conflict situation model in a way to encapsulate the conflict components in a clear manner.

In practice, if opinions of agents on issues are expressed by Pythagorean fuzzy sets, then they are more effective than intuitionistic fuzzy sets for describing imprecise information. But little effort focus on conflict analysis of Pythagorean fuzzy information systems now. Much research [4–8,10,18,20] has illustrated three-way decision theory and matrix theory are effective for knowledge discovery of information systems, we will study conflict analysis of Pythagorean fuzzy information systems based on decision-theoretic rough sets. The contributions of this paper are as follows. Firstly, we provide the concept of Pythagorean fuzzy information system, Pythagorean matrix, Pythagorean closeness index matrix, whole Pythagorean closeness index, and whole Pythagorean closeness index matrix. Secondly, we provide the concepts of maximum positive alliance, central alliance, and negative alliance with the thresholds α and β. Thirdly, we investigate how to compute the thresholds α and β based on decision-theoretic rough sets. We also employ examples to illustrate how to conduct conflict analysis of Pythagorean fuzzy information systems.

The rest of this paper is shown as follows. Section 2 reviews the basic concepts of Pythagorean fuzzy sets and decision-theoretic rough sets. Section 3 provides conflict analysis models for Pythagorean fuzzy information systems. The conclusion is given in Sect. 4.

2 Preliminaries

In this section, we review concepts of Pythagorean fuzzy sets and decision-theoretic rough sets.

Definition 1 [19]. *Let U be an arbitrary non-empty set, a Pythagorean fuzzy set (PFS) P is a mathematical object of the form as follows: $P = \{< x, (\mu(x), \nu(x)) > | x \in U\}$, where $\mu(x), \nu(x) : U \to [0,1]$ such as $\mu^2(x) + \nu^2(x) \leq 1$, for every $x \in U$, $\mu(x)$ and $\nu(x)$ denote the membership degree and the non-membership degree of the element x to U in P, respectively.*

By Definition 1, we see that an intuitionstic fuzzy set is a Pythagorean fuzzy set, but a Pythagorean fuzzy set is not always an intuitionstic fuzzy set, and Pythagorean fuzzy sets are generalizations of intuitionstic fuzzy sets. Furthermore, the hesitant degree of $x \in U$ is defined as $\pi(x) = \sqrt{1 - \mu^2(x) - \nu^2(x)}$. For convenience, we denote the Pythagorean fuzzy number (PFN) as $\gamma = P(\mu_\gamma, \nu_\gamma)$ satisfying $\mu_\gamma, \nu_\gamma \in [0,1]$ and $\mu_\gamma^2 + \nu_\gamma^2 \leq 1$, and the hesitant degree $\pi_\gamma(x) = \sqrt{1 - \mu_\gamma^2(x) - \nu_\gamma^2(x)}$.

Definition 2 [21]. *Let $\gamma_1 = (\mu_{\gamma_1}, \nu_{\gamma_1})$ and $\gamma_2 = (\mu_{\gamma_2}, \nu_{\gamma_2})$ be PFNs. Then the Euclidean distance between γ_1 and γ_2 is defined as: $d(\gamma_1, \gamma_2) = \frac{1}{2}(|\mu_{\gamma_1}^2 - \mu_{\gamma_2}^2| + |\nu_{\gamma_1}^2 - \nu_{\gamma_2}^2| + |\pi_{\gamma_1}^2 - \pi_{\gamma_2}^2|)$.*

By Definition 2, we get the Euclidean distance between two Pythagorean fuzzy numbers, which describes the similarity degree between Pythagorean fuzzy numbers. Then we provide the concept of the closeness index of a Pythagorean fuzzy number.

Definition 3 [21]. *Let $\gamma = (\mu_\gamma, \nu_\gamma)$ be a PFN, $\mathcal{O}^+ = (1,0)$ be the positive ideal PFN, and $\mathcal{O}^- = (0,1)$ be the negative ideal PFN. Then the closeness index of γ is defined as: $\mathcal{P}(\gamma) = \frac{d(\gamma, \mathcal{O}^-)}{d(\gamma, \mathcal{O}^+) + d(\gamma, \mathcal{O}^-)} = \frac{1 - \nu_\gamma^2}{2 - \mu_\gamma^2 - \nu_\gamma^2}$.*

By Definition 3, we have the closeness index of a Pythagorean fuzzy number, and obtain the relationship between the Pythagorean fuzzy number and the positive ideal PFN, the negative ideal PFN.

Definition 4 [20]. *Let $S = (U, A)$ be an information system, and $X \subseteq U$. Then the probabilistic lower and upper approximations of X are defined as follows: $\underline{apr}_{(\alpha,\beta)}(X) = \{x \in U \mid P(X|[x]) \geq \alpha\}; \overline{apr}_{(\alpha,\beta)}(X) = \{x \in U \mid P(X|[x]_A) \geq \beta\}$, where $P(X|[x]_A) = \frac{|[x]_A \cap X|}{|[x]_A|}$, $[x]_A$ is the equivalence class of x with respect to A, and $0 \leq \beta \leq \alpha \leq 1$.*

The probabilistic lower and upper approximation operators are better than Pawlak's model for handling the uncertain and imprecise information. By Definition 4, Prof. Yao presented the concepts of the probabilistic positive, boundary, and negative regions as follows.

Definition 5 [20]. *Let $S = (U, A)$ be an information system, $X \subseteq U$, and $0 \leq \beta \leq \alpha \leq 1$. Then the probabilistic positive, boundary, and negative regions of X are defined as: $POS_{(\alpha,\beta)}(X) = \{x \in U \mid P(X|[x]) \geq \alpha\}, BND_{(\alpha,\beta)}(X) = \{x \in U \mid \beta < P(X|[x]) < \alpha\}, NEG_{(\alpha,\beta)}(X) = \{x \in U \mid P(X|[x]) \leq \beta\}$.*

3   Conflict Analysis for Pythagorean Fuzzy Information Systems

In this section, we provide conflict analysis models for Pythagorean fuzzy information systems.

Definition 6. *A Pythagorean fuzzy information system is a 4-tuple $S = (U, A, V, f)$, where $U = \{x_1, x_2, \ldots, x_n\}$ is a finite set of objects, $A = \{c_1, c_2, \ldots, c_m\}$ is a finite set of attributes, $V = \{V_a \mid a \in A\}$, where V_a is the set of attribute values on a, all attribute values are PFNs, and f is a function from $U \times A$ into V.*

Pythagorean fuzzy information systems are generalizations of intuitionistic fuzzy information systems, which are more effective for depicting uncertain information in practical situations.

Table 1. The Pythagorean fuzzy information system for the middle east conflict.

U	c_1	c_2	c_3	c_4	c_5
x_1	$(1.0, 0.0)$	$(0.9, 0.3)$	$(0.8, 0.2)$	$(0.9, 0.1)$	$(0.9, 0.2)$
x_2	$(0.9, 0.1)$	$(0.5, 0.5)$	$(0.1, 0.9)$	$(0.3, 0.8)$	$(0.1, 0.9)$
x_3	$(0.1, 0.9)$	$(0.1, 0.9)$	$(0.2, 0.8)$	$(0.1, 0.9)$	$(0.5, 0.5)$
x_4	$(0.5, 0.5)$	$(0.1, 0.9)$	$(0.3, 0.7)$	$(0.5, 0.5)$	$(0.1, 0.9)$
x_5	$(0.9, 0.2)$	$(0.4, 0.6)$	$(0.1, 0.9)$	$(0.1, 0.9)$	$(0.3, 0.9)$
x_6	$(0.0, 1.0)$	$(0.9, 0.1)$	$(0.2, 0.9)$	$(0.5, 0.5)$	$(0.8, 0.4)$

Example 1. Table 1 depicts the Pythagorean fuzzy information system for the Middle East conflict, which is given by experts. Concretely, x_1, x_2, x_3, x_4, x_5, and x_6 denotes Israel, Egypt, Palestinians, Jordan, Syria, and Saudi Arabia, respectively. Moreover, c_1 means Autonomous Palestinian state on the West Bank and Gaza; c_2 denotes Israeli military outpost along the Jordan River; c_3 stands for Israeli retains East Jerusalem; c_4 is Israeli military outposts on the Golan Heights; c_5 notes Arab countries grant citizenship to Palestinians who choose to remain with their borders.

Definition 7. *Let $S = (U, A, V, f)$ be a Pythagorean fuzzy information system. Then the Pythagorean matrix $M(S)$ is defined as follows:*

$$M(S) = \begin{bmatrix} (\mu_{11}, \nu_{11}) & (\mu_{12}, \nu_{12}) & \cdot & (\mu_{1m}, \nu_{1m}) \\ (\mu_{21}, \nu_{21}) & (\mu_{22}, \nu_{22}) & \cdot & (\mu_{2m}, \nu_{2m}) \\ & \cdot & \cdot & \cdot \\ (\mu_{n1}, \nu_{n1}) & (\mu_{n2}, \nu_{n2}) & \cdot & (\mu_{nm}, \nu_{nm}) \end{bmatrix}.$$

By Definition 7, we have the matrix representation of a Pythagorean fuzzy information system, which is helpful for dealing with uncertain information with computers.

Example 2 (Continuation from Example 1). By Definition 7, we have the Pythagorean matrix $M(S)$ as follows:

$$M(S) = \begin{bmatrix} (1.0,0.0) & (0.9,0.3) & (0.8,0.2) & (0.9,0.1) & (0.9,0.2) \\ (0.9,0.1) & (0.5,0.5) & (0.1,0.9) & (0.3,0.8) & (0.1,0.9) \\ (0.1,0.9) & (0.1,0.9) & (0.2,0.8) & (0.1,0.9) & (0.5,0.5) \\ (0.5,0.5) & (0.1,0.9) & (0.3,0.7) & (0.5,0.5) & (0.1,0.9) \\ (0.9,0.2) & (0.4,0.6) & (0.1,0.9) & (0.1,0.9) & (0.3,0.9) \\ (0.0,1.0) & (0.9,0.1) & (0.2,0.9) & (0.5,0.5) & (0.8,0.4) \end{bmatrix}.$$

Definition 8. *Let $S = (U, A, V, f)$ be a Pythagorean fuzzy information system. Then the Pythagorean closeness index matrix $MP(S)$ is defined as follows:*

$$MP(S) = \begin{bmatrix} \mathscr{P}(\gamma_{11}) & \mathscr{P}(\gamma_{12}) & . & \mathscr{P}(\gamma_{1m}) \\ \mathscr{P}(\gamma_{21}) & \mathscr{P}(\gamma_{22}) & . & \mathscr{P}(\gamma_{2m}) \\ . & . & . & . \\ \mathscr{P}(\gamma_{n1}) & \mathscr{P}(\gamma_{n2}) & . & \mathscr{P}(\gamma_{nm}) \end{bmatrix},$$

where $\gamma_{ij} = (\mu_{ij}, \nu_{ij})$ denote the attribute value of x_i with respect to c_j.

By Definition 8, we get the matrix representation of Pythagorean closeness indexes for the Pythagorean fuzzy information system, which is helpful for conducting conflict analysis.

Example 3 (Continuation from Example 1). By Definition 8, we have the Pythagorean closeness index matrix $MP(S)$ as follows:

$$MP(S) = \begin{bmatrix} 1.000 & 0.827 & 0.727 & 0.839 & 0.835 \\ 0.839 & 0.500 & 0.161 & 0.283 & 0.161 \\ 0.161 & 0.161 & 0.273 & 0.161 & 0.500 \\ 0.500 & 0.161 & 0.359 & 0.500 & 0.161 \\ 0.835 & 0.432 & 0.161 & 0.161 & 0.173 \\ 0.000 & 0.839 & 0.165 & 0.500 & 0.700 \end{bmatrix}.$$

Definition 9. *Let $S = (U, A, V, f)$ be a Pythagorean fuzzy information system, γ_i denotes the attribute value of $x \in U$ on $c_i \in A$, $0 \le w_j \le 1$ and $\sum_{j=1}^{m} w_j = 1$. Then the whole Pythagorean closeness index of x on A is defined as: $D(x) = \sum_{i=1}^{m} w_i \mathscr{P}(\gamma_i) = \sum_{i=1}^{m} \frac{w_i(1-\nu_{\gamma_i}^2)}{2-\mu_{\gamma_i}^2 - \nu_{\gamma_i}^2}.$*

By Definition 9, we get the whole Pythagorean closeness index of each object with respect to all attributes and present the concept of the whole Pythagorean closeness index matrix $CP_A(S)$ as follows.

Definition 10. *Let $S = (U, A, V, f)$ be a Pythagorean fuzzy information system, $0 \le w_j \le 1$, and $\sum_{j=1}^{m} w_j = 1$. Then the whole Pythagorean closeness index matrix $CP_A(S)$ is defined as follows:*

$$CP_A(S) = \begin{bmatrix} D(x_1) \\ D(x_2) \\ . \\ D(x_n) \end{bmatrix} = \begin{bmatrix} w_1 \mathscr{P}(\gamma_{11}) + w_2 \mathscr{P}(\gamma_{12}) + . + w_m \mathscr{P}(\gamma_{1m}) \\ w_1 \mathscr{P}(\gamma_{21}) + w_2 \mathscr{P}(\gamma_{22}) + . + w_m \mathscr{P}(\gamma_{2m}) \\ . \\ w_1 \mathscr{P}(\gamma_{n1}) + w_2 \mathscr{P}(\gamma_{n2}) + . + w_m \mathscr{P}(\gamma_{nm}) \end{bmatrix}.$$

By Definition 10, we have the matrix representation of the whole Pythagorean closeness indexes of all objects with respect to all attributes.

Example 4 (Continuation from Example 3). By Definition 10, we get the whole Pythagorean closeness index matrix $CP_A(S)$ as follows:

$$CP_A(S) = \begin{bmatrix} 0.8456 & 0.3888 & 0.2512 & 0.3362 & 0.3524 & 0.4408 \end{bmatrix}^T.$$

By Definition 9, we provide the concepts of the maximum positive alliance, central alliance, and negative alliance as follows.

Definition 11. *Let $S = (U, A, V, f)$ be a Pythagorean fuzzy information system, and $0 \leq \beta \leq \alpha \leq 1$. Then the maximum positive alliance, central alliance, and negative alliance are defined as: $POA_{(\alpha,\beta)}(U) = \{x \in U \mid D(x) \geq \alpha\}$; $CTA_{(\alpha,\beta)}(U) = \{x \in U \mid \beta < D(x) < \alpha\}; NEA_{(\alpha,\beta)}(U) = \{x \in U \mid D(x) \leq \beta\}.$*

By Definition 11, we see that the universe is divided into three parts: the maximum positive alliance, central alliance, and negative alliance using two thresholds α and β.

Example 5 (Continuation from Example 5). By Definition 11, we have $POA_{(\alpha,\beta)}(U) = \{x_1\}, CTA_{(\alpha,\beta)}(U) = \{x_2, x_3, x_4, x_5, x_6\}$, and $NEA_{(\alpha,\beta)}(U) = \emptyset$.

Thirdly, we calculate the parameters α and β for conflict analysis based on decision-theoretic rough set theory.

Table 2. Loss function for Pythagorean fuzzy information systems.

Action	$x \in POA_{(\alpha,\beta)}(U)$	$x \in NEA_{(\alpha,\beta)}(U)$
a_P	λ_{PP}	λ_{PN}
a_C	λ_{CP}	λ_{CN}
a_N	λ_{NP}	λ_{NN}

Theorem 1. *Let $S = (U, A, V, f)$ be a Pythagorean fuzzy information system, and the losses $\lambda_{PP}, \lambda_{CP}, \lambda_{NP}, \lambda_{NN}, \lambda_{CN}$, and λ_{PN}, where $0 \leq \lambda_{PP} \leq \lambda_{CP} \leq \lambda_{NP}$ and $0 \leq \lambda_{NN} \leq \lambda_{CN} \leq \lambda_{PN}$. Then*
(1) If $D_A(x) > \alpha$, then $x \in POA_{(\alpha,\beta)}(U)$;
(2) If $\alpha \geq D_A(x) \geq \beta$, then $y \in CTA_{(\alpha,\beta)}(U)$;
(3) If $D_A(x) < \beta$, then $y \in NEA_{(\alpha,\beta)}(U)$, where

$$\alpha = \frac{\lambda_{PN} - \lambda_{NN}}{\lambda_{PN} - \lambda_{CN} + \lambda_{CP} - \lambda_{PP}}, \beta = \frac{\lambda_{CN} - \lambda_{NN}}{\lambda_{CN} - \lambda_{NN} + \lambda_{NP} - \lambda_{CP}}.$$

Proof. By Table 2, we have the expected losses $R(a_P|x)$, $R(a_C|x)$, and $R(a_N|x)$ associated with taking the individual actions for the object x as follows:

$$R(a_P|x) = \lambda_{PP} * D_A(x) + \lambda_{PN} * (1 - D_A(x));$$
$$R(a_C|x) = \lambda_{CP} * D_A(x) + \lambda_{CN} * (1 - D_A(x));$$
$$R(a_N|x) = \lambda_{NP} * D_A(x) + \lambda_{NN} * (1 - D_A(x)).$$

The Bayesian decision procedure suggests the following minimum-cost decision rules:

(P): If $R(a_P|x) \le R(a_C|x)$ and $R(a_P|x) \le R(a_N|x)$, then $x \in POA_{(\alpha,\beta)}(U)$;
(N): If $R(a_C|x) \le R(a_P|x)$ and $R(a_C|x) \le R^x(a_N|x)$, then $x \in CTA_{(\alpha,\beta)}(U)$;
(A): If $R(a_N|x) \le R(a_P|x)$ and $R(a_N|x) \le R(a_C|x)$, then $x \in NEA_{(\alpha,\beta)}(U)$.
Suppose $\lambda_{PP} \le \lambda_{CP} \le \lambda_{NP}$, we simplify the rules $(P),(C)$, and (N) as follows:
(C): If $D_A(x) > \alpha$, then $x \in POA_{(\alpha,\beta)}(U)$;
(N): If $\beta \le D_A(x) \le \alpha$, then $x \in CTA_{(\alpha,\beta)}(U)$;
(A): If $D_A(x) < \beta$, then $x \in NEA_{(\alpha,\beta)}(U)$.

Table 3. Loss function for Pythagorean fuzzy information systems.

Action	$x \in POA_{(\alpha,\beta)}(U)$	$x \in NEA_{(\alpha,\beta)}(U)$
a_P	$\lambda_{PP} = 0$	$\lambda_{PN} = 10$
a_C	$\lambda_{CP} = 4$	$\lambda_{CN} = 4$
a_N	$\lambda_{NP} = 10$	$\lambda_{NN} = 0$

By Theorem 1, we get the two thresholds α and β for computing the maximum positive alliance, central alliance, and negative alliance using loss functions, which supplies a theoretical foundation for decision making with reasonable thresholds α and β.

Example 6 (Continued from Example 5). By Theorem 1, we have the thresholds α and β using Table 3 as follows:

$$\alpha = \frac{\lambda_{PN} - \lambda_{CN}}{\lambda_{PN} - \lambda_{CN} + \lambda_{CP} - \lambda_{PP}} = \frac{5 - 2}{5 - 2 + 2 - 0} = \frac{3}{5},$$
$$\beta = \frac{\lambda_{CN} - \lambda_{NN}}{\lambda_{CN} - \lambda_{NN} + \lambda_{NP} - \lambda_{CP}} = \frac{2 - 0}{2 - 0 + 6 - 2} = \frac{1}{3}.$$

By Definition 11, we get $POA_{(\alpha,\beta)}(U) = \{x_1\}$, $CTA_{(\alpha,\beta)}(U) = \{x_2, x_4, x_5, x_6\}$, and $NEA_{(\alpha,\beta)}(U) = \{x_3\}$.

In Example 6, we compute the thresholds $\alpha = \frac{3}{5}$ and $\beta = \frac{1}{3}$ for computing the maximum positive alliance, central alliance, and negative alliance using loss functions in Table 3, and give a theoretical foundation for decision making with reasonable thresholds.

4   Conclusions

In this paper, we have introduced the concepts of the maximum positive alliance, central alliance, and negative alliance. Furthermore, we have shown how to compute the thresholds for conflict analysis of Pythagorean fuzzy information systems. Finally, we have employed several examples to illustrate how to conduct conflict analysis of Pythagorean fuzzy information systems from the view of matrix.

In practice, Pythagorean fuzzy information systems are effective for describing uncertain information, and there will be more Pythagorean fuzzy information systems, and we will further study conflict analysis of Pythagorean fuzzy information systems in the future.

Acknowledgments. We would like to thank the reviewers very much for their professional comments and valuable suggestions. This work is supported by the National Natural Science Foundation of China (Nos. 61603063, 61673301, 11526039), Doctoral Fund of Ministry of Education of China (No. 20130072130004), China Postdoctoral Science Foundation (No. 2015M580353), China Postdoctoral Science special Foundation (No. 2016T90383).

References

1. Beliakov, G., James, S.: Averaging aggregation functions for preferences expressed as Pythagorean membership grades and fuzzy orthopairs. In: Proceedings of 2014 IEEE International Conference on Fuzzy Systems (FUZZ-IEEE), pp. 298–305. IEEE (2014)
2. Bustince, H., Barrenechea, E., Pagola, M., Fernandez, J., Xu, Z.S., Bedregal, B., Montero, J., Hagras, H., Herrera, F., DeBaets, B.: A historical account of types of fuzzy sets and their relationships. IEEE Trans. Fuzzy Syst. **24**(1), 179–194 (2016)
3. Deja, R.: Conflict Analysis, Rough Set Methods and Applications. Studies in Fuzzyness and Soft Comput. Physica, Heidelberg (2000). 491–520
4. Ju, H.R., Li, H.X., Yang, X.B., Zhou, X.Z.: Cost-sensitive rough set: a multi-granulation approach. Knowl.-Based Syst. (2017). http://dx.doi.org/10.1016/j.knosys.2017.02.019
5. Kang, X.P., Miao, D.Q.: A variable precision rough set model based on the granularity of tolerance relation. Knowl.-Based Syst. **102**, 103–115 (2016)
6. Khan, M.T., Azam, N., Khalid, S., Yao, J.T.: A three-way approach for learning rules in automatic knowledge-based topic models. Int. J. Approx. Reason. **82**, 210–226 (2017)
7. Lang, G.M., Miao, D.Q., Yang, T., Cai, M.J.: Knowledge reduction of dynamic covering decision information systems when varying covering cardinalities. Inf. Sci. **346–347**, 236–260 (2016)
8. Li, H.X., Zhang, L.B., Zhou, X.Z., Huang, B.: Cost-sensitive sequential three-way decision modeling using a deep neural network. Int. J. Approx. Reason. (2017). http://dx.doi.org/10.1016/j.ijar.2017.03.008
9. Lin, T.Y.: Granular computing on binary relations analysis of conflict and chinese wall security policy. In: Alpigini, J.J., Peters, J.F., Skowron, A., Zhong, N. (eds.) RSCTC 2002. LNCS, vol. 2475, pp. 296–299. Springer, Heidelberg (2002). doi:10.1007/3-540-45813-1_38

10. Liu, G.L.: The axiomatization of the rough set upper approximation operations. Fundam. Informaticae **69**(3), 331–342 (2006)
11. Maeda, Y., Senoo, K., Tanaka, H.: Interval density functions in conflict analysis. In: Zhong, N., Skowron, A., Ohsuga, S. (eds.) RSFDGrC 1999. LNCS, vol. 1711, pp. 382–389. Springer, Heidelberg (1999). doi:10.1007/978-3-540-48061-7_46
12. Pawlak, Z.: Some remarks on conflict analysis. Eur. J. Oper. Res. **166**(3), 649–654 (2005)
13. de Oliveira Silva, L.G., de Almeida-Filho, A.T.: A multicriteria approach for analysis of conflicts in evidence theory. Inf. Sci. **346**, 275–285 (2016)
14. Ramanna, S., Skowron, A.: Requirements interaction and conflicts: a rough set approach. In: Proceedings of IEEE Symposium Series on Foundations of Computational Intelligence (2007)
15. Reformat, M.Z., Yager, R.R.: Suggesting recommendations using pythagorean fuzzy sets illustrated using netflix movie data. In: Laurent, A., Strauss, O., Bouchon-Meunier, B., Yager, R.R. (eds.) IPMU 2014. CCIS, vol. 442, pp. 546–556. Springer, Cham (2014). doi:10.1007/978-3-319-08795-5_56
16. Sun, B.Z., Ma, W.M., Zhao, H.Y.: Rough set-based conflict analysis model and method over two universes. Inf. Sci. **372**, 111–125 (2016)
17. Skowron, A., Deja, R.: On some conflict models and conflict resolutions. Rom. J. Inf. Sci. Technol. **5**(1–2), 69–82 (2002)
18. Song, J.J., Tsang, E.C.C., Chen, D.G., Yang, X.B.: Minimal decision cost reduct in fuzzy decision-theoretic rough set model. Knowl.-Based Syst. (2017). http://dx.doi.org/10.1016/j.knosys.2017.03.013
19. Yager, R.R.: Pythagorean membership grades in multicriteria decision making. IEEE Trans. Fuzzy Syst. **22**, 958–965 (2014)
20. Yao, Y.Y.: Probabilistic rough set approximations. Int. J. Approx. Reason. **49**, 255–271 (2008)
21. Zhang, X.L., Xu, Z.S.: Extension of TOPSIS to multiple criteria decision making with Pythagorean fuzzy sets. Int. J. Intell. Syst. **29**, 1061–1078 (2014)

Attribute Reduction in Utility-Based Decision-Theoretic Rough Set Models

Nan Zhang[1,2(✉)], Lili Jiang[1,2], and Caihui Liu[3]

[1] School of Computer and Control Engineering,
Yantai University, Yantai 264005, Shandong, China
zhangnan0851@163.com, ytjianglili0919@163.com
[2] Key Lab for Data Science and Intelligent Technology of Shandong Higher
Education Institutes, Yantai University, Yantai 264005, Shandong, China
[3] Department of Mathematics and Computer Science,
Gannan Normal University, Ganzhou 341000, Jiangxi, China
liu_caihui@163.com

Abstract. Decision-theoretic rough set (DTRS) model, proposed by Yao in the early 1990's, introduces Bayesian decision procedure and loss function in rough set theory. Considering utility function in decision processing, utility-based decision-theoretic rough set model (UDTRS) is given in this paper. The utility of the positive region, the boundary region and the negative region are obtained respectively. We provide a reduction definition which can obtain the maximal utility in decisions. A heuristic reduction algorithm with respect to the definition is proposed. Finally, experimental results show the proposed algorithm is effective.

Keywords: Attribute reduction · Utility theory · Decision-theoretic rough sets

1 Introduction

Decision-theoretic rough set (DTRS) model was firstly introduced by Yao et al. [1] in the early 1990's. As a probabilistic rough set model, it has been successfully used in many research areas, such as knowledge presentation [2–4], data mining [5], machine learning [6], artificial intelligence [7, 8] and pattern recognition.

Attribute reduction [9–14] aims to remove the unnecessary attributes from the information system while keeping the particular property, and becomes one of the hottest issues in rough set theory. Yao and Zhao [9] studied attribute reduction in decision-theoretic rough set models with respect to the different classification properties, confidence, coverage, decision-monotocity, generality and cost, they also gave a general definition of probabilistic attribute reduction. Jia et al. [10] provided a minimum cost attribute reduction in decision-theoretic rough set model, and decision cost induced from the reduct is minimum. Dou et al. proposed a parameterized decision-theoretic rough set model in the paper [11]. In the proposed model, the smallest possible cost and the largest possible cost are computed respectively. Li et al. [12] introduced a non-monotonic attribute reduction for decision-theoretic rough set model. The expanded positive region can be kept by the non-monotonic attribute

© Springer International Publishing AG 2017
L. Polkowski et al. (Eds.): IJCRS 2017, Part II, LNAI 10314, pp. 368–375, 2017.
DOI: 10.1007/978-3-319-60840-2_27

reduction in an information system. To extend classical indiscernibility relation in Yao's decision-theoretic rough sets, Ju et al. [13] gave the δ-cut decision-theoretic rough set. In the proposed decision-theoretic rough set model, attribute reduction of the decision-monotonicity criterion and the cost minimum criterion are proposed respectively in the paper. By constructing variants of conditional entropy in decision-theoretic rough set model, Ma et al. [14] proposed solutions to the attribute reduction based on decision region preservation.

The remaining parts of this paper are arranged as follows. Some basic notions with respect to utility-based decision-theoretic rough set (UDTRS) model are briefly recalled in Sect. 2. Definition of attribute reduction in UDTRS and relative heuristic reduction algorithm are investigated respectively in Sect. 3. We give the experimental analysis in Sect. 4. The paper is summarized in Sect. 5.

2   Utility-Based Decision-Theoretic Rough Sets

By considering the subjective factors in risk decision, Zhang et al. [15] proposed utility-based decision-theoretic rough set (UDTRS) model based on Yao's decision-theoretic rough set model [1]. In this section, we briefly recall some basic notions about utility-based decision-theoretic rough set model. Detailed information about UTRS can be found in the paper [15].

A decision system is defined as the 3-tuple $S = (U, AT = C \cup D, V_a)$. Universe U is the finite set of the objects; AT is a nonempty set of the attributes, such that for all $a \in AT$; C is the set of conditional attribute and D is the set of decision attribute; V_a is the domain of attribute a.

For each nonempty subset $A \subseteq AT$, the indiscernibility relation $IND(A)$ is defined as: $IND(A) = \{(x, y) \in U^2, a(x) = a(y), \forall a \in A\}$. Two objects in U satisfy $IND(A)$ if and only if they have the same value in $\forall a \in A$. U is divided into a family of disjoint subsets $U/IND(A)$ defined a quotient set of U as $U/IND(A) = \{[x]_A : x \in U\}$, where $[x]_A = \{y \in U : (x, y) \in IND(A)\}$ denotes the equivalence class determined by x with respect to A. The set of states is given by $\Omega = U/D = \{X, X^c\}$ indicating that an object is in state X or X^c.

Utility is an important economic concept, and it reflects degree of one's satisfaction related to the cost or profit in decision procedure. For $\forall x \in U$ and $[x] \in U/\pi$, $u(\lambda)$ is utility function, λ denotes the cost of taking action. The expected utilities for different actions can be expressed as:

$$\Psi(a_P|[x]) = u(\lambda_{PP})P(X|[x]) + u(\lambda_{PN})P(X^c|[x])$$
$$\Psi(a_N|[x]) = u(\lambda_{NP})P(X|[x]) + u(\lambda_{NN})P(X^c|[x])$$
$$\Psi(a_B|[x]) = u(\lambda_{BP})P(X|[x]) + u(\lambda_{BN})P(X^c|[x])$$

According to maximal utility in Bayesian procedures, we have the following as:

If $\Psi(a_P|[x]) \geq \Psi(a_N|[x])$ and $\Psi(a_P|[x]) \geq \Psi(a_B|[x])$, then $[x] \subseteq POS_\pi(X)$,

If $\Psi(a_N|[x]) \geq \Psi(a_P|[x])$ and $\Psi(a_N|[x]) \geq \Psi(a_B|[x])$, then $[x] \subseteq NEG_\pi(X)$,

If $\Psi(a_B|[x]) \geq \Psi(a_P|[x])$ and $\Psi(a_B|[x]) \geq \Psi(a_N|[x])$, then $[x] \subseteq BND_\pi(X)$.

If $P(X|[x]) = P$ then $P(X^c|[x]) = 1 - P$, then we derived the following decision rules:

$$\text{If } P(X|[x]) \geq \alpha_u, \text{ then } [x] \subseteq POS_\pi(X),$$
$$\text{If } P(X|[x]) \leq \beta_u, \text{ then } [x] \subseteq NEG_\pi(X),$$
$$\text{If } \beta_u < P(X|[x]) < \alpha_u, \text{ then } [x] \subseteq BND_\pi(X);$$

where

$$\alpha_u = \frac{u(\lambda_{BN}) - u(\lambda_{PN})}{(u(\lambda_{BN}) - u(\lambda_{PN})) + (u(\lambda_{PP}) - u(\lambda_{BP}))},$$

$$\beta_u = \frac{u(\lambda_{NN}) - u(\lambda_{BN})}{(u(\lambda_{NN}) - u(\lambda_{BN})) + (u(\lambda_{BP}) - u(\lambda_{NP}))}.$$

Since $u(\lambda_{PP}) \geq u(\lambda_{BP}) > u(\lambda_{NP})$, $u(\lambda_{NN}) \geq u(\lambda_{BN}) > u(\lambda_{PN})$, $\alpha_u \in (0, 1]$, $\beta_u \in [0, 1)$ Then, we can obtain

$$\alpha_u = \frac{1}{1 + \Delta(\alpha_u)} = \frac{1}{1 + \frac{u(\lambda_{PP}) - u(\lambda_{BP})}{u(\lambda_{BN}) - u(\lambda_{PN})}},$$

$$\beta_u = \frac{1}{1 + \Delta(\beta_u)} = \frac{1}{1 + \frac{u(\lambda_{BP}) - u(\lambda_{NP})}{u(\lambda_{NN}) - u(\lambda_{BN})}}.$$

For $\forall X \subseteq U$, (α_u, β_u) -upper and lower approximations in utility-based decision-theoretic rough set model are presented as:

$$\underline{apr}_{(\alpha_u,\beta_u)}(X) = \{x \in U | P(X|[x]) \geq \alpha_u\},$$

$$\overline{apr}_{(\alpha_u,\beta_u)}(X) = \{x \in U | P(X|[x]) > \beta_u\}.$$

Based on the definition of rough approximations in UDTRS, the positive, boundary and negative regions are defined as

$$POS_\pi(X) = \underline{apr}_{(\alpha_u,\beta_u)}(X),$$

$$BND_\pi(X) = \overline{apr}_{(\alpha_u,\beta_u)}(X) - \underline{apr}_{(\alpha_u,\beta_u)}(X),$$

$$NEG_\pi(X) = U - \overline{apr}_{(\alpha_u,\beta_u)}(X).$$

3 Attribute Reduction in UDTRS

In this section, we will give the definition of attribute reduction based on maximal utility in UDTRS. By attribute reduction, the maximal utility will be obtain in decisions. According to the proposed definition of reduction, a heuristic algorithm with respect to the maximal utility will be investigated in this section.

Similar to the Bayesian expected cost [10] in decision-theoretic rough set model, the Bayesian expected utility [15] of each rule is expressed as:

$$\text{Utility of the positive rule} : p \cdot u(\lambda_{PP}) + (1 - p) \cdot u(\lambda_{PN});$$
$$\text{Utility of the negative rule} : p \cdot u(\lambda_{BP}) + (1 - p) \cdot u(\lambda_{BN});$$
$$\text{Utility of the boundary rule} : p \cdot u(\lambda_{NP}) + (1 - p) \cdot u(\lambda_{NN}).$$

From above, we can easily get the Bayesian expected utility of decision rules:
Utility of positive rules:

$$Utility_A^{POS} = \sum_{x_i \in POS_{(\alpha_u, \beta_u)}(\pi_D / \pi_A)} (p_i \cdot u(\lambda_{PP}) + (1 - p_i) \cdot u(\lambda_{PN}));$$

Utility of boundary rules:

$$Utility_A^{BND} = \sum_{x_j \in BND_{(\alpha_u, \beta_u)}(\pi_D / \pi_A)} (p_j \cdot u(\lambda_{BP}) + (1 - p_j) \cdot u(\lambda_{BN}));$$

Utility of negative rule:

$$Utility_A^{NEG} = \sum_{x_k \in NEG_{(\alpha_u, \beta_u)}(\pi_D / \pi_A)} (p_k \cdot u(\lambda_{NP}) + (1 - p_k) \cdot u(\lambda_{NN})).$$

For any subset $A \subseteq AT$, the whole utility is composed of three parts: utility of positive region, utility of boundary region and utility of negative region. Then, we have the whole utility of all decision rules in decision systems as follows [15]:

$$
\begin{aligned}
Utility_A &= Utility_A^{POS} + Utility_A^{BND} + Utility_A^{NEG} \\
&= \sum_{x_i \in POS_{(\alpha_u, \beta_u)}(\pi_D / \pi_A)} (p_i \cdot u(\lambda_{PP}) + (1 - p_i) \cdot u(\lambda_{PN})) \\
&+ \sum_{x_j \in BND_{(\alpha_u, \beta_u)}(\pi_D / \pi_A)} (p_j \cdot u(\lambda_{BP}) + (1 - p_j) \cdot u(\lambda_{BN})) \\
&+ \sum_{x_k \in NEG_{(\alpha_u, \beta_u)}(\pi_D / \pi_A)} (p_k \cdot u(\lambda_{NP}) + (1 - p_k) \cdot u(\lambda_{NN}))
\end{aligned}
$$

In real applications, it is better to obtain more utility in decision procedures. Thus, according to "non-decreasing" principle, we define attribute reduction in utility-based decision-theoretic rough set model as follows:

Definition 1. A decision system $S = (U, C \cup D, V_a)$, $R \subseteq C$ is a reduct of C with respect to D if it satisfies the following two conditions:

(1) $Utility_R \geq Utility_C$;
(2) $\forall Rh' \subset R$, $Utility_{R'} < Utility_R$.

From Definition 1, the decision utility will be increased or unchanged by the reduction. Condition (1) is the jointly sufficient condition and condition (2) is the individual necessary condition. Condition (1) guarantees that the utility induced from the reduct is maximal, and condition (2) guarantees the reduct is minimal.

The fitness function, which shows the significance of an attribute, is usually used to construct a heuristic algorithm in rough set theory. In UTRS model, the fitness function is defined as:

Definition 2. A decision system $S = \{U, C \cup D, V_a\}$, $A \subseteq C$ The utility fitness function of attribute $a_i \in A$ is defined as:

$$Sig_{Utility}(A, a_i) = \frac{Utility_{A-\{a_i\}} - Utility_A}{Utility_A}.$$

The three strategies in heuristic algorithm is summarized in paper [9]. In this paper, we take deletion strategy to give an algorithm in UDTRS. The heuristic algorithm (The algorithm of maximal-utility attribute reduction, **AMUAR**) based on the utility fitness function is described as follows:

Algorithm: The Algorithm of Maximal-Utility Attribute Reduction, **AMUAR**

```
Input:  A decision system S = {U, C ∪ D, V}
Output: A reduct R
1    B = C , A = C ;
2    While A ≠ ∅
     Compute the fitness for each attribute a_i ∈ A using
     fitness function Sig_Utility(A, a_i); Find the minimal
     Sig_Utility(B, a_i) ≥ 0 and the corresponding attribute a_i ;
     A = A - {a_i}; If Utility_{B-{a_i}} ≥ Utility_C , B = B - {a_i};
3    Output B = R .
```

The fitness function shows the significance of an attribute. In the processing of deleting attributes, if $Utility_B \geq Utility_C$, the algorithm will stop the deleting procedure and output reduct of decision systems.

4 Experimental Analysis

In this section, we will verify effectiveness of the algorithm AMUAR and the monotonicity of utility with attributions by experiments. All the experiments have been carried out on a personal computer with Windows 7, Intel (R) Pentium (R) CPU G640 (2.8 GHz) and 6.00 GB memory. The programming language is Matlab 2010b.

We take $u(\lambda) = a(-\lambda + c)^b$ as the utility function. If $0 < b < 1$, then UDTRS model is risk aversion; If $b = 1$, UDTRS model is risk neutrality; If $b > 1$, UDTRS model is risk loving; Six data sets from the UCI Machine Learning Repository are used. For each data set, the utility functions are randomly generated in interval value [100, 1000]. Their values meet the following constraint conditions: $u(\lambda_{BP}) > u(\lambda_{NP})$, $u(\lambda_{BN}) > u(\lambda_{PN})$, $u(\lambda_{PP}) = u(\lambda_{NN}) = 1$. 10 different groups of utility functions are randomly generated. Table 1 shows the average length of the derived reduct with different data sets.

Table 1. Average length of a reduct

Data sets	Attributes	Samples	Risk aversion	Risk neutrality	Risk loving
credit_a	15	690	7.0 ± 0.0	7.0 ± 0.0	7.0 ± 0.0
forestfires	12	517	4.0 ± 0.0	4.0 ± 0.0	4.0 ± 0.0
german	20	1000	12.0 ± 0.0	12.0 ± 0.0	12.0 ± 0.0
heart_statlog	13	270	6.0 ± 0.0	6.0 ± 0.0	6.0 ± 0.0
lymph	18	148	8.0 ± 0.0	8.0 ± 0.0	8.0 ± 0.0
vote	16	435	11.9 ± 0.3	11.9 ± 0.3	11.8 ± 0.4
breast_cancer	9	286	7.9 ± 0.3	8.0 ± 0.0	7.9 ± 0.3
fertility	9	100	6.9 ± 0.3	6.9 ± 0.3	6.8 ± 0.4

To validate the monotonicity of utility with attributes, utility is calculated with the increasing number of attributes from 1 to the total attribute number in each data set. In Fig. 1, the x-coordinate represents the number of attributes, and the y-coordinate represents the utility of three models. Figure 1 shows the utility of three models do not strictly increase with the increasing of attribute numbers. For example, the utility decrease with adding an attribute in data set credit_a, forestfires and vote. The utility with the number of attributes increasing do not present monotonicity strictly.

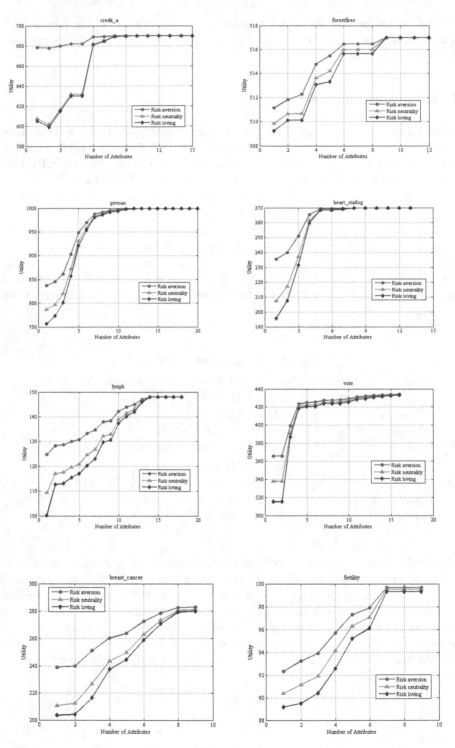

Fig. 1. Utility comparison of three attribute reductions

5   Conclusions

Utility-based decision-theoretic rough set model is introduced in this paper. The utility of the positive region, the boundary region and the negative region are given respectively. We provide a definition of reduction which aims to obtain the maximal utility in decisions. A heuristic reduction algorithm with respect to the definition is proposed. Finally, experimental results show the proposed algorithm is effective.

Acknowledgements. This work was partially supported by the National Natural Science Foundation of China (Nos. 61403329, 61572418, 61663002, 61502410, 61572419), the Natural Science Foundation of Shandong Province (No. ZR2013 FQ020).

References

1. Yao, Y.Y., Wong, S.K.M., Lingras, P.: A decision-theoretic rough set model. In: Ras, Z.W., Zemankova., M., and Emrichm M.L. (eds.) Proceedings of the 5th International Symposium on Methodologies for Intelligent Systems, 25–27 October 1990. North-Holland, New York (1990)
2. Liu, D., Liang, D.C., Wang, C.C.: A novel three-way decision model based on incomplete information system. Knowl.-Based Syst. **91**, 32–45 (2016)
3. Deng, X.F., Yao, Y.Y.: Decision-theoretic three-way approximations of fuzzy sets. Inf. Sci. **279**, 702–715 (2014)
4. Herbert, J.P., Yao, J.T.: Game-theoretic rough sets. Fundamenta Informaticae **108**, 267–286 (2011)
5. Yu, H., Liu, Z.G., Wang, G.Y.: An automatic method to determine the number of clusters using decision-theoretic rough set. Int. J. Approx. Reason. **55**, 101–115 (2014)
6. Zhang, H.R., Min, F.: Three-way recommender systems based on random forests. Knowl.-Based Syst. **91**, 275–286 (2016)
7. Zhou, B., Yao, Y.Y., Luo, J.G.: Cost-sensitive three-way email spam filtering. J. Intell. Inf. Syst. **42**, 19–45 (2014)
8. Liang, D.C., Pedrycz, W., Liu, D., Hu, P.: Three-way decisions based on decision-theoretic rough sets under linguistic assessment with the aid of group decision making. Appl. Soft Comput. **29**, 256–269 (2015)
9. Yao, Y.Y., Zhao, Y.: Attribute reduction in decision-theoretic rough set model. Inf. Sci. **178**, 3356–3373 (2008)
10. Jia, X.Y., Liao, W.H., Tang, Z.H., Shang, L.: Minimum cost attribute reduction in decision-theoretic rough set models. Inf. Sci. **219**, 151–167 (2013)
11. Dou, H.L., Yang, X.B., Song, X.N., et al.: Decision-theoretic rough set: a multicost strategy. Knowl.-Based Syst. **91**, 71–83 (2016)
12. Li, H.X., Zhou, X.Z., Zhao, J.B.: Non-monotonic attribute reduction in decision-theoretic rough sets. Fundamenta Informaticae **126**, 415–432 (2013)
13. Ju, H.R., Dou, H.L., Qi, Y., Yu, H.L., Yu, D.J., Yang, J.Y.: δ-cut decision-theoretic rough set approach: model and attribute reductions. Sci. World J. **2014**, 1–12 (2014)
14. Ma, X.A., Wang, G.Y., Yu, H., Li, T.R.: Decision region distribution preservation reduction in decision-theoretic rough set model. Inf. Sci. **278**, 614–640 (2014)
15. Zhang, N., Jiang, L.L., Yue, X.D., Zhou, J.: Utility-based three-way decisions model. CAAI Trans. Intell. Syst. **11**, 459–468 (2016)

Dynamic Three Way Decisions and Its Application Based on Two-Direction PS-Probabilistic Rough Set

Chunying Zhang[1,2], Liya Wang[1,2(✉)],
and Baoxiang Liu[1,2(✉)]

[1] College of Science, North China University of Science and Technology,
No. 46. Xinhua Road, Tangshan 063009, People's Republic of China
wang_liya@126.com
[2] Hebei Province Key Lab of Data Science and Application, Tangshan 063009,
People's Republic of China

Abstract. In order to solve the issue of three way decisions under set's dynamic changing, we put forward a model of three way decisions model based on two-direction PS-probabilistic rough set by analyzing the theory and properties of two-direction PS-probabilistic rough set. Firstly, according to the upper and lower approximation of two-direction PS-probabilistic rough set, we deduce the boundary region, negative region and boundary region, explain the rules of three way decisions and analyze the properties of confidence coefficient and error rate. Then, we define decision metric function and decision loss function of three way decisions based on two-direction PS-probabilistic rough set, and infer the estimation method of the threshold value based on the minimum risk decision rules of Bayesian decision theory. Finally, the properties of this dynamic model are discussed; the example shows the correctness and feasibility of this model.

Keywords: Two-direction PS-probabilistic rough set · Three-Way decisions · Dynamic decision

1 Introduction

Based on rough set [1] and probabilistic rough set [2], three way decisions theory is raised by Yao, and it is the generalization of two way decisions and is one of the methods for dealing with the imprecise or incomplete information. It uses the deferment decision as the third decision behavior and has wide application on medical diagnosis, paper review, emotion classification, incremental learning, text recognition, etc. [3].

For the problem of decision rules based on three way decisions, many scholars have come up with lots of models on basis of probabilistic rough set, such as decision-theoretic rough set model, variable precision rough set model [4], Bayesian rough set model [5, 6], interval-valued decision-theoretic rough set [7]. According to probabilistic rough set model, the equivalence class with higher threshold value is classified into positive region, the equivalence class not meeting the lower threshold value into negative region; others are classified to boundary region. Probabilistic rough

© Springer International Publishing AG 2017
L. Polkowski et al. (Eds.): IJCRS 2017, Part II, LNAI 10314, pp. 376–389, 2017.
DOI: 10.1007/978-3-319-60840-2_28

set model has better fault-tolerant ability. For the next decision of objects in boundary region, the three-way decisions model based on constructive covering algorithm [8] is constructed, and it provides two further decision schemes for the object in boundary region. According to the parent-children relationships of interval concept lattice [9], a three way decisions model is built to deal with the objects in boundary region and it reduces the loss of incorrect decisions effectively. The methods above built on basis of that objects in set are constant. Actually, the set is dynamically changing, which includes immigration and emigration of elements. Both of the dynamic property of set X and the statistical information of knowledge base can be considered by using two-direction PS-probabilistic rough set [10], which can build a bridge between of three way decisions and dynamic set. So in this paper, a three way decisions based on two-direction PS-probabilistic rough set is put forward.

The rest of the paper is organized as follows. In Sect. 2, we review the main ideas of decision rough set and the associated three-way decisions. In Sect. 3, we introduce the theory of two-direction PS-probabilistic rough set and its some theorems. In Sect. 4, we provide the detailed analysis of the three way decisions model based on two-direction PS-probabilistic rough set. In Sect. 5, a case is discussed which shows the validity and feasibility of the model.

2 Decision-Theoretic Rough Set and Three Way Decisions

2.1 Decision-Theoretic Rough Set

The approximation of rough set is defined on the qualitative relationship among concepts. However, without considering the intersection of concepts, there are many problems cannot be solved by rough set. Thus many scholars put forward various rough set models combining with probability theory. In 1990, Yao Yiyu proposed decision-theoretic rough set (DTRS), which expands the 0.5-probabilistic rough set model.

Suppose quaternion $S = (U, A, V, I)$ is a decision table, in which, $U = \{x_1, x_2, \ldots, x_n\}$ is a nonempty finite set of objects; $A = C \cup D$ is an attribute set (C is a condition attribute set, D is decision attribute set, and $C \cap D = \emptyset$); V is an attribute values set; I is an information function to assign the attribute value of each object.

Definition 1. Suppose U is a universe, $X \subseteq U$, and R is an equivalence relationship, $[x]_R$ is X's equivalence class in terms of R. To depict X, a pair of upper approximation and lower approximation are defined as follow:

$$\overline{R}(X) = \{x | x \in U, [x]_R \cap X \neq \emptyset\}$$

$$\underline{R}(X) = \{x | x \in U, [x]_R \subseteq X\}$$

Definition 2. Suppose U is a universe, $X \subseteq U$, and R is an equivalence relationship. U is partitioned based on $X's$ upper approximation and lower approximation

$$POS(X) = \underline{R}(X) = \{x | x \in U, [x]_R \subseteq X\}$$

$$NEG(X) = \mathrm{U} - \overline{R}(X) = \{x | x \in U, [x]_R \cap X = \emptyset\}$$

$$BND(X) = \overline{R}(X) - \underline{R}(X) = \{x | x \in U, [x]_R \cap X \neq \emptyset \wedge \neg([x]_R \subseteq X)\}$$

The three subsets above are called $X's$ positive region, negative region and boundary region, respectively.

Pawlak rough set is a qualitative approximation which cannot accept any uncertainty. So it has limitation in some ways. In order to promote the faults tolerant capability, Wong and Ziarko introduced the probability approximation space to rough set, and purposed 0.5-probabilistic rough set model [3].

Definition 3. Suppose U is a universe, $X \subseteq U$. Let $Pr(X|[x]_R)$ denote the conditional probability of each object belonging to X given that the object belongs to $[x]_R$, then the positive region, negative region and boundary region of X under 0.5 are defined as follow:

$$\mathrm{POS}_{0.5}(X) = \{x | x \in U, \mathrm{Pr}(X|[x]_R) > 0.5\}$$

$$\mathrm{NEG}_{0.5}(X) = \{x | x \in U, \mathrm{Pr}(X|[x]_R) < 0.5\}$$

$$\mathrm{BND}_{0.5}(X) = \{x | x \in U, \mathrm{Pr}(X|[x]_R) = 0.5\}$$

The threshold value 0.5 can depict majority rule quantitatively. While the majority rule cannot explain the general threshold value (α, β). Yiyu Yao put forward decision-theoretic rough set based on Bayesian decision theory which can achieve all the positive region, negative region and boundary region of threshold value (α, β).

Definition 4. Suppose U is a universe, $X \subseteq U$. One may choose a pair of thresholds (α, β) with $0 \leq \beta \leq \alpha \leq 1$, and introduce three probabilistic regions:

$$\mathrm{POS}_{(\alpha,\beta)}(X) = \{x | x \in U, \mathrm{Pr}(X|[x]_R) \geq \alpha\}$$

$$\mathrm{BND}_{(\alpha,\beta)}(X) = \{x | x \in U, \beta < \mathrm{Pr}(X|[x]_R) < \alpha\}$$

$$\mathrm{NEG}_{(\alpha,\beta)}(X) = \{x | x \in U, \mathrm{Pr}(X|[x]_R) \leq \beta\}$$

When $\alpha = 0, \beta = 1$, the Pawlak rough set is achieved.

2.2   Three Way Decisions

The positive region, negative region and boundary region of rough set provide the theoretical basis of three way decisions to a great extent. Suppose $Des(x)$ denotes the logic formula defining the equivalence class $[x]_R$, which is typically a conjunction of attribute-value pairs in an information table. For the Pawlak rough set models, the following positive, negative and boundary rules can be introduced:

$$\text{Positive rule} : Des(x) \rightarrow \text{accept}, x \in X, [x]_R \subseteq POS(X)$$

$$\text{Negative rule} : Des(x) \rightarrow \text{reject}, x \in X, [x]_R \subseteq NEG(X)$$

$$\text{Boundary rule} : Des(x) \rightarrow \text{defer a decision}, x \in X, [x]_R \subseteq BND(X)$$

For positive rule, confidence coefficient is $\delta = Pr(X|[x]_R) = 1$, error rate is $1 - \delta = 0$; For negative rule, confidence coefficient is $\delta' = Pr(X^C|[x]_R) = 1$, error rate is $1 - \delta' = 0$; For boundary rule, confidence coefficient and error rate are between 0 and 1.

As positive region and negative region do not get wrong results, three way decisions model based on Pawlak rough set is a qualitative decision rule.

For the decision-theoretic rough set, the following positive, negative and boundary rules can be introduced:

$$\text{Positive rule} : Des(x) \rightarrow \text{accept}, x \in X, [x]_R \subseteq POS_{(\alpha,\beta)}(X)$$

$$\text{Negative rule} : Des(x) \rightarrow \text{reject}, x \in X, [x]_R \subseteq NEG_{(\alpha,\beta)}(X)$$

$$\text{Boundary rule} : Des(x) \rightarrow \text{defer a decision}, x \in X, [x]_A \subseteq BND_{(\alpha,\beta)}(X)$$

For positive rule, confidence coefficient is $\delta = Pr(X|[x]_A) \geq \alpha$, error rate is $1 - \delta = 1 - \alpha$. For negative rule, confidence coefficient is $\delta' = Pr(X^C|[x]_A) = 1 - Pr(X|[x]_A) = 1 - \beta$.

3   Two-Direction PS-Probabilistic Rough Set

Whether Pawlak rough set or decision-theoretic rough set, the subset X is constant. Actually, $X \subseteq U$ is dynamically changing, including immigration and emigration of elements. In this context, Professor Shi Kaiquan of Shandong University proposes S-rough set, two direction Singular Sets [11]. Based on probabilistic rough set and S-rough set, a two-direction PS-probabilistic rough set is put forward, which allows for the probability of two-direction transfer. It can describe the probability of X of $[x]_R$.

Definition 5   [10]. For any X subset of U. $F = \{f_1, f_2, \ldots, f_m\}$ and $\overline{F} = \{\overline{f}_1, \overline{f}_2, \ldots, \overline{f}_m\}$ is the element transfer family. The element transfers are defined as

$$f_i \in F : \exists u \in U, u \notin X \Rightarrow f_i(u) = x \in X$$

$$\overline{f}_j \in \overline{F} : \exists x \in X \Rightarrow \overline{f}_j(x) = y \notin X$$

$F = \{f_1, f_2, \ldots, f_m\}$ means some objects move into X, on the contrary, $\overline{F} = \{\overline{f}_1, \overline{f}_2, \ldots, \overline{f}_m\}$ means some objects move out of X.

Definition 6 [10]. For any X subset of U, the two-direction S-set is defined as

$$X^* = X' \cup \{u | u \in U, u \notin X, f(u) = x \in X\}$$

$$X' = X - \{x | x \in X, \overline{f}(x) = u \notin X\}$$

X' is called loss set of $X \subseteq U$.

Definition 7 [10]. For any X subset of U, X^* is the two-direction S-set. The lower approximation of $X^* \subseteq U$ is defined as

$$F_-(X^*) = \{x | x \in U, [x]_R \subseteq X^*\}$$

The upper approximation of $X^* \subseteq U$ is defined as

$$F^-(X^*) = \{x | x \in U, [x]_R \cap X^* \neq \emptyset\}$$

$(F_-(X^*), F^-(X^*))$ is called S-rough set of X^*.

Definition 8 [10]. For any X subset of U, X^* is the two-direction S-set. Based on the upper and lower approximation of X^*, positive region, negative region and boundary region are defined as follow:

$$POS(X^*) = F_-(X^*) = \{x | x \in U, [x]_R \subseteq X^*\}$$

$$NEG(X^*) = U - F^-(X^*) = \{x | x \in U, [x]_R \cap X^* = \emptyset\}$$

$$BND(X^*) = F^-(X^*) - F_-(X^*) = \{x | x \in U, [x]_R \cap X^* \neq \emptyset \wedge \neg([x]_R \subseteq X^*)\}$$

When $F = \emptyset$, then $X^* = X$, the positive region, negative region and boundary region of X^* are the same to the ones of X. Two-direction S-rough set degenerates to Pawlak rough set. In one form or another, Pawlak rough set is a particular case of two-direction S-rough set.

Definition 9 [10]. For any X subset of U, X^* is the two-direction S-set. $f \in F$ is an element transfer defined in U. Given a pair of threshold values (α, β) which meet $0 \leq \beta \leq \alpha \leq 1$. $F_-(X^*)_{(\alpha,\beta)}$ is called probability PS-lower approximation of X^* in parameters (α, β), if $F_-(X^*)_{(\alpha,\beta)} = \{x | x \in U, Pr(X^* | [x]_R) \geq \alpha\}$, $F^-(X^*)_{(\alpha,\beta)}$ is called probability PS-upper approximation of X^* in parameters (α, β), if $F^-(X^*)_{(\alpha,\beta)} = \{x | x \in U, Pr(X^* | [x]_R) \rangle \beta\}$, $(F_-(X^*)_{(\alpha,\beta)}, F^-(X^*)_{(\alpha,\beta)})$ is called probability PS-rough set of X^* in parameters (α, β).

Positive region $POS_{(\alpha,\beta)}(X^*)$, negative region $NEG_{(\alpha,\beta)}(X^*)$, boundary region $BND_{(\alpha,\beta)}(X^*)$ of two-direction S-set are defined as follow:

$$POS_{(\alpha,\beta)}(X^*) = F_-(X^*)_{(\alpha,\beta)} = \{x | x \in U, Pr(X^* | [x]_R) \geq \alpha\}$$

$$NEG_{(\alpha,\beta)}(X^*) = U - F^-(X^*)_{(\alpha,\beta)} = \{x | x \in U, Pr(X^* | [x]_R) \leq \beta\}$$

$$BND_{(\alpha,\beta)}(X^*) = F^-(X^*)_{(\alpha,\beta)} - F_-(X^*)_{(\alpha,\beta)} = \{x | x \in U, \beta < Pr(X^* | [x]_R) < \alpha\}$$

When (α, β) is $(1, 0)$, probability PS-rough set degenerates to S-rough set; when $X^* = X$ and $0 \leq \beta \leq \alpha \leq 1$, probability PS-rough set becomes probabilistic rough set; when $X^* = X$ and (α, β) is $(1, 0)$, probability PS-rough set becomes Pawlak rough set.

Definition 10 [10]. When $BND_{(\alpha,\beta)}(X^*) = \emptyset$, X^* is called "can be defined in parameters (α, β)". Otherwise X^* is called "can not be defined in parameters (α, β)" or "two-direction probability PS-rough set".

Theorem 1. Suppose $X_1, X_2 \subseteq U$, if there are migrating elements, X_1^* is the two-direction S-set of X_1, X_2^* is the two-direction S-set of X_2, and $X_1^* \subseteq X_2^*$, then

$$F_-(X_1^*)_{(\alpha,\beta)} \subseteq F_-(X_2^*)_{(\alpha,\beta)}$$

$$F^-(X_1^*)_{(\alpha,\beta)} \subseteq F^-(X_2^*)_{(\alpha,\beta)}$$

Theorem 2. Suppose $X_1, X_2 \subseteq U$, if there are migrating elements, X_1^* is the two-direction S-set of X_1, X_2^* is the two-direction S-set of X_2, and $X_1^* \subseteq X_2^*$, then

$$POS_{(\alpha,\beta)}(X_2^*) \supseteq POS_{(\alpha,\beta)}(X_1^*)$$

$$NEG_{(\alpha,\beta)}(X_2^*) \subseteq NEG_{(\alpha,\beta)}(X_1^*)$$

$$BND_{(\alpha,\beta)}(X_2^*) \subseteq BND_{(\alpha,\beta)}(X_1^*)$$

4 Three Way Decisions Based on Probability PS-Rough Set

4.1 Three Way Rules in X^*

Suppose two-direction S-set X^*. And the positive region, negative region, boundary region of its probability PS-rough set in parameters (α, β) are $POS_{(\alpha,\beta)}(X^*)$, $NEG_{(\alpha,\beta)}(X^*)$ and $BND_{(\alpha,\beta)}(X^*)$. Then there are:

Positive rule : $Des(x) \rightarrow$ accept, $x \in X^*$, $[x]_R \subseteq POS_{(\alpha,\beta)}(X^*)$

Negative rule : $Des(x) \rightarrow$ reject, $x \in X^*$, $[x]_R \subseteq NEG_{(\alpha,\beta)}(X^*)$

Boundary rule : $Des(x) \rightarrow$ defer a decision, $x \in X^*$, $[x]_R \subseteq BND_{(\alpha,\beta)}(X^*)$

For positive rule, its confidence coefficient is $\delta = Pr(X^*|[x]_R) \geq \alpha$, error rate is $e = 1 - \delta \leq 1 - \alpha$. For negative rule, its confidence coefficient is $\delta' = Pr(X^{*C}|[x]_R) = 1 - Pr(X^*|[x]_R) \geq 1 - \beta$, error rate is $1 - \delta' < \beta$. For boundary rule, its confidence coefficient and error rate are between α and β.

Theorem 3. Suppose $X_1, X_2 \subseteq U$, if there are migrating elements, X_1^* is the two-direction S-set of X_1, X_2^* is the two-direction S-set of X_2, $X_1^* \subseteq X_2^*$, δ_1 is the confidence coefficient of X_1^*, δ_2 is the confidence coefficient of X_2^*, e_1 is the error rate of X_1^*, and e_2 is the error rate of X_2^*, then $\delta_1 \leq \delta_2$, $e_1 \geq e_2$.

Proof. $X_1^* \subseteq X_2^*$, so $X_1^* \cap [x]_R \subseteq X_2^* \cap [x]_R$.

Then $|X_1^* \cap [x]_R| \leq |X_2^* \cap [x]_R|$, $\delta_1 = Pr(X_1^*|[x]_R) = \frac{|X_1^* \cap [x]_R|}{|[x]_R|} \leq \delta_2 = Pr(X_2^*|[x]_R) = \frac{|X_2^* \cap [x]_R|}{|[x]_R|}$, $e_1 = 1 - \delta_1 \geq e_2 = 1 - \delta_2$.

Inference 1. Suppose $X \subseteq U, X_1^*, X_2^*, \ldots X_m^*$ are the two-direction S-set of X in different time, $X_i^* \subseteq X_j^* (1 \leq i < j \leq m)$. The confidence coefficient of X_i^*'s positive rule is δ_i, and the error rate is e_i $(1 \leq i \leq m)$. Then $\delta_1 \leq \delta_2 \leq \ldots \leq \delta_m$, $e_1 \geq e_2 \geq \ldots \geq e_m$.

Theorem 3 and Inference 1 show that if there is more information, the accuracy of decision is higher, and the error rate is lower.

Inference 2. Suppose $X \subseteq U, X_1^*, X_2^*, \ldots X_m^*$ are the two-direction S-set of X in different time, $X_i^* \supseteq X_j^* (1 \leq i < j \leq m)$. The confidence coefficient of X_i^*'s positive rule is δ_i, and the error rate is e_i $(1 \leq i \leq m)$. Then $\delta_1 \geq \delta_2 \geq \ldots \geq \delta_m$, $e_1 \leq e_2 \leq \ldots \leq e_m$.

4.2   Computing of Threshold Value (α, β)

For $X \subseteq U$, its two-direction S-set is X^*. A states set $\Omega = (X^*, X^{*C})$ is constructed, where X^* and X^{*C} are complementary. For the positive region, negative region and boundary region of probability PS-rough set, the actions set $A^* = \{a_P^*, a_N^*, a_B^*\}$ is constructed, where a_P^*, a_N^*, a_B^* represent the three actions in classifying an object x. The different decision actions will lead to different results, and all the 6 loss functions are shown in Table 1.

Table 1. Loss function

	X^* (positive)	X^{*C} (negative)
a_P^*	$\lambda_{PP}^* = \lambda^*(a_P^*|X^*)$	$\lambda_{PN}^* = \lambda^*(a_P^*|X^{*C})$
a_N^*	$\lambda_{NP}^* = \lambda^*(a_N^*|X^*)$	$\lambda_{NN}^* = \lambda^*(a_N^*|X^{*C})$
a_B^*	$\lambda_{BP}^* = \lambda^*(a_B^*|X^*)$	X^{*C} (negative)

The conditional risks of the three actions given an equivalence class $[x]_R$ are computed as:

$$L(a_P^*|[x]_R) = \lambda_{PP}^* Pr(X^*|[x]_R) + \lambda_{PN}^* Pr(X^{*C}|[x]_R)$$

$$L(a_N^*|[x]_R) = \lambda_{NP}^* Pr(X^*|[x]_R) + \lambda_{NN}^* Pr(X^{*C}|[x]_R)$$

$$L(a_B^*|[x]_R) = \lambda_{BP}^* Pr(X^*|[x]_R) + \lambda_{BN}^* Pr(X^{*C}|[x]_R)$$

Bayesian decision procedure gives rise to three minimum-risk decision rules:

(P^*)If $L(a_P^*|[x]_R) \leq L(a_N^*|[x]_R)$ and $L(u_P^*|[x]_R) \leq L(a_B^*|[x]_R)$, decide $x \in POS_{(\alpha,\beta)}(X^*)$

(N^*)If $L(a_N^*|[x]_R) \leq L(a_P^*|[x]_R)$ and $L(a_N^*|[x]_R) \leq L(a_B^*|[x]_R)$, decide $x \in NEG_{(\alpha,\beta)}(X^*)$

(B^*)If $L(a_B^*|[x]_R) \leq L(a_P^*|[x]_R)$ and $L(a_B^*|[x]_R) \leq L(a_N^*|[x]_R)$, decide $x \in BND_{(\alpha,\beta)}(X^*)$

In order to ensure that each object can be classified into a only region, a decisive rule need to be introduce when the risks of two actions are same. In two-direction S-rough set, although there are migrating elements in X, the universe U is invariant, namely, $X^* \cup X^{*C} = U$. So $Pr(X^*|[x]_R) + Pr(X^{*C}|[x]_R) = 1$. Hence, $r(X^*|[x]_R)$ and loss function λ^* can be used to simplify the rule $(P^*) \sim (B^*)$. Actually, an object x belonging to X^* is classified to positive region $POS_{(\alpha,\beta)}(X^*)$, that means $\lambda_{PP}^* \leq \lambda_{BP}^* \leq \lambda_{NP}^*$; an object x belonging to X^* is classified to negative region $NEG_{(\alpha,\beta)}(X^*)$, that means $\lambda_{NN}^* \leq \lambda_{BN}^* \leq \lambda_{PN}^*$. On this basis, three threshold values with $(P^*) \sim (B^*)$ can be got:

$$\alpha = \frac{(\lambda_{PN}^* - \lambda_{BN}^*)}{(\lambda_{PN}^* - \lambda_{BN}^*) + (\lambda_{BP}^* - \lambda_{PP}^*)}$$

$$\beta = \frac{(\lambda_{BN}^* - \lambda_{NN}^*)}{(\lambda_{BN}^* - \lambda_{NN}^*) + (\lambda_{NP}^* - \lambda_{BP}^*)}$$

$$\gamma = \frac{(\lambda_{PN}^* - \lambda_{NN}^*)}{(\lambda_{NP}^* - \lambda_{PP}^*) + (\lambda_{PN}^* - \lambda_{NN}^*)}$$

Obviously, $\alpha \in (0,1], \beta \in [0,1], \gamma \in (0,1)$. If the loss functions meet that $(\lambda_{PN}^* - \lambda_{BN}^*) \cdot (\lambda_{NP}^* - \lambda_{BP}^*) > (\lambda_{BP}^* - \lambda_{PP}^*) \cdot (\lambda_{BN}^* - \lambda_{NN}^*)$, $\alpha > \gamma > \beta$ can be proved. Then γ is not needed. The rule $(P^*) \sim (B^*)$ can be simplified as follow:

(P_1^*) If $Pr(X^*|[x]_R) \geq \alpha$, then $x \in POS_{(\alpha,\beta)}(X^*)$

(N_1^*) If $Pr(X^*|[x]_R) \leq \beta$, then $x \in NEG_{(\alpha,\beta)}(X^*)$

(B_1^*) If $\beta < Pr(X^*|[x]_R) < \alpha$, then $x \in BND_{(\alpha,\beta)}(X^*)$

Suppose $Pr(X^*|[x]_R) = p^*$, then the risks of $(P_1^*) \sim (B_1^*)$ can be shown as follow:

Risk of positive rule $(P_1^*) : R(P_1^*) = \lambda_{PP}^* \cdot p^* + \lambda_{PN}^* \cdot (1 - p^*)$

Risk of negative rule $(N_1^*) : R(N_1^*) = \lambda_{NP}^* \cdot p^* + \lambda_{NN}^* \cdot (1 - p^*)$

Risk of boundary rule $(B_1^*) : R(B_1^*) = \lambda_{BP}^* \cdot p^* + \lambda_{BN}^* \cdot (1 - p^*)$

Usually in the learning process, we set $\lambda_{PP}^* = 0, \lambda_{NN}^* = 0$.

4.3   Properties of Dynamic Decision

Theorem 4. Suppose $X \subseteq U$ on t_0. If there are migrating elements, X_1^* is the two-direction S-set of X on t_1, and $X \subseteq X_1^*$, then

$$Pr(X_1^*|[x]_R) \geq Pr(X|[x]_R)$$

Proof. $X \subseteq X_1^*$, so $X \cap [x]_R \subseteq X_1^* \cap [x]_R$, then $|X \cap [x]_R| \leq |X_1^* \cap [x]_R|$,

$$Pr(X|[x]_R) = \frac{|X \cap [x]_R|}{|[x]_R|} \leq Pr(X_1^*|[x]_R) = \frac{|X_1^* \cap [x]_R|}{|[x]_R|}$$

Inference 3. Suppose $X \subseteq U$ on t_0. Let $1 \leq i < j \leq n$, and $t_0 \leq t_i < t_j \leq t_n$. If there are migrating elements, X_i^* is the two-direction S-set of X on t_i, X_j^* is the two-direction S-set of X on t_j, and $X \subseteq X_i^* \subseteq X_j^*$. Then

$$Pr(X_1^*|[x]_R) \leq \ldots \leq Pr(X_i^*|[x]_R) \leq \ldots \leq Pr(X_j^*|[x]_R) \leq \ldots \leq Pr(X_n^*|[x]_R).$$

Inference 4. Suppose $X \subseteq U$ on t_0, $Pr(X|[x]_R) \geq \alpha$, and decide $x \in POS_{(\alpha,\beta)}(X)$. Let $1 \leq i < j \leq n$, and $t_0 \leq t_i < t_j \leq t_n$. If there are migrating elements, X_i^* is the two-direction

S-set of X on t_i, X_j^* is the two-direction S-set of X on t_j, and $X \subseteq X_i^* \subseteq X_j^*$ Then on each $t_k(1 \leq k \leq n)$, decide $x \in POS_{(\alpha,\beta)}(X_k^*)$.

Inference 5. Suppose $X \subseteq U$ on t_0, $Pr(X|[x]_R) \geq \alpha$. Let $1 \leq i < j \leq n$, and $t_0 \leq t_i < t_j \leq t_n$. If there are migrating elements, X_i^* is the two-direction S-set of X on t_i; X_j^* is the two-direction S-set of X on t_j, and $X \subseteq X_i^* \subseteq X_j^*$. $R_i(P_1^*)$ is the risk of X_i^*'s positive rule (P_1^*), and $R_j(P_1^*)$ is the risk of X_j^*'s positive rule (P_1^*). Then

$$R_1(P_1^*) \geq \ldots R_i(P_1^*) \geq \ldots R_j(P_1^*) \geq \ldots \geq R_n(P_1^*)$$

Inference 6. Suppose $X \subseteq U$ on t_0, $\beta < Pr(X|[x]_R) < \alpha$, and decide $x \in BND_{(\alpha,\beta)}(X)$. Let $1 \leq i < j \leq n$, and $t_0 \leq t_i < t_j \leq t_n$. If there are migrating elements, X_i^* is the two-direction S-set of X on t_i ; X_j^* is the two-direction S-set of X on t_j, and $X \subseteq X_i^* \subseteq X_j^*$. If on t_i, $Pr(X_i^*|[x]_R) \geq \alpha$, and decide $x \in POS_{(\alpha,\beta)}(X_i^*)$. Then on each $t_k(i \leq k \leq n)$, decide $x \in POS_{(\alpha,\beta)}(X_k^*)$.

Theorem 5. Suppose $X \subseteq U$ on t_0. If there are migrating elements, X_1^* is the two-direction S-set of X on t_1, and $X \supseteq X_1^*$, then

$$Pr(X_1^*|[x]_R) \leq Pr(X|[x]_R)$$

Proof. $X \supseteq X_1^*$, so $X \cap [x]_R \supseteq X_1^* \cap [x]_R$, then $|X \cap [x]_R| \geq |X_1^* \cap [x]_R|$,

$$Pr(X|[x]_R) = \frac{|X \cap [x]_R|}{|[x]_R|} \geq Pr(X_1^*|[x]_R) = \frac{|X_1^* \cap [x]_R|}{|[x]_R|}$$

Inference 7. Suppose $X \subseteq U$ on t_0. Let $1 \leq i < j \leq n$, and $t_0 \leq t_i < t_j \leq t_n$. If there are migrating elements, X_i^* is the two-direction S-set of X on t_i, X_j^* is the two-direction S-set of X on t_j, and $X \supseteq X_i^* \supseteq X_j^*$. Then

$$Pr(X_1^*|[x]_R) \geq \ldots \geq Pr(X_i^*|[x]_R) \geq \ldots \geq Pr(X_j^*|[x]_R) \geq \ldots \geq Pr(X_n^*|[x]_R).$$

Inference 8. Suppose $X \subseteq U$ on t_0, $Pr(X|[x]_R) \leq \beta$, and decide $x \in NEG_{(\alpha,\beta)}(X)$. Let $1 \leq i < j \leq n$, and $t_0 \leq t_i < t_j \leq t_n$. If there are migrating elements, X_i^* is the two-direction S-set of X on t_i, X_j^* is the two-direction S-set of X on t_j, and $X \supseteq X_i^* \supseteq X_j^*$ Then on each $t_k(1 \leq k \leq n)$, decide $x \in NEG_{(\alpha,\beta)}(X_k^*)$.

Inference 9. Suppose $X \subseteq U$ on t_0, $Pr(X|[x]_R) \leq \beta$, and decide $x \in NEG_{(\alpha,\beta)}(X)$. Let $1 \leq i < j \leq n$, and $t_0 \leq t_i < t_j \leq t_n$. If there are migrating elements, X_i^* is the two-direction S-set of X on t_i ; X_j^* is the two-direction S-set of X on t_j, and $X \supseteq X_i^* \supseteq X_j^*$. $R_i(N_1^*)$ is the risk of X_i^*'s negative rule $\left(N_1^*\right)$, and $R_j\left(N_1^*\right)$ is the risk of X_j^*'s negative rule $\left(N_1^*\right)$. Then

$$R_1\left(N_1^*\right) \geq \ldots R_i\left(N_1^*\right) \geq \ldots R_j\left(N_1^*\right) \geq \ldots \geq R_n\left(N_1^*\right)$$

Inference 10. Suppose $X \subseteq U$ on t_0, $\beta < Pr\left(X|[x]_R\right) < \alpha$, and decide $x \in BND_{(\alpha,\beta)}(X)$. Let $1 \leq i < j \leq n$, and $t_0 \leq t_i < t_j \leq t_n$. If there are migrating elements, X_i^* is the two-direction S-set of X on t_i; X_j^* is the two-direction S-set of X on t_j, and $X \supseteq X_i^* \supseteq X_j^*$. If on t_i, $Pr\left(X_i^*|[x]_R\right) \geq \alpha$, and decide $x \in NEG_{(\alpha,\beta)}\left(X_i^*\right)$. Then on each $t_k (i \leq k \leq n)$, decide $x \in NEG_{(\alpha,\beta)}\left(X_k^*\right)$.

5   Case Study

In a venture capital management system, all risk factors affecting the system are regarded as the universe $= \{x_1, x_2, x_3, x_4, x_5, x_6, x_7, x_8, x_9, x_{10}, x_{11}, x_{12}\}$. For some investment project, the risk factors affecting it form the set $X = \{x_1, x_3, x_5, x_{10}, x_{11}\}$. According to the investors' experience and knowledge, $U/d = \{D_1, D_2, D_3\}$, where, $D_1 = \{x_1, x_2, x_3, x_4, x_5\}$, $D_2 = \{x_6, x_7, x_8\}$, $D_3 = \{x_9, x_{10}, x_{11}, x_{12}\}$.

Suppose $(\alpha, \beta) = (0.55, 0.35)$, then the conditional probability is as follow:

$$Pr(X|D_1) = 3/5 > 0.55 = \alpha$$

$$Pr(X|D_2) = 0 < 0.35 = \beta$$

$$\beta = 0.35 < Pr(X|D_3) = 1/2 < 0.55 = \alpha$$

The probabilistic rough three way approximates are defined as follow with Definition 5:

$$POS_{(\alpha,\beta)}(X) = \{x_1, x_2, x_3, x_4, x_5\}$$

$$BND_{(\alpha,\beta)}(X) = \{x_9, x_{10}, x_{11}, x_{12}\}$$

$$NEG_{(\alpha,\beta)}(X) = \{x_6, x_7, x_8\}$$

In X, x_1, x_2, x_3, x_4, x_5 certainly affect the risk project (accept action); $x_9, x_{10}, x_{11}, x_{12}$ may affect the risk project (defer a decision); x_6, x_7, x_8 certainly don't affect the risk project (reject action).

5.1   Three Way Decisions Based on Probability PS-Rough Set

With the development of the system, the risk factors x_1, x_3 have no impact on the project, while the risk factors $x_2, x_6, x_8, x_9, x_{12}$ become the new risk factors of the project. Then a two-direction S-set $X^* = \{x_2, x_5, x_6, x_8, x_9, x_{10}, x_{11}, x_{12}\}$ is achieved. Then the conditional probabilities are as follow:

$$\beta = 0.35 < Pr(X^*|D_1) = 2/5 < 0.55 = \alpha$$

$$Pr(X^*|D_2) = 2/3 > 0.55 = \alpha$$

$$Pr(X^*|D_3) = 1 > 0.55 = \alpha$$

For the decision concepts D_1, D_2, D_3 of subset X^*, probability PS-rough set of X^* in parameters (α, β) is $(F\_(X^*)_{(\alpha,\beta)} = \{x_6, x_7, x_8, x_9, x_{10}, x_{11}, x_{12}\}, F^-(X^*)_{(\alpha,\beta)} = \{x_1, x_2, x_3, x_4, x_5, x_6, x_7, x_8, x_9, x_{10}, x_{11}, x_{12}\})$, and the three regions are defined as follow:

$$POS_{(\alpha,\beta)}(X^*) = \{x_6, x_7, x_8, x_9, x_{10}, x_{11}, x_{12}\}$$

$$BND_{(\alpha,\beta)}(X^*) = \{x_1, x_2, x_3, x_4, x_5\}$$

$$NEG_{(\alpha,\beta)}(X^*) = \emptyset$$

In X^*, $x_6, x_8, x_9, x_{10}, x_{11}, x_{12}$ certainly affect the risk project (accept action); x_2, x_5 may affect the risk project (defer a decision).

5.2   Properties of Dynamic Decision

On t_1, x_6, x_9 and x_{12} become the new risk factors of the project. Suppose $X_1^* = \{x_1, x_3, x_5, x_{10}, x_{11}\} \cup \{x_6, x_9, x_{12}\} = \{x_1, x_3, x_5, x_6, x_9, x_{10}, x_{11}, x_{12}\}$, then the conditional probabilities are as follow:

$$Pr(X_1^*|D_1) = 3/5$$

$$Pr(X_1^*|D_2) = 1/3$$

$$Pr(X_1^*|D_3) = 1$$

For the decision concepts D_1, D_2, D_3 of subset X_1^*, on t_1, the probabilistic rough three way approximates are defined as follow:

$$POS_{(\alpha,\beta)}(X_1^*) = \{x_1, x_2, x_3, x_4, x_5, x_9, x_{10}, x_{11}, x_{12}\}$$

$$BND_{(\alpha,\beta)}(X_1^*) = \emptyset$$

$$NEG_{(\alpha,\beta)}(X_1^*) = \{x_6, x_7, x_8\}$$

By this time, for $x_{10} \in X_1^*$, the "accept action" is made; for $x_6 \in X_1^*$, the "reject action" is made still.

On t_2, x_2 and x_8 become the new risk factors of the project. Suppose $X_2^* = \{x_1, x_3, x_5, x_6, x_9, x_{10}, x_{11}, x_{12}\} \cup \{x_2, x_8\} = \{x_1, x_2, x_3, x_5, x_6, x_8, x_9, x_{10}, x_{11}, x_{12}\}$. Then the conditional probabilities are as follow:

$$Pr(X_2^* | D_1) = 4/5$$

$$Pr(X_2^* | D_2) = 2/3$$

$$Pr(X_2^* | D_3) = 1$$

For the decision concepts D_1, D_2, D_3 of subset X_2^*, on t_2, the probabilistic rough three way approximates are defined as follow:

$$POS_{(\alpha,\beta)}(X_2^*) = \{x_1, x_2, x_3, x_4, x_5, x_6, x_7, x_8, x_9, x_{10}, x_{11}, x_{12}\}$$

$$BND_{(\alpha,\beta)}(X_2^*) = \emptyset$$

$$NEG_{(\alpha,\beta)}(X_2^*) = \emptyset$$

By this time, for $x_6 \in X_2^*$, the "accept action" is made.
Thus it can be seen that if $X_2 \supseteq X_1 \supseteq X_0$, there are:

$$Pr(X_2^* | [x]_R) \geq Pr(X_1^* | [x]_R) \geq Pr(X | [x]_R)$$

$$POS_{(\alpha,\beta)}(X_2^*) \supseteq POS_{(\alpha,\beta)}(X_1^*) \supseteq POS_{(\alpha,\beta)}(X)$$

$$NEG_{(\alpha,\beta)}(X_2^*) \subseteq NEG_{(\alpha,\beta)}(X_1^*) \subseteq NEG_{(\alpha,\beta)}(X)$$

Namely, when increasing number of elements move into X, the positive region becomes wider and the negative region becomes smaller. For the same element, as time goes on, the decision is changing, which can become "accept action" from "defer a decision" or "reject action". It conforms to the decision reality that with more information understood, confidence of decision will be bigger. Thus with the help of this theory, decision-makers can make decisions more reasonably.

In a similar way, increasing number of elements move out of X, there are dynamic changes according to Theorem 5 and Inferences 7–10.

6   Conclusions

A three way decisions based on two-direction probability PS-rough set is put forward, which allows for dynamic change of set. Firstly, the positive region, negative region and boundary region are divided according to two-direction probability PS-rough set, and the decision rules are given by these regions. Secondly, the measurement and loss functions of this model are given, on this basis, the method of computing threshold value (α, β) is discussed. Finally, the validity is shown by a case. There are many problems of this model to be discussed much further/needing further discussion: the optimized processing of the boundary objects, the application of specific decision, etc.

Acknowledgements. This work is partially supported by the National Natural Science Foundation of China (Grant No. 61370168,61472340), Natural Science Foundation of Hebei Province (Grant No. F2016209344), Young Scientist Fund of North China University of Science and Technology (Grant No. Z201621). The authors also gratefully acknowledge the helpful comments and suggestions of the reviewers, which have improved the presentation.

References

1. Yao, Y.: Decision-Theoretic Rough Set Models. In: Yao, J., Lingras, P., Wu, W.-Z., Szczuka, M., Cercone, Nick J., Ślęzak, D. (eds.) RSKT 2007. LNCS (LNAI), vol. 4481, pp. 1–12. Springer, Heidelberg (2007). doi:10.1007/978-3-540-72458-2_1
2. Yiyu, Y.: Three-Way Decisions with Probabilistic Rough Sets. Inf. Sci. **180**, 341–353 (2010)
3. Dun, L., Duoqian, M., Guoyin, W., Jiye, L.: Three-way Decisions and Granular Computing. Science Press, Beijing (2013)
4. Ziarko, W.: Variable Precision Rough Set Model. J. Comput. Syst. Sci. **46**, 39–59 (1993)
5. Ślęzak, D.: Rough Sets and Bayes Factor. In: Peters, James F., Skowron, A. (eds.) Transactions on Rough Sets III. LNCS, vol. 3400, pp. 202–229. Springer, Heidelberg (2005). doi:10.1007/11427834_10
6. Slezak, D., Ziarko, W.: The investigation of the Bayesian rough set model. Int. J. Approx. Reason. **40**, 81–91 (2005)
7. Dun, L., Tianrui, L., Huaxiong, L.: Interval decision rough set. computer. Science **39**(7), 178–181 (2012)
8. Hang, X.: Three Decision Models Based on Constructive Covering Algorithm. Anhui University, Hefei (2014)
9. Liya, W., Chunying, Z., Baoxiang, L.: Dynamic strategy regulation model of three-way decisions based on interval concept lattice and its application. Comput. Eng. Appl. **52**(24), 80–84 (2016)
10. Yanjun, Z., Chunying, Z.: Model and application of bidirectional transfer probabilistic ps-rough sets. Comput. Eng. Appl. **48**(14), 148–151 (2012)
11. Kaiquan, S., Yuquan, C.: S-rough Set and Rough Decision. Science Press, Beijing (2008)

Recent Advances in Biomedical Data Analysis, Trends in Multi-Agent Systems, Formal Concept Analysis, Rough Set Theory and Their Applications

Robust Sigmoidal Control Response
of *C. elegans* Neuronal Network

Rahul Badhwar[1] and Ganesh Bagler[1,2(✉)]

[1] Department of Bioscience and Bioengineering, Indian Institute of Technology
Jodhpur, Jodhpur, Rajasthan, India
pg201384010@iitj.ac.in
[2] Center for Computational Biology, Indraprastha Institute of Information
Technology Delhi (IIIT-Delhi), New Delhi, India
bagler@iiitd.ac.in

Abstract. Biological systems are known to evolve mechanisms for acquiring robust response under uncertainty. Brain is a complex adaptive system characterized with system specific network features, at global as well as local level, critical for its function and control. We studied controllability response in *C. elegans* neuronal network with change in number of functionally important feed-forward motifs, due to synaptic rewiring. We find that this neuronal network has acquired a sigmoidal control response with a robust regime for saturation of feed-forward motifs and an extremely fragile response for their depletion. Further we show that, to maintain controllability this neuronal network must rewire following a power law distance constraint. Our results highlight distance constrained synaptic rewiring as a robust evolutionary strategy in the presence of sigmoidal control response.

Keywords: *C. elegans* neuronal network · Controllability · Feed-forward motifs · Synaptic rewiring · Optimization

1 Introduction

Brain networks are characterized with non-trivial topological features, on global as well as local level, that are key to their function and control [1]. Typical to a complex adaptive system, the neuronal map is known to be plastic, and undergoes synaptic rewiring [2]. Under such dynamic synaptic reorganizations, it is important to know how the brain maintains functionally important topological features. We investigated this question in *C. elegans* neuronal network (CeNN), the most complete neuronal wiring diagram available till date [3, 4]. CeNN is a small world network, characterized with over-representation of feed-forward motifs (FFMs) and distributed control architecture [5–8]. FFMs represent functional building blocks of this system, a fine-grained feature that potentially gives rise to coarse-grained properties specifying network control [9].

A system is said to be controllable if it can be driven from any initial state to a desired final state in finite amount of time. For a linear time-invariant system, the necessary conditions to achieve structural control were specified by Lin in 1974 [10].

© Springer International Publishing AG 2017
L. Polkowski et al. (Eds.): IJCRS 2017, Part II, LNAI 10314, pp. 393–402, 2017.
DOI: 10.1007/978-3-319-60840-2_29

To achieve full control with least efforts, minimum input theorem requires identification of a minimal subset of 'driver nodes'. Maximal matching algorithm facilitates computation of the number of driver nodes (D_n) in a network [7]. Lesser the number of inputs, the more centralized is the control [8].

CeNN is known to have distributed control with higher number of driver neurons than its random counterpart [7, 8, 11]. By studying genotypic and phenotypic aspects of CeNN, in our earlier study we have shown that 'driver neurons' are associated with important biological functions such as reproduction, signaling processes and anatomical structural development [11]. The CeNN has been shown to have a bimodal control architecture which is sensitive to edge plasticity [8]. Synaptic plasticity can influence the number of driver neurons and hence control mechanisms in CeNN. Hence, we probed relationship between number of FFMs and number of driver neurons under synaptic rewiring. While the saturation of feed-forward motifs in CeNN is of functional consequence [6, 12, 13], it is not clear whether the system optimizes for the number of FFMs.

Interestingly, our studies suggest that the controllability (number of driver neurons) is sensitive to not 'the absolute number of FFMs' but to 'change in FFMs', exhibiting an asymmetric, sigmoidal response. We also find that the distance constrained synaptic rewiring can explain preservation of FFMs as well as robust controllability response of the network.

2 Materials and Methods

Towards investigations done as part of this work, we compiled data of *C. elegans* nervous system to construct its network model as well as its controls. Apart from enumerating its motifs and driver nodes, we also designed an algorithm for implementing motifs tuning.

2.1 *C. elegans* Neuronal Network

The nervous system of *C. elegans* consists of around 302 neurons which are interconnected via chemical synapses and gap junctions [3, 14]. We constructed CeNN, a network model of *C. elegans* neuronal network, using neuronal connectivity data of 277 somatic neurons [4]. Multiple synaptic connections between two neurons were merged to represent a single edge between them. Thus neuronal connectivity data were represented as a directed unweighted graph, where neurons represent nodes and synaptic connections represent links between them. We also constructed a random control of CeNN viz. Erdős-Rényi random control (ER) in which the number of nodes and edges were kept identical but wiring pattern was randomized [15]. Among topological properties of CeNN, we computed clustering coefficient and characteristic path-length which represent global features of the network [5, 9].

2.2   Analysis of Motifs

Network sub-structures that are significantly over-represented in networks compared to their random counterparts are known as motifs [6]. Some of these motifs are known to be of functional significance to the system [6, 12, 16]. A directed binary graph can have 13 types of three node sub-structures. These three node sub-graphs could further be divided into angular and triangular motifs. Angular motifs are linear three node sub-structures, whereas triangular motifs comprise of three nodes sub-graphs with either unidirectional or bidirectional edges. Following the methodology of Milo *et al.*, we computed the number of sub-structures and their over-representation using $Z-\text{score} = \frac{X-\mu}{\sigma}$ [6].

2.3   Number of Driver Neurons

In a network where every node can be in one of the multiple states, it has been shown that the state of the network can be controlled with the help of driver nodes [7, 11, 17]. Aligned with this notion, driver neurons are those neurons which when controlled with an external input can provide full control over the state of the network [7]. Due to their role in control of network 'number of driver neurons' (D_n) are of functional relevance to the neuronal network [11]. To find the minimum number of driver neurons we used maximum matching criterion [7]. A pair of edges were matched if they share start and end nodes [18]. A node is said to be matching if any matching edge points towards it and is unmatched if no matching edge is directed towards it.

2.4   Motif Tuning Algorithm

Feed forward motifs are three neuron sub-graphs composed of two input neurons, one of which regulates the other and both jointly regulating a third target neuron. FFMs are known to be of critical functional relevance for CeNN [6]. To observe the effect of increase/decrease (MTA +/MTA-) of FFMs on controllability of CeNN, we devised a Motif Tuning Algorithm (MTA). This strategy achieves maximum increase/decrease in the number of FFMs (n_{FFM}) with minimal rewiring. Starting from a random neuron in CeNN, MTA looks for a three node linear chain ($A \rightarrow B \rightarrow C$). In case of finding such a linear chain, it adds a feed-forward link from $A \rightarrow C$ if it doesn't exist already. To preserve the number of edges, it removes an edge randomly from the network, while ensuring the connectedness of CeNN. An inverse procedure of searching for an FFM and removing the feed-forward link was implemented to decrease the number of motifs. The detailed logic of motif tuning algorithm is depicted in Fig. 1. Through monotonous increase/decrease of number of FFMs, MTA achieves the desired tuning of motifs in the network. The motif tuning was implemented enough number of times till the saturation of the number of FFMs.

(a)   (b)

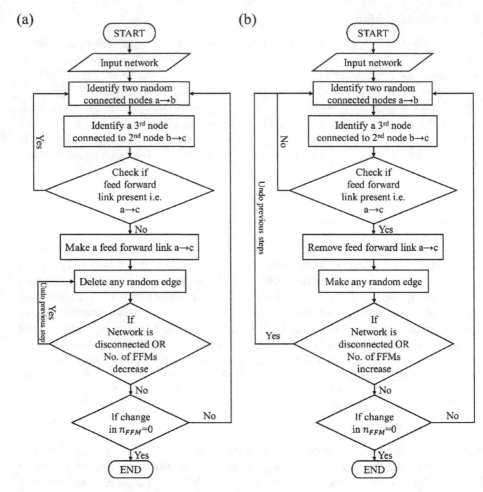

Fig. 1. Motif tuning algorithm. Strategy implemented to (a) increase and to (b) decrease the number of feed-forward motifs.

2.5   Strategies for Synaptic Rewiring

Two types of strategies were implemented for simulating the synaptic rewiring: (a) Random rewiring and (b) Distance constrained rewiring (DC).

(a) **Random Rewiring:** In this strategy it was assumed that, neurons rewire completely randomly under the influence of synaptic plasticity. Every synapse was swapped randomly without affecting the number of nodes and edges [15].

(b) **Distance Constrained Rewiring:** In this strategy, while maintaining the number of synapses of each neuron, the synapses were rewired such that the probability of two neurons being connected to each other is proportional to $d^{-\beta}$, where d is the distance between two nodes and β is the distance constrain parameter. Despite randomization of synapses, this strategy imposes a power law distance constraint.

3   Results and Discussion

A networked entity could be studied as a linear time invariant system to assess its control architecture. A system could have centralized control with a small number of nodes critical for driving its dynamics. The structural features of CeNN could be probed at the coarse grained as well as fine grained levels to adjudge their connection to control of the system. We investigated the control response of CeNN for change in in number of feed-forward motifs to identify rewiring mechanisms that render it robust.

3.1   Topological Properties of CeNN

CeNN encodes the structural and functional correlates of the neuronal wiring of *C. elegans* which are reflected in its topological features. These features could be enumerated at coarse-grained level as well as at a fine-grained level. Consistent with previous observations [5, 9, 11, 19, 20], we found that *C. elegans* neuronal network is a small world network by virtue of high average clustering coefficient ($\bar{C} = 0.172$) and small characteristic path length ($L = 4.02$), when compared to its randomized counterpart ($\overline{C_{rand}} = 0.028 \pm 0.001$ and $L_{rand} = 2.97 \pm 0.01$).

CeNN is characterized with a distributed control architecture with higher number of driver neurons compared to its random control. Knowing that driver neurons are of biological significance to *C. elegans* [11] and that CeNN is over represented with feed-forward motifs (Fig. 2) [6], we investigated their interrelationship that could be of central importance for control of CeNN.

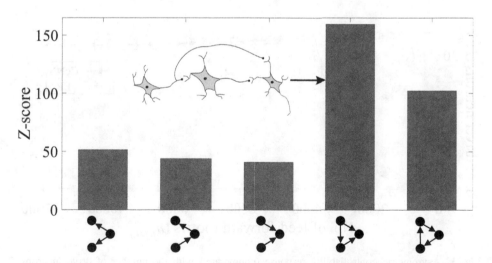

Fig. 2. Feed-forward motifs are significantly over-represented in CeNN, followed by feedback motifs, as measured in terms of Z-score against a background of random networks.

CeNN has significantly large number of driver neurons ($D_n = 34$) compared to that of its randomized counterpart (0.26 ± 0.44). Connectivity of neurons is one of the key factors in specification of number of driver neurons, as preservation of degree distribution leads to its increases (22.38 ± 1.15) [7, 11]. Driver neurons in CeNN are genotypically and phenotypically associated with various functions such as reproduction and maintenance of cellular processes of the organism [11]. CeNN is characterized with distributed control with a large number of driver neurons [8]. Synaptic rewiring, a common features in neuronal systems, could alter the motif saturation in CeNN with repercussions for control mechanisms. To probe the response of CeNN with increase/decrease of FFMs, we devised the motif tuning algorithm.

3.2 CeNN Shows Sigmoidal Controllability Response with Change in FFMs

We used motif tuning algorithm (see Methods) to simulate monotonous increase/decrease in number of FFMs due to synaptic plasticity. Interestingly, we observed that the CeNN shows an asymmetric, sigmoidal response with a clear division between a robust regime in which the number driver neurons (hence, the distributed control) is maintained with monotonic increase in FFMs, and a fragile regime in which it rapidly loses the distributed control with decrease in FFMs (Fig. 3). This implies that to maintain the distributed control (through large number of driver neurons), the neuronal system would need to maintain the number of FFMs. Prevalence of certain connectivity patterns is associated with evolution and development [21]. Starting from the random counterpart of CeNN, systematic monotonic increase/decrease was found to have no

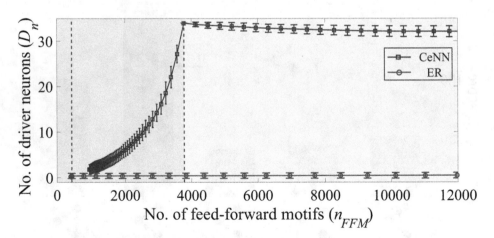

Fig. 3. Asymmetric controllability response (enumerated with the number of driver neurons, D_n) of *C. elegans* neuronal network with monotonic increase/decrease in number of FFMs (n_{FFM}). The random control (ER), on the other hand, does not show any change in D_n. This implies that while CeNN exhibits robust control response to systematic increase in FFMs, it is extremely sensitive to systematic depletion of FFMs. Dashed lines represent the starting points for the models. Error bars indicate standard deviation over 1000 instances.

impact on number of driver nodes (Fig. 3), indicating that neuronal architecture of *C. elegans* has evolved to achieve an optimum structure with distributed control as well as asymmetric response to change in number of key network motifs (FFMs).

Aligned with our observations, we hypothesize that the synaptic rewiring mechanisms in *C. elegans* must have adapted a robust strategy to avoid depletion of FFMs, and hence to maintain distributed control. Rooted in our distance constraint synaptic plasticity model [9], we propose that the mechanisms of synaptic rewiring are not random, but are dictated by distance constraint. We investigated effect of random rewiring versus distance constrained rewiring on change in number of feed-forward motifs (Δn_{FFM}), for which the network control was found to have sensitive dependence (Fig. 3).

3.3   Response of CeNN to Random Versus Distance Constrained Rewiring

Neuronal networks evolving under cognitive stresses show a remarkable property of forming new synapse and deleting older obsolete ones known as neuronal rewiring [22]. To simulate neuronal plasticity in CeNN we implemented different strategies to identify the best strategy the system may have evolved.

To assess the control response of different kind of rewiring mechanisms (MTA+, MTA−, random and distance constrained), we measured the change in number of feedforward motifs for every step of rewiring, Δn_{FFM} (Fig. 4). Positive value of Δn_{FFM} indicates that such a mechanism yields robust control response by maintaining the number of driver neurons (see Fig. 3). On the contrary, negative values suggest fragile response. This is corroborated by observations made with MTA + and MTA- rewiring strategies. MTA + and MTA- are artificial strategies implementing monotonous increase and decrease of FFMs, respectively. While the rewiring mechanisms of CeNN are not expected to follow such artificial processes, any process the brain network may have evolved is expected to show robust controllability response.

Random Rewiring

The easiest way to simulate a natural phenomenon, such as synaptic rewiring, is to assume that it is dictated by random processes. We observed that random rewiring is expected to induce loss of FFMs over time, hence is fragile (Fig. 4). Such a strategy is also expected to cause loss of clustering, an important topological feature which renders the network small-world [5, 9]. Randomized synaptic rewiring has been reported to result in loss of number of driver neurons as well as FFMs [9]. Hence, we conclude that such a mechanism could not have evolved through natural selection as it yields loss of structurally important features as well as leads to fragile control response.

Distance Constrained Rewiring

The neuronal connectivity of CeNN is known to follow a scale free distribution suggesting a deviation from random connectivity pattern [23, 24]. Further, it is also observed that, in this spatially laid network, distance between two neurons is critical in specifying probability of they being connected with a synapse [9]. The probability of two neurons being linked with each other, interestingly, decreases as a power law. This suggests that while increasing distance between neurons is a constraint in their

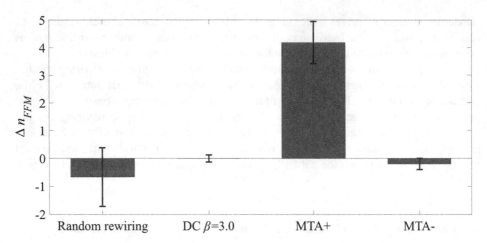

Fig. 4. Change in n_{FFM} per rewiring for different strategies. DC and MTA + show a positive Δn_{FFM}, whereas random and MTA- were presented with negative Δn_{FFM}. This implies that MTA + and distance constrained rewiring induce robust response.

connection, it still allows for more number of neuronal connections than expected by exponential decay. Such a distance constraint has also been reported to be central in determining the location of neurons in the body of organism [25–27].

With this premise, we modeled the synaptic rewiring in CeNN following the power law distance constraint. In this model every neuron maintains its connections (degree) and every synapse is rewired following power law distribution, $P(k) \sim k^{-\beta}$. We implemented the model for varying values of the exponent $\beta (0 \leq \beta \leq 3)$, such that with increasing value of β, chances of observing a synaptic connection are higher for a given distance between neurons. We find that distance constrained rewiring is expected to maintain the FFMs yielding robust response, unlike random rewiring (Fig. 4, DC for $\beta = 3$).

To further probe the response to distance constrained rewiring, we studied the change in number of FFMs (n_{FFM}) and number of driver nodes (D_n) with increasing number of rewiring for different values of exponent β (Fig. 5(a) and (b)). We also computed the average change in number of FFMs (Δn_{FFM}) with changing β (Fig. 5(c)). Consistent with the observation made from Fig. 4, we find that number of FFMs drops marginally regardless of the value of exponent, with better response observed for higher values of β (Fig. 5(a)). Despite large number of rewirings, the number of driver nodes is preserved to maintain the distributed control (Fig. 5(b)). The performance improves with increasing values of β, suggesting that following a strong power law in synaptic rewiring promotes robust controllability response.

In summary, we investigated the control response of CeNN, measured in terms of the number of driver neurons, with varying number of FFMs known to be of functional relevance. By implementing MTA, we surmise that monotonous increase or decrease of FFMs shows an interesting asymmetric, sigmoidal response divided into robust and fragile regimes, respectively. We find that, while random synaptic rewiring would lead to fragile control response, distance constrained rewiring is expected to yield robust response.

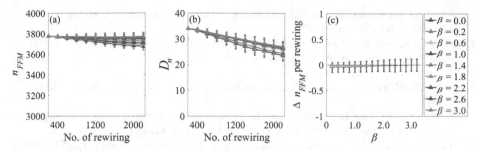

Fig. 5. Robust control response of CeNN under distance constrained rewiring. (a) With increasing extent of rewiring, the number of FFMs are preserved. The stronger the constraint, the better is the response. (b) Correspondingly, the number of driver nodes is preserved with distance constrained rewiring. (c) With increasing power law exponent the average change in number of FFMs (Δn_{FFM}) is diminished.

Acknowledgements. Ganesh Bagler acknowledges the seed grant support from Indian Institute of Technology Jodhpur (IITJ/SEED/2014/0003), and support from Indraprastha Institute of Information Technology Delhi (IIIT-Delhi). Rahul Badhwar thanks Ministry of Human Resource Development, Government of India and Indian Institute of Technology Jodhpur for the senior research fellowship.

References

1. Sporns, O.: Networks of the Brain. MIT Press, Cambridge (2011)
2. Kandel, E.R., Schwartz, J.H., Jessel, T.M.: Principles of Neural Science. McGraw-Hill, New York (2000)
3. White, J.G., Southgate, E., Thomson, J.N., Brenner, S.: The structure of the nervous system of the nematode caenorhabditis elegans. Philos. Trans. R. Soc. Lond. B Biol. Sci. **314**, 1–340 (1986)
4. Choe, Y., McCormcik, B.H., Koh, W.: Network connectivity analysis on the temporally augmented C. elegans web: a pilot study. Soc. Neurosci. Abstr. **30**(921.9) (2004)
5. Watts, D.J., Strogatz, S.H.: Collective dynamics of "small-world" networks. Nature **393**, 440–442 (1998)
6. Milo, R., Shen-Orr, S., Itzkovitz, S., Kashtan, N., Chklovskii, D., Alon, U.: Network motifs: simple building blocks of complex networks. Science **298**, 824–827 (2002)
7. Liu, Y.-Y., Slotine, J.-J., Barabási, A.-L.: Controllability of complex networks. Nature **473**, 167–173 (2011)
8. Jia, T., Liu, Y.-Y., Csoka, E., Posfai, M., Slotine, J.-J., Barabasi, A.-L.: Emergence of bimodality in controlling complex networks. Nat. Commun. **4**, 2002 (2013)
9. Badhwar, R., Bagler, G.: A distance constrained synaptic plasticity model of C. elegans neuronal network. Phys. A Stat. Mech. Appl. **469**, 313–322 (2017)
10. Lin, C.T.: Structural Controllability. IEEE Trans. Automat. Contr. **19**, 201–208 (1974)
11. Badhwar, R., Bagler, G.: Control of neuronal network in Caenorhabditis elegans. PLoS ONE **10**, e0139204 (2015)
12. Mangan, S., Alon, U.: Structure and function of the feed-forward loop network motif. PNAS **100**, 11980–11985 (2003)

13. Alon, U.: An Introduction to Systems Biology: Design Principles of Biological Circuits. CRC Press, Boca Raton (2006)
14. Hall, D., Russell, R.: The posterior nervous system of the nematode Caenorhabditis elegans: serial reconstruction of identified neurons and complete pattern of synaptic interactions. J. Neurosci. **11**, 1–22 (1991)
15. Erdös, P., Rényi, A.: The evolution of random graphs. Trans. Am. Math. Soc. **286**, 257 (1984)
16. Azulay, A., Itskovits, E., Zaslaver, A.: The C. elegans connectome consists of homogenous circuits with defined functional roles. PLoS Comput. Biol. **12**, e1005021 (2016)
17. Tang, E., Bassett, D.S.: Control of Dynamics in Brain Networks. arXiv:1701.01531 (2017)
18. Pothen, A., Fan, C.-J.: Computing the block triangular form of a sparse matrix. ACM Trans. Math. Softw. **16**, 303–324 (1990)
19. Chatterjee, N., Sinha, S.: Understanding the mind of a worm: hierarchical network structure underlying nervous system function in C. elegans. Prog. Brain Res. **168**, 145–153 (2008)
20. Pan, R.K., Chatterjee, N., Sinha, S.: Mesoscopic organization reveals the constraints governing Caenorhabditis elegans nervous system. PLoS ONE **5**, e9240 (2010)
21. MacKay, D.: The Brain and Conscious Experience. Springer, Berlin Heidelberg (1988)
22. Kandel, E.R., Dudai, Y., Mayford, M.R.: The molecular and systems biology of memory. Cell **157**, 163–186 (2014)
23. Esposito, U., Giugliano, M., van Rossum, M., Vasilaki, E., Sporns, O., Tononi, G., Ktter, R., Lichtman, J., Sanes, J., Smith, S., Luo, L., Callaway, E., Svoboda, K., Seung, H., White, J., Southgate, E., Thomson, J., Brenner, S., Varshney, L., Chen, B., Paniagua, E., Hall, D., Chklovskii, D., Briggman, K., Helmstaedter, M., Denk, W., Bock, D., Lee, W., Kerlin, A., Andermann, M., Hood, G., Koetter, R., Insel, T., Volkow, N., Li, T., Battey, J., Landis, S., Briggman, K., Denk, W., Song, S., Sjstrm, P., Reigl, M., Nelson, S., Chklovskii, D., Wang, Y., Markram, H., Goodman, P., Berger, T., Ma, J., Silberberg, G., Markram, H., Perin, R., Berger, T., Markram, H., Clopath, C., Buesing, L., Vasilaki, E., Gerstner, W., Lefort, S., Tomm, C., Sarria, J., Petersen, C., Vasilaki, E., Giugliano, M., Babadi, B., Abbott, L., Bourjaily, M., Miller, P., Bourjaily, M., Miller, P., Vasilaki, E., Fusi, S., Wang, X., Senn, W., Vasilaki, E., Fremaux, N., Urbanczik, R., Senn, W., Gerstner, W., Richmond, P., Buesing, L., Giugliano, M., Vasilaki, E., Pfister, J., Gerstner, W., Clopath, C., Ziegler, L., Vasilaki, E., Bsing, L., Gerstner, W., Hines, M., Morse, T., Migliore, M., Carnevale, N., Shepherd, G.: Measuring symmetry, asymmetry and randomness in neural network connectivity. PLoS ONE **9**, e100805 (2014)
24. Varshney, L.R., Chen, B.L., Paniagua, E., Hall, D.H., Chklovskii, D.B.: Structural properties of the Caenorhabditis elegans neuronal network. PLoS Comput. Biol. **7**, e1001066 (2011)
25. Chen, B.L., Hall, D.H., Chklovskii, D.B.: Wiring optimization can relate neuronal structure and function. PNAS **103**, 4723–4728 (2006)
26. Ahn, Y.Y., Jeong, H., Kim, B.J.: Wiring cost in the organization of a biological neuronal network. Phys. A Stat. Mech. Appl. **367**, 531–537 (2006)
27. Gushchin, A., Tang, A.: Total wiring length minimization of C. elegans neural network: a constrained optimization approach. PLoS ONE **10**, e0145029 (2015)

Resolving the Conflicts Between Cuts in a Decision Tree with Verifying Cuts

Sylwia Buregwa-Czuma[1(✉)], Jan G. Bazan[1], Stanislawa Bazan-Socha[2],
Wojciech Rzasa[1], Lukasz Dydo[1], and Andrzej Skowron[3,4]

[1] Interdisciplinary Centre for Computational Modelling,
University of Rzeszow, Pigonia 1, 35-310 Rzeszow, Poland
{sczuma,bazan,wrzasa,ldydo}@ur.edu.pl
[2] II Department of Internal Medicine, Jagiellonian University Medical College,
Skawinska 8, 31-066 Krakow, Poland
mmsocha@cyf-kr.edu.pl
[3] Institute of Mathematics, The University of Warsaw,
Banacha 2, 02-097 Warsaw, Poland
skowron@mimuw.edu.pl
[4] Systems Research Institute Polish Academy of Sciences,
Newelska 6, 01-447 Warsaw, Poland

Abstract. A decision tree with verifying cuts, called V-tree, uses additional knowledge encoded in many attributes to classify new objects. The purpose of the verifying cuts is to confirm the correctness of the partitioning of tree nodes based on the (semi)-optimal cut determined by a greedy approach. The confirmation may be relevant because for some new objects there are discrepancies in the class prediction on the basis of the individual verifying cuts. In this paper we present a new method for resolving conflicts between cuts assigned to node. The method uses an additional local discretization classifier in each node where there is a conflict between the cuts. The paper includes the results of experiments performed on data sets from a biomedical database and machine learning repositories. In order to evaluate the presented method, we compared its performance with the classification results of a local discretization decision tree, well known from literature and called here C-tree, as well as a V-tree with previous simple conflict resolution method. Our new approach outperforms the C-tree, although it does not produce better results than V-tree with simple method of conflict resolution for the surveyed data sets. However, the proposed method is a step toward a deeper analysis of conflicts between rules.

Keywords: Rough sets · Discretization · Classifiers · Conflict resolution

1 Introduction

In a classic local discretization tree [11], node divisions are based on only one cut, i.e., one value of one of the attributes, that best divides objects in a node,

© Springer International Publishing AG 2017
L. Polkowski et al. (Eds.): IJCRS 2017, Part II, LNAI 10314, pp. 403–422, 2017.
DOI: 10.1007/978-3-319-60840-2_30

in the sense of the chosen cut quality. All the knowledge related to divisions of objects, contained in other attributes, is therefore lost at every stage of the tree construction. To use this additional knowledge, we have developed a method for inducing trees with verifications of cuts defined on many attributes. In each node of a tree created using this method, called V-tree [1], the distribution of objects based on the optimal cut is confirmed by other cuts on different attributes that divide objects in a similar way. Such an approach mimics the behaviour of domain experts who make decisions based on many aspects at the same time during the decision-making process. The previous experiments with V-tree have shown that such an application of the additional knowledge hidden in attributes gives better results than a local discretization tree using node splitting based on only one cut.

When using V-tree to classify new objects, the predicted decision class is indicated by all cuts in the nodes. When all the cuts in a node are consistent, we have more certainty (than with one cut) that the predicted decision is correct. However, for some new objects there are discrepancies in the predicted class indicated by the individual verification cuts. So far in such cases, we have used a simple conflict resolution method to select the predicted decision class among the decisions coming from the left and right subtrees. The method consists in selecting the class that is indicated by the prevailing number of the cuts in the node. This simplest method of resolving conflicts (the majority voting), presented in [1], was additionally modified by taking into account the size of nodes from which the decisions originate. With such a way of resolving conflicts, the question arises whether other ways of dissolving it would give better results. In particular, the question arises as to whether the general method of resolving such a conflict with a classifier would improve the quality of the V-tree classification.

To answer this question in this paper we propose a new classifier based on the V-tree. In order to construct it, the training data is divided into two parts. Part one, called the basic training part, is used to build a V-tree classifier. Part two, called the validation part, is used to construct classifiers, which resolve conflicts at each node. When applying the proposed V-tree to classify new objects, in situations where a conflicts between a right and a left subtree appears in a given node, an additional (judging) classifier built for that node is used to determine the final decision.

In this paper we consider the supervised discretization, i.e. the discretization methods using the values of decision attribute for training cases. There are many methods of supervised discretization, which are based on various heuristics. We use an approach based on the generation of the so-called decision tree of the local discretization (see, e.g., [2,5,7,11]). This is a binary tree, created by multiple binary partitions of the set into two groups of objects (e.g., cases, states, processes, patients, observations, vehicles) with the value of the selected attribute. The decision tree of local discretization can be applied not only for discretization but also can be treated as a classifier (see Sect. 2).

However, there are serious doubts as to the validity of this approach for classifier induction, especially in case of a large number of attributes in a dataset.

Therefore in [1] we proposed a method of a V-tree construction using additional cuts to evaluate of quality of cuts in tree nodes (see Sect. 3). Here, we propose a new approach of building V-tree with a more advanced method of resolving conflicts.

To illustrate the method and to verify the effectiveness of presented classifiers, we have performed several experiments on the data sets obtained from Kent Ridge Biomedical Dataset, UC Irvine Machine Learning repository and the website of The Elements of Statistical Learning book (see Sect. 5).

2   The Discretization Tree

In this paper, we consider the supervised discretization based on the decision tree over the local discretization (see, e.g., [2]). This is a binary tree, created by multiple binary partitions of the set into two groups of objects with the value of the selected attribute. Because this method is well known from literature (see, e.g., [5,11]), in this paper we call this method as the *classic method*.

2.1   Cuts and Templates

Selection of an attribute and its value (for numeric attributes often called the cut) during divisions of nodes is a key element of the local discretization tree construction method and should involve the analysis of values of the decision attribute for training objects.

Formally, a *cut* is a pair (a, v) that is defined for a given *decision table* $\mathbf{A} = (U, A, d)$ in Pawlak's sense (see, e.g., [12]), where $a \in A$ (A is a set of attributes or columns in the data table) and v is the value of the attribute a. For numeric attributes, a cut (a, v) defines a partition of a set of objects into two subsets, the first set, denoted by $L(a, v)$, is the set of objects for which the value of attribute a is less than v, and the second set of objects, denoted by $R(a, v)$, for which the value of attribute a is greater than or equal to v. Instead, for symbolic attributes the $L(a, v)$ is a set of objects for which the value of the attribute a is equal to v, and the $R(a, v)$ is a set of objects for which the value of attribute a is different from v.

Moreover, any cut (a, v) defines two templates, where by a template we understand a description of a set of objects, that are defined in different ways for numerical and symbolical attributes. In case of numerical attributes, if we define templates for a cut $c = (a, v)$, the first template, called *a left template*, is described by a formula: $TL(c) = \{u \in U : a(u) < v\}$, while the second template, called *a right template*, is described by a formula: $TR(c) = \{u \in U : a(u) \geq v\}$. An object $u \in U$ matches the template $TL(c)$, if $a(u) < v$ holds, that is the value of the attribute $a \in A$ of this object u is less than v, otherwise the object u does not match the template $TL(c)$. Whereas, an object $u \in U$ matches the template $TR(c)$, if it satisfies a descriptor $a(u) \geq v$, that is the value of the attribute $a \in A$ of this object u is greater than or equal to v, otherwise the object u does not match the template $TR(c)$. In case of symbolic

attributes, the first template, called also *a left template*, is described by a formula: $TL(c) = \{u \in U : a(u) = v\}$, while the second template, called also *a right
template*, is described by a formula: $TR(c) = \{u \in U : a(u) \neq v\}$. An object
$u \in U$ matches the template $TL(c)$, if it satisfies a descriptor $a(u) = v$, that
is the value of the attribute $a \in A$ of this object u is equal to v, otherwise the
object u does not satisfy the template $TL(c)$. Finally, an object $u \in U$ matches
the template $TR(c)$, if it satisfies a descriptor $a(u) \neq v$ that is the value of the
attribute $a \in A$ of this object u is not equal to v, otherwise the object u does
not satisfy the template $TR(c)$.

If c is a cut, we denote in general by $T(c)$ the template defined by the c,
keeping in mind that it might be one of two following templates $TL(c)$ or $TR(c)$.
In addition, to simplify the description, instead of $T(c)$, we sometimes write T,
when the cut c is established. Besides, if T is a template defined for some cut
c, by $\neg T$ we understand the template $TR(c)$ when $T = TL(c)$, or the template
$TL(c)$ when $T = TR(c)$. Finally, if T is a template defined for the decision table
$\mathbf{A} = (U, A, d)$, by $\mathbf{A}(T)$ we denote a subtable of $\mathbf{A}$ containing all objects from
U matching the template T.

A pair of objects $(u_1, u_2) \in U \times U$ is discerned by the cut which defines the
template T, if u_1 matches the template T and u_2 does not match the template T,
or vice versa, u_2 matches the template T and u_1 does not match the template T.
By $Dis(c)$ we denote the number of pairs of objects from the different decision
classes discerned by the cut c that defines the template T. After calculation of
a value of this measure for all possible cuts, one can greedily choose one of the
cuts and divide the entire set of objects into two parts on its basis. Of course,
this approach can be easily generalized to the case of more than two decision
classes. In our approach, the value of $Dis(c)$ is treated as the quality of the cut
c for classic discretization tree.

It should be noted that above quality measure $Dis(c)$ can be calculated for
the given cut in time $O(n)$, where n is the number of objects in the decision table
(see, e.g., [5]). But the determination of the optimal cut requires the calculation
of quality measures for all the potential cuts. For this purpose it is necessary to
check all potential cuts, including all conditional attributes in a specific order.
This can be done using various methods. One of such methods for numerical
attributes firstly sorts the objects of the given attribute for which we seek the
optimal partition. This allows to determine the optimal cut in linear time.

Sorting a collection of objects results in the fact that the calculation of the
optimal partition is done in time $O(n \cdot log\, n \cdot m)$, where n is the number of objects,
and m is the number of conditional attributes. This method is implemented in
our own RS-lib computational library, which is an extension of the RSES-lib
library forming the kernel of the RSES system [6].

Let us now introduce the concept of simultaneous discerning of pairs of
objects by two cuts. This concept will be used in Sect. 3. A pair of objects
$(u_1, u_2) \in U \times U$ is discerned simultaneously by the cuts c_1 and c_2 that define
templates $T1$ and $T2$ respectively, if u_1 matches $T1$ and $T2$, but u_2 matches
neither $T1$ nor $T2$, or vice versa, u_2 matches $T1$ and $T2$, but u_1 matches neither

$T1$ nor $T2$. By $Dis(c_1, c_2)$ we denote the number of pairs of objects from the different decision classes (of a given decision table) discerned simultaneously by the cuts c_1 and c_2.

2.2   Construction of the Classic Decision Tree

The quality of cuts may be computed for any subset of a given set of objects. In the local strategy of discretization, after finding the best cut and dividing the objects set into two subsets of objects (matching both templates mentioned above for a given cut), this procedure is repeated for each set of objects separately until a stop condition is met.

At the beginning of the procedure we have the whole set of objects at the root of the tree. Then, we recursively apply the same splitting procedure to the emerging parts that we assigned to tree nodes at higher levels. Stop condition of partition is designed so that the given part is not divided (becomes a tree leaf), if it contains only objects of one decision class (optionally the objects of the given class constitute a certain percentage, which is treated as a parameter of the method) or the considered cut does not have any effect, i.e., there are no new pairs of objects of different decision classes separated by the cut. In this paper, we assume that the partition stops when all objects from the current set of objects belong to the same decision class. A simple method for constructing the tree described above can be configured in many ways. For example, one can change the cut quality, which may also be made by introducing the domain

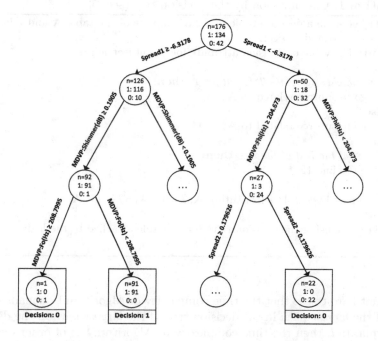

Fig. 1. A fragment of an exemplary C-tree classifier

knowledge. This often leads to the improvement of the classifier performance (see [2,4]). The quality of a given cut computed as a number of object pairs discerned by this cut and belonging to different decision classes was used in [3] and the classifier constructed using this method we call here as the *C-tree* classifier.

Figure 1 presents an exemplary fragment of a decision tree classifier for the problem of forecasting Parkinson's disease on the basis of voice measurements. Note that the above decision tree can be treated directly as a classifier, as test objects can be classified by stating to which leaf of the tree they belong. This is possible because, thanks to the designated partitions, one can trace membership of an object in the path from the root to the leaf, and then classify the object to the decision class whose objects dominate in the leaf.

2.3 The Decision Tree as a Classifier

The decision tree computed during the local discretization can be treated as a classifier for the concept C represented by the decision attribute from a given decision table $\mathbf{A}$. Let $\mathbf{A}(T)$ be a subtable containing all objects matching the template T defined by the cut from the current node of a given decision tree (at the beginning of an algorithm run, T is the template defined by the cut from the root). We classify a tested object starting from the root of the tree using Algorithm 1.

Algorithm 1. Classification by the decision tree (see [5])

Input: Let $\mathbf{A}$ be a decision table, T be a template of the table $\mathbf{A}$ and u be a new (tested) object.

Output: The value of decision attribute for the object u.

1 **begin**
2   **if** *u matches template T found for* $\mathbf{A}$ **then**
3 | go to subtree related to $\mathbf{A}(T)$
4   **else**
5 | go to subtree related to $\mathbf{A}(\neg T)$
6   **end**
7   **if** *u is at the leaf of the tree* **then**
8 | go to line 12
9   **else**
10 | repeat lines 2–11 substituting $\mathbf{A}(T)$ (or $\mathbf{A}(\neg T)$) for $\mathbf{A}$
11   **end**
12   Classify u using the decision rules for subtable attached to the leaf;
13 **end**

It is not hard to see that the time complexity of Algorithm 1 depends on the length of the largest path in the decision tree. If the largest path in the decision tree is equal to l, then the time complexity of Algorithm 1 is of order $O(l \cdot m)$, where m is the number of conditional attributes in the table $\mathbf{A}$.

3 The Decision Tree with Verifying Cuts

We now present an approach to the decision tree construction, which introduces the so-called verifying cuts.

3.1 Motivation

When applying the approach described in the previous section to the construction of classifiers for the case of data with a large number of attributes, there are serious doubts as to the validity of this approach. The point is that the method chooses only one split with the best quality based on the selected measure, at the given step of searching for optimal binary partitions. In other words, just one from among perhaps many partitions with the high quality is chosen, while the others are ignored. Obviously, in the next step, the subsequent optimal binary split is selected, but not for the entire input set of objects, but only for each previously obtained part separately. Such an approach is often effective leading to efficient classifiers, if the number of attributes is small and the attributes carry diverse information (e.g., in terms of diverse positive areas relative to the decision attribute). However, data sets with a large number of attributes can contain a lot of attributes that bear similarity with respect to the quality of potential cuts but differ significantly with respect to domain knowledge represented by the attributes. These attributes will be here called additional or redundant attributes. The domain experts (such as medical doctors) who in their daily work observe the redundancy of attributes, realize that and use it, e.g., making diagnosis more secure through the use of several such attributes simultaneously. Meanwhile, the above-mentioned greedy method, out of the plurality of redundant attributes selects only one, eliminating others. However, in practice, the classification of the test objects may reveal the object that for some reason should not be classified according to the partition specified by the greedy algorithm (e.g., an outlier, from the point of view of an attribute selected by the greedy algorithm in the current node of the decision tree).

Therefore, the possibility of the object classification by greedily designated binary partition would require a confirmation by other attributes, which in the above method is not done. As a consequence, a situation may occur where, e.g. for the microarray data with very many attributes and few objects the method finds only a few partitions (on several attributes), that are sufficient to create a tree allowing us for an unambiguous classification of objects from the training sample. This situation is very difficult to be accepted by the domain experts who are not able to come to terms with such a large reduction of the knowledge encoded in the attributes and not using the rejected redundant attributes in the tree construction.

Serious doubts arise also from a statistical point of view. Typically, a set of objects is too small to call it representative. Therefore, the disposal of the information contained in the rejected attributes may lead to overfitting of the constructed tree to the objects from the training sample.

Some might say that the problem could be solved by a method calculating greedily k-partitions in one step, which at any given stage of the algorithm best distinguish pairs of the objects in terms of the fixed criterion (for one or more attributes). Unfortunately, no such algorithm is known with the time complexity less than the square (of the number of objects). Such an algorithm would have to optimize k at a given stage of its operation, examining different subsets of potential partitions, which would increase its complexity. Due to the required efficiency, in the work we are interested in the complexity of the algorithms of the order at most $n \cdot log\ n$ relative to the number of objects n.

One of the approaches attempting to overcome the disadvantages of greedy methods is to use ensemble methods, such as random forests (see, e.g. [8]) which use random data samples in the learning step in order to produce several different decision tree models and then to combine the predictions of those models to form the prediction of the ensemble. The ensemble made of the individual models built from many different data samples may provide a better approximation of the concepts that any of the single models, which is the key for generalization.

3.2   Construction of the Decision Tree with Verifying Cuts

The basic idea of the V-tree lies in the fact that at a given stage of searching for partitions of a set of objects, after determining the optimal binary partition, the family of k-binary verifying partitions is determined (for other attributes than the attribute used in the optimal partition).

The idea behind it is as follows. As discussed above, the optimal partition is a tool for partial classification of the test object, i.e., it provides information specifying where the test object should be sent for the classification: to the right subtree or to the left one. Each partition from the family of verifying k-partitions divides objects from the training table analogously to the optimal partition. Thus, if a test object to be classified will be submitted for further classification by the optimal partition to the left tree, there is a presumption that it should be directed analogously by the verifying partition. If so, this increases our confidence that the optimal partition correctly classified the test object (as it is possible in a given node).

However, if it is not so, i.e., for instance, the optimal partition directs the test object into the left tree, and the verifying partition to the right, then there may be uncertainty about the performance of our classifier. Therefore, in this situation, a caution is recommended in planning further classifier actions. This precaution in the case of our method is revealed by the fact that the object is recommended to the classification by both the left and right subtree. After receiving the results of the classification, the possible conflict between the received decisions is resolved. Of course, there may be more than one verifying partition, and therefore the methodology outlined above must take this into account.

Another issue is the question of how verifying partitions interfere with the formation of the tree for a training table. In the classic method of tree construction (see Sect. 2), on a given stage of the tree construction, the optimal partition of a set of objects into two disjoint sets is determined, for which subtrees are separately created in the subsequent stages. However, in the V-tree, the split of a set of objects may not be a partition. On the one hand, as before, the optimal partition divides a set of training objects into two disjoint sets, but on the second hand there may be a number of objects matching the template defined on the basis of the optimal partition, but not matching many of the templates defined by verifying partitions. Analogously, there may be objects that do not match the template defined on the basis of the optimal partition, but match sufficiently many of the patterns defined for the verifying partitions.

One can claim about such objects that already at the stage of the tree construction, it is doubtful that the template based on the determined optimal partition is appropriate to classify this type of objects. Therefore, when creating a tree, the objects will be included into both sets of objects, the one intended to create a left subtree, as well as the set of objects intended to create a right subtree. This corresponds to the intuition that learning to classify this type of object is somehow postponed and transferred to both subtrees, where for their classification new partitions will be counted (perhaps better suited to these objects than optimal partition counted in the current tree node).

3.3   The Algorithm of the V-Tree Construction

In this section, we present the algorithm for construction of a decision tree, based on the above considerations (see Algorithm 2). Due to the fact that the algorithm uses verifying cuts, the decision tree produced by this algorithm is called the V-tree or V-decision tree. During the construction of V-tree we select verifying cuts using a special measure of quality. The quality of a verifying cut c_i relative to a given optimal cut c is computed by the measure: $VQ(c, c_i) = \frac{Dis(c,c_i)}{Dis(c)}$, where $Dis(c)$ is the number of pairs of objects from different decision classes discerned by the cut c, and $Dis(c, c_i)$ is the number of pairs of objects from different decision classes discerned simultaneously by the cuts c and c_i (see Sect. 2.1). In construction of the V-tree we only use these verifying cuts c_i, the quality of which is greater than a fixed threshold t, i.e., c_i satisfying the following condition: $VQ(c, c_i) > t$.

The stop condition in Algorithm 2 is the same as in the algorithm discussed in Sect. 2. Note that the only element of the algorithm, which would increase the time complexity compared to the classical algorithm from Sect. 2 is step 3, in which the collection of k verifying cuts for a given cut c is computed. We show in Sect. 3.4 that this step can be accomplished in time $O(n \cdot log\ n \cdot m)$, where n is the number of objects and m is the number of conditional attributes and therefore it does not increase the computational time complexity of the algorithm compared to the algorithm from Sect. 2.

It's not hard to see that for the symbolic attributes, which typically have a small number of values, the determination of the best verification split can be done in time $O(n \cdot l)$, where l is the number of values of symbolic attribute. Somewhat more difficult situation occurs when the cut for numerical attribute is computed.

Algorithm 2. Construction of the V-decision tree

Input: Let $\mathbf{A} = (U, A, d)$ be a decision table, k be a parameter belonging to
natural numbers and t be a fixed threshold (t was equal to 0.9 in our
experiments).
Output: The V-decision tree computed for the table $\mathbf{A}$.

1 **begin**
2   Find the optimal cut c in the table $\mathbf{A}$ and assign the template $T = TL(c)$
     (and $\neg T = TR(c)$).
3   Find a collection of verifying cuts $c_1, ..., c_k$ in the table $\mathbf{A}$ which verify the
     cut c and a collection of templates $VTC(T) = \{T\} \cup \{T_1, ..., T_k\}$ associated
     with verifying cuts, such that $VQ(c, c_i) > t$, for $i \in \{1, ..., k\}$ (this is the
     collection of templates with maximal possible value of VQ, greater than t;
     if the number of all such templates for a given T is less than k, the
     collection can be smaller, but non-empty because T always belongs to it).
4   Split the table $\mathbf{A}$ into two subtables $\mathbf{A}(T)$ and $\mathbf{A}(\neg T)$ such that $\mathbf{A}(T)$
     contains the objects matching a template T, and $\mathbf{A}(\neg T)$ contains the
     objects matching a template $\neg T$.
5   Assign $\mathbf{A}_l = \mathbf{A}(T)$ and $\mathbf{A}_r = \mathbf{A}(\neg T)$.
6   Determine all the objects in the table $\mathbf{A}$, which match the template T and
     do not match a template T_i (for some $i \in \{1, ..., k\}$) or match the template
     $\neg T$ and do not match a template $\neg T_i$ (for some $i \in \{1, ..., k\}$), and attach
     these objects both to the table $\mathbf{A}_l$ and $\mathbf{A}_r$ (if they are not there yet)
7   If the tables $\mathbf{A}_l$ and $\mathbf{A}_r$ satisfy the stop condition, then finish the tree
     construction else repeat steps 2–6 for all the subtables which do not satisfy
     the stop condition.

8 **end**

3.4 Calculation of Verifying Cuts

In this section, we present the algorithm for selection of verification cuts for
the computed earlier cut c_b (c_b is a cut for an attribute b), assuming that the
verification split is determined by a selected numerical attribute a different then
b (see Algorithm 3). In order to find globally the best verification cuts for the
cut c_b, this algorithm can be executed for all numerical attributes different then
b. For ease of discussion, we assume that there are only two decision classes C_0
and C_1 in the data set. This approach can be easily generalized to the case of
more than two decision classes.

     Assuming that the information about cuts from the memory M is accessible
in constant time, Algorithm 3 runs in time $O(n \cdot log\ n)$, where n is the number
of objects (due to the sorting time of objects on the basis of the attribute a).

3.5 Classification by the V-Tree

Now we provide the classification algorithm, based on a tree with verifying cuts.
Suppose we classify the object u at a node where the optimal cut $c = (a, v)$

Algorithm 3. Computation of verifying cuts for a given cut on the basis of selected attribute

---

Input: Let $\mathbf{A} = (U, A, d)$ be a decision table with decision classes C_0 and C_1, a be an attribute of the table $\mathbf{A}$ and c_b be a cut of the table $\mathbf{A}$ based on the attribute b (where $a \neq b$).

Output: The computed collection of verifying cuts on the basis of the attribute a for the cut c_b with selection for every verifying cut c a proper left or right template ($TL(c)$ or $TR(c)$)

1 **begin**

2   Sort the values of the numerical attribute a.

3   Browsing the values of the attribute a from the smallest to the largest, determine for $i = 0, 1$, for each appearing cut c on a the following numbers and store them in a memory M:

     $LL(a, c, C_i), LR(a, c, C_i)$ - numbers of objects from decision class C_i with values of attribute a smaller than c and at the same time matching the templates $TL(c_b), TR(c_b)$, respectively.

4   Browsing the values of attribute a from the highest to the lowest, determine for $i = 0, 1$, for each appearing cut c on a the following numbers and store them in a memory of information about cuts M:

     $HL(a, c, C_i), HR(a, c, C_i)$ - numbers of objects from decision class C_i with values of attribute a greater than or equal to c and at the same time matching $TL(c_b), TR(c_b)$, respectively.

5   Using information from the memory M, determine the quality of cuts on a by the following formula $Dis(c_b, c) = max\{QL(c), QR(c)\}$, where:

     $QL(c) = LL(a, c, C_0) \cdot HR(a, c, C_1) + LL(a, c, C_1) \cdot HR(a, c, C_0)$ and
     $QR(c) = LR(a, c, C_0) \cdot HL(a, c, C_1) + LR(a, c, C_1) \cdot HL(a, c, C_0)$;
     also $TL(c)$ is assigned to c if $QL(c) > QR(c)$, otherwise $TR(c)$ is assigned to c.

6 **end**

---

and the family of verifying cuts $c_1, \ldots, c_k$ were found. Besides, let T denote the template assigned to c, and $T_1, \ldots, T_k$ the templates for cuts $c_1, \ldots, c_k$, where for any $i \in \{1, \ldots, k\}$ the template $T_i = TL(c_i)$ or $T_i = TR(c_i)$, depending on a type of template selected for a given c_i by the Algorithm 3. The classification is performed according to Algorithm 4 with $t = 0.9$.

In order to demonstrate classification by the Algorithm 4, let us consider a decision table $\mathbf{A} = (U, A, z)$, such that $A = \{a, b, c, d, e, f\}$ and the decision attribute z has two values 0 and 1, that is, there are only two decision classes Z_0 and Z_1. Figure 2 illustrates the V-decision tree computed for the table $\mathbf{A}$ using the Algorithm 2.

Algorithm 4. Classification by the V-tree

Input: Let u be a new (tested) object and $VT(\mathbf{A})$ be a V-decision tree
computed for a decision table $\mathbf{A}$; besides by T and $VTC(T)$ we denote
the template for an optimal cut and the collection of templates
proposed by Algorithm 2 for the current node of $VT(\mathbf{A})$, respectively.

Output: The value of decision for the object u.

1 **begin**

2   If a node satisfies the stop condition, return the decision fixed in the tree
node and terminate.

3   Assign $l_1 := $ the number of templates from the collection $VTC(T)$, to which
the object u fits.

4   Assign $l_2 = l - l_1$, where $l = card(VTC(T))$.

5   **if** *object u matches the template T and $l_1 = l$* **then**

6   Send it for classification by the subtree constructed for the table $\mathbf{A}(T)$,
to obtain the value of the decision d_1, and return d_1.

7   **else**

8   **if** *the object u does not match the template T, and $l_2 = l$,* **then**

9   Send u for classification by subtree designed for a table $\mathbf{A}(\neg T)$, to
obtain the value of the decision d_2, and return d_2.

10   **else**

11   Classify object u by node $\mathbf{A}(T)$ to obtain the value of decision d_1

12   Classify object u by node $\mathbf{A}(\neg T)$ to obtain the value of decision d_2

13   **if** $d_1 = d_2$ **then**

14   return d_1

15   **else**

16   //Simple method of conflict resolving between d_1 and d_2

17   Assign $p_1 := $ (leaf size of the left tree)$/|\mathbf{A}|$

18   Assign $p_2 := $ (leaf size of the right tree)$/|\mathbf{A}|$

19   **if** $(\frac{l_1}{l} * p_1) > (\frac{l_2}{l} * p_2)$ **then**

20   return d_1

21   **else**

22   **if** $(\frac{l_1}{l} * p_1) < (\frac{l_2}{l} * p_2)$ **then**

23   return d_2

24   **else**

25   //Decides the main cut

26   **if** *object u matches the template T* **then**

27   return d_1.

28   **else**

29   return d_2.

This V-decision tree consists of a root-node N_1, two internal nodes N_2 and
N_3, and four leaf-nodes N_4, N_5, N_6 and N_7. In the node N_1 there are the template
T related to the main cut from this node and two templates T_1 and T_2 related

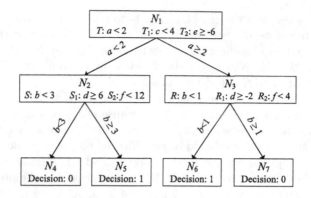

Fig. 2. Visualization of an exemplary V-decision tree

to verifying cuts. At the same time, in the node N_2 there are the template S related to the main cut from this node and two templates S_1 and S_2 related to verifying cuts. Finally, in the node N_3 there are the template R related to the main cut from this node and two templates R_1 and R_2 related to verifying cuts. We will examine how the Algorithm 4 classifies three test objects from the Table 1.

The classification of all objects starts in the node N_1. An object u_1 matches the template T, because $a(u_1) = 1 < 2$. At the same time, object u_1 matches the template T_1, because $c(u_1) = 3 < 4$ and matches the template T_2, because $e(u_1) = -5 \geq -6$. It means that templates T, T_1 and T_2 suggest that object u_1 should be classified by node N_2. In the node N_2, the object u_1 does not match the template S, because $b(u_1) = 4 \geq 3$. At the same time, object u_1 does not match the template S_1, because $d(u_1) = -7 < 6$ and does not match the template S_2, because $f(u_1) = 14 \geq 12$. It means that the object u_1 is directed to classification by the node N_5 and is classified to the decision class Z_1.

Table 1. Three test objects.

Test objects	a	b	c	d	e	f
u_1	1	4	3	-7	-5	14
u_2	3	0	5	-3	-7	5
u_3	1	4	3	-5	-8	10

An object u_2 does not match the template T, because $a(u_2) = 3 \geq 2$. At the same time, object u_2 does not match the template T_1, because $c(u_2) = 5 \geq 4$ and does not match the template T_2, because $e(u_2) = -7 < -6$. It means that templates T, T_1 and T_2 suggest that object u_1 should be classified by node N_3. Hence, the object u_2 is directed to classification by the node N_3. In the node N_3, the object u_2 matches the template R, because $b(u_2) = 0 < 1$. At the same time, object u_2 does not match the template R_1, because $d(u_2) = -3 < -2$ and does not match the template R_2, because $f(u_2) = 5 \geq 4$. It means that the object u_2 should be directed to classification by both nodes N_6 and N_7. However, more templates from the node N_3 suggest classification by the node N_7. Therefore the object u_2 is classified to the decision class Z_0.

An object u_3 matches the template T, because $a(u_3) = 1 < 2$. At the same time, object u_3 matches the template T_1, because $c(u_3) = 3 < 4$ and does not match the template T_2, because $e(u_3) = -8 < -6$. It means that templates T and T_1 suggest that object u_3 should be classified by node N_2, while the template T_2 suggests that object u_3 should be classified by node N_3. Hence, the object u_3 is directed to classification by the node N_2. In the node N_2, the object u_3 does not match the template S, because $b(u_3) = 4 \geq 3$. At the same time, object u_3 does not match the template S_1, because $d(u_3) = -5 < 6$ and matches the template S_2, because $f(u_3) = 10 < 12$. It means that the object u_3 should be directed to classification by both nodes N_4 and N_5. However, more templates from the node N_2 suggest classification by the node N_5. Therefore the object u_3 is classified to the decision class Z_1.

The classifier constructed with the use of V-tree will be called here the *V-tree* classifier. Note that the above algorithm to classify the object in the node utilizes a single tree only when all verifying splits classify the object just as the main cut c. In other cases, the classification is done by both subtrees. Then the following two cases are considered. The first case refers to the situation when the two subtrees returned the same decision value. Then the value from any node is returned as the decision. The second case refers to a situation where one of the subtrees returned one decision value, and the second subtree the other one. Then that node returns a decision coming from the subtree, which is associated with a greater number of such verifying templates that classify a test object for this tree. This is a simple method to resolve the conflict between decisions generated by two subtrees. The classification made by each subtree is performed recursively, that is at each node the stop condition is checked to find out whether the node is the leaf. If so, the algorithm returns the decision assigned to that node and terminates.

4   Classification by the RV-Tree with Resolving Conflicts by a Judging Classifier

Due to the inconsistency of cuts indications that appear in V-tree nodes for some test objects we developed more advanced method of resolving this conflicts. The section discusses the construction of a V-tree with a new method of resolving conflicts between left and right subtrees, if such conflicts arise. A new tree constructed in this way will be called a RV-tree or RV-decision tree.

First, based on the basic training set, a V-tree is built, according to the Algorithm 2. Then, the objects from the validation set (mentioned in Sect. 1) are used to build classifiers that resolve conflicts. Each object of this set is tested for matching with templates defined by the cuts for subsequent nodes of RV-tree.

If the object fits all templates in the node, it is routed to the left subtree, while in the opposite situation (it does not fit any pattern), it is moved to the right subtree, until it reaches the leaf.

However, we are interested in the case when there is a conflict of cut indications, so that the object matches a part of templates and does not match the rest of the templates. Then such an object is used to construct an additional classifier aimed at resolving such conflicts. As the additional classifier in the tree node, we used a local discretization tree with the number of pairs of objects from the different decision classes discerned by the cut as a cut quality measure (see Sect. 2.2). To build such a classifier, we create a decision table for it, in each conflicting node. Such a table consists of all objects of the validation set for which there is a conflict in the given node. Figure 3 presents the schema of such a resolving table, used to build a classifier for conflict resolution. The decision attribute of this table corresponds to the indication of the subtree to which the object should be directed so as to obtain the correct decision class (for the object from the validation set, the value of the decision class is known). The decision is therefore estimated based on the cuts indications for the validation objects. The larger the set, the more accurate the RV-tree response prediction. As the conditional attributes, used to build decision rules, information such as: left and right subtree decisions, the number of cuts leading the object to the left and right subtree, the percentage of objects in the leaf from the left and right subtree (in the validation set) and a strength of decision from the left and from the right subtree, are used. The decision strength of a given subtree is calculated as the product of the percentage of cuts that direct the object to that subtree and the percentage of objects in the leaf of the subtree (from which the decision originates), out of the entire validation set.

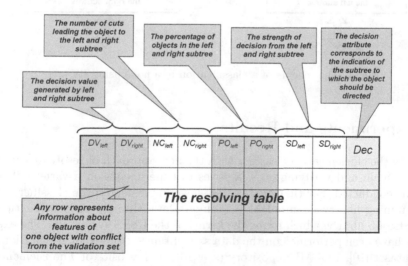

Fig. 3. The schema of a resolving table

The classification using a RV-tree is performed according to Algorithm 5 and the scheme of the process in one node is presented on Fig. 4. When applying the RV-tree to classify a new object, in nodes where a conflict between the right and left subtree appears, directing such an object to the corresponding subtree is indicated by the decision of an additional classifier referred to as a judging classifier.

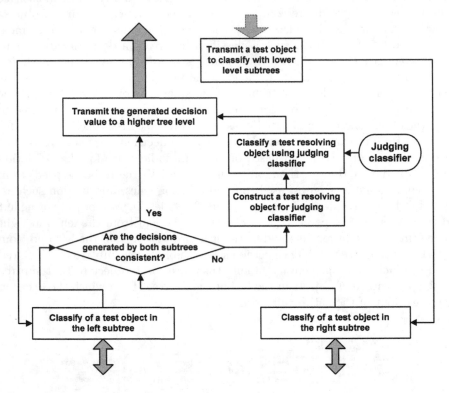

Fig. 4. The schema of a classification in a node using RV-tree

5   Experiments and Results

To verify the efficiency of a classifier with the new approach of resolving conflicts between main and verifying cuts, a series of experiments on a variety of data sets was conducted. For that purpose, we have implemented the classifier in the programming library CommoDM (Common Data Mining) - a continuation of the RSES-lib library, which forms the kernel of the RSES system [6]. The experiments have been performed on the data sets obtained from Kent Ridge Biomedical Dataset [10], UCI ML repository (see [13]) and website of The Elements of Statistical Learning book (Statweb) (see [9]). Six data collections from the first source relates to microarray experiments and they are characterized by a large

---

Algorithm 5. Classification by the RV-decision tree

Input: Let u be a new (tested) object, $RVT(\mathbf{A})$ be a RV-decision tree
computed for a decision table $\mathbf{A}$ (based on training set) and $JT(\mathbf{B})$ be a
classic decision tree computed for a decision table $\mathbf{B}$ (based on
validation set) in a conflict node of $RVT(\mathbf{A})$; besides by T and
$RVTC(T)$ we denote the template for an optimal cut and the collection
of templates proposed by Algorithm 2 for the current node of $RVT(\mathbf{A})$,
respectively.

Output: The value of decision for the object u.

1 **begin**
2   If a node satisfies the stop condition, return the decision fixed in the tree
       node and terminate.
3   Assign $l_1 := $ the number of templates from the collection $RVTC(T)$, to
       which the object u fits.
4   Assign $l_2 = l - l_1$, where $l = card(RVTC(T))$.
5   **if** *object u matches the template T and $l_1 = l$* **then**
6   Send it for classification by the subtree constructed for the table $\mathbf{A}(T)$,
         to obtain the value of the decision d_1, and return d_1.
7   **else**
8   **if** *the object u does not match the template T, and $l_2 = l$,* **then**
9   Send u for classification by subtree designed for a table $\mathbf{A}(\neg T)$, to
           obtain the value of the decision d_2, and return d_2.
10   **else**
11   //Classify u with judging classifier $JT(\mathbf{B})$ according to Algorithm 1
12   **if** *decision returned by $JT(\mathbf{B})$ indicates right subtree* **then**
13   Classify object u by node $\mathbf{A}(T)$ to obtain the value of the
             decision d_1, and return d_1.
14   **else**
15   Classify object u by node $\mathbf{A}(\neg T)$ to obtain the value of the
             decision d_2, and return d_2.
16   **end**
17   **end**
18   **end**
19 **end**

---

number of attributes. Our experiments were conducted on the merged original
training and testing data sets. Our goal was to verify whether the new approach
to resolving conflicts between cuts, which is based on knowledge acquired in the
validation process, performs better than the previous method. Table 2 presents
the experimental results received for given data sets and three classifiers: classic decision tree (marked as *C-tree classifier*), decision tree with verifying cuts
that uses the old method of resolving conflicts (marked as *V-tree classifier*), and
approach described in this paper (marked as *RV-tree classifier*). Each of them
utilizes the measure for determining the quality of cuts defined as the number
of pairs of objects from the different decision classes discerned by the cut). In

Table 2. The average ACC and COV with standard deviations of data sets with classification algorithms based on 10 fold CV.

Dataset	No of objects	No of attr.	No of classes	C-Tree classifier				V-Tree classifier				RV-Tree classifier			
				Acc	Std dev	Cov	Std dev	Acc	Std dev	Cov	Std dev	Acc	Std dev	Cov	Std dev
Lymphoma	47	4026	2	0.802	0.046	0.943	0.01	**0.891**	0.045	1.0	0.0	0.743	0.048	0.957	0.052
Leukemia	72	7129	2	0.824	0.037	1.0	0.0	**0.901**	0.021	1.0	0.0	**0.906**	0.032	0.96	0.025
Colon	62	2000	2	0.739	0.046	1.0	0.0	**0.818**	0.03	1.0	0.0	**0.742**	0.037	0.966	0.03
Lung_cancer	181	12533	2	0.918	0.013	1.0	0.0	0.94	0.012	1.0	0.0	**0.96**	0.01	0.963	0.019
Prostate	136	12600	2	0.807	0.042	1.0	0.0	**0.868**	0.015	1.0	0.0	0.77	0.029	0.999	0.004
Ovarian_cancer	253	15154	2	0.981	0.003	1.0	0.0	**0.985**	0.008	1.0	0.0	0.965	0.009	0.992	0.006
Audiology	200	71	24	0.524	0.012	0.955	0.012	0.515	0.018	1.0	0.002	**0.691**	0.029	0.981	0.012
Biodeg	1055	41	2	0.808	0.004	1.0	0.0	**0.821**	0.008	1.0	0.0	**0.812**	0.007	0.993	0.003
Connectionist_bench	208	61	2	0.755	0.022	1.0	0.0	**0.762**	0.022	1.0	0.0	0.734	0.033	0.977	0.017
Cylinder_bands	540	40	2	0.682	0.015	0.86	0.01	0.679	0.01	1.0	0.0	**0.691**	0.01	0.99	0.005
Dermatology	366	35	6	0.921	0.007	1.0	0.0	**0.933**	0.007	1.0	0.0	**0.928**	0.011	0.987	0.007
Mushroom_agaricus-lepiota	8124	24	2	1.0	0.0	1.0	0.0	1.0	0.0	1.0	0.0	1.0	0.0	1.0	0.0
Flags	194	30	8	0.578	0.019	1.0	0.0	0.578	0.024	1.0	0.0	0.555	0.021	0.961	0.017
Ozone	2536	74	2	0.948	0.004	0.825	0.003	**0.961**	0.002	1.0	0.0	**0.958**	0.003	0.997	0.001
Parkinsons	185	23	2	0.88	0.019	1.0	0.0	**0.892**	0.014	1.0	0.0	**0.882**	0.016	0.987	0.011
SAheart	462	9	2	0.638	0.018	1.0	0.0	**0.646**	0.016	1.0	0.0	0.634	0.02	0.999	0.001
Segmentation	2310	20	7	0.955	0.002	1.0	0.0	0.949	0.003	1.0	0.0	**0.958**	0.004	0.991	0.002
Spam	4601	58	2	0.896	0.002	1.0	0.0	**0.899**	0.003	1.0	0.0	0.889	0.005	0.996	0.001

case of classifiers with verifying cuts, the minimum quality of redundant cut was equal to 0.9 in our experiments, and also the maximum number of redundant cuts was set to 10.

For determining quality of the classifiers we applied 10 fold cross-validation (CV) technique, which was repeated 10 times for every data set (i.e., 100 cycles of a train-and-test scheme was conducted). Moreover, at each iteration of 10 fold CV technique, the nine-folds data set was additionally divided into two parts: the training set and the validation set, with splitting ratio equal to 0.75. So the percentage of validation objects constituted 25% of the total training set. The final result of the algorithm is the average of 100 cycles. Popular parameters, i.e. accuracy (ACC) and coverage (COV) were used to measure the classification success.

6   Conclusion

We presented a new method for resolving conflicts between cuts in a node of the V-tree with verifying cuts. The method involves a judging classifier construction in the nodes where the conflicts arise.

The assessment of the approach was conducted using eighteen datasets. The experimental results show that the employment of the knowledge embedded in the redundant attributes increases the quality of the classifiers. However, the simple method of resolving conflicts, based on a majority voting, does well or even slightly better than more advanced method of resolving conflicts.

Results indicate that in most cases of data sets the accuracy of the proposed RV-tree classifier was better compared to the classical method, from an insignificant increase (0.2%) to almost 32%. The biggest increase of ACC was observed for a multi-class set ("audiology" with 24 classes). But although the new approach is superior to the classical one, it does not always produce better results than a simple method of solving conflicts for the surveyed data sets. One of the reasons for this may be the size of the validation set which is used to build a judging classifier. The average size of this set was about 260 objects in our experiments. Assuming that only some objects encounter conflicts in tree nodes and that the object is assigned only to one of all nodes, the effective number of objects taking part in building a judging tree for one node was much lower than the mean size. In the optimal case, it corresponds to the size of a validation set divided by the number of RV-tree nodes. In case of several examined datasets, the decision table for the judging classifier was ranged from a few to a dozen or so. Perhaps this is why the average accuracy of the RV-tree for microarray datasets (84.4%) is smaller than for V-tree (90.1%), but it is the highest (81.1%) of all three tested methods for the remaining, much larger collections (79.9% for C-tree and 80.3% for V-tree).

This approach may be good for some kind of data (e.g. with multiple decision classes) and we plan to more accurate verify what properties of datasets suggest the use of each particular method. One of the proposals for further research is to test the approach, applying methods for inducing judging classifiers different from the used in this paper.

Acknowledgement. This work was partially supported by two following grants of the Polish National Science Centre: DEC-2013/09/B/ST6/01568, DEC-2013/09/B/NZ5/ 00758, and also by the Centre for Innovation and Transfer of Natural Sciences and Engineering Knowledge of University of Rzeszów, Poland.

References

1. Bazan, J.G., Bazan-Socha, S., Buregwa-Czuma, S., Dydo, L., Rzasa, W., Skowron, A.: A classifier based on a decision tree with verifying cuts. Fundam. Inform. **143**(1–2), 1–18 (2016)
2. Bazan, J.G., Bazan-Socha, S., Buregwa-Czuma, S., Pardel, P.W., Sokolowska, B.: Predicting the presence of serious coronary artery disease based on 24 hour Holter ECG monitoring. In: Ganzha, M., Maciaszek, L., Paprzycki, M. (eds.) Proceedings of the Federated Conference on Computer Science and Information Systems, pp. 279–286. IEEE Xplore - digital library (2012)
3. Bazan, J.G., Bazan-Socha, S., Buregwa-Czuma, S., Pardel, P.W., Sokolowska, B.: Prediction of coronary arteriosclerosis in stable coronary heart disease. In: Greco, S., Bouchon-Meunier, B., Coletti, G., Fedrizzi, M., Matarazzo, B., Yager, R.R. (eds.) IPMU 2012. CCIS, vol. 298, pp. 550–559. Springer, Heidelberg (2012). doi:10. 1007/978-3-642-31715-6_58 ·
4. Bazan, J.G., Buregwa-Czuma, S.: A domain knowledge as a tool for improving classifiers. Fundam. Inform. **127**(1–4), 495–511 (2013)
5. Bazan, J.G., Nguyen, H.S., Nguyen, S.H., Synak, P., Wróblewski, J.: Rough set algorithms in classification problems. In: Polkowski, L., Lin, T.Y., Tsumoto, S. (eds.) Rough Set Methods and Applications: New Developments in Knowledge Discovery in Information. Systems Studies in Fuzziness and Soft Computing, vol. 56, pp. 49–88. Springer/Physica, Heidelberg (2000). doi:10.1007/978-3-7908-1840-6_3
6. Bazan, J.G., Szczuka, M.: The rough set exploration system. In: Peters, J.F., Skowron, A. (eds.) Transactions on Rough Sets III. LNCS, vol. 3400, pp. 37–56. Springer, Heidelberg (2005). doi:10.1007/11427834_2
7. Buregwa-Czuma, S., Bazan, J.G., Zareba, L., Bazan-Socha, S., Pardel, P., Sokolowska, B., Dydo, L.: The method for describing changes in the perception of stenosis in blood vessels caused by an additional drug. Fundam. Inform. **147**, 193–207 (2016)
8. Breiman, L.: Random forests. Mach. Learn. **45**, 5–32 (2001)
9. The Elements of Statistical Learning Repository: http://statweb.stanford.edu/ ~tibs/ElemStatLearn/datasets/
10. Kent Ridge Biomedical Dataset Repository: http://datam.i2r.a-star.edu.sg/ datasets/krbd/
11. Nguyen, H.S.: Approximate boolean reasoning: foundations and applications in data mining. In: Peters, J.F., Skowron, A. (eds.) Transactions on Rough Sets V. LNCS, vol. 4100, pp. 334–506. Springer, Heidelberg (2006). doi:10.1007/ 11847465_16
12. Pawlak, Z., Skowron, A.: Rudiments of rough sets. Inf. Sci. **177**, 3–27 (2007)
13. UC Irvine Machine Learning Repository: http://archive.ics.uci.edu/ml/

Depression Behavior Detection Model Based on Participation in Serious Games

Rytis Maskeliūnas[1], Tomas Blažauskas[2],
and Robertas Damaševičius[2(✉)]

[1] Department of Multimedia Engineering, Faculty of Informatics,
Kaunas University of Technology, Kaunas, Lithuania
[2] Department of Software Engineering, Faculty of Informatics,
Kaunas University of Technology, Kaunas, Lithuania
robertas.damasevicius@ktu.lt

Abstract. Managing depression is one of the main challenges that health specialists have to deal with. Due to the cumulative nature of depression, the major problem is that a long-term observation of symptoms is required to make an accurate decision about an individual's state. The depressed mood rate of an individual can be estimated according to recorded physiological and emotional information. We propose a mobile health monitoring system using wearable smart identification sensors (EEG, ECG, EMG, gaze tracking, and physical activity data) that capture stress and specific subject behaviors as a result of the participation in a serious game. The main objective is to study the impact of serious games on the human cognitive system in treating the early signs of depression by using a multi-level systems approach for representing the structure and dynamics of human cognitive functions. Our initial findings show that subjects with negative moods have been characterized by psychomotor retardation and lower correlation between the neural and cardiac systems.

Keywords: Depression modeling · EEG · Cognitive functions · Serious games

1 Introduction

Mental health conditions account for 13% of the global disease burden, with depression being the main cause of disability and the fourth largest burden of disease worldwide, while not all potential patients favor or can access existing modes of treatment delivery. Depression affects more than 300 million people worldwide. Europe also faces a high number (25%) of persons affected by depression, and the associated cost is about 170B EUR per year [1]. Therefore, managing depression is one of the main challenges that national health systems face. The detection and treatment of early stages of depression is a worldwide concern as the governmental institutions not only aim to decrease the number of depressed persons and the negative impact of depression on life quality but also to save a lot of money spent on its treatment.

Integrating user-driven options into general community-level settings is one of the strategies promoted by the WHO Mental Health Action Plan 2013–2020 [1]. Computer-based therapies have been effective in reducing depression and anxiety

© Springer International Publishing AG 2017
L. Polkowski et al. (Eds.): IJCRS 2017, Part II, LNAI 10314, pp. 423–434, 2017.
DOI: 10.1007/978-3-319-60840-2_31

symptoms in adults, adolescents, and children [2, 3], there are problems with user engagement in current computerized cognitive behavioral therapy programs [4]. Cognitive rehabilitation shows increased potential for use in neuropsychological evaluation allowing to be more engaging and user friendly [5]. Integration of EEG modality in serious games (i.e., games with a more serious purpose than entertainment) can help establishing a usable depression model [6] helping to understand etiology and pathophysiology of depression.

Due to the cumulative nature of depression, the major problem is that a long-term examination of the symptoms and observation of the recorded physiological and emotional information is required to make an accurate decision about an individual's state of depression.

Our main objective is to study the impact of serious games on the human cognitive system in treating the early signs of depression by using a multi-level systems approach for representing the structure and dynamics of human cognitive functions.

This research brings researchers a step closer to continuous, real-time systemic monitoring that will allow one to analyze the dynamic human physiology and understand, diagnosis, and treat mood disorders. The structure of the remaining parts of the paper is as follows. Section 2 discusses state-of-the-art works related to the considered problem. Section 3 described the proposed model and architecture of a depression monitoring system. Section 4 presents some preliminary results. Finally, Sect. 5 presents conclusions and discusses future work.

2 State-of-the-Art

Major depression is a debilitating condition characterized by diverse neurocognitive and behavioral deficits. The EEG based depression research is far from new (reported already 80 years from now [7]), ranging from general measurements to detection of neuropsychiatric disorders underpinning EEG as one of the most heritable biomarkers [8]. Chemistry based model such as based on monoamine depletion are generally accepted. Severity of depression has a moderate positive correlation with left parieto-occipital upper alpha event-related synchronization during the maintenance period of a working memory task [9]. EEG based models investigate models of affect: relationships among EEG alpha band asymmetry, depression, and anxiety [10]. So far the more promising research data come from the sleep brain flow analysis [11], providing effective biomarkers [12], revealing an altered interaction between cardiac vagal influence and delta sleep [13].

For example, Kim et al. [14] investigated statistical associations between momentary depressive mood and behavioral dynamics measured in patients with major depressive disorder (MDD). A small watch-type computer was used as an electronic diary to record self-reported symptoms and as locomotor activity recorder through an acceleration sensor. The constructed statistical model indicated that worsening of depression was associated with increased intermittency of locomotor activity characterized by lower mean and higher skewness. Findings suggest there are associations between momentary depressive mood and behavioral dynamics in patients with depression, which may motivate the continuous monitoring of the states of depression.

Yang et al. [15] has investigated the relation between vocal prosody and change in depression severity over time. Findings suggest that analysis of vocal prosody could assist in depression screening and monitoring over the course of depressive disorder and recovery.

The LiveNet system uses mobile physiologic sensors to track depression symptoms over time and to measure objective measures of depression. The measured data included skin conductance response, heart rate variability, movements, and vocal characteristics [16].

Massey et al. [17] propose techniques to improve communication in Body Sensor Network (BSN) that gathers data (accelerometers, galvanic response, electrocardiogram, audio sensor) on the affective states of the patient. These BSNs can continuously monitor, discretely quantify, and classify a patient's depressive states. In addition, data on the patient's lifestyle can be correlated with his/her physiological conditions to identify how various stimuli trigger symptoms.

A real-time depression monitoring system for the home has been developed to detect the early signs of a depression episode [18]. The data collected are multi-modal, spanning a number of different behavioral domains including sleep, weight, activities of daily living, and speech prosody.

An application based on smartphone behavior and activity monitoring proposed in [19] is able to recognize depressive and manic states and detect state changes of patients suffering from bipolar disorder and helps to detect state changes in order to guarantee the availability of in-time treatment.

Other studies outline the associations between depression and cardiac outcomes, as well as the mechanisms that may mediate these links [20, 21], and aims at investigating how the autonomic nervous system, in terms of electrodermal activity (EDA), responds to specific controlled emotional stimuli in bipolar patients [22].

Serious games have been shown to support improved outcomes of depression in several health conditions [23] even in severe cases such as Alzheimer's [24]. Appealing to a user's sense of self or agency and connectedness with others has been suggested to improve uptake and support engagement of computer-delivered therapies for depression and anxiety [25]. Combining data obtained from EEG brain monitoring and other physiological data such ECG, EMG and gait parameters, along with provocations provided by involving in serious games [26], physiological activity models of depression can be established.

3   Model and Methodology

The background of our research is Physiological Computing (PC), which uses physiological data of the users as input during computing tasks. Using such inputs, PC systems are becoming able to monitor, diagnose and respond to the cognitive, emotional and physical states of persons in real time. The physiological measures are measured from sensors attached to the body and include Electroencephalography (EEG), Electrocardiography (ECG), Electromyography (EMG), Heart Rate Variability

(HRV), etc. The measured data can be used to determine the internal changes and events occurring within the human body, including the involuntary reactions of the autonomic nervous system (ANS). As a PC system monitors the user's state that it improves, it creates a bio-cybernetic feedback loop [27], which allows to produce a more accurate representation of the user's state.

Affective Computing (AC) is a related paradigm of computing that is measuring the emotional state of a human through behavioral and physiological signals and developing computational models for the emotional state [28]. One of the key elements in AC is emotion recognition that estimates the emotional state of users from their behavioral and physiological responses. The principles of Physiological/Affective Computing are summarized in Fig. 1.

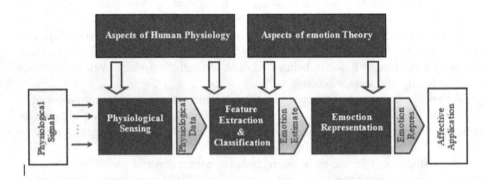

Fig. 1. Model of a system based on physiological/affective computing paradigm

The proposed mobile health monitoring system using wearable smart identification sensors (based on EEG, EMG and Physical Activity analysis) that capture stress and specific behaviors as a result of participation in a serious game, are enhanced with a knowledge based rule system to interpret the data and characterize depression symptom trajectories. Depression is associated with a number of affective, motor, and physiological changes that can be detected using the wearable device. We focus on the following parameters that can be monitored remotely:

1. General level of activity as measured using physical activity sensors (accelerometers, inclinometers and gravity sensors);
2. Analysis of physiological signals (including ECG, EMG and EEG) for identification of specific biomarkers for mental/affective states for diagnosis of stress, anxiety and mood disorders.
3. Gaze tracking data during the execution of an on-screen task.

We aim to develop a pervasive and personalized monitoring system for care assessment in mental health, providing parameters, indices and trends in order to better assess pathological mood states. The system is to provide a continuous communication and feedback to the patient and physician through a closed loop in order to facilitate disease management by fostering an innovative way to manage the illness, to help patients, to facilitate interaction between patient and physician, as well as to alert professionals in case of relapse and depressive or manic episodes. The closed-loop system is implemented on the patient side through a noninvasive wearable platform to acquire physiological signals from the patient as well as from a mobile platform. It records the physiological signals during a dedicated serious game task based on a prototype described in [29], allows patients to fill out a mood agenda and daily self-administered questionnaires, and finally, sends data to a remote server wherein the processing block is located. On the professional side, a central remote server is dedicated to analyze the data acquired from the patients and to provide results to clinicians for future evaluations. These data are used, together with other data of the same patient already present in the management platform to extract data mining results that will be shown to the attending physician, who will use them to optimize patient's therapy, thus closing the loop.

The methodology of research includes (1) Evaluation of user affective state using standard questionnaires; (2) Serious game; (3) Data acquisition; (4) Data analysis using advanced computing techniques; (5) Research architecture; and is summarized below.

Evaluation of User Affective State

An electronic diary is used to provide a computerized mood chart. To keep users interested in filling the test and to prevent from random filling, several tests are provided as a part of a serious game. The initial psychological state of the users is be evaluated using Social Readjustment Rating Scale (SRRS) [30]. A short test is used each time a user feels exceptional symptoms of stress/anxiety/mood-change, while a longer and more detailed test is used to evaluate the state of the user at the end of the day. A longer and more detailed test is used to evaluate the state of the user at the end of each week. In case of the occasional changes in the life of the users during the survey, their state is evaluated using the SRRS. The results of the test survey is used to find statistically significant biomarkers in physiological date that match the time and severity of mood disorders across the participant population.

Serious Game

We introduce a serious game as a means to collect data in an engaging and controlled environment which allows for introduction of mood affecting elements and measurement of human reaction. We have developed a market simulation game based on a Minority Game model [31], called OilTrader, which allows for users to experience simplified market conditions while trading the digital shares of the fantasy company OilFund. It involves seeing historical game outcomes and trying to predict outcome of the next round. In each round, a player decides to sell or buy the OilFund shares, or is not to place any trades in that round. Winning a game requires enabling complex cognitive functions, while a limited response time ensures that an element of stress is introduced.

Data Acquisition

For the daily monitoring of the state of a human, we use biomarkers. A biomarker is a biological indicator that reflects underlying physiological processes, including both normative processes and pathogenic states [32]. Our aim is to capture allostatic load, which is a summary measure of the cumulative biological burden of the repeated attempts to adapt to daily stress [33]. The allostatic load is "the fatigue of the body" which grows over time when the individual is exposed to repeated or chronic stress. It represents the physiological consequences of chronic exposure to fluctuating or heightened neural or neuroendocrine response that results from repeated or chronic stress. In our case, the stress is induced and simulated by a serious game.

Data acquisition is performed using smart textiles. Clothes are natural possessions and are part of the processes and routines in our daily life. A wearable shirt is used for measuring the physiological parameters as well as physical activities (posture [34] and gait [35]) help to detect the patient's state. It is such a comfortable device that a patient does not feel the presence of any sensor or other components in the shirt. The smart shirt also ensures a wide range of mobility.

The main data that is registered using a smart shirt is electromyography (EMG). EMG is a product of recruited muscle fibers by descending motor commands, driven from higher neural centers. EMG analysis is used to evaluate the function of the neuromuscular sub-systems and identify kinetic related muscular fatigue. EMG recording may be considered a sensitive technique for inferring subjective mood states or affective responses. The differences in EMG features between rest and stress conditions indicate that EMG is a useful parameter to detect stress levels and assess the state of discomfort as has been demonstrated in [36]. However, identification of allostatic fatigue require gathering of data for much longer periods (days instead of minutes) than existing EMG studies perform. ECG and HRV is also a good indicator of overall activity levels, with a high heart rate associated with an anxious state and a low rate with a relaxed state [37]. EEG patterns obtained during execution of several different tasks is also used as an accurate diagnostic marker of Major Depression Disorder (MDD) as suggested in [38]. The eye movement data captured by gaze tracking is used as an indicator of an emotional state. Eye movements during the execution of a task show an increase in reaction time in prosaccade and antisaccade movements for subjects who report sad mood, which can be associated with depression [39].

Data Processing and Analysis
First, data is denoised using an extension of the Empirical Mode Decomposition (EMD) method [40]. Data analysis methods include phase space reconstruction and correlation analysis. Phase space reconstruction deals with a phase space of a dynamical system is a space in which all possible states of a system are represented, with each possible state of the system corresponding to one unique point in the phase space. The method is useful for detecting the dynamical structure and evolution of a system. The analysis of periodic and aperiodic orbits in the reconstructed phase space helps to determine specific mental/affective states of subjects. We use a modified phase space reconstruction methods that is based on fractional time differences, which allows extraction of more accurate signal trajectories [41]. Correlation analysis is used to identify correlations between different physiological signals. It is expected that a person in a depressive state would have lower levels of correlation (we specifically use

Pearson correlation and Granger causality [42]) than a person in a normal emotional state. For classification, nonlinear operators [43] are applied and signals are compressed to extract features [44–47] before a custom class-adaptive classification method [48] is applied to assign the correct affective state.

Research Architecture

The architecture of the system is based on the personalized health monitoring framework [49]. The sensorized smart shirt with wireless Body Area Network (BAN) is interfaced with a smartphone application, for the subject's usage at home, as well as the online database for remote supervision. It also stores the data from the smart shirt and sends them to the server. The components are:

(1) Wearable Smart Shirt System: contains a hooded shirt with integrated BAN, transmitter and a server computer for distant monitoring. Smart Shirt is used to provide the individual physiological data. Then this data is transmitted in ad-hoc wireless communication for further processing using a wireless link.
(2) Wearable Sensor Node: wearable EMG/ECG sensors acquire physiological data from human body and transmit it through a wireless link.
(3) Consumer-grade EEG device integrated into the hood of a shirt to record the brain activity of a subject [50].
(4) Gaze tracker to follow the eye landing sites and dwelling time [51].
(5) Smartphone that remains in communication with a central server using the GPRS technology. Smartphone app provides the audio-visual biofeedback to the user.
(6) Central Server receives sensor data from all subjects and store it in database.

The acquired physiological signals are pre-processed at each node and transmitted to the wearable data acquisition hardware (sink node) for further processing and transmitted wireless to a remote monitoring station.

4 Preliminary Results

Our preliminary results include the analysis of Pearson correlations between ECG and EEG (Fig. 2), analysis of Granger causality at different frequencies between ECG and EEG (Fig. 3), and Granger causality demonstration on a head model of a subject (Fig. 4). Here Fp1, ..., O2 are stand for scalp electrode positions according to the International 10–20 electrode placement system.

The results show an increased level of Pearson correlation and Granger causality associated with frontal, vision association and cognitive processing areas of human brain. The maximal value of Granger causality obtained at 16–20 Hz can be associated with the presence of beta waves, which normally are linked with active thinking, focus, and high alert.

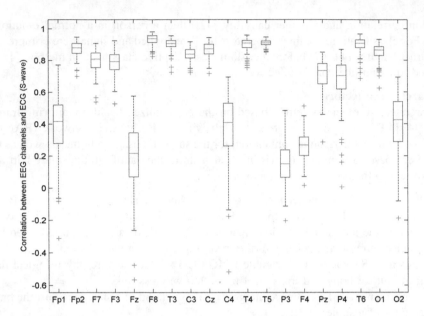

Fig. 2. Correlation between ECG (S-wave) and EEG channels

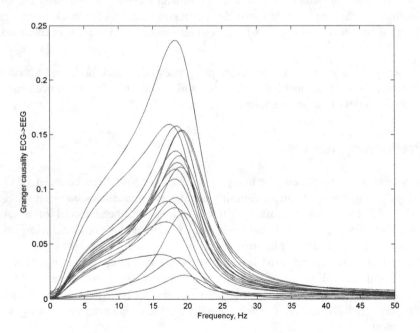

Fig. 3. Granger causality between ECG and EEG

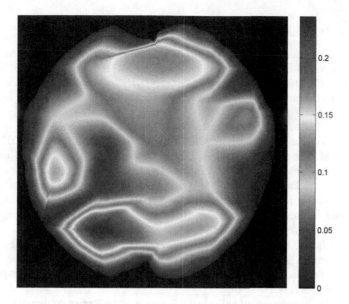

Fig. 4. Granger causalities on a head model

5 Evaluation and Conclusion

The study of EEG and ECG in psychiatric disorders has previously been established, and these physiological parameters are considered as promising biomarkers for the detection and monitoring of affective disorders. The technology for the measurement of the respective parameters is available and the methodology for the analysis and interpretation of the data collected is established.

We propose the depression behavior measurement model and the system to measure these biological parameters, and prospectively test the sensitivity of the device in the early detection of the depressive symptoms. The proposed system will integrate the measurement of these physiological parameters in a single wearable system, and deploy the necessary IT systems to store, transmit, and analyze the data that will be used in future studies to trigger an alarm at a central monitoring station of a possible event (onset of depression). The envisioned usage scenario for the depressive behavior recognition system is to provide daily updates to the doctors and, possibly, the patients who would then look at the trend evolving on the scale of a few days and, if the trend points toward a negative change of state, make sure that a medical examination is scheduled.

Our initial findings show that subjects with negative moods have been characterized by psychomotor retardation and lower correlation between neural and cardiac systems. The obtained data may be useful for understanding the link between emotion regulation and mood disorders.

Future work will focus on the analysis of EEG-ECG discordance in the beta band of EEG and its association with the recorded evidence of mood disorders.

References

1. World Health Organisation (WHO): Mental health action plan 2013–2020. In: Mental Health Action Plan. WHO Document Production Services (2013)
2. Calear, A.L., Christensen, H.: Review of internet-based prevention and treatment programs for anxiety and depression in children and adolescents. Med. J. Aust. **192**(11 Suppl.), S12–S14 (2010)
3. Richards, D., Richardson, T.: Computer-based psychological treatments for depression: a systematic review and meta-analysis. Clin. Psychol. Rev. **32**(4), 329–342 (2012)
4. Melville, K.M., Casey, L.M., Kavanagh, D.J.: Dropout from internet-based treatment for psychological disorders. Br. J. Clin. Psychol. **49**(Pt. 4), 455–471 (2010)
5. Tarnanas, I., Tsolakis, A., Tsolaki, M.: Assessing virtual reality environments as cognitive stimulation method for patients with MCI. In: Brooks, A.L., Brahnam, S., Jain, L.C. (eds.) Technologies of Inclusive Well-Being. SCI, vol. 536, pp. 39–74. Springer, Heidelberg (2014). doi:10.1007/978-3-642-45432-5_4
6. Lee, C.S., Chui, C.K., Guan, C., Eu, P.W., Tan, B.L., Leong, J.J.Y.: Integrating EEG modality in serious games for rehabilitation of mental patients. In: Cai, Y., Goei, S.L. (eds.) Simulations, Serious Games and Their Applications. GMSE. Springer, Singapore (2014). doi:10.1007/978-981-4560-32-0
7. Lemere, F.: The significance of individual differences in the Berger rhythm. Brain **5**(9), 366–375 (1936)
8. De Gennaro, L., Marzano, C., Fratello, F., Moroni, F., Pellicciari, M.C., Ferlazzo, F., Rossini, P.M.: The electroencephalographic fingerprint of sleep is genetically determined: a twin study. Ann. Neurol. **64**, 455–460 (2008)
9. Segrave, R.A., Thomson, R.H., Cooper, N.R., Croft, R.J., Sheppard, D.M., Fitzgerald, P.B.: Upper alpha activity during working memory processing reflects abnormal inhibition in major depression. J. Affect. Disord. **127**, 191–198 (2010)
10. Mathersul, D., Williams, L.M., Hopkinson, P.J., Kemp, A.H.: Investigating models of affect: relationships among EEG alpha asymmetry, depression, and anxiety. Emotion **8**(4), 560–572 (2008)
11. Steiger, A., Pawlowski, M., Kimura, M.: Sleep electroencephalography as a biomarker in depression. Chronophysiol. Ther. **2015**(5), 15–25 (2015)
12. Steiger, A., Kimura, M.: Wake and sleep EEG provide biomarkers in depression. J. Psychiatr. Res. **44**(4), 242–252 (2010)
13. Jurysta, F., Kempenaers, C., Lancini, J., Lanquart, J.-P., van de Borne, P., Linkowski, P.: Altered interaction between cardiac vagal influence and delta sleep EEG suggests an altered neuroplasticity in patients suffering from major depressive disorder. Acta Psychiatr. Scand. **121**, 236–239 (2010)
14. Kim, J., Nakamura, T., Kikuchi, H., Yoshiuchi, K., Yamamoto, Y., Kim, J.: Co-variation of depressive mood and spontaneous physical activity evaluated by ecological momentary assessment in major depressive disorder, pp. 6635–6638 (2014)
15. Yang, Y., Fairbairn, C., Cohn, J.F.: Detecting depression severity from vocal prosody. IEEE Trans. Affect. Comput. **4**(2), 142–150 (2013)
16. Sung, M., Marci, C., Pentland, A.S.: Objective Physiological and Behavioral Measures for Identifying and Tracking Depression State in Clinically Depressed Patients. Institute of Technology Media Laboratory, Cambridge (2005)
17. Massey, T., Marfia, G., Potkonjak, M., Sarrafzadeh, M.: Experimental analysis of a mobile health system for mood disorders. IEEE Trans. Inf. Technol. Biomed. **14**(2), 241–247 (2010)

18. Dickerson, F.: Empath: a continuous remote emotional health monitoring system for depressive illness. In: Proceedings of the 2nd Conference on Wireless Health (Wireless Health 2011) (2011). Article No. 5
19. Grunerbl, A., Muaremi, A., Osmani, V., Bahle, G., Ohler, S., Troster, G., Mayora, O., Haring, C., Lukowicz, P.: Smartphone-based recognition of states and state changes in bipolar disorder patients. IEEE J. Biomed. Health Inform. **19**(1), 140–148 (2015)
20. Huffman, J.C., Celano, C.M., Beach, S.R., Motiwala, S.R., Januzzi, J.L.: Depression and cardiac disease: epidemiology, mechanisms, and diagnosis. Cardiovasc. Psychiatry Neurol. **2013**, 14 (2013). Article ID 695925
21. Iverson, G.L., Gaetz, M.B., Rzempoluck, E.J., Mclean, P., Linden, W., Remick, R.: A new potential marker for abnormal cardiac physiology in depression. J. Behav. Med. **28**(6), 507 (2005)
22. Greco, A., Lanat, A., Valenza, G., Rota, G., Vanello, N., Scilingo, E.P.: On the deconvolution analysis of electrodermal activity in bipolar patients. In: Annual International Conference of the IEEE Engineering in Medicine and Biology Society (EMBC), pp. 6691–6694 (2012)
23. Fleming, T., Cheek, C., Merry, S., Thabrew, H., Bridgman, H., Stasiak, K., Shepherd, M., Perry, Y., Hetrick, S.: Serious games for the treatment or prevention of depression: a systematic review. Revista de Psicopatología y Psicología Clínica **19**(3), 227–242 (2014)
24. Férnandez-Calvo, B., Rodriguez-Pérez, R., Contador, I., Rubio-Santorum, A., Ramos, F.: Efficacy of cognitive training programs based on new software technologies in patients with Alzheimer-type dementia. Psicothema **23**, 44–50 (2011)
25. Noar, S.M., Benac, C.N., Harris, M.S.: Does tailoring matter? Meta-analytic review of tailored print health behavior change interventions. Psychol. Bull. **133**(4), 673–693 (2007)
26. Derbali, L., Frasson, C.: Players' motivation and EEG waves patterns in a serious game environment. In: Aleven, V., Kay, J., Mostow, J. (eds.) ITS 2010. LNCS, vol. 6095, pp. 297–299. Springer, Heidelberg (2010). doi:10.1007/978-3-642-13437-1_50
27. Serbedzija, N.B., Fairclough, S.H.: Biocybernetic loop: from awareness to evolution. In: IEEE Congress on Evolutionary Computation, pp. 2063–2069 (2009)
28. Picard, R.W.: Affective Computing. MIT Press, Cambridge (1997)
29. Martisius, I., Damasevicius, R.: A prototype SSVEP based real time BCI gaming system. Comput. Intel. Neurosci. **2016**, 15 (2016). Article ID 3861425
30. Holmes, T.H., Rahe, R.H.: The social readjustment rating scale. J. Psychosom. Res. **11**(2), 213–218 (1967)
31. Damaševičius, R., Ašeriškis, D.: Visual and computational modelling of minority games. TEM J. **6**(1), 108–116 (2017). UIKTEN, Novi Pazar
32. Baum, A., Grunberg, N.: Measurement of stress hormones. In: Cohen, S., Kessler, R.C., Gordon, L.U. (eds.) Measuring Stress: A Guide for Health and Social Scientists, pp. 175–192. Oxford University Press, Oxford (1997)
33. Djuric, Z., Bird, C.E., Furumoto-Dawson, A., Rauscher, G.H., Ruffin, M.T., Stowe, R.P., Tucker, K.L., Masi, C.M.: Biomarkers of psychological stress in health disparities research. Open Biomark. J. **1**, 7–19 (2008)
34. Damasevicius, R., Vasiljevas, M., Salkevicius, J., Wozniak, M.: Human activity recognition in AAL environments using random projections. Comput. Math. Methods Med. **2016**, 17 (2016). Article ID 4073584
35. Damasevicius, R., Maskeliunas, R., Venckauskas, A., Wozniak, M.: Smartphone user identity verification using gait characteristics. Symmetry **8**(10), 100 (2016)
36. Kolich, M., Taboun, S.M.: Combining psychophysical measures of discomfort and electromyography for the evaluation of a new automotive seating concept. Int. J. Occup. Saf. Ergon. **8**(4), 483–496 (2002)

37. Frijda, N.H.: The Emotions. Cambridge University Press, Cambridge (1986)
38. Hahn, T., Marquand, A.F., Ehlis, A.C., Dresler, T., Kittel-Schneider, S., Jarczok, T.A., Lesch, K.P., Jakob, P.M., Mourao-Miranda, J., Brammer, M.J., Fallgatter, A.J.: Integrating neurobiological markers of depression. Arch. Gen. Psychiatry **68**, 361–368 (2011)
39. Carvalho, N., Laurent, E., Noiret, N., Chopard, G., Haffen, E., Bennabi, D., Vandel, P.: Eye movement in unipolar and bipolar depression: a systematic review of the literature. Front. Psychol. **6**, 1809 (2015)
40. Damaševičius, R., Vasiljevas, M., Martišius, I., Jusas, V., Birvinskas, D., Wozniak, M.: BoostEMD: an extension of EMD method and its application for denoising of EMG signals. Electron. Electr. Eng. **21**(6), 57–61 (2015)
41. Damaševičius, R., Martišius, I., Jusas, V., Birvinskas, D.: Fractional delay time embedding of EEG signals into high dimensional phase space. Electron. Electr. Eng. **20**(8), 55–58 (2014)
42. Kaminski, M., Ding, M., Truccolo, W.A., Bressler, S.L.: Evaluating causal relations in neural systems: granger causality, directed transfer function and statistical assessment of significance. Biol. Cybern. **85**, 145–157 (2001)
43. Martišius, I., Damaševičius, R., Jusas, V., Birvinskas, D.: Using higher order nonlinear operators for SVM classification of EEG data. Electron. Electr. Eng. **3**(119), 99–102 (2012)
44. Birvinskas, D., Jusas, V., Martisius, I., Damasevicius, R.: EEG dataset reduction and feature extraction using discrete cosine transform. In: Sixth UKSim/AMSS European Symposium on Computer Modeling and Simulation, pp. 199–204 (2012). doi:10.1109/EMS.2012.88
45. Birvinskas, D., Jusas, V., Martišius, I., Damaševičius, R.: Data compression of EEG signals for artificial neural network classification. Inf. Technol. Control **42**(3), 238–241 (2013)
46. Martisius, I., Birvinskas, D., Damasevicius, R., Jusas, V.: EEG dataset reduction and classification using wave atom transform. In: Mladenov, V., Koprinkova-Hristova, P., Palm, G., Villa, A.E.P., Appollini, B., Kasabov, N. (eds.) ICANN 2013. LNCS, vol. 8131, pp. 208–215. Springer, Heidelberg (2013). doi:10.1007/978-3-642-40728-4_26
47. Birvinskas, D., Jusas, V., Martisius, I., Damasevicius, R.: Fast DCT algorithms for EEG data compression in embedded systems. Comput. Sci. Inf. Syst. **12**(1), 49–62 (2015)
48. Martišius, I., Damaševičius, R.: Class-adaptive denoising for EEG data classification. In: Rutkowski, L., Korytkowski, M., Scherer, R., Tadeusiewicz, R., Zadeh, L.A., Zurada, J.M. (eds.) ICAISC 2012. LNCS, vol. 7268, pp. 302–309. Springer, Heidelberg (2012). doi:10.1007/978-3-642-29350-4_36
49. Venčkauskas, A., Štuikys, V., Toldinas, J., Jusas, N.: A model-driven framework to develop personalized health monitoring. Symmetry. **8**(7), 65, 1–18 (2016). MDPI AG, Basel
50. Maskeliūnas, R., Damaševičius, R., Martišius, I., Vasiljevas, M.: Consumer grade EEG devices: are they usable for control tasks? PeerJ. **4**, e1746, 1–27 (2016)
51. Vasiljevas, M., Gedminas, T., Ševčenko, A., Jančiukas, M., Blažauskas, T., Damaševičius, R.: Modelling eye fatigue in gaze spelling task. In: IEEE 12th International Conference on Intelligent Computer Communication and Processing (ICCP), pp. 95–102 (2016)

Persuasive Strategies in Dialogue Games with Emotional Reasoning

Magdalena Kacprzak[✉]

Faculty of Computer Science, Bialystok University of Technology,
Bialystok, Poland
m.kacprzak@pb.edu.pl

Abstract. The paper presents a formal system for describing dialogues with emotional reasoning. This system has been proposed in order to develop methods of analyzing and searching for dialogue participant's optimal strategy. The methodology used draws from a tradition of dialogue in games and game theory. Moreover the formal mathematical model is applied towards designing and implementation of a software tool. The aim of this tool is to improve communication skills during parent-child dialogues, and will be an invaluable support for learning how to talk to children. Developed formalism will also constitute the basis for semantic verification dialogue protocols (e.g. model checking).

Keywords: Strategy · Persuasive dialogue game · Dialogue protocol · Emotions

1 Introduction

Decades ago, having a meaningful conversation with a friend was an enjoyable experience. People loved meeting, chatting and listening to long stories about distant lands. Nowadays, one of the most popular forms of communication is a text conversation. It replaces phone calls and person-to-person conversations, even with those people you really care about, which are family and friends. Young people use texting as a way to share or solve some very difficult personal problems like breaking up. Technology has transformed the way we communicate but communicating is still one of the best ways to strengthen your connection with someone. Even though the communication channels have changed, the message should stay the same. Therefore, to keep a good relationship with someone you should focus on asking and answering appropriate questions, engage in conversations that offer solutions, learn more about your interlocutor and his/her behavior, what he/she likes, and what topics grab his/her attention. Multi-agent systems provide the most natural and persistent methodologies for designing and implementing an interactive tool that support studying and teaching of conversational abilities, which is the purpose of our research.

© Springer International Publishing AG 2017
L. Polkowski et al. (Eds.): IJCRS 2017, Part II, LNAI 10314, pp. 435–453, 2017.
DOI: 10.1007/978-3-319-60840-2_32

1.1 Aim and Challenge

In this work we focus on dialogues, in particular those between a human being and a software agent playing the role of the opponent in a discussion. As an example, we analyze the specific type of dialogue between a parent and a child. Such a dialogue should not be considered as some intentional attempt to reach conclusions or express mere points of view, but as the very prerequisite of authentic relationships between people. As a starting point, we have chosen argumentation dialogues. Argumentation is the act of forming reasons, drawing conclusions, and applying them to a case in a discussion. It can be an element of persuasion. The aim of persuasion is to cause someone to do or believe something by asking, arguing, or giving reasons. The range of possibilities is large. One of them is the attempt to use argumentation to convince an opponent, without using force. One of the most important elements of the persuasion process are emotions. Both the influence of emotions on the process of giving reasons for and against something as well as the influence of specific arguments on emotions and the change of their intensity are significant in persuasion. It's necessary to recognize, name, and manage emotions to have a productive conversation. Ignoring emotions interferes with reaching an agreement.

The aim of this paper is to propose a formal system which serves as a base for human-machine tools for implementing persuasive dialogue. These tools will be a support in the education of communication skills. It can also assist in parents' self-develop- ment, or in the training of teachers. Incorporating emotions into this system allows systemization and automation while still have a personal touch. Such a system will allow automation, but yet the feel of a more personal message. The tool must be based on a specified protocol. Therefore, analyzed dialogue must be structured. This means that it is subject to the rules adopted. It won't reduce significantly analyzed dialogues but reject those that do not bring anything new to the study because this dialogue contains a lot of redundant information or indicates a very irrational behavior of the participants in the dialogue. This is not of interest in this study. The tools are designed to help consolidate the desired behavior.

The main question is what we seek in the analyzed dialogues, and why such an analysis is needed? To answer this question let us consider two examples. The first one concerns teams. The most common hazard for teams is a lack of consensus. It is a particularly thorny problem, and brings a lot of teams to heated arguments, division and disasters. Therefore, the task of the leader of such a group is to find a solution and use tools which help to build consensus. The second example concerns marketing strategies and building relationships with a customer. The seller should use special techniques to keep clients excited about participating in the sales process. People want to feel special. Therefore, there is a need to learn more about interested buyers and their behaviors. Who influences them? Who they follow, etc. so they are all looking for the optimal strategy and the factors impacting it. They need to know when the persuasion is impactful and how to convince the recipient to achieve the intended goal.

The same features can be found in a dialogue with a child. Many parents would like to know how to talk to their children and which strategy to choose for reaching an agreement. Do such strategies exist? Are there rules that can help and assist parents? Systematic and automatic analysis can give us an answer to these and similar questions and assist parents in choosing effective strategies tailored to the personality of the child, family relationships, and the situation. The success of a dialogue with the child also strengthens relationships within the family. Multi-agent systems can offer great assistance in improving communication skills.

The original contribution of this paper consists in (a) defining a formal system suitable for modeling the parent-child dialogue game which uses the concept of the Nash-style game and (b) introducing a game-theoretic description of strategies that players can choose in this game. For the first time, game theory is used to characterize games in which emotions play a crucial role. Furthermore, the game-theoretic concept of solutions like dominant strategies or Nash equilibrium is used to explore strategic properties of the parent-child dialogue game. As a result, we get a system that allows to examine the effectiveness of parent's strategies. This innovative approach is a great theoretical base for the tool designed for training communication skills.

There are two key questions in this training: (1) Which strategy should you choose to achieve the intended success? and (2) Does the winning strategy exist? In response to these questions, it may be helpful to use a tool for automated verification of dialogue systems. A new description language for such a tool is introduced in the paper [39]. Developing a verifier relevant for dialogue games is a big challenge. This verification differs from the typical verification of multi-agent systems, where the analysis is performed on paths composed of the global states of the system. In dialogue systems we analyze sequences of actions (dialogue histories) rather than sequences of states. Obviously, the sequence of actions determines a sequence of states, but vice versa is not necessarily. The parent-child dialogue game can be an input of the tool described in [39]. This tool is designed to verify a wide variety of games, not just the parent-child dialogue.

The rest of the paper is organized as follows. Section 1.2 discusses the related work. In Sect. 2 the running example is presented. In Sect. 3 the game-theoretic model for dialogues with emotional reasoning is introduced. Section 4 studies two types of solutions for the parent-child dialogue game: dominant strategies and Nash equilibrium. Section 5 concludes the paper.

1.2   Related Work

Dialogue Games. A software tool supporting learning how to conduct conversations with elements of persuasion should be equipped with a well defined mathematical model. To give the theoretical background, we use the terminology of persuasive dialogue games. Such games are played between two players, of the kind where one plays the role of proponent and argues for some thesis, and one is the opponent. The specification of these systems typically is given by defining the set of locution rules, protocol and the set of effect rules. Locution rules indicate what kind of actions players can use. They are typically called locutions and include speech acts such as: *claim, concede, why, question,* and *since.* A protocol defines conditions under which specific actions can be executed and which actions can go next. In [20,21] protocol is defined by means of *legal answer function* and *protocol function*. Effect rules define results of actions and in [21] are given by means of *global evolution function*.

Dialogue games can be intended to examine dialogue types that meet conditions of some policies like prohibition of formal fallacies [19,22] or other dialogue fallacies (see e.g. [12,42]) or can concentrate on the requirements that dialogical interaction must meet in order to serve specific goals, such as persuasion, negotiation, information-seeking, and other discourses [2,13,32]. In the current article a dialogue system which describes parent-child persuasive conversation is presented. The important part of this kind of a dialogue is to show empathy to the recipient and understanding and acceptance of his/her emotions. The key is to ask follow-up questions and without being intrusive, dig deep to find the real motivations of unsuitable behavior in a child. The parent acts as a coach, who must choose the appropriate strategy to solve a difficult situation and lead to approval. Searching for this strategy is the main reason for designing the dialogue game. To this end, players are equipped with emotional reasoning ability [18]. Then some elements of game-theoretic framework are employed to study which choices constitute the effective strategy [9].

Strategies in Dialogues. Much work has been devoted to strategies [8,35]. However only few of them discuss a Nash-style game-theoretic approach in the context of dialogue games. Rahwan and Larson [34] focus on constructing a new dialogue game that satisfy some selected properties but do not analyze the game-theoretic features like Nash equilibrium for some existing game. The authors of [33,37] also study the game they construct and study other game-theoretic features like subgame perfect equilibria. In [17] the DC game introduced by Mackenzie is taken into consideration. Players' strategies have a game-theoretic description and solutions for dominant strategies and Nash equilibrium are analyzed. In current work the similar analysis is performed for very special type of game, that is parent-child persuasive dialogue. This analysis has lead to finding the optimal strategy. Mackenzie's DC game is also studied in [43] where the authors show weaknesses of this game in preventing fallacious arguments and common errors. Black and Hunter's work [2] offers a dialogue-game-style protocol for inquiry dialogue. Emele et al. [11] introduce a theoretical account which allows players to build flexible and adaptive strategies for agent's arguing in information-seeking domains. A logical system for specification and verification of strategies is discussed in [16]. It enables to reason about the persuasive properties and develop winning strategies. Although an effort has been devoted to strategies in games, only a few works employ game-theoretic approach [23,33,34].

The research on the optimization of persuasive strategies in argumentative dialogues has two main streams. The first one refers to the tradition of game theory where players maximize their utility and act optimally. The second uses heuristic-based methods in which players use a strategy following a principle which is not based on exact calculations, but rather on experience [38]. This paper fits in the first approach since we assume, study and compute optimal and monolithic strategies. This is justified in our system because we focus on behavior of leaders in dialogues which is assumed to be rational. A methodology for predicting people's argumentative choices during a dialogue using Machine Learning techniques is described in [38]. It uses the approach which does not force an opponent to act strategically nor optimally.

The development of automated argumentation-based agents combines argumentation theory and methods of multi-agent systems to propose logical systems, protocols for dialogues or policies for artificial agents to ensure correct and effective argumentation [3, 24]. Much less attention is paid to models of argumentation that can be applied to humans. Only few of them address this topic [6].

Models of Emotions. Many of the works devoted to formal modeling of emotions in multi-agent systems appeals to appraisal theory of emotions [30, 40] where the main cause of changes in intensity of emotions are the beliefs and intentions of the agents. The same emotions depend mainly on some events and their consequences, that is how they impact beliefs, especially those concerning the possibilities to achieve the intended goal [5, 7]. Therefore in formal systems, emotions are often determined by the mental states of the agents [4].

In our approach, the intensity of emotions also depend on events. It's just that these events are verbal actions, spoken during the dialogue. Emotions change not only under the influence of content of speech acts, but also their type and intent. For example locution *scold* is an action expressing frustration and annoyance of the performer while the recipient feels in connection with this extreme discomfort. It can turn into anger or aggression, but also sadness or withdrawal. To a large extent, it depends on the player's profile and preferences. In addition, the change of emotions depends on commitments and public declarations rather then the beliefs of the agents.

The BDI-like formal model of emotions, which merge both empirical and theoretical approaches, is given in [29]. The authors introduce the semantically grounded formal representation of rational dialogue agents, and implements agents which can express empathy and recognize situations where this should be shown. BDI description is also used in [14] for deducing and understanding user's emotions during interaction with a pedagogical virtual agent. In [26] the communication theory of emotion [28] is applied. In this model emotional behavior is based on selected mental attitudes expressed in modal logic and emotions which indicate which actions should be performed by the agent. In many works (see e.g. [1]) to generate emotions the Ortony, Clore and Collinss (OCC) model is used [30]. It states that the strength of an agent's emotion depends on the events, other agents and objects found in the multi-agent environment. The model distinguishes 22 emotion categories and five processes which determine the behavior of the agent.

In recent times, more and more systems are equipped with agents with emotional interactions. This feature significantly improves the expressiveness, adaptability, and credibility of agents. This is very important in the design of virtual, embodied agents, the aim of which is to keep human-machine interaction. Other applications can be found in verification of hypotheses in theories of emotions, developing new techniques for computer games or improvement of decision-making mechanisms [27, 41].

2   Parent-Child Persuasive Dialogue

This section shows a dialogue that will become the basis for further discussion. It is a dialogue between a parent (P) and his 10 year old child (C). Dialogue is presented in 3 different versions. The beginning of all the dialogues is the same. Later the parent chooses one of the three strategies. The result of these dialogues is of course different. Dialogues are included in the following tables with their description in a formal dialogue system.

Dialogue 1

Player	Utterance	Locution	Locution's name
P:	*Dinner is ready. Come and get it.*	*claim* α_1	a_1
C:	*This is dinner? It isn't ready.*	*claim* $\neg\alpha_1$	a_2
P:	*Why isn't it ready?*	*why* $\neg\alpha_1$	a_3
C:	*Oh, these are whole pieces of food that you've just cooked*	$\neg\alpha_1$ *since* $\{\alpha_2\}$	a_4
P:	*That's right*	*concede* α_2	a_5
C:	*Do you think I'll eat it?*	*question* α_3	a_6
P:	*Yes*	*claim* α_3	a_7
C:	*Why would I want to eat it?*	*why* α_3	a_8
P:	*Because today we're eating something healthy for dinner*	α_3 *since* $\{\alpha_4\}$	a_9
C:	*How can I be sure this is healthy?*	*why* α_4	a_{10}
P:	*Because I said so*	α_4 *since* $\{\alpha_5\}$	a_{11}
C:	*I had pizza for breakfast, and then I got a 5 in math*	*claim* α_6	a_{12}
P:	*That's not the way it works!*	*scold* $\neg\alpha_7$	a_{13}
C:	*I think it's cold*	*claim* α_8	a_{14}
P:	*It's not cold*	*scold* $\neg\alpha_8$	a_{15}
C:	*Look at it. It's gone cold*	*scold* α_8	a_{16}
P:	*Obey, it's not cold.*	*scold* $\neg\alpha_8$	a_{17}
C:	*I'll eat it if you let me play on the computer.*	*claim* α_9	a_{18}
P:	*I don't agree*	*claim* $\neg\alpha_9$	a_{19}
C:	*Why?*	*why* $\neg\alpha_9$	a_{20}
P:	*Because I'm the grown-up and I said so. Now quit asking me and go do something else besides talking to me, for the love of God!*	$\neg\alpha_9$ *since* $\{\alpha_{10}\}$	a_{21}
C:	*Why are you yelling these things at me?*	*why* α_{11}	a_{22}
P:	*I'm sorry, I didn't mean to yell.*	*retract* α_{11}	a_{23}
C:	*I'm not going to eat this meat.*	*claim* α_{12}	a_{24}
P:	*I'll order pizza*	*claim* α_{13}	a_{25}

In this version, the child is trying to convince the parent that pizza is the best for lunch. He asks a lot of questions, has a lot of responses and leads the parent to irritation. The parent feels a sense of guilt because of screaming at the child and decides to order pizza. The child wins the dialogue.

Dialogue 2

Player	Utterance	Locution	Locution's name
P:	*Dinner is ready. Come and get it.*	*claim* α_1	a_1
C:	*This is dinner? It isn't ready.*	*claim* $\neg\alpha_1$	a_2
P:	*Why isn't it ready?*	*why* $\neg\alpha_1$	a_3
C:	*Oh, these are whole pieces of food that you've just cooked*	$\neg\alpha_1$ *since* $\{\alpha_2\}$	a_4
P:	*You always complain about food!*	*scold* α_{14}	a_{26}
C:	*If you cooked like John's mom, I won't complain!*	*scold* α_{15}	a_{27}
P:	*So go to John's mom!*	*scold* α_{16}	a_{28}
C:	*I'll eat potato chips!*	*claim* α_{17}	a_{29}
P:	*You never eat anything healthy!*	*scold* α_{18}	a_{30}

In the second version of the dialogue, the parent often uses the action *scold*. The response of the child who feels cornered is screaming and wailing. As a result, no one wins. For both this situation is not favorable.

Dialogue 3

Player	Utterance	Locution	Locution's name
P:	*Dinner is ready. Come and get it.*	*claim* α_1	a_1
C:	*This is dinner? It isn't ready.*	*claim* $\neg\alpha_1$	a_2
P:	*Why isn't it ready?*	*why* $\neg\alpha_1$	a_3
C:	*Oh, these are whole pieces of food that you've just cooked*	$\neg\alpha_1$ *since* $\{\alpha_2\}$	a_4
P:	*I see that you don't like turkey.*	*claim* α_{19}	a_{31}
C:	*Exactly!*	*nod* α_{19}	a_{32}
P:	*I understand, but you can eat it or go to sleep hungry*	*claim* α_{20}	a_{33}
C:	*No, I'll just eat potato chips!*	$\neg\alpha_{20}$ *since* $\{\alpha_{17}\}$	a_{34}
P:	*You can't. We don't have any.*	$\neg\alpha_{17}$ *since* $\{\alpha_{21}\}$	a_{35}
C:	*OK, I'll eat this meat if I have to.*	*concede* α_1	a_{36}

In the last version, the parent shows interest, understanding and acceptance of the child's emotions. Simultaneously, he is consistent and gives the child a choice. The child agrees to eat dinner, though he prefers something else. The parent's goal is reached. The child doesn't protest, because his need for acceptance is satisfied.

The above dialogues can be played in a single dialogue game. In this game there are two players P and C. They perform alternate actions. There are 36 actions, $Act = \{a_1, \ldots, a_{36}\}$. Each action consists of locution and its content. The used speech acts are: *claim, why, since, concede, question, scold, retract, nod*. There are 21 applied contents, $S_0 = \{\alpha_1, \ldots, \alpha_{21}\}$, of the form '*Dinner is ready. Come and get it.*', '*This is dinner? It isn't ready.*', '*Why isn't it ready?*', '*Oh, these are whole pieces of food that you've just. . . cooked.*', etc.

3   A Game-Theoretic Model

In this section the model of a parent-child game is described in the game-theoretic terminology. The model is a dialogue game formalizing persuasive dialogue with elements of argumentation. When defining the model we use the following standard notation. Given a set Σ, the set of all finite sequences over Σ is denoted by Σ^* and the set of all infinite sequence over Σ is denoted by Σ^ω. The empty sequence is denoted by ε and the operation of concatenation is denoted by $\cdot$. Given sets A, B, $C \subseteq A$, $D \subseteq B$, and a function $f : A \to B$, we use $\overrightarrow{f}(C)$, to denote the image of C, and $\overrightarrow{f}^{-1}(D)$ to denote the inverse image of D. Before we define the game, we need to define the following parameters of the game: the set of statements, and the set of locutions.

Let S_0 be a non-empty and countable set called the *set of atomic statements*. The *set of statements, $FORM[S_0]$*, is a minimal set such that:

- $S_0 \subseteq FORM[S_0]$.
- If $s \in FORM[S_0]$, then $\neg s \in FORM[S_0]$. (Negation)
- If $T \subseteq FORM[S_0]$, then $\bigwedge T \in FORM[S_0]$. (Conjunction)
- If $T \subseteq FORM[S_0]$, then $\bigvee T \in FORM[S_0]$. (Alternative)
- If $s, t \in FORM[S_0]$, then $s \to t \in FORM[S_0]$. (Conditional)

The *set of locutions, $L[S_0]$*, is then defined as follows:

$$L[S_0] = \{\varepsilon\} \cup \{claim\ \varphi : \varphi \in FORM[S_0]\} \cup \{concede\ \varphi : \varphi \in FORM[S_0]\} \cup$$

$$\{why\ \varphi : \varphi \in FORM[S_0]\} \cup \{scold\ \varphi : \varphi \in FORM[S_0]\} \cup \{nod\ \varphi : \varphi \in FORM[S_0]\} \cup$$

$$\{\varphi\ since\ \{\psi_1, \ldots, \psi_n\} : \varphi, \psi_1, \ldots, \psi_n \in FORM[S_0]\} \cup \{retract\ \varphi : \varphi \in FORM[S_0]\} \cup$$

$$\{question\ \varphi : \varphi \in FORM[S_0]\}.$$

All the expression from the set $FORM[S_0]$, which have been spoken are treated as public declarations of players and are called *commitments*. The commitments of player i are stored in the *commitment set C_i*. This set changes during the course of the dialogue.

A key element of an effective strategy is to influence the change of the opponent's emotions. There are five emotions considered in this dialogue system: *fear*, *disgust, joy, sadness*, and *anger*. These emotions are recognized by Ekman [10] as emotions which are universal despite the cultural context. They are universal for all human beings and are experienced and recognized in the same way all around the world. Other emotions are mixed and built from those basic emotions.

The strength (intensity) of emotions is represented by natural numbers from the set $\{1, 2, \ldots, 10\}$. Thus, the emotion vector E_i is a 5-tuple consisting of five values which refer to *fear, disgust, joy, sadness*, and *anger*, respectively. The change in the intensity of the emotions is dependent on the type of the performed locution as well as on its content.

Given a set of atomic statements, S_0, the *parent-child persuasive game* is a tuple

$$\Gamma_{[S_0]} = \langle Pl, \pi, H, T, (\precsim_i)_{i \in Pl}, (A_i)_{i \in Pl}, (AAF_i)_{i \in Pl}, (C_i)_{i \in Pl}, (E_i)_{i \in Pl}, (Init_i)_{i \in Pl} \rangle$$

where

- $Pl = \{P, C\}$ is the set of players.
- $H \subseteq L[S_0]^* \cup L[S_0]^\omega$ is the *set of histories*. A history is a (finite or infinite) sequence of locutions from $L[S_0]$. The set of finite histories in H is denoted by $\bar{H}$.
- $\pi : \bar{H} \to Pl \cup \{\varnothing\}$ is the *player function* assigning to each finite history the player who moves after it, or $\varnothing$, if no player is to move. The set of histories at which player $i \in Pl$ is to move is $H_i = \overrightarrow{\pi}^{-1}(i)$.
- $T = \overrightarrow{\pi}^{-1}(\varnothing) \cup (H \cap L[S_0]^\omega)$ is the set of *terminal histories*. A terminal history is a history after which no player is to move, hence it consists of the set of finite histories mapped to $\varnothing$ by the player function and the set of all infinite histories.
- $\precsim_i \subseteq T \times T$ is the *preference relation* of player i defined on the set of terminal histories. The preference relation is a total preorder, i.e. it is total and transitive.
- $A_i = L[S_0]$ is the *set of actions* of player $i \in Pl$.
- $AAF_i : H_i \to 2^{A_i}$ is the *admissible actions function* of player $i \in Pl$, determining the set of actions that i can choose from after history $h \in H_i$.
- $C_i : L[S_0]^* \to 2^{FORM[S_0]}$ is the *commitment set function* of player $i \in Pl$, designating the change of commitments.
- $E_i : L[S_0]^* \to Emotion_i$ is the *emotion intensity function* of player $i \in Pl$, designating the change of emotions where $Emotion_i$ is the set of possible emotional states of i.
- $Init_i$ determines the initial attributes of player i and consists of the set of initial commitments IC_i and the initial state of emotions IE_i.

In what follows we will assume that the set of atomic statements S_0 is fixed and omit it, writing $FORM$ rather than $FORM[S_0]$ and L rather than $L[S_0]$. We start by defining the properties of the player function. In the case of parent-child persuasive dialogue system, $\pi(h) \in \{P, \varnothing\}$ if $|h|$ is odd and $\pi(h) \in \{C, \varnothing\}$ if $|h|$ is even.

Having defined the sets of actions for the players and the player function, we move on to define the admissible actions functions of the players. The functions are determined by the rules of dialogue. In the case of parent-child dialogue system, the rules of dialogue are defined using the notion of players' commitment sets and emotion levels.

The *commitment set function* of player i is a function

$$C_i : L^* \to 2^{FORM},$$

assigning to each finite sequence of locutions $h \in L^*$ the *commitment set* $C_i(h)$ of i at h. The commitment set function of $i \in Pl$ is defined inductively as follows.

CR_0 $C_i(\varepsilon) = IC_i$.
CR_1 If $h \in L^*$, $\varphi \in FORM$ and $i = \pi(h)$, then

$$C_i(h \cdot a) = C_i(h) \text{ for } a \in \{why\ \varphi, question\ \varphi\}.$$

CR_2 If $h \in L^*$, $\varphi \in FORM$ and $i = \pi(h)$, then

$$C_i(h \cdot a) = C_i(h) \cup \{\varphi\} \text{ for } a \in \{claim\ \varphi,\ scold\ \varphi,\ concede\ \varphi, nod\ \varphi\}.$$

CR_3 If $h \in L^*$, $\varphi, \psi_1, \ldots, \psi_n \in FORM$ and $i = \pi(h)$, then

$$C_i(h \cdot a) = C_i(h) \cup \{\varphi, \psi_1, \ldots, \psi_n\} \text{ for } a \in \{\varphi\ since\{\psi_1, \ldots, \psi_n\}\}.$$

CR_4 If $h \in L^*$, $\varphi \in FORM$ and $i = \pi(h)$, then

$$C_i(h \cdot a) = C_i(h) \setminus \{\varphi\} \text{ for } a \in \{retract\ \varphi\}.$$

The *emotion intensity function* of player i is a function

$$E_i : L^* \to Emotion_i,$$

assigning to each finite sequence of locutions $h \in L^*$ the *emotion vector* $E_i(h)$ of i at h. The set $Emotion_i$ consists of all possible 5-tuples for levels of emotions, i.e.,

$$Emotion_i = \{(n_1, \ldots, n_5) : n_k \in \{1, \ldots, 10\} \wedge k \in \{1, \ldots, 5\}\}.$$

The emotion intensity function of $i \in Pl$ determines the change of intensity of emotions and is defined inductively as follows.

ER_0 $E_i(\varepsilon) = IE_i$.
ER_1 If $h \in L^*$, $a \in L$ and $j = \pi(h)$, then

$$E_i(h \cdot a) = EMOT_i(E_i(h), j, a),$$

where $EMOT_i : Emotion_i \times Pl \times L \to Emotion_i$ is a function which shows how emotions of player i can change if player j performs action a after the history h. This function is defined for each specific application and depends on player's profile and character.

The admissible actions function AAF_i of player $i \in Pl$ is defined below, where, for $i \in Pl$, $-i \in Pl\backslash\{i\}$ denotes the opponent for i. Given $h \in H_i$, $AAF_i(h)$ is a maximal set of locutions satisfying the following:

R_0 $AAF_i(\varepsilon) = InitActions$,

where $InitActions$ are locutions that can begin a dialogue. It is mostly a collection of actions of the type $claim, question, since$. Therefore $InitActions \subseteq \{claim\ \varphi, question\ \varphi, \varphi\ since\ \{\psi_1,\dots,\psi_n\} : \varphi, \psi_1, \dots, \psi_n \in FORM\}$.

R_1 If $h = h' \cdot claim\ \varphi$, $i \in \pi(h)$, $\psi \notin C_i(h)$ then

$$AAF_i(h) = \{why\ \varphi, concede\ \varphi, claim\ \psi, \neg\varphi\ since\ \{\psi_1, \dots, \psi_n\}\}$$

for some $\psi, \psi_1, \dots, \psi_n \in FORM$. Moreover, the set is extended to the following actions, if the following conditions are met:
- if $E_i(h)[k] > 5$ for $k \in \{1, 5\}$, then $scold\ \psi \in AAF_i(h)$ for some $\psi \in FORM$,
- if $E_i(h)[k] < 5$ for $k \in \{2, 3, 4\}$, then $nod\ \psi \in AAF_i(h)$ for some $\psi \in FORM$.

R_2 If $h = h' \cdot scold\ \varphi$, $i \in \pi(h)$, $\psi \notin C_i(h)$, then

$$AAF_i(h) = \{why\ \varphi, concede\ \varphi, claim\ \psi, scold\ \psi,\ \neg\varphi\ since\ \{\psi_1, \dots, \psi_n\}\}$$

for some $\psi, \psi_1, \dots, \psi_n \in FORM$.

R_3 If $h = h' \cdot \varphi\ since\ \{\psi_1, \dots, \psi_n\}$, $i \in \pi(h)$, $\psi \notin C_i(h)$ then

$$AAF_i(h) = \{why\ \varphi, concede\ \varphi, claim\ \psi,\ \neg\varphi\ since\ \{\psi_1, \dots, \psi_n\}\}$$

for some $\psi, \psi_1, \dots, \psi_n \in FORM$. Moreover, the set is extended to the following actions, if the following conditions are met:
- if $E_i(h)[k] > 5$ for $k \in \{1, 5\}$, then $scold\ \psi \in AAF_i(h)$ for some $\psi \in FORM$,
- if $E_i(h)[k] < 5$ for $k \in \{2, 3, 4\}$, then $nod\ \psi \in AAF_i(h)$ for some $\psi \in FORM$,
- if $\psi \in C_{-i}(h)$ and $E_i(h)[k] > 5$ for $k \in \{1, 5\}$, then $concede\ \psi \in AAF_i(h)$ for some $\psi \in FORM$.

R_4 If $h = h' \cdot why\ \varphi$, $i \in \pi(h)$, then

$$AAF_i(h) = \{retract\ \varphi, \varphi\ since\ \{\psi_1, \dots, \psi_n\}\}$$

for some $\psi, \psi_1, \dots, \psi_n \in FORM$.

R_5 If $h = h' \cdot question\ \varphi$, $i \in \pi(h)$, then

$$AAF_i(h) = \{retract\ \varphi,\ claim\ \varphi,\ claim\ \neg\varphi\}.$$

R_6 If $h = h' \cdot a$, $a \in \{concede\ \varphi,\ nod\ \varphi,\ retract\ \varphi\}$, $i \in \pi(h)$, $\psi \notin C_i(h)$, then

$$AAF_i(h) = \{claim\ \psi,\ nod\ \psi,\ scold\ \psi,\ \psi\ since\ \{\psi_1, \dots, \psi_n\}\}$$

for some $\psi, \psi_1, \dots, \psi_n \in FORM$.

The set of histories, H, is the maximal set of sequences from $L^* \cup L^\omega$ satisfying the following:

- $\varepsilon \in H$.
- For any $h_1 \cdot h_2 \in H$ with $h_1 \in L^*$ and $h_2 \in L^* \cup L^\omega$, $h_1 \in H$.
- For any $h_1 \cdot s \cdot h_2 \in H$ with $h_1 \in L^*$, $h_2 \in L^* \cup L^\omega$ and $s \in L$, $s \in AAF_{\pi(h_1)}(h_1)$.

The last two elements of the game are player preferences and the termination rules that describe which finite histories are mapped to $\varnothing$. The definition of termination rules and preferences on terminal histories depend on the type of dialogue the system is applied to and also some other application-dependent considerations (some players could prefer histories which are shorter, as long as they attain their objectives in the end). The parent-child dialogue system is a pure persuasion system [32]. Therefore, the game should end if one of the following happens: (i) The commitment sets of both players contain some expression t which is the agreement of both players that, for example, the child is ready to eat the dinner, or (ii) neither player's commitment set contains the expression t.

Although the purpose of the parent is to influence on behavior of the child, this may not be the result of intimidation. A wise parent tries to explain or justify their decisions. However, the use of violence, even verbal is unacceptable. The parent's victory also means that the child is not scared or upset. Therefore, the level of child's emotions like fear, sadness, and anger may not exceed the value 5. Likewise, it can be concluded that the child is successful when the parent interrupts convincing, but does not do it with anger and aggression.

Formally, this amounts to a definition of finite terminal histories, which are defined as follows. A finite history $h \in \bar{H}$ is terminal, i.e. $\pi(h) = \varnothing$, if one of the following conditions is satisfied:

$$T_{\text{Parent}} : E_C(h)[k] \leq 5 \text{ for } k \in \{1,4,5\} \text{ and } t \in C_P(h) \cap C_C(h),$$
$$T_{\text{Child}} : E_P(h)[k] \leq 5 \text{ for } k \in \{1,4,5\} \text{ and } t \notin C_P(h) \cup C_C(h).$$

Note that, since in the parent-child system the set of admissible actions at each non-terminal history is non-empty, a finite history can be terminal only if one of the above conditions is satisfied.

Having defined finite terminal histories we will now define the preferences of the players. Let H_P^{win} denote the set of finite histories for which condition T_{Parent} is satisfied and let H_C^{win} denote the set of finite histories for which condition T_{Child} is satisfied. Set H_P^{win} contains the terminal histories at which player P, the proponent, is the winner, and set H_C^{win} contains the terminal histories at which player P, the opponent, is the winner.

We assume the following preference relation on terminal histories. Given $h_1, h_2 \in T$,

$$h_1 \precsim_P h_2 \text{ if } h_2 \in H_P^{\text{win}} \text{ or } h_2 \notin H_C^{\text{win}} \text{ and } h_1 \in H_C^{\text{win}} \text{ or}$$

$$h_1, h_2 \notin H_P^{\text{win}} \cup H_C^{\text{win}} \text{ and } E_C(h_1)[k] < E_C(h_2)[k] \text{ for at least one } k \in \{1,4,5\} \text{ and}$$

$$h_1 \precsim_C h_2 \text{ if } h_2 \in H_C^{\text{win}} \text{ or } h_2 \notin H_P^{\text{win}} \text{ and } h_1 \in H_P^{\text{win}} \text{ or}$$

$$h_1, h_2 \notin H_P^{\text{win}} \cup H_C^{\text{win}} \text{ and } E_P(h_1)[k] < E_P(h_2)[k] \text{ for at least one } k \in \{1,4,5\}.$$

In other words, each player prefers a terminal history at which he wins to that at which he does not win, and each player prefers a history at which the opponent does not win to one at which the opponent wins. Moreover, both players prefer histories after which the interlocutor is not scared, sad or angry, i.e. the levels of this emotions are as low as possible.

4   Player's Persuasive Strategy

A *strategy* of a player i is a function from player i's histories to the set of actions $S_i : H_i \rightarrow L$, such that for all $h \in H_i$, $S_i(h) \in AAF_i(h)$. Thus a strategy is a contingent plan that determines a player's move at each of his histories. The set of strategies of player i is denoted by $\mathbf{S}_i$. A *strategy profile* $\bar{S} = (S_i, S_{-i})$ is a pair of strategies chosen by each of the players, $\bar{S} \in \mathbf{S}_i \times \mathbf{S}_{-i}$. Every strategy profile $\bar{S} = (S_i, S_{-i})$ determines a unique terminal history $h_{\bar{S}}$ such that for each strategy $s \in \mathbf{S}_i \cup \mathbf{S}_{-i}$, finite history $h' \in \bar{H}$ and history $h'' \in H$ with $h_{\bar{S}} = h' \cdot a \cdot h''$, $a = S_{\pi(h')}(h')$. Player $i \in P$ prefers strategy profile $\bar{S}$ to strategy profile $\bar{S}'$, $\bar{S}' \precsim_i \bar{S}$, if $h_{\bar{S}'} \precsim_i h_{\bar{S}}$. Solution concepts define sets of strategy profiles which represent stable outcomes of the game. Below we define two basic solution concepts and illustrate them in the context of pure persuasion.

A strategy S_i is *dominant* for player i if for all $S_i' \in \mathbf{S}_i$ and all $S_j \in \mathbf{S}_j$ with $j = -i$,

$$(S_i', S_j) \precsim_i (S_i, S_j).$$

A strategy is *strictly dominant* if the property above holds with strict inequality. A strategy profile $\bar{S} = (S_i, S_{-i})$ is a *solution in (strictly) dominant strategies* iff S_i is dominant for player i and S_{-i} is dominant for player $-i$. The solution in strictly dominant strategies, if it exists, is unique.

A strategy profile $\bar{S} = (S_i, S_{-i})$ is a *Nash equilibrium* if for all $i \in P$ and for all $S_i' \in \mathbf{S}_i$,

$$(S_i', S_{-i}) \precsim_i (S_i, S_{-i}).$$

Note that if the game has a solution in dominant strategies, then it also has a Nash equilibrium (but the reverse is not necessarily true).

Consider a parent-child game $\Gamma_{[S_0]}$ defined for the set of atomic statements $S_0 = \{\alpha_1, \dots, \alpha_{21}\}$ such as in Sect. 2. The initial attributes of players are defined below. The sets of initial commitments are $IC_P = C_P(\emptyset) = \emptyset$, $IC_C = C_C(\emptyset) = \emptyset$. The vectors of initial emotions which determine intensity of fear, disgust, joy, sadness, and anger are $IE_P = E_P(\emptyset) = (1, 2, 7, 2, 3)$, $IE_C = E_C(\emptyset) = (3, 4, 6, 3, 4)$. The initial action is only one $InitActions = \{a_1\} = \{claim(\alpha_1)\}$. Other actions $Act = L[S_0] = \{a_2, \dots, a_{36}\}$ are described is Sect. 2. The admissible action functions for players given in Sect. 3 define very liberal dialogue system. Let us limit them here to the following:

$$AAF_P(h' \cdot a_i) = \begin{cases} \{a_5, a_{26}, a_{31}\} & if \ i = 4 \\ a_{i+1} & otherwise, \end{cases}$$

$$AAF_C(h' \cdot a_i) = a_{i+1} \text{ for any history } h' \cdot a_i \in H_C.$$

Table 1. Player's emotions during the dialogue 1.

Dialogue 1 (history h^1)

$EMOT_P$ (F,D,J,S,A)	action	$EMOT_C$ (F,D,J,S,A)	$EMOT_P$ (F,D,J,S,A)	action	$EMOT_C$ (F,D,J,S,A)
(1,2,7,2,3)	a_1	(3,4,6,3,4)	(3,6,4,5,8)	a_{14}	(4,9,5,5,6)
(1,2,7,2,3)	a_2	(3,4,7,3,4)	(3,6,4,5,9)	a_{15}	(4,9,4,6,6)
(1,3,6,2,4)	a_3	(3,8,6,3,5)	(3,6,3,5,9)	a_{16}	(5,9,4,6,7)
(1,3,6,2,4)	a_4	(3,8,6,4,5)	(3,6,2,5,9)	a_{17}	(5,9,4,6,7)
(1,4,5,3,5)	a_5	(3,8,6,4,6)	(3,6,3,5,9)	a_{18}	(6,9,4,6,7)
(1,4,5,3,5)	a_6	(3,9,6,4,6)	(3,7,3,6,9)	a_{19}	(6,9,4,6,7)
(1,4,4,3,5)	a_7	(3,9,6,4,6)	(3,7,3,5,9)	a_{20}	(6,9,4,6,7)
(1,4,4,4,5)	a_8	(3,9,6,4,6)	(3,7,2,5,10)	a_{21}	(7,9,3,6,8)
(1,4,4,4,6)	a_9	(4,9,5,4,7)	(4,6,2,6,9)	a_{22}	(6,9,3,6,7)
(1,4,4,4,7)	a_{10}	(3,9,5,4,6)	(4,6,2,6,9)	a_{23}	(6,9,3,6,7)
(2,4,4,4,7)	a_{11}	(3,9,5,4,6)	(4,6,2,6,9)	a_{24}	(5,8,4,5,7)
(2,5,4,5,7)	a_{12}	(4,9,5,5,6)	(4,6,3,6,7)	a_{25}	(6,9,3,6,7)
(2,5,4,5,8)	a_{13}	(4,9,5,5,6)	(4,6,3,7,7)		**(4,5,6,5,6)**

Therefore, only three histories are legal:

$$h^1 = (a_1, a_2, a_3, a_4, a_5, \ldots, a_{25}),$$
$$h^2 = (a_1, a_2, a_3, a_4, a_{26}, a_{27}, \ldots, a_{30}),$$
$$h^3 = (a_1, a_2, a_3, a_4, a_{31}, a_{32}, \ldots, a_{36}).$$

They are presented in Sect. 2. According to them players have the following strategies. The parent has 3 strategies:

$S_P^1(h' \cdot a_4) = a_5$ and $S_P^1(h' \cdot a_i) = a_{i+1}$ for any history h' and $i = \{2, 6, 8, 10, \ldots, 24\}$.

$S_P^2(h' \cdot a_4) = a_{26}$ and $S_P^2(h' \cdot a_i) = a_{i+1}$ for any history h' and $i = \{2, 27, 29\}$.

$S_P^3(h' \cdot a_4) = a_{31}$ and $S_P^3(h' \cdot a_i) = a_{i+1}$ for any history h' and $i = \{2, 32, 34\}$.

The child has one strategy:

$S_C^1(h' \cdot a_i) = a_{i+1}$ for any history h' and $i = \{1, 3, \ldots, 23, 26, 28, 31, 33, 35\}$.

Assume that the commitment set function, players' preferences and finite terminal histories are as defined in Sect. 3. The $EMOT_p$ and $EMOT_C$ functions are determined by Tables 1 and 2 where the change of players' emotions in the course of the dialogue is described. The first action is performed by the parent. Next, players make their moves alternately.

Note that after the history h^3, the commitment sets of both players contain α_1:

$$\alpha_1 \in C_P(h^3) \cap C_C(h^3).$$

The parent claims α_1 at the first move and the child concedes it in the last move. Furthermore, the levels of child's fear, sadness, and anger are lower then 5 (see Table 2):

$$E_C(h^3)[1] = 2, E_C(h^3)[4] = 4, E_C(h^3)[5] = 4.$$

Table 2. Player's emotions during the dialogues 2 and 3.

Dialogue 2 (history h^2)

$EMOT_P$ (F,D,J,S,A)	action	$EMOT_C$ (F,D,J,S,A)
(1,2,7,2,3)	a_1	(3,4,6,3,4)
(1,2,7,2,3)	a_2	(3,4,7,3,4)
(1,3,6,2,4)	a_3	(3,8,6,3,5)
(1,3,6,2,4)	a_4	(3,8,6,4,5)
(1,4,5,3,5)	a_{26}	(3,8,6,4,6)
(1,4,5,3,5)	a_{27}	(3,9,5,4,7)
(1,4,4,3,6)	a_{28}	(3,9,5,4,7)
(1,4,4,3,7)	a_{29}	(4,9,4,4,8)
(1,4,3,4,8)	a_{30}	(5,9,3,5,8)
(1,4,3,4,9)		(**6,9,3,6,9**)

Dialogue 3 (history h^3)

$EMOT_P$ (F,D,J,S,A)	action	$EMOT_C$ (F,D,J,S,A)
(1,2,7,2,3)	a_1	(3,4,6,3,4)
(1,2,7,2,3)	a_2	(3,4,7,3,4)
(1,3,6,2,4)	a_3	(3,8,6,3,5)
(1,3,6,2,4)	a_4	(3,8,6,4,5)
(1,4,5,3,5)	a_{31}	(3,8,6,4,6)
(1,4,5,3,5)	a_{32}	(3,7,6,4,5)
(1,3,6,2,4)	a_{33}	(3,7,6,4,5)
(1,3,5,2,4)	a_{34}	(3,6,6,4,5)
(1,3,5,2,4)	a_{35}	(3,6,8,3,5)
(1,3,5,2,4)	a_{36}	(3,6,5,4,4)
(1,3,9,2,2)		(**2,5,5,4,4**)

Whereas, after the histories h^1 and h^2, α_1 is only in the commitment set of the parent:

$$\alpha_1 \in C_P(h^i) \text{ and } \alpha_1 \notin C_C(h^i) \text{ for } i = 1, 2$$

and most of levels of child's fear, sadness, and anger are greater than 5:

$$E_C(h^1)[1] = 4, E_C(h^1)[4] = 5, E_C(h^1)[5] = 6,$$
$$E_C(h^2)[1] = 6, E_C(h^2)[4] = 6, E_C(h^2)[5] = 9.$$

Comparing these levels, we find that the history 2 leads to a state in which the child is more frightened and upset than after the history 1. However, the parent prefers situations in which the child is happy than situations where he is sad and scared.

Thus, for the strategy S_P^3, the outcome most preferred by player P is obtained. Moreover, for any strategy S_C of player C, the outcome of the game from strategy profile (S_P^3, S_C) is the same, i.e., the commitment sets of both players contain α_1. Taking all this into account, we can conclude that strategy 3 is dominant for the parent since

$$(S_P^2, S_C^1) \precsim_P (S_P^1, S_C^1) \precsim_P (S_P^3, S_C^1)$$

and at the same time the strategy profile (S_P^3, S_C^1) is a Nash equilibrium of the game and leads to an outcome whereby the parent wins. This means that the parent should choose the strategy S_P^3 to be successful.

The aim of the above example is to show the idea of the presented formal model and its analysis. The functions $EMOT$ and AAF for real scenarios which we want to study are much more complex and will be the subject of future research. All aspects related to the change of emotions are consulted with a group of psychologists who specialize in this subject.

5   Conclusion

Designing conversational agents is one of the strongest trends in artificial intelligence. The paradigm of multi-agent systems as well as methods and techniques commonly used for construction and analysis of these systems can be successfully used to construct a computer program that simulates human conversation. More and more chatbots are engineered. They represent online stores, City offices, insurance companies, telecommunications companies, etc. Problems associated with speech recognition, speech synthesis, text recognition, text synthesis are very excited but many of them still remains a challenge.

Learning effective persuasion can also be realized using the conversational platform that provides tools for learning and training rules governing the conversation and looking for optimal or winning strategies. The large database of examples is the excellent background of such a system. In this paper a formal basis for a system which simulates human conversation using text messages was proposed. This is a mathematical model which will be used in implementation of a software tool. Furthermore, the protocols concerning persuasive dialogues will be verified by means of symbolic model checking techniques [25,44]. We plan to apply bounded model checking (BMC) and other techniques used for verification multi-agent systems with knowledge and group strategies [15,31,36]. The mathematical model constitutes a theoretical base for an automatic verification tool. The prototype of this system was presented in [18]. This time the focus was on building and analyzing strategies. Therefore our approach combines argumentation theory, the paradigm of multi-agent systems and formal model of emotions. All the above is incorporated into the formalism of dialogue systems described in the game-theory terminology. The goal of our research is to construct a dialogue agent that will support learning how a wise parent should talk to the child.

Acknowledgment. The research by Kacprzak have been carried out within the framework of the work S/W/1/2014 and funded by Ministry of Science and Higher Education.

References

1. Adam, C., Gaudou, B., Herzig, A., Longin, D.: OCC's emotions: a formalization in a BDI logic. In: Euzenat, J., Domingue, J. (eds.) AIMSA 2006. LNCS, vol. 4183, pp. 24–32. Springer, Heidelberg (2006). doi:10.1007/11861461_5
2. Black, E., Hunter, A.: An inquiry dialogue system. Auton. Agent. Multi-Agent Syst. **19**(2), 173–209 (2009)
3. Budzyńska, K., Kacprzak, M., Rembelski, P.: Perseus. Software for analyzing persuasion process. Fundam. Inf. **93**(1–3), 65–79 (2009)
4. Carofiglio, V., De Rosis, F.: In favour of cognitive models of emotions. Virtual Soc. Agents 171 (2005)
5. Castelfranchi, C.: Affective appraisal *versus* cognitive evaluation in social emotions and interactions. In: Paiva, A. (ed.) IWAI 1999. LNCS, vol. 1814, pp. 76–106. Springer, Heidelberg (2000). doi:10.1007/10720296_7

6. Cerutti, F., Tintarev, N., Oren, N.: Formal arguments, preferences, and natural language interfaces to humans: an empirical evaluation. In: ECAI (2014)
7. De Rosis, F., Pelachaud, C., Poggi, I., Carofiglio, V., De Carolis, B.: From Greta's mind to her face: modelling the dynamics of affective states in a conversational embodied agent. Int. J. Hum.-Comput. Stud. **59**(1), 81–118 (2003)
8. Devereux, J., Reed, C.: Strategic argumentation in rigorous persuasion dialogue. In: McBurney, P., Rahwan, I., Parsons, S., Maudet, N. (eds.) ArgMAS 2009. LNCS (LNAI), vol. 6057, pp. 94–113. Springer, Heidelberg (2010). doi:10.1007/978-3-642-12805-9_6
9. Dziubiński, M., Goyal, S.: Network design and defence. Games Econ. Behav. **79**(1), 30–43 (2013)
10. Ekman, P.: An argument for basic emotions. Cognit. Emot. **6**, 169–200 (1992)
11. Emele, D.C., Guerin, F., Norman, T.J., Edwards, P.: A framework for learning argumentation strategies. In: Proceedings of the Third International Workshop on Argumentation in Multi-agent Systems, pp. 151–154 (2006)
12. Hamblin, C.L.: Fallacies. Methuen and Co. Ltd., London (1970)
13. Hussain, A., Toni, F.: Bilateral agent negotiation with information-seeking. In: Proceedings of the 5th European Workshop on Multi-Agent Systems (2007)
14. Jaques, P.A., Viccari, R.M.: A BDI approach to infer student's emotions. In: Lemaître, C., Reyes, C.A., Gonsálon, J.A. (eds.) IBERAMIA 2004. LNCS, vol. 3315, pp. 901–911. Springer, Heidelberg (2004). doi:10.1007/978-3-540-30498-2_90
15. Jones, A.V., Lomuscio, A.: Distributed BDD-based BMC for the verification of multi-agent systems. In: van der Hoek, W., Kaminka, G.A., Lespérance, Y., Luck, M., Sen, S. (eds.), 9th International Conference on Autonomous Agents and Multiagent Systems (AAMAS 2010), Toronto, Canada, May 10–14, 2010, vol. 1–3, pp. 675–682. IFAAMAS (2010)
16. Kacprzak, M., Budzynska, K.: Reasoning about dialogical strategies. In: Graña, M., Toro, C., Howlett, R.J., Jain, L.C. (eds.) KES 2012. LNCS (LNAI), vol. 7828, pp. 171–184. Springer, Heidelberg (2013). doi:10.1007/978-3-642-37343-5_18
17. Kacprzak, M., Dziubinski, M., Budzynska, K.: Strategies in dialogues: a game-theoretic approach. In: Parsons, S., Oren, N., Reed, C., Cerutti, F. (eds.) Computational Models of Argument - Proceedings of COMMA 2014, Atholl Palace Hotel, Scottish Highlands, UK, September 9–12, 2014, Frontiers in Artificial Intelligence and Applications, vol. 266, pp. 333–344. IOS Press (2014)
18. Kacprzak, M., Rzenca, K., Sawicka, A.Z.A., Zukowska, K.: A formal model of an argumentative dialogue in the management of emotions. In: Poznan Reasoning Week, L&C 2016/14th ArgDiap/QuestPro 2016 Abstracts (2016)
19. Kacprzak, M., Sawicka, A.: Identification of formal fallacies in a natural dialogue. Fundam. Inform. **135**(4), 403–417 (2014)
20. Kacprzak, M., Sawicka, A., Zbrzezny, A.: Dialogue systems: modeling and prediction of their dynamics. In: Abraham, A., Wegrzyn-Wolska, K., Hassanien, A.E., Snasel, V., Alimi, A.M. (eds.) Proceedings of the Second International Afro-European Conference for Industrial Advancement AECIA 2015. AISC, vol. 427, pp. 421–431. Springer, Cham (2016). doi:10.1007/978-3-319-29504-6_40
21. Kacprzak, M., Sawicka, A., Zbrzezny, A.: Towards verification of dialogue protocols: a mathematical model. LNAI **9693**, 329–339 (2016)
22. Kacprzak, M., Yaskorska, O.: Dialogue protocols for formal fallacies. Argumentation **28**(3), 349–369 (2014)

23. Matt, P.-A., Toni, F.: A game-theoretic measure of argument strength for abstract argumentation. In: Hölldobler, S., Lutz, C., Wansing, H. (eds.) JELIA 2008. LNCS (LNAI), vol. 5293, pp. 285–297. Springer, Heidelberg (2008). doi:10.1007/978-3-540-87803-2_24

24. McBurney, P., Parsons, S.: Dialogue games for agent argumentation. In: Simari, G., Rahwan, I. (eds.) Argumentation in Artificial Intelligence, pp. 261–280. Springer US, New york (2009). doi:10.1007/978-0-387-98197-0_13

25. Meski, A., Penczek, W., Szreter, M., Wozna-Szczesniak, B., Zbrzezny, A.: BDD-versus SAT-based bounded model checking for the existential fragment of linear temporal logic with knowledge: algorithms and their performance. Auton. Agents Multi-agent Syst. **28**(4), 558–604 (2014)

26. Meyer, J.-J.C.: Reasoning about emotional agents. In: Proceedings of the 16th European Conference on Artificial Intelligence, pp. 129–133. IOS Press (2004)

27. Nawwab, F.S., Dunne, P.E., Bench-Capon, T.: Exploring the role of emotions in rational decision making. In: Proceedings of COMMA (2010)

28. Oatley, K.: Best Laid Schemes: The Psychology of the Emotions. Cambridge University Press, Cambridge (1992)

29. Ochs, M., Sadek, D., Pelachaud, C.: A formal model of emotions for an empathic rational dialog agent. Auton. Agents Multi-agent Syst. **24**(3), 410–440 (2012)

30. Ortony, A., Clore, G.L., Collins, A.: The Cognitive Structure of Emotions. Cambridge University Press, United Kingdom (1998)

31. Penczek, W., Lomuscio, A.: Verifying epistemic properties of multi-agent systems via bounded model checking. Fundam. Inform. **55**(2), 167–185 (2003)

32. Prakken, H.: Models of persuasion dialogue. In: Simari, G., Rahwan, I. (eds.) Argumentation in AI, pp. 281–300. Springer US, New York (2009). doi:10.1007/978-0-387-98197-0_14

33. Procaccia, A.D., Rosenschein, J.S.: Extensive-form argumentation games. In: Gleizes, M.P., Kaminka, G.A., Nowé, A., Ossowski, S., Tuyls, K., Verbeeck, K. (eds.) EUMAS, pp. 312–322 (2005)

34. Rahwan, I., Larson, K.: Argumentation and game theory. In: Simari, G., Rahwan, I. (eds.) Argumentation in AI, pp. 321–339. Springer US, New york (2009). doi:10.1007/978-0-387-98197-0_16

35. Rahwan, I., Larson, K., Tohme, F.: A characterisation of strategy-proofness for grounded argumentation semantics. In: Proceedings of the 21st International Joint Conference on Artificial Intelligence (IJCAI) (2009)

36. Raimondi, F., Lomuscio, A.: Automatic verification of multi-agent systems by model checking via ordered binary decision diagrams. J. Appl. Logic **5**(2), 235–251 (2007). (Logic-Based Agent Verification)

37. Riveret, R., Prakken, H., Rotolo, A., Sartor, G.: Heuristics in argumentation: a game theory investigation. In: Besnard, P., Doutre, S., Hunter, A. (eds.) COMMA, Frontiers in Artificial Intelligence and Applications, vol. 172, pp. 324–335. IOS Press (2008)

38. Rosenfeld, A., Kraus, S.: Strategical argumentative agent for human persuasion. In Proceedings of European Conference on Artificial Intelligence (2016)

39. Sawicka, A., Kacprzak, M., Zbrzezny, A.: A novel description language for two-agent dialogue games. In: Proceedings of IJCRS 2017, Olsztyn, Poland, 3–7 July 2017 (This issue)

40. Scherer, K.R., Schorr, A., Johnstone, T.: Appraisal Processes in Emotion: Theory, Methods, Research. Oxford University Press, Oxford (2001)

41. Silveira, R., da Silva Bitencourt, G.K., Gelaim, T., Marchi, J., de la Prieta, F.: Towards a model of open and reliable cognitive multiagent systems: dealing with trust and emotions. ADCAIJ: Adv. Distrib. Comput. Artif. Intell. J. 4(3) (2016)

42. Walton, D.N.: Logical Dialogue-Games and Fallacies. University Press of America, Lanham (1984)

43. Yuan, T., Moore, D., Grierson, A.: A conversational agent system as a test-bed to study the philosophical model DC. In: Proceedings of CMNA 2003 (2003)

44. Zbrzezny, A.M., Woźna-Szcześniak, B., Zbrzezny, A.: SMT-based bounded model checking for weighted epistemic ECTL. In: Pereira, F., Machado, P., Costa, E., Cardoso, A. (eds.) EPIA 2015. LNCS (LNAI), vol. 9273, pp. 651–657. Springer, Cham (2015). doi:10.1007/978-3-319-23485-4_65

An Approach for Hospital Planning with Multi-Agent Organizations

John Bruntse Larsen and Jørgen Villadsen[✉]

DTU Compute, Technical University of Denmark,
2800 Kongens Lyngby, Denmark
{jobla,jovi}@dtu.dk

Abstract. The background for this paper is a development that the Danish hospitals are undertaking which requires the establishment of a common emergency department. It is uncertain exactly what and how many resources the department needs and so resources are assigned dynamically as seen necessary by the staff. Such dynamic adjustments pose a challenge in predicting what consequences these adjustments may lead to. We propose an approach to deal with this challenge that applies simulation with intelligent agents and logics for organizational reasoning. We present some of the expected obstacles with this approach and potential ways to overcome them.

Keywords: Multi-agent organizations · Logic · Simulation · Soft computing · Process mining

1 Introduction

One of the fundamental ideas behind multi-agent systems is that agents act autonomously but in practice the agents are often encoded with rules for coordination that limit their ability to do so. A recent approach to address this issue is by *agent organizations* [5]. The agents in an organization are aware of the norms of the organization but may choose to go against rigorous rules decided by the organization.

Our work is motivated by a recent development in how the Danish hospitals manage acute patients. We consider agent based simulation as a tool for forecasting delayed treatments and expected waiting times. We argue that agent organizations are appropriate for simulating human behavior because of the normative aspect: humans generally act according to the norms of the hospital and may act against rigorous rules that have been decided at a top level.

Inspired by the approach for agent simulation of an emergency department by Taboada et al. [10], we propose an approach in which we distinguish between three types of agents in the hospital organization: those are the *active*, the *passive*, and the *external* agents. For modeling the relationship between the agents we use AORTA, a logical framework for agent organizations developed by Jensen et al. [6]. We argue that a formalization of the framework in the proof assistant

© Springer International Publishing AG 2017
L. Polkowski et al. (Eds.): IJCRS 2017, Part II, LNAI 10314, pp. 454–465, 2017.
DOI: 10.1007/978-3-319-60840-2_33

Isabelle/HOL [15,16] can be useful in verifying properties of the framework and potential new extensions that we make during the project.

Finally we propose ideas on using KPIs to measure the 'distance' between the expected global behavior, as expressed in the organization model, and the actual global state as expressed by staff activity logs. The motivation is to automatically extend the organizational model in the simulation from the data that the hospital produces. In this way, the simulation should adjust itself to changes in the behavior of the people at a given hospital and reduce some of the complexity in the initial hand-crafted model.

2   Background

Traditionally, an emergency department takes care of acute patients and acts as an entrance to further treatment in hospital. The acute treatment is taken care of by acute doctors and the further treatment is taken care of by specialists. The Danish hospitals are undergoing a reform in which they establish a common emergency department (FAM, Danish: Fælles AkutModtagelse) where all acute patients can receive treatment from both specialists and acute doctors [1]. The vision is to put the patient in focus and plan the staff for the treatment of the patient. A straightforward way to achieve this vision would be to hire more staff for the FAM but it is not a feasible solution due to the cost and the constrained budget. As a consequence, the FAM draws on staff from the specialized departments that carry out operations, patient status check-ups and other scheduled activities. It also means that the scheduled activities may be delayed because the specialists are called to the FAM for an acute patient or that an acute patient may have to wait for a long time because a specialist is not available. The scenario is illustrated in Fig. 1.

2.1   Agent-Based Simulation

In our work, we will attempt to simulate the consequences of the actions of the agents in the FAM and forecast likely delayed treatments and expected waiting times for the acute patients. Simulation has been found useful for planning physical resources and staff for the FAM as it produces more accurate results than traditional analytic approaches which tend to oversimplify the processes that go on in the department [1,2]. Following the arguments presented at the UK Operational Research Societys Simulation Workshop 2010 [4] and in the work of Zhengchun Liu et al. [3], we believe that agent-based simulation is a promising alternative for simulating a complex system with conflicting goals like the FAM scenario.

2.2   Modeling Human Behavior

In general, hospital regulations describe best practice in an open manner and it is then up to the individual staff members to determine the exact work processes

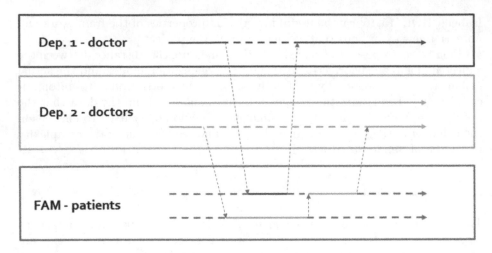

Fig. 1. A case in the FAM scenario. Two doctors from department 1 were called for FAM to assist with two acute patients. As a result, the treatments that they were scheduled for were delayed.

that also fit within the individual hospital. Thus the regulations are not sufficient for making a process model for an emergency department and a process model that is accurate across different hospitals easily grows highly complicated to maintain manually. With the advent of powerful computers that allow analysis on big data, there has been an increasing focus on systems that learn from human behavior, and soft computing systems that are inspired by human behavior. Process mining is an approach for discovering process models, checking conformance of models and extending models for such systems based on event logs generated by an actual organization. In the context of healthcare, process mining has been studied with the purpose of providing insight into the complex system of a hospital that deals with a lot of human behavior and human values. Typically the hospital model is based on a top-down analysis of the processes that result from the interaction between the individuals in the hospital [11–13]. In our approach, we combine a top-down model that describes the organization with a bottom-up model that describes the interaction between individuals. Considering the high amount of uncertainty in the FAM environment that depends on eventualities and causalities, we expect our approach to provide better insight into the processes of the environment than with a pure top-down approach.

3   The Hospital as a Multi-Agent Organization

A multi-agent system is specified at two levels: the agent level and the system level. At agent level, an agent architecture defines the behavior of the agent. At system level, a framework defines the world that the agents are acting within. The framework includes the environment and interaction protocols. Ideally, the agent architectures and the system framework should be loosely coupled such that new agents can enter the system with only local changes to the system, and so that the agents can act independently no matter what architecture they use.

A key challenge in multi-agent systems is to make the agents able to act in a coordinated fashion without limiting their ability to act autonomously. A recent approach to achieve this is by applying frameworks that model the interaction and dependencies between the agents as an organization. In a multi-agent organization, the agent is aware of its role in the organization and the norms for 'common good practice' in the organization. Agents can enter and exit the organization freely, and there is an explicit model of the expected behavior that the agents can choose to go against if deemed necessary [5]. At agent level, the agents distinguish between personal and organizational goals. At system level, there is a framework for defining expected behavior of the agents.

Given the complex flow of information and the independent actors in FAM, we believe that multi-agent organizations can provide insight into the relation between micro-behavior of the agents and the macro-behavior of the system in an agent-based simulation. In this section we propose our approach for modeling the hospital setting as a multi-agent organization. We define three types of agents, and introduce the framework that we later use to model the hospital organization.

3.1 Agent Model

As detailed below, we follow the analysis of Taboada et al. [10] that introduces two distinct types of agents for an emergency department. We have *active* agents that represent individuals and *passive* agents that represent services and other reactive systems. We also introduce a third distinct type of agent for the FAM scenario, the *external agent*, that represent an entire specialized department.

Active Agents. Active agents represent individuals that act on their own initiative toward achieving specific goals. A knee specialist that can diagnose the pains that a patient feels is an example of an active agent. For the active agents, we use a Belief-Desire-Intention (BDI) model that allows us inspect the beliefs that the agent has about its current state, the goals that it would like to achieve and the goal that it is currently working towards achieving. In each step of the simulation, the agent takes an input vector of percepts and messages from other agents, update its beliefs, desires and current goal, and then outputs an action toward achieving its current goal.

Passive Agents. Passive agents represent passive entities that only react to the other agents and they do not work toward achieving a goal on their own. An IT-system that the nurses must register data with is an example of a passive agent. For the passive agents we use a rule-based model, in which the agent has a rule base that maps messages to actions. In each step of the simulation, the agent takes an input vector of messages from other agents, selects a corresponding rule for each message and then outputs the vector of actions for all messages.

External Agents. External agents represent an entity that acts towards achieving vague goals. A specialized department that requests assistant nurses for a scheduled treatment is an example of an external agent. The agent is external from the point of view of the FAM. For the external agents we use a BDI model where the goals and actions are generated from a statistical model that corresponds to the average behavior of the agent. The actions that it outputs are in the form of requests for resources. In each step of the simulation, the agent takes an input vector of messages from other agents, updates its beliefs and goals, generates new goals from the statistical model and then outputs the vector of requests.

3.2   AORTA

We investigate the logical framework AORTA for modeling organization-aware agents as presented in [7,8]. In the framework, the agents are assumed to be BDI-agents that each receives an additional module that allows it to include organizational beliefs and goals in its reasoning. The module defines three phases of organizational reasoning that are used in addition to the reasoning that the agent already uses: the *obligation check*, the *option generation*, and the *action execution*.

Step 1: obligation check. The agent updates the status of its obligation state: it checks if an obligation has been satisfied (objective completed) or violated (deadline reached before objective completed). The agent also checks for new obligations.

Step 2: option generation. The agent generates options for what it can do regarding the organization. It considers these aspects in the option generation: *role enactment*, *role deactment*, *obligations* (obligation state), *delegation* (based on role dependency relations), *information* (exchange).

Step 3: action execution. The agent selects a single action to execute based on rules of the form

$$option : context \rightarrow action$$

By separating the organizational reasoning from the reasoning about the personal goals and beliefs, the agents are able to take into account how they are expected to behave, given the role they enact, while also able to reason about personal goals independently. In this fashion, the model of the organization is distributed among the agents so it is possible that the agents have different models of the organization.

The three steps of organizational reasoning in AORTA are based on an *organizational metamodel* defined by the predicates in Table 1. In a later section, we construct a metamodel that describes a simplified version of the situation in the FAM.

Table 1. Predicates of the AORTA metamodel and their informal meaning.

Predicate	Informal meaning
role($Role, Objs$)	$Role$ is the name of a role and $Objs$ is a set of *main* objectives of that role
obj($Obj, SubObjs$)	Obj is an objective that has $SubObjs$ as a set of sub-objectives
dep($Role_1, Role_2, Obj$)	$Role_1$ depends on $Role_2$ in order to complete Obj
rea($Ag, Role$)	Agent Ag enacts $Role$
cond($Role, Obj, Deadline, Cond$)	When the condition $Cond$ holds, $Role$ is obliged to complete Obj before the objective $Deadline$
obl($Ag, Role, Obj, Deadline$)	Agent Ag is obliged to enact $Role$ to complete Obj before $Deadline$
viol($Ag, Role, Obj$)	Agent Ag enacting $Role$ has violated the obligation to complete Obj

3.3 Formalization of AORTA in Isabelle/HOL

AORTA can be viewed as a large logical framework. A formalization of the most relevant parts of AORTA in a proof assistant like Isabelle/HOL [15,16] will allow us to verify the logical framework and will also be useful for showing properties of the logical framework. As we work with applying the logical framework for organizational reasoning, we may also find that we want to extend the framework with features that are needed or useful for the FAM scenario. For that purpose, the formalization will allow us to extend the framework in a verified manner. Verification of agents using AORTA has been investigated in [9].

4   Modeling a FAM in AORTA

In this section we present our approach to applying the AORTA framework to the FAM scenario. To get started, we make a metamodel of a FAM based on basic assumptions about what processes go on in and around the department with inspiration from the work by Taboada et al. [10] about a conventional emergency department. We will revise this model based on data from interviews and observations from an actual FAM; for this purpose we have a collaboration agreement with the hospitals in the capital area of Denmark.

Based on the descriptions of a FAM in [2] and the scenario described in [10] we assume that the FAM scenario consists of the following stages:

1. *Admission.* Arrival of the patient in the department; check in at reception.
2. *Triage.* A nurse carries out the triage process on the patient.
3. *Diagnosis and Treatment.* A doctor performs a diagnosis and initial treatment on the patient.
4. *Round-up.* The patient receives a plan for further treatment and leaves the department.

Additionally, we assume the following norms in the FAM scenario:

a. Patients arrive in the admission area, either by their own means or by ambulance.
b. Patients must wait in the admission area until they have been attended to by the reception.
c. After the admission, patients must wait in a designated room until called by a triage nurse.
d. The nurse who carries out the triage must fill out a triage form for the patient.
e. After the triage, patients must wait in a designated room until called by a doctor.
f. Patients are involved in making their plan for further treatment.
g. The doctors in the specialized departments take care of scheduled treatments.
h. The initial treatment of patients may require assistance from doctors from specialized departments.

We translate the informal description of the scenario (1–4) and (a–h) into a formal AORTA metamodel as follows. The complete AORTA metamodel is shown in Table 2. This metamodel is the basis for the AORTA module that allows each agent in the simulation to perform organizational reasoning.

4.1 Roles

The roles in the metamodel are defined by the role-predicate. We use roles to formalize what kinds of actors are involved in the scenario and what their main objectives are. Stages 1–4 mention these roles and their objectives: a *patient* that receives treatment, a *receptionist* that admits patients, a *nurse* that carries out triage, and an *acute doctor* that carries out acute treatment and gives the patient a plan for further treatment. For example we formalize the patient role as such:

role(*patient*, {*acute_treatment*(*Patient*), *treatment_plan*(*Patient*, *Plan*)})

Additionally, the norm (g) mentions a *specialized department* that carries out scheduled treatments and *specialized doctors* that work in the department. As mentioned in (h), the doctors are also sometimes needed in the acute department, but we choose to not model it as their main objective.

role(*specialized_doctor*, {*scheduled_treatment*(*Department*, *Patient*)})
role(*specialized_department*, {*scheduled_treatment*(*Department*, *Patient*)})

4.2 Objectives

The objectives in the metamodel are defined by the obj-predicate. We use objectives to formalize what objectives the roles have and what sub-objectives must be solved with each objective. Stages 1–4 mention 4 objectives that are completed in sequence: (1) *admission*, (2) *triage*, (3) *acute treatment*, and (4) *treatment plan*. We define the sequence in AORTA as objectives that depend on the completion of the previous objective: (4) depends on (3), (3) depends on (2), (2) depends on

Table 2. Predicates of the AORTA metamodel for the FAM scenario. The "role" predicate defines the roles and the objective of each role. The "obj" predicate defines sub-objectives of each objective. Notice that the first four "obj" predicates form a sequence of objectives. The "dep" predicate defines which other roles a role depends on in order to complete an objective. The "cond" predicate defines conditional objectives that should be fulfilled before a role completes an objective. For example, the first predicate says that a patient should wait in the admission area until admission no matter if they arrive by themselves or by ambulance. The end of each line shows the part of the informal description the predicate corresponds to (1–4 or a–h).

role($patient$, {$acute\_treatment(Patient)$, $treatment\_plan(Patient, Plan)$})	
role($receptionist$, {$admission(Patient)$})	1
role($nurse$, {$triage(Patient)$})	2
role($acute\_doctor$, {$acute\_treatment(Patient)$, $treatment\_plan(Patient)$})	3, 4
role($specialized\_doctor$, {$scheduled\_treatment(Department, Patient)$})	g
role($specialized\_department$, {$scheduled\_treatment(Department, Patient)$})	g
obj($treatment\_plan(Patient)$, {$acute\_treatment(Patient)$})	4
obj($acute\_treatment(Patient)$, {$triage(Patient)$})	3
obj($triage(Patient)$, {$admission(Patient)$})	2
obj($admission(Patient)$, {})	1
obj($scheduled\_treatment(Department, Patient)$, {})	g
dep($patient$, $receptionist$, $admission(Patient)$)	1
dep($patient$, $nurse$, $triage(Patient)$)	2
dep($patient$, $acute\_doctor$, $acute\_treatment(Patient)$)	3
dep($patient$, $acute\_doctor$, $treatment\_plan(Patient)$)	4
dep($specialized\_department$, $specialized\_doctor$, $scheduled\_treatment(Department, Patient)$)	g
cond($patient$, $wait\_in(Admission\_area)$, $admission(Patient)$, $arrivedBy(Patient, Self) \lor arrivedBy(Patient, Ambulance)$)	a, b
cond($patient$, $wait\_in(Room)$, $triage(Patient)$, $admission(Patient)$)	c
cond($nurse$, $fill\_form(Patient, Nurse)$, $triage(Patient)$, $admission(Patient)$)	d
cond($patient$, $wait\_in(Room)$, $acute\_treatment(Patient)$, $triage(Patient)$)	e
cond($acute\_doctor$, $involve\_patient(Patient, Plan)$, $treatment\_plan(Patient, Plan)$, $acute\_treatment(Patient)$)	f
cond($acute\_doctor$, $specialized\_treatment(Patient, specialized\_doctor)$, $acute\_treatment(Patient)$, $specialistNecessary(Patient, specialized\_doctor)$)	h

(1), and (1) does not depend on any sub-objective so that an acute patient can be admitted at any time. For example we formalize the last step in the sequence as such:

$$obj(treatment\_plan(Patient), \{acute\_treatment(Patient)\})$$

Additionally, the norm (g) mentions that there are also scheduled treatments that should be taken care of but the details about what those treatments involve have been omitted from the description. We model a scheduled treatment as an objective without sub-objectives:

$$\text{obj}(scheduled\_treatment(Department, Patient), \{\})$$

4.3 Dependencies

The dependencies in the metamodel are defined by the dep-predicate. We use dependencies to formalize which roles depend on other roles to complete their objectives. Stage 1 mentions that the *patient* depends on the *receptionist* in order to be *admitted*. Stage 2 mentions that the *patient* depends on the *nurse* in order to receive *triage*. Stages 3–4 mention that the *patient* depends on the *acute doctor* in order to receive *acute treatment* and a *treatment plan*. Finally norm (g) mentions that the *specialized department* depends on *specialized doctors* in order to carry out *scheduled treatments*. For example we formalize the dependency between the patient and the receptionist as such:

$$\text{dep}(patient, receptionist, admission(Patient))$$

4.4 Conditions

The conditions in the metamodel are defined by the cond-predicate. We use conditions to formalize the norms about how the roles are expected to complete their main objectives. Norms (a) and (b) mention that *patients* should *wait in the admission area* until they are *admitted* when they have *arrived by themselves or by ambulance*. We formalize this norm as such:

$$\text{cond}(patient, wait\_in(Admission\_area), admission(Patient),$$
$$arrivedBy(Patient, Self) \lor arrivedBy(Patient, Ambulance))$$

Norm (c) mentions that *patients* should *wait in a room* before *triage* when they have been *admitted*:

$$\text{cond}(patient, wait\_in(Room), triage(Patient), admission(Patient))$$

Norm (d) mentions that *nurses* should *fill in the triage form* before they finish the *triage* when a patient has been *admitted*:

$$\text{cond}(nurse, fill\_form(Patient, Nurse), triage(Patient), admission(Patient))$$

Norm (e) mentions that *patients* should *wait in a room* until they receive *acute treatment* when they have gone through *triage*:

$$\text{cond}(patient, wait\_in(Room), acute\_treatment(Patient), triage(Patient))$$

Norm (f) mentions that *acute doctors* should *involve the patient* when they make the *treatment plan* during the *acute treatment*:

cond(*acute_doctor*, *involve_patient*(*Patient*, *Plan*),

treatment_plan(*Patient*, *Plan*), *acute_treatment*(*Patient*))

Finally norm (h) mentions that *acute doctors* should involve *specialized doctors for specialized treatment* in the *acute treatment* if a *specialist is necessary*:

cond(*acute_doctor*, *specialized_treatment*(*Patient*, *specialized_doctor*),

acute_treatment(*Patient*), *specialistNecessary*(*Patient*, *specialized_doctor*))

On top of using the AORTA metamodel we also will investigate KPIs for measuring the distance between the expected global behavior, as expressed by the organization in the model, and the actual global state as expressed by event logs. The goal of this investigation will be to repair the metamodel based on the event logs with the process mining tool *Prom*. In order to get the event logs for the evaluation, we need to analyze the current systems that they use to register activity and assess that the additional necessary activity can be registered in a feasible manner.

5   Related Work

Making autonomous agents has been a major focus in the academic *Multi-Agent Programming Contest* that has taken place each year since 2005. Each year the contest organizers adjust the contest to further promote solutions that take advantage of distributed decision making and autonomous agents. The winning team from 2016 used the multi-agent programming framework JaCaMo which combines the multi-agent programming frameworks of Jason and Cartago with the multi-agent organization framework of Moise made by Hübner et al. [14]. JaCaMo is based on the A&A approach which distinguishes between two types of entities: agents and artifacts. An agent is a *goal-oriented pro-active* entity where as an artifact is a *non-autonomous function-oriented* entity. The motivation for this approach is inspired by human organizations that are populated by humans who assume roles and are responsible to obligations and permissions of those roles in the organization, and artifacts that have a designated purpose in the organization. Typical examples of such artifacts are whiteboards and telephones that the agents can use to coordinate with, and access cards that enables agents with certain permissions and obligations. In comparison, AORTA does not distinguish artifacts from agents at a fundamental level. They are considered primarily reactive agents and, like in JaCaMo, are designated with certain roles.

In 2009 Mans et al. [11] showed initial work on the feasibility of applying the prominent process mining tool *Prom* in the hospital environment with a focus on discovering a process model. In 2013 Kirchner et al. [12] noted the problem of sparse event logs that are common in the hospital environment which increases the importance of clearly defined clinical pathways in the hospital in order to apply process mining successfully. In the works of [11,12], the models produced and treated with *Prom* were based on highly procedural modeling languages which are difficult to fit across multiple hospitals with different execution paths. In 2015 Rovani et al. [13] proposed an approach that applied the declarative process modeling language *Declare* which is based on linear temporal logic. In this language, the model only specifies constraints within finite traces on the processes rather than concrete execution paths, which enables a Declare model to allow multiple execution paths. They applied a cross validation methodology for automatically creating a repaired model from a manually created model and an event log.

6 Conclusion and Future Work

We have introduced and modeled the new kind of emergency department, FAM, that is being implemented at Danish hospitals, as a multi-agent organization in the agent organization framework AORTA. Our goal with this approach is to use the model for simulating the activity that goes on in the department and calculate consequences based on the predicted behavior of the agents in the simulation. We have shown a model of the FAM in the framework. The model is based on previous work on agent simulation for emergency departments and the official descriptions of the FAM and its purposes.

In future work we will use proof assistants to verify properties of the AORTA framework and implement the AORTA model in an agent simulation framework. That way we may get a model that can adjust itself automatically to the soft aspects of human behavior that influence the activity in an actual department.

Acknowledgements. This work is part of the Industrial PhD project *Hospital Planning with Multi-Agent Goals* between PDC A/S and Technical University of Denmark. We are grateful to Innovation Fund Denmark for funding and the governmental institute Region H, which manages the hospitals in the Danish capital region, for being a collaborator on the project. We would like to thank PDC A/S for providing feedback on the ideas described in this paper. We would also like to thank Virginia Dignum and Anders Schlichtkrull for comments on a draft.

References

1. Pedersen, K.M., Petersen, N.C.: Fremtidens Hospital. Munksgaard, Copenhagen (2014)
2. Hansen-Nord, M., Steensen, J.P., Holm, S.: Process driven patient tracks in FAM. Scand. J. Trauma, Resusc. Emerg. Med. **18**(Suppl. 1), P27 (2010)
3. Liu, Z., Cabrera, E., Rexachs, D., Epelde, F., Luque, E.: Simulation modelling in healthcare: challenges and trends, simulating the micro-level behavior of emergency department for macro-level features prediction. In: Winter Simulation Conference (2015)
4. Siebers, P.O., Macal, C.M., Garnett, J., Buxton, D., Pidd, M.: Discrete-event simulation is dead, long live agent-based simulation!. J. Simul. **4**(3), 204–210 (2010). doi:10.1057/jos.2010.14

5. Weiss, G. (ed.): Multiagent Systems, 2nd edn. MIT Press, Cambridge (2013)
6. Jensen, A.S., Dignum, V., Villadsen, J.: A framework for organization-aware agents. In: Autonomous Agents and Multi-Agent Systems, pp. 1–36 (2016)
7. Jensen, A.S., Dignum, V.: AORTA: adding organizational reasoning to agents. In: International Conference on Autonomous Agents and Multi-Agent Systems, AAMAS, pp. 1493–1494 (2014)
8. Jensen, A.S., Dignum, V., Villadsen, J.: The AORTA architecture: integrating organizational reasoning in *Jason*. In: Dalpiaz, F., Dix, J., Riemsdijk, M.B. (eds.) EMAS 2014. LNCS, vol. 8758, pp. 127–145. Springer, Cham (2014). doi:10.1007/978-3-319-14484-9_7
9. Jensen, A.S.: Model Checking AORTA: Verification of Organization-Aware Agents. CoRR, 1503.05317 (2015)
10. Taboada, M., Cabrera, E., Iglesias, M.L., Epelde, F., Luque, E.: An agent-based decision support system for hospitals emergency. Procedia Comput. Sci. 4, 1870–1879 (2011)
11. Mans, R.S., Schonenberg, M.H., Song, M., Aalst, W.M.P., Bakker, P.J.M.: Application of process mining in healthcare – a case study in a Dutch hospital. In: Fred, A., Filipe, J., Gamboa, H. (eds.) BIOSTEC 2008. CCIS, vol. 25, pp. 425–438. Springer, Heidelberg (2008). doi:10.1007/978-3-540-92219-3_32
12. Kirchner, K., Herzberg, N., Rogge-Solti, A., Weske, M.: Embedding conformance checking in a process intelligence system in hospital environments. In: Lenz, R., Miksch, S., Peleg, M., Reichert, M., Riaño, D., Teije, A. (eds.) KR4HC/ProHealth -2012. LNCS, vol. 7738, pp. 126–139. Springer, Heidelberg (2013). doi:10.1007/978-3-642-36438-9_9
13. Rovani, M., Maggi, F.M., de Leoni, M., van der Aalst, W.M.P.: Declarative process mining in healthcare. Expert Syst. Appl. 42, 9236–9251 (2015)
14. Hübner, J.F., Kitio, O.B.R., Ricci, A.: Instrumenting multi-agent organisations with organisational artifacts and agents. Auton. Agents Multi-Agent Syst. 20, 369–400 (2010)
15. Geuvers, H.: Proof assistants: history, ideas and future. Sadhana 34(1), 3–25 (2009)
16. Nipkow, T., Wenzel, M., Paulson, L.C. (eds.): Isabelle/HOL: A Proof Assistant for Higher-Order Logic. LNCS, vol. 2283. Springer, Heidelberg (2002)

A Novel Description Language for Two-Agent Dialogue Games

Anna Sawicka[1], Magdalena Kacprzak[2(✉)], and Andrzej Zbrzezny[3]

[1] Polish-Japanese Academy of Information Technology, Warsaw, Poland
asawicka@pja.edu.pl
[2] Bialystok University of Technology, Bialystok, Poland
m.kacprzak@pb.edu.pl
[3] Jan Długosz University, Częstochowa, Poland
a.zbrzezny@ajd.czest.pl

Abstract. Every day we use protocols unconsciously during the conversations and the ability to abide by them is an important part of our communication skills (e.g. questioning the question is neither contributing to the conversation nor polite). The protocols can support dialogue to achieve the goal of the conversation (e.g. a compromise, a persuasion). In the paper, we focus on argumentative dialogues and we propose a description language for an argumentative dialogue game in which players can perform actions representing speech acts like *claim*, *question*, *scold* etc. We introduce a Game with Emotional Reasoning Description Language (GERDL), since some of the speech acts introduced by us have an emotional undertow. It will be used in our system for semantic verification of properties of dialogue games with emotional reasoning. This framework is based on interpreted system designed for a dialogue protocol in which participants have emotional skills. To represent the verified properties of the protocol we use the extension of CTL logic with commitment and emotion modalities (formulated in [8]).

Keywords: Dialogue game · Description language · Dialogue protocol · Emotions

1 Introduction

Dialogues are certainly the most popular form of communication, but also - the most complex one. To capture some aspects of the dialogue, we can formalize it by defining e.g. a set of participants, a set of possible actions, a set of rules, and so on.

Argumentation systems are formal frameworks for describing games where participants try to reach an agreement, solve a conflict or convince somebody and one of such systems is called a dialogue game [3,19]. A dialogue can be treated as a two-player game, rules of which are intended to formalize and ensure correctness of the communication [9,12,21]. Formal dialogue systems can be also used as a schema for dialogues reasoning about emotions [11].

© Springer International Publishing AG 2017
L. Polkowski et al. (Eds.): IJCRS 2017, Part II, LNAI 10314, pp. 466–486, 2017.
DOI: 10.1007/978-3-319-60840-2_34

However, the question arises, what are the properties of such a dialogue game? We may wonder whether some of them are true e.g. that one of the players eventually have to admit that the other one was right. Currently, with increasing size and complexity of many systems, there is also a growing demand for the verification of properties of these systems. It is crucial to avoid unforeseen behaviours and to be sure, that the design meet some requirements. One of the solutions is to use formal verification, which takes the form of some logic-based technique e.g. theorem proving or model checking. Model checking [1, 4, 14, 16, 22, 23], which we decided to use, is an automatic verifying technique for concurrent systems such as distributed systems, real-time systems, multi-agent systems, protocols, concurrent programs, and many others. To use this method, we can describe properties of dialogue protocols using propositional temporal logics e.g. linear temporal logic (LTL), computation tree logic (CTL), an extended computation tree logic (CTL*), the universal and existential fragments of these logics, and other extended logics.

Our goal is to adapt existing methods of verification to a new field - dialogue games and to show what mechanisms occur in human argumentative dialogues. In our case, we focus on the dialogue games intended for human-computer communication, but there are also other approaches (e.g. [2]). This paper is a continuation of our earlier work, where we introduced a formal system for verification dialogue games. We want to combine two approaches, dialogue games and model checking techniques used in multi-agent systems, and adapt them to our system designed for verification of dialogue games with emotional reasoning. We consulted the psychological aspect of such a reasoning with a group of psychologists, and our current model of emotions is an effect of this collaboration. We develop a system which can be used to extract elements of dialogue which relate to emotion. The main contribution of this paper is a new description language that meets our needs of describing rules of the dialogue game with emotional reasoning - Game with Emotional Reasoning Description Language (GERDL). This language will specify required aspects of the dialogue game on the input of our system. We will also use it for describing players' strategies and preferences. We need a new language because the languages used in systems, which were our inspirations, are not equipped in some specific for our domain features. The first system, the Model Checker for Multi-Agent Systems (MCMAS) introduced by Raimondi and Lomuscio [13, 18] does not enable dialogue game description. The second one, the Dialogue Game Description Language (DGDL) proposed by Wells and Reed [20], is a language for describing dialectical games in order to play these games in the Dialogue Game Execution Platform (DGEP). This language also does not consider emotional aspects of dialogues. In contrast to our language, DGDL language was created to play dialogue games, not to verify their properties. We will discuss these systems in more detail in the next section.

Our aim is to create a universal tool, which allows verification and simulation of different dialogue systems. We present an example of such a dialogue game, both the model and the description in GERDL. In this paper, we do not propose a new model, but we use the presented one to explain the input specification of our tool, which will be used in the verification of properties of the given dialogue system described in GERDL.

The paper is structured as follows. In Sect. 2 we present our background and inspirations. Section 3 describes interpreted system for dialogue games with emotional reasoning, Kripke model as a basis for the application of model checking. In Sect. 4 we present the Game with Emotional Reasoning Description Language (GERDL) and a general input file structure in this language, as well as short description of the language used for defining properties to be verified. Section 5 contains the GERDL usage example with some specific properties of the dialogue game we want to verify. Conclusions are given in Sect. 6.

2   Background

Our goal is to build a novel system for dialogue systems verification, which was inspired by existing concepts, such as dialogue systems, multi-agent systems, and model checking. Below we briefly describe mentioned approaches.

2.1   Dialogue Games

As we mentioned, in dialogue games, a dialogue is treated as some kind of a game played between two parties. A dialogue game can take place both between artificial agents or between the man and the machine. In argumentative dialogues, players can perform actions affecting commitments. In our case, we need an argumentative dialogue model which takes into account also their emotions. Our model, which is designed for human-computer communication, is based on strict rules (same as [3,7]). On one hand, it makes a game protocol a little trivial, but on the other hand we can extract and focus on most important features of the game.

The dialogue game is specified by three basic categories of rules. *Locution rules* define a set of locutions (actions, speech acts) the player is allowed to utter during the game. Locutions express communication intentions of interlocutors. Such rules specify for example that player can claim, argue, justify, question, concede something etc.

The *structural rules* specify available responses for each specific locution. For example, after one interlocutor claims something, the other one can concede it (by performing *concede*), claim the opposite (by performing *claim* with the opposite content) or ask for justification (by performing *why*).

The *effect rules* defines effects of actions. Due to performing some action a set of commitments (public declarations) of the player can change. The result of an action is a change in the commitments set of the player, i.e. addition or removal of some statement.

To define a dialogue game, we must specify there three sets of rules, which allow to determine available moves for each player at every point of the dialogue. Even though every dialogue game must meet above general requirements, each one is unique and we want to verify some properties of the dialogue games by the means of model checking method. Main approaches in this matter combine bounded model checking (BMC) with symbolic verification using translations to either ordered binary decision diagrams (BDDs) [6] or propositional logic (SAT) [15]. This paper is a continuation of our work on the mathematical model of dialogue inspired by Prakken's argumentative dialogue games [10,17]. We want to use this model as a base for our work on the verification of properties of dialogue protocols.

2.2   MCMAS

One of our inspirations is MCMAS - the Model Checker for Multi-Agent Systems [13,18]. Verification is very important for multi-agent systems, which are intended to capture complex properties of large, distributed, autonomous systems. There are many frameworks and languages able to describe a multi-agent system (MAS), but what distinguish the concept of MCMAS is that it extends the idea of interpreted systems by defining the Interpreted Systems Programming Language (ISPL) dedicated to MAS characterization.

Given a MAS specification, MCMAS verifies a set of specified formulae. The mentioned specification is provided using a dedicated language (ISPL), which allows to describe agents and their behaviour using variables and Boolean expressions. The evaluation of formulae uses algorithms based on Ordered Binary Decision Diagrams (OBDDs). MCMAS shows witnesses for true formulae and counterexamples for false formulae. It provides many modalities e.g. CTL operators, epistemic operators, and so on. In ISPL, there are two kinds of agents: standard agents, and the optional environment agent, which represents common properties of the system. Each agent is characterised by: a set of local states, a set of actions, a protocol describing which actions can be performed by an agent in a given local state, and an evolution function, describing change of the local state of the agent according to the current local state and other agents actions.

Each agent has a set of local variables, some of them can be defined as a visible for other agents. All the Environment's variables are visible for other agents. Each of the local states of an agent contains a valuation of its local variables. ISPL allows three types of variables: Boolean, enumeration and bounded integer. The set of agent's states is divided into two parts - green and red states, which are used to check correct behaviour properties.

If we define a set of actions for an agent, we can use these actions to describe some condition. Such a condition is represented by local states that satisfy the condition and the list of actions allowed to be performed in local states specified by the condition. There can be many conditions for each agent. If there are many actions possible in one condition, the agent has non-deterministic behaviour and all these actions are considered possible.

The definition of the evolution function consists of the elements of the form: a set of assignments of local variables and an enabling condition, which is a Boolean formula over local variables, visible Environment's variables, and actions of all agents. An item is enabled in a state if its enabling condition is satisfied in that state.

The specification of the evaluation function consists of a group of atomic propositions, which are defined over global states. Each atomic proposition is associated with a Boolean formula over local variables of all agents and observable variables in the Environment. The proposition is evaluated to true in all the global states that satisfy the Boolean formula.

The ISPL specification contains also the definition of initial states, propositions, groups, fairness formulae and formulae to be checked. A fairness formula is a Boolean formula over atomic propositions, there are a few Boolean operators allowed (and, or, ! as a negation, $\rightarrow$ as a implication). A formula to be checked is defined over atomic propositions and one can use above operators but also it can use following ones: AG, EG, AX, EX, AF, EF, AU, EU, K, GK, GCK, DK and some other group operators.

The main reason ISPL was not sufficient in our case is the domain we are considering. Probably the most important difference between multi-agent systems and dialogue games is a need for referring to the history of the dialogue. In dialogue games, the history of moves is often crucial for the decision about a current move. In opposition to MCMAS, our rules are based not only on the last/next action of the agent but potentially on the whole history of the dialogue between players. Therefore, we have to make some extensions to ISPL, which enable such references.

Although to express the concept of the set of commitments it was enough to use boolean variables introduced in ISPL, such a mechanism is not suitable for the other sets, especially if the specified set is supposed to be changed during the dialogue. That is why we decided to add the possibility to specify our own sets of specific types. Thanks to that, we can base some decision (e.g. about current move or change in variables) on the content of such a set, and indirectly on the history of the dialogue.

Sometimes it is not the action itself that is interesting for us, but some of its attributes, e.g. player which performed this action or the action it refers to. In order to be able to use this information, we provided two additional variable types (Action and Player). This way, we can catch more aspects of the dialogue.

Also, in ISPL we cannot specify any emotion-dependent conditions or properties because agents cannot refer to the other agent's variables. They need a special agent called Environment to convey the communication between agents. In our solution there is no such a need, the players can make some of their variables directly visible for the other players (read-only). While maintaining the general structure of the ISPL input file and most of the operators, we extended ISPL to suit our needs of expressing emotions and players' preferences. We also omitted some elements of this language, which are irrelevant in our domain (e.g. groups, red/green states). It seems that the verification method will be different, MCMAS uses OBDDs and we plan to use SMT.

2.3   DGDL

Our second inspiration was the Dialogue Game Description Language (DGDL), and also its refined version - DGDL+, which is a language for describing dialectical games [20]. Dialectical games are one of the kinds of multi-player argumentative dialogue games, which provide argumentative behaviours. The DGDL determines whether a game description is syntactically correct. This language was created for describing the features of some commonly used dialectical games and also to be able to describe other games. DGDL takes into account the most important aspects of dialogue games: moves per turn, turn organization, dialogue magnitude, move types, move content, openers, stores, store contents, store visibility, move legality, move effects, participants, roles, and rules.

In DGDL the user can define a single dialectical game or a collection of dialectical games with rules for enabling shifts between them (they form a single system). Each game is specified by describing attributes of the game such as turns, players, and so on. One can define a mandatory set of interactions and an optional set of rules.

Turns control the alternations of players' moves. Turns consist of a single move, a defined set of moves, or any number of moves. There are two types of turn orderings: a strict ordering (after each turn the speaker role is changed) and a liberal ordering (after each turn the next player to move is chosen on the basis of the previous moves).

The user can define the minimum and maximum numbers of players and for each one of them, we specify an identifier and initial role. The players can be referred by roles in different contexts in the rules of the game. Typical roles are e.g. speaker, listener, initiator, respondent, proponent, and opponent.

Stores are collections (sets, stacks or queues) of game artifacts (e.g. commitments or claimed facts). Each store is owned by a player, a group of players, or shared by all players. The user can specify the visibility of the store (public/private). They are usually used to follow the progress of the game.

Interactions take the form of locutions uttered during a dialogue, they change the game components e.g. stores and they allow the player to interact with the game components. Interactions are formed from a move ID, specification of content and opener, and a body. On the other hand, the optional rules allow to define effects of reaching a particular game state. The difference between rules and interactions is that rules' requirements are checked at discrete time-points (e.g. after each turn) and interactions' effect is a result of a specific move. Rules are formed from a rule ID, specification of the scope with which the rule should be checked, and a body. The structure in these two cases is similar and consist of either a set of effects or a conditional statement setting out the conditions under which various sets of effects can occur. Conditions and effects are both predicate statements having a condition ID/effect ID followed by a list of elements. The conditions support a lot of features (e.g. inspecting previous moves or the content/ attributes of specified store, roles of the players, comparing stores, checking the number of played turns, etc.). The user can also define responses, changes in stores, updates to the status of a specific system or game, he can assign a role to a player or swap of roles between players.

Despite large possibilities, DGDL does not suit our needs. There are no means to express emotions and their changes. This language was not created to specify and verify properties, we can rather play specified games using Dialogue Game Execution Platform. In our system, we need to have the possibility of expressing properties of the game and verifying them by the means of the model checking and we are not only interested in simulation of the dialogue game. We are interested in some mechanism that will allow us to describe the intensity and the changes of emotions and use it in the player's preferences notation.

3   Model

We start out by defining a mathematical model for argumentation dialogue games, which uses the concept of interpreted systems and Kripke structures. Obtained Kripke structure and model checking techniques allow us to perform automatic verification of dialogue protocols. In this model formulas of a modal logic adequate to express properties of dialogues are interpreted. This is an example of the dialogue game, which can be realized and verified by our tool. The tool itself is supposed to be universal and take any dialogue game described in GERDL as an input.

First, we assume that the set of players of a dialogue game consists of two players: White (W) and Black (B), $Pl = \{W, B\}$. To each player $p \in Pl$, we assign a set of possible local states L_p and a set of actions Act_p. Player's local state $l_p \in L_p$ consists of the player's *commitments* and *emotions*, $l_p = (C_p, E_p)$.

Players' commitments are elements of a fixed topic language, which allows expressing the content of locutions. They are understood as public declarations of players but we do not assume their honesty and truthfulness. Thus, C_p are sets of such expressions. These sets may be subject to change after a player's action. More specifically, the player can add or delete the selected expression. Formally we assume a finite set $FORM$ of expressions which can be used as a content of a locution and thereby express some commitment of a player. We do not assume that this set is closed under logical or material implication and it can contain conflict expressions.

Emotions which we consider are *fear*, *disgust*, *joy*, *sadness*, and *anger*, and their strength (intensity) is represented by natural numbers from the set $\{1, 2, \ldots, 10\}$. Thus, E_p is a 5-tuple consisting of five values, which may also change after a certain action. It is worth highlighting here that a change in the intensity of the emotions is dependent on the type of locution and, perhaps even more, on its content.

Every action from Act_p can influence participant's commitments and emotions. We assume that the set Act_p contains also the special empty (null) action ε. Every action (except null action) is synonymous with locution expressed by the specific player. In argumentation systems the most commonly used locutions are: *claim* - some statement, *concede* - confirmation, *since* - justification, *why* - the request for justification, *retract* - revocation, and *question* about some fact. Thus, in argumentation dialogues, a player can *claim* some facts, *concede* with the opponent or change his mind performing action *retract*. To challenge the opponent's statement, he may ask *why*, or ask whether the opponent commits to something, i.e., perform action *question*. For defence he can use the action *since*. It is the kind of reasoning and argumentation. To these typical actions, we added two, which we believe allow better describe dialogues and changes in the intensity of players' emotions. These are *scold* and *nod*. They express reprimand and approval, respectively. Results of locutions are determined by *evolution function* and are specified afterwards.

Let $\alpha, \beta, \varphi, \psi_1, \ldots, \psi_n, \gamma_1, \ldots, \gamma_n \in FORM$. Locutions used in players' actions are the same for both players:

$$Act_W = Act_B = \{\varepsilon, \; claim \; \varphi, \; concede \; \varphi, \; why \; \varphi,$$

$$scold \; \varphi, \; nod \; \varphi, \; \varphi \; since \; \{\psi_1, \ldots, \psi_n\}, \; retract \; \varphi, \; question \; \varphi\}.$$

Next, *Act* denotes a subset of the Cartesian product of the players' actions such that:

$$Act = \{(a, \varepsilon) : a \in Act_W\} \cup \{(\varepsilon, a) : a \in Act_B\}.$$

The global action $a \in Act$ is a pair of actions $a = (a_W, a_B)$, where $a_W \in Act_W$, $a_B \in Act_B$ and at least one of these actions is the empty action. This means that players cannot speak at the same time. Moreover, a player cannot reply to his own moves. Thus, the empty action is performed alternately by players W and B.

Also, we need to order performed global actions and indicate which actions correspond with which ones and therefore we define *double-numbered global actions* set $Num_2Act = \mathbb{N} \times \mathbb{N} \times Act$. During the dialogue, we assign to each performed global action two numbers: the first one (ascending) indicates order (starting from the value 1). The second one points out to which earlier action this action is referring (0 at the beginning of the dialogue means that we are not referring to any move).

Furthermore, we define *numbered global actions* set $Num_1Act = \mathbb{N} \times Act$. Each element of this set is a pair (n, a) consisting of an action $a \in Act$ and the identifier of the action it refers to, $n \in \mathbb{N}$. If we want to find out whether we can use some global action one more time, we should check if the possible move containing the same global action refers to the different earlier move.

We define function $Denum : Num_2Act \rightarrow Num_1Act$, $Denum(n_1, n_2, a) = (n_2, a)$, which maps double-numbered global action to the numbered global action. We understand dialogue d as a sequence of moves and in particular, we denote $d_{1..n} = d_1, \ldots, d_n$, where $d_i \in Num_2Act$, $d_i = (i, j, a), j \in \mathbb{N}, j < i$, $a \in Act$.

A global state g is a triple consisting of dialogue history and players' local states corresponding to a snapshot of the system at a given time point $g = (d(g), l_W(g), l_B(g))$, $g \in G$ where G is the set of global states. Given a global state g, we denote by $d(g)$ a sequence of moves executed on a way to state g and by $l_p(g)$ - the local state of player p in g.

An *interpreted system* for a dialogue game is a tuple $IS = (I, \{L_p, Act_p\}_{p \in Pl})$ where $I \subseteq G$ is the set of initial global states.

Now we define *legal answer function* $F_{LA} : Num_2Act \rightarrow 2^{Num_1Act}$, which maps a double-numbered action to the set of possible numbered actions. This function is symmetrical for both players and determines for every action a set of legal actions which can be performed next:

- $F_{LA}(i, j, (\varepsilon, \varepsilon)) = \emptyset$,
- $F_{LA}(i, j, (\alpha, \varepsilon)) = \{(i, (\varepsilon, \beta)) : \beta \in LEGAL(\alpha)\}$,

where $LEGAL(\alpha)$ is defined in Table 1:

Table 1. Definition of $LEGAL$ function.

α	$LEGAL(\alpha)$
claim φ	*why* φ, *concede* φ, *claim* $\neg\varphi$, *nod* ψ, *scold* ψ, for some $\psi \in FORM$
scold φ	*why* φ, *concede* φ, *claim* $\neg\varphi$, *nod* ψ, *scold* ψ, for some $\psi \in FORM$
φ *since* $\{\psi_1, \ldots, \psi_n\}$	*why* α, *concede* β, $\neg\varphi$ *since* $\{\gamma_1, \ldots, \gamma_n\}$, *nod* ψ, *scold* ψ, where $\alpha \in \{\psi_1, \ldots, \psi_n\}$, $\beta \in \{\varphi, \psi_1, \ldots, \psi_n\}$, and $\psi \in FORM$
why φ	φ *since* $\{\psi_1, \ldots, \psi_n\}$, *retract* φ
question φ	*retract* φ, *claim* φ, *claim* $\neg\varphi$
concede φ	ε, *claim* α, *nod* α, *scold* α, α *since* $\{\psi_1, \ldots, \psi_n\}$, for some $\alpha, \psi_1, \ldots, \psi_n \in FORM$
nod φ	ε, *claim* α, *nod* α, *scold* α, α *since* $\{\psi_1, \ldots, \psi_n\}$, for some $\alpha, \psi_1, \ldots, \psi_n \in FORM$
retract φ	ε, *claim* α, *nod* α, *scold* α, α *since* $\{\psi_1, \ldots, \psi_n\}$, for some $\alpha, \psi_1, \ldots, \psi_n \in FORM$

The actions executed by players are selected according to a *protocol function* $Pr : G \rightarrow 2^{Num_2Act}$, which maps a global state g to the set of possible double-numbered global actions. The function Pr satisfies the following rules.

(R1) For $\iota \in I$ $Pr(\iota) =$
$\{(1, 0, (claim\ \varphi, \varepsilon)), (1, 0, (question\ \varphi, \varepsilon)), (1, 0, (\varphi\ since\ \{\psi_1, \ldots, \psi_n\}, \varepsilon))\}$.

(R2) $Pr((d_{1..k-1}, (k, l, (a, \varepsilon)), l_W(g), l_B(g))) = \{(k+1, numact) :$
$numact \in F_{LA}(k, l, (a, \varepsilon))\}$, for $a \in \{\varepsilon,\ claim\ \varphi,\ scold\ \varphi,\ why\ \varphi,$
$question\ \varphi,\ \varphi\ since\ \{\psi_1, \ldots, \psi_n\}\}$.

(R3) $Pr((d_{1..k-1}, (k, l, (a, \varepsilon)), l_W(g), l_B(g))) = \{(k+1, numact) : numact \in$
$((\bigcup_{i<=k} F_{LA}(d_i) \cap \{(n, (\varepsilon, \alpha)) : n < k, \alpha \in Act_B\}) \setminus \{Denum(d_i) : i = 1, ..,$
$k\})\}$, for $a \in \{concede\ \varphi,\ nod\ \varphi\}$.

(R4) $Pr((d_{1..k-1}, (k, l, (retract\varphi, \varepsilon)), l_W(g), l_B(g))) = \{(k+1, numact) : numact$
$\in ((\bigcup_{i<=k} F_{LA}(d_i) \cap \{(n, (\varepsilon, \alpha)) : n < k, \alpha \in Act_B\}) \setminus \{Denum(d_i) : i =$
$1, .., k\})\} \cup \{(k+1, x, (\varepsilon, why\ \beta)) : \exists_{x<k}\ d_x = (x, y, (\beta\ since\ \varphi, \varepsilon))\}$ for
some $\varphi, \beta \in FORM$.

These rules for player B are analogous. The protocol is a crucial element of the model since it gives strict rules which determine the behaviour of players. In other words, it formally describes who, when and which action can perform. Rule (R1) defines the actions that can begin a dialogue. Rule (R2) states that after locutions *claim, scold, why, question, since* and the empty action, only actions determined by the legal answer function can be used. According to rule (R3) actions *concede* and *nod* end one of the threads of dialogue. Therefore, the next action can start a new thread or return to one of the unfinished. After opponent's locutions *concede, nod* or *question* the player can use one from possible answers for all previous opponent's moves, excluding these ones which he has already used since this protocol does not allow the repetition of the same part of the dialogue, if it is not caused by new locutions. Actions *nod* and *scold* act similarly to actions *concede* and *claim*, but what distinguishes these actions is their emotional charge. Rule (R4) expresses that after opponent's locution *retract* φ the player can use one from the possible answers for all previous opponent's previous moves, excluding those which he has already used, but also he can ask for the reason for β if φ was previously used to justify β. In other words, the player can challenge the statement β, which was defended by the previously withdrawn statement φ.

To express how locutions and their contents affect players' emotions during the dialogue we define a function, which determines the change of intensity of emotions: $EMOT_p : Act_p \times Emotion_p \rightarrow Emotion_p$ where $p \in Pl$ and $Emotion_p$ is a set of all possible 5-tuples for emotions, i.e., $Emotion_p = \{(n_1, \ldots, n_5) : n_i \in \{1, \ldots, 10\} \wedge i \in \{1, \ldots, 5\}\}$.

Finally, we define *global* (partial) *evolution function* $t : G \times Num_2 Act \rightarrow G$, which determines results of actions. This function is symmetrical for both players. Let $d(g) = d(g)_{1,\ldots,m}$, then:

- $t(g, (m+1, j, (\alpha, \varepsilon))) = g'$ iff $RESULT(\alpha) \wedge E_W(g') = EMOT_W(\alpha, E_W(g)) \wedge$
  $d(g') = (d(g)_{1,\ldots,m}, (m+1, j, (\alpha, \varepsilon)))$,

where $RESULT(\alpha)$ is defined in Table 2.
Global evolution function defines results of actions. In particular, actions *claim, concede, scold, nod* and *since* add an expression to the commitments set while action *retract* deletes it. Actions *why* and *question* do not modify this set. The t function also takes into account the changes in the levels of emotions that are

Table 2. Definition of *RESULT* function

α	$RESULT(\alpha)$
claim φ, *scold* φ	$C_W(g') = C_W(g) \cup \{\varphi\}$
φ *since* $\{\psi_1, \ldots, \psi_n\}$	$C_W(g') = C_W(g) \cup \{\varphi, \psi_1, .., \psi_n\}$
concede φ, *nod* φ	$C_W(g') = C_W(g) \cup \{\varphi\}$
why φ, *question* φ	$C_W(g') = C_W(g)$
retract φ	$C_W(g') = C_W(g) \setminus \{\varphi\}$

determined by the function $EMOT$. Thus, the sets of emotions in the new state of the system are results of this function having as the input the previous state. Moreover, the history of the dialogue is extended with the last move.

The application of the model checking requires a *model* of the system under consideration. We associate with the given interpreted system a *Kripke structure*, that is the basis for the application of model checking. A Kripke structure is defined as a tuple $M = (G, Act, T, I)$ consisting of a set of global states G, a set of actions Act (in our approach $Num_2 Act$), a set of initial states $I \subseteq G$, a transition relation $T \subseteq G \times Act \times G$ such that T is left-total. Relation T is defined as follows $(g, a, g') \in T$ *iff* $g' \in t(g, a)$. By T^* we will denote the relation $T^* \subseteq G \times G$ defined as follows: $(g', g) \in T^*$ if there exist $a_1, a_2, \ldots, a_n \in Num_2 Act$ and there exists $g_1, g_2, \ldots, g_{n-1}$ such that $(g', a_1, g_1) \in T$, $(g_{n-1}, a_n, g) \in T$, and for $i = 1, 2, \ldots, n-2$ it holds that $(g_i, a_{i+1}, g_{i+1}) \in T$.

Also, we need to formulate *properties* of the dialogue protocol to be checked, we present a suitable language in the next section.

4   Description Language

In this section, we introduce the Game with Emotional Reasoning Description Language (GERDL) developed on the basis of the presented model. This language is designed to describe a dialogue game on the input of the framework, which will be focused on model checking of the properties of this dialogue game. We present a few details about each section of the GERDL input file. In the next section, we show an example the input file in GERDL based on the mentioned model.

In contrast to MCMAS, there is no special agent Environment included, since there is no such a concept in the context of dialogue games. A dialogue game is specified by a set of players and some attributes of the game background (e.g. turns' rules, commitments). We focus on two-players games and one action per turn, but we assume that we are going to extend this framework e.g. to allow more players.

Below is the general structure of the input file in GERDL and descriptions of each section. All of the sections and attributes are obligatory. First, there is global settings section, in which we declare commitments (public declarations) of players. After that, we specify the players, each one in his own *Player* section. It contains the specification of the locutions available to this player, his variables (subsections PublicVars and PrivateVars), protocol and evolution function (subsections Protocol and Evolution respectively).

After the declaration of players, we have to complete the input file by adding InitStates and Formulae sections. The first one describes which states are initial and the second one specifies properties of the dialogue game to be verified.

A single line comment in GERDL starts with #.
Commitments={ ... };

Player P1

Locutions = { ...};

PublicVars:

...

end PublicVars

PrivateVars

...

end PrivateVars

Protocol:

...

end Protocol

Evolution

...

end Evolution

end Player

Player P2

...

end Player

InitStates

...

end InitStates

Formulae

...

end Formulae

Specification of the Game

We assume that players can perform one action per turn and after each turn, the next player in the players' list speaks (the ordering of the list is consistent with the order of players in the input file). By "the action of the player" we understand hereafter a global action, where only one of the players is making an utterance.

We do not limit the number of turns since the real life dialogues usually do not have such limitations and the players can continue the argumentation as long as they have a valid argument.

We assume that the locutions are speech acts uttered during a dialogue. The set of possible locutions (Locutions = { ... }) is declared inside of the player's section and it specifies the specific locutions of this player. To show the structure of the locution we use the notation, where capital letters X, Y, Z, ... symbolize some content of the locution, the notation X1...XN symbolizes the set of contents (of non-zero length), and Z1|...|ZN symbolizes one element from such a set.

Players' commitments are elements of a fixed topic language, which allows expressing the content of locutions. We specify the sets of possible commitments by listing them in the form of strings e.g. "alpha". They represent some facts players would like to talk about and they might as well be whole sentences expressed in the natural language e.g. "I'm hungry". These sets are also defined outside the players' section because the commitments are public and each player is aware of other player's utterances.

For each player, there are boolean variables representing all possible commitments and we can refer to it by Black."alpha" where "alpha" is in the commitments set. If the player Black has committed to "alpha", then Black."alpha" is true, otherwise - it is false.

In our system, we have six types of variables. You can see below typical declarations and possible operations for these types (= and != always denote respectively equality and inequality).

- a: boolean; - boolean variables with possible operators: =, !=, negation ($\tilde{\ }$), conjunction (&), inclusive disjunction (|), exclusive disjunction (^),
- b: {m, n, p}; - enumeration variables with possible operators: =, != (comparable if they have the same type, or one's type is a subset of the type of the other),
- c: 1..10; - bounded integer variables with possible arithmetic operators: =, !=, <, <=, >, >=,
- A: Action; - action variables with possible operators: =, != and attributes: number (in the dialogue), locution (performed speech act e.g. *claim*), content (elementary expression based on commitments), player (reference to the player), referringTo (number of the action it refers to);
- P: Player; - player variables with possible operators: =, != and attribute lastAction, which refers to the last action of this player (e.g. Black.lastAction is the last action used by the player Black),
- S: set of Action; - set of elements of one of the above types with possible operators: union (+), intersection (&), difference (-), membership *in*.

In the dialogue game specification we can use a few predefined variables:

- actionNumber - the integer variable describing a number of the action, which is about to be executed,
- initialState - the boolean variable, which is true before the first action was executed in the dialogue,
- lastAction - the action variable referring to the last action in the dialogue, e.g. in condition lastAction.player=Black we check whether the player of the last action is player Black,
- lastPlayer - the player variable referring to the player of the last action in the dialogue.

Specification of Players

Each player has two sets of variables: private and public one. Private variables are not visible for the other players, the public ones are visible, but read only. Each local state of a player contains a valuation of all its variables.

Each player has also his own set of locutions, which can be uttered, a protocol function, and an evolution function. The set of player's possible commitments is already specified before the player's description.

Specification of protocol function is composed of the conditions, which are Boolean formulae over global states, and after each condition, there is a list of actions which can be used, if a condition is fulfilled. The condition represents all global states that satisfy the condition.

For example, in this line of protocol function

Black.lastAction=claim.X: why.X, concede.X, claim.(!X),nod.Y, scold.Y

We state that if the last action of the player Black was *claim* with some content (X), the player White can reply with *why* or *concede* (with the same content), *claim* (with the negation of the content) or *nod/scold* with any content.

Notation Z1...ZN refers to the set (e.g. premises) and means "the set {Z1,...,ZN}" ("all from the set {Z1,...,ZN}"). Z1|...|ZN means "one of the set {Z1,...,ZN}", for example:

Black.lastAction=X.since.Z1...ZN:{ why.Z1|...|ZN, concede.X,

concede.Z1|...|ZN, (!X).since.Y1...YN, claim.X, claim.(!X), nod.Y, scold.Y}

By notation Before(White, claim.X)=true we understand that there is White's action in the dialogue history and this action was of the form *claim*.X.

If there are many matching rules, actions from all of them are considered available. With many global states, we do not have to specify actions for every state and we can encode all remaining states (except those specified before) by defining optional section Other (Other: list of actions;). This section is the last one in a protocol function.

An evolution function line consists of a set of assignments of variables (accessible for the specific player ones) and an enabling condition, which is a Boolean formula over variables of the player, public variables of the other players and actions of all players. An item is enabled in a state if its enabling condition is satisfied in that state. Below we have an example of such a line of an evolution function:

Black.joy=Black.joy+1 if Black.joy<10 and White.lastAction=nod.X

This is interpreted as: "in the next step, the value of Black.joy is increased by 1 if the current value of Black.joy is lower that 10 and the last action of the player White was action *nod*". Some of these rules can be interpreted as properties of the dialogue game itself and the other ones as elements of player's profile.

The input specification in GERDL contains also the definition of initial states and formulae to be verified.

Specification of Initial States

The section InitStates defines the set of initial states using a Boolean formula over variables (public and predefined ones). The propositions in this formula can take the form:

var = value or *var1 = var2*

where var, var1, var2 can be public variables of the player (e.g. P1.x) or predefined ones (e.g. initialState). Allowed Boolean operators are *and*, *or* and ! (negation). Value and variable (or two variables) must be a matching type to enable the comparison.

Specification of Formulae to be Verified

The section Formulae contains the properties of dialogue systems to be verified, expressed in language based on CTL logic introduced by Emerson and Clarke [5] enriched with commitment and emotion components (presented at [8]). Usually, properties we want to verify are used to reason about desirable behaviour of the system e.g. the safety property expresses that something bad cannot happen or that something good is always true, the guarantee property can ensure that something eventually happens, the response property expresses the fact that some property is a guaranteed response to specific condition, and so on.

Below, we present a few details about the mentioned language. Examples of the expressed properties are shown in the next section. Let $Pl = \{W, B\}$ be a set of players. The set of formulas is defined inductively as follows:

- *true* is a formula.
- if $\varphi \in FORM$, $p \in Pl$ and $e \in \{fear, disgust, joy, sadness, anger\}$ then $COM_p(\varphi)$ and $EMO_p(e)$ are formulas.
- if α and β are formulas, then so are $\neg\alpha$, $\alpha \wedge \beta$, $EX\alpha$, $EG\alpha$, $E(\alpha U\beta)$.

The boolean connectives $\alpha \vee \beta$, $\alpha \Rightarrow \beta$, $\alpha \Leftrightarrow \beta$, and the formula *false* are defined in the standard manner. The remaining temporal modalities are defined by derivation: $EF\alpha \overset{def}{=} E(true\ U\ \beta)$, $AX\alpha \overset{def}{=} \neg EX\neg\alpha$, $AG\alpha \overset{def}{=} \neg EF\neg\alpha$, $AF\alpha \overset{def}{=} \neg EG\neg\alpha$, $A(\alpha\ U\ \beta) \overset{def}{=} \neg E(\neg\beta\ U\ (\neg\alpha \wedge \neg\beta)) \wedge \neg EG\neg\beta$, $E(\alpha\ R\ \beta) \overset{def}{=} \neg A(\neg\alpha U\neg\beta)$, $A(\alpha\ R\ \beta) \overset{def}{=} \neg E(\neg\alpha U\neg\beta)$.

The formula *true* is used for technical reasons. Formula $COM_p(\varphi)$ expresses that φ is in the set of commitments of player p (φ is not a formula of this language, but a part of a separate structure in which we express the uttered sentences). Modality EMO_p is intended to express properties concerning emotions of player p. The temporal modalities X, G stand for "at the next step", and "forever in the future", respectively. Since the modality E is the existential quantifier ("exists"), EX means "for some next states" and EG means "for all states on some path". The formula $E(\alpha U\beta)$ means that on some path β eventually occurs and that α holds continuously until then.

Semantics of the logic is given by means of interpreted systems. By a *computation* in a Kripke structure $M = (G, Act, T, I)$ we understand a possibly infinite sequence of states $\pi = (g_0, g_1, \ldots)$ such that there exists an action a_m for which $(g_m, a_m, g_{m+1}) \in T$ for each $m \in \mathbb{N}$, i.e., g_{m+1} is the result of applying the transition relation T to the global state g_m, and the action a_m.

In the interpreted systems terminology, a computation is a part of a run. A k-computation is a computation of length k. For a computation $\pi = (g_0, g_1, \ldots)$, let $\pi(k) = g_k$, and $\pi_k = (g_0, \ldots, g_k)$, for each $k \in \mathbb{N}$. By $\Pi(g)$ we denote the set of all the infinite computations starting at g in M, whereas by $\Pi_k(g)$ the set of all the k-computations starting at g.

Let M be a model (Kripke structure), $g \in G$ be a state, π be a computation, and α, β be formulas. $M, g \models \alpha$ denotes that α is true at the state g in the model M. The relation $\models$ is defined inductively as follows:

$$M, g \models true \qquad \text{for all } g \in G,$$
$$M, g \models COM_p(\varphi) \text{ iff } \varphi \in C_p(g),$$
$$M, g \models EMO_p(e) \text{ iff } n_i > 5 \text{ in } E_p(g) = (n_1, .., n_5), \text{ where } e \text{ is fear, disgust, joy,}$$
$$\text{sadness, or anger and } i = 1, 2, 3, 4, 5, \text{ respectively,}$$
$$M, g \models \neg\alpha \qquad \text{iff} \quad M, g \not\models \alpha,$$
$$M, g \models \alpha \land \beta \qquad \text{iff} \quad M, g \models \alpha \text{ and } M, g \models \beta,$$
$$M, g \models EX\alpha \qquad \text{iff} \quad \exists g' \in G \; \exists a \in Num_2 Act((g, a, g') \in T \text{ and } M, g' \models \alpha),$$
$$M, g \models EG\alpha \qquad \text{iff} \quad \exists \pi \in \Pi(g) \; (\forall_{m \geq 0}[M, \pi(m) \models \alpha]),$$
$$M, g \models E(\alpha \, U \, \beta) \text{ iff } \exists \pi \in \Pi(g) \; (\exists_{m \geq 0}[M, \pi(m) \models \beta \text{ and } \forall_{j < m} \; [M, \pi(j) \models \alpha]]).$$

Since the input file is an ordinary text file, we simplified the notation in formulae by replacing some symbols with their text equivalents e.g. $\land$ is replaced with &, $\lor$ with +, and $\neg$ with ~. Also, the symbol after the underscore can be understood as the subscript.

5 Example

In our example, we specify the GERDL input file of the dialogue game modeled in Sect. 3. The players are called White and Black. For each player, we declare five variables responsible for modeling emotions. Additionally, we declare the set variable POSSIBLE_ACTIONS to remember all the unused actions we would like to be able to use at some moment. This set is expanding every time we choose one of the possible actions - the other ones remain available and can be used at certain (specified by the rules of the protocol) points of the dialogue. Even though in the below input file locutions section in players are the same there, we want to emphasize the potential asymmetry of players.

The protocol sections in both players reflect protocol function in our model (Table 1 and R1–R4). Since our modeled dialogue game focus not only on the commitments of the players but also on their emotions, some of the rules of evolution functions represent properties of the dialogue game itself (changes in the sets of commitments, Table 2) and the other ones can be understood as elements of player's emotional profile (changes in the emotions levels of the specific player). In our example, last four rules of evolution function of each player express the specific behaviour of the player. In real-life input files, this section can be much more expanded to prevent too many possible dialogues.

The initial states are defined only be the means of predefined variable initialStates, which is true before the dialogue begins.

The first formula to be verified in the below example is one of the guarantee properties - the *termination* property. Usually, the end of a dialogue means the fulfillment of a certain termination condition e.g. that some player does not feel a strong fear. This specific formula $A(true \, U \, \neg EMO_W(fear))$ claims that every computation contains a state at which the above condition holds and we can assume it is the end of the dialogue.

The second formula, $AG(COM_p(\alpha) \Rightarrow E(true \, U \, \neg \, COM_p(\alpha)))$, is an example of the *response* property - it expresses that even if a player p has committed to α at some point, then during the dialogue he can change his mind and retract this commitment.

Below is the example of the input file in GERDL.

Commitments={ "alpha", "beta", "theta", "phi", "psi", "zeta"};

Player White

Locutions = {claim.X, concede.X, why.X, question.X, X.since.Z1...ZN, retract.X, nod.X, scold.X};

PublicVars:

    fear : 1 .. 10;
    disgust : 1 .. 10;
    joy : 1 .. 10;
    sadness : 1 .. 10;
    anger : 1 .. 10;

end PublicVars

PrivateVars

#the set variable to remember all the unused actions
    POSSIBLE_ACTIONS : set of Actions;

end PrivateVars

Protocol:

    initialState=true : {claim.X, question.X , since.X}
    Black.lastAction=claim.X : { why.X, concede.X, claim.(!X),nod.Y, scold.Y}
    Black.lastAction=scold.X : { scold.Y, why.X, concede.X, claim.X, claim.(!X), nod.Y}
    Black.lastAction=X.since.Z1...ZN : { why.Z1|...|ZN, concede.X, concede.Z1|...|ZN, (!X).since.Y1...YN, claim.X, claim.(!X), nod.Y, scold.Y}
    Black.lastAction=why.X : { retract.X, X.since.Z1...ZN}
    Black.lastAction=question.X : { retract.X, claim.X, claim.(!X)}
    Black.lastAction=concede.X : { claim.Y, nod.Y, scold.Y, X.since.Z1...ZN}
    Black.lastAction=nod.X : { claim.Y, nod.Y, scold.Y, Y.sinceZ1...ZN}
                      +POSSIBLE_ACTIONS
    Black.lastAction=retract.X : { claim.Y, nod.Y, Y.scold.Z1...ZN, since}
                      +POSSIBLE_ACTIONS
    Black.lastAction=retract.X and Before(White, Y.since.X) : {why.Y}

end Protocol

Evolution

    White.X=true if (White.lastAction=claim.X or White.lastAction=scold.X)
    White.X=true and White.Z1...ZN=true if White.lastAction=X.since.Z1...ZN
    White.X=true if (White.lastAction=concede.X or White.lastAction=nod.X)
    White.X=false if White.lastAction=retract.X

    POSSIBLE_ACTIONS=POSSIBLE_ACTIONS+{why.X, concede.X, claim.(!X), nod.Y, scold.Y} - White.lastAction if Black.lastAction=claim.X
    POSSIBLE_ACTIONS=POSSIBLE_ACTIONS+{scold.Y, why.X, concede.X, claim.X, claim.(!X), nod.Y} - White.lastAction if Black.lastAction=scold.X
    POSSIBLE_ACTIONS=POSSIBLE_ACTIONS+{why.Z1|...|ZN, concede.X, concede.Z1|...|ZN, (!X).since.Y1...YN , claim.X, claim.(!X), nod.Y, scold.Y} - White.lastAction if Black.lastAction=X.since.Z1...ZN
    POSSIBLE_ACTIONS=POSSIBLE_ACTIONS+{retract.X, X.since.Z1...ZN} - White.lastAction if Black.lastAction=question.X

POSSIBLE_ACTIONS=POSSIBLE_ACTIONS+
  {retract.X, claim.X, claim.(!X)} - White.lastAction if Black.lastAction=why.X
POSSIBLE_ACTIONS=POSSIBLE_ACTIONS+
  {claim.Y, nod.Y, scold.Y, Y.since.Z1...ZN} -White.lastAction
  if Black.lastAction=concede.X

Below are examples of rules describing White's emotional profile

White.joy=White.joy-1 if lastAction=scold.X
  and lastPlayer=White and White.joy>1 and Black.anger<10

White.joy=White.joy+1 if White.disgust<5
  and White.joy<9 and lastAction=nod."beta" and lastPlayer=Black

White.anger=White.anger+1
  if Before(White, scold."alpha")=true and White.anger<10
    and lastAction=question."beta" and lastPlayer=Black

White.fear=White.fear+1
  if lastAction=scold.X and lastPlayer=Black and White.fear<10

end Evolution

end Player

Player Black

Locutions = {claim.X, concede.X, why.X, question.X, X.since.Z1...ZN, retract.X,
nod.X, scold.X};

PublicVars:

  fear : 1 .. 10;
  disgust : 1 .. 10;
  joy : 1 .. 10;
  sadness : 1 .. 10;
  anger : 1 .. 10;

end PublicVars

PrivateVars

#the set variable to remember all the unused actions
  POSSIBLE_ACTIONS : set of Actions;

end PrivateVars

Protocol:

  initialState=true : {claim.X, question.X , X.since.Z1...ZN}
  White.lastAction=claim.X : { why.X, concede.X, claim.(!X),nod.Y, scold.Y}
  White.lastAction=scold.X : { scold.Y, why.X, concede.X, claim.X, claim.(!X),
    nod.Y}
  White.lastAction=X.since.Z1...ZN : { why.Z1|...|ZN, concede.X,
    concede.Z1|...|ZN, (!X).since.Y1...Y2, claim.X, claim.(!X), nod.Y, scold.Y}
  White.lastAction=why.X : { retract.X, X.since.Z1...ZN}
  White.lastAction=question.X : { retract.X, claim.X, claim.(!X)}
  White.lastAction=concede.X : { claim.Y, nod.Y, scold.Y, Y.since.Z1...ZN}
  White.lastAction=nod.X : { claim.Y, nod.Y, scold.Y, Y.since.Z1...ZN}
                    +POSSIBLE_ACTIONS
  White.lastAction=retract.X : { claim.Y, nod.Y, scold.Y, Y.since.Z1...ZN}
                    +POSSIBLE_ACTIONS

White.lastAction=retract.X and Before(White, Y.since.X) : {why.Y}

end Protocol

Evolution

Black.X=true **if** (Black.lastActioĥ=claim.X or Black.lastAction=scold.X)
Black.X=true and Black.Z1...ZN=true **if** Black.lastAction=X.since.Z1...ZN
Black.X=true **if** (Black.lastAction=concede.X or Black.lastAction=nod.X)
Black.X=false **if** Black.lastAction=retract.X

POSSIBLE_ACTIONS=POSSIBLE_ACTIONS+{why.X, concede.X,
  claim.(!X), nod.Y, scold.Y} - Black.lastAction **if** White.lastAction=claim.X
POSSIBLE_ACTIONS=POSSIBLE_ACTIONS+{scold.Y, why.X, concede.X,
  claim.X, claim.(!X), nod.Y} - Black.lastAction **if** White.lastAction=scold.X
POSSIBLE_ACTIONS=POSSIBLE_ACTIONS+{why.Z1|...|ZN, concede.X,
  concede.Z1|...|ZN, (!X).since.Y1...YN , claim.X, claim.(!X), nod.Y, scold.Y}
  - Black.lastAction **if** White.lastAction=X.since.Z1...ZN
POSSIBLE_ACTIONS=POSSIBLE_ACTIONS+{retract.X, X.since.Z1...ZN} -
  Black.lastAction **if** White.lastAction=question.X
POSSIBLE_ACTIONS=POSSIBLE_ACTIONS+
  {retract.X, claim.X, claim.(!X)} - Black.lastAction **if** White.lastAction=why.X
POSSIBLE_ACTIONS=POSSIBLE_ACTIONS+{claim.Y, nod.Y, scold.Y,
  Y.since.Z1...ZN} - Black.lastAction **if** White.lastAction=concede.X

\# Below there are rules specific for the player Black

Black.anger=Black.anger+1 **if** lastAction=question.X
  and lastPlayer=White and Before(Black, claim.X)=true and Black.anger<10

Black.joy=Black.joy-1 **if** Black.disgust>5 and Before(White, scold.X)=true
  and Black.joy>1 and lastAction=scold.Y

Black.joy=Black.joy-2 and Black.anger=Black.anger+2
  if Before(White, scold."alpha")=true and Black.joy>2 and Black.anger<9

Black.anger=Black.anger+1 **if** lastAction=scold.X
  and lastPlayer=White and White.joy>1 and Black.anger<10

end Evolution

end Player

InitStates

  initialState=true;

end InitStates

Formulae

  A($true$ U $\tilde{\ }EMO\_W(fear)$)
  AG($COM\_p(\alpha)$ − > E($true$ U $\tilde{\ }$ $COM\_p(\alpha)$))

end Formulae

6   Conclusion

The goal of our work is the specification and semantic verification of protocols for
dialogue games with a fixed protocol. We believe that it can show how important
is the role of emotions in the argumentative discourse. In this paper, as the

next stage of this work, we introduced the Game with Emotional Reasoning Description Language. The GERDL is essential to describe the verified dialogue game on the input of our framework, which will be focused on model checking of the properties of this dialogue game. We described the most important features of dialogue games we wanted to capture in our specification. To represent the verified properties of the protocol we used the extension of CTL logic with commitment and emotion modalities (formulated in [8]).

We were inspired by existing frameworks which demand a similar specification, whether it is for multi-agent systems or dialogue games. We pointed out main differences in our approaches, what features of these systems we accommodated and which ones did not have an application in our domain. Next step of our work on dialogue games verification will be focused on the design and the implementation of model checker that will use presented in this paper GERDL file as the input file and verify whether specified properties are true.

Acknowledgment. The research by Kacprzak have been carried out within the framework of the work S/W/1/2014 and funded by Ministry of Science and Higher Education.

References

1. Baier, C., Katoen, J.P.: Principles of Model Checking. MIT Press, Cambridge (2008)
2. Bentahar, J., Ch. Meyer, J.-J., Wan, W.: Model checking agent communication. In: Dastani, M., Hindriks, K.V., Charles Meyer, J.-J. (eds.) Specification and Verification of Multi-agent Systems, pp. 67–102. Springer US, Boston (2010). doi:10. 1007/978-1-4419-6984-2_3
3. Budzynska, K., Kacprzak, M., Sawicka, A., Yaskorska, O.: Dialogue Dynamics: Formal Approach. IFS PAS (2015)
4. Clarke, E.M., Grumberg, O., Peled, D.A.: Model Checking. MIT Press, Cambridge (2001)
5. Emerson, E.A., Clarke, E.: Using branching-time temporal logic to synthesize synchronization skeletons. Sci. Comput. Program. **2**(3), 241–266 (1982)
6. Jones, A.V., Lomuscio, A.: Distributed BDD-based BMC for the verification of multi-agent systems. In: van der Hoek, W., Kaminka, G.A., Lespérance, Y., Luck, M., Sen, S. (eds.) 9th International Conference on Autonomous Agents and Multiagent Systems (AAMAS 2010) Toronto, Canada, 2010, vol. 1–3, pp. 675–682. IFAAMAS, Richland (2010)
7. Kacprzak, M., Dziubinski, M., Budzynska, K.: Strategies in dialogues: a game-theoretic approach. In: Parsons, S., Oren, N., Reed, C., Cerutti, F. (eds.) Computational Models of Argument - Proceedings of COMMA 2014, Scottish Highlands, UK, 2014, Frontiers in Artificial Intelligence and Applications, vol. 266, pp. 333–344. IOS Press, Amsterdam (2014)
8. Kacprzak, M., Rzenca, K., Sawicka, A., Zbrzezny, A., Zukowska, K.: A formal model of an argumentative dialogue in the management of emotions, Poznan Reasoning Week, L&C 2016/14th ArgDiap/QuestPro 2016 Abstracts (2016). http://poznanreasoningweek.files.wordpress.com/2016/09/ prw2016abstracts.pdf. Accessed 05 Mar 2017

9. Kacprzak, M., Sawicka, A.: Identification of formal fallacies in a natural dialogue. Fundam. Inform. **135**(4), 403–417 (2014)

10. Kacprzak, M., Sawicka, A., Zbrzezny, A.: Dialogue systems: modeling and prediction of their dynamics. In: Abraham, A., Wegrzyn-Wolska, K., Hassanien, A.E., Snasel, V., Alimi, A.M. (eds.) Proceedings of the Second International Afro-European Conference for Industrial Advancement AECIA 2015. AISC, vol. 427, pp. 421–431. Springer, Cham (2016). doi:10.1007/978-3-319-29504-6_40

11. Kacprzak, M., Sawicka, A., Zbrzezny, A.: Towards model checking argumentative dialogues with emotional reasoning (extended abstract). In: Proceedings of the 25th International Workshop on Concurrency, Specification and Programming, pp. 257–268 (2016)

12. Kacprzak, M., Yaskorska, O.: Dialogue protocols for formal fallacies. Argumentation **28**(3), 349–369 (2014)

13. Lomuscio, A., Qu, H., Raimondi, F.: MCMAS: an open-source model checker for the verification of multi-agent systems. Int. J. Softw. Tools Technol. Transf. **19**(1), 9–30 (2017)

14. Meski, A., Penczek, W., Szreter, M., Wozna-Szczesniak, B., Zbrzezny, A.: BDD-versus SAT-based bounded model checking for the existential fragment of linear temporal logic with knowledge: algorithms and their performance. Auton. Agents Multi-agent Syst. **28**(4), 558–604 (2014)

15. Penczek, W., Lomuscio, A.: Verifying epistemic properties of multi-agent systems via bounded model checking. Fundam. Inform. **55**(2), 167–185 (2003)

16. Penczek, W., Wozna-Szczesniak, B., Zbrzezny, A.: Towards SAT-based BMC for LTLK over interleaved interpreted systems. Fundam. Inform. **119**(3–4), 373–392 (2012)

17. Prakken, H.: Models of persuasion dialogue. In: Simari, G., Rahwan, I. (eds.) Argumentation in Artificial Intelligence, pp. 281–300. Springer, Heidelberg (2009). doi:10.1007/978-0-387-98197-0_14

18. Raimondi, F., Lomuscio, A.: Automatic verification of multi-agent systems by model checking via ordered binary decision diagrams. J. Appl. Logic **5**(2), 235–251 (2007). Logic-Based Agent Verification

19. Visser, J., Bex, F., Reed, C., Garssen, B.: Correspondence between the pragma-dialectical discussion model and the argument interchange format. Stud. Logic, Gramm. Rhetor. **23**(36), 189–224 (2011)

20. Wells, S., Reed, C.A.: A domain specific language for describing diverse systems of dialogue. J. Appl. Logic **10**(4), 309–329 (2012)

21. Yaskorska, O., Budzynska, K., Kacprzak, M.: Proving propositional tautologies in a natural dialogue. Fundam. Inform. **128**(1–2), 239–253 (2013)

22. Zbrzezny, A.M., Woźna-Szcześniak, B., Zbrzezny, A.: SMT-based bounded model checking for weighted epistemic ECTL. In: Pereira, F., Machado, P., Costa, E., Cardoso, A. (eds.) EPIA 2015. LNCS (LNAI), vol. 9273, pp. 651–657. Springer, Cham (2015). doi:10.1007/978-3-319-23485-4_65

23. Zbrzezny, A.M., Zbrzezny, A., Raimondi, F.: Efficient model checking timed and weighted interpreted systems using SMT and SAT solvers. In: Jezic, G., Chen-Burger, Y.-H.J., Howlett, R.J., Jain, L.C. (eds.) Agent and Multi-Agent Systems: Technology and Applications. SIST, vol. 58, pp. 45–55. Springer, Cham (2016). doi:10.1007/978-3-319-39883-9_4

Simple SMT-Based Bounded Model Checking for Timed Interpreted Systems

Agnieszka M. Zbrzezny[✉] and Andrzej Zbrzezny

IMCS, Jan Długosz University, Al. Armii Krajowej 13/15,
42-200 Częstochowa, Poland
{agnieszka.zbrzezny,a.zbrzezny}@ajd.czest.pl

Abstract. The paper deals with symbolic approach to bounded model checking (BMC) for metric temporal logic with epistemic operators (MTLK) that is interpreted over timed interpreted systems (TIS). We present an SMT-based BMC method based on the translation of MTLK formulae to LTL_qK formulae. We show how to implement the bounded model checking technique for LTL_qK logic and timed interpreted systems, and we present full translation to SMT problem for LTL_qK. As a case study, we apply the technique in the analysis of the Timed Generic Pipeline Paradigm modelled by TIS. We also present the differences between the old translation of MTLK and the new one. The theoretical description is supported by the experimental results that demonstrate the efficiency of the method.

1 Introduction

The formalism of *interpreted systems* (IS) was introduced in [5] to model multi-agent systems (MAS) [10], which are intended for reasoning about the agents' epistemic and temporal properties. The formalism of timed interpreted systems (TIS) was presented in [11] extends IS to make the reasoning possible about not only temporal and epistemic properties, but also about real-time aspects of MASs.

Multi-agent systems (MASs) are composed of many intelligent agents that interact with each other. The agents can share a common goal or they can pursue their own interests. Also, the agents may have deadline or other timing constraints to achieve in- tended targets. As it was shown in [5], knowledge is a useful concept for analysing the information state and the behaviour of agents in multi-agent systems. In particular, it is useful to reason about and to verify the evolution over time of epistemic states [6].

Model checking [2] is an automatic method for formally verifying systems, in particular, multi-agent systems. To check automatically whether the system satisfies a given property, one must first create a formal model of the system, and then describe the property in a modal logic [4].

Partly supported by National Science Centre under the grant No. 2014/15/N/ST6/05079.

L. Polkowski et al. (Eds.): IJCRS 2017, Part II, LNAI 10314, pp. 487–504, 2017.
DOI: 10.1007/978-3-319-60840-2_35

Bounded model checking [1,9] (BMC) is one of the symbolic model checking techniques designed for finding witnesses for existential properties or counterexamples for universal properties. Its main idea is to consider a model reduced to a specific depth, which means that we consider only finite prefixes of the paths in the model. The SMT-BMC method works by mapping a bounded model checking problem to the satisfiability modulo theories problem (SMT). For metric temporal logic with epistemic operators (MTLK) [7,11] and timed interpreted systems [11] the BMC method can by described as follows: given a model $\mathcal{M}$ for a timed interpreted system, an MTLK formula φ, and a bound k, a model checker creates a quantifier-free first-order formula $[\mathcal{M}, \varphi]_k$ that is satisfiable if and only if the formula φ is true in the model $\mathcal{M}$.

The original contributions of the paper are as follows. First of all, we define a translation of the existential model checking problem for MTLK to the existential model checking problem for linear temporal logic with additional propositional variables q_I. This logic is denoted by $\mathrm{LTL_q K}$. Secondly, we define bounded semantics for $\mathrm{LTL_q K}$ and define the BMC algorithm. Finally, we define the translation of $\mathrm{LTL_q K}$ formula to SMT problem and implement the new method.

The translation from MTLK to $\mathrm{LTL_q K}$ requires neither new clocks nor new transitions, whereas the translation to HLTLK [11] requires as many new clocks as there are intervals in a given formula. It also requires an exponential number of resetting transitions. Moreover, our BMC method needs only one path for temporal operators, whereas the BMC method from [11] needs a number of paths depending on a given formula φ. Thus, one may expect that our method is much more effective since intuition is that an encoding which results in fewer variables and clauses is usually easier to solve.

Finally, we evaluate the BMC method experimentally by means of a timed generic pipeline paradigm (TGPP), which we model by a TIS, and then we compare it with the corresponding SAT-based BMC method [14].

The rest of the paper is structured as follows. In Sect. 2 we briefly recall the basic notion used through the paper. In Sect. 3 we define the translation to $\mathrm{LTL_q K}$. In Sect. 4 we define the BMC method for $\mathrm{LTL_q K}$. In Sect. 5 we discuss our experimental results. In Sect. 6 we conclude the paper.

2   Preliminaries

In this section we introduce the basic definitions used in the paper. In particular, we define the semantics of timed interpreted systems and syntax and semantics of MTLK. The semantics of timed interpreted systems provides a setting to reason about MAS by means of specifications based on knowledge and discrete time.

2.1   Timed Interpreted System

Let us start by fixing some notation used through the paper. Let $\mathbb{N}$ be a set of natural numbers. We assume a finite set $\mathcal{X} = \{x_0, \ldots, x_{n-1}\}$ of variables, called *clocks*. Each clock is a variable ranging over a set of non-negative natural numbers.

A *clock valuation* is a total function $v : \mathcal{X} \mapsto \mathbb{N}$ that assigns to each clock x a non-negative integer value $v(x)$. The set of all the clock valuations is denoted by $\mathbb{N}^n$. For $X \subseteq \mathcal{X}$, the valuation $v' = v[X := 0]$ is defined as: $\forall x \in X, v'(x) = 0$ and $\forall x \in \mathcal{X} \setminus X, v'(x) = v(x)$. For $\delta \in \mathbb{N}_+, v + \delta$ denotes the valuation v'' such that $\forall x \in \mathcal{X}, v''(x) = v(x) + \delta$. Let $x \in \mathcal{X}, c \in \mathbb{N}$. The set $\mathcal{C}(\mathcal{X})$ of *clock constraints* over the set of clocks $\mathcal{X}$ is defined by the following grammar:

$$\mathfrak{cc} := true \mid x < c \mid x \leq c \mid x = c \mid x \geq c \mid x > c \mid \mathfrak{cc} \wedge \mathfrak{cc}.$$

Let v be a clock valuation, and $\mathfrak{cc} \in \mathcal{C}(\mathcal{X})$. A clock valuation v satisfies a clock constraint $\mathfrak{cc}$, written as $v \models \mathfrak{cc}$, iff $\mathfrak{cc}$ evaluates to true using the clock values given by the valuation v.

We begin by assuming a MAS to be composed of n agents $\mathcal{A}$. Let $\mathcal{E}$ be a special agent that is used to model the environment in which the agents operate, and $\mathcal{AP} = \bigcup_{i \in \mathcal{A} \cup \{\mathcal{E}\}} \mathcal{AP}_i$ be a set of atomic formulae, such that $\mathcal{AP}_{i_1} \cap \mathcal{AP}_{i_2} = \emptyset$ for all $i_1, i_2 \in \mathcal{A} \cup \{\mathcal{E}\}$.

Timed Interpreted Systems were proposed in [11] to extend interpreted systems (ISs) in order to make possible reasoning about real-time aspects of MASs. A *timed interpreted system* is a tuple

$$\text{TIS} = (\{L_i, Act_i, \mathcal{X}_i, P_i, \mathcal{V}_i, Inv_i, \iota_i\}_{i \in \mathcal{A} \cup \{\mathcal{E}\}}, \{t_i\}_{i \in \mathcal{A}}, \{t_{\mathcal{E}}\}),$$

where:

- L_i is a non-empty set of *locations* of the agent i,
- $\iota_i \subseteq L_i$ is a non-empty set of initial locations,
- Act_i is a non-empty set of *possible actions* of the agent i, $Act = Act_1 \times \ldots \times Act_n \times Act_{\mathcal{E}}$ is the set of *joint actions*. We assume that the special action - called "null", or "silent" action of agent i -ϵ_i belongs to Act_i,
- $\mathcal{X}_i$ is a non-empty set of *clocks*,
- $P_i : L_i \to 2^{Act_i}$ is a *protocol function* modelling the program the agent is executing. Formally, for any agent i, the actions of the agents are selected according to a local protocol.
- $t_i : L_i \times L_{\mathcal{E}} \times \mathcal{C}(\mathcal{X}_i) \times 2^{\mathcal{X}_i} \times Act \to L_i$ is a (partial) *evolution function* for agents. The evolution function determines how local states "evolve", based on the agent's local state, on other agents' actions, on the local state of a special agent used to model the environment, on the clock constraints of agent i, and on the set of clocks;
- $t_{\mathcal{E}} : L_{\mathcal{E}} \times \mathcal{C}(\mathcal{X}_{\mathcal{E}}) \times 2^{\mathcal{X}_{\mathcal{E}}} \times Act \to L_{\mathcal{E}}$ is a (partial) *evolution function* for environment,
- $\mathcal{V}_i : L_i \to 2^{\mathcal{AP}_i}$ is a *valuation function* assigning to each location a set of atomic formulae that are assumed to be true at that location,
- $Inv_i : L_i \to \mathcal{C}(\mathcal{X}_i)$ is an *invariant function*, that constraints the amount of time the agent i may spend in a given location.

It is assumed that locations, actions and clocks for the environment are "public", which means that all the agents know the current location, the action, and the clock valuation of the environment.

We also assume that if $\epsilon_i \in P_i(\ell_i)$, then $t_i(\ell_i, \ell_{\mathcal{E}}, cc_i, \mathcal{X}, (a_1, \ldots, a_n, a_{\mathcal{E}})) = \ell_i$ for $a_i = \epsilon_i$, any $cc_i \in \mathcal{C}(\mathcal{X}_i)$, and any $\mathcal{X} \subseteq \mathcal{X}_i$. Each element t of t_i is denoted by $< \ell_i, \ell_{\mathcal{E}}, cc_i, \mathcal{X}', a, \ell'_i >$, where ℓ_i is the source location, ℓ'_i is the target location, a is an action, cc_i is the enabling condition for cc_i, and $\mathcal{X}' \subseteq \mathcal{X}_i$ is the set of clocks to be reset after performing t. An invariant condition allows the TIS to stay at the location ℓ as long as the constraint $Inv_i(\ell_i)$ is satisfied. The guard cc_i has to be satisfied to enable the transition.

2.2   Timed Model

For a given TIS let the symbol $S = \prod_{i \in \mathcal{A} \cup \{\mathcal{E}\}} (L_i \times \mathbb{N}^{\mathcal{X}_i})$ denote the non-empty set of all the *global states*. Moreover, for a given global state $s = ((\ell_1, v_1), \ldots, (\ell_n, v_n), (\ell_{\mathcal{E}}, v_{\mathcal{E}})) \in S$, let the symbols $l_i(s) = \ell_i$ and $v_i(s) = v_i$ denote, respectively, the local component and the clock valuation of agent $i \in \mathcal{A} \cup \{\mathcal{E}\}$ in s. Now, for a given TIS we define a *timed model* (or a *model*) as a tuple $\mathcal{M} = (S, Act, \iota, T, \mathcal{V})$, where: $Act = Act_1 \times \ldots \times Act_n \times Act_{\mathcal{E}}$ is the set of all the joint actions, $\iota = \prod_{i \in \mathcal{A} \cup \{\mathcal{E}\}} (\iota_i \times \{0\}^{\mathcal{X}_i})$ is the set of all the *initial* global states, $\mathcal{V} : S \to 2^{\mathcal{AP}}$ is the valuation function defined as $\mathcal{V}(s) = \bigcup_{i \in \mathcal{A} \cup \{\mathcal{E}\}} \mathcal{V}_i(l_i(s))$, $T \subseteq S \times (Act \cup \mathbb{N}) \times S$ is a transition relation defined by action and time transitions. Let s and s' be two global states. For $\tilde{a} \in Act$:

1. Action transition: $(s, \tilde{a}, s') \in T$ (or $s \xrightarrow{\tilde{a}} s'$) iff for all $i \in \mathcal{A} \cup \{\mathcal{E}\}$, there exists a local transition $t_i(l_i(s), cc_i, \mathcal{X}', \tilde{a}) = l_i(s')$ such that $v_i(s) \models cc_i \wedge Inv(l_i(s))$ and $v'_i(s') = v_i(s)[\mathcal{X}' := 0]$ and $v'_i(s') \models Inv(l_i(s'))$ $(v_i(s)[\mathcal{X}' := 0]$ denotes the clock valuation which assigns 0 to each clock in $\mathcal{X}'$ and agrees with $v_i(s)$ over the rest of the clocks).
2. Time transition: let $\delta \in \mathbb{N}$, $(s, \delta, s') \in T$ iff for all $i \in \mathcal{A} \cup \mathcal{E}$, $l_i(s) = l_i(s')$ and $v_i(s) \models Inv(l_i(s))$ and $v'_i(s') = v_i(s) + \delta$ and $v'_i(s') \models Inv(l_i(s'))$.

Given a TIS, one can define for any agent i the indistinguishability relation $\sim_i \subseteq S \times S$ as follows: $s \sim_i s'$ iff $l_i(s') = l_i(s)$ and $v_i(s') = v_i(s)$. We assume the following definitions of epistemic relations: $\sim_{\Gamma}^{E} \overset{def}{=} \bigcup_{i \in \Gamma} \sim_i$, $\sim_{\Gamma}^{C} \overset{def}{=} (\sim_{\Gamma}^{E})^+$ (the transitive closure of $\sim_{\Gamma}^{E}$), $\sim_{\Gamma}^{D} \overset{def}{=} \bigcap_{i \in \Gamma} \sim_i$, where $\Gamma \subseteq \mathcal{A}$.

A run in $\mathcal{M}$ is an infinite sequence $\rho = s_0 \xrightarrow{\delta_0, a_0} s_1 \xrightarrow{\delta_1, a_1} s_2 \xrightarrow{\delta_2, a_2} \ldots$ of global states such that the following conditions hold for all $i \in \mathbb{N} : s_i \in S, a_i \in Act, \delta_i \in \mathbb{N}_+$, and there exists $s'_i \in S$ such that $(s_i, \delta_i, s'_i) \in T$ and $(s_i, a_i, s_{i+1}) \in T$.

Observe that the above definition of the run ensures that the first transition is the time one, and between each two action transitions at least one time transition appears.

The set of all the runs starting at $s \in S$ is denoted by $\Pi(s)$, and the set of all the runs starting at an initial state is denoted by $\Pi = \bigcup_{s^0 \in \iota} \Pi(s^0)$. Moreover, for $\tilde{a} \in Act \cup \{\tau\}$, we sometimes write $s \xrightarrow{\tilde{a}} s'$ instead of $(s, \tilde{a}, s') \in T$.

2.3   MTLK

Let $p \in \mathcal{AP}$, and I be an interval in $\mathbb{N}$ of the form: $[a, b)$ or $[a, \infty)$, for $a, b \in \mathbb{N}$ and $a \neq b$. The MTLK in negation normal form is defined by the following grammar:

$$\alpha := \textbf{true} \mid \textbf{false} \mid p \mid \neg p \mid \alpha \wedge \alpha \mid \alpha \vee \alpha \mid \alpha \textbf{U}_I \alpha \mid \textbf{G}_I \alpha \mid \text{K}_i \varphi \mid \overline{\text{K}}_i \varphi.$$

Intuitively, $\textbf{U}_I$ and $\textbf{G}_I$ are the operators for *bounded until* and for *bounded always*. The formula $\alpha \textbf{U}_I \beta$ is true in a computation if β is true in the interval I at least in one state and always earlier α holds. The formula $\textbf{G}_I \alpha$ is true in a computation if α is true at all states of the computation that are in the interval I. The derived basic modality $\textbf{F}_I$ for *bounded eventually* is defined as follows: $\textbf{F}_I \alpha \stackrel{def}{=} \textbf{true} \textbf{U}_I \alpha$. $\overline{\text{K}}_i$ is the operator dual for the standard epistemic modality K_i ("agent i knows"), so $\overline{\text{K}}_i \alpha$ is read as "agent i does not know whether or not α holds".

The EMTLK in the existential fragment of MTLK defined as:

$$\alpha := \textbf{true} \mid \textbf{false} \mid p \mid \neg p \mid \alpha \wedge \alpha \mid \alpha \vee \alpha \mid \alpha \textbf{U}_I \alpha \mid \textbf{G}_I \alpha \mid \overline{\text{K}}_i \varphi.$$

Observe that we assume that MTLK (and so EMTLK) formulae are given in the negation normal form, in which the negation can be only applied to propositional variables. Moreover, EMTLK is existential only w.r.t. the epistemic modalities.

In order to define the satisfiability relation for MTLK, we need to define the notion of a *discrete path* λ_ρ *corresponding to run* ρ [11]. This can be done in a unique way because of the assumption that $\delta_i \in \mathbb{N}_+$. First, define the sequence $\Delta_0 = [b_0, b_1), \Delta_1 = [b_1, b_2), \Delta_2 = [b_2, b_3), \dots$ of pairwise disjoint intervals, where: $b_0 = 0$, and $b_i = b_{i-1} + \delta_{i-1}$ if $i > 0$. Now, for each $t \in \mathbb{N}$, let $idx_\rho(t)$ denote the unique index i such that $t \in \Delta_i$. A *discrete path* (or *path*) λ_ρ *corresponding to* ρ is a mapping $\lambda_\rho : \mathbb{N} \mapsto S$ such that $\lambda_\rho(t) = (\ell_i, v_i + t - b_i)$, where $i = idx_\rho(t)$. Given $t \in \mathbb{N}$, the suffix λ_ρ^t of a path λ_ρ at time t is a path defined as: $\forall i \in \mathbb{N}, \lambda_\rho^t(i) = \lambda_\rho(t + i)$.

In order to improve readability, in the following definition we write $\lambda_\rho^t \models_{MTLK} \varphi$ instead of $\widehat{\mathcal{M}}, \lambda_\rho^t \models_{MTLK} \varphi$, for any MTLK formula φ.

Definition 1. *The* satisfiability *relation* $\models_{MTLK}$, *which indicates truth of an MTLK formula in the model $\mathcal{M}$ along a path λ_ρ at time $t \in \mathbb{N}$, is defined inductively as follows:*

- $\lambda_\rho^t \models_{MTLK} \textbf{true}, \lambda_\rho^t \not\models_{MTLK} \textbf{false}$,
- $\lambda_\rho^t \models_{MTLK} p$ iff $p \in \mathcal{V}(\lambda_\rho(t))$, $\lambda_\rho^t \models_{MTLK} \neg p$ iff $p \notin \mathcal{V}(\lambda_\rho(t))$,
- $\lambda_\rho^t \models_{MTLK} \alpha \wedge \beta$ iff $\lambda_\rho^t \models_{MTLK} \alpha$ and $\lambda_\rho^t \models_{MTLK} \beta$,
- $\lambda_\rho^t \models_{MTLK} \alpha \vee \beta$ iff $\lambda_\rho^t \models_{MTLK} \alpha$ or $\lambda_\rho^t \models_{MTLK} \beta$,
- $\lambda_\rho^t \models_{MTLK} \alpha \textbf{U}_I \beta$ iff $(\exists t' \in I)(\lambda_\rho^{t+t'} \models_{MTLK} \beta$ and $(\forall 0 \leqslant t'' < t')\lambda_\rho^{t+t''} \models_{MTLK} \alpha)$,
- $\lambda_\rho^t \models_{MTLK} \textbf{G}_I \beta$ iff $(\forall t' \in I)(\lambda_\rho^{t+t'} \models_{MTLK} \beta)$,
- $\lambda_\rho^t \models_{MTLK} \text{K}_i \alpha$ iff $(\forall \pi' \in \Pi)(\forall i \geq 0)(\pi'(i) \sim_i \pi(t)$ implies $\mathcal{M}, \pi'^i \models \alpha)$,
- $\lambda_\rho^t \models_{MTLK} \overline{\text{K}}_i \alpha$ iff $(\exists \pi' \in \Pi)(\exists i \geq 0)(\pi'(i) \sim_i \pi(t)$ and $\mathcal{M}, \pi'^i \models \alpha)$.

As $\lambda_\rho^0 = \lambda_\rho$, we shall write $\mathcal{M}, \lambda_\rho \models_{MTLK} \varphi$ for $\mathcal{M}, \lambda_\rho^0 \models_{MTLK} \varphi$. An MTLK formula φ is *existentially valid* in the model $\mathcal{M}$, denoted $\mathcal{M} \models_{MTLK} \textbf{E}\varphi$, if, and only if $\mathcal{M}, \lambda_\rho \models_{MTLK} \varphi$ for some path λ_ρ starting in the initial state of $\mathcal{M}$. Determining whether an MTLK formula φ is existentially valid in a given model is called the *existential model checking problem*.

3   Translation from MTLK to LTL_qK

3.1   Abstract Model

The set of all the clock valuations is infinite which means that a model has an infinite set of states. We need to abstract the proposed model before we can apply the bounded model checking technique.

Let φ be an MTLK formula and TIS $= (\{L_i, Act_i, \mathcal{X}_i, P_i, \mathcal{V}_i, I_i, \iota_i\}_{i \in \mathcal{A} \cup \{\mathcal{E}\}}$, $\{t_i\}_{i \in \mathcal{A}}, \{t_\mathcal{E}\})$ be a timed interpreted system with $\mathcal{X} = \{x_0, \ldots, x_n\}$. For each $i \in \mathcal{A} \cup \{\mathcal{E}\}$, let c_i^{max} be the largest constant appearing in intervals of φ and in any enabling condition involving the clock x_i and used in the state invariants and guards of TIS. For two clock valuations v and v' in $\mathbb{N}^{|\mathcal{X}|}$, we say that $v \simeq v'$ iff for each agent i either $v(x_i) > c_i^{max}$ and $v'(x_i) > c_i^{max}$ or $v(x) \leqslant c_i^{max}$ and $v'(x) \leqslant c_i^{max}$ and $v(x) = v'(x)$.

It is well known, that the relation $\simeq$ is an equivalence relation, what gives rise to construct an finite abstract model. To this end we define the set of possible values of the clock x_i in the abstract model as $\mathbb{D}_i = \{0, \ldots, c_i^{max} + 1\}$. Moreover, for two clock valuations v and v' in $\mathbb{D}_0 \times \ldots \times \mathbb{D}_n \times \mathbb{D}_\mathcal{E}$, we say that v' is the *time successor* of v (denoted $succ(v)$) as follows: for each $x \in \mathcal{X}$,

$$succ(v)(x_i) = \begin{cases} v(x_i) + 1, & \text{if } v(x_i) \leqslant c_j^{max}, \\ c_i^{max} + 1, & \text{if } v(x_i) = c_i^{max} + 1. \end{cases}$$

Definition 2. *A tuple* $\widehat{\mathcal{M}} = (\widehat{S}, Act, \widehat{\iota}, \widehat{T}, \widehat{\mathcal{V}})$, *is an* abstract model, *where*

- $\widehat{\iota} = \prod_{i \in \mathcal{A} \cup \mathcal{E}} (\iota_i \times \{0\}^{|\mathcal{X}_i|})$ *is the set of all the initial global states,*
- $\widehat{S} = \prod_{i \in \mathcal{A} \cup \mathcal{E}} (L_i \times \mathbb{D}_i^{|\mathcal{X}_i|})$ *is the set of all the abstract global states.*
- $\widehat{\mathcal{V}} : \widehat{S} \to 2^{\mathcal{AP}}$ *is the valuation function such that:* $p \in \widehat{\mathcal{V}}(\widehat{s})$ *iff* $p \in \bigcup_{i \in \mathcal{A} \cup \mathcal{E}} \mathcal{V}_i(l_i(\widehat{s}))$ *for all* $p \in \mathcal{AP}$; *and*
- $\widehat{T} \subseteq \widehat{S} \times (Act \cup \tau) \times \widehat{S}$. *Let* $\widetilde{a} \in Act$. *Then,*
  - *action transition is defined as* $(\widehat{s}, \widetilde{a}, \widehat{s}') \in \widehat{T}$ *iff* $\forall_{i \in \mathcal{A}} \exists_{\phi_i \in \mathcal{C}(\mathcal{X}_i)} \exists_{\mathcal{X}_i' \subseteq \mathcal{X}_i}$ $(t_i(l_i(\widehat{s}), \phi_i, \mathcal{X}_i', \widetilde{a}) = l_i(\widehat{s}')$ *and* $v_i \models \phi_i \wedge Inv(l_i(\widehat{s}))$ *and* $v_i'(\widehat{s}') = v_i(\widehat{s})[\mathcal{X}_i' := 0]$ *and* $v_i'(\widehat{s}') \models Inv(l_i(\widehat{s}')))$;
  - *time transition is defined as* $(\widehat{s}, \tau, \widehat{s}') \in \widehat{T}$ *iff* $\forall_{i \in \mathcal{A} \cup \mathcal{E}} (l_i(\widehat{s}) = l_i(\widehat{s}'))$ *and* $v_i(\widehat{s}) \models Inv(l_i(\widehat{s}))$ *and* $succ(v_i(\widehat{s})) \models Inv(l_i(\widehat{s})))$ *and* $\forall_{i \in \mathcal{A}} (v_i'(\widehat{s}') = succ(v_i(\widehat{s}')))$ *and* $(v_\mathcal{E}'(\widehat{s}') = succ(v_\mathcal{E}(\widehat{s})))$.

Definition 3. *A path in* $\widehat{\mathcal{M}}$ *is a sequence* $\pi = (s_0, s_1, \ldots)$ *of states such that for each* $j \in \mathbb{N}$, *either* $(s_j \xrightarrow{\tau} s_{j+1})$ *or* $(s_j \xrightarrow{\widetilde{a}} s_{j+1})$ *for some* $\widetilde{a} \in Act$, *and every action transition is preceded by at least one time transition.*

The above definition of the path ensures that the first transition is the time one, and that between each two action transitions at least one time transition appears.

For a path π, $\pi(j)$ denotes the j-th state s_j of π, $\pi[..j] = (\pi(0), \ldots, \pi(j))$ denotes the j-th prefix of π ending with $\pi(j)$, and $\pi^j = (s_j, s_{j+1}, \ldots)$ denotes the j-th suffix of π starting with $\pi(j)$.

Given a path π one can define a function $\zeta_\pi : \mathbb{N} \mapsto \mathbb{N}$ such that for each $j \geqslant 0, \zeta_\pi(j)$ is equal to the number of time transitions on the prefix $\pi[..j]$. Let us note that for each $j \geqslant 0, \zeta_\pi(j)$ gives the value of the global time in the j-th state of the path π.

3.2   Example of MAS and Its Model

The Timed Generic Pipeline Paradigm (TGPP) TIS model shown in Fig. 1 consists of Producer producing data within the certain time interval ($[a, b]$) or being inactive, Consumer receiving data within the certain time interval ($[c, d]$) or being inactive within the certain time interval ($[g, h]$), and a chain of n intermediate Nodes which can be ready for receiving data within the certain time interval ($[c, d]$), processing data within the certain time interval ($[e, f]$) or sending data. We assume that $a = c = e = g = 1$ and $b = d = f = h = 2 \cdot n + 2$, where n represents number of nodes in the TGPP.

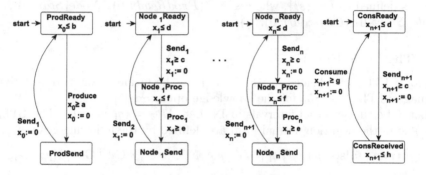

Fig. 1. The TGPP system.

Each agent of the scenario can be modelled by considering its local states, the local actions, the local protocol, the local evolution function, the local clocks, the clock constraints, the invariants, and the local valuation function. Figure 1 shows the local states, the possible actions, and the protocol, the clock constraints, invariants and weights for each agent. Null actions are omitted in the figure. For environment, we shall consider just one local state: $L_\mathcal{E} = \{\cdot\}$. The set of actions for $\mathcal{E}$ is $Act_\mathcal{E} = \{\epsilon_\mathcal{E}\}$. The local protocol of $\mathcal{E}$ is the following: $P_\mathcal{E}(\cdot) = Act_\mathcal{E}$. The set of clocks of $\mathcal{E}$ is empty, and the invariant function is defined as follows: $Inv_\mathcal{E}(\cdot) = true$.

Given Fig. 1, the local evolution functions of TGPP are straightforward to infer. Moreover, we assume the following set of propositional variables: $\mathcal{AP} = \{ProdReady, ProdSend, ConsReady, ConsReceived\}$ with the following definitions of local valuation functions:

$$\widehat{\mathcal{V}}_P(ProdReady) = \{ProdReady\}, \widehat{\mathcal{V}}_P(ProdSend) = \{ProdSend\};$$
$$\widehat{\mathcal{V}}_C(ConsReady) = \{ConsReady\}, \widehat{\mathcal{V}}_C(ConsReceived) = \{ConsReceived\}.$$

Let $Act = Act_P \times \prod_{i=1}^{n} Act_{N_i} \times Act_C \times Act_\mathcal{E}$, with $Act_P = \{Produce, Send_1, \epsilon_P\}$, $Act_C = \{Start_{n+1}, Consume, Send_{n+1}, \epsilon_C\}$, $Act_{N_i} = \{Start_i, Send_i, Send_{i+1}, Proc_i, \epsilon_{N_i}\}$, and $Act_\mathcal{E} = \{\epsilon_\mathcal{E}\}$ defines the set of joint actions for the scenario. For $\tilde{a} \in Act$ let $act_P(\tilde{a})$ denotes an action of Producer, $act_C(\tilde{a})$ denotes an action of Consumer, $act_{N_i}(\tilde{a})$ denotes an action of Node i, and $act_{\mathcal{E}}(\tilde{a})$ denotes an action of environment $\mathcal{E}$. We assume the following local evolution functions:

- $t_P(ProdReady, \cdot, x_0 \geq a, \emptyset, \tilde{a}) = ProdSend$, if $act_P(\tilde{a}) = Produce$;
- $t_P(ProdSend, \cdot, true, \{x_0\}, \tilde{a}) = ProdReady$, if $act_P(\tilde{a}) = Send_1$ and $act_{N_i}(\tilde{a}) = Send_1$;
- $t_C(ConsStart, \cdot, true, \{x_{n+1}\}, \tilde{a}) = ConsReady$, if $act_C(\tilde{a}) = Start_{n+1}$;
- $t_C(ConsReady, \cdot, x_{n+1} \geq c, \{x_{n+1}\}, \tilde{a}) = ConsReceived$, if $act_C(\tilde{a}) = Send_{n+1}$ and $act_{N_n}(\tilde{a}) = Send_{n+1}$;
- $t_C(ConsReceived, \cdot, x_{n+1} \geq g, \{x_{n+1}\}, \tilde{a}) = ConsReady$, if $act_C(\tilde{a}) = Consume$.

The set of all the global states $\widehat{S}$ for the scenario is defined as the product $(L_P \times \mathbb{D}_P^{|\mathcal{X}_P|}) \times \prod_{i=1}^{n}(L_{N_i} \times \mathbb{D}_{N_i}^{|\mathcal{X}_{N_i}|}) \times (L_C \times \mathbb{D}_{L_C}^{|\mathcal{X}_{L_C}|}) \times L_{\mathcal{E}}$. The set of the initial states is defined as $\widehat{\imath} = \{s^0\}$, where $s^0 = ((ProdReady, 0), (Node_1 Start, 0), \ldots, (Node_n Start, 0), (ConsStart, 0), (\cdot))$.

3.3 The Logic $LTL_q K$

The logic LTL_q was defined in [13]. $LTL_q K$ is the fusion of the two underlying languages: LTL_q and $S5_n$ for the knowledge operators [5].

Let $\mathcal{I}$ be the set of all intervals in $\mathbb{N}$. Let $\mathcal{AP}_{\mathcal{I}} = \{q_I \mid I \in \mathcal{I}\}$. The $LTL_q K$ formulae in the negation normal form are defined by the following grammar:

$$\psi ::= \textbf{true} \mid \textbf{false} \mid p \mid \neg p \mid q_I \mid \neg q_I \mid \psi \wedge \psi \mid \psi \vee \psi \mid \psi \textbf{U} \psi \mid \textbf{G} \psi \mid \textbf{K}_i \varphi \mid \overline{\textbf{K}}_i \varphi,$$

where $p \in \mathcal{AP}$ and $q_I \in \mathcal{AP}_{\mathcal{I}}$. The temporal modalities $\textbf{U}$ and $\textbf{G}$ are, respectively, named as the *until* and the *always*. The derived basic temporal modality for *eventually* is defined in the standard way: $\textbf{F}\psi \overset{def}{=} \textbf{true} \textbf{U} \psi$.

In order to improve readability, in the following definition we write $\langle \pi, m \rangle \models_k \psi$ instead of $\widehat{\mathcal{M}}, \langle \pi, m \rangle \models_k \psi$, for any $LTL_q K$ formula ψ.

Definition 4. *The satisfiability relation $\models^d$, which indicates truth of an $LTL_q K$ formula in the abstract model $\widehat{\mathcal{M}}$ along the path π with the starting point m and at the depth $d \geq m$, is defined inductively as follows:*

- $\langle \pi, m \rangle \models^d \textbf{true}$, $\langle \pi, m \rangle \not\models^d \textbf{false}$,
- $\langle \pi, m \rangle \models^d p$ iff $p \in \mathcal{V}(\pi(d))$, $\langle \pi, m \rangle \models^d \neg p$ iff $p \notin \mathcal{V}(\pi(d))$,
- $\langle \pi, m \rangle \models^d q_I$ iff $\zeta_\pi(d) - \zeta_\pi(m) \in I$,
- $\langle \pi, m \rangle \models^d \neg q_I$ iff $\zeta_\pi(d) - \zeta_\pi(m) \notin I$,
- $\langle \pi, m \rangle \models^d \alpha \wedge \beta$ iff $\langle \pi, m \rangle \models^d \alpha$ and $\langle \pi, m \rangle \models^d \beta$,
- $\langle \pi, m \rangle \models^d \alpha \vee \beta$ iff $\langle \pi, m \rangle \models^d \alpha$ or $\langle \pi, m \rangle \models^d \beta$,
- $\langle \pi, m \rangle \models^d \alpha \textbf{U} \beta$ iff $(\exists j \geq d)(\langle \pi, d \rangle \models^j \beta$ and $(\forall d \leq i < j) \langle \pi, d \rangle \models^i \alpha)$,
- $\langle \pi, m \rangle \models^d \textbf{G}\beta$ iff $(\forall j \geq d) \langle \pi, d \rangle \models^j \beta$,
- $\langle \pi, m \rangle \models^d \textbf{K}_i \alpha$ iff $(\forall \pi' \in \Pi)(\forall j \geq d)(\langle \pi', j \rangle \sim_i \langle \pi, d \rangle$ implies $\langle \pi', d \rangle \models^j \alpha)$,
- $\langle \pi, m \rangle \models^d \overline{\textbf{K}}_i \alpha$ iff $(\exists \pi' \in \Pi)(\exists j \geq d)(\langle \pi', j \rangle \sim_i \langle \pi, d \rangle$ and $' \langle \pi', d \rangle \models^j \alpha)$.

An LTL$_q$K formula ψ *existentially holds* in the model $\widehat{\mathcal{M}}$, written $\widehat{\mathcal{M}} \models \mathbf{E}\psi$, if, and only if $\widehat{\mathcal{M}}, \langle \pi, 0 \rangle \models^0 \psi$ for some path π starting at the initial state. The *existential model checking problem* asks whether $\widehat{\mathcal{M}} \models \mathbf{E}\psi$.

3.4   Translation

The translation from MTLK to LTL$_q$K is based on translation presented in [13]. Let $p \in \mathcal{AP}, \alpha$ and β be formulae of MTLK. We define the translation from MTLK into LTL$_q$K as a function tr : MTLK $\rightarrow$ LTL$_q$K in the following way:

- tr($\mathbf{true}$) = $\mathbf{true}$,
- tr($\mathbf{false}$) = $\mathbf{false}$,
- tr(p) = p,
- tr($\neg p$) = $\neg p$,
- tr($\alpha \wedge \beta$) = tr(α) $\wedge$ tr(β),
- tr($\alpha \vee \beta$) = tr(α) $\vee$ tr(β),
- tr($\alpha \mathbf{U}_I \beta$) = tr($\alpha$)$\mathbf{U}(q_I \wedge$ tr(β)),
- tr($\mathbf{F}_I \alpha$) = $\mathbf{F}$tr($q_I \wedge \alpha$),
- tr($\mathbf{G}_I \beta$) = $\mathbf{G}(\neg q_I \vee$ tr(β))
- tr($\alpha \mathbf{R}_I \beta$) = $\mathbf{G}(\neg q_I \vee$ tr(α)) $\vee$ tr(α)$\mathbf{U}(q_I \wedge$ tr($\alpha \vee \beta$)),
- tr($\mathbf{K}\alpha$) = $\mathbf{K}\alpha$,
- tr($\overline{\mathbf{K}}\alpha$) = $\overline{\mathbf{K}}\alpha$.

Observe that the translation of literals as well as logical connectives and epistemic operators is straightforward. The translation of the $\mathbf{U}_I$ operator ensures that β holds somewhere in the interval I (this is expressed by the requirement $q_I \wedge$ tr(β)), and α holds always before β. Similarly, the translation of the $\mathbf{G}_I$ operator ensures that β always holds in the interval I (this is expressed by the requirement $\neg q_I \vee$ tr(β)).

Now we show how to apply our new translation for a timed interpreted system to verify a version of the *timed generic pipeline paradigm* (TGPP).

Example 1. *Consider TGPP described in Sect. 3.2 for one node and the MTLK formula* $\varphi = \mathbf{G}_{[3,4)}\mathbf{F}_{[0,7)}(ProdReady \vee ProdSend)$ *(Fig. 2).*

Assume the following run ρ *with the following prefix:*

$((ProdReady, 0)(NodeReady, 0)(ConsReady, 0)) \overset{1,Produce}{\longrightarrow}$

$((ProdSend, 0)(NodeReady, 1)(ConsReady, 1)) \overset{1,Send_1}{\longrightarrow}$

$((ProdReady, 0)(NodeProc, 0)(ConsReady, 2)) \overset{1,Proc_1}{\longrightarrow}$

$((ProdReady, 1)(NodeSend, 1)(ConsReady, 3)) \overset{1,Send_2}{\longrightarrow}$

$((ProdReady, 2)(NodeReady, 0)(ConsFree, 0)) \overset{}{\longrightarrow} \ldots$

The corresponding path λ_ρ *is constructed as follows. First we take* $\Delta_0 = [0, 1)$, $\Delta_1 = [1, 2)$, $\Delta_2 = [2, 3)$, $\Delta_3 = [3, 4)$, $\Delta_4 = [4, 5)$, $\Delta_5 = [6, 7)$.... *Next we have* $idx_\rho(0) = 0$ *since* $0 \in \Delta_0$, $idx_\rho(1) = 1$ *since* $1 \in \Delta_1$, $idx_\rho(2) = 2$ *since* $2 \in \Delta_2$, $idx_\rho(3) = 3$ *since* $3 \in \Delta_3$, $idx_\rho(4) = 4$ *since* $4 \in \Delta_4$, $idx_\rho(5) = 5$ *since* $5 \in \Delta_5$ *etc. Finally, we get the following discrete path* λ_ρ *corresponding to the run* ρ:

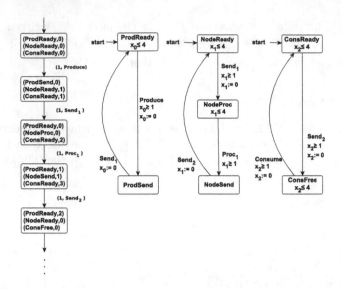

Fig. 2. The TGPP system with one node and an example run.

$\lambda_\rho^0 = ((ProdReady, 0)(NodeReady, 0)(ConsReady, 0)),$
$\lambda_\rho^1 = ((ProdSend, 0)(NodeReady, 1)(ConsReady, 1)),$
$\lambda_\rho^2 = ((ProdReady, 0)(NodeProc, 0)(ConsReady, 2)),$
$\lambda_\rho^3 = ((ProdReady, 1)(NodeSend, 1)(ConsReady, 3)),$
$\lambda_\rho^4 = ((ProdReady, 2)(NodeReady, 0)(ConsFree, 0)),$ *etc.*
From the semantics of MTLK we have that:
$\lambda_\rho^t \models_{MTLK} \mathbf{G}_{[3,4)}\mathbf{F}_{[0,7)}(ProdReady \vee ProdSend)$ *iff*
$(\forall t' \in [3,4))(\exists t'' \in [0,7))(\lambda_\rho^{t+t'+t''} \models_{MTLK} ProdReady\vee$
$\lambda_\rho^{t+t'+t''} \models_{MTLK} ProdSend)).$
Observe that following is true: $\mathcal{V}(\lambda_\rho^3) = ProdReady.$ *Therefore we have that*
$\lambda_\rho^3 \models_{MTLK} \mathbf{G}_{[3,4)}\mathbf{F}_{[0,7)}(ProdReady \vee ProdSend).$
The $\mathrm{tr}(\varphi)$ *is calculated as follows:* $\mathrm{tr}(\mathbf{G}_{[3,4)}\mathbf{F}_{[0,7)}(ProdReady \vee ProdSend))) =$
$\mathbf{G}(\neg q0_{[3,4)} \vee \mathrm{tr}(\mathbf{F}_{[0,7)}(ProdReady \vee ProdSend))) =$
$\mathbf{G}(\neg q0_{[3,4)} \vee \mathbf{F}(q1_{[0,7)} \wedge \mathrm{tr}(ProdReady \vee ProdSend))) =$
$\mathbf{G}(\neg q0_{[3,4)} \vee \mathbf{F}(q1_{[0,7)} \wedge (ProdReady \vee ProdSend))).$
From the semantics of $\mathrm{LTL_q}$ *we have that:*
$\langle \pi, m \rangle \models^d \mathbf{G}(\neg q0 \vee \mathbf{F}(q1 \wedge (ProdReady \vee ProdSend))) \Leftrightarrow$
$(\forall j \geqslant d)(\langle \pi, d \rangle \models^j \neg q0 \vee \langle \pi, d \rangle \models^j \mathbf{F}(q1 \wedge (ProdReady \vee ProdSend))) \Leftrightarrow$
$(\forall j \geqslant d)(\langle \pi, d \rangle \models^j (\neg q0 \vee (\exists i \geqslant j)(\langle \pi, j \rangle \models^i q1 \wedge (ProdReady \vee ProdSend)))) \Leftrightarrow$
$(\forall j \geqslant d)(\langle \pi, d \rangle \models^j \neg q0 \vee (\exists i \geqslant j)(\langle \pi, j \rangle \models^i q1 \wedge \langle \pi, j \rangle \models^i (ProdReady \vee ProdSend))).$

Now we show how to check where $q0_{[3,4)}$ is true. We check $q0_{[3,4)}$ at the starting point $m = 0$:

- at the depth $d = 0$: $\zeta_\pi(0) - \zeta_\pi(0) = 0 - 0 = 0, 0 \notin [3,4)$

- at the depth $d = 1$: $\zeta_\pi(1) - \zeta_\pi(0) = 1 - 0 = 1, 1 \notin [3, 4)$
- at the depth $d = 2$: $\zeta_\pi(2) - \zeta_\pi(0) = 1 - 0 = 1, 1 \notin [3, 4)$
- at the depth $d = 3$: $\zeta_\pi(3) - \zeta_\pi(0) = 2 - 0 = 2, 2 \notin [3, 4)$
- at the depth $d = 4$: $\zeta_\pi(4) - \zeta_\pi(0) = 2 - 0 = 2, 2 \notin [3, 4)$
- at the depth $d = 5$: $\zeta_\pi(5) - \zeta_\pi(0) = 3 - 0 = 3, 3 \in [3, 4)$.

It follows that the formula in question is true in the model under consideration.

Theorem 1. *Let* TIS *be a timed interpreted system,* φ *an* MTLK *formula, and* $\mathcal{M}$ *the model for the timed interpreted system* TIS*, and* $\widehat{\mathcal{M}}$ *the abstract model for the timed interpreted system* TIS *and the formula* φ*. Then,* $\mathcal{M} \models \mathbf{E}\varphi$ *if, and only if* $\widehat{\mathcal{M}} \models \mathbf{E}\mathrm{tr}(\varphi)$.

4 Bounded Model Checking

In this section we define a *bounded semantics* for $\mathrm{LTL_q K}$ in order to translate the *existential model checking problem* for $\mathrm{LTL_q K}$ into the satisfiability problem.

4.1 Bounded Semantics

To define the bounded semantics one needs to represent infinite paths in a model in a special way. To this aim, we recall the notions of *k-paths* and *loops* [12].

Definition 5. *Let* $\widehat{\mathcal{M}}$ *be the abstract model,* $k \in \mathbb{N}$*, and* $0 \leqslant l \leqslant k$*. A* k-path *is a pair* (π, l)*, also denoted by* π_l*, where* π *is a finite sequence* $\pi = (s_0, \ldots, s_k)$ *of states such that for each* $0 \leqslant j < k$*, either* $(s_j \xrightarrow{\tau} s_{j+1})$ *or* $(s_j \xrightarrow{\tilde{a}} s_{j+1})$ *for some* $\tilde{a} \in Act$*, and every action transition is preceded by at least one time transition. A* k-path π_l *is a* loop*, written* $\eth(\pi_l)$ *for short, if* $l < k$ *and* $\pi(k) = \pi(l)$*.*

If a k-path π_l is a loop it represents the infinite path of the form uv^ω, where $u = (\pi(0), \ldots, \pi(l))$ and $v = (\pi(l+1), \ldots, \pi(k))$. We denote this unique path by $\tilde{\pi}_l$. Note that for each $j \in \mathbb{N}$, $\tilde{\pi}_l^{l+j} = \tilde{\pi}_l^{k+j}$.

In the definition of bounded semantics for variables from $\mathcal{AP}_\mathcal{I}$ one needs to use only a finite prefix of the sequence $(\zeta_{\tilde{\pi}_l}(0), \zeta_{\tilde{\pi}_l}(1), \ldots)$. Namely, for a k-path π_l that is not a loop the prefix of the length k is needed, and for a k-path π_l that is a loop the prefix of the length $k + k - l$ is needed.

In order to improve readability, in the following definition we write $\langle \pi_l, m \rangle \models_k \psi$ instead of $\widehat{\mathcal{M}}, \langle \pi_l, m \rangle \models_k \psi$, for any $\mathrm{LTL_q K}$ formula ψ.

Definition 6 (Bounded semantics). *Let* $\widehat{\mathcal{M}}$ *be the abstract model,* π_l *be a* k-path *in* $\widehat{\mathcal{M}}$*, and* $0 \leqslant m, d \leqslant k$*. The relation* $\models_k^d$ *is defined inductively as follows:*

- $\langle \pi_l, m \rangle \models_k^d$ **true***,*
- $\langle \pi_l, m \rangle \not\models_k^d$ **false***,*

$- \langle \pi_l, m \rangle \models_k^d p \ iff \ p \in \mathcal{V}(\pi_l(d)),$

$- \langle \pi_l, m \rangle \models_k^d \neg p \ iff \ p \notin \mathcal{V}(\pi_l(d)),$

$- \langle \pi_l, m \rangle \models_k^d q_I \ iff \begin{cases} \zeta_{\widetilde{\pi}_l}(d) - \zeta_{\widetilde{\pi}_l}(m) \in I, & if \ \pi_l \ is \ not \ a \ loop, \\ \zeta_{\widetilde{\pi}_l}(d) - \zeta_{\widetilde{\pi}_l}(m) \in I, & if \ \pi_l \ is \ a \ loop \ and \ d \geqslant m, \\ \zeta_{\widetilde{\pi}_l}(d + k - l) - \zeta_{\widetilde{\pi}_l}(m) \in I, & if \ \pi_l \ is \ a \ loop \ and \ d < m, \end{cases}$

$- \langle \pi_l, m \rangle \models_k^d \neg q_I \ iff \ \langle \pi_l, m \rangle \not\models_k^d q_I,$

$- \langle \pi_l, m \rangle \models_k^d \alpha \wedge \beta \ iff \ \langle \pi_l, m \rangle \models_k^d \alpha \ and \ \langle \pi_l, m \rangle \models_k^d \beta,$

$- \langle \pi_l, m \rangle \models_k^d \alpha \vee \beta \ iff \ \langle \pi_l, m \rangle \models_k^d \alpha \ or \ \langle \pi_l, m \rangle \models_k^d \beta,$

$- \langle \pi_l, m \rangle \models_k^d \alpha \mathbf{U} \beta \ iff \ (\exists_{d \leqslant j \leqslant k})\big(\langle \pi_l, d \rangle \models_k^j \beta \ and \ (\forall_{d \leqslant i < j}) \langle \pi_l, d \rangle \models_k^j \alpha \big)$

$\quad or \ (\partial(\pi_l)) \ and \ (\exists_{l < j < d}) \langle \pi_l, d \rangle \models_k^j \beta \ and \ (\forall_{l < i < k}) \langle \pi_l, d \rangle \models_k^j \alpha$

$\quad and \ (\forall_{d \leqslant i \leqslant k}) \langle \pi_l, d \rangle \models_k^j \alpha),$

$- \langle \pi_l, m \rangle \models_k^d \mathbf{G} \beta \ iff \partial(\pi_l) \ and \ (\forall_{j \leqslant k}) j \geqslant \min(d, l) \ implies \ \langle \pi_l, d \rangle \models_k^j \beta,$

$- \langle \pi_l, m \rangle \models_k^d \overline{\mathbf{K}}_\mathbf{i} \alpha \ iff \ (\exists \pi'_{l'} \in \Pi_k)(\exists d \leq j \leq k)(\langle \pi_l, d \rangle \models_k^j \alpha \ and \ \pi(d) \sim_\mathbf{i} \pi'(j)).$

An $\mathrm{LTL_q K}$ formula ψ *existentially* k-*holds* in the model $\widehat{\mathcal{M}}$, written $\widehat{\mathcal{M}} \models_k \mathbf{E}\psi$, if, and only if $\widehat{\mathcal{M}}, \langle \pi, 0 \rangle \models_k^0 \psi$ for some path π starting at the initial state.

Theorem 2. *Let* TIS *be a timed interpreted system,* φ *an MTLK formula, and* $\widehat{\mathcal{M}}$ *the abstract model for the timed interpreted system* TIS *and the formula* φ. *Moreover, let* $\psi = \mathrm{tr}(\varphi)$. *Then,* $\widehat{\mathcal{M}} \models \mathbf{E}\psi$ *if, and only if there exists* $k \geqslant 0$ *such that* $\widehat{\mathcal{M}} \models_k \mathbf{E}\psi$.

4.2 Translation to SMT

The presented SMT encoding of the BMC problem for $\mathrm{LTL_q K}$ and for TIS is based on the SAT encoding presented in [9, 12] and it relies on defining a quantifier-free first-order formula. It consists in encoding the transition relation of $\widehat{\mathcal{M}}$ and the $\mathrm{LTL_q K}$ formula $\mathrm{tr}(\varphi)$. The only novelty lies in encoding of the finite prefix of the sequence $(\zeta_{\widetilde{\pi}_l}(0), \zeta_{\widetilde{\pi}_l}(1), \ldots)$.

Let $\widehat{\mathcal{M}}$ be an abstract model for the timed interpreted system and an MTLK formula $\varphi, \mathrm{tr}(\varphi)$ the $\mathrm{LTL_q K}$ formula, and $k \in \mathbb{N}$ a bound. It is well known that the main idea of the SMT-based BMC method consists in translating the bounded model checking problem, i.e., $\widehat{\mathcal{M}} \models_k \mathrm{tr}(\varphi)$, to the problem of checking the satisfiability of the following quantifier-free first-order formula:

$$[\widehat{\mathcal{M}}, \varphi]_k^{\mathrm{SMT}} := [\widehat{\mathcal{M}}^{\varphi, \widehat{\iota}}]_k^{\mathrm{SMT}} \wedge [\varphi]_{\widehat{\mathcal{M}}, k}^{\mathrm{SMT}}.$$

The definition of the formula $[\widehat{\mathcal{M}}, \mathrm{tr}(\varphi)]_k^{\mathrm{SMT}}$ assumes that each abstract global state $\widehat{s} \in \widehat{S}$ of $\widehat{\mathcal{M}}$ can be represented by a valuation of a symbolic state $\overline{\mathbf{w}} = ((w_1, v_1), \ldots, (w_n, v_n), (w_\mathcal{E}, v_\mathcal{E}))$ that consists of symbolic local states. Each symbolic local state is a pair $(w_\mathbf{i}, v_\mathbf{i})$ of individual variables ranging over the natural numbers that consists of a local state of the agent $\mathbf{i}$ and a clock valuation.

Similarly, each action can be represented by a valuation of a symbolic joint action $\overline{a}$ that is a vector of the individual variables ranging over the natural number.

The formula $[\widehat{\mathcal{M}}^{\mathrm{tr}(\varphi),\widehat{\iota}}]^{\mathrm{SMT}}_k$ constrains the $f_k(\varphi)$ symbolic k-paths to be valid k-paths of $\widehat{\mathcal{M}}$, while the formula $[\mathrm{tr}(\varphi)]_{\widehat{\mathcal{M}},k}$ encodes a number of constraints that must be satisfied on these sets of k-paths for $\mathrm{tr}(\varphi)$ to be satisfied. Note that the exact number of necessary symbolic k-paths depends on the checked formula $\mathrm{tr}(\varphi)$, and it can be calculated by means of the function $f_k : \mathrm{LTL_qK} \to \mathbb{N}$ which is an auxiliary function defined in [9,12]. Now, since in the BMC method we deal with existential validity, the number of k-paths sufficient to validate φ is given by the function $\widehat{f}_k : \mathrm{LTL_qK} \to \mathbb{N}$ that is defined as $\widehat{f}_k(\mathrm{tr}(\varphi)) = f_k(\mathrm{tr}(\varphi)) + 1$.

Let $\overline{w}$ and $\overline{w}'$ be two different symbolic states, $\overline{a}$ a symbolic action, δ a symbolic time passage, and u be a symbolic number. We assume definitions of the following auxiliary quantifier-free first-order formulae:

- $I_{\widehat{s}}(\overline{w})$ - it encodes the state $\widehat{s}$ of the abstract model $\widehat{\mathcal{M}}$,
- $\mathcal{T}_i(w_i, (a_i, \delta), w'_i)$ encodes the local evolution function of agent i; We assume that the first transition is the time one, and between each two action transitions at least one time transition appears.
- $\mathcal{A}(\overline{a})$ encodes that each symbolic local action a_i of $\overline{a}$ has to be executed by each agent in which it appears, and
- $\mathcal{T}(\overline{w}, (\overline{a}, \delta), \overline{w}') := \mathcal{A}(\overline{a}) \wedge \bigwedge_{i \in \mathcal{A} \cup \{\mathcal{E}\}} \mathcal{T}_i(w_i, (a_i, \delta, w'_i)$,
- $Gt^m(\pi_n)$ is a function which encodes a global time at the symbolic path π_n at the depth m.

Thus, given the above, one can define the formula $[\widehat{\mathcal{M}}^{\mathrm{tr}(\varphi),\widehat{\iota}}]^{\mathrm{SMT}}_k$ as follows:

$$[\widehat{\mathcal{M}}^{\mathrm{tr}(\varphi),\widehat{\iota}}]^{\mathrm{SMT}}_k := \bigvee_{s \in \widehat{\iota}} I_s(\overline{w}_{0,0}) \wedge \bigvee_{j=1}^{\widehat{f}_k(\mathrm{tr}(\varphi))} \overline{w}_{0,0} = \overline{w}_{0,j} \wedge$$

$$\bigwedge_{j=1}^{\widehat{f}_k(\mathrm{tr}(\varphi))} \bigvee_{l=0}^{k} l = u_j \wedge \bigwedge_{j=1}^{\widehat{f}_k(\mathrm{tr}(\varphi))} \bigwedge_{i=0}^{k-1} \mathcal{T}\left(\overline{w}_{i,j}, (\overline{a}_{i,j}, \delta_{i,j}), \overline{w}_{i+1,j}\right)$$

where $\overline{w}_{i,j}, \overline{a}_{i,j}$, and $\delta_{i,j}$ are, respectively, symbolic states, symbolic actions, and symbolic time passage for $0 \leq i \leq k$ and $1 \leq j \leq \widehat{f}_k(\mathrm{tr}(\varphi))$.

The formula $[\mathrm{tr}(\varphi)]^{\mathrm{SMT}}_{\widehat{\mathcal{M}},k}$ encodes the bounded semantics of a $\mathrm{LTL_qK}$ formula $\mathrm{tr}(\varphi)$, and it is defined on the same sets of individual variables as the formula $[\widehat{\mathcal{M}}^{\mathrm{tr}(\varphi),\widehat{\iota}}]^{\mathrm{SMT}}_k$. Moreover, it uses the auxiliary quantifier-free first-order formulae defined in [12].

Let $F_k(\mathrm{tr}(\varphi)) = \{j \in \mathbb{N} \mid 1 \leq j \leq \widehat{f}_k(\mathrm{tr}(\varphi))\}$, and $[\mathrm{tr}(\varphi)]^{[m,n,A]}_k$ denote the translation of $\mathrm{tr}(\varphi)$ along the n-th symbolic path π^m_n with the starting point m by using the set $A \subseteq F_k(\mathrm{tr}(\varphi))$. Then, the next step is a translation of a $\mathrm{LTL_qK}$ formula $\mathrm{tr}(\varphi)$ to a quantifier-free first-order formula $[\mathrm{tr}(\varphi)]^{\mathrm{SMT}}_{\widehat{\mathcal{M}},k} := [\mathrm{tr}(\varphi)]^{[0,1,F_k(\mathrm{tr}(\varphi))]}_k$.

Definition 7 (Translation of the LTL$_q$K formula). *Let $\widehat{\mathcal{M}}$ be an abstract model, α and β an LTL$_q$K formula, and $k \geq 0$ a bound. We define inductively the translation of α over a path number $n \in F_k(\alpha)$ starting at the symbolic state $\overline{w}_{m,n}$ at the depth m as shown below, where $n' = min(A)$, $h_U = h_U(A, \widehat{f}_k(\phi))$, and $h_R = h_R(A, \widehat{f}_k(\alpha))$.*

$$[\mathbf{true}_{k,m}^{[d,n,A]}] := \mathbf{true},$$

$$[\mathbf{false}_{k,m}^{[d,n,A]}] := \mathbf{false},$$

$$[p_{k,m}^{[d,n,A]}] := p(\overline{\mathbf{w}}_{d,n}),$$

$$[\neg p_{k,m}^{[d,n,A]}] := \neg p(\overline{\mathbf{w}}_{d,n}),$$

$$[q_{\mathrm{I}\,k,m}^{[d,n,A]}] := \begin{cases} \bigvee\limits_{l=0}^{k-1} \left(Gt^d(\boldsymbol{\pi}_n) - Gt^m(\boldsymbol{\pi}_n) \in \mathrm{I} \wedge \overline{\mathbf{w}}_{k,n} \neq \overline{\mathbf{w}}_{l,n} \right) \\ \bigvee\limits_{l=0}^{k-1} \left(Gt^d(\boldsymbol{\pi}_n) - Gt^m(\boldsymbol{\pi}_n) \in \mathrm{I} \wedge \overline{\mathbf{w}}_{k,n} = \overline{\mathbf{w}}_{l,n} \right) \\ \quad \text{if } m \geq d \\ \bigvee\limits_{l=0}^{k-1} \left(Gt^{d+k-l}(\boldsymbol{\pi}_n) - Gt^m(\boldsymbol{\pi}_n) \in \mathrm{I} \wedge \overline{\mathbf{w}}_{k,n} = \overline{\mathbf{w}}_{l,n} \right) \\ \quad \text{if } d < m \end{cases}$$

$$[\neg q_{\mathrm{I}\,k,m}^{[d,n,A]}] := \neg [q_{\mathrm{I}\,k,m}^{[d,n,A]}],$$

$$[\alpha \wedge \beta_{k,m}^{[d,n,A]}] := [\alpha_{k,m}^{[d,n,g_l(A,f_k(\alpha))]}] \wedge [\beta_{k,m}^{[d,n,g_r(A,f_k(\beta))]}],$$

$$[\alpha \vee \beta_{k,m}^{[m,n,A]}] := [\alpha_{k,m}^{[m,n,g_l(A,f_k(\alpha))]}] \vee [\beta_{k,m}^{[m,n,g_l(A,f_k(\beta))]}],$$

$$[\alpha \mathbf{U} \beta]_{k,m}^{[d,n,A]} := \bigvee\limits_{j=d}^{k} \left([\beta]_{k,m}^{[j,n,h_U(A,f_k(\beta))(k)]} \wedge \bigwedge\limits_{i=d}^{j-1} [\alpha]_{k,m}^{[i,n,h_U(A,f_k(\beta))(i)]} \right) \vee$$

$$\left(\bigvee\limits_{l=0}^{d-1} \left(j > u_n \wedge \overline{\mathbf{w}}_{k,n} = \overline{\mathbf{w}}_{l,n} \right) \wedge \bigvee\limits_{j=0}^{d-1} \left(j > u_n \wedge \right. \right.$$

$$[\beta]_{k,m}^{[j,n,h_U(A,f_k(\beta))(k)]} \wedge \bigvee\limits_{i=0}^{j-1} (i > u_n \rightarrow [\alpha]_{k,m}^{[i,n,h_U(A,f_k(\beta))(i)]}) \wedge$$

$$\left. \bigwedge\limits_{i=d}^{k} [\alpha]_{k,m}^{[i,n,h_U(A,f_k(\beta))(i)]} \right) \Big),$$

$$[\alpha \mathbf{R} \beta]_{k,m}^{[d,n,A]} := \bigvee\limits_{j=d}^{k} \left([\alpha]_{k,m}^{[j,n,h_R(A,f_k(\alpha))(k+1)]} \wedge \bigwedge\limits_{i=d}^{j} [\beta]_{k,m}^{[i,n,h_R(A,f_k(\alpha))(i)]} \right)$$

$$\vee \left(\bigvee\limits_{l=0}^{d-1} \left(j > u_n \wedge \overline{\mathbf{w}}_{k,n} = \overline{\mathbf{w}}_{l,n} \right) \wedge \bigvee\limits_{j=0}^{d-1} \left(j > u_n \wedge \right. \right.$$

$$[\alpha]_{k,m}^{[j,n,h_{\mathbf{R}}(A,f_k(\alpha))(k+1)]} \wedge \bigwedge_{i=0}^{j-1} \left(i > u_n \rightarrow [\beta]_{k,m}^{[i,n,h_{\mathbf{R}}(A,f_k(\alpha))(i)]}\right)$$

$$\wedge \bigwedge_{i=d}^{k} [\beta]_{k,m}^{[i,n,h_{\mathbf{R}}(A,f_k(\alpha))(i)]}\bigg)\bigg) \vee \left(\bigvee_{l=0}^{k-1} \left(\overline{\mathbf{w}}_{k,n} = \overline{\mathbf{w}}_{l,n}\right)\right) \wedge$$

$$\bigwedge_{j=l}^{k} \left(i \geq u_n \rightarrow [\beta]_{k,m}^{[j,n,h_{\mathbf{R}}(A,f_k(\alpha))(j)]}\right) \bigwedge_{j=d}^{k} [\beta]_{k,m}^{[j,n,h_{\mathbf{R}}(A,f_k(\alpha))(j)]}\bigg),$$

$$[\mathbf{K_i}\alpha_{k,m}^{[d,n,A]}] := \bigvee_{s\in\iota} I_s(\overline{\mathbf{w}}_{0,n'}) \wedge \bigvee_{j=0}^{k} \left([\alpha]_{k,m}^{[j,n',g_s(A)]} \wedge H_{\mathbf{i}}(\overline{\mathbf{w}}_{d,n}, \overline{\mathbf{w}}_{j,n'})\right),$$

The theorem below states the correctness and the completeness of the presented translation. It can be proven by induction on the complexity of the given LTL$_q$K formula.

Theorem 3. *Let $\widehat{\mathcal{M}}$ be an abstract model for the timed interpreted system and MTLK formula φ, and let $\mathrm{tr}(\varphi)$ be a LTL$_q$K formula. Then, for every $k \in \mathbb{N}, \widehat{\mathcal{M}} \models_k^d \mathbf{E}\mathrm{tr}(\varphi)$ if, and only if, the quantifier-free first-order formula $[\widehat{\mathcal{M}}, \mathrm{tr}(\varphi)]_k$ is satisfiable.*

5 Experimental Results

In this section we experimentally evaluate the performance of our new translation. We have conducted the experiments using Timed Generic Pipeline Paradigm (TGPP) [13].

We have tested the TGPP timed interpreted system model, scaled in the number of intermediate nodes on the following MTLK formulae that existentially hold in the model of TGPP (n is the number of nodes):

- $\varphi_1 = \mathbf{G}(\mathrm{K}_P(ProdSend \Rightarrow \mathbf{F}_{[0,2n+2)}(ConsReceived)))$. It expresses that Producer knows that each time Producer produces data, then Consumer receives this data not later than in $2n + 1$ time units.
- $\varphi_2 = \mathrm{K}_P(\mathbf{F}_{[0,2n+1)}(ConsReceived))$. It states that Producer knows that eventually Consumer will receive data not later than in $2n + 1$ time units.
- $\varphi_3 = \mathrm{K}_C(\mathrm{K}_P(\mathbf{F}_{[0,2n+2)}(ConsReceived)))$. It expresses that Consumer knows that Producer knows that eventually Consumer will receive data not later than in $2n + 2$ time units.
- $\varphi_4 = \mathrm{K}_P(ConsReceived \Rightarrow \mathbf{F}_{[0,2n+1)}(\neg ConsReceived))$. It states that Producer knows that time Consumer receives data, then Consumer is ready to receive data no later than $2n + 1$ time units after that Consumer will receive data.

5.1   Performance Evaluation

We have performed our experimental results on a computer equipped with I7-3770 processor, 32 GB of RAM, and the operating system Linux. Our SMT-based BMC algorithm are implemented as standalone program written in the programming language C++. We used the state of the art SMT-solvers Z3 [8] and Yices2 [3], and the state of the art SAT-solver CryptoMiniSAT.

All the benchmarks together with instructions on how to reproduce our experimental results can be found at the web page tinyurl.com/smt-bmc-tis-emtlk.

The number of considered k-paths for the properties φ_1, φ_2, and φ_4, is equal to 2, and for the property φ_3 is equal to 3.

The line charts in Figs. 3, 4, 5 and 6 showing the total time and the memory consumption for all the tested properties. In general, the experimental results show that the SAT-based BMC outperforms the SMT-based BMC in the execution time (as shown below in the line charts), but the SMT-based BMC outperforms the SAT-based BMC in the memory consumption.

The reason of the higher efficiency of the SAT-based BMC method is small number of arithmetic operations and small number of k-paths with a long length.

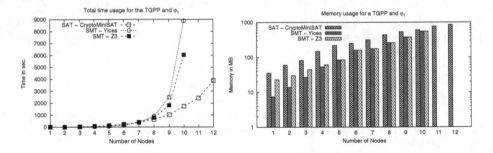

Fig. 3. TGPP with n nodes.

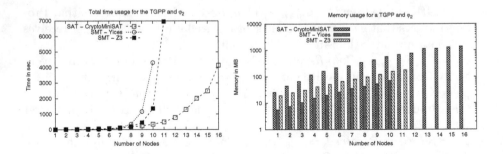

Fig. 4. TGPP with n nodes.

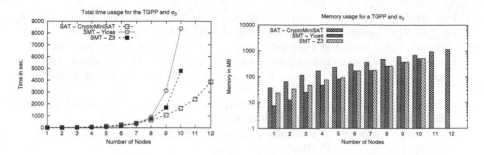

Fig. 5. TGPP with n nodes.

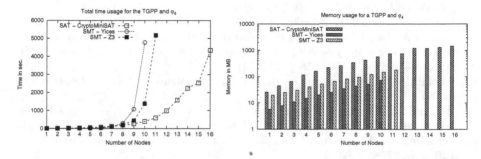

Fig. 6. TGPP with n nodes.

6   Conclusions

We have proposed, implemented, and experimentally evaluated SMT-based BMC method for timed interpreted systems and for properties expressible in MTLK with the semantics over timed interpreted systems. The method is based on a translation of the existential model checking for MTLK to the existential model checking for LTL_qK, and then on the translation of the existential model checking for LTL_qK to the quantifier-free first-order formula.

We believe that our approach is much better than the approach based on translation to HLTLK as we could see in [13]. The reason is that the new method needs only one new path for temporal operators, does not need any new clocks, and does not need any new transitions. The paper presents preliminary experimental results only, but they show that the proposed verification method is quite efficient and worth exploring especially if memory usage is the priority.

References

1. Biere, A., Cimatti, A., Clarke, E., Zhu, Y.: Symbolic model checking without BDDs. In: Cleaveland, W.R. (ed.) TACAS 1999. LNCS, vol. 1579, pp. 193–207. Springer, Heidelberg (1999). doi:10.1007/3-540-49059-0_14
2. Clarke, E., Grumberg, O., Peled, D.: Model Checking. MIT Press, Cambridge (1999)

3. Dutertre, B.: Yices 2.2. In: Biere, A., Bloem, R. (eds.) CAV 2014. LNCS, vol. 8559, pp. 737–744. Springer, Cham (2014). doi:10.1007/978-3-319-08867-9_49

4. Emerson, E.A.: Temporal and modal logic. In: Handbook of Theoretical Computer Science. Formal Methods and Semantics, vol. B, pp. 995–1067. Elsevier (1990)

5. Fagin, R., Halpern, J.Y., Moses, Y., Vardi, M.Y.: Reasoning About Knowledge. MIT Press, Cambridge (1995)

6. Halpern, J.Y., Vardi, M.Y.: The complexity of reasoning about knowledge and time. i. lower bounds. J. Comput. Syst. Sci. **38**(1), 195–237 (1989)

7. Koymans, R.: Specifying real-time properties with metric temporal logic. Real-Time Syst. **2**(4), 255–299 (1990)

8. De Moura, L., Bjørner, N.: Z3: an efficient SMT solver. In: Ramakrishnan, C.R., Rehof, J. (eds.) TACAS 2008. LNCS, vol. 4963, pp. 337–340. Springer, Heidelberg (2008). doi:10.1007/978-3-540-78800-3_24

9. Męski, A., Penczek, W., Szreter, M., Woźna-Szcześniak, B., Zbrzezny, A.: BDD-versus SAT-based bounded model checking for the existential fragment of linear temporal logic with knowledge: algorithms and their performance. Auton. Agent. Multi-Agent Syst. **28**(4), 558–604 (2014)

10. Wooldridge, M.: An Introduction to Multi-agent Systems, 2nd edn. Wiley, Hoboken (2009)

11. Woźna-Szcześniak, B., Zbrzezny, A.: Checking EMTLK properties of timed interpreted systems via bounded model checking. Stud. Logica. **104**(4), 641–678 (2016)

12. Zbrzezny, A.: A new translation from ECTL* to SAT. Fundam. Informaticae **120**(3–4), 377–397 (2012)

13. Zbrzezny, A.M., Zbrzezny, A.: Simple bounded MTL model checking for discrete timed automata (extended abstract). In: Proceedings of CS&P 2016, pp. 37–48 (2016)

14. Zbrzezny, A.M., Zbrzezny, A.: Simple bounded MTLK model checking for timed interpreted systems. In: Jezic, G., Kusek, M., Chen-Burger, Y.-H.J., Howlett, R.J., Jain, L.C. (eds.) KES-AMSTA 2017. SIST, vol. 74, pp. 88–98. Springer, Cham (2018). doi:10.1007/978-3-319-59394-4_9

A Neural Network Pattern Recognition Approach to Automatic Rainfall Classification by Using Signal Strength in LTE/4G Networks

Francesco Beritelli[1], Giacomo Capizzi[1], Grazia Lo Sciuto[1],
Francesco Scaglione[1], Dawid Połap[2], and Marcin Woźniak[2(✉)]

[1] Department of Electrical, Electronics, and Informatics Engineering,
University of Catania, Viale A. Doria 6, 95125 Catania, Italy
gcapizzi@diees.unict.it, glosciuto@dii.unict.it
[2] Institute of Mathematics, Silesian University of Technology,
Kaszubska 23, 44-100 Gliwice, Poland
{dawid.polap,marcin.wozniak}@polsl.pl

Abstract. Accurate and real time rainfall levels estimations are very useful in various applications of hydraulic structure design, agriculture, weather forecasting, climate modeling, etc. An accurate measurement of rainfall with high spatial resolution is possible with an appropriate positioned set of rainfall gauge, but an alternative method to estimate the rainfall is the analysis of electromagnetic wave, in particular the microwave attenuation. Mainly this is done concerning impact of rain on transmission of electromagnetic waves at the level of radio frequency above 10 GHz. In this paper we investigate a new method to estimate rainfall level using the analysis of received signal strength and its variance in mobile LTE/4G terminal to produce a map of prediction.

Keywords: Rainfall estimation · LTE · Radio signal attenuation · Neural network

1 Introduction

In meteorology rainfall levels are important climatologic features for weather forecast affecting humans, industries, and harvesting in agriculture. Intense rainfall events in Italy have sparked shallow landslides leading to serious consequences. The rainfall level is not easy to measure due to many factors such as the intermittent nature, the spatial and temporal variability, and the sensitivity to environmental conditions [1]. In order to provide accurate rainfall estimations, many studies focus on hybrid solutions incorporating rain gauges and weather radar.

The first attempt to rainfall estimation based on microwave attenuation was carried out by Atlas and Ulbrich [2]. The research has investigated the relation between microwave attenuation and rainfall rate pointing out a nearly linear relation in 10–35 GHz range frequency. We can find several studies on rainfall estimation based on microwave attenuation analysis using commercial microwave links [3, 5–7]. In addition to higher spatial resolution rainfall estimation based on study of the electromagnetic waves attenuation allows to increase temporal resolution [8]. However attenuation

© Springer International Publishing AG 2017
L. Polkowski et al. (Eds.): IJCRS 2017, Part II, LNAI 10314, pp. 505–512, 2017.
DOI: 10.1007/978-3-319-60840-2_36

becomes considerable for frequencies higher than 10 GHz. Empirical results have shown that at low frequencies signal attenuation is significantly higher than theoretical attenuation model. In particular there are some studies on Global System for Mobile (GSM) at 1.8 GHz to analyze effects of rain on signal propagation [9, 10]. Unfortunately the GSM signals received by mobile terminal is affected by a considerable attenuation and a mismatching levels due to the rain attenuation at these frequencies [11]. An interesting approach to estimate rainfall level from data collected by a mobile terminal is proposed in [12], while efficient programming approaches are in [4].

In this paper the rain condition effects on 4G/LTE mobile radio wave signal propagation are analyzed, in particular we have examined the received signal strength (RSS) from the Mobile Terminal (MT) for which proposed neural classifier is analyzing meteoric precipitation levels by LTE Received Signal Strength.

2   The Rain Attenuation Model

The rain attenuation depends on the frequency and on the rainfall level due to the absorption and the rain scattering. Radio wave attenuation increases with number of raindrops along path, as well as drop size and radio path length through rain [9]. If the wavelength is larger than raindrop size, scattering is the predominant factor. Several attenuation models have been proposed. In particular in this section we analyze the model indicated by the International Telecommunication Union for the Radiocommunication (ITU-R), whose purpose is to provide frequency management service for radiocommunications to ensure optimal and rational use of radio-frequency spectrum.

According to rain attenuation model provided by ITU-R recommendation, the specific attenuation γ_R (dB/km) is obtained from rain rate R (mm/h) using power-law relation:

$$\gamma_r = kR^\alpha \tag{1}$$

The total attenuation A (dB) in a link of length L can be calculated as:

$$A = L\gamma_r \tag{2}$$

The values of coefficients k and α are determined as functions of frequency f (GHz) in the range from 1 to 1000 GHz. The following equations have been developed from curve-fitting to power-law coefficients derived from scattering calculations:

$$\log_{10} k = \sum_{j=1}^{4} a_j \exp\left[-\left(\frac{\log_{10} f - b_j}{c_j}\right)^2\right] + m_k \log_{10} f + c_k \tag{3}$$

$$\alpha = \sum_{j=1}^{5} a_j \exp\left[-\left(\frac{\log_{10} f - b_j}{c_j}\right)^2\right] + m_\alpha \log_{10} c_\alpha \tag{4}$$

where f is frequency (GHz), k is either k_H or k_V and α is either α_H or α_V. The values of the coefficient k constants (k_H for horizontal polarization and k_V for vertical polarization) and the coefficient α constants (α_H for horizontal polarization and α_v for vertical polarization) are given in the appropriate tables in [13]. For linear and circular polarization, and for all path geometries, coefficients in Eq. (1) can be calculated from values obtained from Eqs. (3) and (4) using the following equation:

$$k = \frac{[k_h + K_v + (k_h - k_v)cos^2\theta\,cos2\tau]}{2}, \alpha = \frac{[k_h + k_v + (k_h - k_v)cos^2\theta\,cos2\tau]}{2} \quad (5)$$

where Θ is path elevation angle and τ is polarization tilt angle relative to horizontal ($\tau = 45°$ for circular polarization). ITU-R state that this attenuation model provides sufficient accuracy up to 55 GHz. Theoretical attenuation is 0.002 dB for rain rate of 15 mm/h, although empirical results indicate 12 dB for measured attenuation [13].

3   The Scenario

In this paper we have analyzed the impact of weather conditions on LTE signal. Smartphone with dedicated application to report ID and received signal strength was used for data collection. In our case, knowledge of cell ID allows to verify received signal measured by a mobile terminal which is referred to base station.

The wireless network application has provided collected data with programmable frequency each 60 s. In Fig. 1 is shown the tested scenario in which distance between base station and mobile terminal was about 200 m. The collected data are provided with 5 min temporal resolution.

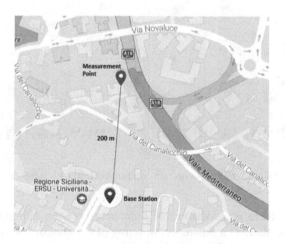

Fig. 1. The test-bed scenario

4   The Signal Analysis

In this paper we classified the rainfall levels according to classification shown in Table 1.

Table 1. Rainfall classification.

Rain classification	mm/h
No rain	0 mm/h
Light Rain	<2.5 mm
Moderate rain	2.5–5 mm/h
Heavy rain	6–10 mm/h
Very heavy rain	11–30 mm/h
Cloudburst	>30 mm/h

We have analyzed three weather conditions: no rain, light rain and moderate rain. In Fig. 2 is reported the measured signal strength in no-rain condition (left) and in light rain condition (right) while Fig. 3 the measured signal strength with moderate rain. All the results were obtained with one hour of measurements collected every 60 s. Figure 4 shows the average values of received signal strength measured by a mobile terminal. The average level of the received signal in no-rain conditions is −77.41 dBm, while for other two rain conditions, i.e. light rain and moderate rain the average level of the received signal is almost the same (−85.66 dBm for light rain and −85.86 dBm for moderate rain).

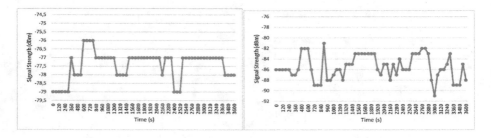

Fig. 2. The received signal strength in no-rain conditions (left) and in light rain condition (right)

It is clear that there is a considerable difference between rain and no-rain conditions. In particular, there is a difference, in terms of attenuation, of about 8 dB. From the analysis of the average signal level values we can discriminate between rain and no-rain conditions. Although the analysis of the average signal level values may not be sufficient to discriminate between light rain and moderate rain.

The probability distribution of received signal strength is represented in Fig. 5. The probability distribution of received signal strength in light rain conditions is different from moderate rain condition. Signal strength in light rain is more variable and presents

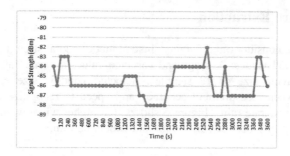

Fig. 3. The received signal strength in moderate rain condition.

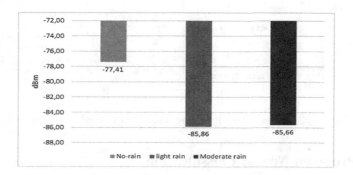

Fig. 4. The average values of received signal strength.

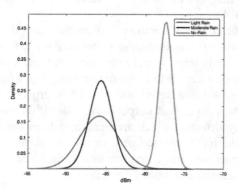

Fig. 5. Probability density of signal strength: no-rain, light rain, moderate rain.

higher variance. Then, on the basis of the signal strength analysis, in particular instantaneous value in correlation with average value and variance, we can discriminate between weather conditions.

5   The Feature Extraction

In the research we consider three features: instantaneous signal strength value, average and variance rainfall values. Average and variance values are calculated using sliding window filter having size of 12 samples. Selected window size establishes good compromise between measurement accuracy and speed to recognize change of state (i.e. light rain – moderate rain). Figure 6 shows that higher window size allows better discrimination capacity between light rain and moderate rain.

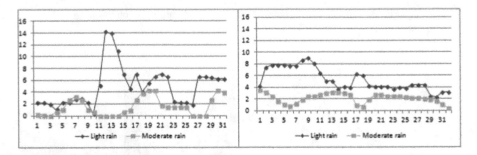

Fig. 6.   The variance calculated using sliding window size equals 5 (left) and 12 (right).

6   The Proposed Neural Classification

The proposed classifier is trained to recognize three weather condition: clear weather, light and moderate rainfall. For the process we have used daily power attenuation data of 4G Received Signal Strength.

To perform classification task we use a probabilistic neural network (PNN). This kind of network can classify various input patterns. Also it is possible to associate categories, which essentially improve performance with respect to particular statistical parameters. PNN utilizes a kernel to discriminate operating within a multilayer feed forward network. There are four layers within a PNN structure namely: input layer, pattern layer, summation layer and output layer. The PNN is created by a set of multivariate probability densities which are generated from the training vectors presented to the PNN. The input instance with unknown category is propagated to the pattern layer. The outputs are a linear combination of the hidden nodes' outputs. More specifically, the k-th network output has the form:

$$y_k(x(t)) = \sum_{j=1}^{M} w_{kj}\Phi_j(x(t)) \tag{6}$$

where

$$\Phi_j(x(t)) = exp\left\{-\frac{1}{2\sigma_j}(x(t) - \mu_j)^T \Sigma_j^{-1}(x(t) - \mu_j)\right\} \tag{7}$$

We restricts Σ to three global and scalar smoothing parameter, σ_1, σ_2 and σ_3, where σ_1 is used in those basis functions that have centers coming from the first class (clear weather), σ_2 for the second class (light rainfall) while σ_3 for the third class (moderate rainfall). The determination of the smoothing parameters is done by calculating the spreads of the training data set belonging to the reference classes for σ_1, σ_2 and σ_3 respectively. The third layer (summation layer) performs an weighted average of the outputs from the second layer for each class. The fourth layer (output layer) performs a vote, selecting the largest value for each class. The resulting network after the training phase is shown in Fig. 7). It consists of 399 neurons (133 of them represent the clear weather, 133 represent the light rainfall and 133 represent the moderate rainfall). To evaluate the pattern recognition algorithm, we have been used a test set composed of 57 patterns (different from that used for the training).

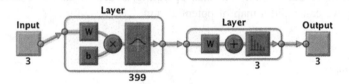

Fig. 7. The proposed neural classifier.

As shown by Fig. 8, a correct classification rate of 93% average has been obtained. Out of 57 test patterns we had 4 misclassification. In all four cases the network confuses the light rainfall with the moderate rainfall.

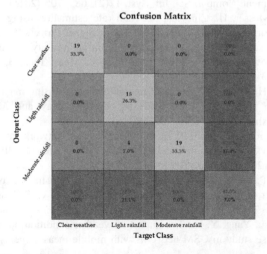

Fig. 8. The confusion matrix of the rain classification.

7 Conclusion

In this paper the rain condition effects on 4G/LTE mobile radio wave signal propagation were analyzed in particular three weather conditions: no rain, light rain and moderate rain. Other weather conditions are not analyzed due to a limited amount of data collected. To discriminate between these conditions we have considered three features: the instantaneous signal strength value, the average and variance values. The average and variance values are calculated using sliding window filter having size of 12 samples. The results obtained in this paper show that the weather conditions have noticeable impact on LTE signal propagation. On the basis of features extracted from received signal by a mobile terminal (instantaneous, average and variance values) it is possible to develop a relation with rainfall levels, providing rainfall information with a higher spatial resolution than classical rainfall measurement methods. Therefore with possibility to have each mobile terminal operating as sensor able to ensure real-time rainfall data we can build a map of potential rain.

References

1. Pascual, M., Guichard, F.: Criticality and disturbance in spatial ecological systems. Trends Ecol. Evol. **20**(2), 88–95 (2005)
2. Atlas, D., Ulbrich, C.W.: Path and area-integrated rainfall measurement by microwave attenuation in the 1–3 cm band. J. Appl. Meteorol. **16**, 1322–1331
3. Messer, H., Zinevich, A., Alpert, P.: Environmental monitoring by wireless communication networks. Science **312**, 713 (2006). doi:10.1126/science.1120034
4. Porubaen, J., Bačíková, M., Chodarev, S., Nosal, M.: Teaching pragmatic model-driven software development. Comput. Sci. Inf. Syst. **12**(2), 683–705 (2015)
5. Goldshtein, O., Messer, H., Zinevich, A.: Rain rate estimation using measurements from commercial telecommunications links. IEEE Trans. Signal Process. **57**, 1616–1625 (2009)
6. Zinevich, A., Messer, H., Alpert, P.: Prediction of rainfall intensity measurement errors using commercial microwave communication links. Atmos. Meas. Tech. **3**, 1385–1402 (2010). doi:10.5194/amt-3-1385-2010
7. Ostrometzky, J., Hagit, M.: Accumulated rainfall estimation using maximum attenuation of microwave radio signal. In: 2014 IEEE 8th Sensor Array and Multichannel Signal Processing Workshop (SAM). IEEE (2014)
8. Messer, H., Zinevich, A., Alpert, P.: Environmental sensor networks using existing wireless communication systems for rainfall and wind velocity measurements. IEEE Instrum. Meas. Mag. **15**, 32–38 (2012). doi:10.1109/MIM.2012.6174577
9. Sharma, A., Jain, P.: Effect of rain on radio propagation in GSM. Int. J. Adv. Eng. Appl. (2010)
10. Kumar, V.: Effect of environmental parameters on GSM and GPS. Indian J. Sci. Technol. **7**(8), 1183–1188 (2014)
11. Fang, S.-H., Sylvia Yang, Y.-H.: The impact of weather condition on radio-based distance estimation: a cause study in GSM networks with mobile measurements. IEEE Trans. Veh. Technol. (2016)
12. Brito, L., Albertini, M.: Data mining of meteorological-related attributes from smartphone data. INFOCOMP **15**(2), 1–9 (2016)
13. ITU-R RECOMMENDATION P.838-3

Attribute Reduction in Rough Set Theory and Formal Concept Analysis

María José Benítez-Caballero, Jesús Medina, and Eloísa Ramírez-Poussa[✉]

Departament of Mathematics, Universidad de Cádiz, Cádiz, Spain
{mariajose.benitez,jesus.medina,eloisa.ramirez}@uca.es

Abstract. Rough Set Theory (RST) and Formal Concept Analysis (FCA) are two mathematical tools for data analysis which, in spite of considering different philosophies, are closely related. In this paper, we study the relation between the attribute reduction mechanisms in FCA and in RST. Different properties will be introduced which provide a new size reduction mechanism in FCA based on the philosophy of RST.

Keywords: Formal Concept Analysis · Rough Set Theory · Attribute reduction · Reduct

1 Introduction

Two fundamental mathematical tools for modeling and processing incomplete information in databases are Rough Set Theory (RST) and Formal Concept Analysis (FCA). Both theories extract information from databases composed by a set of objects, a set of attributes and a relationship between them.

One of the principal targets in both theories is to reduce the number of attributes, preserving the main information that can be obtained from the database. To this end, reducts (minimal set of attributes preserving the information in the database) have been studied in a number of papers, in these two frameworks [4–7,10,11,13,15,16,19,20,24].

In addition, these theories have been related in different papers but few of them have studied the connections between the attribute reduction mechanisms given in both frameworks. For example, in [3], the authors reduce the number of attributes of a formal context using equivalence class as covering generalized in Rough Set Theory. With this covering of objects, they compute the same reduction as Wille [13] and Medina [18] did, however, they do not introduce a proper relationship between the attribute reduction given currently in both framework. In [23], the obtained results are interesting although a proper relation is not completely studied. Hence, a deeper comparison should be given.

In this paper, we relate information systems to the formal contexts in FCA, establishing a way of obtaining an information system from a formal context and

Partially supported by the State Research Agency (AEI) and the European Regional Development Fund (FEDER) project TIN2016-76653-P.

L. Polkowski et al. (Eds.): IJCRS 2017, Part II, LNAI 10314, pp. 513–525, 2017.
DOI: 10.1007/978-3-319-60840-2_37

vice versa. We also present diverse interesting properties about the relationship between the usual attribute reduction mechanisms in FCA and in RST. From this relation, we will consider the philosophy of attribute reduction in RST, in order to obtain a new mechanism of attribute reduction in FCA. Hence, this paper introduces a new and different way of reducing a formal context in FCA, which contributes with a new vision of reduction in this mathematical area from the point of view of RST. The results and this mechanism has been illustrated in an example.

This paper is organized as follows. Section 2 recalls some necessary definitions and results. Section 3 presents the reduction mechanism considered in this work together with some properties and examples, and finally Sect. 4 shows some conclusions and prospects for future works.

2 Preliminaries

In this section, we will recall the basic notions of RST and FCA.

2.1 Rough Set Theory

In RST a relational database can be seen as a decision system or as an information system, depending on the problem to be solve. In this paper we will consider information systems, since these systems are the natural ones used when RST and FCA are compared.

Definition 1. *An* information system $(U, \mathcal{A})$ *is a tuple, such that the sets* $U = \{x_1, x_2, \ldots, x_n\}$ *and* $\mathcal{A} = \{a_1, a_2, \ldots, a_m\}$ *are finite, non-empty sets of objects and attributes, respectively, in which, each* $a \in \mathcal{A}$ *corresponds to a mapping* $\bar{a} : U \to V_a$, *where* V_a *is the value set of* a *over* U. *For every subset* D *of* $\mathcal{A}$, *the* D-indiscernibility relation, $Ind(D)$, *is defined as the equivalence relation*

$$Ind(D) = \{(x_i, x_j) \in U \times U \mid for\,all\,a \in D, \bar{a}(x_i) = \bar{a}(x_j)\}$$

where each class given by this relation can be written as $[x]_D = \{x_i \mid (x, x_i) \in Ind\,(D)\}$. *$Ind(D)$ produces a partition on* U *denoted as* $U/Ind(D) = \{[x]_D \mid x \in U\}$.

If we have that the value set of a *is* $V_a = \{0, 1\}$, *for all* $a \in \mathcal{A}$, $(U, \mathcal{A})$ *is called* a boolean information system.

Now, we will recall the definitions of consistent set and reduct of an information system. These notions will be essential in the relationship between RST and FCA considered in this paper.

Definition 2. *Let* $(U, \mathcal{A})$ *be an information system and a subset of attributes* $D \subseteq \mathcal{A}$. *D is a* consistent set *of* $(U, \mathcal{A})$ *if*

$$Ind(D) = Ind(\mathcal{A})$$

Moreover, if for each $a \in D$ *we have that* $Ind(D \setminus \{a\}) \neq Ind(\mathcal{A})$, *then* D *is called* reduct *of* $(U, \mathcal{A})$.

In order to characterize the reducts in RST, the notions of discernibility matrix and discernibility function [20], are presented in the next definition.

Definition 3. *Given an information system $(U, \mathcal{A})$, its* discernibility matrix *is a matrix of order $|U| \times |U|$, denoted as $M_{\mathcal{A}}$, in which the element $M_{\mathcal{A}}(i, j)$ for each pair of objects (i, j) is defined by:*

$$M_{\mathcal{A}}(i, j) = \{a \in \mathcal{A} \mid \bar{a}(i) \neq \bar{a}(j)\}$$

and the discernibility function *of $(U, \mathcal{A})$ is defined by:*

$$\tau_{\mathcal{A}} = \bigwedge \left\{ \bigvee (M_{\mathcal{A}}(i, j)) \mid i, j \in U \text{ and } M_{\mathcal{A}}(i, j) \neq \varnothing \right\}$$

The following result relates the discernibility function to the reducts of an information system. This result shows a simple mechanism to obtain reducts of an information system.

Theorem 1. *Given a boolean information system $(U, \mathcal{A})$. An arbitrary set D, where $D \subseteq \mathcal{A}$, is a reduct of the information system if and only if the cube $\bigwedge_{a \in D} a$ is a cube in the restricted disjunctive normal form[1] (RDNF) of $\tau_{\mathcal{A}}$.*

2.2 Formal Concept Analysis

As we previously mentioned, another theory applied to the extraction of information from databases is FCA. In this section, the basic definitions of this mathematical tool will be recalled.

In this environment, we consider a set of attributes A, a set of objects B, both of them non empty, and a crisp relationship between them $R: A \times B \rightarrow \{0, 1\}$. We define for each $a \in A$ and $b \in B$ the relation as $R(a, b) = 1$, if a and b are related and $R(a, b) = 0$, otherwise. We will also write aRb when $R(a, b) = 1$. A *context* is the triple (A, B, R) and we can define the mappings[2] $\uparrow: 2^B \rightarrow 2^A$, $\downarrow: 2^A \rightarrow 2^B$, for each $X \subseteq B$ and $Y \subseteq A$, as follows:

$$X^{\uparrow} = \{a \in A \mid \text{for all } b \in X, aRb\} = \{a \in A \mid \text{if } b \in X, \text{ then } aRb\} \quad (1)$$
$$Y^{\downarrow} = \{b \in B \mid \text{for all } a \in Y, aRb\} = \{b \in B \mid \text{if } a \in Y, \text{ then } aRb\} \quad (2)$$

A *concept* in the context (A, B, R) is a pair (X, Y), where $X \subseteq B$, $Y \subseteq A$, $X^{\uparrow} = Y$ and $Y^{\downarrow} = X$ hold. The subset of objects X of the concept (X, Y) is called *extent* and the *intent* is the subset of attributes Y.

The set of all the concepts is denoted as $\mathcal{B}(A, B, R)$. This set has a complete lattice structure [8, 13], when we consider the inclusion ordering on the left

---

[1] We assume that the reader is familiar with the notions related to classical theory of propositional logic [8, 12].

[2] Originally these operators were denoted as $'$ by Ganter and Wille and they were called derivation operators. In order to differentiate between the mapping on the set of objects and on the set of attributes, we have changed the notation.

argument (or, equivalently, the opposite of the inclusion ordering on the right argument). That means, for each $(X_1, Y_1), (X_2, Y_2) \in \mathcal{B}(A, B, R)$, we have that $(X_1, Y_1) \leq (X_2, Y_2)$, if $X_1 \subseteq X_2$ (or, equivalently, $Y_2 \subseteq Y_1$). We define the meet $(\wedge)$ and join $(\vee)$ operators by:

$$(X_1, Y_1) \wedge (X_2, Y_2) = (X_1 \wedge X_2, (Y_1 \vee Y_2)^{\downarrow\uparrow})$$
$$(X_1, Y_1) \vee (X_2, Y_2) = ((X_1 \vee X_2)^{\uparrow\downarrow}, Y_1 \wedge Y_2)$$

for all $(X_1, Y_1), (X_2, Y_2) \in \mathcal{B}(A, B, R)$.

Note that the operators defined in Eqs. (1) and (2) form a Galois connection. Given an attribute $a \in A$, the concept generated by a, that is $(a^{\downarrow}, a^{\downarrow\uparrow})$, will be called *attribute-concept*. Note that this pair is really a concept due to $(\uparrow, \downarrow)$ is a Galois connection [8,9]. Similarly, given an object $b \in B$, the concept generated by b, that is $(b^{\uparrow\downarrow}, b^{\uparrow})$, will be called *object-concept*.

On the other hand, reducing the set of attributes without modifying the structure of the concept lattice is pursued by attribute reduction theory in formal concept analysis. That means, obtaining a new concept lattice isomorphic to the original one. Now, we recall some necessary definitions related to attribute reduction in FCA.

Definition 4. *Given two concept lattices $\mathcal{B}(A_1, B, R_1)$ and $\mathcal{B}(A_2, B, R_2)$. If for any $(X, Y) \in \mathcal{B}(A_2, B, R_2)$ there exists $(X', Y') \in \mathcal{B}(A_1, B, R_1)$ such that $X = X'$, then we say that $\mathcal{B}(A_1, B, R_1)$ is* finer *than $\mathcal{B}(A_2, B, R_2)$ and we will write:*

$$\mathcal{B}(A_1, B, R_1) \leq \mathcal{B}(A_2, B, R_2)$$

We said two concept lattices $\mathcal{B}(A_1, B, R_1), \mathcal{B}(A_2, B, R_2)$ are *isomorphic* if $\mathcal{B}(A_1, B, R_1) \leq \mathcal{B}(A_2, B, R_2)$ and $\mathcal{B}(A_2, B, R_2) \leq \mathcal{B}(A_1, B, R_1)$ hold; and we will write

$$\mathcal{B}(A_1, B, R_1) \cong \mathcal{B}(A_2, B, R_2)$$

If we consider a context (A, B, R), a subset of attributes, $Y \subseteq A$ and the restricted relation $R_{|Y} = R \cap (Y \times B)$ then, the triple $(Y, B, R_{|Y})$ is also a formal context. We can interpret it as a *subcontext* of the original one. Therefore, the mappings $\downarrow$ and $\uparrow$ introduced in Eqs. (1) and (2) can be defined in this subcontext, they will be denoted as $\downarrow^Y$ and $\uparrow^Y$ in order to avoid some confusion. It is clear that, given $X \subseteq B$, we obtain that $X^{\uparrow_Y} = X^{\uparrow} \cap Y$. Note that, when we consider a subset $Y_1 \subseteq Y$, then $Y_1^{\downarrow_Y} = Y_1^{\downarrow}$.

Considering a formal context (A, B, R), it is easy to verify that for any $Y \subseteq A$, such that $Y \neq \varnothing$, $\mathcal{B}(A, B, R) \leq \mathcal{B}(Y, B, R_{|Y})$ holds.

Definition 5. *Let (A, B, R) be a context, if there exists a set of attributes $Y \subseteq A$ such that $\mathcal{B}(A, B, R) \cong \mathcal{B}(Y, B, R_{|Y})$, then Y is called a* consistent set *of (A, B, R). Moreover, if $\mathcal{B}(Y \smallsetminus \{y\}, B, R_{|Y \smallsetminus \{y\}}) \ncong \mathcal{B}(A, B, R)$, for all $y \in Y$, then Y is called* reduct *of (A, B, R).*

The core *of (A, B, R) is the intersection of all the reducts of (A, B, R).*

Finally, we will recall the notions of meet-irreducible and join-irreducible elements of a lattice, since these definitions will also be considered later.

Definition 6. *Given a lattice* $(L, \preceq)$, *such that* $\wedge, \vee$ *are the meet and the join operators, and an element* $x \in L$ *verifying*

1. *If* L *has a top element* $\top$, *then* $x \neq \top$.
2. *If* $x = y \wedge z$, *then* $x = y$ *or* $x = z$, *for all* $y, z \in L$.

we call x meet-irreducible ($\wedge$-irreducible) element *of* L. *Condition* (2) *is equivalent to*

2′. *If* $x < y$ *and* $x < z$, *then* $x < y \wedge z$, *for all* $y, z \in L$.

A join-irreducible ($\vee$-irreducible) element *of* L *is defined dually.*

Once the basic definitions on attribute reduction in RST and FCA have been recalled we can relate both reductions since the study given in [23].

3 Attribute Reduction in RST and FCA

Only a few number of papers have worked in the relationship between the attribute reduction in FCA and in RST [3,23]. In [3] the authors rewrite the attribute reduction in FCA using covering sets and they do not introduce a proper relationship between the attribute reduction currently given in both frameworks. On the other hand, the authors in [23] introduce a real relationship, although they only provides an interesting result which proves that a consistent set in FCA is also a consistent set in RST. They also show that the counterpart does not hold. Hence, the consideration of the RST attribute reduction in a FCA framework will provide a different reduction mechanism from the usual attribute reduction in FCA. Therefore, we can consider that we have another new attribute reduction mechanism in FCA. However, before doing this consideration we must study more useful properties and analyze whether this reduction is meaningful and useful.

From now on, as it is usual in real-life knowledge systems, the sets of attributes and the set of objects will be considered finite. Furthermore, in order to highlight what notion of reduct is considered (in RST or in FCA), a reduct of the information system $(U, \mathcal{A})$ will be called *RS-reduct* and a reduct of the context (A, B, R) as *CL-reduct*. In a similar way, a consistent set of the information system $(U, \mathcal{A})$ will be written in short as *RS-consistent set* and a consistent set of the context (A, B, R) as *CL-consistent set*.

First of all, we will recall the result given in [23], which shows in some sense that the attribute reduction in FCA implies an attribute reduction in RST. For that, we need the definition of information system from a formal context and a technical lemma.

Definition 7. *Let* (A, B, R) *be a context, a* context information system *is defined as the pair* (B, A) *where the mappings* $\bar{a} : B \rightarrow V_a$, *with* $V_a = \{0, 1\}$, *are defined as* $\bar{a}(b) = R(a, b)$, *for all* $a \in A, b \in B$.

From the previous definition, the following result straightforwardly holds.

Lemma 1. *Given a context (A, B, R) and the corresponding context informa-tion system (B, A), the following equality holds, for each $a \in A$:*

$$a^{\downarrow} = \bar{a}$$

The following result given in [23] shows that a CL-consistent set of a context provides an RS-consistent set of the context information system.

Theorem 2 [23]. *Given a context (A, B, R) and the corresponding context infor-mation system (B, A). If $D \subseteq A$ is a CL-consistent set then D is an RS-consistent set.*

Note that the previous result is not valid if we consider reducts instead of consistent sets as the following simple example shows.

Example 1. Let us consider a context (A, B, R) with two objects $b_1, b_2 \in B$, two attributes $a_1, a_2 \in A$, and the following relation between them:

$$\begin{array}{c|cc} R & a_1 & a_2 \\ \hline b_1 & 1 & 0 \\ b_2 & 0 & 1 \end{array}$$

In this case, we have that $a_1^{\downarrow} = \{b_1\}$ and $a_2^{\downarrow} = \{b_2\}$ and the associated concept lattice is shown in Fig. 1. Note that, the concepts $C_1 = (a_1^{\downarrow}, a_1^{\downarrow\uparrow})$ and $C_2 = (a_2^{\downarrow}, a_2^{\downarrow\uparrow})$ are both meet-irreducible elements of the concept lattice. There-fore, these concepts cannot be removed and so, the attributes a_1 and a_2 cannot be removed either. Hence, we have that the set $\{a_1, a_2\}$ is a CL-reduct of the context. Indeed, it is the unique CL-reduct.

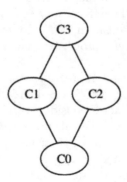

Fig. 1. Concept lattice of the context of Example 1.

On the other hand, if we consider the context information system associated with the context (A, B, R), we have that the discernibility matrix is

$$\begin{pmatrix} \varnothing & \{a_1, a_2\} \\ \{a_1, a_2\} & \varnothing \end{pmatrix}$$

Therefore, the discernibility function is $\tau_{\mathcal{A}} = \{a_1\} \vee \{a_2\}$, which shows that we only need a_1 or a_2 in order to discern the objects b_1 and b_2 (that is, $\text{Ind}(D_1) = \text{Ind}(D_2) = \text{Ind}(\mathcal{A})$) and so, we obtain the RS-reducts $D_1 = \{a_1\}$ and $D_2 = \{a_2\}$, whereas in FCA we need both attributes. □

Consequently, as we previously commented, the counterpart of Theorem 2 is not true, even though considering a small information system. Example 1 also provides that, given an information system $(U, \mathcal{A})$, an RS-consistent set (resp. RS-reduct) may not be a CL-consistent set (resp. CL-reduct) in the information context $(\mathcal{A}, U, R)$. Nevertheless, this fact can be positive if the use of RS-consistent sets in FCA can provide a new and useful reduction mechanism in FCA.

Hereon, we will prove interesting properties of the contexts associated with an information system and an RS-consistent set. Before that, we need to present how to consider a context from an information system.

Definition 8. *Given a boolean information system $(U, \mathcal{A})$, an information context is defined as the triple $(\mathcal{A}, U, R)$, where the relation $R \colon \mathcal{A} \times U \to V_a$, with $V_a = \{0, 1\}$, is defined as $R(a, b) = \bar{a}(b)$, for all $a \in \mathcal{A}$, $b \in U$.*

This is a dual notion of the definition of context information system. The following result proves that different object-concepts in an information context provides different object-concepts in the reduced information context, which implies that the reduction given by an RS-consistent set preserves the number of object-concepts.

Proposition 1. *Given a boolean information system $(U, \mathcal{A})$, $D \subseteq \mathcal{A}$ an RS-consistent set of $(U, \mathcal{A})$, the corresponding information contexts $(\mathcal{A}, U, R)$ and $(D, U, R_{|D})$, and the objects $k, j \in U$. If $k^{\uparrow} \neq j^{\uparrow}$, then $k^{\uparrow_D} \neq j^{\uparrow_D}$.*

The following proposition shows that the reduction given by a RS-consistent set also preserves the (strict) inequality between object-contexts.

Proposition 2. *Let $(U, \mathcal{A})$ be a boolean information system, $D \subseteq \mathcal{A}$ an RS-consistent set of $(U, \mathcal{A})$ and the objects $k, j \in U$. If we have that $k^{\uparrow} \subset j^{\uparrow}$ in the information context $(\mathcal{A}, U, R)$, then $k^{\uparrow_D} \subset j^{\uparrow_D}$ in $(D, U, R_{|D})$.*

Hence, if we consider an RS-consistent set, the ordering among the object-concepts in the corresponding information context is practically preserved. The unique possibility is that incomparable object-concepts in the original information context can be comparable in the reduced one. This fact and other features will be observed in Example 2.

Taking into account the previous result, the following theorem proves that the join-irreducible elements in the reduced concept lattice by an RS-consistent set are also join-irreducible elements of the original concept lattice.

Theorem 3. *Given an information system $(U, \mathcal{A})$ and a RS-consistent set $D \subseteq \mathcal{A}$. If an object $j \in U$ generates a join-irreducible concept in the corresponding information context $(D, U, R_{|D})$, then it also generates a join-irreducible concept in $(\mathcal{A}, U, R)$.*

From the previous results, we have that the consideration of an RS-consistent set does not introduce new join-irreducible elements in the lattice and the strict inclusions between the join-irreducible elements must also be preserved. Therefore, if an object does not generate a join-irreducible concept in the original context, then we have that it cannot generate a join-irreducible concept in the reduced context.

As a consequence, although the notion of RS-consistent set does not imply the notion of CL-consistent set, it has interesting properties to be considered in a reduction mechanism in the FCA framework. Specifically, this reduction mechanism in FCA consists in, given a formal context (A, B, R), computing the RS-reducts $D_1, \ldots, D_n$ of the information context associated with (A, B, R), and then the obtained reduced contexts are: $(D_1, B, R_{|D_1 \times U}), \ldots, (D_n, B, R_{|D_1 \times U})$.

In the following example, we will apply the proposed reduction mechanism using RS-reducts in the FCA framework and we present several comments related to other results introduced in this paper. The context considered in this example has been extracted from [23].

Example 2. Let us consider the formal context (A, B, R), where B represents a group of patients, $B = \{1, 2, 3, 4, 5, 6\}$, A is the set of symptoms (attributes) $A = \{\text{low fever(lf)}, \text{high fever(hf)}, \text{cough(c)}, \text{tonsil inflam.(ti)}, \text{ache muscle(am)}\}$ and R is the relation given by Table 1. The concept lattice associated with this context is displayed in Fig. 2.

Table 1. Relation of Example 2.

R	low fever(lf)	high fever(hf)	cough(c)	tonsil inflam.(ti)	ache muscle(am)
1	0	1	0	0	0
2	0	1	0	1	1
3	1	0	1	1	0
4	1	0	1	1	0
5	0	1	1	1	1
6	0	0	1	1	0

Now, we will reduce the context taking into account RS-reducts. In order to obtain RS-reducts, we have to consider the associated context information system (B, A), to obtain the discernibility matrix and the corresponding discernibility function, according to Definition 3.

In this case, from the relation presented in Table 2, we obtain the following discernibility matrix:[3]

---

[3] Note that the discernibility matrix is symmetric due to the discernibility relation is reflexive.

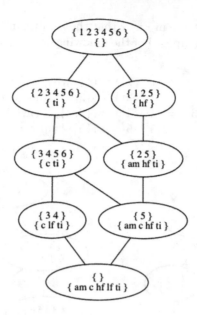

Fig. 2. Concept lattice of the context of Example 2.

$$
\begin{pmatrix}
\varnothing \\
\{\text{ti}, \text{am}\} & \varnothing \\
\{\text{lf}, \text{hf}, \text{c}, \text{ti}\} & \{\text{lf}, \text{hf}, \text{c}, \text{am}\} & \varnothing \\
\{\text{lf}, \text{hf}, \text{c}, \text{ti}\} & \{\text{lf}, \text{hf}, \text{c}, \text{am}\} & \varnothing & \varnothing \\
\{\text{c}, \text{ti}, \text{am}\} & \{\text{c}\} & \{\text{lf}, \text{hf}, \text{am}\} & \{\text{lf}, \text{hf}, \text{am}\} & \varnothing \\
\{\text{hf}, \text{c}, \text{ti}\} & \{\text{hf}, \text{c}, \text{am}\} & \{\text{lf}\} & \{\text{lf}\} & \{\text{hf}, \text{am}\} & \varnothing
\end{pmatrix}
$$

From this matrix, we obtain the discernibility function,

$$
\begin{aligned}
\tau_A = {}& \{\text{ti} \vee \text{am}\} \wedge \{\text{lf} \vee \text{hf} \vee \text{c} \vee \text{ti}\} \wedge \{\text{c} \vee \text{ti} \vee \text{am}\} \wedge \{\text{hf} \vee \text{c} \vee \text{ti}\} \\
& \wedge \{\text{lf} \vee \text{hf} \vee \text{c} \vee \text{am}\} \wedge \{\text{c}\} \wedge \{\text{hf} \vee \text{c} \vee \text{am}\} \wedge \{\text{lf} \vee \text{hf} \vee \text{am}\} \\
& \wedge \{\text{lf}\} \wedge \{\text{hf} \vee \text{am}\} \\
= {}& \{\text{lf} \wedge \text{c} \wedge \text{am}\} \vee \{\text{lf} \wedge \text{hf} \wedge \text{c} \wedge \text{ti}\}
\end{aligned}
$$

Consequently, by Theorem 1, we have two RS-reducts:

$$
\begin{aligned}
D_1 &= \{\text{low fever}, \text{cough}, \text{ache muscle}\} \\
D_2 &= \{\text{low fever}, \text{high fever}, \text{cough}, \text{tonsil inflam.}\}
\end{aligned}
$$

The concept lattices built from the two RS-reducts are shown in Fig. 3. As it is natural, we can see that the structure of the original concept lattice is not necessarily preserved when we consider RS-reducts. In this case, the original structure is not preserved when we consider D_1, whereas we obtain an isomorphic concept lattice to the original one from D_2, that is, D_2 is also a CL-reduct.

Moreover, we can observe in Fig. 2 that the set of join-irreducible elements of the concept lattice are composed of the following concepts, generated by objects 1, 2, 3, 4 and 5:

$$(1^{\uparrow\downarrow}, 1^{\uparrow}) = (\{1, 2, 5\}, \{hf\})$$
$$(2^{\uparrow\downarrow}, 2^{\uparrow}) = (\{2, 5\}, \{am, hf, ti\})$$
$$(3^{\uparrow\downarrow}, 3^{\uparrow}) = (4^{\uparrow\downarrow}, 4^{\uparrow}) = (\{3, 4\}, \{c, lf, ti\})$$
$$(5^{\uparrow\downarrow}, 5^{\uparrow}) = (\{5\}, \{am, c, hf, ti\})$$

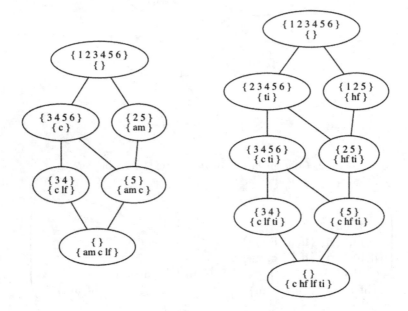

Fig. 3. Concept lattices built from the RS-reducts D_1 (left) and D_2 (right).

Firstly, we will analyze the obtained result considering the RS-reduct D_2. In this case, the object-concepts generated after the reduction of the context from this reduct are given in the following list[4]:

$$(1^{\uparrow_2\downarrow^2}, 1^{\uparrow_2}) = (\{1, 2, 5\}, \{hf\})$$
$$(2^{\uparrow_2\downarrow^2}, 2^{\uparrow_2}) = (\{2, 5\}, \{hf, ti\})$$
$$(3^{\uparrow_2\downarrow^2}, 3^{\uparrow_2}) = (4^{\uparrow_2\downarrow^2}, 4^{\uparrow_2}) = (\{3, 4\}, \{c, lf, ti\})$$
$$(5^{\uparrow_2\downarrow^2}, 5^{\uparrow_2}) = (\{5\}, \{c, hf, ti\})$$

As we previously mentioned, considering D_2 we do not alter the original structure of the concept lattice since this RS-reduct is also a CL-reduct. Hence, Propositions 1, 2 and Theorem 3 trivially hold.

---

[4] In order to simplify the notation, we will write $(^{\uparrow_1}, ^{\downarrow^1})$ and $(^{\uparrow_2}, ^{\downarrow^2})$, instead of $(^{\uparrow_{D_1}}, ^{\downarrow^{D_1}})$ and $(^{\uparrow_{D_2}}, ^{\downarrow^{D_2}})$ to denote the concept-forming operators in the reduced contexts by D_1 and D_2, respectively.

On the other hand, when we consider the concept lattice obtained from the RS-reduct D_1, displayed in left side of Fig. 3, we have that the join-irreducible concepts are $(\{3,4\},\{c,lf\})$, $(\{5\},\{am,c\})$ and $(\{2,5\},\{am\})$ and they are generated by objects 2, 3, 4 and 5:

$$(2^{\uparrow_1\downarrow^1}, 2^{\uparrow_1}) = (\{2,5\},\{am\})$$
$$(3^{\uparrow_1\downarrow^1}, 3^{\uparrow_1}) = (4^{\uparrow_1\downarrow^1}, 4^{\uparrow_1}) = (\{3,4\},\{c,lf\})$$
$$(5^{\uparrow_1\downarrow^1}, 5^{\uparrow_1}) = (\{5\},\{am,c\})$$

which are a subset of the join-irreducible concepts of the original context, as Theorem 3 asserts.

We can observe that Proposition 2 is also satisfied in this case. For example, we have that $2^{\uparrow} < 1^{\uparrow}$ in the original context, and the inequality $2^{\uparrow_1} < 1^{\uparrow_1}$ holds after the reduction.

Besides, we can also note that two incomparable object-concepts in the original information context can become comparable concepts in the reduced one. For instance, the object-concept generated by 1 is not comparable with the object-concept generated by 3 in the original context. Whereas, if we consider the RS-reduct D_1, the object-concepts generated by these objects are comparable.

Moreover, in this reduced context, we have that the concept generated by the object 1 has become the top element $((1^{\uparrow_1\downarrow^1}, 1^{\uparrow_1}) = (\{1,2,3,4,5,6\},\{\}))$ which is not a join-irreducible element. Therefore, we have lost the join-irreducible concept generated by object 1 in the original context, that is, the set of join-irreducible elements is not preserved after the reduction process, which is also natural. Hence, the converse of Theorem 3 is not true in general.

The most important property is that no new join-irreducible element is created from the reduction. We have that objects $2,3,4,5$ generate join-irreducible concepts of the concept lattice $\mathcal{B}(D_1, B, R_{|D_1})$ and they also generate join-irreducible concepts of $\mathcal{B}(A, B, R)$, according to Theorem 3.

Thus, the new mechanism introduced in this paper to reduce contexts in FCA, provides a significant reduction, since it satisfies useful properties and preserves the necessary information to distinguish the objects. Specifically, in this example, we have removed attributes ensuring that patients with different symptoms will continue to be different.

4   Conclusions and Future Work

We have shown in this paper that the attribute selection procedure given in RST is not equivalent to the attribute reduction in FCA, continuing the results given in [23]. Although both procedures are not equivalent, we have proven that the attribute selection mechanism given in RST has different interesting properties when it is applied in the FCA framework. Diverse properties have been introduced relating the object-concepts of the original concept lattice to the object-concepts obtained from the reduced context given by the rough set reduction mechanism. The most important result shows that the join-irreducible elements of the reduced concept lattice must be associated with the join-irreducible elements in the original one. Hence, this mechanism does not produce new join-irreducible concepts.

These interesting properties provide the possibility of applying the philosophy of RST in order to obtain a reduction in the number of attributes of a context in FCA, offering a new perspective in the attribute reduction removing the unnecessary attributes to distinguish the objects of the initial context. This new mechanism has been illustrated by a detailed example.

Bireducts have recently been presented in RST as a new reduction procedure providing more flexibility, with the possibility of also reducing attributes and registering objects for which information is lost [1,2,14,17,21,22]. In the future, we will apply the philosophy of bireducts within the FCA framework and we will also analyze the possible interpretation of this kind of reduction.

References

1. Benítez, M., Medina, J., Ślęzak, D.: Delta-information reducts and bireducts. In: Alonso, J.M., Bustince, H., Reformat, M. (eds.) 2015 Conference of the International Fuzzy Systems Association and the European Society for Fuzzy Logic and Technology (IFSA- EUSFLAT 2015), Gijón, Spain, pp. 1154–1160. Atlantis Press (2015)
2. Benítez, M., Medina, J., Ślęzak, D.: Reducing information systems considering similarity relations. In: Kacprzyk, J., Koczy, L., Medina, J. (eds.) 7th European Symposium on Computational Intelligence and Mathematices (ESCIM 2015), pp. 257–263 (2015)
3. Chen, J., Li, J., Lin, Y., Lin, G., Ma, Z.: Relations of reduction between covering generalized rough sets and concept lattices. Inf. Sci. **304**, 16–27 (2015)
4. Cornejo, M.E., Medina, J., Ramírez-Poussa, E.: Irreducible elements in multi-adjoint concept lattices. In: International Conference on Fuzzy Logic and Technology, EUSFLAT 2013, pp. 125–131 (2013)
5. Cornejo, M.E., Medina, J., Ramírez-Poussa, E.: Attribute reduction in multi-adjoint concept lattices. Inf. Sci. **294**, 41–56 (2015)
6. Cornelis, C., Jensen, R., Hurtado, G., Ślęzak, D.: Attribute selection with fuzzy decision reducts. Inf. Sci. **180**, 209–224 (2010)
7. Cornelis, C., Medina, J., Verbiest, N.: Multi-adjoint fuzzy rough sets: definition, properties and attribute selection. Int. J. Approx. Reason. **55**, 412–426 (2014)
8. Davey, B., Priestley, H.: Introduction to Lattices and Order, 2nd edn. Cambridge University Press, Cambridge (2002)
9. Denecke, K., Erné, M., Wismath, S.L. (eds.): Galois Connections and Applications. Kluwer Academic Publishers, Dordrecht (2004)
10. Dias, S., Vieira, N.: Reducing the size of concept lattices: the JBOS approach. In: 7th International Conference on Concept Lattices and Their Applications (CLA 2010), vol. 672, pp. 80–91 (2010)
11. Elloumi, S., Jaam, J., Hasnah, A., Jaoua, A., Nafkha, I.: A multi-level conceptual data reduction approach based on the Lukasiewicz implication. Inf. Sci. **163**(4), 253–262 (2004). Information Technology
12. Gabbay, D.M., Guenthner, F. (eds.): Handbook of Philosophical Logic. Volume I: Elements of Classical Logic. Springer, Netherlands (1983)

13. Ganter, B., Wille, R.: Formal Concept Analysis: Mathematical Foundation. Springer, Heidelberg (1999)
14. Janusz, A., Ślęzak, D., Nguyen, H.S.: Unsupervised similarity learning from textual data. Fundam. Informaticae **119**, 319–336 (2012)
15. Li, J., Kumar, C.A., Mei, C., Wang, X.: Comparison of reduction in formal decision contexts. Int. J. Approx. Reason. **80**, 100–122 (2017)
16. Li, M., Wang, G.: Approximate concept construction with three-way decisions and attribute reduction in incomplete contexts. Knowl.-Based Syst. **91**, 165–178 (2016)
17. Mac Parthalain, N., Jensen, R.: Simultaneous feature and instance selection using fuzzy-rough bireducts. In: IEEE International Conference on Fuzzy Systems (FUZZ-IEEE 2013), pp. 1–8, July 2013
18. Medina, J.: Multi-adjoint property-oriented and object-oriented concept lattices. Inf. Sci. **190**, 95–106 (2012)
19. Medina, J.: Relating attribute reduction in formal, object-oriented and property-oriented concept lattices. Comput. Math. Appl. **64**(6), 1992–2002 (2012)
20. Pawlak, Z.: Rough sets. Int. J. Comput. Inf. Sci. **11**, 341–356 (1982)
21. Ślęzak, D., Janusz, A.: Ensembles of bireducts: towards robust classification and simple representation. In: Kim, T., Adeli, H., Slezak, D., Sandnes, F.E., Song, X., Chung, K., Arnett, K.P. (eds.) FGIT 2011. LNCS, vol. 7105, pp. 64–77. Springer, Heidelberg (2011). doi:10.1007/978-3-642-27142-7_9
22. Stawicki, S., Ślęzak, D.: Recent advances in decision bireducts: complexity, heuristics and streams. In: Lingras, P., Wolski, M., Cornelis, C., Mitra, S., Wasilewski, P. (eds.) RSKT 2013. LNCS, vol. 8171, pp. 200–212. Springer, Heidelberg (2013). doi:10.1007/978-3-642-41299-8_19
23. Wei, L., Qi, J.-J.: Relation between concept lattice reduction and rough set reduction. Knowl.-Based Syst. **23**(8), 934–938 (2010)
24. Yao, Y.-Q., Mi, J.-S., Li, Z.-J.: Attribute reduction based on generalized fuzzy evidence theory in fuzzy decision systems. Fuzzy Sets Syst. **170**(1), 64–75 (2011)

Toward Interactive Attribute Selection
with Infolattices – A Position Paper

Dominik Ślęzak$^{(\boxtimes)}$, Marek Grzegorowski, Andrzej Janusz,
and Sebastian Stawicki

Institute of Informatics, University of Warsaw,
ul. Banacha 2, 02-097 Warsaw, Poland
slezak@mimuw.edu.pl

Abstract. We discuss a new approach to interactive exploration of high-dimensional data sets which is aimed at building human's understanding of the data by iterative additions of recommended attributes and objects that can together represent a context in which it may be useful to analyze the data. We identify challenges and expected benefits that our methodology can bring to the users. We also show how our ideas got inspired by Formal Concept Analysis (FCA) and Rough Set Theory (RST). It is though worth emphasizing that this particular paper is not aimed at investigating relationships between FCA and RST. Instead, the goal is to discuss which algorithmic methods developed within FCA and RST could be reused for the purpose of our approach.

Keywords: Attribute selection · Data visualization · User interaction

1 Introduction

There are plenty of methods aimed at data-based derivation of attributes that can be useful for a variety of data mining and business intelligence purposes [1]. Our goal in this paper is to discuss how to design an interactive framework which supports domain specialists in browsing through a realm of attribute subsets and takes advantage of their knowledge while resolving attribute selection problems. The motivation for this kind of investigation is that it is still challenging to represent the data-driven meaning of derived attributes to the users. The users are often able to interpret the meaning of a few attributes at a time but navigation through their larger set and the corresponding interdependencies becomes harder. To address this aspect of complexity, one can operate with clusters of attributes that induce similar information (e.g. similar partitions or rankings [2]) or employ some techniques of attribute selection which aim at replacing large sets of attributes with their minimal subsets providing comparable information about the data. Searching for such subsets is a well-established task within Rough Set Theory (RST) [3]. Given an initial set of attributes, one can search for so called (approximate) *reducts* or *bireducts* which induce (almost) the same data-based level of information as all considered attributes. A number

© Springer International Publishing AG 2017
L. Polkowski et al. (Eds.): IJCRS 2017, Part II, LNAI 10314, pp. 526–539, 2017.
DOI: 10.1007/978-3-319-60840-2_38

of heuristic methods were invented to search for the most valuable reducts and ensembles of diversified reducts from complex data sets [4].

We would like to discuss how to enrich the aforementioned attribute selection approaches with some elements of user interaction. Our assumption is that the users (domain experts, data analysts, people responsible for data model design, etc.) are able to understand practical meaning of particular attributes but they would find it problematic to choose their best subsets manually. Thus, it may be helpful for them to work with a kind of interactive recommendation framework that – starting from the empty set – would suggest adding subsequent (sets of) attributes, each time presenting several options and following user selections. More precisely, the idea is to generate and recommend several possible extensions to any set of attributes selected by a user and then let the user decide which of them should be considered for further investigation. During such process, the user should be able to interact with a kind of information lattice – *infolattice* for short – whose nodes correspond to attribute subsets explored up to now, whereby their cardinalities keep growing from layer to layer. Infolattice nodes should also include information about examples of objects representing different combinations of attribute values, i.e., every node should correspond to a pair (X, B) consisting of a subset of objects X whose elements are (sufficiently) *discerned* from each other using the subset of attributes B.

As an illustrative example, let us consider a repository of scientific publications and a student who wants to make her first steps in understanding, e.g., the theory and applications of RST. One might expect that she would query the repository so as to search for some specific topics, using keywords translated to some semantic indices [5]. Query outcomes might be then provided as a collection of publications, optionally categorized with respect to some measures, like in the faceted search applications [6]. On the other hand, let us imagine a student who does not have crystalized interests yet, so he cannot formulate any specific query. In this case, the idea of our approach is to let the student navigate through the incrementally constructed infolattice of possible subsets of attributes representing semantic indices and objects representing publications labeled with different combinations of attribute values. This way, the student could eventually discover a suitable context for looking at the repository content, i.e., a set of attributes discriminating articles that he is (not) interested in.

The above way of operating with attributes and objects is similar to Formal Concept Analysis (FCA) which has brought significant contributions in the areas of data understanding, data visualization and user interaction [7]. As we will see in further sections, there are analogies between our lattice-related ideas and FCA principles with regards to conceptual and graphical data representation. This is an important reference because various methods of constructing lattices of concepts emerged, basing on both intuitive meaning of lattice structures and mathematical properties of formal concepts represented by lattice nodes. It is particularly worth mentioning FCA-based techniques developed for the unstructured data, including investigation reported in [8] on how to represent FCA-related articles using FCA methods. In that paper, like in our example above, articles were represented as objects and their indices – produced using well-known semantic tools – were defined as their attributes.

We rely on both FCA and RST to better specify the requirements related to implementation of our approach to interactive attribute selection. We are certainly aware of strong mathematical connections between these two method-ologies that allow, e.g., to interpret reducts in terms of concept lattice character-istics or introduce lattice simplification and approximation criteria by extending the classical rough set notions. However, our goal in this particular study is to avoid direct "FCA versus RST" comparisons and, instead, concentrate on specific algorithmic developments in both of these domains that could be most useful to design new tools for interactive data exploration. The presented mate-rial is a continuation of our previous short communications referring to the use cases in the area of data modelling processes [9]. In our opinion, the framework discussed in this paper can be used together with other well-known methodolo-gies of data analysis and information retrieval such as already mentioned faceted search or, e.g., Online Analytical Processing (OLAP) which was also thoroughly investigated within the framework of FCA [10]. The OLAP tools usually require the users to interact with the data by selecting attributes and their values which becomes difficult for more dimensions. On the other hand, our approach assumes that attributes are recommended to the users automatically. Thus, we believe that the infolattice framework could be actually useful also as a support to search for attribute subsets that are a good basis for the OLAP cubes.

Let us think about an analyst who is supposed to design an intelligent services layer in a risk monitoring system. In particular, the need is to model attribute subsets that the users will work with once the system is put into production. A lattice-based way of exploring attributes and objects can help the analyst to understand dependencies in the data. Moreover, the ability to edit, delete and expand the infolattice nodes can facilitate the data modeling process. As yet another example, let us imagine a coal mine expert who is requested to define attributes that will be used to train sensor-based prediction models. The role of our framework in that case would be to recommend a variety of temporal attributes labeling time windows extracted from historical logs. Then, step by step again, one could collect attributes that discriminate different characteristics of sensor measurements or – what may be especially helpful to support inter-actions with domain specialists – information sources (e.g. types of sensors and time interval lengths) that are sufficient to build those attributes [11]. Further-more, the infolattice framework could be utilized to build interactively several subsets of attributes that collectively represent the required data characteristics as if they were the basis for an ensemble of rule-based classifiers [12].

The proposed framework should consist of (at least) three components. The first one is a front-end allowing to display, modify and grow infolattices, starting from a root-node that refers to an empty set of attributes. Although the mean-ings of nodes in infolattices and concept lattices are different from a mathemat-ical viewpoint, the experiences related to development of FCA-based interactive retrieval tools may be helpful with this respect [13]. The framework is required to deliver several sets of attributes (together with object examples) that are its initial recommendations. Next, a user should be able to mark relevant nodes or to ask for more suggestions. The framework recommends further extensions of chosen nodes and the process repeats until the user becomes satisfied with its outputs. The second component refers to algorithms generating the aforementioned ensembles of new recommendations (X, B) whenever a user wishes to expand an infolattice for some of its nodes. To provide a good variety of recommendations, it is important for generated pairs (X, B) to be diverse with respect to both X and B. Moreover, they should include objects and attributes present in their parent nodes. This leads to quite a complex optimization problem which is, fortunately, similar to the tasks considered earlier in the literature [14]. Lastly, the third component corresponds to attribute engineering mechanisms which may vary between application areas. We would like to keep our algorithms domain-agnostic, so they can work similarly in many scenarios. However, we also have to embed domain-dependent attribute specifications. More research is needed to make this component efficient enough for real-world applications.

The rest of the paper is organized as follows: In Sect. 2, we introduce basic assumptions related to our framework's functionality. In Sect. 3, we outline the main challenges that need to be addressed to implement it in practice. In Sects. 4 and 5, we discuss to what extent the existing FCA and RST methods can be adapted for our purposes. Section 6 concludes the paper.

2   Preliminaries

Let us refer to the data in a standard tabular form as used, e.g., in RST [3]. By an information system we will mean a pair (U, A) of non-empty sets U and A, where U is a universe of objects, and A is a set of attributes such that every $a \in A$ is a function $a : U \to V_a$, where V_a is called a value set of a. This way of looking at the data is equivalent also to some other popular representations such as relations in relational database systems [15] or many-valued contexts in Formal Concept Analysis (FCA) [16]. In any case – whatever the underlying representation is – the users think about their analytical tasks by means of objects and attributes that are more or less explicitly formulated.

Table 1 illustrates an example of an information system. This is a data set that was used in [17] as an illustration for studying functional dependencies within RST framework. This is a simple example including a small amount of objects and attributes. In [17], we assumed that attributes are categorical, i.e., one can consider partitions induced by their values over U. In real world applications, one can expect millions of objects and hundreds of attributes with various kinds of value sets [2]. Objects can correspond to (parts of) texts, (parts of) images, (time windows of) sensor measurements, etc. Attributes can take a form of domain-specific indices, often coming with additional parameters deciding about specifics of how to calculate their values for particular objects [18].

We are interested in specifying requirements for software environment which would support the users in an interactive selection of attributes. Figure 1 depicts

Table 1. A data table with 7 objects $U = \{u_1, \ldots, u_7\}$ and 6 attributes $A = \{a, \ldots, f\}$.

	a	b	c	d	e	f
u_1	1	1	1	1	1	1
u_2	0	0	0	1	1	1
u_3	1	0	1	1	0	1
u_4	0	1	0	0	0	0
u_5	1	0	0	0	0	1
u_6	1	1	1	1	1	0
u_7	0	1	1	0	1	2

Fig. 1. Three attribute recommendations for information system in Table 1. Objects $\{u_1, u_2\}$, $\{u_1, u_4\}$ and $\{u_1, u_3\}$ are representatives of partition classes induced by attribute subsets $\{a\}$, $\{d\}$ and $\{e\}$, respectively. Representatives are chosen according to a natural order of objects in U. Recommendations are chosen to possibly maximize diversity of displayed representative objects. An arrow symbolizes a hypothetical user choice of $\{e\}$ as the most interesting subset for further expansion.

an information structure that such framework could work with. Each node corresponds to a subset of attributes and to examples of objects representing particular groups of objects that behave comparably with respect to selected attributes. Such understood infolattice can be built incrementally as a result of interaction between the users and a GUI layer. A user can start with a node corresponding to the empty set of attributes and a single object representing all objects. Our framework should then compute and present a certain amount of attribute subsets that are its recommendations for the beginning. Then, the user can choose a node which seems to be the most relevant according to her needs. Let us imagine that someone selects attribute subset $\{e\}$ as illustrated by an arrow in Fig. 1. In the next step, as shown in Fig. 2, our framework should recommend extensions of the selected subset and the process should iteratively continue until the user becomes satisfied with the resulting subset.

In our opinion, displaying the examples of objects is as important as displaying the examples of attributes. This differs from OLAP, where the object groups are usually represented by some aggregated measures. In our approach one can utilize measures too, although they would be used to select objects rather than to compute aggregations. For instance, for each group of scientific publications, one can display its most frequently cited element. Actually, one can set up a linear order over objects and utilize it to display them while adding

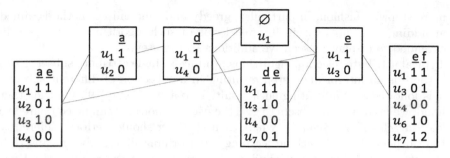

Fig. 2. Three further recommendations how to extend attribute subset $\{e\}$ selected in Fig. 1 – $\{a, e\}$, $\{d, e\}$ and $\{e, f\}$. Representatives of corresponding partition classes are chosen along the same order as in Fig. 1. Connections between nodes symbolize inclusions of both attribute and object subsets. Although $\{a, e\}$ and $\{d, e\}$ occurred as a result of choosing node $\{e\}$ in previous iteration, they might be also reached by a user through nodes corresponding to $\{a\}$ and $\{d\}$, respectively.

attributes. If such order is the same for all visible nodes, then a connection between them implies inclusion with respect to both attributes and objects. It can be observed in Fig. 2. For instance, attribute subset $\{a, e\}$ corresponds to representatives $\{u_1, u_2, u_3, u_4\}$, i.e., a superset of $\{u_1, u_3\}$ displayed earlier for $\{e\}$. More advanced scenarios of choosing objects will be discussed in Sect. 5.

3   Framework Components

There are a number of tasks to be addressed to make our interactive framework useful in practice. From a software design perspective, it is important to think about the following three well-abstracted components that cooperate with each other by means of internal interfaces. These components have been already sketched in Sect. 1. Below we proceed with a few more details.

The first component is a GUI-based navigation front-end which should allow to display structures like those in Figs. 1 and 2 in a clear form, supporting incremental process of constructing attribute subsets. Such GUI layer should let the users look at detailed formulations of attributes and summarized information about objects. It should also let the users move and remove previously generated nodes. Any other GUI features need to be carefully discussed to provide the users with reasonably (but not overwhelmingly) rich functionality [9].

The second component is a layer of fast algorithms that recommend additions of attributes whenever a user selects one of displayed nodes. Such algorithms should have certainly a lot in common with the tasks of attribute selection [1], though there are some specific aspects worth remembering about:

– Typical attribute selection algorithms produce final outcomes rather than ascending attribute subsets that converge to final outcomes. However, it could be relatively easy to change some of their parameters to let them work in a more stepwise fashion. In particular, greedy and randomized methods aimed at adding attributes within internal loops of such algorithms can be easily extended to display consecutive additions to the users.

– Typical attribute selection algorithms produce a single attribute subset. Even if there is an intermediate step resulting in a collection of different subsets, it is followed by aggregating such results into a single one [19]. On the other hand, we need several subsets to give the users a choice. It can be compared to learning classifier ensembles, where each classifier should perform differently than others [20]. In machine learning, "performing differently" means that classifiers should not repeat similar mistakes. In our case, recommendations should be diversified with respect to attributes, basing on their semantic meaning and a way they partition the data.

The third component refers to the attribute generation mechanisms which may vary significantly depending on application domain. Let us consider an attribute selection algorithm that iteratively utilizes some data-based test measures to decide whether randomly chosen attributes should be added to its outcomes. On the one hand, we would like to keep such algorithm as "domain-agnostic", so it can be applied similarly in many scenarios. On the other hand, we need to be able to somehow "plug in" a domain-specific space of possible attributes, so it can work with above components of our framework. A reasonable solution is to design a kind of "get attribute" function which generates a collection of object-value pairs for a randomly chosen attribute. Domain-specific random selection and value computation are then encapsulated within such function's implementation while higher-level algorithms responsible for attribute recommendations and user interactions work with its standardized outcomes.

4   FCA Background

As mentioned in Sect. 1, our ideas are partially inspired by [8], where concept lattices were used to visualize FCA-related scientific publications. However, comparing to that study, we would like to show objects that differ from each other by means of considered many-valued attributes rather than regularity patterns expressed in classical FCA [21]. From this perspective, it is useful to refer to FCA techniques working with partitions [16] which can be represented by replacing original objects with their pairs and redefining attributes $a \in A$ as an FCA-specific attributes having a cross over a pair of objects $u, u' \in U$, if and only if $a(u) = a(u')$. Then, concepts encode partitions corresponding to functional-dependency-related closures. Herein, it is also worth referring to multi-valued contexts and their connections to, e.g., triadic concept analysis [22].

Figure 3 shows a partition-based FCA lattice representation of the data set introduced in Table 1. For simplicity, only subsets of attributes, i.e., intents of partition-based formal concepts are presented. Additionally, in order to support the data understanding, it can be truly useful to present the examples of objects in particular partition classes, similarly as we did in Figs. 1 and 2. Moreover, as

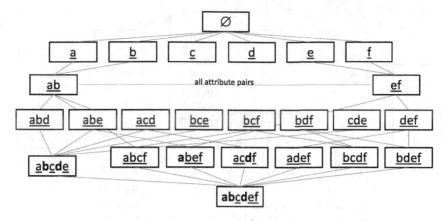

Fig. 3. Intents of concepts in partition-based lattice for the data set in Table 1. Extents are omitted – they could be reported as sets of pairs of indistinguishable objects, sets of partition classes, or sets of examples of objects from different classes.

it will be discussed in Sect. 6, we could also consider displaying examples representing groups of objects that are not necessarily equivalence classes such as, e.g., centers of tolerance classes or fuzzy equivalence classes. This would correspond to operating with pairs of objects whose attribute values are compared by means of similarity relations rather than crisp equalities [23].

Figure 3 shows also additional information that can be represented by two ways of marking attributes. Within each node, bolded attributes can be derived from underlined ones. An intent of every partition-based concept may include multiple subsets of attributes which determine others. For instance, subset $\{a, b, e, f\}$ is an intent of formal concept corresponding to partition classes $\{u_1\}$, $\{u_2\}$, $\{u_3, u_5\}$, $\{u_4\}$, $\{u_6\}$ and $\{u_7\}$. The same partition can be obtained for $\{a, b, f\}$, $\{a, e, f\}$ and $\{b, e, f\}$ which corresponds to functional dependencies $abf \to e$, $aef \to b$ and $bef \to a$, respectively [15]. Although such information could be determined from a lattice structure, a more explicit representation of dependencies may help the users who are not familiar with FCA.

The above observations lead towards some questions about algorithms aimed at the formal concept lattice construction. One of them is whether it is worth searching for attributes that should be marked as underlined for the previously found concepts or maybe rather searching for subsets of non-inter-dependent attributes that can be further "closed" by adding bolded attributes. Such questions become even more interesting when our task is to deal with bigger lattice fragments rather than their single components [24]. More generally, these are examples of questions related to derivation and representation of concept lattice structures corresponding to large and complex data sets [7].

In summary, Fig. 4 shows that our approach discussed in the previous sections can be really easily interpreted in terms of the FCA lattices with many-valued attributes. Let us go back to the example illustrated by Figs. 1 and 2 and imagine that a user selects the attribute subset $\{e, f\}$ for further expansion. Suppose

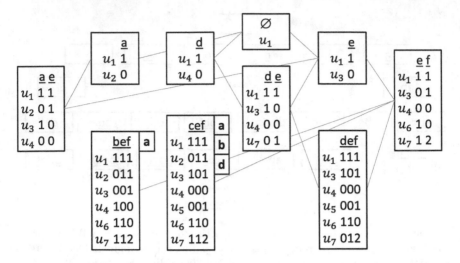

Fig. 4. Continuation of Fig. 2 – three further recommendations how to extend attribute subset $\{e, f\}$. The considered infolattice structure is enriched by showing functionally dependent attributes in right-side tabs of particular nodes.

that subsets $\{b, e, f\}$, $\{c, e, f\}$ and $\{d, e, f\}$ are recommended. Let us extend the previously discussed functionality and, for each particular node, display on its right side all attributes that are functionally determined by those in the main node's box. This way, we actually obtain a piece of partition-based lattice. A difference is that only the underlined attributes and only single examples of partition classes are presented in detail. Such correspondence allows us to better leverage methods developed within the FCA literature, even though we concentrate on slightly different aspects of data representation.

5   RST Background

As already mentioned, there are a number of efficient attribute selection algorithms developed according to RST principles. Complexity problems addressed by most of them refer to the fact that, for a given set of attributes, there may exist multiple irreducible subsets – called reducts – that induce (almost) the same level of information [3]. The meaning of an information level may vary for particular RST-based methods. In some scenarios, it is worth looking at a quality of approximations of some predefined subsets of objects. In other cases, it is more applicable to rely on attributes' ability to distinguish between arbitrary objects. That latter interpretation of information level has strong relationships to FCA models for many-valued attributes [16] and discernibility-based formulation of the notion of functional dependency in relational databases [15].

Most of RST techniques have been developed for a supervised learning framework, where we search for decision reducts, i.e., optimal subsets of attributes determining a special decision attribute. Among a number of extensions of classical RST, there are fuzzy-rough attribute reduction methods, where objects supporting different decision classes need to be discerned to a satisfactory degree based on a distance between numeric attribute values [4]. However, in this paper we should refer rather to RST-based methods specialized in unsupervised learning for which there are no predefined decision attributes.

Let us go back one more time to Fig. 3. A task of finding – for a given node – a subset of attributes inducing unchanged partition over the universe of objects is equivalent to finding an information reduct in the information system restricted to a given set of attributes. For example, consider an information system obtained from that presented in Table 1 by taking into account only attributes $\{a, b, e, f\}$. It has three information reducts – $\{a, b, f\}$, $\{a, e, f\}$ and $\{b, e, f\}$. It is also worth recalling the notion of an association reduct which is a pair of attribute subsets (B, C) such that there is functional dependency $B \rightarrow C$ and there are neither proper subsets $B' \subsetneq B$ nor proper supersets $C' \supsetneq C$ such that $B' \rightarrow C$ or $B \rightarrow C'$ [17]. Actually, every node in Fig. 3 corresponds to an association reduct for original information system illustrated by Table 1, where B and C gather underlined and bolded attributes, respectively.

Functional-dependency-related analogies between FCA and RST are important from computational perspective, e.g., to adapt heuristic algorithms that search for association reducts to incrementally build partition-based lattices. However, in this paper, our goal is to represent the data by means of combinations of attributes and objects. In RST, this can be addressed by bireducts [12]. For information system (U, A), a pair (X, B), where $X \subseteq U$ and $B \subseteq A$, is called an information bireduct, if and only if the following is satisfied:

(1) B discerns all pairs $u, u' \in X$, i.e., there is $a \in B$ such that $a(u) \neq a(u')$;
(2) There is no proper subset $C \subsetneq B$ such that C discerns all pairs $u, u' \in X$;
(3) There is no proper superset $Y \supsetneq X$ such that B discerns all pairs $u, u' \in Y$.

Information bireducts were utilized in [14] for a purpose of defining similarity between objects in high-dimensional spaces, specifically to analyze texts basing on their semantic indices. Therefore, one may say that this idea goes well together with our previously mentioned case study related to scientific publications as well as with RST-based and FCA-based methods considered in [5] and [8], respectively. On the other hand, a usage of bireducts can easily go beyond text processing. Actually, information bireducts can be studied as a counterpart to formal concepts understood as non-extendable subsets of objects that are indiscernible with respect to non-extendable subsets of attributes. In contrast, information bireducts correspond to non-extendable subsets of objects that can be said as pairwise different using irreducible subsets of attributes.

Actually, every node in Figs. 1, 2 and 4 corresponds to an information bireduct. For instance, pair $(\{u_1, u_3, u_4, u_6, u_7\}, \{e, f\})$ cannot be extended with respect to its objects and reduced with respect to its attributes without losing the above condition (1). Let us note that navigation principles described in Sects. 2 and 3 do not explicitly require displayed combinations of attributes and objects to be information bireducts. However, underlying algorithms are supposed to recommend subsets of attributes that are not redundant and subsets of objects that "cover" all significant combinations of attribute values. Thus, at each step of interaction, new recommendations may indeed take a form of bireducts. Recommendations should be diverse, letting the users look at the data by means of possibly different attributes and objects. This is in line with optimization principles defined in [12] with respect to searching for ensembles of bireducts, inspired by well-known ensembles of classifiers [20].

Let us slightly modify a bireduct derivation algorithm introduced in [14]. Let us begin with (X, B), where $X = U$ and $B = \emptyset$, and keep removing objects from X and adding attributes to B in a random order, until the above condition (1) starts holding. In the second phase, begin removing previously added attributes and adding previously removed objects under constraint of satisfying (1). After examining all attributes and objects, obtained (X, B) will hold conditions (2) and (3) too. This approach creates some interesting opportunities:

- We can use function "get attribute" (see Sect. 3) to add elements to B.
- We can follow a measure-based order (see Sect. 2) to remove/add objects.
- We can replace $a(u) \neq a(u')$ in condition (1) by, e.g., a dissimilarity relation.

Following the idea of using function "get attribute", we do not need all attributes to be materialized prior to computations of bireducts. This is convenient especially for data sets with huge cardinalities of A related, e.g., to biomedicine [2], texts [5], sensors [11], images [18], etc. Further, thanks to combining bireduct derivation algorithms with an idea of using measures to order objects, we can be sure that elements of X correspond to most valuable representatives of some blocks of objects. Finally, working with (dis)similarities instead of (in)equalities makes it possible for our framework to handle complex attributes, whose values do not necessarily induce any meaningful data partitions. In such cases, outcomes are still in form of pairs (X, B) but elements of X may not correspond to representatives of equivalence classes any longer. They rather correspond to the most representative examples as it was discussed for FCA in Sect. 4.

6 Future Directions

We discussed the idea of a new interactive attribute selection framework helping the users to specify a scope of their exploratory and modelling tasks. We based it on an intuitive lattice-like data representation, whereby nodes correspond to automatically generated attribute recommendations that are illustrated by examples of objects available in the data. We showed that such data representation – referred to as infolattice – and the algorithms aimed at its iterative construction, can refer to methods developed in FCA [21] and RST [3].

FCA is a great source of inspiration from knowledge representation and conceptual exploration points of view. Although our infolattices – as illustrated by Figs. 1, 2 and 4 – are not equivalent to formal concept lattices, they can be still interpreted using the FCA terminology which makes it possible to adapt some useful algorithmic solutions [24]. On the other hand, RST is helpful when formulating and addressing the optimization goals for local expansion of attribute subsets selected by the users, by following advances in the RST-based attribute selection [4] and the attribute/object diversification [14].

We present just a draft of how our interactive attribute selection framework should look like. Apart from a discussion related to FCA and RST, we also made an attempt to specify software components that must be developed in next steps. An important part is a GUI layer that needs to encourage the users to work with ˌit, basing on its graphical and functional features. It is tempting to provide the users with a wide spectrum of ways of using our framework to understand the data. However, any extension of functionality presented in Sects. 2 and 3 needs to be carefully investigated to avoid making it too complex.

An example of such functionality can be seen in Fig. 4, where each node is additionally equipped with right-side tabs including derivable attributes. The amount of such attributes can be treated as one more parameter while evaluating recommendations. Moreover, in high-dimensional data sets, it is often useful to group together attributes which induce similar partitions in the data [19]. Then, recommendations can include representatives of such attribute clusters, while right-side tabs may contain more general cluster descriptions.

Examining dependencies is also important when producing new recommendations. It may happen that previously recommended attributes become functionally dependent from the added ones, so they should be moved to right-side tabs in new nodes. The users should be also able to remove attributes from already generated nodes or replace them with other attributes visible in right-side tabs [2]. All those operations need to be designed in such a way that our infolattice structure based on attribute/object subset inclusions is maintained and the users do not feel lost when the number of nodes increases.

Another important aspect is to continue comparing our framework with other methods. We should refer, e.g., to analytical environments based on FCA/RST as well as to the principles of faceted search [6], OLAP [10] and interactive retrieval [18]. Although functionality proposed in Sects. 2 and 3 seems to be relevant mainly to data modeling, it can be extended toward search support too. As illustrated by Figs. 5 and 6, it would be quite straightforward to enrich our GUI layer to let the users select particular objects in particular nodes. Then,

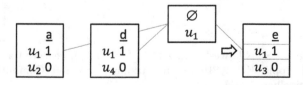

Fig. 5. Three attribute recommendations for information system in Table 1. Unlike in Fig. 1, the arrow symbolizes a hypothetical user choice of a group of objects represented by u_1 to be further analyzed in context of attributes including e.

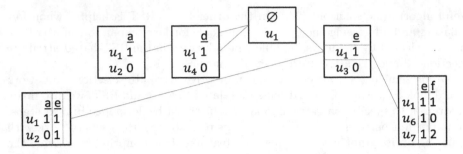

Fig. 6. Two further recommendations how to extend attribute subset $\{e\}$ within its partition class represented by object u_1. There is no connection between nodes corresponding to $\{a\}$ and $\{a, e\}$ because they are built for different sets of objects.

further recommendations can be generated for a corresponding group of similar objects, where similarity is defined by a given node's attributes.

Besides things that can be seen by the users, there are also some decisions to be made for internal algorithms. In Sect. 5, it was suggested that one can adapt heuristics searching for ensembles of information bireducts – i.e., irreducible subsets of attributes which make it possible to tell a difference between non-extendable subsets of objects [14] – to generate several new attribute/object-based recommendations whenever a user chooses one of visible nodes to be further expanded. However, such algorithms have a number of tunable parameters responsible for average cardinality and pairwise diversity of generated subsets. Moreover, there is a question whether it is enough for new recommendations to be reasonably different from each other or whether their diversity should be measured also with respect to other leaves in a current structure.

Last but not least, in high-dimensional data sets there are usually some semantic hierarchies, i.e., meanings of some attributes may be relatively similar to each other, even if they do not partition the data identically. In such cases, different recommendations should be based on "semantically distant" attributes. One can say that this kind of diversity might be addressed by appropriate implementation of function "get attribute" discussed in Sects. 3 and 5. On the other hand, it is important for our framework to memorize the user choices and – over time – learn their favorite descriptions of the data.

References

1. Guyon, I., Gunn, S., Nikravesh, M., Zadeh, L.A. (eds.): Feature Extraction: Foundations and Applications. Studies in Fuzziness and Soft Computing, vol. 207. Springer, Heidelberg (2006)
2. Grużdź, A., Ihnatowicz, A., Ślęzak, D.: Interactive gene clustering: a case study of breast cancer microarray data. Inf. Syst. Front. **8**(1), 21–27 (2006)
3. Pawlak, Z.: Rough Sets: Theoretical Aspects of Reasoning about Data. System Theory, Knowledge Engineering and Problem Solving, vol. 9. Kluwer, Dorchelt (1991)

4. Riza, L.S., Janusz, A., Bergmeir, C., Cornelis, C., Herrera, F., Ślęzak, D., Benítez, J.M.: Implementing algorithms of rough set theory and fuzzy rough set theory in the R package "RoughSets". Inf. Sci. **287**, 68–89 (2014)
5. Suraj, Z., Grochowalski, P.: About new version of RSDS system. Fundam. Informaticae **135**(4), 503–519 (2014)
6. Tunkelang, D.: Faceted Search. Synthesis Lectures on Information Concepts Retrieval, and Services, vol. 1. Morgan & Claypool, San Rafael (2009)
7. Carpineto, C., Romano, G.: Concept Data Analysis - Theory and Applications. Wiley, Hoboken (2005)
8. Poelmans, J., Ignatov, D.I., Kuznetsov, S.O., Dedene, G.: Formal concept analysis in knowledge processing: a survey on applications. Expert Syst. Appl. **40**(16), 6538–6560 (2013)
9. Ślęzak, D., Grzegorowski, M., Janusz, A., Stawicki, S.: Interactive data exploration with infolattices. Abstract Materials of BAFI 2015. http://www.sistemasdeingen ieria.cl/BAFI2015/ProceedingsBAFI.pdf
10. Stumme, G.: On-line analytical processing with conceptual information systems. In: Proceedings of FODO 1998, pp. 117–126 (1998)
11. Nguyen, S.H., Szczuka, M.: Feature selection in decision systems with constraints. In: Flores, V., et al. (eds.) IJCRS 2016. LNCS, vol. 9920, pp. 537–547. Springer, Cham (2016). doi:10.1007/978-3-319-47160-0_49
12. Stawicki, S., Ślęzak, D., Janusz, A., Widz, S.: Decision bireducts and decision reducts - a comparison. Int. J. Approx. Reason. **84**, 75–109 (2017)
13. Codocedo, V., Napoli, A.: Formal concept analysis and information retrieval – a survey. In: Baixeries, J., Sacarea, C., Ojeda-Aciego, M. (eds.) ICFCA 2015. LNCS, vol. 9113, pp. 61–77. Springer, Cham (2015). doi:10.1007/978-3-319-19545-2_4
14. Janusz, A., Ślęzak, D., Nguyen, H.S.: Unsupervised similarity learning from textual data. Fundam. Informaticae **119**(3–4), 319–336 (2012)
15. Maier, D.: The Theory of Relational Databases. Computer Science Press, Rockville (1983)
16. Baixeries, J., Kaytoue, M., Napoli, A.: Characterizing functional dependencies in formal concept analysis with pattern structures. Ann. Math. Artif. Intell. **72**(1–2), 129–149 (2014)
17. Ślęzak, D.: Rough sets and functional dependencies in data: foundations of association reducts. In: Gavrilova, M.L., Tan, C.J.K., Wang, Y., Chan, K.C.C. (eds.) Transactions on Computational Science V. LNCS, vol. 5540, pp. 182–205. Springer, Heidelberg (2009). doi:10.1007/978-3-642-02097-1_10
18. Osman, T., Thakker, D., Schaefer, G.: Utilising semantic technologies for intelligent indexing and retrieval of digital images. Computing **96**(7), 651–668 (2014)
19. Abeel, T., Helleputte, T., de Peer, Y.V., Dupont, P., Saeys, Y.: Robust biomarker identification for cancer diagnosis with ensemble feature selection methods. Bioinformatics **26**(3), 392–398 (2010)
20. Kuncheva, L.I.: Combining Pattern Classifiers: Methods and Algorithms, 2nd edn. Wiley, Hoboken (2014)
21. Ganter, B., Wille, R.: Formal Concept Analysis: Mathematical Foundations. Springer, Heidelberg (1998)
22. Kaytoue, M., Kuznetsov, S.O., Macko, J., Napoli, A.: Biclustering meets triadic concept analysis. Ann. Math. Artif. Intell. **70**(1–2), 55–79 (2014)
23. Díaz, J.C., Medina, J.: Solving systems of fuzzy relation equations by fuzzy property-oriented concepts. Inf. Sci. **222**, 405–412 (2013)
24. Dias, S.M., Vieira, N.J.: Concept lattices reduction: definition, analysis and classification. Expert Syst. Appl. **42**(20), 7084–7097 (2015)

AFS-Based Formal Concept Analysis on Multi-valued Context

Lidong Wang[1(✉)], Xiaodong Liu[1], and Jinhai Li[2]

[1] Department of Mathematics, Dalian Maritime University,
Dalian 116026, Liaoning, People's Republic of China
ldwang@dlmu.edu.cn
[2] Faculty of Science, Kunming University of Science and Technology,
Kunming 650500, Yunnan, People's Republic of China

Abstract. Non-symmetric indiscernibility preorders, arising naturally from hierarchically structured data, are general methods of conceptual scaling for multi-valued data. Based on the original idea of Ganter on non-symmetric indiscernibility preorders and the AFS (Axiomatic Fuzzy Sets) theory, this paper investigates a multi-valued formal concept analysis, in which multi-granule concept lattice is established on multi-valued context, and the membership function is directly determined from the original data of the multi-valued context. Compared with symmetric indiscernibility relations, the main advantage of the proposed method is capable of dealing with information table with fuzzy attributes, Boolean attributes, and intuition order attributes, and describing the uncertainty relations between the objects and the attributes for formal context with complex data.

Keywords: Multi-valued context · Concept lattice · Membership function · Axiomatic fuzzy sets

1 Introduction

Formal Concept Analysis (FCA) was originally proposed by Rudolf Wille in 1980s [12]. In classical FCA approaches, the notion of indiscernibility is a fundamental tool. If two objects have same values for all the attributes under consideration, they are called indiscernible [14]. In the language of FCA, one expresses this setting as follows: for a given formal context $(X, M, \mathbb{I})$, define the indiscernibility equivalence relation on X by

$$g \sim h :\Leftrightarrow g' = h',$$

Supported by the Natural Science Foundation of China (No. 61203283), the Macau Science and Technology Development Fund (No. 081/2015/A3), Liaoning Provincial Natural Science Foundation of China (No. 2014025004) and the Fundamental Research Funds for the Central Universities (Nos. 3132016306, 3132017048).

L. Polkowski et al. (Eds.): IJCRS 2017, Part II, LNAI 10314, pp. 540–557, 2017.
DOI: 10.1007/978-3-319-60840-2_39

where g and h belong to X and "$/$" is the concept forming operator. Ganter suggested a generalised notion of indiscernibility by dropping the condition of symmetry [14]. In the past three decades, FCA has had great development in both theory and application fields. Nowadays, FCA has been used in various fields such as data analysis, information retrieval, and knowledge processing [21, 30, 31, 34]. In artificial intelligence community, FCA has been used as a knowledge representation mechanism [18, 44, 45] as well as a conceptual clustering method [7, 27] for crisp concepts. In database theory, FCA has been extensively applied to class hierarchy design and management [15, 28, 35]. Its effectiveness in the relationship analysis of databases has been demonstrated by the commercial management system TOSCANA for conceptual information systems [38].

Currently, complex data widely exist in the current popular relational database, in which the yes/no binary relations are not enough to describe the information between the objects and the attributes. By introducing the yes/no binary relations among three data sets, triadic formal concept is proposed to describe the multi-relational setting on more than two data sets [8, 9, 46]. To cope with imprecise and incomplete information, fuzzy sets and rough sets are introduced in FCA to improve the ability on dealing with uncertain data [32]. Poelmans et al. gave an overview of the literature on extending FCA with fuzzy logic and rough set theory [32]. For most of information systems, the value domains of attributes are recorded by some real numbers, in which the ternary relationship of object-attribute-value is employed to store data. In the concept lattice theory, such a formal context is known as the multi-valued context $(X, M, W, \mathbb{I})$ [47]. The rows correspond to objects, the columns correspond to (multi-valued) attributes, and the entries correspond to attribute values. Incidence $(x, m, w) \in \mathbb{I}$ is read as "the value of object x on attribute m is w" and abbreviated as $m(x) = w$ [14,43]. Multi-valued formal concepts of a multi-valued context have been applied in extracting knowledge from observation data [16, 36, 43], conceptual information retrieval [2, 20], switching signal [29], etc.

Table 1. Descriptions of contexts [37]

	Color	Max.Speed		Light Color	Dark Color
Car1	Red	100	Red	×	
Car2	Green	120	Green	×	
Car3	Black	160	Black		×

Owing to its structural characteristic, the construction of the concept lattice is based on the single-valued context. Multi-valued contexts are usually translated into a single-valued context to build the concept lattice. The traditional discretization methods include two categories, (1) transforming multi-valued context into single-valued context by introducing some threshold values (when the attribute value is greater than the specified "degree", we call that the object has the attribute; on the contrary, the object does not have the attribute [47]) and (2) scaling multi-valued attribute into a single-valued context for each attribute $m \in M$ [47] (In Table 1, on the left a multi-valued context has been drawn and on the right it is a scale for the color attribute).

However, transforming and scaling method mentioned above may bring new problems about threshold selection and the loss of associated information. There are many methods to directly deal with multi-valued context with complex data in FCA. Gugisch introduced formal description to deal with multi-valued concept analysis, which avoids generating huge single valued contexts by mapping the set of attributes to the power set of the values [17]. Pattern structures have been proposed as a generalization of formal contexts [1]. By defining an appropriate semi-lattice operation, pattern structures translate FCA to any partially ordered data descriptions to deal with complex data [13]. Symbolic Data Analysis(SDA) has been introduced to build concept lattices, which can better deal with formal context with different type values by formalizing symbolic objects and defining Galois connections symbolic objects and their descriptions [1,6]. Functional dependency is another method of extracting knowledge from formal context and multi-valued formal context. By using functional dependencies, Ganter established a new formal context from multi-valued context $(X, M, W, \mathbb{I})$ as follows [12]:

$$(X \times X, M, \mathbb{J}), (g, h)\mathbb{J}m :\Leftrightarrow m(g) = m(h).$$

In fact, the implications of the latter are the functional dependencies of the former. In the concept lattice of the formal context $(X \times X, M, \mathbb{J})$, concept extents are subsets of $X \times X$, and concept intents are the maximal attribute sets corresponding to a given indiscernibility relation "Coreducts" [14]. In order to deal with non-numerical ("unprecise") data, Ganter introduced ordinal dependencies in ordinally scaled multi-valued attributes, and established the formal context

$$(X \times X, M, \mathbb{K}), (x, h)\mathbb{K}m :\Leftrightarrow m(x) \leq m(h).$$

In $(X \times X, M, \mathbb{K})$, concept extents are the ordinal indiscernibility relations that can be obtained by shortening the attribute set. These relations are preorders. Concept intents are the maximal attribute sets corresponding to a given ordinal indiscernibility relation [14]. Baixeries et al. introduced pattern structures to characterize functional dependencies for dealing with complex data, which provides a new conceptual structure with better computational properties [3].

Fuzzy formal concept analysis (FFCA) is another important method to represent multi-valued attributes with vague information, in which fuzzy logic can be incorporated into FCA to handle uncertainty information for conceptual clustering and concept hierarchy generation [4,5,11,19,33]. Most of FFCA approaches usually assume that the relationship between a given object and property is a matter of degree in a scale L (generally [0,1]) [10]. Humans interpretation is usually also required to define the membership function of the fuzzy set I for FFCA. However, the extent to which "object o has property a" may be sometimes hardly assessed precisely [10]. Different people have different opinions on the same attribute (or feature). For example, for evaluating the car, someone feels comfortable, while others do not think so. So it is very important for both the structure of FFCA and decision making to determine the reasonable membership function. Besides, in the real-world applications, based on humans interpretation, it is also difficult to define the fuzzy set I for describing the uncertainty relations between the objects in X and the attributes in M.

The main purpose of the current study is to establish the multi-granule concept lattice on multi-valued context and a method to determine the uncertainty relations between the objects in X and the attributes in M from the original data within the framework of the AFS (Axiomatic Fuzzy Sets) theory. The rest of this paper is organized as follows: Sect. 2 introduces AFS algebra by an illustrative example. In Sect. 3, the AFS-based concept lattice on multi-valued context is presented. In Sect. 4, the membership function of fuzzy formal concept is discussed. Section 5 concludes the paper.

2   Preliminaries

In this section, we briefly introduce some basic notions related to AFS algebras and coherence membership functions of fuzzy sets.

2.1   Introduction to the AFS Algebras by an Example

AFS (Axiomatic Fuzzy Sets) theory was firstly proposed by Liu in 1998 [22,26], which provides an effective tool to convert the information by training examples and databases into the membership functions and their fuzzy logic operations. The following example, which employs the information table, serves as an introductory illustration of the set EM^* and EM^*/R used in AFS.

Example 1 [42]. Let $X = \{x_1, x_2, \ldots, x_{10}\}$ be a set of 10 people with feature set $F = \{f_1, f_2, \ldots, f_{10}\}$, where the features are described by real numbers (f_1: age, f_2: height, f_3: weight, f_4: salary, f_5: estate), Boolean values (f_6: male, f_7: female), and order relation (f_8: black hair, f_9: white hair, f_9: yellow color). Here, the number i in the "hair color" column, which corresponds to some $x \in X$, implies that the hair color of x is ordered as the i-th following our perception of the color. For example, as to the numbers in the column "hair black", $x_i < x_j$ (e.g., $x_7 < x_{10}$) means that the hair of x_i is closer to the color black than that of individual x_j. The relationship $x_i = x_j$ (e.g., $x_4 = x_8$) means that the hair of x_i looks as black as that of x_j. Let $M = \{m_1^1, m_2^1, m_1^2, m_2^2, m_1^3, m_2^3, m_1^4, m_2^4, m_1^5, m_2^5, m_1^6, m_1^7, m_1^8, m_1^9, m_1^{10}\}$, in which m_j^i is the j-th assertion about f_i, $m_1^1 = $ large, $m_2^1 = $ small, ($i = 1, 2, 3, 4, 5$), $m_1^6 = $ male, $m_1^7 = $ female, $m_1^8 = $ black, $m_1^9 = $ white, and $m_1^{10} = $ yellow.

Let F_i be the set of feature values on the i-th feature f_i, and ϕ_i be the partial function $\phi_i : X \rightarrow F_i$. The elements of M are viewed as "single" (or "simple") assertions because each of them associates to a single feature. Each $m \in M$ is an assertion of a feature value about an object x, that is $m_i^j(x) = $ '$\phi_i(x)$ should be taken the j-th assertion value'. For instance, for object x_1, denote $m_1^1(x_1) = $ '$\phi_1(x_1)$ is large', and $m_1^2(x_1) = $ '$\phi_2(x_1)$ is large'. However, in many real-world applications, an assertion on x may associate to more than one feature.

For example, $\gamma = m_1^1 m_1^4 + m_1^1 m_1^7$ ("+" denotes a disjunction of the assertions about features) is a complex assertion, and $\gamma(x) =$ '$\phi_1(x)$ is large and $\phi_4(x)$ is large' or '$\phi_1(x)$ is large and $\phi_7(x)$ is female'. For $A_i \subseteq M, i \in I, \sum_{i \in I}(\prod_{m \in A_i} m)$ has a well-defined semantic meaning such as the one we have discussed above.

Let M be a nonempty set. The set EM^* is defined by

$$EM^* = \{\sum_{i \in I}(\prod_{m \in A_i} m) \mid A_i \subseteq M, i \in I, I \text{ is any nonempty indexing set}\}. \quad (1)$$

In [22], Liu established the quotient set EM^*/R by introducing the binary relation R on EM^*. Moreover, Liu established EI algebra $(EM^*/R, \vee, \wedge)$ by introducing the algebra operations $\vee$ ("or") and $\wedge$ ("and") on the set EM^*/R.

Theorem 1 [22]. *Let M be a non-empty set. Then $(EM^*/R, \vee, \wedge)$ forms a complete distributive lattice under the binary compositions $\vee$ and $\wedge$ defined as follows. For any $\sum_{i \in I}(\prod_{m \in A_i} m)$, $\sum_{j \in J}(\prod_{m \in B_j} m) \in EM^*/R$,*

$$\sum_{i \in I}(\prod_{m \in A_i} m) \vee \sum_{j \in J}(\prod_{m \in B_j} m) = \sum_{k \in I \sqcup J}(\prod_{m \in C_k} m), \quad (2)$$

$$\sum_{i \in I}(\prod_{m \in A_i} m) \wedge \sum_{j \in J}(\prod_{m \in B_j} m) = \sum_{i \in I, j \in J}(\prod_{m \in A_i \cup B_j} m), \quad (3)$$

where for any $k \in I \sqcup J$ (the disjoint union of I and J, i.e., an element in I and an element in J are always regarded as different elements in $I \sqcup J$), $C_k = A_k$ if $k \in I$, and $C_k = B_k$ if $k \in J$.

In what follows, we introduce another AFS algebra — $E^{\#}I$ algebra over X, which will play the role of the extents of AFS-based formal concepts.

The set EX^* is defined by $EX^* = \{\sum_{i \in I} a_i \mid a_i \in 2^X, I$ is any non-empty indexing set$\}$.

In [26], Liu established the quotient set EX^*/R by introducing the binary relation $R^{\#}$ on EX^* and $E^{\#}I$ algebra $(EX^*/R^{\#}, \vee, \wedge)$ by introducing the algebra operations $\vee$ and $\wedge$ as follows:

Theorem 2 [22]. *For any $\sum_{i \in I} a_i, \sum_{j \in J} b_j \in EX^*/R^{\#}$, then $(EX^*/R^{\#}, \vee, \wedge)$ forms a complete distributive lattice under the binary compositions $\vee$, $\wedge$ defined as follows:*

$$\sum_{i \in I} a_i \vee \sum_{j \in J} b_j = \sum_{k \in I \sqcup J} c_k, \quad \sum_{i \in I} a_i \wedge \sum_{j \in J} b_j = \sum_{i \in I, j \in J}(a_i \cap b_j), \quad (4)$$

where for any $k \in I \sqcup J$ (the disjoint union of I and J, i.e., an element in I and an element in J are always regarded as different elements in $I \sqcup J$), $c_k = a_k$ if $k \in I$, and $c_k = b_k$ if $k \in J$. $(EX^*/R^{\#}, \vee, \wedge)$ is called $E^{\#}I$ algebra over X.

For $\mu = \sum_{i \in I} a_i$, $\nu = \sum_{j \in J} b_j \in EX^*/R^{\#}$, $\mu \leq \nu \iff \mu \vee \nu = \nu \Leftrightarrow$ for any a_i $(i \in I)$, $\exists b_h$ $(h \in J)$ such that $a_i \subseteq b_h$. Just as shown in the Example 1, EI algebra can be represented by the fuzzy terms, and the membership can be defined in the sequel.

2.2   Coherence Membership Functions of Fuzzy Terms

Let X be a set and M be a set of fuzzy terms on X. For $A \subseteq M$, $x \in X$, define

$$A^{\succeq}(x) = \{y \in X \mid x \succeq_m y \text{ for any } m \in A\} \subseteq X. \tag{5}$$

For $m \in M$, "$x \succeq_m y$" implies that the degree of x belonging to m is larger than or equal to that of y. $A^{\succeq}(x)$ is the set of all elements in X whose degrees of belonging to $\prod_{m \in A} m$ are less than or equal to that of x. $A^{\succeq}(x)$ is determined by the semantic of fuzzy set A and the probability distribution of observed data set.

For fuzzy term $\xi \in EM^*/R$, let $\mu_\xi : X \to [0,1]$. $\{\mu_\xi(x) | \xi \in EM^*/R\}$ is called a set of *coherence membership functions* in the AFS algebra system $(EM^*/R, \vee, \wedge)$, if the following conditions are satisfied [26]:

1. For $\alpha, \beta \in EM^*/R$, if $\alpha \leq \beta$ in $(EM^*/R, \vee, \wedge)$, then $\mu_\alpha(x) \leq \mu_\beta(x)$ for any $x \in X$;
2. for $x \in X$, $\eta = \sum_{i \in I}(\Pi_{m \in A_i} m) \in EM^*/R$, if $A_i^{\succeq}(x) = \emptyset$ for all $i \in I$ then $\mu_\eta(x) = 0$;
3. for $x, y \in X$, $A \subseteq M$, $\eta = \prod_{m \in A} m \in EM^*/R$, if $A^{\succeq}(x) \subseteq A^{\succeq}(y)$, then $\mu_\eta(x) \leq \mu_\eta(y)$; if $A^{\succeq}(x) = X$ then $\mu_\eta(x) = 1$, where $A^{\succeq}(x)$ is defined by Eq. (5).

The coherence membership function is associated with a measure over X. Liu et al. proposed two types of measures for fuzzy terms, which can be constructed by taking the semantics of the fuzzy terms and the probability distribution of the feature values of the data [26].

Definition 1 [26]. *Let ν be a fuzzy term on X, $\rho_\nu : X \to R^+ = [0, \infty)$. ρ_ν is called a weight function of the fuzzy term ν if ρ_ν satisfies the following conditions:*

1. $\rho_\nu(x) = 0 \Leftrightarrow x \nsucceq_m x$, *for any $x \in X$;*
2. $\rho_\nu(x) \geq \rho_\nu(y) \Leftrightarrow x \succeq_m y$, *for any $x, y \in X$.*

In what follows, we discuss how to define the coherence membership functions in a probability measure space.

Theorem 3 [26]. *Let $(\Omega, \mathcal{F}, \mathcal{P})$ be a probability measure space and M be a set of fuzzy terms on Ω. Let ρ_γ be the weight function for a fuzzy term $\gamma \in M$. Let $X \subseteq \Omega$ be a finite set of observed samples from the probability space $(\Omega, \mathcal{F}, \mathcal{P})$. If for any $m \in M$ and $x \in \Omega$, $\{m\}^{\succeq}(x) \in \mathcal{F}$, then the following assertions hold:*

1. *$\{\mu_\xi(x) | \xi \in EM^*/R\}$ is a set of coherence membership functions of $(EM^*/R, \wedge, \vee)$, provided that the membership function for each $\xi = \sum_{i \in I}(\Pi_{m \in A_i} m) \in EM^*/R$ is defined as follows:*

$$\xi(x) = \sum_{i \in I} A_i^{\succeq}(x) \in EX^*/R^{\#}. \tag{6}$$

$$\mu_\xi(x) = ||\xi(x)||_\rho = \left|\left| \sum_{i \in I} A_i^{\succeq}(x) \right|\right|_\rho = \sup_{i \in I} \inf_{\gamma \in A_i} \frac{\sum_{u \in A_i^{\succeq}(x)} \rho_\gamma(u) N_u}{\sum_{u \in X} \rho_\gamma(u) N_u} \in [0,1], \tag{7}$$

$$\mu_\xi(x) = ||\xi(x)||_\rho = ||\sum_{i\in I} A_i^\succeq(x)||_\rho = \sup_{i\in I} \inf_{\gamma\in A_i} \frac{\int_{A_i^\succeq(x)} \rho_\gamma(t)dP(t)}{\int_\Omega \rho_\gamma(t)dP(t)} \in [0,1], \quad (8)$$

where $||\xi(x)||_\rho$ is a norm of $\xi(x)$, and N_u is the number of times that $u \in X$ is observed.

2. If for every $\gamma \in M$, $\rho_\gamma(x)$ is continuous on Ω and X is a set of samples randomly drawn from the probability space $(\Omega, \mathcal{F}, \mathcal{P})$, then the membership function defined by (7) converges to the membership function defined by (8), for all $x \in \Omega$ as $|X|$ approaches to infinity.

Remark 1. Theorem 3 defines the membership functions based on the fuzzy logic operations and the overall space by taking both fuzziness and randomness into account via $\rho_\gamma(x)$. The following practical relevance of the coherence membership functions can be ensured by Theorem 3.

In this study, let $\rho_\gamma(u) \equiv 1$ for any $x \in X$, and for the complex assertion (feature) $\eta = \sum_{i\in I}(\prod_{m\in A_i} m) \in EM^*/R$, the coherence membership function of η is defined as follows:

$$\mu_\eta(x) = ||\eta(x)||_\rho = ||\sum_{i\in I} A_i^\succeq(x)||_\rho = \sup_{i\in I} \frac{|A_i^\succeq(x)|}{|X|}, \text{for any } x \in X. \quad (9)$$

Example 2. Let $X = \{x_1, x_2, \ldots, x_{10}\}$ be a set of 10 persons with the features described by real numbers (i.e. age, height, weight, salary, estate), Boolean values (i.e., male, female) and the order relations (hair black, hair white, hair yellow), which are shown in Table 2.

By a straightforward comparison of the two assertion expressions $\gamma_1 = m_1^1 m_1^4 + m_1^1 m_1^7$ and $\gamma_2 = m_1^1 m_1^4 + m_1^1 m_1^7 + m_1^1 m_2^2 m_1^7$, we conclude that their

Table 2. Descriptions of features [26]

		Appearance		Wealth		Gender		Hair color		
	Age	Height	Weight	Salary	Estate	Male	Female	Black	White	Yellow
x_1	20	1.9	90	1	0	1	0	6	1	4
x_2	13	1.2	32	0	0	0	1	4	3	1
x_3	50	1.7	67	140	34	0	1	6	1	4
x_4	80	1.8	73	20	80	1	0	3	4	2
x_5	34	1.4	54	15	2	1	0	5	2	2
x_6	37	1.6	80	80	28	0	1	6	1	4
x_7	45	1.7	78	268	90	1	0	1	6	4
x_8	70	1.65	70	30	45	1	0	3	4	2
x_9	60	1.82	83	25	98	0	1	4	3	1
x_{10}	3	1.1	21	0	0	0	1	2	5	3

left and right sides are equivalent. Considering the terms on the left side of the assertion expression, for any x, the degree of x belonging to the fuzzy complex assertion $m_1^1 m_2^2 m_1^7$ is always less than or equal to the degree of x belonging to the fuzzy complex assertion $m_1^1 m_1^7$. Therefore, the term $m_1^1 m_2^2 m_1^7$ is redundant when forming the left side of the fuzzy complex assertion.

Let us take two assertion expressions into consideration, which are $\psi_1 = m_2^1 m_1^7 + m_1^2 m_1^3 m_1^6$ and $\psi_2 = m_1^2 m_1^6 + m_1^6 m_1^8 \in EM^*/R$, respectively, as in Example 2. The semantic content of the fuzzy complex assertions "ψ_1 or ψ_2" and "ψ_1 and ψ_2" can be expressed as follows:

"ψ_1 or ψ_2'' : $m_2^1 m_1^7 + m_1^2 m_1^6 + m_1^6 m_1^8 + m_1^2 m_1^3 m_1^6$
equivalent to $m_2^1 m_1^7 + m_1^2 m_1^6 + m_1^6 m_1^8$,
"ψ_1 and ψ_2'' : $m_2^1 m_1^2 m_1^6 m_1^7 + m_2^1 m_1^6 m_1^7 m_1^8 + m_1^2 m_1^3 m_1^6 + m_1^2 m_1^3 m_1^6 m_1^8$
equivalent to $m_2^1 m_1^2 m_1^6 m_1^7 + m_2^1 m_1^6 m_1^7 m_1^8 + m_1^2 m_1^3 m_1^6$.

Accordingly, "and", "or", and "equivalent to" correspond to $\wedge$, $\vee$, and the equivalence R in EI algebra, respectively. The algebra operations of them are shown as follows:

$$\psi_2 \wedge \psi_2 = m_2^1 m_1^7 + m_1^2 m_1^6 + m_1^6 m_1^8 + m_1^2 m_1^3 m_1^6 = m_2^1 m_1^7 + m_1^2 m_1^6 + m_1^6 m_1^8,$$
$$\psi_1 \vee \psi_2 = m_2^1 m_1^2 m_1^6 m_1^7 + m_2^1 m_1^6 m_1^7 m_1^8 + m_1^2 m_1^3 m_1^6 + m_1^2 m_1^3 m_1^6 m_1^8$$
$$= m_2^1 m_1^2 m_1^6 m_1^7 + m_2^1 m_1^6 m_1^7 m_1^8 + m_1^2 m_1^3 m_1^6.$$

For each fuzzy complex assertion $\alpha = \sum_{i \in I} A_i \in EM^*/R$, one can get another kind of L-fuzzy set representation of α, i.e., the $E^{\#} I$ algebra. For any $x \in X$

$$\alpha(x) = \sum_{i \in I} A^{\succeq}(x) \in EX^*/R^{\#}. \tag{10}$$

In [26], the authors proposed a special family of measures using the $E^{\#} I$ algebra with norms, by which we can convert the $E^{\#} I$ algebra represented membership degrees into [0,1]. In the AFS-based formal concept [39], $EX^*/R^{\#}$ plays the role of the extents of AFS-based formal concepts, and $E(X \times X)^*/R^{\#}$ over $X \times X$ plays the role of the extents of AFS-based fuzzy formal concepts in the sequel.

Recently, AFS theory has been further developed and applied to fuzzy clustering analysis [23,24], fuzzy decision trees [25], concept representations [24,39,40], decision management [48], set approximation [42], etc. About the detailedly mathematical properties and operations of AFS algebras, please refer to [26].

3 Multi-valued Formal Concept Based on AFS Theory

To develop multi-granule concept lattice and AFS-based formal concept [39,41] within multi-valued context $(X, M, W, \mathbb{I})$, we shall propose a new AFS-based multi-valued formal concept analysis, in which the extents are defined on

$E(X \times X)^*/R^\#$. Intents are defined on EM^*/R. This study extends AFS-based formal concept from single context to multi-valued context, and establishes a method to describe the uncertainty relations between the objects in X and the attributes in M, which can deal with the information table with fuzzy terms, Boolean terms, and intuition order terms.

3.1 AFS-Based Multi-valued Formal Concept

Let X be a set of objects and M be a set of simple assertions. Define the map $\tau : X \times X \to 2^M$ as follows: for any $(x, y) \in X \times X$,

$$\tau(x, y) = \{m | m \in M, y \in m^{\succeq}(x)\} \in 2^M, \tag{11}$$

where $m^{\succeq}(x)$ is defined by Eq. (5) and 2^M is the power set of M. Furthermore, it follows from Eq. (11) directly that the following propositions hold for τ.

Proposition 1. *Let X, M be sets, $\tau : X \times X \to 2^M$ be defined as Eq. (11). Then τ satisfies the following conclusions:*
  AX1: for any $(x_1, x_2) \in X \times X$, $\tau(x_1, x_2) \subseteq \tau(x_1, x_1)$;
  AX2: for any $(x_1, x_2), (x_2, x_3) \in X \times X$, $\tau(x_1, x_2) \cap \tau(x_2, x_3) \subseteq \tau(x_1, x_3)$.

In the sequel, we explore multi-valued formal concept by using non-symmetric indiscernibility preorders and AFS structure, in which each element in concept intent EM^*/R is a fuzzy complex assertion with a definite semantic interpretation.

Definition 2. *Let X, M be two sets. The relationship $\mathbb{I}_\tau$ between $X \times X$ and M is defined as follows: for $(x, y) \in X \times X, m \in M$,*

$$((x, y), m) \in \mathbb{I}_\tau \Leftrightarrow m \in \tau(x, y) \Leftrightarrow y \in m^{\succeq}(x). \tag{12}$$

$(X \times X, M, \mathbb{I}_\tau)$ *is called the formal context based on AFS theory.*

As a matter of fact, the formal context based on AFS theory can be viewed as the result of applying the ordinal dependencies in ordinally scaled multi-valued attributes proposed by Ganter [14] to the AFS algebra systems.

In [39], Wang and Liu proposed AFS-based formal concept, which extends the Galois connection formed by Wille [12] on the single-valued context $(X, M, \mathbb{I})$ to the one between two AFS algebra systems $(EM^*/R, \vee, \wedge)$ and $(EX^*/R^\#, \vee, \wedge)$. The intent of an AFS-based formal concept is an element of the EI algebra $(EM^*/R, \vee, \wedge)$—a kind of AFS algebra over M; correspondingly, the extent of the AFS-based formal concept is an element of the $E^\#I$ algebra $(EX^*/R^\#, \vee, \wedge)$—another kind of AFS algebra over X. The extent and intent of an AFS-based formal concept are uniquely determined by each other. Thus, the intent of an AFS-based formal concept not only generalizes that of the formal concept, but also has a well-defined semantic interpretation. Unfortunately, AFS-based formal concept proposed in [39] cannot be applied to fuzzy context and multi-valued context.

Based on the above mentioned works, we establish a new multi-granule concept lattice by introducing the new context $(X \times X, M, \mathbb{I}_\tau)$ on the multi-valued context $(X, M, \mathbb{I})$. The Galois connection is extended to the connection between the EI algebra $(EM^*/R, \vee, \wedge)$ and the $E^\# I$ algebra $(E(X \times X)^*/R^\#, \vee, \wedge)$, which are shown as follows: for any $\sum_{i \in I}(\prod_{m \in A_i} m) \in EM^*/R$, $\sum_{j \in J} a_j \in E(X \times X)^*/R^\#$,

$$\alpha(\sum_{i \in I}(\prod_{m \in A_i} m)) = \sum_{i \in I} A_i' \in E(X \times X)^*/R^\#, \tag{13}$$

$$\beta(\sum_{j \in J} a_j) = \sum_{j \in J}(\prod_{m \in a_j'} m) \in EM^*/R. \tag{14}$$

In the following, we denote the subsets of X with the lower case letters and the subsets of M with the capital letters, in order to distinguish the subsets of X from those of M.

Definition 3. *Assume that* $(X \times X, M, \mathbb{I}_\tau)$ *be context on the multi-valued context* $(X, M, \mathbb{I})$, *and* $(EM^*/R, \wedge, \vee)$ *be the EI algebra over* M *and* $(E(X \times X)^*/R^\#, \wedge, \vee)$ *be the $E^\# I$ algebra over* $X \times X$. *Let* $\zeta = \sum_{i \in I}(\prod_{m \in A_i} m) \in EM^*/R$, $\nu \in \sum_{j \in J} a_j \in E(X \times X)^*/R^\#$. (ν, ζ) *is called an AFS-based multi-valued formal concept of the context* $(X \times X, M, \mathbb{I}_\tau)$, *if* $\alpha(\zeta) = \nu$, $\beta(\nu) = \zeta$. *Then* ν *is called the extent of the AFS-based multi-valued formal concept* (ν, ζ) *and* ζ *is called the intent of the AFS-based multi-valued formal concept* (ν, ζ).

Theorem 4. *Let* $(X \times X, M, \mathbb{I})$ *be context on the multi-valued context* $(X, M, \mathbb{I})$ *and* $\mathcal{B}(E(X \times X)^*/R^\#, EM, \mathbb{I}_\tau)$ *be the set of all AFS-based multi-valued formal concepts of the context* $(X \times X, M, \mathbb{I}_\tau)$. *Then, for any* $(\nu, \zeta) \in \mathcal{B}(E(X \times X)^*/R^\#, EM^*/R, \mathbb{I}_\tau)$, ν *and* ζ *are uniquely determined by each other.*

Definition 4. *Let* $(\nu_1, \zeta_1), (\nu_2, \zeta_2) \in \mathcal{B}(E(X \times X)^*/R^\#, EM^*/R, \mathbb{I}_\tau)$. *Define* $(\nu_1, \zeta_1) \leq (\nu_2, \zeta_2)$ *if and only if* $\nu_1 \leq \nu_2$ *in lattice* $E(X \times X)^*/R^\#$ *(or equivalently* $\zeta_1 \leq \zeta_2$ *in lattice* EM^*/R).

It is obvious that $\leq$ defined in Definition 4 is a partial order relation on $\mathcal{B}(E(X \times X)^*/R^\#, EM^*/R, \mathbb{I}_\tau)$. The following theorem shows that the set $\mathcal{B}(E(X \times X)^*/R^\#, EM^*/R, \mathbb{I}_\tau)$ forms a complete lattice under the partial order relation $\leq$.

Theorem 5. *Let* $(X \times X, M, \mathbb{I}_\tau)$ *be context on the multi-valued context* $(X, M, \mathbb{I})$ *and* $\mathcal{B}(E(X \times X)^*/R^\#, EM^*/R, \mathbb{I}_\tau)$ *be the set of all AFS-based multi-valued formal concepts of* $(X \times X, M, \mathbb{I}_\tau)$. *Then* $(\mathcal{B}(E(X \times X)^*/R^\#, EM^*/R, \mathbb{I}_\tau), \leq)$ *is a complete lattice, in which suprema and infima are given as follows: for any* $(\nu_k, \zeta_k) \in \mathcal{B}(E(X \times X)^*/R^\#, EM^*/R, \mathbb{I}_\tau)$,

$$\vee_{k \in K}(\nu_k, \zeta_k) = (\vee_{k \in K}\alpha(\zeta_k), \beta(\vee_{k \in K}\alpha(\zeta_k))), \tag{15}$$

$$\wedge_{k \in K}(\nu_k, \zeta_k) = (\wedge_{k \in K}\alpha(\zeta_k), \beta(\wedge_{k \in K}\alpha(\zeta_k))). \tag{16}$$

where $k \in K$, *and* K *is any non-empty indexing set.*

$(\mathcal{B}(E(X \times X)^*/R^{\#}, EM^*/R, \mathbb{I}_\tau), \leq)$ forms a complete lattice, and M can be a fuzzy term set, Boolean term set or intuition order set. However, how to determine the membership of x belonging to $\sum_{i \in I} \prod_{m \in A_i} m$ is a key problem. In the sequel, we shall explore how to obtain the membership function for FFCA from the origin data within the framework of AFS algebras.

3.2 Membership Function Based on Lattice $E(X \times X)^*/R^{\#}$

In this subsection, we show that the lattice $EX^*/R^{\#}$ can be used in representation of each fuzzy set $\gamma = \sum_{i \in I} a_i \in E(X \times X)^*/R^{\#}$ based on the coherence membership functions [26].

Based on the semantics of the fuzzy terms and logic operations discussed in Sect. 2.1, Liu et al. proposed the coherence membership functions, which are associated with a measure over X [26]. The membership functions and the fuzzy logic operations are determined by the observed data and drawn from a probability space. An example was presented in [26] to demonstrate the approach of computing the membership functions. In Example 2, let $\eta_1 = m_1^1$, $\eta_2 = m_1^4$, $\eta_3 = m_1^1 m_1^4$, $\eta_4 = m_1^1 + m_1^4 \in EM^*/R$, $\rho_m(x) = 1$ for any $x \succeq_m x, x \in X$. By Eq. (7), we can get that

for η_1, $A = \{m_1^1\}$, $A^{\succeq}(x_3) = \{x_1, x_2, x_3, x_5, x_6, x_7, x_{10}\}$, $\mu_\eta(x_3) = \frac{|A_i^{\succeq}(x_3)|}{|X|} = \frac{7}{10} = 0.7$;

for η_2, $A = \{m_4\}$, $A^{\succeq}(x_3) = \{x_1, \ldots, x_6, x_8, x_9, x_{10}\}$, $\mu_\eta(x_3) = \frac{|A^{\succeq}(x_4)|}{|X|} = \frac{8}{10} = 0.8$;

for η_3, $A = \{m_1^1, m_1^4\}$, $A^{\succeq}(x_3) = \{x_1, x_2, x_3, x_5, x_6, x_{10}\}$, $\mu_\eta(x_3) = \frac{|A^{\succeq}(x_3)|}{|X|} = \frac{6}{10} = 0.6$;

for η_4, $A_1 = \{m_1^1\}$, $A_2 = \{m_1^4\}$, $A_1^{\succeq}(x_3) = \{x_1, \ldots, x_6, x_7, x_{10}\}$, $A_2^{\succeq}(x_3) = \{x_1, \ldots, x_6, x_8, x_9, x_{10}\}$, $\mu_\eta(x_3) = \sup_{i \in \{1,2\}} \frac{|A_i^{\succeq}(x_3)|}{|X|} = \sup\{0.7, 0.8\} = 0.8$.

Definition 5. Let X be a set and $(E(X \times X)^*/R^{\#}, \wedge, \vee)$ be the $E^{\#}I$ algebra on $X \times X$. For any $a \subseteq X \times X$, $x \in X$, denote

$$a^R(x) = \{y \in X \mid (x, y) \in a\} \subseteq X. \tag{17}$$

For any $\gamma = \sum_{i \in I} a_i \in E(X \times X)^*/R^{\#}$ and $x \in X$, the $E^{\#}I$ algebra valued membership function $\gamma^R : X \to EX^*/R^{\#}$ is defined as follows:

$$\gamma^R(x) = \sum_{i \in I} a_i^R(x) \in EX^*/R^{\#}, \tag{18}$$

and the membership function $\mu_{\gamma^R}(x)$ of γ^R is defined as follows:

$$\mu_{\gamma^R}(x) = \|\gamma^R(x)\|_\rho = \|\sum_{i \in I} a_i^R(x)\|_\rho \in [0, 1], \tag{19}$$

where $\|\cdot\|_\rho$ is called a norm of $\xi(x)$. Every $\gamma \in E(X \times X)^*/R^{\#}$ is called a fuzzy set on $X \times X$, whose membership function is defined by Eq. (18) or (19).

Since $EX^*/R^{\#}$ is a lattice, hence for each $\gamma \in E(X \times X)^*/R^{\#}$, $\gamma^R : X \to EX^*/R^{\#}$ defined by Definition 5 is a lattice-valued fuzzy set. One can easily verify that for $\gamma, \eta \in E(X \times X)^*/R^{\#}$, if $\gamma \leq \eta$ in lattice $E(X \times X)^*/R^{\#}$, then for any $x \in X$, $\gamma^R(x) \leq \eta^R(x)$ in lattice $EX^*/R^{\#}$. Thus in $(X \times X, M, \mathbb{I}_\tau)$, for each $\eta \in EM^*/R$, $\alpha(\eta)$ is a fuzzy set on X with the membership function defined by Eq. (18) or (19). Contrastively, for any $\gamma \in E(X \times X)^*/R^{\#}$ as a fuzzy set defined by Eq. (18) or (19), $\beta(\gamma)$ is an attribute in EM^*/R. If (γ, η) is an AFS-based multi-valued formal concept, then the fuzzy set γ is the extent of (γ, η), and the attribute η is the AFS logic combination of the simple attributes in M and has a definite semantic interpretation.

4   Membership Function of FFCA

Theorem 6. *Let X be a set and M be a set of simple assertions on X. Let $\tau(x, y)$ be specified by Eq. (11) and $(X \times X, M, \mathbb{I}_\tau)$ be the formal context defined by Definition 2. Then for $\zeta, \varsigma \in EM^*/R$, if $\beta(\alpha(\zeta)) = \beta(\alpha(\varsigma))$, then for any $x \in X$, $\zeta(x) = \varsigma(x)$ and $\mu_\zeta(x) = \mu_\varsigma(x)$, where for any fuzzy complex assertion $\gamma = \sum_{u \in U}(\prod_{m \in C_u} m) \in EM^*/R$, $\gamma(x) = \sum_{u \in U} C_u^{\succeq}(x) \in E^{\#}X$ is the $E^{\#}I$ valued membership function of γ defined by Eq. (18) and $\mu_\gamma(x) = \|\sum_{u \in U} C_u^{\succeq}(x)\|_\rho \in [0, 1]$ is the membership function of γ defined by Eq. (7).*

Proof: By the definition of $(X \times X, M, \mathbb{I}_\tau)$ and Eq. (18), we can verify that for any $A \subseteq M$, $x \in X$,

$$\alpha(A)^R(x) = (\cap_{m \in A} \alpha(m))^R(x)$$
$$= (\cap_{m \in A}\{(x, y) \in X \times X \mid m \in \tau(x, y)\})^R(x)$$
$$= (\{(x, y) \in X \times X \mid A \subseteq \tau(x, y)\})^R(x). \tag{20}$$

By Eqs. (11) and (17), we have

$$(\{(x, y) \in X \times X \mid A \subseteq \tau(x, y)\})^R(x) = A^{\succeq}(x). \tag{21}$$

Furthermore, for any $\gamma = \sum_{u \in U}(\prod_{m \in C_u} m) \in EM^*/R$ and $x \in X$, it follows from Eqs. (7) and (18), one has

$$\alpha(\gamma)^R(x) = \sum_{u \in U} \alpha(C_u)^R(x) = \sum_{u \in U} C_u^{\succeq}(x) = \gamma(x). \tag{22}$$

For $\zeta, \varsigma \in EM^*/R$, if $\beta(\alpha(\zeta)) = \beta(\alpha(\varsigma))$, then

$$\alpha(\zeta) = \alpha(\beta(\alpha(\zeta))) = \alpha(\beta(\alpha(\varsigma))) = \alpha(\varsigma).$$

Therefore, for any $x \in X$, it follows

$$\zeta(x) = \alpha(\zeta)^R(x) = \alpha(\varsigma)^R(x) = \varsigma(x),$$

and $\mu_\zeta(x) = ||\zeta(x)||_\rho = ||\varsigma(x)||_\rho = \mu_\varsigma(x)$. $\square$

Assume that each element in M is a crisp assertion. Then, for any $x \in X$, either $x \succeq_m y$ or $x \not\succeq_m y$ for any $y \in X$. By Eq. (17), either $\{m\}^R(x) = X$ or $\{m\}^R(x) = \emptyset$. This also implies that for any $A \subseteq M$, $x \in X$, either $A^R(x) = X$ or $A^R(x) = \emptyset$. Furthermore, by Eqs. (18) and (19), for any $\zeta \in E^\#(X \times X)$, $x \in X$, either $\zeta^R(x) = X$ or $\zeta^R(x) = \emptyset$, and either $\mu_{\zeta^R}(x) = 1$ or $\mu_{\zeta^R}(x) = 0$, i.e., $\mu_{\zeta^R}(x)$ is the characteristic function of a crisp set $C_\zeta \subseteq X$. In [26], the authors proved that the AFS logic system can be reduced to Boolean logic system if every element in M is a crisp assertion. Therefore, in the framework of AFS-based formal concept analysis, the AFS-based formal concept lattice of an AFS structure (M, τ, X) will be reduced to the classic formal concept lattice of the context $(X, M, \mathbb{I})$, where for $x \in X$ and $m \in M$, $(x, m) \in \mathbb{I} \Leftrightarrow ((x, y), m) \in \mathbb{I}_\tau$ for any $y \in X \Leftrightarrow x \succeq_m y$ for any $y \in X$.

Example 3. From Table 2, one can verify that each element $m \in M$ is a simple assertion. Let $\rho(x) = 1$, for any $x \in X$. Then, for any fuzzy complex assertion $\eta = \sum_{i \in I}(\prod_{m \in A_i} m) \in EM^*/R$, the membership function of η defined by Eq. (7) is as follows:

$$\mu_\eta(x) = ||\eta(x)||_\rho = ||\sum_{i \in I} A_i^\succeq(x)||_\rho \in [0, 1], \quad \text{for any } x \in X, \tag{23}$$

where $\eta(x)$ is defined by Eq. (6).

There are 24 fuzzy concepts generated by $\{x_1, x_2, \cdots, x_{10}\}$ and m_1^1, m_1^2, m_1^3, m_1^6, m_1^7, and the membership for any $x \in X$ is shown in Table 3, where m_1^1, m_1^2, m_1^3 are fuzzy complex assertions, while m_6, m_7 are crisp assertions. By using these fuzzy terms, we can obtain many multi-valued formal concepts, which can provide a new method to determine the membership function for FFCA from original data with fuzzy, crisp and order information.

Moreover, the above theorem can be applied to discuss the reducing problem of elements in EM^*/R. For example, let

$$\zeta = m_1^1 m_1^3 m_1^4 + m_1^1 m_1^3 m_1^7, \ \xi = m_1^1 m_1^2 m_1^3 m_1^4 + m_1^1 m_1^2 m_1^3 m_1^7$$

be two fuzzy complex assertions in EM^*/R. Then

$$\alpha(m_1^1 m_1^3 m_1^4) = \{(x_1, x_1), (x_1, x_2), (x_1, x_{10}), (x_3, x_2), (x_3, x_3), (x_3, x_5), (x_3, x_{10}),$$
$$(x_4, x_2), (x_4, x_4), (x_4, x_5), (x_4, x_{10}), (x_5, x_2), (x_5, x_5), (x_5, x_{10}),$$
$$(x_6, x_2), (x_6, x_5), (x_6, x_6), (x_6, x_{10}), (x_7, x_2), (x_7, x_5), (x_7, x_7),$$
$$(x_7, x_{10}), (x_8, x_2), (x_8, x_5), (x_8, x_8), (x_8, x_{10}), (x_9, x_2), (x_9, x_5),$$
$$(x_9, x_9), (x_9, x_{10})\}$$
$$\alpha(m_1^1 m_1^3 m_1^7) = \{(x_2, x_2), (x_2, x_{10}), (x_3, x_2), (x_3, x_3), (x_3, x_5), (x_3, x_{10}), (x_6, x_2),$$
$$(x_6, x_5), (x_4, x_8), (x_4, x_{10}), (x_6, x_{10}), (x_9, x_2), (x_9, x_3), (x_9, x_5),$$
$$(x_9, x_6), (x_9, x_7), (x_9, x_9), (x_9, x_{10}), (x_{10}, x_{10})\}$$
$$\beta(\alpha(m_1^1 m_1^3 m_1^4)) = \{m_1^1, m_1^2, m_1^3, m_1^4\}$$
$$\beta(\alpha(m_1^1 m_1^3 m_1^7)) = \{m_1^1, m_1^2, m_1^3, m_1^7\}$$

Table 3. Membership about fuzzy complex assertions generated by $X, m_1, m_2, m_3,$ m_6, m_7

	x_1	x_2	x_3	x_4	x_5	x_6	x_7	x_8	x_9	x_{10}
$\mu_{m_1^1}(\cdot)$	0.3	0.2	0.7	1	0.4	0.5	0.6	0.9	0.8	0.1
$\mu_{m_1^1 m_1^2}(\cdot)$	0.3	0.2	0.6	0.8	0.3	0.4	0.5	0.5	0.7	0.1
$\mu_{m_1^1 m_1^3}(\cdot)$	0.3	0.2	0.4	0.6	0.3	0.4	0.4	0.5	0.7	0.1
$\mu_{m_1^1 m_1^6}(\cdot)$	0.3	0	0	1	0.4	0	0.6	0.9	0	0
$\mu_{m_1 m_7}(\cdot)$	0	0.2	0.7	0	0	0.5	0	0	0.8	0.1
$\mu_{m_1 m_2 m_3}(\cdot)$	0.3	0.2	0.4	0.6	0.3	0.4	0.4	0.4	0.7	0.1
$\mu_{m_1^1 m_1^2 m_1^6}(\cdot)$	0.3	0	0	0.8	0.3	0	0.5	0.5	0	0
$\mu_{m_1^1 m_1^2 m_1^7}(\cdot)$	0	0.2	0.6	0	0	0.4	0	0	0.7	0.1
$\mu_{m_1^1 m_1^3 m_1^6}(\cdot)$	0.3	0	0	0.6	0.3	0	0.4	0.5	0	0
$\mu_{m_1^1 m_1^2 m_1^3 m_1^6}(\cdot)$	0.3	0	0	0.6	0.3	0	0.4	0.4	0	0
$\mu_{m_1^1 m_1^2 m_1^3 m_1^7}(\cdot)$	0	0.2	0.4	0	0	0.4	0	0	0.7	0.1
$\mu_{m_1^2}(\cdot)$	1	0.2	0.7	0.8	0.3	0.4	0.7	0.5	0.9	0.1
$\mu_{m_1^2 m_1^3}(\cdot)$	1	0.2	0.4	0.6	0.3	0.4	0.6	0.4	0.9	0.1
$\mu_{m_1^2 m_1^6}(\cdot)$	1	0	0	0.8	0.3	0	0.7	0.5	0	0
$\mu_{m_1^2 m_1^7}(\cdot)$	0	0.2	0.7	0	0	0.4	0	0	0.9	0.1
$\mu_{m_1^2 m_1^3 m_1^6}(\cdot)$	1	0	0	0.6	0.3	0	0.6	0.4	0	0
$\mu_{m_1^2 m_1^3 m_1^7}(\cdot)$	0	0.2	0.4	0	0	0.4	0	0	0.9	0.1
$\mu_{m_1^3}(\cdot)$	1	0.2	0.4	0.6	0.3	0.8	0.7	0.5	0.9	0.1
$\mu_{m_1^3 m_1^6}(\cdot)$	1	0	0	0.6	0.3	0	0.7	0.5	0	0
$\mu_{m_1^3 m_1^7}(\cdot)$	0	0.2	0.4	0	0	0.8	0	0	0.9	0.1
$\mu_{m_1^6}(\cdot)$	1	0	0	1	1	0	1	1	0	0
$\mu_{m_1^7}(\cdot)$	0	1	1	0	0	1	0	0	1	1

while

$$\beta(\alpha(m_1^1 m_1^2 m_1^3 m_1^4)) = m_1^1 m_1^2 m_1^3 m_1^4, \ \beta(\alpha(m_1^1 m_1^2 m_1^3 m_1^7)) = m_1^1 m_1^2 m_1^3 m_1^7.$$

From Table 4, one can get $\mu_{m_1^1 m_1^3 m_1^4}(x) = \mu_{m_1^1 m_1^2 m_1^3 m_1^4}(x)$, $\mu_{m_1 m_3 m_7}(x) = \mu_{m_1 m_2 m_3 m_7}(x)$ for any $x \in X$. So, the fuzzy assertion $m_1^1 m_1^3 m_1^4$ is equivalent to $m_1^1 m_1^2 m_1^3 m_1^4$, and the fuzzy complex assertion $m_1^1 m_1^3 m_1^7$ is equivalent to $m_1^1 m_1^2 m_1^3 m_1^7$. Consequently, the fuzzy complex assertion ζ is equivalent to ξ, and $\mu_\zeta(x) = \mu_\xi(x)$ for any $x \in X$.

Remark:

1. For two fuzzy complex attributes $\zeta, \xi \in EM^*/R$, $\zeta(x) = \xi(x)$ for any $x \in X$ if and only if $\beta(\alpha(\zeta)) = \beta(\alpha(\xi))$. Therefore, we can find the simplest reduced form for each attribute in EM^*/R.

Table 4. Membership about fuzzy complex assertions

	$m_1^1 m_1^3 m_1^4$	$m_1^1 m_1^2 m_1^3 m_1^4$	$m_1^1 m_1^3 m_1^7$	$m_1^1 m_1^2 m_1^3 m_1^7$	ζ	ξ
x_1	0.3	0.3	0	0	0.3	0.3
x_2	0	0	0.2	0.2	0.2	0.2
x_3	0.4	0.4	0.4	0.4	0.4	0.4
x_4	0.4	0.4	0	0	0.4	0.4
x_5	0.3	0.3	0	0	0.3	0.3
x_6	0.4	0.4	0.4	0.4	0.4	0.4
x_7	0.4	0.4	0	0	0.4	0.4
x_8	0.4	0.4	0	0	0.4	0.4
x_9	0.4	0.4	0.7	0.7	0.7	0.7
x_{10}	0	0	0.1	0.1	0.1	0.1

2. For any $\gamma \in EM^*/R$, let $\gamma = \sum_{u \in U}(\prod_{m \in A_u} m)$ be the simplest reduced form. Then for any $u \in U$, $A_u'' = A_u$ in the context $(X \times X, M, I_\tau)$.
3. Let $\mathcal{B} = \{\mathcal{A}|\mathcal{A} \subseteq \mathcal{M}, \mathcal{A} = \mathcal{A}''\}$. For any fuzzy attribute $\gamma \in EM^*/R$, there exists $\eta \in EB^*/\mathcal{R}$, such that $\gamma(x) = \eta(x)$, for any $x \in X$ under $EX^*/R^\#$. Thus $\mathcal{B}$ is the dimension to measure the complexity of (M, τ, X).

5   Conclusions

This current study mainly focuses on the applications of multi-valued context to the AFS algebra systems. Concretely, this paper explores multi-valued concept lattices within the framework of AFS theory, in which non-symmetric indiscernibility preorders are introduced to deal with conceptual scaling for multi-valued data. The proposed method can be used to deal with the multi-valued information with fuzzy attributes, Boolean attributes and intuition order attributes. Besides, a method to determine membership function is proposed, which is directly determined by the original data and does not need additional humans interpretation to describe the uncertainty relations between the objects and the attributes. This paper provides a new approach to explore the mathematization of formal concepts of a multi-valued context from point of view of algebraic logics.

References

1. Agarwal, P., Kaytoue, M., Kuznetsov, S.O., Napoli, A., Polaillon, G.: Symbolic galois lattices with pattern structures. In: Kuznetsov, S.O., Ślęzak, D., Hepting, D.H., Mirkin, B.G. (eds.) RSFDGrC 2011. LNCS (LNAI), vol. 6743, pp. 191–198. Springer, Heidelberg (2011). doi:10.1007/978-3-642-21881-1_31
2. Baixeries, J.: Lattice characterization of Armstrong and symmetric dependencies. Ph.D. thesis, Universitat Politècnica de Catalunya, Spain (2007)

3. Baixeries, J., Kaytoue, M., Napoli, A.: Characterizing functional dependencies in formal concept analysis with pattern structures. Ann. Math. Artif. Intell. **72**, 129–149 (2014)
4. Belohlavek, R.: Lattices generated by binary fuzzy relations. Tatra Mt. Math. Publ. **16**(1), 11–19 (1999)
5. Belohlavek, R.: Fuzzy Galois connections. Math. Log. Q. **45**(4), 497–504 (1999)
6. Bock, H.H., Diday, E. (eds.): Analysis of Symbolic Data C Exploratory Methods for Extracting Statistical Information from Complex Data. Springer, Heidelberg (2000)
7. Carpineto, C., Romano, G.: A lattice conceptual clustering system and its application to browsing retrieval. Mach. Learn. **24**(2), 95–122 (1996)
8. Ignatov, D.I., et al.: Can triconcepts become triclusters? Int. J. Gen Syst **42**(6), 572–593 (2013)
9. Ignatov, D.I., et al.: Triadic formal concept analysis and triclustering: searching for optimal patterns. Mach. Learn. **101**(1–3), 271–302 (2015)
10. Djouadi, Y.: Interval-valued fuzzy Galois connections: algebraic requirements and concept lattice construction. Fundam. Inform. **99**(2), 169–186 (2010)
11. Fan, S., Zhang, W., Xu, W.: Fuzzy inference based on fuzzy concept lattice. Fuzzy Sets Syst. **157**(24), 3177–3187 (2006)
12. Ganter, B., Wille, R.: Formal Concept Analysis: Mathematical Foundations. Springer, Berlin (1999)
13. Ganter, B., Kuznetsov, S.O.: Pattern structures and their projections. In: Delugach, H.S., Stumme, G. (eds.) ICCS-ConceptStruct 2001. LNCS (LNAI), vol. 2120, pp. 129–142. Springer, Heidelberg (2001). doi:10.1007/3-540-44583-8_10
14. Ganter, B.: Non-symmetric indiscernibility. In: Wolff, K.E., Palchunov, D.E., Zagoruiko, N.G., Andelfinger, U. (eds.) KONT/KPP -2007. LNCS (LNAI), vol. 6581, pp. 26–34. Springer, Heidelberg (2011). doi:10.1007/978-3-642-22140-8_2
15. Godin, R., Mili, H., Mineau, G., Missaoui, R., Arfi, A., Chau, T.: Design of class hierarchies based on concept Galois lattices. TAPOS **4**(2), 117–134 (1998)
16. Grosser, D., Ralambondrainy, H.: Concept analysis on structured, multi-valued and incomplete data. In: Eklund, P.W., Diatta, J., Liquiere, M. (eds.) Proceedings of the Fifth International Conference on Concept Lattices and Their Applications, CLA 2007, France, Montpellier, 24–26 October (2007)
17. Gugisch, R.: Many-valued context analysis using descriptions. In: Delugach, H.S., Stumme, G. (eds.) ICCS-ConceptStruct 2001. LNCS, vol. 2120, pp. 157–168. Springer, Heidelberg (2001). doi:10.1007/3-540-44583-8_12
18. Harms, S., Deogun, J.: Sequential association rule mining with time lags. J. Intell. Inform. Syst. **22**(1), 7–22 (2004)
19. Huynh, V., Nakamori, Y.: Fuzzy concept formation based on context model. In: Baba, N., et al. (eds.) Knowledge-Based Intelligent Information Eng. Systems and Allied Technologies (IOS Press, 2001), pp. 687–691 (2001)
20. Ignatov, D.I., Kuznetsov, S.O., Magizov, R.A., Zhukov, L.E.: From triconcepts to triclusters. In: Kuznetsov, S.O., Ślęzak, D., Hepting, D.H., Mirkin, B.G. (eds.) RSFDGrC 2011. LNCS (LNAI), vol. 6743, pp. 257–264. Springer, Heidelberg (2011). doi:10.1007/978-3-642-21881-1_41
21. Kuznetsov, S.O., Poelmans, J.: Knowledge representation and processing with formal concept analysis. Wiley Interdiscip. Rev. Data Min. Knowl. Discov. **3**(3), 200–215 (2013)
22. Liu, X.: The fuzzy theory based on AFS algebras and AFS structure. J. Math. Anal. Appl. **217**(2), 459–478 (1998)

23. Liu, X., Wang, W., Chai, T.: The fuzzy clustering analysis based on AFS theory. IEEE Trans. Syst. Man Cybern. Part B **35**(5), 1013–1027 (2005)
24. Liu, X., Chai, T., Wang, W.: Approaches to the representations and logic operations of fuzzy concepts in the framework of axiomatic fuzzy set theory I. Inform. Sci. **177**(4), 1007–1026 (2007)
25. Liu, X., Pedrycz, W.: The development of fuzzy decision trees in the framework of axiomatic fuzzy set logic. Appl. Soft Comput. **7**(1), 325–342 (2007)
26. Liu, X., Pedrycz, W.: Axiomatic fuzzy set theroy and its applications. Springer, Heidelberg (2009)
27. Mineau, G., Godin, R.: Automatic structuring of knowledge bases by conceptual clustering. IEEE Trans. Knowl. Data Eng. **7**(5), 824–829 (1995)
28. Missikoff, M., Scholl, M.: An algorithm for insertion into a lattice: application to type classification. In: Litwin, W., Schek, H.-J. (eds.) FODO 1989. LNCS, vol. 367, pp. 64–82. Springer, Heidelberg (1989). doi:10.1007/3-540-51295-0_119
29. Nakatani, Y., Hariyama, M., Kameyama, M.: Architecture of a multi-context FPGA using a hybrid multiple-valued/binary context switching signal. In: 20th International Parallel and Distributed Processing Symposium, IPDPS 2006, pp. 25–29, April 2006
30. Poelmans, J., Ignatov, D.I., Kuznetsov, S.O., Dedene, G.: Formal concept analysis in knowledge processing: a survey on applications. Expert Syst. Appl. **40**(16), 6538–6560 (2013)
31. Poelmans, J., Ignatov, D.I., Kuznetsov, S.O., Dedene, G.: Formal Concept Analysis in knowledge processing: a survey on models and techniques. Expert Syst. Appl. **40**(16), 6601–6623 (2013)
32. Poelmans, J., Ignatov, D.I., Kuznetsov, S.O., Dedene, G.: Fuzzy and rough formal concept analysis: a survey. Int. J. Gen Syst **43**(2), 105–134 (2014)
33. Pollandt, S.: Fuzzy-Begriffe: Formale Begriffsanalyse Unscharfer Daten. Springer, Heidelberg (1996)
34. Stumme, G., Wille, R.: Begriffliche Wissensverarbeitung-Methoden und Anwendungen. Springer, Heidelberg (2000)
35. Stumme, G., Taouil, R., Bastide, Y., Pasquier, N., Lakhal, L.: Computing iceberg concept lattices with TITANIC. Data Knowl. Eng. **42**(2), 189–222 (2002)
36. Tang, Y., Fan, M., Li, J.: An information fusion technology for triadic decision contexts. Int. J. Mach. Learn. Cybern. **7**(1), 13–24 (2016)
37. Tilly, T.: Formal concept analysis and formal methods, submitted in partial fulfilment of the requirements for PhD candidature, Grifith University (2000)
38. Vogt, F., Wille, R.: TOSCANA — a graphical tool for analyzing and exploring data. In: Tamassia, R., Tollis, I.G. (eds.) GD 1994. LNCS, vol. 894, pp. 226–233. Springer, Heidelberg (1995). doi:10.1007/3-540-58950-3_374
39. Wang, L., Liu, X.: Concept analysis via rough set and AFS algebra. Inform. Sci. **178**(21), 4125–4137 (2008)
40. Wang, L., Liu, X., Cao, J.: A new algebraic structure for formal concept analysis. Inform. Sci. **180**(24), 4865–4876 (2010)
41. Wang, L., Liu, X., Wang, X.: AFS-based formal concept analysis within the logic description of granules. In: Yao, J.T., Yang, Y., Słowiński, R., Greco, S., Li, H., Mitra, S., Polkowski, L. (eds.) RSCTC 2012. LNCS (LNAI), vol. 7413, pp. 323–331. Springer, Heidelberg (2012). doi:10.1007/978-3-642-32115-3_38
42. Wang, L., Liu, X., Qiu, W.: Nearness approximation space based on axiomatic fuzzy sets. Int. J. Approx. Reason. **53**, 200–211 (2012)
43. Wei, L., Qian, T., Wan, Q., Qi, J.: A research summary about triadic concept analysis. Int. J. Mach. Learn. Cybern. (2016). doi:10.1007/s13042-016-0599-7

44. Wille, R.: Restructuring lattice theory: an approach based on hierarchies of concepts. In: Ivan Rival, R. (ed.) Ordered Sets, pp. 445–470. Reidel, Boston (1982)
45. Wille, R.: Knowledge acquisition by methods of formal concept analysis. In: Diday, E. (ed.) Data Analysis, Learning Symbolic and Numeric Knowledge, pp. 365–380. Nova Science, NewYork (1989)
46. Wille, R.: The basic theorem of triadic concept analysis. Order **12**, 149–158 (1995)
47. Wu, S., Li, M., Tang, Y., Xu, L., Wei, D.: The data scales in multi-valued context based on formal concept analysis. In: IEEE Ninth International Conference on Computer and Information Technology, pp. 278–282 (2009)
48. Xu, X., Liu, X., Chen, Y.: Applications of axiomatic fuzzy set clustering method on management strategic analysis. Eur. J. Oper. Res. **198**, 297–304 (2009)

Turning Krimp into a Triclustering Technique on Sets of Attribute-Condition Pairs that Compress

Maxim Yurov and Dmitry I. Ignatov$^{(\boxtimes)}$

National Research University Higher School of Economics, Moscow, Russia
dignatov@hse.ru

Abstract. Mining ternary relations or triadic Boolean tensors is one of the recent trends in knowledge discovery that allows one to take into account various modalities of input object-attribute data. For example, in movie databases like IMBD, an analyst may find not only movies grouped by specific genres but see their common keywords. In the so called folksonomies, users can be grouped according to their shared resources and used tags. In gene expression analysis, genes can be grouped along with samples of tissues and time intervals providing comprehensible patterns. However, pattern explosion effects even with one more dimension are seriously aggravated. In this paper, we continue our previous study on searching for a smaller collection of "optimal" patterns in triadic data with respect to a set of quality criteria such as patterns' cardinality, density, diversity, coverage, etc. We show how a simple data preprocessing has enabled us to use the frequent itemset mining algorithm KRIMP based on MDL-principle for triclustering purposes.

Keywords: Itemsets that compress · Triclustering · MDL principle · Frequent patterns

1 Introduction

Frequent pattern mining is one of the major topics in Data Mining, which dates back to early 1990s [1]. The classic level-wise Apriori approach to enumerate frequent itemsets exploits antimonotonicity property between the itemset size and the number of containing transactions [2]. However, even for relatively small transaction datasets the number of frequent itemsets may be humongous up to 2^m, where m is the number of transactions or items. The well-known remedy is the usage of closed itemsets, i.e. itemsets with no superset of the same support (the number of containing transactions). One can store only closed itemsets to count the support of any other itemset contained in the input database. In case this number is very high to generate frequent patterns within reasonable time and limited memory, then only top-k frequent closed itemsets or maximal ones can be obtained. However, there is another view on the way of generating relevant

© Springer International Publishing AG 2017
L. Polkowski et al. (Eds.): IJCRS 2017, Part II, LNAI 10314, pp. 558–569, 2017.
DOI: 10.1007/978-3-319-60840-2_40

itemsets. One can apply minimal description length (MDL) principle to select only a limited amount of itemsets to cover the original transaction database w.r.t. set inclusion. This approach can be efficiently implemented by means of simple sorting heuristics like ordering such coding itemsets by size, support, or lexicographically [3,4]. In Formal Concept Analysis (FCA), an applied branch of Lattice Theory, a convenient language for the problem formulation can be found in terms of concepts and their hierarchies over object-attribute binary relations [5].

Later, more complex data came to the stage like sequences, graphs, linked relational tables, and n-ary relations, in particular. n-ary relations (aka Boolean tensors) can relate more than two entities; one of the famous examples are the so-called Folksonomies, ternary relations, where users, resources, and tags are tied by assignment relation. Similarly, in transactional or object-attribute binary data, one can try to find frequent bisets like (tags, resources) that have been frequently related, i.e. the tags that have been assigned to the resources by sufficiently large number of users. However, the number of outputted frequent bisets (or n-sets, to be more general) increases as n^m in the worst case, where m is the number of different input entities in the first component of the original n-ary relation (m should be no greater than the total number of other related entities of each type, respectively). Frequent closed bisets or, more generally, closed n-sets can be a tool of choice to select only limited amount of potentially interesting n-sets [6].

FCA proposes the so-called triadic formal concepts (or triconcepts), i.e. maximal cuboids in ternary relations w.r.t. possible permutations along the interrelated dimensions [7]; triadic formal concepts are also known as closed trisets in Data Mining community [8]. One way to reduce the number of outputted patterns is to consider a relaxation of their definition. While maximality of a frequent trisets already allows to reduce the number of patterns in comparison to all the frequent trisets of a given ternary relation, trisets with some triples missing may help to do it more efficiently [9,10]. To study those two ways of searching for relevant patterns on common grounds, we treated trisets (not necessarily closed) and trisets with missing triples as triclusters [10]. Moreover, we proposed a reasonable set of criteria to select such relevant patterns like their cardinality, density, diversity, coverage, and their variations. However, among the five compared approaches (formal triconcepts TRIAS, least-square based triclusters TRIBOX, two variants of FCA-based OAC-triclustering, and spectral triclustering SPECTRIC) there were no a winner according to the whole set of criteria. Only incomparable and non-dominated, i.e. Pareto-optimal solutions, have been identified. Therefore, we are continuing our findings by investigation of other prospective candidates into "optimal" patterns.

In fact, the aforementioned triclustering approaches have been rather well studied, but MDL-based KRIMP algorithm seems to be not even tested in triadic setting, i.e. on ternary relations like Bibsonomy[1]. Since the resulting bisets (or sets of pairs) are not necessarily closed but uniquely determine the supporting

---

[1] There exists a version of KRIMP for mining linked relation tables, which seems to be suitable for n-ary relations as well [11].

entities and thus similar, we would refer to the whole resulting triset as a tri-cluster. Note that while closed trisets are well-known under the name of formal triconcepts, closed bisets for binary relations are formal concepts.

In this short paper, we compare several triclustering algorithms, including those for generation of formal triconcepts, against triclusters (in fact, bisets or sets of pairs) generated by KRIMP, according to the aforementioned criteria.

The remaining sections are organised as follows. In Sect. 2, we give a short overview of the KRIMP methodology for compressing itemset mining based on paper [3]. Section 3 introduces the necessary notions from triadic data analysis and describes the underlying data transformation from an input ternary relation to the corresponding binary one; this section also presents the quality criteria to assess the resulting patterns. Section 4 presents the results of experiments with the original KKRIMP implementation and several triclustering algorithms along with the examples of outputted patterns. The last section concludes the paper.

2   Krimp Approach for Itemsets Compression

Let us briefly recall the idea of KRIMP algorithm [3] in terms or FCA[2].

Let $\mathbb{K} = (G, M, I)$ be a formal context, where G is a set of objects (e.g., transactions), M is a set of attributes (e.g., items), and $I \subseteq G \times M$. This is a more general mathematical representation of a transactional data table.

A code table consists of two columns. In the left column, sets of attributes are listed (say, in lectic order) per row, in the right one the corresponding code words are placed. The left column contains at least all 1-itemsets. All the code words are unique. An example of a code table (CT) for $M = \{a, b, c\}$ is given in Table 1. Note that the Usage column is not a part of the code table and the codes are ordered by their lengths, e.g. $L(\alpha) < L(\beta) < L(\gamma) < \dots$.

Table 1. An example of a formal context (left) and the corresponding code table.

	a	b	c
1	×	×	×
2	×	×	×
3	×	×	×
4	×	×	×
5	×	×	×
6	×	×	
7	×		
8		×	

Attribute set (itemset)	Code	Usage
$\{a, b, c\}$	α	5
$\{a, b\}$	β	1
$\{a\}$	γ	1
$\{b\}$	δ	1
$\{c\}$	-	0

The context encoded by the code table from Table 1 is given in Table 2. The $cover(CT, g)$ is a subset of CS, the coding set of CT such that the union of all $X \in cover(CT, g)$ equals g' and elements of $cover(CT, g)$ do not overlap, i.e. it returns a unique partition of g', $g' = \bigsqcup_{X \in cover(CT,g)} X$.

---

[2] FCA basics can found in books [5, 12] or tutorial [13].

Table 2. The database (context), its cover with the code table (CT), and the encoded database.

Object intents, g'	Cover with CT	Encoded database
$\{a, b, c\}$	$\{a, b, c\}$	α
$\{a, b, c\}$	$\{a, b, c\}$	α
$\{a, b, c\}$	$\{a, b, c\}$	α
$\{a, b, c\}$	$\{a, b, c\}$	α
$\{a, b, c\}$	$\{a, b, c\}$	α
$\{a, b\}$	$\{a, b\}$	β
$\{a\}$	$\{a\}$	γ
$\{b\}$	$\{b\}$	δ

A special type of code table, standard code table, contains only sets of size one. The example of the standard code table for the context from Table 2 is given in Table 3.

Table 3. The database cover with the standard code table (ST) and the encoded database.

Attribute set (1-itemset)	Code	Usage
$\{a\}$	α	7
$\{b\}$	β	7
$\{c\}$	γ	5

Cover with ST	Encoded database
$\{a\}, \{b\}, \{c\}$	$\alpha\beta\gamma$
$\{a\}, \{b\}, \{c\}$	$\alpha\beta\gamma$
$\{a\}, \{b\}, \{c\}$	$\alpha\beta\gamma$
$\{a\}, \{b\}, \{c\}$	$\alpha\beta\gamma$
$\{a\}, \{b\}, \{c\}$	$\alpha\beta\gamma$
$\{a\}, \{b\}$	$\alpha\beta$
$\{a\}$	α
$\{b\}$	β

It is clear that ST is not always optimal. Hence, the main problem here is to find a Minimal Coding Set. Let $\mathbb{K} = (G, M, I)$ be a formal context, *cover* be a cover function, and $\mathcal{F}$ be a set of candidates to cover $\mathbb{K}$. We need to find the minimal coding set $CS \subseteq \mathcal{F}$ such that the resulting code table CT has the minimal size $L(\mathbb{K}, CT)$.

The total compressed size of the encoded database and the code table is computed as follows:

$$L(\mathbb{K}, CT) = L(\mathbb{K} \mid CT) + L(CT \mid \mathbb{K}), \text{ where}$$

$L(\mathbb{K} \mid CT)$ is the size of the encoded context $\mathbb{K}$ and $L(CT \mid \mathbb{K})$ is the size of the code table CT, in bits.

The size of the code table CT is computed as follows:

$$L(CT \mid \mathbb{K}) = \sum_{X \in CT: usage_{\mathbb{K}}(X) \neq 0} L(code_{ST}(X)) + L(code_{CT}(X))), \text{ where}$$

$L(code_{ST}(X))$ and $L(code_{CT}(X))$ are the lengths of the codes of itemset X with respect to the standard code table ST and the code table CT. The usage of an itemset is the number of objects such that their intent contains this itemset as a covering block:

$$usage_{\mathbb{K}}(X) = |\{g \in G \mid X \in cover(CT, g)\}|.$$

The size of the encoded $\mathbb{K}$ is computed as the sum over all object intents:

$$L(\mathbb{K}|CT) = \sum_{g \in G} L(g|CT), \text{ where}$$

$$L(g|CT) = \sum_{X \in cover(CT, g)} L(code_{CT}(X)).$$

Concrete examples of computations with code lengths in bits can be found in [3].

Let us shortly discuss algorithmic strategy of KRIMP (see Algorithm 1).

It starts with the standard code table ST that contains only sets of single attributes $\{m\}$, where $m \in M$. Then KRIMP adds one-by-one candidate itemsets from $\mathcal{F}$. If the resulting code table provides better compression, keep the candidate and continue search; otherwise remove the candidate.

The KRIMP algorithm uses several heuristics, first, the so called standard cover order. That is it orders $X \in CT$ by decreasing cardinality, then by decreasing support, and then by increasing position w.r.t. lexicographic order:

$$|X| \downarrow \quad supp_{\mathbb{K}}(X) \downarrow \quad lexicographically \uparrow.$$

Second, KRIMP exploits the standard order of candidates. Large and then frequent sets are of priority:

$$supp_{\mathbb{K}}(X) \downarrow \quad |X| \downarrow \quad lexicographically \uparrow.$$

Algorithm 1. Krimp Algorithm.

Input: $\mathbb{K} = (G, M, I)$ is a context, $\mathcal{F} \subseteq M$ is a set of candidates.
Output: A heuristic solution to the Minimal Coding Set Problem, code table CT.
1: $CT \leftarrow$ **StandardCodeTable**$(\mathbb{K})$
2: $F_0 \leftarrow F$ in **Standard Candidate Order**
3: **for all** $F \in \mathcal{F}_0 \setminus \{\{m\} \mid m \in M\}$ **do**
4:     $CT_c \leftarrow (CT \cup F)$ in **Standard Cover Order**
5:     **if** $L(\mathbb{K}, CT_c) < L(\mathbb{K}, CT)$ **then**
6:         $CT \leftarrow CT_c$
7:     **end if**
8: **end for**
9: **return** CT

---

3   Triadic Data and Their Transformation

Let us consider, a *triadic (formal) context* denoted by $(G, M, B, I \subseteq G \times M \times B)$. Here, sets G, M, and B are interpreted as objects, attributes, and conditions, respectively, while $(g, m, b) \in I$ means that the object g has the attribute m under the condition b [7].

A triadic context $\mathbb{K} = (G, M, B, I)$ gives rise to the following dyadic context $\mathbb{K}^{(1)} = (X_1, X_2 \times X_3, I^{(1)})$, where $gI^{(1)}(m, b) :\Leftrightarrow (g, m, b) \in I$. We use such contexts as an input for KRIMP for mining triclusters in them.

Example 1. **Triadic Data.**

1. A sample of *Top-250 movies from* www.IMDB.com.
   The objects are movie titles, the attributes are keywords, and the conditions are genres.
2. A sample from *bibliography sharing system* BibSonomy.org.
   The objects are users, the attributes are tags, and the conditions are electronic bookmarks.

Example 2. **Transformation of a triadic relation to a dyadic relation.**
If there is a movie description in terms of keywords and genres

$$\{Star\ Wars\} \times \{Princess, Empire\} \times \{Adventure, Sci\text{-}Fi, Action\},$$

then these data can be transformed into object-attribute form as follows:

$$\{Star\ Wars\} \times \left\{ \begin{array}{c} (Princess, Adventure), (Princess, Sci\text{-}Fi) \\ (Princess, Action), (Empire, Adventure) \\ (Empire, Sci\text{-}Fi), (Empire, Action) \end{array} \right\}.$$

Here, the role of new attributes is played by the original (attribute, condition) pairs.

Consider $\mathbb{K} = (G, M, B, I)$, a triadic context; in what follows we will refer to a trisets $T = (X, Y, Z)$ with $Z \subseteq G, Y \subseteq M, Z \subseteq B$ as an object-attribute-condition tricluster or simply *tricluster*.

These triclusters are triadic patterns that we are going to find with KRIMP on a transformed triadic data.

Each encoding set of (object, attribute) pairs found by KRIMP is contained as a coding block in the description of some object $g \in G$. Let S be a coding set returned by KRIMP that consists of n attribute-condition pairs from $M \times B$. Then the first component X of the corresponding tricluster is $\{g \mid (g, m, b) \in I\,forall(m, b) \in S\}$. The remaining two components are $Y = \{m \mid \forall(m, b) \in S\}$ and $Z = \{b \mid \forall(m, b) \in S\}$. It is clear that S is not necessarily equal to $Y \times Z$, so, some amount of missing triples is allowed inside $T = (X, Y, Z)$. The quality of such a tricluster can be assessed by its density.

The quality metrics that we use to compare triclusters and their collections are below.

Density. The *density* of a tricluster $T = (X, Y, Z)$ is defined as the fraction of all triples of I in $X \times Y \times Z$:

$$\rho(T) = \frac{|I \cap (X \times Y \times Z)|}{|X||Y||Z|}.$$

For a tricluster collection $\mathcal{T}$ its average density is defined as follows:

$$\rho(\mathcal{T}) = \frac{\sum_{T_i \in \mathcal{T}} \rho(T_i)}{|\mathcal{T}|}.$$

If $T = (X, Y, Z) \subseteq I$, then $\rho(T) = 1$.

Coverage. Coverage is defined as a fraction of the triples of the context (alternatively, objects, attributes or conditions) included in at least one of the triclusters of their resulting collection $\mathcal{T}$:

$$coverage(\mathcal{T}, \mathbb{K}) = \frac{|\bigcup_{(X,Y,Z) \in \mathcal{T}} X \times Y \times Z \cap I|}{|I|}.$$

Diversity. To define diversity of triclusters we use a binary function that equals to 1 if the intersection of triclusters T_i and T_j is not empty, and 0 otherwise. For the whole tricluster the diversity is defined as follows:

$$diversity(\mathcal{T}) = 1 - \frac{\sum_j \sum_{i<j} intersect(T_i, T_j)}{\frac{|\mathcal{T}|(|\mathcal{T}|-1)}{2}},$$

where

$$intersect(T_i, T_j) = \begin{cases} 1, & G_{T_i} \cap G_{T_j} \neq \emptyset \wedge \\ & \wedge M_{T_i} \cap M_{T_j} \neq \emptyset \wedge \\ & \wedge B_{T_i} \cap B_{T_j} \neq \emptyset \\ 0, & \text{otherwise.} \end{cases}$$

Thus, one may assume that a not that large collection of triclusters, with high average density, coverage, and diversity is a good alternative, for example, to a large collection of absolutely dense triclusters of low coverage and diversity.

Now, having the definition of extracted patterns and the quality criteria, let us test the KRIMP-based triclustering approach on a real dataset of moderate size against the triclustering techniques compared in [10].

4   Experiments

To perform experiments with KRIMP on triadic data we have selected the IMDB dataset with top-250 movies from [14][3]; its basic statistics are given in Table 4.

---

[3] http://bit.ly/triMLData.

As for the triclustering approaches for comparison, we have selected five triclustering methods from [10]. The OAC-triclustering methods OAC-BOX [15] and OAC-PRIME [10] are based on the idea of relaxation of the triadic formal concept definition to allow missing triples. The TRIBOX follows the notion of box tricluster based on the conventional least-squares criterion [14]. The SPECTRIC triclustering approach is based on the adaptation of spectral clustering to the triadic setting [15]. TRIAS is one of the first efficient algorithms for large triadic contexts [8].

Table 4. Basic statistics of the IMDB dataset with top-250 movies.

Context	$|G|$	$|M|$	$|B|$	# triples	Density
IMDB	250	795	22	3818	0.00087

All the methods, except of KRIMP, have been implemented by the authors of [10] and incorporated into a single triclustering toolbox. The toolbox has been implemented in C# using MS Visual Studio 2010/2012. All the experiments have been performed on Windows 7 SP1 x64 system equipped with an Intel Core i7-2600 @ 3.40 GHz processor and 8 GB of RAM. AlgLib[4] library was used for performing eigenvalue decomposition. The KRIMP implementation has been taken from http://www.cs.uu.nl/groups/ADA/krimp/.

Technically, as we could see, this is possible to restore the movie component of a KRIMP-based tricluster in one pass over the initial data checking the presence (keyword, genre) pairs taken from the KRIMP output, i.e. the corresponding code table. According to the results summary in Table 5, the used KRIMP implementation is the fastest; due to technical reasons we start only with $minsup = 2$ (KRIMP has not terminated correctly in our experiments). While the number of generated triclusters without singletons, i.e. pairs of (keyword, genre), is the lowest, for arbitrary coding sets of pairs, this number is the highest. The density is equal to 1 and the diversity is close to 1. However, the coverage is one of the lowest for non-singletons. There is a trade-off between the coverage and the number of triclusters outputted by KRIMP.

To provide the reader with examples of the extracted triclusters, we have selected three triclusters found by KRIMP.

Example 3. Three triclusters extracted by KRIMP from IMDB dataset.
Tricluster 1.
Keyword-genre component:

```
{(Princess,Adventure), (Princess,Fantasy), (Empire,Sci-Fi),
(Empire,Adventure), (Empire,Action), (Princess,Sci-Fi),
(Princess,Action), (Empire,Fantasy), (Death Star,Sci-Fi),
(Death Star,Fantasy), (Death Star,Adventure), (Death Star,Action)},
(2,2)
```

---

[4] http://www.alglib.net/.

Table 5. Time, cardinality, density, coverage and diversity of the resulting triclustering collection for Top-250 IMDB movies dataset.

Algorithm	t, ms	N, number of triclusters	ρ, %	Cov, %	Div, %
IMDB					
OAC ($\square$)	2314	1500	1.84	100	15.650
OAC ($/$)	547	1274	53.85	100	96.550
SPECTRIC	98799	21	17.07	20.88	100
TRIBOX	197136	328	91.65	98.90	98.890
TRIAS	102554	1956	100	100	99.890
KRIMP ($minsup = 2$, only non-singletons)	87	152	100	24.04	99.556
KRIMP ($minsup = 2$, $usage \neq 0$)	87	2859	100	99.97	99.997
KRIMP ($minsup = 3$, only non-singletons)	46	57	100	12.07	98.684
KRIMP ($minsup = 3$, $usage \neq 0$)	46	2966	100	99.97	99.998

Movies component:

{Star Wars: Episode VI ? Return of the Jedi (1983), Star Wars (1977)}

Tricluster 2.
Keyword-genre component:

{(Future,Sci-Fi), (Future,Thriller), (Future,Action), (Cyborg,Thriller),
(Cyborg,Sci-Fi), (Cyborg,Action), (The Terminator,Thriller),
(The Terminator,Sci-Fi), (The Terminator,Action) },
(2,2)

Movies component:

{The Terminator (1984), Terminator 2: Judgment Day (1991)}

Tricluster 3.
Keyword-genre component:

{Gotham,Thriller), (Gotham,Drama), (Gotham,Crime), (Gotham,Action),
(Batman,Thriller), (Batman,Drama), (Batman,Crime), (Batman,Action)},
(2,2)

Movies component:

{Batman Begins (2005), The Dark Knight (2008)}.

The numbers in brackets like (2,2) after the keyword-genre component of a tricluster represent the current count of this particular pattern in the cover and the total number of occurrences of this pattern in the original database, respectively. As it is clear from the example, the corresponding encoding sets of attribute-condition pairs form biset; this is also confirmed by the density of triclusters $\rho = 1$. Such triclusters can be used to provide a user by relevant recommendations based not only on movie genres but on the extra dimension of keywords, which may result in more focused recommendations via this enriched semantic.

5   Conclusion

The performed experiments allow us to say that KRIMP can be considered as a prospective method for triadic data analysis.

There are its positive features that we have seen:

- fast computational time (although on the dataset of rather moderate size with the lowest minimal support $minsup = 2$);
- absolutely dense triclusters (however, this may not be the case for sparse and noisy datasets);
- we can select a rather small set of "large" triclusters (e.g., by imposing higher support for non-singletons).

The negative features that we have seen are the following:

- the strong trade-off between coverage and the number of triclusters (switching from coding sets with singletons to itemsets of higher size);
- even higher number of triclusters than the number of triconcepts with the usage of singletons is allowed.

So, now we have one more Pareto-suboptimal triclustering algorithm (there is no a winner according to the chosen quality criteria) obtained by combining a straightforward data transformation and the MDL-based KRIMP approach for sets of attribute-condition pairs that compress. Note that, a backward transformation from object-attribute data to ternary ones may have sense, e.g. for biclustering in numeric setting replaced by triclustering (triconcepts search) in the transformed binary triadic relation [16].

A more detailed study involving comparison with Boolean tensor factorisation [17,18] to find tricluster cover close to the optimal one can be considered as future prospects of the approach as well as its testing on n-ary relations with direct usage of $(n - 1)$-sets.

Among the prospective applications of triclustering one may consider grouping by similarity and subsequent recommendations for medical informatics purposes, where ternary relations can be composed by triples of patients, symptoms, and diagnoses. From Rough Set Theory perspective, triclustering being tolerant to missing triples can produce a tricluster in a rough manner with its core, i.e. the indispensable absolutely dense part, within the boundary region [15,19].

Acknowledgements. We would like to thank our colleagues, Rakesh Agrawal, Arno Siebes (for the introduction to KRIMP), and Jean-François Boulicaut, for their piece of advice on pattern mining.

The article chapter was prepared within the framework of the Basic Research Program at the National Research University Higher School of Economics (HSE) and supported within the framework of a subsidy by the Russian Academic Excellence Project '5-100'. The second co-author was also supported by the Russian Foundation for Basic Research, grants no. 16-29-12982 and 16-01-00583.

References

1. Agrawal, R., Imielinski, T., Swami, A.N.: Mining association rules between sets of items in large databases. In: Proceedings of the 1993 ACM SIGMOD International Conference on Management of Data, Washington, D.C., 26–28 May 1993, pp. 207–216 (1993)
2. Agrawal, R., Srikant, R.: Fast algorithms for mining association rules in large databases. In: Proceedings of 20th International Conference on Very Large Data Bases, VLDB 1994, 12–15 September 1994, Santiago de Chile, Chile, pp. 487–499 (1994)
3. Vreeken, J., van Leeuwen, M., Siebes, A.: Krimp: mining itemsets that compress. Data Min. Knowl. Discov. **23**(1), 169–214 (2011)
4. Siebes, A.: MDL in pattern mining a brief introduction to KRIMP. In: Glodeanu, C.V., Kaytoue, M., Sacarea, C. (eds.) ICFCA 2014. LNCS (LNAI), vol. 8478, pp. 37–43. Springer, Cham (2014). doi:10.1007/978-3-319-07248-7_3
5. Ganter, B., Wille, R.: Formal Concept Analysis: Mathematical Foundations, 1st edn. Springer-Verlag New York Inc., Secaucus (1999)
6. Cerf, L., Besson, J., Robardet, C., Boulicaut, J.F.: Closed patterns meet n-ary relations. ACM Trans. Knowl. Discov. Data **3**, 3:1–3:36 (2009)
7. Lehmann, F., Wille, R.: A triadic approach to formal concept analysis. In: Ellis, G., Levinson, R., Rich, W., Sowa, J.F. (eds.) ICCS-ConceptStruct 1995. LNCS, vol. 954, pp. 32–43. Springer, Heidelberg (1995). doi:10.1007/3-540-60161-9_27
8. Jäschke, R., Hotho, A., Schmitz, C., Ganter, B., Stumme, G.: TRIAS-an algorithm for mining iceberg tri-lattices. In: Proceedings of the Sixth International Conference on Data Mining, ICDM 2006, Computer Society, pp. 907–911. IEEE, Washington, DC (2006)
9. Cerf, L., Besson, J., Nguyen, K.N., Boulicaut, J.F.: Closed and noise-tolerant patterns in n-ary relations. Data Min. Knowl. Discov. **26**(3), 574–619 (2013)
10. Ignatov, D.I., Gnatyshak, D.V., Kuznetsov, S.O., Mirkin, B.G.: Triadic formal concept analysis and triclustering: searching for optimal patterns. Mach. Learn. **101**(1–3), 271–302 (2015)
11. Koopman, A., Siebes, A.: Characteristic relational patterns. In: Proceedings of the 15th ACM SIGKDD International Conference on Knowledge Discovery and Data Mining, KDD 2009, pp. 437–446. ACM, New York (2009)
12. Ganter, B., Obiedkov, S.A.: Conceptual Exploration. Springer, Heidelberg (2016)
13. Ignatov, D.I.: Introduction to formal concept analysis and its applications in information retrieval and related fields. In: Braslavski, P., Karpov, N., Worring, M., Volkovich, Y., Ignatov, D.I. (eds.) RuSSIR 2014. CCIS, vol. 505, pp. 42–141. Springer, Cham (2015). doi:10.1007/978-3-319-25485-2_3

14. Mirkin, B.G., Kramarenko, A.V.: Approximate bicluster and tricluster boxes in the analysis of binary data. In: Kuznetsov, S.O., Ślęzak, D., Hepting, D.H., Mirkin, B.G. (eds.) RSFDGrC 2011. LNCS (LNAI), vol. 6743, pp. 248–256. Springer, Heidelberg (2011). doi:10.1007/978-3-642-21881-1_40

15. Ignatov, D.I., Kuznetsov, S.O., Poelmans, J., Zhukov, L.E.: Can triconcepts become triclusters? Int. J. Gen. Syst. **42**(6), 572–593 (2013)

16. Kaytoue, M., Kuznetsov, S.O., Macko, J., Napoli, A.: Biclustering meets triadic concept analysis. Ann. Math. Artif. Intell. **70**(1–2), 55–79 (2014)

17. Miettinen, P., Vreeken, J.: MDL4BMF: minimum description length for Boolean matrix factorization. TKDD **8**(4), 18:1–18:31 (2014)

18. Belohlávek, R., Trnecka, M.: From-below approximations in Boolean matrix factorization: geometry and new algorithm. J. Comput. Syst. Sci. **81**(8), 1678–1697 (2015)

19. Lingras, P., Peters, G.: Rough clustering. Wiley Interdisc. Rev.: Data Min. Knowl. Disc. **1**(1), 64–72 (2011)

Classification Model Based on Topological Approximation Space

Bożena Staruch[(⊠)]

Faculty of Mathematics and Computer Science,
University of Warmia and Mazury in Olsztyn,
ul. Słoneczna 54, 10-710 Olsztyn, Poland
bostar@matman.uwm.edu.pl

Abstract. In this paper we present an application of a topological approximation space and a rough fuzzy membership function in aim to get classification models. We propose a model of obtaining coverings based on statistical methods applied to attributes in decision systems (where missing values are also considered). We include in this paper experimental results on classification of Horse Colic, Diabetes and Austra data sets, and compare the results with classifiers built in RSES2.

Keywords: Topological approximation space · Coverings · Rough fuzzy membership function · Classification

1 Introduction

We consider a topological approach to rough approximation space. In this paper we assume that a covering of the finite set is given. In [1,2] a topological approximation space based on coverings, where the lower approximation of a set X is given by the topological interior of X and its upper approximation coincides with the least open set that includes X. Minimal neighbourhoods of objects are treated as information granules. A generalization of an approximation space via the information granulation approach can be found in [3–5]. In [2] we define a rough fuzzy membership function based on information granules. We also propose there, an extended rough fuzzy membership function, which is used to classify 'new' (testing) objects.

There are many approaches to classification problem, e.g. [6,7] present rough set based approach, while [8,9] are based on formal concept analysis, fuzzy approach can be found in [10–13], and symbolic data analysis is in [14].

Section 2 recalls definitions and useful facts. In Sect. 3 the classification model is described. The intuitive meaning of covering subsets is as similarity classes i.e. objects in the same covering subset are similar under some (possibly hidden) property. So, to simulate such a meaning we decided to create covering subsets based on statistical frequency distribution and two thresholds *high* and *low*. Given a covering of the set of training objects we calculate values of the rough

© Springer International Publishing AG 2017
L. Polkowski et al. (Eds.): IJCRS 2017, Part II, LNAI 10314, pp. 570–578, 2017.
DOI: 10.1007/978-3-319-60840-2_41

fuzzy membership function. The next step is getting an open neighbourhood for testing objects. Finally, after calculating values of an extended rough fuzzy membership function we classify the testing objects. We also present experimental results for Horse Colic, Diabetes and Austra data sets (available in the open repository UCI [15]) with their comparison with RSES2 classifier [16].

2   Covering Based Granulation and Topological Approximation Spaces

The terminology and facts of this section are taken from [2]. Let U be a finite non-empty set of objects (training objects). A non-empty family $\mathcal{C}$ of subsets of U is *a covering on U (or covers U)* if and only if $\bigcup \mathcal{C} = U$. Every $C \in \mathcal{C}$ will be called *a covering subset*. Any covering $\mathcal{C}$ on U can be represented as a table which is determined by a function $F_{\mathcal{C}} : U \times \mathcal{C} \longrightarrow \{0,1\}$ such that $F_{\mathcal{C}}(u, C) = 1$ if and only if $u \in C$. Every column C in the latter table is determined by the characteristic function of the covering subset C. Any family of subsets of U can be extended to a covering by adding the set U to this family.

A family T of subsets of a finite set U is *a topology* on U if and only if $\emptyset, U \in T$ and for any $X, Y \in T$, $X \cap Y \in T$ and $X \cup Y \in T$. Given any family $\mathcal{A}$ of subsets of U there exists the least topology $T(\mathcal{A})$ containing $\mathcal{A}$.

Let $\mathcal{T} = T(\mathcal{C})$. For any object $u \in U$ the family $\mathcal{N}_{\mathcal{C}}(u) = \{C \in \mathcal{C}: u \in C\}$ is a family of all its neighbourhoods. Then $g_{\mathcal{C}}(u) = \bigcap \mathcal{N}_{\mathcal{C}}(u)$ is the least neighbourhood of u in $T(\mathcal{C})$ and is called *an information granule* about u in the covering $\mathcal{C}$. The set $Gran_{\mathcal{C}}(U) = \{g_{\mathcal{C}}(u): u \in U\}$ is a covering of U and will be called *a granulation set*.

We define a topological approximation space $TAS = (U, \mathcal{T})$ as a topology $\mathcal{T}$ on U with operators of the lower and upper approximation of subsets of U as follows:

1. $L(X)$ is the greatest open set Y such that $Y \subseteq X$,
2. $UP(X)$ is the least open set Y such that $X \subseteq Y$.

If $\mathcal{C}$ is a covering then $T(\mathcal{C}) = T(Gran_{\mathcal{C}}(U))$ and $UP(X) = \bigcup\{g_{\mathcal{C}}(x) : x \in X\}$.

Let $\mathcal{T} = T(\mathcal{C})$ for a covering $\mathcal{C}$. Then for any $u \in U$ and $X \subseteq U$, $X' = U \setminus X$ we define *a rough fuzzy membership functions* $\mu(u, X)$ as follows:

$$\mu(u, X) = \begin{cases} 0, & \text{for } u \in U \setminus UP(X) \\ \frac{card(X \cap g_{\mathcal{C}}(u))}{card(g_{\mathcal{C}}(u))}, & \text{for } u \in UP(X) \cap UP(X') \\ 1, & \text{for } u \in U \setminus UP(X') \end{cases}$$

If $X \subseteq U$ and $V \in \mathcal{T}$, we can propose different kinds of rough inclusion measure based on values of the rough fuzzy membership function for objects from V and then we can use this measure to classification of new (testing) objects. Depending on the specific application, statistical measures of central tendency can be used as well as other 'aggregation' methods, like maximal/minimal value. Let $\mu(V, X)$ denote any such aggregated measure. If t is a testing object and $\mathcal{N}(t)$ is its open neighbourhood then we define *an extended rough fuzzy membership function* as $\mu(t) = \mu(\mathcal{N}(t), X)$.

3 Classification Model

In this section, we present the application of topological approximation spaces in building classifiers of new objects to decision classes. A *decision system* is a pair $DS = (U, A \cup \{d\})$, where A is a set of conditional attributes such that for every $a \in A$ there is a partial 'onto' function $a : U \to Val_a$ and d is the decision attribute with a function $d : U \to Val_d$, where Val_d is a finite set that determines m decision classes (categories of objects) $D_1, \ldots, D_m \subseteq U$. Every decision class can be represented as a binary decision attribute d_i such that $d_i(u) = 1$ if and only if $u \in D_i$.

We assume that the data set is divided into two parts: U is the set of training objects and T is the set of testing objects and that the information about objects is described in a form of a decision system DS, where the decision attribute d is binary. Let $D = \{u \in U : d(u) = 1\}$.

For every $a \in A$ the set $PVal_a = \{a(u) : u \in U, d(u) = 1\}$ will be called *an a-positive decision values set* and every object $u \in U$ such that $a(u) \in PVal_a$ will be called *an a-positive decision object*. The set of all a-positive decision objects is denoted by Pos_a.

The procedure of classification is based on the following steps:

1 Preparation of the covering $\mathcal{C}$ based on conditional attribute values of DS and the decision attribute.
2 Calculation of the granules table and the values of the rough fuzzy membership function $\mu(u, D)$ for every $u \in U$.
3 Determination of open neighbourhoods $\mathcal{N}(t)$ for $t \in T$.
4 Calculation of the measure $\mu(t)$ for $t \in T$ and classification of t.

I - Preparation of the Covering $\mathcal{C}$. The ideal situation in preparation of the covering of U would be if the data set is collecting and preparing having in mind the future coverings, for example, the covering subsets can be indicated by experts' decisions or human recognizing of pictures, sounds, smell and so on.

As an exemplary method of covering the training set U we use statistical frequency distributions of the values of every conditional attribute $a \in A$ as follows:

1. The limits of distribution classes are determined by discrete values of a if $card(Val_a) \leq 10$, and by deciles values $dec(i)$ of a, in the opposite case. More precisely, the different values of deciles are taken and the classes are intervals in the form: $\langle min, dec(1) \rangle, (dec(1), dec(2)), \ldots$
2. Let $class(i)$ for $i = 1, \ldots, k$ be distribution classes. We calculate the following two frequency distributions:
   (a) the distribution frequency $n(i)$ of Val_a (we omit missing values),
   (b) the distribution frequency $nPos_a(i)$ of $PVal_a$.
3. We calculate $n_a = card(Val_a)$, $nPos_a = card(PVal_a)$ and the following values:
   (a) the fraction of 1's $p_a = \frac{nPos_a}{n_a}$ i.e. the probability of the positive decision,
   (b) the conditional fraction of 1's $pPos_a(i) = \frac{nPos_a(i)}{n_a(i)}$ i.e. the conditional probability of the positive decision in each distribution class,

Table 1. Distribution frequency for rectal temperature and nasogastric tube, and values calculated according to 3

classes	$n_a(i)$	$nPos_a(i)$	$pPos_a(i)$	$factor_a(i)$
Rectal temperature				
$\langle 35.40, 37.30 \rangle$	27	18	0.67	1.11
$(37.30, 37.60)$	22	14	0.64	1.06
$(37.60, 37.80)$	24	14	0.58	0.97
$(37.80, 38.00)$	33	20	0.61	1.01
$(38.00, 38.10)$	12	9	0.75	1.25
$(38.10, 38.30)$	34	18	0.53	0.8
$(38.30, 38.50)$	30	18	0.60	1.00
$(38.50, 38.70)$	19	6	0.32	0.53
$(38.70, 39.17)$	16	12	0.75	1.25
$(39.17, 40.80)$	23	15	0.65	1.09
Nasogastric tube				
1	120	72	0.60	0.80
2	35	29	0.83	1.21
3	39	33	0.82	1.20

(c) the factor $factor_a(i) = \frac{pPos_a(i)}{p_a}$, which compares the fraction of 1's in the given class with the fraction of 1's in the whole sample.

4. A decision which distribution class should be labelled by 1, is made by using two thresholds $low < high$. Then we obtain the two covering subsets:

   (a) *the high covering* is obtained by giving the value 1 for every distribution class such that $factor_a(i) \geq high$ and the 0 value in the opposite case,

   (b) *the low covering* is obtained by giving the value 1 for every distribution class such that $factor_a(i) \leq low$ and the 0 value in the opposite case.

Repeating the above procedure for every attribute and adding the set U, we get the covering C consisting of the obtained covering subsets and the set U.

We have used deciles to determining distribution classes but other types of quantiles can be also used. The property of quantiles that they divide the sample into parts of almost equal cardinality is why we use such kind of statistical parameters, although other methods of distribution frequency can be used. It is worth of effort to decide which method gives the best classification results. It is worth mentioning here that the value 0 for missing values can be understand as 'if we don't know what is the value of the given attribute for the given object then we do not use this object in any covering subset corresponding to this attribute'.

Table 1 contains an example of calculation of the above values for two attributes of 'Horse Colic' (from UCI repository [15]). For 'Rectal Temperature' we have $n_a = 240$, $nPos_a = 144$, $p_a = 0, 6$, number of missing values = 60. For 'Nasogastric Tube' we have $n_a = 194$, $nPos_a = 133$, $pPos = 0, 69$, number of missing values = 106.

Table 2. Nasogastric tube(NT) and rectal temperature(RT) with their values, the covering and decision values

U	NT	RT	C_1	C_2	C_3	C_4	C_5	D
u_1	2	?	1	1	0	0	0	0
u_2	1	39.2	1	0	1	0	0	0
u_3	3	38.3	1	1	0	0	1	1
u_4	1	38	1	0	1	0	0	1
u_5	1	37.3	1	0	1	0	0	1
u_6	2	?	1	1	0	0	0	1
u_7	3	37.9	1	1	0	0	0	0
u_8	3	?	1	1	0	0	0	1
u_9	2	?	1	1	0	0	0	1

Table 2 contains a part of the Horse Colic data set and the induced covering based on the distribution frequencies from Table 1, where $high = 1.2$ and $low = 0.83$ ($1.2 \times 0.83 \approx 1$). To explain the role of the thresholds low and $high$ notice that if $factor_a(i) = 1$ then the class i has the same fraction of positive decisions as the whole sample has, so this class does not carry much information on the decision. If $factor_a(i) > 1$ then it is more probable to get the positive decision, while $factor_a(i) < 1$ indicates that it is more probable to get the negative decision. Objects with a high value of $factor_a$ are similar under the property that the probability of positive decision is high, while objects with a low value of $factor_a$ are similar under the property that the probability of negative decision is high.

Table 3. Calculation of the values of the rough fuzzy membership function

U	Granulation table										D	D'	$UP(D)$	$UP(D')$	$UP(D) \cap UP(D')$	$\mu(u, D)$
u_1	1	0	0	0	0	1	1	1	1	1	0	1	1	1	1	0.67
u_2	0	1	0	1	1	0	0	0	0	0	0	1	1	1	1	0.67
u_3	1	0	1	0	0	1	1	1	1	1	1	0	1	1	1	1.00
u_4	0	1	0	1	1	0	0	0	0	0	1	0	1	1	1	0.67
u_5	0	1	0	1	1	0	0	0	0	0	1	0	1	1	1	0.67
u_6	1	0	0	0	0	1	1	1	1	1	0	1	1	1	1	0.67
u_7	1	0	0	0	0	1	1	1	1	1	0	1	1	1	1	0.67
u_8	1	0	0	0	0	1	1	1	1	1	0	1	1	1	1	0.67
u_9	1	0	0	0	0	1	1	1	1	1	0	1	1	1	1	0.67

II - Calculation of Granules and $\mu(u, D)$. Table 3 contains the granulation for the covering from Table 2 and the values that are used for calculating the values of the rough fuzzy membership function for all training objects.

III - Determination of $\mathcal{N}(t)$ for Every $t \in T$. Basing on attribute values of the given testing object we associate the values 0 or 1 depending on the distribution class to which the attribute value belongs. In Table 4 there are six testing objects with their attribute values, 0–1 values and decision values.

Table 4. Testing objects with values of Nasogastric Tube (NT) and Rectal Temperature (RT), 0–1 values and decision values

T	NT	RT	0-1 values						D
t_1	1	38.3	1	0	1	0	0		1
t_2	2	38.1	1	1	0	1	0	0	0
t_3	2	39.1	1	1	0	1	0	1	1
t_4	3	37.2	1	1	0	0	0	0	0
t_5	?	38.0	1	0	0	0	0	0	1
t_6	2	38.2	1	1	0	0	1	1	1

The next step is obtaining the neighbourhood of each testing object as the intersection of all covering subsets which are 'similar' to the testing object i.e. the columns in the covering table corresponding to units in 0–1 values. Notice that neighbourhoods obtaining this way are open sets as an intersection of covering subsets (Table 5).

Table 5. The neighbourhood calculated for t_1, the right part contains neighbourhoods for the testing objects

U	C_1	C_4	$\mathcal{N}(t_1)$	$\mathcal{N}(t_2)$	$\mathcal{N}(t_3)$	$\mathcal{N}(t_4)$	$\mathcal{N}(t_5)$	$\mathcal{N}(t_6)$
u_1	1	0	0	0	0	1	1	0
u_2	1	1	1	0	0	0	1	0
u_3	1	0	0	0	0	1	1	1
u_4	1	1	1	0	0	0	1	0
u_5	1	1	1	0	0	0	1	0
u_6	1	0	0	0	0	1	1	0
u_7	1	0	0	0	0	1	1	0
u_8	1	0	0	0	0	1	1	0
u_9	1	0	0	0	0	1	1	0
t_1	1	1						

IV - An extended Membership Function for Testing Objects and Their Classification. Having an open neighbourhood $\mathcal{N}(t)$ of the testing object t we calculate a value of an extended membership function to the positive decision class D in two ways:

1. $\mu_{av}(t, D)$ as the average value of $\{\mu(u, D) : u \in \mathcal{N}(t)\}$,
2. $\mu_{max}(t, D)$ as the maximal value of $\{\mu(u, D) : u \in \mathcal{N}(t)\}$.

The last step is classification of objects based on some a priori chosen satisfiability threshold $0 < \mu \le 1$ such that $d(t) = 1$ if and only if $\mu(t) \ge \mu$.

Experimental Results. An experimental session was made for three of data sets with randomly chosen training objects and testing objects:

1. Austra – $card(U) = 490, card(T) = 200$. There was no missing values.
2. Diabetes – $card(U) = 615, card(T) = 153$. There was no missing values.
3. Horse Colic – $card(U) = 300, card(T) = 100$. The average fraction of missing values for conditional attributes is $\frac{1}{3}$.

Table 6. Average classification accuracy

Low	High	μ_{av}			μ_{max}		
		$\mu = 0.4$	$\mu = 0.5$	$\mu = 0.6$	$\mu = 0.4$	$\mu = 0.5$	$\mu = 0.6$
Low	High	Austra					
0.6	1.6	0.83	0.83	**0.85**	0.51	0.51	0.51
0.7	1.4	0.84	0.82	0.81	0.65	0.65	0.65
0.8	1.25	0.81	0.80	0.81	0.71	0.71	0.71
Low	High	Diabetes					
0.6	1.6	0.70	0.70	0.68	0.64	0.63	0.64
0.7	1.4	0.71	**0.73**	0.71	0.65	0.71	0.71
0.8	1.25	0.70	0.69	0.69	0.66	0.69	0.68
Low	High	Horse colic					
0.6	1.6	0.72	0.73	0.50	0.69	0.70	0.72
0.7	1.4	**0.76**	**0.76**	0.60	0.68	0.67	0.68
0.8	1.25	0.59	0.57	0.58	0.54	0.59	0.58

For each of these data sets there were used three pairs of thresholds, two types of measure and three of satisfiability. The accuracies (the number of properly classified testing objects factored by the number of testing objects) of every of the 54 classification tests are presented in Table 6.

4   Conclusion

We compared our results with RSES2 (see [16]) classifier based on rules generated from decision tables of the training objects. The chosen parameters were: 'calculate Rules by Exhaustive algorithm - Don't discern with misssing values' applied to the training objects and 'test table using rule sets, generate confusion matrix' applied to the testing objects with two options 'Simple voting' and 'Standard voting'. The results are presented in Table 7.

Table 7. Average classification accuracy

Data set	RSES simplevoting	RSES standardvoting	Our best
Austra	0.80	0.82	**0.85**
Diabetes	0.65	0.68	**0.73**
Horse colic	**0.77**	0.68	0.76

References

1. Kumar, A., Banerjee, M.: Definable and rough sets in covering-based approximation spaces. In: Li, T., Nguyen, H.S., Wang, G., Grzymala-Busse, J., Janicki, R., Hassanien, A.E., Yu, H. (eds.) RSKT 2012. LNCS (LNAI), vol. 7414, pp. 488–495. Springer, Heidelberg (2012). doi:10.1007/978-3-642-31900-6_60
2. Staruch, B., Staruch, B.: A topological approximation space based on open sets of topology generated by coverings. In: Polkowski, L., Yao, Y., Artiemjew, P., Ciucci, D., Liu, D., Ślęzak, D., Zielosko, B. (eds.) IJCRS 2017, Part II. LNCS (LNAI), vol. 10314, pp. 130–137. Springer, Cham (2017)
3. Szczuka, M., Jankowski, A., Skowron, A., Ślęzak, D.: Building granular systems - from concepts to applications. In: Yao, Y., Hu, Q., Yu, H., Grzymala-Busse, J.W. (eds.) RSFDGrC 2015. LNCS, vol. 9437, pp. 245–255. Springer, Cham (2015). doi:10.1007/978-3-319-25783-9_22
4. Polkowski, L., Skowron, A.: Rough mereology: a new paradigm for approximate reasoning. Int. J. Approx. Reas. **15**(4), 333–365 (1996). Elsevier
5. Polkowski, L., Artiemjew, P.: Granular Computing in Decision Approximation. An Application of Rough Mereology. Intelligent Systems Reference Library, vol. 77. Springer, Heidelberg (2015)
6. Artiemjew, P.: On classification of data by means of rough mereological granules of objects and rules. In: Wang, G., Li, T., Grzymala-Busse, J.W., Miao, D., Skowron, A., Yao, Y. (eds.) RSKT 2008. LNCS (LNAI), vol. 5009, pp. 221–228. Springer, Heidelberg (2008). doi:10.1007/978-3-540-79721-0_33
7. Bazan, J.G., Nguyen, H.S., Nguyen, S.H., Synak, P., Wróblewski, J.: Rough set algorithms in classification problems. In: Polkowski, L., Tsumoto, S., Lin, T.Y. (eds.) RSMA New Developments in Knowledge Discovery in Information Systems 56, pp. 49–88. Physica Verlag, Heidelberg (2000)
8. Kuznetsov, S.O.: Machine Learning and Formal Concept Analysis. In: Eklund, P. (ed.) ICFCA 2004. LNCS (LNAI), vol. 2961, pp. 287–312. Springer, Heidelberg (2004). doi:10.1007/978-3-540-24651-0_25
9. Ganter, B., Kuznetsov, S.O.: Scale coarsening as feature selection. In: Medina, R., Obiedkov, S. (eds.) ICFCA 2008. LNCS (LNAI), vol. 4933, pp. 217–228. Springer, Heidelberg (2008). doi:10.1007/978-3-540-78137-0_16
10. Belohlavek, R., Klir, G.J., Way, E.C., Lewis, H.: Concepts and fuzzy sets: misunderstandings, misconceptions, and oversights. Int. J. Approx. Reas. **51**(1), 23–34 (2009). Elsevier
11. Poelmans, J., Ignatov, D.I., Kuznetsov, S.O., Dedene, G.: Fuzzy and rough formal concept analysis: a survey. Int. J. Gen Syst **43**(2), 105–134 (2014)

12. Dubois, D., Prade, H.: Formal concept analysis from the standpoint of possibility theory. In: Baixeries, J., Sacarea, C., Ojeda-Aciego, M. (eds.) ICFCA 2015. LNCS (LNAI), vol. 9113, pp. 21–38. Springer, Cham (2015). doi:10.1007/978-3-319-19545-2_2
13. Buzmakov, A.V., Napoli, A.: How fuzzy FCA and pattern structures are connected?. In: Proceedings of the International Workshop "What can FCA do for Artificial Intelligence?" (FCA4AI at ECAI), pp. 89–96. HSE Publishing House, Moscow (2016)
14. Brito, P., Polaillon, G.: Structuring probabilistic data by Galois lattices. Math. Soc. Sci. **1**(169), 77–104 (2005)
15. https://archive.ics.uci.edu/ml/datasets.html
16. http://logic.mimuw.edu.pl/rses/

Author Index

Printed in the United States
By Bookmasters